MILLER'S

YEARBOOK & PRICE GUIDE

collectors cars

2002

MILLER'S

YEARBOOK & PRICE GUIDE

collectors cars

GENERAL EDITOR
Dave Selby

FOREWORD
Johnny Herbert

2002

MILLER'S COLLECTORS CARS YEARBOOK & PRICE GUIDE 2002

Created and designed by
Miller's Publications
The Cellars, High Street
Tenterden, Kent TN30 6BN
Telephone: 01580 766411
Fax: 01580 766100

General Editor: Dave Selby
Project Co-ordinator: Philip Hannath
Editorial Assistants: Rosemary Cooke, Maureen Horner, Lalage Johnstone
Designer: Kari Reeves
Advertisement Designer: Simon Cook
Jacket Design: Colin Goody
Advertising Executive: Jo Hill
Advertising Assistant: Melinda Williams
Production Assistants: Caroline Bugeja, Ethne Tragett
Additional Photography: Jacques Chevalier, Guy Griffiths, GPL,
David Hawtin, Haynes Motor Museum, Brian Jocelyne, LAT Photographic Library,
Bob Masters, Peter Nygaard, Robin Saker, William Taylor
Indexer: Hilary Bird

First published in Great Britain in 2001
by Miller's, a division of Mitchell Beazley,
imprints of Octopus Publishing Group Ltd,
2–4 Heron Quays, London E14 4JP

A CIP catalogue record for this book is
available from the British Library

ISBN 1 84000 440 1

Illustrations and film output by CK Litho, Whitstable, Kent
Printed and bound by Toppan Printing Co (HK) Ltd, China

Front cover illustration:

1968 Aston Martin DB6 Mk 1 Volante
£71,900–86,250 / $104,250–125,000 ⚒ BKS

Contents

Acknowledgements

The publishers would like to acknowledge the great assistance given by our consultants:

Malcolm Barber	Montpelier Street, Knightsbridge SW7 1HH Tel: 020 7393 3900
Tom Falconer	Claremont Corvette, Snodland, Kent ME6 5NA
Simon Johnson	Military Vehicle Trust, 7 Carter Fold, Mellor, Lancs BB2 7ER
Brian Page	Classic Assessments, Stonechat House, Moorymead Close, Watton-at-Stone, Herts SG14 3HF
Mike Penn CEI, Tech Eng ITE, Mairso	Haynes Motor Museum, Sparkford, Nr Yeovil, Somerset BA22 7LH
Mike Smith	Chiltern House, Ashendon, Aylesbury, Bucks HP18 0HB
Neil Tuckett	Marstonfields, North Marston, Bucks MK18 3PG
Peter W. Card BSc	Bonhams & Brooks, 65 Lots Road, Chelsea, London SW10 1HH

We would like to extend our thanks to all auction houses, their press offices, and dealers who have assisted us in the production of this book, along with the organisers and press offices of the following events:

Beaulieu September Autojumble & Automart
Louis Vuitton Classic
Goodwood Festival of Speed
Foster's British Grand Prix
Coys Historic Festival at Rockingham Motor Speedway
Rétromobile, Paris
The War & Peace Show

How to use this book

It is our aim to make the guide easy to use. Marques are listed alphabetically and then chronologically. Commercial Vehicles, Children's Cars, Replica Vehicles, Restoration Projects, Racing & Rallying and Military Vehicles are located after the marques, towards the end of the book. In the Automobilia section, objects are grouped alphabetically by type. If you cannot find what you are looking for, please consult the index on page 348.

ALFA ROMEO 27

1973 Alfa Romeo Montreal, coachwork by Bertone, 2593cc V8 engine, fuel injection, 230bhp, 5-speed ZF manual gearbox, finished in red.
£6,000–7,000 / $8,700–10,200 POU

1973 Alfa Romeo Montreal, coachwork by Bertone, 2.6 litre double-overhead-camshaft V8, fuel injection, electronic ignition, dry-sump lubrication, 5-speed ZF gearbox, 137mph top speed, left-hand drive, resprayed in silver, red cloth/leather upholstery, fewer than 16,000 miles from new, well maintained.
£6,500–7,500 / $9,500–10,800 BKS

1969 Alfa Romeo 1750 Spider Veloce, coachwork by Pininfarina, 1 of 633 factory right-hand-drive models, restored.
£8,000–9,500 / $11,600–13,800 BKS
A modern classic by Pininfarina, the simple yet elegant Spider bodywork premiered on the 1966 Duetto would prove enduringly popular, lasting into the 1990s. The Spider's mechanics were essentially those of the Giulia saloon, comprising independent front suspension, coil-suspended live rear axle and four-wheel, servo-assisted disc brakes, while the engine was the Giulia Sprint GTV's 1.6 litre, double-overhead-camshaft four. The Duetto was made for just two years before being superseded, in 1967, by the 1.8 litre 1750 Spider Veloce.

Miller's Starter Marque

Starter Alfa Romeos: *1750 & 2000 GTV; 1300 Junior Spider, 1600 Duetto Spider, 1750 & 2000 Spider Veloce; 1300 & 1600 GT Junior; Alfasud ti & Sprint*

- Responsive, eager and sweet twin-cam engines, finely balanced chassis, nimble handling and delightful looks are just some of the character traits of classic Alfas from the mid-sixties onward. They are also eminently affordable.
For the kind of money that gets you an MGB or TR Triumph, you could be a little more adventurous and acquire an engaging Alfa Romeo sporting saloon or convertible.
- That's the good news; the bad new is that the unfortunate reputation Alfas of the 1960s and 1970s earned for rusting was deserved. Take a magnet along. Classic Alfa owners – *Alfisti* as they prefer to call themselves – have a saying: 'You pay for the engineering and the engine, but the body comes free.' Bear in mind too that maintenance costs are likely to be pricier than those of an MG or TR Triumph.

1968 Alfa Romeo Duetto Spider, regularly serviced by specialists, complete brake overhaul, approximately 55,000 miles from new.
£4,500–6,000 / $6,500–8,700 COYS
Perspex headlamp covers give smoother air-flow and raise top speed a little. However, they were banned in the USA.

Duetto Spider

When the new Spider was first seen at the Geneva Motor Show in 1966 Alfa launched a competition to name the car. After ploughing through 140,000 entries with suggestions like Lollobrigida, Bardot and Nuvolari, they chose Duetto, which neatly summed up the two's-company-three's-a-crowd image.

ALFA ROMEO Model	ENGINE cc/cyl	DATES	CONDITION 1	2	3
24hp	4084/4	1910–11	£25,000	£16,000	£12,000
12hp	2413/4	1910–11	£18,000	£11,000	£8,000
40–60	6028/4	1913–15	£32,000	£24,000	£14,000
RL/RLSS	2916/6	1921–22	£40,000	£24,000	£14,000
RM	1944/4	1924–25	£28,000	£17,000	£13,000
6C 1500	1487/6	1927–28	£50,000*	£20,000+	£10,000+
6C 1750	1752/6	1923–33	£100,000+	£80,000+	-
6C 1900	1917/6	1933	£18,000	£15,000	£12,000
6C 2300	2309/6	1934	£30,000+	£18,000	£15,000
6C 2500 SS Cabriolet/Spider	2443/6	1939–45	£100,000	£50,000	£40,000
6C 2500 SS Coupé	2443/6	1939–45	£60,000	£40,000	£30,000
8C 2300 Monza/Short Chassis	2300/8	1931–34	£1,500,000+	£400,000+	-
8C 2900	2900/8	1935–39	£1,500,000+	£1,000,000	-

Value is very dependent on sporting history, body style and engine type.
*The high price of this model is dependent on whether it is 1500 supercharged/twin overhead cam, and with or without a racing history.

Caption
provides a brief description of the vehicle or item, and could include comments on its history, mileage, any restoration work carried out and current condition.

Source Code
refers to the 'Key to Illustrations' on page 330 that lists the details of where the item was sourced. Advertisers are also indicated on this page. The icon indicates the item was sold at auction. The icon indicates the item originated from a dealer. The icon indicates the item belonged to a member of a car club; see Directory of Car Clubs on page 336.

Miller's Starter Marque
refers to selected marques that offer affordable, reliable and interesting classic motoring.

Information Box
covers relevant information on marques, designers, racing drivers and special events.

Price Guide
these are based on actual prices realised shown in £sterling with a US$ conversion. Remember that Miller's is a PRICE GUIDE not a PRICE LIST and prices are affected by many variables such as location, condition, desirability and so on. Don't forget that if you are selling, it is quite likely you will be offered less than the price range. Price ranges for items sold at auction include the buyer's premium.

Price Boxes
give the value of a particular model, dependent on condition and are compiled by our team of experts, car clubs and private collectors.
Condition 1 refers to a vehicle in top class condition, but not concours d'élégance standard, either fully restored or in very good original condition.
Condition 2 refers to a good, clean roadworthy vehicle, both mechanically and bodily sound.
Condition 3 refers to a runner, but in need of attention, probably to both bodywork and mechanics. It must have a current MOT.
Restoration projects are vehicles that fail to make the Condition 3 grading.

Foreword

Everything about *Miller's Collectors Cars Yearbook & Price Guide* is fascinating - not least the memorabilia section. I notice in the 2000 edition that a replica of my 1994 helmet, when I was driving for Lotus and signed by me, was valued at between £600 and £800! I notice also that Ayrton Senna's overalls and helmet in JPS livery were between £30,000 and £35,000.

Miller's seems to reflect the growth and changes in motoring with great accuracy. When I had my first Formula 1 test, in a Benetton at Brands Hatch in the late 1980s, no special seat was made (I had to use somebody else's) and they packed me in with pillows. This is as unthinkable now as paying £35,000 for a pair of overalls would have been then.

The past is not a foreign country. We all lived there once and, on each page of *Miller's*, it can be revisited. Here are all the cars of your childhood, and your father's childhood, too. What intrigues me, as someone whose life has been so close to cars, is how (comparatively) affordable so many of them are to the enthusiast.

What fascinates me just as much is, as with racing cars, beautiful shapes never date. Look at any of the Ferraris or the E-Type Jaguars in *Miller's* and you will see. In fact, *Miller's* is the only Price Guide I have ever seen which you want to read like a book and keep – forever.

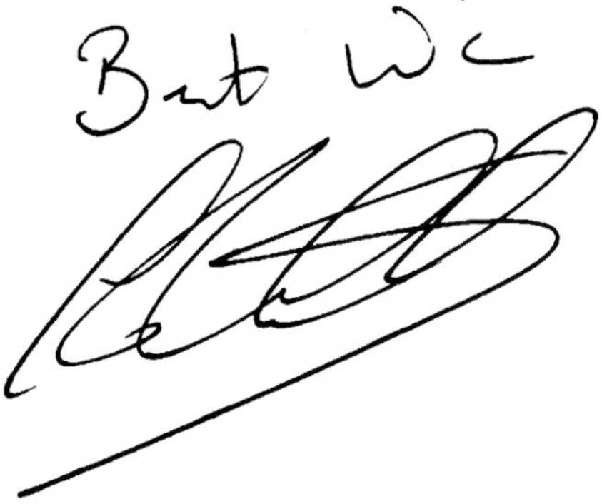

Johnny Herbert

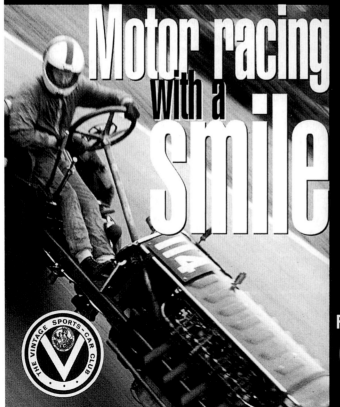

The State of the Market

The past twelve months have seen several momentous developments in the car auction world, and some very exciting sales. Sotheby's, underlining its withdrawal from the market in the UK, closed its automobilia and Formula 1 memorabilia department while forming an alliance in Paris with auctioneers Poulain. Brooks took over the fine art auctioneers Bonhams in October 2000 and subsequently merged with Phillips to rename themselves Bonhams. Coys established a successful new venue at Rockingham Speedway. Its debut sale included the Jaguar Legend collection, with the ex-Hawthorn/Bueb 1955 Le Mans winning D-Type making best price of the day at £392,887 ($570,000).

Bonhams & Brooks has continued to expand in the USA, with four venues: Aurora, Illinois, where the debut sale totalled $1.3 million (£95,000); Hershey Pennsylvania; Quail Lodge Carmel during Pebble Beach weekend; and at The Cavallino Concours, Florida. Bonhams & Brooks' European operation, based in Switzerland, continues to do well. The Ferrari sale at Gstaad in mid-December was one of the most successful of the year, a 1962 250GT California Spyder making best price at £891,261 ($1,292,400). At Monaco, on 21 May, 84 per cent of cars offered sold, and £480,000 ($696,000) was paid for a 1959 Ferrari 410 Super America.

Christie's sale held at the Pebble Beach Concours proved to be the highlight of the year in the USA. The sale totalled $26,497,000, (£18,250,000): a 1966 Ferrari P3 Le Mans two-seater made $5.6 million (£3,752,000); a 1928 Maserati Tipo 26, $1.65 million (£1,105,500); and a 1932 Maserati 8C 3000 Grand Prix two-seater, $1,084,000 (£726,280). In the UK, Christies sold 20 of Sir Elton John's cars at practically double pre-sale estimates.

By the middle of 2000, the E-commerce boom was approaching its height – US auctioneers Kruse had been taken over by E-bay and, in the UK, Sothebys was using the internet for automobilia sales. In the event, the outcome followed the general trend in the dot-com industry, with sales declining. It remains to be seen whether there will be a recovery.

In the provinces, H&H continued to be the most successful of the smaller houses, with sales continuing to achieve at least 70 per cent of entries sold, and with some inroads into the higher-priced vehicle category formerly the exclusive province of the London houses. Barons made steady progress at Sandown Park, but despite all its efforts – and at least one sale topping £100,000 ($145,000) – is still not enjoying the success it deserves. Purely Classics in Southend continues to hold regular modest sales catering mainly for classics under £5,000 ($7,250), while BCA, with its purpose-built venue at Blackbushe and others in the provinces, has held some moderately successful sales, albeit tending to concentrate on classics under £10,000 ($14,500) with few exceptions.

Cheffins, in the Cambridge area, has made quite an impression in the short time it has been holding regular sales, and some excellent prices have included £79,410 ($115,145) for a 1922 Rolls-Royce Silver Ghost and £50,500 ($73,225) for a 1932 Rolls-Royce 20/25 drophead. Bonhams & Brooks' sales at Harrogate have proved so successful that summer and autumn events are now held at the Great Yorkshire Showground.

In North America, Ontario based RM Auctions has held some successful sales on Amelia Island, at the Waldorf Astoria, New York, and in Monterey. Bonhams & Brooks' sale at Quail Lodge in August at the Pebble Beach weekend totalled over $10 million (£6.66 million) and brought a record price of $3,082,500 (£2,077,913) for a Mille Miglia winning 1938 Alfa Romeo 8C 2900. Racing provenance adds premium to prices, and this was true at Coys' Rockingham sale and Christies' London sale, where a 1960 Maserati Tipo 60 Birdcage sports racer realised £1,433,750 ($2,078,937).

Bonhams & Brooks' flagship sale in December at Olympia totalled £2.2 million ($3.3 million). This included £230,000 ($333.500) for a rare 1965 Bizzarrini 5300. Coys also ended the year with its 'True Greats' sale in the same month and achieved some good prices, a 1962 Mercedes-Benz 300SL topping the list at £128,000 ($185,600). This was followed by a sale at the NEC in January, which included Formula 1 memorabilia. A bronze of Stirling Moss in a Maserati brought £3,823 ($5,500), while top car price was the £57,638 ($83,575) paid for a 1972 Ferrari Daytona.

The Bonhams & Brooks Rolls-Royce sale held at the RREC annual rally in April included the collection of the late Terry Cohn, which helped achieve a £1.2 million ($1.75 million) sold figure. Days later, the same team was at the Goodwood Festival of Speed with a £2.7 million ($3.91 million) sale total. The highest price for a car was £265,000 ($282,750) for a 1904 Mercedes Simplex tourer and a selection of Bugatti spares realising £330,000 ($478,500).

After a rather faltering start over the first five months of 2001, mainly due to the crisis in the countryside and the hesitation preceding the general election in the UK, the market picked up well. The Aston Martin marque continued to flourish, the sale held by Bonhams & Brooks at the factory in May seeing the ex-works Gatsonides Monte Carlo Rally class winning 1954 DB 2/4 making £95,000 ($137,750), and the late King Hussein of Jordan's 1993 Virage Volante selling for £73,000 ($105,850). American bidding has been a feature in the market, despite the predictions of recession in the USA, and some of the best sales have been held there. We look forward to the future with confidence. Clearly, quality is required – Ferrari, Aston Martin, Jaguar and other exotica all show signs of a slight rise, and classic marques remain fairly stable.

Malcolm Barber

Stars' Cars

Some cars are stars in their own right. Others are stars' cars and when the seat-squab of a classic car has been caressed by famous buttocks, celebrity trophy hunters can push prices sky high.

At UK and international auctions over the past year there's been a frenzy of celebrity trophy buying that culminated early in June with the spectacular sale of Elton John's car collection by Christie's in London. Unfortunately, the sale took place just after our print deadline, but the results were remarkable. Not only did every one of his 20 cars sell, but they soared way beyond their estimated values, realising £1.95 million ($2.83 million) against pre-sale estimates of less than half that sum.

One of the star lots was a beautiful 1973 Rolls-Royce Phantom VI that sold for a staggering £223,000 ($323,400) (including premium) against an estimate of £110,000 to £150,000 ($159,500 to $217,500). Likewise, Elton John's Jaguar XJ220, driven a total of just 852 miles, sold for £234,750 ($340,425), twice the price of XJ220s not belonging to Elton John. A very nice but not perfect 1965 Jaguar E-Type roadster sold for £80,750 ($117,100) – just compare that with our price guide on page 135. A really lovely Bentley S1 Continental fastback commanded £196,000 ($284,250) against an estimate of £50,000 to £70,000 ($72,500 to $101,500). It was the same story throughout, with a series of V8 Aston Martins, Rolls-Royces, including an £86,000 ($124,750) Silver Cloud 3, and Bentleys from the 1950s through to a 1997 Bentley Turbo R 400 for £83,000 ($120,400).

It was little wonder that Elton John later commented: 'When the bidding kept going up and up, way above the estimates, I was both thrilled and surprised. There's obviously a lot of money to be made from second-hand cars!'

That seems to be true enough – if your name's Elton John, or James Bond, Elvis Presley, James Cagney or John Lennon. These are just a few of the famous folk – dead, alive and fictional – whose cars have come up at auction over the last year.

At the beginning of 2001, a 'double 0' movie association more than doubled the value of an Aston Martin DB5 when the hammer fell at a staggering £140,000 at a Christie's auction of James Bond memorabilia on Valentine's Day. With buyer's premium the sum paid totted up to £157,750 ($228,800), which in the real world would be enough to buy two superb restored DB5s, with change left over. This DB5, however, was a *Goldeneye* Aston. Three were used in the filming of Pierce Brosnan's 1995 Bond debut movie and this one, known as the 'chase car' featured in the famous duel with a Ferrari 355GTS in the hills above Monte Carlo. Imagine then, how much an original Sean Connery Aston Martin from the 1964 *Goldfinger* movie might be worth.

This 'star-car' phenomenon is not confined to the UK. In January 2001, a 1940 Lincoln Continental convertible came up at RM Auctions in the US. It's a blue-chip US classic, for sure, worth perhaps £30,000 to £45,000 ($43,500 to $65,250) in the normal run of things. But this particular car was originally owned by American baseball legend Babe Ruth and that association saw the Lincoln soar to £77,000 ($111,650). And that's by no means unusual in the star car world. In September 2000, a 1961 Bentley S2 owned by screen legend James Cagney soared to £37,000 ($53,650) at Doyle New York. Without the Cagney connection it might not have been worth even half that.

More recently, also in the USA, Elvis Presley's 1975 Lincoln Continental Mk IV, notably the very last Lincoln he owned, sold for £45,000 at a Barrett-Jackson sale. Again, that's way over market value as a car. But on occasion celebrity motoring artefacts don't even have to include the car to command high prices. In March, Fleetwood-Owen, the entertainment memorabilia auction house founded by legendary drummer Mick Fleetwood, offered a pair of vehicle tax discs once attached to a Rolls-Royce Corniche belonging to Who drummer Keith Moon. The pair of discs (for 1973 and 1974) sold for £1,035 ($1,550).

However, a celebrity name-tag doesn't always live up to expectations. At the same sale John Lennon's 1970 Mercedes-Benz 600 Pullman failed to sell, with a top bid of £190,000 ($275,000). Curiously, a few weeks after that sale, George Harrison's Mercedes-Benz 600 also came up for sale at a Cheffins' auction.

Harrison's 1967 car, an 18ft 600 saloon as opposed to Lennon's 20ft 600 Pullman, failed to sell, with a top bid of £19,500 ($28,300). However, a sale was later agreed at that rather modest price to a Danish fan.

To the classic-car enthusiast this is all a bit dizzying. You might be asking yourself, how can one Mercedes-Benz 600 sell for £19,500 and another not sell for ten times that?

Douglas Jamieson, chairman of London based Coys Auctioneers, assesses the celebrity car market thus: 'Cars with a history of famous ownership bridge two fields of collecting and that makes it difficult to pinpoint values. While there are established values for cars, the added value of a celebrity association is much harder to quantify, particularly as fame can be so fleeting. I suppose that's why many appear at auction, where it's left to the market to establish their value.'

For me, this star-car spectacle is a diverting and faintly bewildering side show on the world stage of the classic car market. In truth, it's really not got anything to with cars at all and I'll continue to pursue my driving passions in the same way I always have, by trying to find a car at a price that makes me smile. I hope this edition of the *Miller's Collectors Cars Yearbook & Price Guide* helps you do the same.

Dave Selby

Buying at auction

How can you ignore more than 5,000 cars a year? That's what you're missing out on if you shun the auction arena in the hunt for your next classic car.

Certainly, to the outsider the world of classic car auctions can seem pretty intimidating, a cauldron of adrenalin where a mere twitch or the movement of a bead of sweat on your forehead could commit you to a car you never intended to buy. That's what it's like in the fictional TV world of Lovejoy, where walking into a sale room is akin to swimming with sharks after you've just nicked yourself shaving.

In the real world it's different, but yet to many people their view of auctions remains coloured by inaccurate TV dramas and the occasional news bulletins where a Van Gogh goes into orbit or some mystery telephone bidder shells out a king's ransom for one of Princess Di's frocks.

Well, forget all that. Sure, some of the same auction houses that will sell you a Van Gogh will also sell you a VW Beetle, but you won't be so awestruck if you think of cars not so much as art, not even as used cars, but in most cases as very used cars. Then the intimidating veneer peels back to reveal a world of exciting possibilities and you'll discover the reality that auctions are at once the supermarket, novelty shop and Bond Street jewellers of the classic-car world.

There are pitfalls and you need to exercise common sense and discretion, but the best argument for considering buying a car at auction was once put to me by a very prominent dealer who railed against the 'the general public' for taking 'the bread from his mouth.' And how was 'the general public' doing that? Simply by turning up at what is, after all, a public sale – and actually buying things.

And that's one of the overwhelming attractions of buying at auction; the possibility of picking up a bargain. Of course, there's also the possibility of being landed with a pup, but that's little different from the pitfalls of buying from the private ads.

We've all read those seductive small ads tempting us to drive hundreds of miles to snap up the bargain of the century. When we get there, if it hasn't been sold already, we all too often find that 'must be seen' translates into 'must be seen on a moonless rainy night so the rust doesn't show and what's left of the paint looks shiny.' Then there's that other clichéd come-on: 'one careful owner.' When you turn up you find that rabid heap you're looking at did indeed have one careful owner; it's just that the other 12 didn't give a damn. Furthermore, if the vendor tells you someone else has just offered £200 more, how do you know any other offers exist at all. You didn't see anyone's hand go up in the air.

One of the most hilarious classified ads I saw was for an E-Type Jag described as having 'all matching numbers, just needs engine.'

At least with auctions the car's there when you turn up and there are little things like the Sales of Goods Act to prevent catalogue descriptions soaring too far into the realms of small-ad poetic myth. But the rest is up to you.

The bottom line is this: if you feel confident enough to make a sound buying judgement when shopping in the classifieds – or if you have a friend or colleague whom you trust implicitly

with this faculty – then there's no reason why you shouldn't also consider buying at auction.

If not, you're best buying from reputable dealers. You pay extra, but what you should get for that is the confidence of knowing the car is backed by their good reputation, has been properly prepared for sale, is as described, with known faults declared, and sold to you with a warranty.

Anyone who peruses the regular auction results published in the classic car magazines can't help but be tempted. In short, there seem to be some fantastic and sometimes almost unbelievable bargains out there: seemingly up-together Mk II Jags for well under £10,000 ($14,500); fixed-head E-Types for the same amount, and roadsters at under £20,000 ($29,750).

Jaguar is the single most-prolific marque at auction, followed by MG, with the auction middle-ground for MGB roadsters ranging from under £3,000 to £8,000 ($4,400 to $11,600); likewise for GTs the middle ground is from under £2,000 to £4,000 (2,900 to $5,800). Triumph TR2–6 models are being sold at £3,000 to £10,000 every week. Stags can be even cheaper at auction.

These marques, along with later Rolls-Royces and Bentleys, are the supermarket shelf-fillers, piled high at auction and seemingly priced very competitively when you match them against routinely higher prices in the classifieds.

And, just like in the classifieds, some are bargains and some aren't.

It's good to be sceptical, but you can be too cynical and if you assume that just because a car seems to be cheaper at auction it must therefore be a prettily-bodged lash-up you'll be cutting your nose off to spite your face. One reason is that auctions represent the final reality of the market place for hopelessly optimistic vendors, who seem to retain a nostalgic attachment to peak-market prices and think their car is the only example on earth that has bucked the downward shift that occurred after the boom in the late 1980s and early 1990s.

You see these cars all the time if you study the classifieds, priced far too high, then spiralling down in price, bouncing from one publication to another and back until comes the day of final realisation. The car has now become so tainted in the classified marketplace that there's nowhere else to go but auction. By then the car also has sour associations for the owner who just wants rid of the thing.

It's useful to ponder why anything comes to auction. The old-established auction houses have long prospered on three fundamentals, known to insiders as 'the three Ds' – death, debt and divorce. There's something to that but again, it's a little too cynical. I've sold cars at auction and although I got less than I might have if I'd sold privately, it really was worth it because my working life and leisure time wasn't blighted for weeks on end by aimless tyre-kickers and time-wasters.

If you study the auction results, virtually every week you'll see a car that has been snapped up for less than the cost of its restoration. And when that restoration's just been completed you have to wonder why. Well, it's sad but true that a lot of people get locked into financially unviable restorations with costs spiralling out of control. The trouble is it's very difficult to sell a pile of bits and the vendor often has no alternative but to finish the job to gain any return at all. That car could be a tremendous bargain, but may not be if good early work has later been compromised by the owner's disenchantment, dwindling funds and the desperate need to get the car back together and on the market.

A very different, extreme but pertinent example is a Mk II Jaguar that sold a few years back. The 1963 3.4 model was bought at auction for £6,550 ($9,475). The car came with restoration bills and paid invoices for work done amounting to a staggering £47,631.44 ($68,850+) – that was in addition to whatever the vendor paid to buy the car. The car was bought by a prominent dealer who quickly advertised it for £10,950 ($16.925). If you had paid £6,550 at auction or £10,950 to buy it from the dealer, that still seems an incredible bargain. The dealer later told me that the car had no reverse gear when he bought it, so he had to put that right. Still a bargain.

Let's put that in context. One auctioneer confided to me recently: 'If Mr X [a certain well known dealer] buys it I know it's gone for too little.' He'd be far happier if you bid a little more than the dealer – and so would you, driving off with a good proportion of the dealer's profit margin.

That's the theory. And here are a couple of practical examples. Recently I saw a trophy winning MGB GT, restored at a cost of £18,000 ($26,000), sell at auction for £4,650 ($6,750). A less extreme example was a 1978 MGB GT with £7,600 ($11,020) of paid restoration bills; it sold at auction for £2,500 ($3,600).

Well known TV pundit and market commentator Quentin Willson puts it like this: 'Classic car auctions are the only place you'll find true value in the used-car market. The maths is pretty compelling when you can buy someone else's restoration at a cut price and get a car thrown in for free.'

An analysis of prices achieved in the last year shows that many mainstream classics are at the most affordable they've been for years, with some actually undervalued. As an aside it's worth noting some of the wider economic forces that have created such an enticing buyer's market in the UK. Here's just one example of the 'continental drift' in the old car market caused by fluctuating global economies. Currently the South African economy's really struggling and one consequence is that over the last couple of years over 500 right-hand-drive export Mk II Jags have returned to the UK to add to the pool already here. Additionally the strong pound relative to most European economies has seen fewer continental buyers hopping across the channel for mainstream classics that are more affordable domestically. All of which is actually good news for the UK enthusiast. It means that as far as mainstream classics are concerned there is plentiful supply, and in some cases, such as Mk II Jaguars, possibly even over-supply. Prices are broadly stable and that should be reassuring for enthusiasts who can indulge without fearing that values will plummet or soar beyond reach.

Elsewhere, another factor that has come into play in recent years is the consumer-driven downward pressure on new car prices in the UK. With new car prices coming down, this has exerted downward pressure on the used-car market. You may wonder what this has to do with classic cars. Well, as far as many a borderline enthusiast is concerned, the classic appeal of an E-Type Jaguar roadster, for example, is going to be marginal when there are modern sporting sensations like the Lotus Elise, BMW Z3 roadster, Mazda MX-5 and MGF available for the same kind of money, or in the case of low-mileage used examples, for substantially less. Of course, to committed enthusiasts the new car options make little difference, but it's one more of the pressure points acting on the classic-car market.

That's part of the reality of the modern marketplace, but whether you can take

advantage in the classic-car auction arena is another matter. In practical terms buying at auction all depends on whether you have the wherewithal. A dealer relies on judgement and knowledge that only comes from years of hard-won experience. If they seem casual at an auction it's the end product of a long apprenticeship that has culminated in easy familiarity, confidence, market knowledge and shrewd judgement.

Remember at auction you won't get to drive a car and at all but a few you won't even get to see it run (BCA's drive-through auctions are an exception). It's arguable whether a drive around the block would tell you that much anyway, but at auction you have to find out everything you possibly can about a car, then make an allowance in your estimation of its value to you for what you can't possibly know.

There are two ways to do it. One is like walking into a bookies for the first time in your life, sticking a pin in a paper and then moaning when you haven't won. The other way is to study form, hang around 'the paddock,' listen and learn. It's not very glamorous or even much fun. Then apply your knowledge and you could snap up a rewarding car at a rewarding price. For why? Because, in the first place, you knew it was coming up at auction, and you really did your homework.

Here are a few guide notes for the auction rookie:

• Familiarise yourself with auctions. Visit a few before you go to one to buy – just to soak up the atmosphere, study the etiquette and to find out how it all works.

• Decide what you're after and research the particular make, model and specification you want – and of course, how much it's worth.

• If the car you're after is coming up at auction tell the auction house you are interested and ask them what they know about it – someone at the auction house may well have driven it. Study the catalogue description, both for what's said and what's not said, and pore over the accompanying documentation, making sure the records of work relate to that car and not the vendor's Lada.

• Arrive to view early and crawl over the car, as much as you're allowed.

• If you like what you find you should register to bid and you'll then be given a numbered paddle with which to bid (there's none of this covert winking nonsense at classic-car auctions).

• Take into account the buyer's premium, which can be anything from 0% to 15% of the hammer price. VAT is payable on the premium. Thus with a 15% premium, to a hammer price of £1,000 add £150 premium and £26.25 VAT (17.5% x £150) for a total of £1,176.25 ($1,755).

• Arrange cleared funds. If you do not settle in time, usually 24 hours, you may start to incur storage costs.

• If you want to drive the car away remember to make preliminary insurance arrangements; otherwise, most auction houses can recommend a transport company.

Dave Selby

Abarth

Carlo Abarth's career began with racing motorcycles and sidecars.He moved to Cisitalia after the war, then set up his Turin-based tuning company in 1950, specialising mostly in the Fiat marque, and building a reputation for squeezing out dollops of power from just a few cubic centimetres. His first complete car appeared in 1955, and he went on to produce in limited numbers a distinguished series of small-engined sports racers and competition machines. Throughout the 1960s, Carlo Abarth drew extra performance out of Fiat 500s and 600s. Racing activities propelled the company into liquidation in 1971, when Fiat took over the competition shop and continued to apply the Abarth tag to hot Fiats. You will find some examples in the Fiat section of this book.

◀ **1971 Otas Abarth Scorpione,** coachwork by Lambardi, 4-cylinder engine, 4-speed manual gearbox, 4-wheel independent suspension, Kamm tail, pop-up headlights, low mileage, 2 owners from new.
£5,000–6,000
$7,250–8,750 ⚒ RM

AC

AC started out in 1908 under the name Auto-Carriers, first producing three-wheeled tradesmen's vehicles, then a passenger three-wheeler called The Sociable.They later graduated to four-wheeled cars before WWI, followed by a range of high-quality sporting cars in the 1920s and 1930s. The beautiful Ace of 1954 was a landmark car for the company. Endowed with a mighty American Ford V8, this fine sports car was later transformed into the potent and legendary AC Cobra, whose mechanics and underpinnings also spawned the AC 427 and 428 luxury GT. In 1979 AC introduced the 3 litre V6 mid-engined 300ME. It was never beautiful, but still looked extremely purposeful, although its 120mph stop speed did not live up to its aggressive posture. Only 82 ACs were built and they remain an affordable oddball with a certain 'What is it?' appeal.

AC Model	ENGINE cc/cyl	DATES	CONDITION 1	2	3
Sociable	636/1	1907–12	£13,000	£9,000	£6,000
12/24 (Anzani)	1498/4	1919–27	£14,000	£11,500	£7,500
16/40	1991/6	1920–28	£18,000	£15,000	£11,000
16/60 Drophead/Saloon	1991/6	1937–40	£24,000	£21,000	£15,500
16/70 Sports Tourer	1991/6	1937–40	£35,000	£26,000	£18,000
16/80 Competition 2-Seater	1991/6	1937–40	£55,000	£45,000	£35,000

1958 AC Aceca Coupé, original AC engine replaced by optional Bristol unit, brakes rebuilt, resprayed in maroon, retrimmed in tan leather.
£13,500–16,000 / $19,500–23,200 ⚒ BKS

1961 AC Greyhound, 2500cc 6-cylinder engine, overdrive gearbox, wire wheels, finished in British racing green, valuable 'PP' registration plate, history right back to original sales invoice.
£10,000–12,500 / $14,500–18,125 ⚒ GrM

◀ **1962 AC Ace Bristol,** overdrive, disc brakes, original left-hand drive, completely restored, rebuilt engine, finished in silver with dark green hide interior, limited mileage since restoration.
£45,000–50,000
$65,250–72,500 ⚒ COYS
The Ace's origins lie in a racing design built by John Tojeiro in 1950. This car consisted of a lightweight chassis, high-performance Bristol 2 litre engine and an aluminium body based loosely on the Ferrari 166 MM Barchetta by Touring. During its production life, the Ace was available with AC, Bristol and Ford engines.

1958 AC Ace 'Double Bubble' Berlinetta, coachwork by Zagato, Bristol engine, wire wheels, exterior filler cap, finished in red, black-piped white lightweight interior, good all-round condition.
£150,000–170,000 / $217,000–245,000 ⚒ BKS
The history of this car is sketchy, but it is known to have been owned by Giuseppe 'Jo' Siffert, a very popular racing driver who won World Championship races for Porsche in sports cars, and for BRM in Formula One, in the process earning the nickname 'The last of the late brakers'. Siffert was Swiss and is believed to have been collecting cars associated with his homeland. There is speculation that the Swiss entered AC that finished 22nd at Le Mans in 1960 is this car, but more likely is that it contested various Swiss national events in the first two years of its lifetime. Siffert bought it in a very sorry state, but subsequently it was restored.

AC Model	**ENGINE cc/cyl**	**DATES**	**CONDITION 1**	**2**	**3**
2 litre	1991/6	1947–55	£7,000	£4,000	£1,500
Buckland	1991/6	1949–54	£9,000	£5,500	£2,500
Ace	1991/6	1953–63	£30,000	£25,000	£20,000
Ace Bristol	1971/6	1954–63	£45,000	£30,000	£25,000
Ace 2.6	1553/6	1961–62	£38,000	£32,000	£29,000
Aceca	1991/6	1954–63	£22,000	£16,000	£11,000
Aceca Bristol	1971/6	1956–63	£28,000	£20,000	£12,000
Greyhound Bristol	1971/6	1961–63	£16,000	£12,000	£8,000
Cobra Mk II 289	4735/8	1963–64	£90,000	£80,000	£60,000
Cobra Mk III 427	6998/8	1965–67	£125,000	£100,000	£80,000
Cobra Mk IV	5340/8	1987–92	£55,000	£40,000	£28,000
428 Frua	7014/8	1967–73	£19,000	£15,000	£10,000
428 Frua Convertible	7014/8	1967–73	£28,000	£20,000	£16,000
3000ME	2994/6	1976–84	£15,000	£10,000	£8,000

Racing history for Cobra will put the price to £100,000–120,000+.

Aero

A known continuous history can add value to and enhance the enjoyment of a car.

◀ **1936 Aero Type 30 Saloon,** 996cc 2-cylinder engine, 3-speed manual gearbox, cable-operated drum brakes, left-hand drive, finished in dark blue, chestnut interior.
£2,500–3,000 / $3,600–4,350 ⚒ Pou

Alfa Romeo

Keen drivers have a lot for which to thank Alfa Romeo, for almost from the company's foundation in Milan in 1910, Alfa models have carried sporting genes. The number of lithe, lean and nimble Alfas are simply too many to mention, and for periods in its history its eager road cars have basked in the reflected glory of race-track victories, most notably in the 1920s when Alfa Romeo began a decade of domination of Grand Prix racing. Although after 1945 Alfa Romeo gradually moved toward the automotive mainstream with higher volume production and more affordable models, the sporting genes have persisted to this day. Virtually every Alfa of the 1960s and 1970s was a rewarding driver's car. Although sometimes marred by fragile electrics and readiness to rust, any flaws were generally easily forgiven once you got behind the wheel.

ALFA ROMEO Model	ENGINE cc/cyl	DATES	CONDITION 1	2	3
24hp	4084/4	1910–11	£25,000	£16,000	£12,000
12hp	2413/4	1910–11	£18,000	£11,000	£8,000
40–60	6028/4	1913–15	£32,000	£24,000	£14,000
RL/RLSS	2916/6	1921–22	£40,000	£24,000	£14,000
RM	1944/4	1924–25	£28,000	£17,000	£13,000
6C 1500	1487/6	1927–28	£50,000*	£20,000+	£10,000+
6C 1750	1752/6	1923–33	£100,000+	£80,000+	-
6C 1900	1917/6	1933	£18,000	£15,000	£12,000
6C 2300	2309/6	1934	£30,000+	£18,000	£15,000
6C 2500 SS Cabriolet/Spider	2443/6	1939–45	£100,000	£50,000	£40,000
6C 2500 SS Coupé	2443/6	1939–45	£60,000	£40,000	£30,000
8C 2300 Monza/Short Chassis	2300/8	1931–34	£1,500,000+	£400,000+	-
8C 2900	2900/8	1935–39	£1,500,000+	£1,000,000	-

Value is very dependent on sporting history, body style and engine type.
*The high price of this model is dependent on whether it is 1500 supercharged/twin overhead cam, and with or without a racing history.

1930 Alfa Romeo 6C 1750 3rd Series Turismo Drophead Coupé, coachwork by James Young, Sport model twin-camshaft engine, finished in silver grey with black hood, wind-up windows, external pram hood irons, rear-mounted spare wheel, 2+2 seating, original leather upholstery, wooden dash and door cappings, good order throughout.
£60,000–70,000 / $87,000–108,000 BKS

Tempted to join Alfa Romeo from Fiat in 1923, Vittorio Jano joined the racing department in Milan. His first major project was the six-cylinder P2 racing car, winner of the 1924 European Grand Prix and the AIACR World Championship winning Grand Prix car in 1925. Jano had been briefed in 1924 to develop a medium-capacity light car with brilliant performance, and by the time of the Milan Salon in 1925, the new 6C 1500, then designated the NR, was displayed in chassis form. The new car, although built around a lightweight and nimble-handling chassis, was essentially underpowered, the single-camshaft six-cylinder engine being fundamentally sound, but uninspiring. Before long, a twin-camshaft model, the 1500 Sport, was produced, closely followed by the larger engined 65 x 88mm 6C 1750. This car was to dominate its class in competition from 1929 to 1935, yet it was also a desirable road car for the touring-minded motorist. For 1929, the 6C 1750 was offered in various forms, including the Turismo, a long-wheelbase (10ft 2in), single-overhead-camshaft model; the Sport with 9ft wheelbase; and top of the list, the Super Sport, a supercharged car on the short 9ft wheelbase.

1947 Alfa Romeo 6C 2500 SS Roadster, 2443cc 6-cylinder double-overhead-camshaft engine, 4-speed gearbox with column change, 4-wheel fully independent suspension, 4-wheel hydraulic brakes, 3-passenger front bench seat, faux-yellow ivory control knobs.
£70,000–80,000 / $101,500–116,000 BJ

1949 Alfa Romeo 6C 2500 Super Sport Cabriolet, coachwork by Pinin Farina, 2443cc, double-overhead-camshaft 6-cylinder engine, 110bhp, 4-speed manual gearbox, 4-wheel independent suspension, 4-wheel drum brakes, restored early 1990s.
£80,000–90,000 / $116,000–130,500 RM

The most potent of several 6C 2500 models was the Super Sport. With triple Weber carburettors, it gave 110bhp, even on the low-octane fuel available in Europe at the time. The 6C 2500's relatively stiff chassis and four-wheel independent suspension delivered this power to the road much more effectively than the typical cart-sprung, solid-axle cars of the day.

Alfa Romeo 6C 2500 Deluxe Sales Catalogue, illustrated in full colour, 24 pages with embossed front cover logo, English language, German dealer stamp dated May 1950, excellent condition, 11¾ x 8¼in (30 x 21cm).
£600–700 / $870–1,000 RM

1951 Alfa Romeo 6C 2500 Villa d-Este Cabriolet, coachwork by Touring, original Super Sport engine, 105bhp, standard chassis, 4-seater, disappearing exterior door handles, door pulls, amber window winders and switchgear, bodywork restored 6 years ago, refurbished mechanically, body, paint and brightwork in very good condition.
£55,000–65,000 / $79,750–94,250 BKS
Destined to be the last of the separate-chassis Alfas, the 2500 had debuted in 1939 and was a development of the preceding 2300. The engine was the latest version of Alfa's race-developed twin-cam six, its 2443cc displacement having been arrived at by enlarging the bore of the 2300. Maximum power ranged from 90bhp in single-carburettor Sport guise to 105bhp in the triple-carb Super Sport. 2500 production continued until 1953, by which time a little fewer than 2,200 had been made.

1933 Alfa Romeo 8C 2300 3rd Series Drophead Coupé, coachwork by Castagna, matching numbers car, original specification in all major mechanical respects, apart from non-standard supercharger and distributor, unrestored, engine in need of recommissioning.
£600,000+ / $870,000+ BKS
It was the introduction of the supercharged straight-eight 2.3 engine in 1931 that set Vittorio Jano at the peak of his profession. The engine was so versatile that it was adopted for the Alfa's sporting touring cars as well as their out-and-out Grand Prix racers. It shared the cylinder dimensions of the hugely successful 1750, and in standard form developed 142bhp at 5,000rpm. The engine was constructed in mirrored blocks of four with the camshaft drive gears amidships. The crankshaft was carried in ten plain white-metalled bearings, and the supercharger, water pump and oil pump were driven by helical gears from each crankshaft. The new engine was designed for lightness, featuring detachable alloy cylinder heads and even hollow camshafts. Jano had first used dry-sump lubrication in the P2 models in the 1920s and reverted to this principle for the eight-cylinder cars. The favoured supercharger was a Roots type, and on the standard production engine it produced 9¼lb of boost. The new car was available in two standard chassis lengths, with wheelbases of 9ft and 10ft 2in. The longer-wheelbase cars were generally selected for the more luxuriously appointed coachwork of the drophead coupés and four-seat tourers.

1955 Alfa Romeo 1900 SS, coachwork by Ghia Aigle, earliest of 9 Alfas bodied by Ghia known to survive, restored 1980s, finished in Italian racing red, tan leather upholstery, excellent condition.
£50,000–60,000 / $72,500–87,000 COYS
This car was bodied specifically for the 1955 Geneva Salon.

Miller's is a price GUIDE not a price LIST

An Alfa-Romeo Celebration fibreglass wall plaque, in the shape of a laurel wreath, with armorial in the centre, painted in acrylic and varnish.
£575–675 / $800–1,000 BKS

ALFA ROMEO Model	ENGINE cc/cyl	DATES	CONDITION 1	2	3
2000 Spider	1974/4	1958–61	£14,000	£9,000	£4,000
2600 Sprint	2584/6	1962–66	£11,000	£7,500	£4,000
2600 Spider	2584/6	1962–65	£13,000	£8,000	£5,000
Giulietta Sprint	1290/4	1955–62	£10,000	£7,000	£4,000
Giulietta Spider	1290/4	1956–62	£12,000	£6,000	£4,500
Giulia Saloon	1570/4	1962–72	£5,000	£3,000	£1,500
Giulia Sprint (rhd)	1570/4	1962–68	£10,500	£6,000	£2,000
Giulia Spider (rhd)	1570/4	1962–65	£11,000	£8,000	£4,000
Giulia SS	1570/4	1962–66	£16,000	£11,000	£5,000
GT 1300 Junior	1290/4	1966–77	£7,000	£5,500	£2,000
Giulia Sprint GT	1570/4	1962–68	£7,500	£5,000	£2,000
1600GT Junior	1570/4	1972–75	£7,000	£4,000	£2,000
1750/2000 Berlina	1779/ 1962/4	1967–77	£4,000	£2,000	£1,000
1750GTV	1779/4	1967–72	£7,000	£6,000	£2,000
2000GTV	1962/4	1971–77	£6,500	£4,000	£2,000
1600/1750 (Duetto)	1570/ 1779/4	1966–67	£10,000	£7,500	£5,000
1750/2000 Spider (Kamm)	1779/ 1962/4	1967–78	£9,000	£6,000	£3,000
Montreal	2593/8	1970–77	£9,000	£8,000	£5,000
Junior Zagato 1300	1290/4	1968–74	£7,000	£5,000	£3,000
Junior Zagato 1600	1570/4	1968–74	£8,000	£6,000	£4,000
Alfetta GT/GTV (chrome)	1962/4	1972–86	£4,000	£2,500	£1,000
Alfasud	1186/ 1490/4	1972–83	£2,000	£1,000	£500
Alfasud ti	1186/ 1490/4	1974–81	£2,500	£1,200	£900
Alfasud Sprint	1284/ 1490/4	1976–85	£3,000	£2,000	£1,000
GTV6	2492/6	1981–	£4,000	£2,500	£1,000

Watch for Zagato coachwork on early coupé models – very desirable.

1959 Alfa Romeo Giulietta SZ, coachwork by Zagato, 1290cc double-overhead-camshaft 4-cylinder engine, twin Weber carburettors, 116bhp, 4-speed manual gearbox, 4-wheel finned drum brakes, independent front suspension, live rear axle, original factory lightweight Campagnolo rims on front wheels, aluminium body, racing seats, roll-bar, restored to excellent cosmetic condition, new Rosso Corsa paint.
£35,000–40,000 / $50,750–58,000 ⚒ RM

Two series of the Sprint Zagato were produced between 1959 and 1961. The first series was the round tail model, which featured a smooth flowing body that ended in a short, curved rear end. It was markedly different from the second series, which was redesigned to feature a longer and more abrupt tail. Weighing in at slightly more than 1,700lb, both versions of the SZ were significant performers, a consequence of the excellent power-to-weight ratio.

1961 Alfa Romeo Giulietta SZ Berlinetta, coachwork by Zagato, original 1.3 litre engine, twin Weber 40DCOE4 carburettors with open velocity stacks, lightweight aluminium coachwork, restored mid-1980s, little use since, finished in red , black vinyl interior, correct seats and instruments, smaller-than-standard steering wheel, good all-round condition.
£34,000–38,000 / $49,000–55,000 ⚒ BKS

1962 Alfa Romeo Giulia Spider, 1570cc 4-cylinder engine, twin Weber carburettors, engine rebuilt, suspension uprated with firmer front springs, new black mohair hood, weak synchromesh on second/third gears, otherwise mechanically sound, structurally sound, rev-counter in need of new cable, oil temperature and fuel gauges inoperative.
£6,000–7,000 / $8,700–10,200 ⚒ BRIT

◀ **1963 Alfa Romeo Giulia Spider,** 1570cc 4-cylinder engine, twin Weber carburettors, 140bhp, 5-speed manual gearbox, 4-wheel hydraulic drum brakes, hardtop.
£11,000–13,000 / $16,000–19,000 ⚒ Pou

◄ **1964 Alfa Romeo 2600 Spider,** 2584cc double-overhead-camshaft 6-cylinder engine, triple carburettors, original right-hand drive, 41,000 miles from new.
£11,000–13,000 / $16,000–19,000 H&H

► **1964 Alfa Romeo Giulia Spider,** 1.6 litre engine, 5-speed gearbox, hardtop, just over 25,000 miles from new.
£19,000–21,000 / $27,500–30,500 COYS
This car was the prize in a promotion run by Alfa Romeo on a cruise ship, during which passengers were invited to drive a Spider around the deck, whereupon they were awarded a 'High Seas Driving Licence'. It remained with the winner until sold recently.

1964 Alfa Romeo Giulia Sprint Speciale Coupé, coachwork by Bertone, 1570cc double-overhead-camshaft 4-cylinder engine, front disc brakes, original right-hand drive, older restoration, finished in dark blue with grey/blue interior, good condition throughout.
£14,000–16,000 / $20,300–23,300 BKS
By the time of the Giulia's introduction in 1962, Alfa Romeo's successful 'small car, big performance' formula, initiated by the Giulietta in 1954, was well established. The debutante Sprint Coupé had been joined by Berlina and Spider versions, then in 1959 came the ultimate Giulietta – the Sprint Speciale. These model designations and body styles were carried over into the improved 101 Series, produced from 1959, and continued when the range was upgraded to Giulia status. Only 1,400 of the Bertone-bodied Giulia Sprint Speciales were built between 1963 and 1965.

1965 Alfa Romeo Giulia GTC, coachwork by Touring, 1570cc double-overhead-camshaft 4-cylinder engine, alloy cylinder head, 5-speed gearbox, 4-wheel disc brakes, disappearing top, left-hand drive, 2 owners from new, body restored 1997–98, bare-metal respray in red, new taillights and lenses, door glass and bumpers, tan interior trim, engine completely rebuilt at a cost of over £3,500, approximately 100 miles covered since rebuild.
£7,500–9,000 / $10,800–13,000 BKS
With a total production run of 1,000 units between 1965, when it was launched, and 1966, the Giulia GTC was an exclusive 2+2 convertible derivative of the Bertone-styled Giulia Sprint GT.

1965 Alfa Romeo Giulia TZ Berlinetta, coachwork by Zagato, older restoration, twin-plug ignition, Weber 45DCOE carburettors, choke control for easier starting, Marelli S132 distributor, roadworthy exhaust, Autodelta water radiator, oil catch tank, quick-lift jack supports front and rear, Campagnolo TZ2 wheels, additional set of TZ1 wheels, original double-curvature windscreen, Plexiglas side and rear windows, original front light covers, frames and trim, Hella rear lights, fuel cut-off switch, resprayed in red, black interior, heater, Hellebore wood-rim steering wheel, Jaeger instruments.
£130,000–140,000 / $188,500–203,000 BKS
This car is thought to have competed in the 1965 Targa Florio.

A known continuous history can add value to and enhance the enjoyment of a car.

► **1975 Alfa Romeo 1600 GT Junior,** finished in yellow, grey/black interior, history, excellent condition.
£5,750–6,500 / $8,500–9,500 UMC

1972 Alfa Romeo 2000 GTV, 1962cc 4-cylinder engine, 132bhp, worn synchromesh on second, slight rust bubbling on rear wheel arches, good mechanical order.
£2,000–2,500 / $2,900–3,600 BRIT
Making its first appearance in 1971, the 2000 GTV was an effective development of the original 1750 GTV.

1973 Alfa Romeo Montreal, coachwork by Bertone, 2593cc V8 engine, fuel injection, 230bhp, 5-speed ZF manual gearbox, finished in red.
£6,000–7,000 / $8,700–10,200 Pou

Miller's Starter Marque

Starter Alfa Romeos: *1750 & 2000 GTV; 1300 Junior Spider, 1600 Duetto Spider, 1750 & 2000 Spider Veloce; 1300 & 1600 GT Junior; Alfasud ti & Sprint*

- Responsive, eager and sweet twin-cam engines, finely balanced chassis, nimble handling and delightful looks are just some of the character traits of classic Alfas from the mid-sixties onward. They are also eminently affordable. For the kind of money that gets you an MGB or TR Triumph, you could be a little more adventurous and acquire an engaging Alfa Romeo sporting saloon or convertible.
- That's the good news; the bad new is that the unfortunate reputation Alfas of the 1960s and 1970s earned for rusting was deserved. Take a magnet along. Classic Alfa owners – *Alfisti* as they prefer to call themselves – have a saying: 'You pay for the engineering and the engine, but the body comes free.' Bear in mind too that maintenance costs are likely to be pricier than those of an MG or TR Triumph.

Duetto Spider

When the new Spider was first seen at the Geneva Motor Show in 1966 Alfa launched a competition to name the car. After ploughing through 140,000 entries with suggestions like Lollobrigida, Bardot and Nuvolari, they chose Duetto, which neatly summed up the two's-company-three's-a-crowd image.

1973 Alfa Romeo 2000 GTV, 1962cc 4-cylinder engine, finished in red.
£2,500–3,000 / $3,600–4,300 H&H

1973 Alfa Romeo Montreal, coachwork by Bertone, 2.6 litre double-overhead-camshaft V8, fuel injection, electronic ignition, dry-sump lubrication, 5-speed ZF gearbox, 137mph top speed, left-hand drive, resprayed in silver, red cloth/leather upholstery, fewer than 16,000 miles from new, well maintained.
£6,500–7,500 / $9,500–10,800 BKS

1969 Alfa Romeo 1750 Spider Veloce, coachwork by Pininfarina, 1 of 633 factory right-hand-drive models, restored.
£8,000–9,500 / $11,600–13,800 BKS
A modern classic by Pininfarina, the simple yet elegant Spider bodywork premiered on the 1966 Duetto would prove enduringly popular, lasting into the 1990s. The Spider's mechanics were essentially those of the Giulia saloon, comprising independent front suspension, coil-suspended live rear axle and four-wheel, servo-assisted disc brakes, while the engine was the Giulia Sprint GTV's 1.6 litre, double-overhead-camshaft four. The Duetto was made for just two years before being superseded, in 1967, by the 1.8 litre 1750 Spider Veloce.

1968 Alfa Romeo Duetto Spider, regularly serviced by specialists, complete brake overhaul, approximately 55,000 miles from new.
£4,500–6,000 / $6,500–8,700 COYS
Perspex headlamp covers give smoother air-flow and raise top speed a little. However, they were banned in the USA.

1974 Alfa Romeo Spider Veloce 2000, 2 litre double-overhead-camshaft engine, 5-speed manual gearbox, right-hand drive.
£4,000–5,000 / $5,800–7,200 ⚒ BARO

1978 Alfa Romeo Spider, 1962cc 4-cylinder engine, left-hand drive, finished in silver with blue hood, generally in good condition, but engine oil leak and bodywork in need of attention.
£1,500–1,700 / $2,200–2,500 ⚒ BRIT

1989 Alfa Romeo Spider, converted to right-hand drive, hardtop, finished in silver, 40,700km from new, 1 owner, excellent condition.
£6,000–7,000 / $8,700–10,200 ⚒ BARO

1984 Alfa Romeo Spider 2000, converted to right-hand drive, bodywork restored at a cost of over £3,600.
£6,000–7,000 / $8,700–10,200 ⚒ BARO

The Alfa Romeo Spider has enjoyed a cult following ever since one was driven by Dustin Hoffman to the strains of Simon and Garfunkel in the film The Graduate.

► **1989 Alfa Romeo Spider,** 1962cc 4-cylinder engine, 5-speed manual gearbox, resprayed in silver, very good condition throughout.
£4,500–5,000 / $6,500–7,200 ⚒ H&H

1991 Alfa Romeo SZ Coupé, coachwork by Zagato, finished in red, leather interior, 17,500km from new, 'as-new' condition throughout.
£16,000–18,000 / $23,200–26,200 ⚒ BKS
The limited-production SZ had a dramatic two-seat coupé body, which formed part of its unitary construction. The floorpan and five-speed transaxle were derived from the Alfa Romeo 75 Touring Car contender, while the Alfa Romeo 164 provided the twin-cam 3 litre V6 engine, which was tuned to give 206bhp. Front suspension was by lower front wishbones, coil springs and transverse links, and at the rear was a De Dion axle on coil springs with trailing arms. The SZ boasted a top speed of 253km/h and covered 0–100km/h in under seven seconds, but most impressive was the near-racing-car handling.

Allard

1947 Allard K1, 239cu.in Ford sidevalve V8 engine, belt-driven McCullough supercharger, 3-speed manual gearbox, split-beam independent front suspension, front and rear transverse leaf springs, 4-wheel drum brakes, left-hand drive, finished in black, red leather interior.
£28,000–33,000 / $40,600–50,600 ⚒ RM
Sydney Allard was a trials enthusiast and London Ford dealer who applied the renowned power and torque of the sidevalve Ford V8 and Lincoln Zephyr V12 engines to a series of specials. Using modified Ford chassis with transverse-leaf-spring suspension, Allard split and centre-pivoted the Ford beam front axle to create rudimentary, but effective, independent front suspension. The healthy dose of positive camber, required to offset body-roll-induced camber change became his cars' trademark. Allard began production after WWII with the K1, powered by the Ford V8. Lessons learned with the K1 were applied to the famous J2 and J2X, and established Allard's reputation for solid construction and exceptional performance provided by generous amounts of American V8 cubic inches.

1948 Allard K1, 3600cc sidevalve Ford V8 engine, older restoration, finished in cream with red interior, stored for some time, recently recommissioned.
£16,000–18,000 / $23,200–26,200 ⚒ H&H

1947 Allard L-Type Four-Seat Tourer, 3.6 litre Ford sidevalve V8 engine, 85bhp, 3-speed manual gearbox, transverse leaf springs front and rear, semi-independent front suspension via split front axle, 4-wheel hydraulic drum brakes, restored to factory specification, finished in black with red leather interior.
£13,000–15,000 / $18,800–21,800 ⚒ C
'The new Allard,' said *The Autocar* in February 1946, 'has changed its sporting tweeds for a lounge suit.' There were other changes, too. Allards were no longer specials, for their builders had taken on a new identity. On the strength of a stockpile of Ford V8 engines and parts built up during the war years, Sydney Allard launched into full-scale production of a range of aggressively styled, modern-looking touring cars. It hardly mattered that they were mostly Ford; in the car-starved Britain of the 1940s, there was soon a waiting list for the Allard. The formula was very much as it had been in the 1930s, only now the Ford sidevalve V8 engine was installed well back in a chassis of Allard's own devising. Helped by the excellent Marles steering and that rearward weight bias, the handling was considered to be excellent. The independent front suspension, for all its simplicity, was seen as thoroughly up-to-date. There was power and acceleration in abundance, and the 'long' rear axle ratio of 3.6:1 used at first gave these tourers an easy gait up to a maximum of around 85mph. The L-Type remained in production from late 1946 to 1950, during which time 100 were built.

ALLARD Model	ENGINE cc/cyl	DATES	CONDITION 1	2	3
K/K2/L/M/M2X	3622/8	1947–54	£18,500+	£12,000	£8,000
K3	var/8	1953–54	£24,000	£15,000	£11,000
P1	3622/8	1949–52	£19,500	£13,000	£8,000
P2	3622/8	1952–54	£22,000	£18,000	£11,500
J2/J2X	var/8	1950–54	£60,000+	£50,000	£35,000
Palm Beach	1508/4, 2262/6	1952–55	£12,000	£10,000	£5,500
Palm Beach II	2252/ 3442/6	1956–60	£25,000+	£20,000	£11,000

◀ **1949 Allard M-Type Drophead Coupé,** 5400cc V8 engine, Alvis Speed 25 manual gearbox, 2 owners and 47,000 miles from new, very original, good sound condition, in need of some restoration.
£10,000–11,000 / $14,500–16,000 H&H
Produced from 1947 until 1950, the M-Type drophead coupé was the first truly civilised Allard, although, with only 500 produced, it was possibly not the most successful of the initial post-war series.

1951 Allard J2X, 331cu.in overhead-valve Cadillac V8 engine, 300bhp, 3-speed Hydramatic automatic transmission, semi-independent front suspension via split-front axle, De Dion rear suspension, 4-wheel Lockheed hydraulic drum brakes, finished in British racing green.
£100,000–115,000 / $145,000–167,000 RM

1953 Allard Palm Beach 21C Roadster, 1508cc, Ford overhead-valve 4-cylinder engine, 47bhp, 3-speed manual gearbox, semi-independent front suspension via split beam axle, completely restored, engine rebuilt with period Aquaplane accessories, resprayed, 1 of 8 Consul-engined Palm Beaches built.
£27,000–32,000 / $39,200–46,400 RM
Having built a loyal following with his V8-engined cars, Sydney Allard introduced a smaller model in 1953, the Palm Beach. It was equipped with a fully-enveloping body and a simpler live-axle rear suspension, which replaced the De Dion arrangement of the K and J models. The car retained Allard's characteristic split-beam-axle independent front suspension. Power came from the 1.5 litre, four-cylinder Ford Consul engine or the 2.3 litre, six-cylinder Ford Zephyr engine. Production was modest: only eight Consul-equipped 21Cs and 65 Zephyr-engined 21Zs.

1954 Allard K3, 3622cc Ford sidevalve V8 engine, 95bhp, 3-speed synchromesh gearbox, semi-independent front suspension via split beam axle, De Dion rear suspension, 4-wheel hydraulic drum brakes, inboard at rear, 1 of 2 built with right-hand drive for the home market, restored, finished in original pale blue, 3 owners from new.
£13,000–16,000 / $18,800–23,200 C
Built on what was basically the 2.6 litre Palm Beach tubular chassis, the K3 was designed to receive powerful American V8 power units putting out anything up to 300bhp. It was provided with a version of the De Dion rear suspension developed in the J-Type competition models. As with earlier K-Types, there was a single broad seat with plenty of space for three, four if they were good friends. The remote-control gear lever was beside the seat and there were wind-up side windows to complement an easily lowered, fully disappearing hood. The roomy body was aluminium panelled throughout, supported on steel formers and hoops rising directly from the chassis.

Alvis

Founded in 1919, Alvis soon built a reputation for building fine sporting cars. It was also an early pioneer of front-wheel drive, which featured on the 12/75 model of 1928. In the 1930s, as Alvis added extra luxury, the company's best cars rivalled those of Bentley. After 1945, the cars were initially a little more mundane and sometimes outright quirky, as with the unsuccessful whale-like TB14 and TB21. Elegance returned in 1956 with the Graber-styled TD21, which evolved into the TD, TE, and TF models until Rover took control in 1966 and car production ceased.

ALVIS Model	ENGINE cc/cyl	DATES	CONDITION 1	2	3
12/50	1496/4	1923–32	£20,000	£13,000	£7,000
Silver Eagle	2148	1929–37	£16,000	£12,000	£8,000
Silver Eagle DHC	2148	1929–37	£18,000	£13,000	£9,000
12/60	1645/4	1931–32	£15,000	£10,000	£7,000
Speed 20 (tourer)	2511/6	1932–36	£35,000+	£28,000	£18,000
Speed 20 (closed)	2511/6	1932–36	£25,000	£18,000+	£11,000
Crested Eagle	3571/6	1933–39	£10,000	£7,000	£4,000
Firefly (tourer)	1496/4	1932–34	£14,000+	£10,000	£6,000
Firefly (closed)	1496/6	1932–34	£7,000	£5,000	£4,000
Firebird (tourer)	1842/4	1934–39	£13,000	£10,000	£6,000
Firebird (closed)	1842/4	1934–39	£7,000	£5,000	£4,000
Speed 25 (tourer)	3571/6	1936–40	£38,500	£30,000	£20,000
Speed 25 (closed)	3571/6	1936–40	£23,000	£17,000	£12,000
3.5 Litre	3571/6	1935–36	£35,000	£25,000	£18,000
4.3 Litre	4387/6	1936–40	£44,000+	£30,000	£22,000
Silver Crest	2362/6	1936–40	£14,000	£10,000	£7,000
TA	3571/6	1936–39	£18,000	£12,000	£8,000
12/70	1842/4	1937–40	£10,000	£8,000	£6,000

1928 Alvis TT Supercharged Two-Seater Sports, 1500cc engine, completely restored, Allen crank, high-efficiency radiator, TT-style body built to factory specification, finished in green and black, black interior trim, fewer than 2,000 miles since restoration, concours winner.
£32,000–36,000 / $46,400–52,200 ⚒ H&H

1935 Alvis Silver Eagle 16/95 SG Holbrook Four-Door Saloon, original, with period fittings, history.
£14,000–16,000 / $20,300–23,200 ⊞ UMC

▶ **1938 Alvis 4.3 Short-Chassis Tourer,** coachwork by Whittingham and Mitchell, 4.3 litre high-compression engine, triple carburettors, 123bhp, Dewandre vacuum-servo brakes, Luvax finger-tip-controlled shock absorbers, Phillips radio and stopwatch, adjustable arm rests to both doors, original engine and gearbox, finished in black, brown leather interior.
£55,000–60,000 / $79,750–87,000 ⚒ COYS

ALVIS Model	ENGINE cc/cyl	DATES	CONDITION 1	2	3
TA14	1892/4	1946–50	£9,500	£8,000	£4,500
TA14 DHC	1892/4	1946–50	£14,000	£11,000	£5,000
TB14 Roadster	1892/4	1949–50	£15,000	£10,000	£8,000
TB21 Roadster	2993/6	1951	£16,000	£10,000	£7,000
TA21/TC21	2993/6	1950–55	£12,000	£9,000	£5,000
TA21/TC21 DHC	2993/6	1950–55	£17,000	£13,000	£10,000
TC21/100 Grey Lady	2993/6	1953–56	£13,000	£11,000	£5,000
TC21/100 DHC	2993/6	1954–56	£19,000	£15,000	£9,000
TD21	2993/6	1956–62	£11,000	£8,000	£4,000
TD21 DHC	2993/6	1956–62	£22,000	£16,000	£10,000
TE21	2993/6	1963–67	£15,000	£10,000	£7,000
TE21 DHC	2993/6	1963–67	£22,000	£16,000	£8,000
TF21	2993/6	1966–67	£16,000	£12,000	£8,000
TF21 DHC	2993/6	1966–67	£28,000	£17,000	£13,000

Alvis TD21, TE21 & TF21 (1958–67)

Engine: 2993cc overhead-valve six-cylinder.
Power output: 103–150bhp.
Transmission: Four-speed manual; five-speed manual from 1962, along with optional automatic.
Brakes: Drums all-round to 1959; then front discs; discs all-round from 1962.
Maximum speed: 105–120mph.
0–60mph: 11.5–14 seconds.
Production:1,528.
Pick of the bunch: The last-of-the-line TF21; it's the fastest, with triple-carb 150bhp power, all-round disc brakes and other modernities.
Prices in 1958: Saloon, £2,993, 17s including purchase tax; drophead coupé, £3,293, 17s including purchase tax.

Elvis would never have owned an Alvis – they were just too darned tasteful – and perhaps no Alvis was ever more elegant than the last-of-line TD, TE and TF21 models, which brought car making to a close for the old Coventry firm. Better looking than Bristols, priced on a par with Aston Martins, but less flashy, and with an interior as sumptuous as a Bentley or a Rolls-Royce, Alvis's final flourish was a quintessential understatement of quiet, British establishment old-money confidence. The Duke of Edinburgh owned a TD drophead; actor James Mason also owned a drophead, and World War 2 flying ace Douglas Bader had a TD followed by a TE. You can't get more British than that, yet the shape actually came from Swiss coachbuilder Hermann Graber, who took an Alvis TC21 chassis and transformed it into a beautifully restrained two-door sporting coupé for the 1955 Paris Motor Show. The result was the very pricey, 100mph, hand-built TC108G, of which only 16 or 17 were made, with bodies produced under licence in the UK. In 1958, Park Ward took over body production, and the lightly revised model was named the TD21, evolving gently through the TE to the final TF version. By then, Rover had taken control of Alvis and when, shortly after, Rover was absorbed into British Leyland in 1967, there was no longer any place for anything so individual as an Alvis.

1952 Alvis TA21 Saloon, coachwork by Mulliner, 2993cc 6-cylinder engine, finished in black, tan interior, very good condition throughout.
£4,000–5,000 / $5,800–7,200 H&H

1964 Alvis TE21 Saloon, 5-speed ZF manual gearbox, Kenlowe fan, stainless exhaust, power steering, wire wheels, history.
£10,000–11,000 / $14,500–16,000 UMC

1962 Alvis TD21 Drophead Coupé, automatic transmission, full cosmetic restoration, including complete retrim, new chrome wire wheels and repaint in silver, excellent overall condition.
£15,000–18,000 / $21,750–26,100 COYS
The origins of the TD21/TE21/TF21 series date back to 1953, when sales of Alvis's 3 litre, ladder-chassis cars, such as the TC21/100 Grey Lady, were falling and its planned all-new V8 saloon was scrapped at huge financial cost. The TD21 was announced in October 1958 and benefited from a strengthened chassis, sharper styling and increased interior space. Suspension remained wishbone/coil spring at the front, with a live rear axle and semi-elliptic springs at the rear. Austin-Healey's four-speed manual gearbox became standard, as did front disc brakes on all but the earliest examples.

American La France

◄ **1916 La France Speedster,** 15 litre 6-cylinder engine, converted and fitted with speedster bodywork 1990, finished in yellow, black upholstery.
£18,500–21,000
$26,800–30,500 H&H
This La France Speedster began life as a fire engine, as have most other examples.

Armstrong-Siddeley

The Armstrong-Siddeley name is now just a misty motoring memory, but the Coventry company started making cars way back in 1919 and over the years gained a reputation for producing cars that were solidly built, easy to drive and comfortable rather than sporting.
The company was very quick off the mark after WWII, unveiling the first British line-up of all-new post-war designs in May 1945. Armstrong-Siddeley's evocative model names – Lancaster, Typhoon, Hurricane – referred, of course, to the aviation activities of the parent company, and while the cars weren't exactly flyers, their performance and comfort was what might fairly be described as commendable.
As British manufacturing recovered, Armstrong-Siddeley found itself competing in an increasingly crowded market. Marques like Jaguar, for example, offered luxury saloons with better outright performance at substantially lower prices, and Armstrong-Siddeley finally ceased car production in 1960.

1933 Siddeley Special 5-Litre Four-Door Cabriolet, coachwork by Burlington Tickford, twin side-mounted spares, Lucas lighting including centre spotlight, windscreen-mounted trafficators, 11th car off the production line and believed to be the oldest surviving example, only chassis to be built with Burlington Tickford 4-door cabriolet coachwork, rebuilt late 1980s/early 1990s at a cost of £75,000, finished in red and black , red leather interior, black hood, unused since 1997.
£32,000–35,000 / $52,000–57,000 ⚒ BKS
One of the largest-engined, most powerful and highest-specification touring cars of the 1930s, the Siddeley Special was born out of the 1919 merger of Armstrong-Whitworth's car division with the Coventry-based Siddeley-Deasy. The Armstrong-Siddeley concern had not been noted for performance motoring prior to the debut of the 30hp Siddeley Special in chassis form in 1932. Only 253 chassis were built in the production run, which continued until 1937. Crafted in hiduminium alloy, the Special's six-cylinder overhead-valve engine produced 125bhp at 3,200rpm. This power unit transmitted an abundance of low-speed torque via a Wilson pre-selector gearbox, and the car would accelerate smoothly from walking pace to over 90mph in top gear. The Special's blend of engineering excellence and performance guaranteed its appeal, although the price tag of over £1,000, depending on coachwork chosen, meant that ownership was restricted to a wealthy elite. Among those were Sir Malcolm Campbell and Tommy Sopwith.

1933 Armstrong-Siddeley Landaulette, 20hp, aluminium bodywork, excellent condition.
£12,000–14,000 / $17,400–20,300 ⊞ ASOC

1935 Armstrong-Siddeley 17hp Sports Foursome Saloon, coachwork by Burlington, 2394cc engine, completely restored 1980s, finished in black with maroon trim.
£11,500–13,500 / $16,600–19,500 ⚒ H&H

Miller's is a price GUIDE not a price LIST

► **1959 Armstrong-Siddeley Star Sapphire,** 3.9 litre 6-cylinder engine, automatic transmission, power steering, servo-assisted front disc/rear drum brakes, excellent condition.
£12,000–14,000 / $17,400–20,300 ⊞ ASOC

ARMSTRONG–SIDDELEY Model	ENGINE cc/cyl	DATES	CONDITION 1	2	3
Hurricane	1991/6	1945–53	£10,000	£7,000	£4,000
Typhoon	1991/6	1946–50	£7,000	£3,000	£2,000
Lancaster/Whitley	1991/ 2306/6	1945–53	£8,000	£5,500	£2,500
Sapphire 234/236	2290/4 2309/6	1955–58	£7,500	£5,000	£3,000
Sapphire 346	3440/6	1953–58	£9,000	£5,000	£2,000
Star Sapphire	3990/6	1958–60	£10,000	£7,000	£4,000

Aston Martin

Today, under Ford's ownership, the fabled Aston Martin marque is in the most secure position it has ever been. In fact, in many ways, it is quite remarkable that the company still exists at all, for throughout much of its life it has flirted with extinction on several occasions, with the receivers at the door.

The foundations of the company that became Aston Martin were laid in London's South Kensington in 1913, when engineers Robert Bamford and Lionel Martin, who had met years before through a shared interest in cycling, set themselves up under the name of Bamford as agents for Singer cars. Lionel Martin modified a Singer for competition use, and successes in various trials, hillclimbs and races, including a few outings at Brooklands, prompted interest in his 'hot' Singers. The fledgling company was soon modifying and improving Singers for existing owners, and offering its own tuned Singers for sale. Before long, they set their sights on producing a quality sports car of their own, which took shape in 1915 with a Coventry-Simplex four-cylinder engine fitted to an Isotta-Fraschini racing chassis. That car, in the creation of which Martin played the larger part, was named Aston-Martin (with a hyphen). The name Aston clearly set out the company's sporting and competition aspirations, as it referred to Aston Clinton, near Tring in Buckinghamshire, where Lionel Martin had enjoyed success in hillclimb trials.

Yet that first car remained the only Aston-Martin until about 1920, when a second prototype was produced, with limited production beginning in 1922. Over the next six years, a mere 60 or so Aston-Martins were produced as the company lurched through a series of problems. In 1925, when the firm had already been rescued once, by Lady Dorothea Charnwood, then succumbed to official receivership, its assets were bought by William Renwick and the talented, Italian-born engineer Augustus Bertelli, who set up in Feltham, Middlesex, as Aston Martin Motors Ltd. The hyphen had been dropped and, so too, had Lionel Martin and Robert Bamford.

The Bertelli era, as it has become known, brought a string of racing accomplishments in lower capacity classes at Le Mans and Brooklands, and in the 1935 Mille Miglia, together with a fine string of exclusive sports and competition cars. Yet finances remained on a knife edge as the company reeled from crisis to crisis. Bertelli had gone by 1937, and in 1946 an un-named car company was advertised for sale in *The Times*. The saviour this time was millionaire industrialist and tractor manufacturer David Brown, who early in 1947 bought Aston Martin for £20,000. Later in the year, he bought Lagonda. The chief benefit of the latter acquisition was W. O. Bentley's magnificent twin-cam engine, and thus began the era of the glamorous DB Aston Martins, which took their model names from the company owner's initials. In many ways, these were the glory years. The DB2 of 1950 utilised the 2.6 litre W.O. Bentley-Lagonda engine to full advantage in a surefooted chassis and handsome body with 115mph pace. With the later DB2/4, occasional rear seats were added, along with increasing refinement, both to the interior and exterior. While the DB2 still had a slightly rustic air about it, and even a little clumsiness in external styling detail, the DB2/4 possessed a fully harmonised sophistication. Meanwhile, Aston Martin was also scoring success in top-line competition, both in rallies and on the track, culminating in a 1959 Le Mans win for Carroll Shelby and Roy Salvadori in a DBR1.

Back on the road, the DB4 of 1958 was not just a thing of beauty, with its stunning body designed by Italian styling house Touring; it also offered prodigious performance, for under the bonnet was Tadek Marek's fabulous twin-cam straight-six engine, evolved from Aston's energetic racing programme. In short, the DB4 looked superb and went like stink, all the way to 140mph and beyond. It also stopped, thanks to its all-round servo-assisted disc brakes, and in 1958 David Brown orchestrated a headline grabbing stunt in which a DB4 accelerated to 100mph and braked to a standstill in less than 30 seconds. Back then, that was seriously heady stuff and so too was the price, a whopping £3,976, which in 1958 would have got you two Jaguar XK150s or very nearly nine Ford Populars. With the DB5, Aston Martin went into show business as the preferred transport for the world's most famous big-screen secret agent, James Bond.

Those were heady times, and in 1969 David Brown was knighted for services to the motor industry – and, quite possibly, philanthropy. He reckoned that Aston Martin ran at a loss of around £1 million a year during his ownership, and in 1972 he gave up the unequal struggle, selling the company, and its debts, for a nominal £1. In the next few years, the company came closer than ever to oblivion, closing its doors temporarily at the end of 1974 and calling in the receiver. After a series of twists and turns, Victor Gauntlett joined the board in 1980 and kept the company afloat until 1987, when Ford took control. At the time, there were fears that Ford might devalue the name. In fact, the reverse has happened, and today the legacy of Lionel Martin and David Brown lives on in the cars that bear their name.

ASTON MARTIN Model	ENGINE cc/cyl	DATES	CONDITION 1	2	3
Lionel Martin Cars	1486/4	1921–25	£26,000+	£18,000	£16,000
International	1486/4	1927–32	£40,000	£20,000	£16,000
Le Mans	1486/4	1932–33	£60,000	£40,000	£32,000
Mk II	1486/4	1934–36	£40,000	£30,000	£25,000
Ulster	1486/4	1934–36	£80,000+	£50,000	-
2 Litre	1950/4	1936–40	£40,000	£25,000	£18,000

Value is dependent upon racing history, originality and completeness.
Add 40% if a competition winner or works team car.

1930 Aston Martin International, restored over 30 years, engine with new block converted to shell bearings and uprated pre-war specification, finished in black with dark red wings, matching leather upholstery, 94th 1st-series model built, 1 family ownership for 66 years, excellent condition.
£55,000–60,000 / $79,750–87,000 ⚒ COYS
Designed by Augustus Bertelli, the Aston Martin International was announced at the 1928 Motor Show, where it attracted much attention.
A contemporary road test showed a top speed of 81mph, but 90mph is considered more realistic.

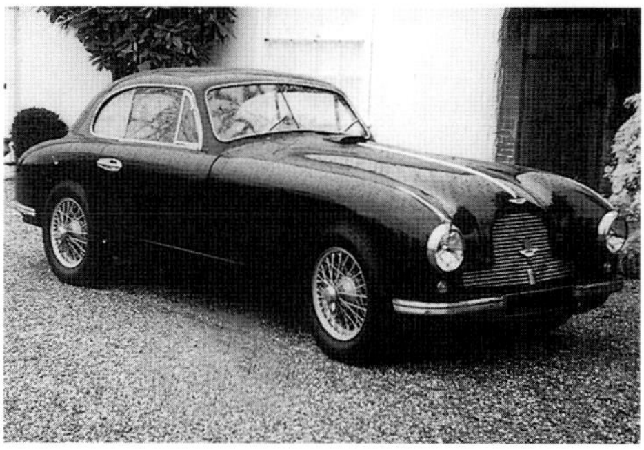

1953 Aston Martin DB2 Vantage, completely restored 1992, finished in dark blue, light blue leather interior, 4,000 miles covered since restoration, excellent condition throughout.
£40,000–45,000 / $58,000–65,250 ⚒ BARO

1937 Aston Martin 15/98 2 Litre Touring Saloon, 2 litre overhead-camshaft 4-cylinder engine, Moss synchromesh gearbox, restored, finished in British racing green, light tan hide interior, good condition throughout.
£14,500–17,000 / $21,000–24,700 ⚒ BKS

1954 Aston Martin DB2/4 Mk II Drophead Coupé, 3 litre double-overhead-camshaft engine, subject of body-off restoration, converted to right-hand drive, Alfin brake drums, new headlights and reflectors, bare-metal respray in white, red hide upholstery.
£37,000–44,000 / $53,500–63,500 ⚒ BKS
Launched in the spring of 1954, the 3 litre engine was initially available only in the drophead model, but by August 1954 it was also offered for the fixed-head coupé. In 1954, the buyer of a drophead coupé would have to spend £2,910, at a time when that amount of money would have bought a very substantial detached property. This car's history includes an appearance in the British film classic *Two Way Stretch*. It is believed also to have been used in 1964 in the film *The Seventh Dawn*.

Aston Martin DB2/4 Mk I & II (1953–57)

Production: 763.
Body styles: Four-seater saloon, fixed-head coupé, drophead coupé.
Engine: Double-overhead-camshaft, six-cylinder, 2580cc; 2922cc from 1954.
Power output: 125bhp @ 5,000rpm for 2580cc; 140bhp @ 5,000rpm for 2992cc.
Transmission: Four-speed manual.
Brakes: Drums all-round.
Maximum speed: 115+mph.
0–60mph: 12.6 seconds for 2580cc; 10 seconds for 2992cc.

Evolved from the two-seat DB2, the 2/4 added two occasional rear seats for practicality. As for the styling, the DB2/4 merely states what it is, suggesting honest durability rather than the Gucci-loafer glitz that came later when Astons clothed themselves in Italian designer wear. Indeed, the whole thing is something of a durable brogue. With its solid chassis and confident gait to match its 115+mph pace, it is also pretty rugged, at least compared with the delicate nerves of later, far more complex and highly strung Astons. In fact, the DB2/4 is the nearest thing to a viable DIY Aston, with an engine that is not as marginally tuned as those of later models and Triumph Herald-like access under that one-piece bonnet. Cheaper to own and run than a Bond-era Aston, understated and, quite possibly, under-valued too, that is the DB2/4.

1956 Aston Martin DB2/4 Mk II Drophead Coupé, coachwork by Tickford, 2.9 litre engine, 140bhp, full chassis and suspension rebuild, engine, gearbox, brakes and rear axle overhauled, new steering box, wheels rebuilt, new wiring loom, bare-metal respray in metallic green, beige Everflex hood, reupholstered in beige hide with beige Wilton carpets, new rubber trim, mouldings and badging, all brightwork polished and replated.
£40,000–45,000 / $58,000–65,250 BKS
Joining the fastback DB2/4 in 1955 was the Tickford-built notchback (with a permanent hardtop) and a drophead coupé, of which few were built. When restoration of this car, which was built as a notchback, began in 1986, a decision was taken not to refit the hardtop. Instead, the normal Tickford-designed folding hood was fitted in its place, carefully retaining all other Tickford features.

1958 Aston Martin DB2/4 Mk III, 2922cc engine, uprated to 178bhp, twin stainless-steel exhausts, manual gearbox with overdrive, restored at a cost of over £30,000, finished in red, grey/red interior, 74,500 miles from new, excellent condition throughout.
£22,000–25,000 / $31,900–36,250 H&H

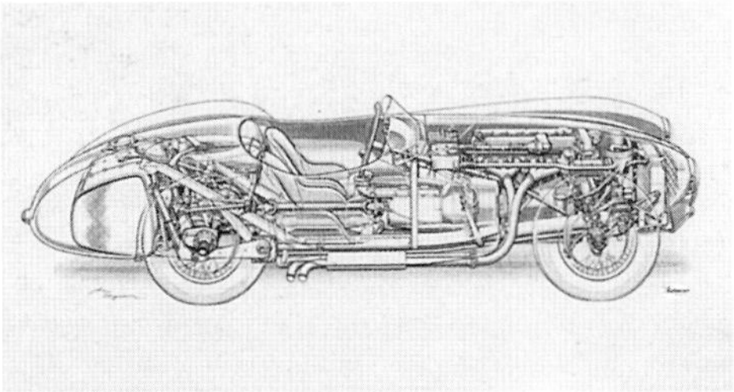

An Aston Martin DB3S pen and Indian ink cut-away, signed by John Ferguson, applied with *The Autocar* copyright stamp and dated in pencil, '5th February 1954', slight damage to edges, 14in x 28in (35 x 71cm).
£450–550 / $650–800 BKS

◀ **1959 Aston Martin DB2/4 Drophead Coupé,** double-overhead-camshaft, 6-cylinder engine, 180bhp, 4-speed manual gearbox, Girling front disc brakes, rear Alfin drum brakes, wire wheels, completely restored, finished in red, tan roof, red interior.
£50,000–55,000
$72,500–79,750 RM

ASTON MARTIN Model	ENGINE cc/cyl	DATES	CONDITION 1	2	3
DB1	1970/4	1948–50	£30,000+	£20,000	£16,000
DB2	2580/6	1950–53	£30,000+	£18,000	£14,000
DB2 Conv	2580/6	1951–53	£45,000+	£28,000+	£17,000
DB2/4 Mk I/II	2580/ 2922/6	1953–57	£30,000	£18,000	£14,000
DB2/4 Mk II Conv	2580/ 2922/6	1953–57	£45,000	£30,000	£15,000
DB Mk III Conv	2922/6	1957–59	£45,000	£28,000	£18,000
DB Mk III	2922/6	1957–59	£30,000	£20,000	£15,000
DB4	3670/6	1959–63	£40,000+	£25,000+	£16,000
DB4 Conv	3670/6	1961–63	£60,000+	£35,000+	-
DB4 GT	3670/6	1961–63	£140,000+	£100,000	-
DB5	3995/6	1964–65	£45,000	£30,000	£20,000
DB5 Conv	3995/6	1964–65	£55,000+	£38,000	-
DB6	3995/6	1965–69	£30,000	£20,000	£16,000
DB6 Mk I auto	3995/6	1965–69	£28,000	£18,000	£14,000
DB6 Mk I Volante	3995/6	1965–71	£50,000+	£32,000+	£28,000
DB6 Mk II Volante	3995/6	1969–70	£60,000+	£40,000+	£30,000
DBS	3995/6	1967–72	£15,000+	£15,000	£9,000
AM Vantage	5340/8	1972–73	£15,000	£12,000	£9,000
V8 Vantage Oscar India	5340/8	1978–82	£30,000+	£20,000	£10,000
V8 Volante	5340/8	1978–82	£45,000+	£30,000	£25,000

Works/competition history is an important factor, as is Vantage specification.

Aston Martin DB4 (1958–63)

Production: 1,040 (fixed-head); 70 (convertible); 95 fixed-head DB4 GT (including 19 Zagato-bodied cars).
Body style: Fixed-head coupé or convertible.
Construction: Pressed-steel and tubular inner chassis frame, aluminium outer panels.
Engine: Double-overhead-camshaft, six-cylinder, 3670cc; 3749cc for some GTs.
Power output: 240bhp @ 5,500rpm.
Transmission: Four-speed manual (with optional overdrive).
Suspension: Front: independent by wishbones, coil springs and telescopic dampers. Rear: live axle located by trailing arms and Watts linkage with coil springs and lever-arm dampers.
Brakes: Servo-assisted Dunlop discs front and rear.
Maximum speed: 140+mph.
0–60mph: 8 seconds (less for GT and GT Zagato).
0–100mph: 20.1 seconds (less for GT and GT Zagato).
Average fuel consumption: 14–22mpg.
The debut of the DB4 in 1958 heralded the beginning of the Aston Martin glory years, ushering in the breed of classic six-cylinder DB Astons that propelled the marque on to the world stage. Earlier post-war Astons were fine sporting enthusiasts' road cars, but with the DB4, Astons acquired a new grace, sophistication and refinement that was, for many, the ultimate expression of the grand tourer theme. Clothed in an Italian designer suit by Touring of Milan, it possessed a graceful, yet powerful, elegance. Under the aluminium body was Tadek Marek's fabulous race-bred, twin-cam straight-six engine.

1961 Aston Martin DB4, manual gearbox with overdrive, chrome wire wheels, original right-hand drive, completely restored 1989–94, finished in pearl blue, cream leather interior, blue carpets.
£50,000–60,000 / $72,500–87,000 ⊞ TSG

1961 Aston Martin DB4, 3.7 litre double-overhead-camshaft 6-cylinder engine, twin SU carburettors, 265bhp, 4-speed manual gearbox, independent front suspension, Salisbury live rear axle located by trailing arms and Watts linkage, 4-wheel disc brakes.
£30,000–35,000 / $43,500–50,000 ⚒ RM

► **1962 Aston Martin DB4,** engine rebuilt, converted to unleaded fuel, overdrive gearbox, handling kit, finished in British racing green, red hide interior.
£70,000–80,000 / $101,500–116,000 ⊞ RSW

Cross Reference
See Colour Review (page 66)

1961 Aston Martin DB4 GT, coachwork by Touring, 4 litre double-overhead-camshaft 6-cylinder engine, new stainless steel silencers, new fuel pump, finished in metallic green, green leather upholstery, factory-fitted rear child seats, excellent condition.
£125,000–140,000 / $182,000–200,000 ⚒ BKS
In 1959, Aston Martin introduced its race-bred DB4 GT, bodied by Touring. The 3.7 litre, twin-cam six-cylinder engine matched the car's fine lines by producing 302bhp at 6,000rpm. A platform-type chassis replaced the multi-tubular structure of the preceding DB2/4 series, which was considered incompatible with Touring's *Superleggera* body construction system, since this employed its own lightweight tubular superstructure to support the aluminium skin. The DB2/4's trailing-link independent front suspension also made way for unequal-length wishbones, while at the rear the DB4 sported a well-located live axle in place of its predecessor's De Dion arrangement. This example was used in the British classic film *The Wrong Arm of the Law*, made in 1962 and starring Peter Sellers.

◄ **1963 Aston Martin DB4 Series IV Convertible,** 3670cc double-overhead-camshaft aluminium 6-cylinder engine, 240bhp, coil spring/wishbone independent front suspension, coil-sprung rear axle located by Watts linkage and parallel trailing arms, 4-wheel disc brakes, aluminium body, converted to unleaded fuel, rear axle rebuilt at a cost of £7,000, finished in light metallic blue, black leather interior, 1 of 70 DB4 convertibles built, of which only 29 were Series IV cars, well maintained.
£60,000–70,000 / $87,000–101,500 ⚒ COYS

1965 Aston Martin DB5, 3670cc double-overhead-camshaft aluminium 6-cylinder engine, uprated to Vantage specification with triple Weber carburettors and Vantage camshafts, cylinder head converted to unleaded fuel, aluminium radiator, Kenlowe fan, upgraded starter, ZF 5-speed gearbox, chrome wire wheels, £30,000 spent on restoration since 1998, finished in metallic light green, interior retrimmed in magnolia leather.
£70,000–80,000 / $101,500–116,000 ⚒ BKS

A JAK cartoon, *'OK 007, where's the fire?'*, depicting a confrontation between the Dallas County Sheriff's Department and an Aston Martin DB5 owner in 1966, 49 x 29in (124.5 x 74cm).
£700–900 / $1,000–1,300 ⚒ BKS

Miller's Compares

I. 1968 Aston Martin DB6 Drophead, 3995cc, manual 5-speed ZF gearbox, power steering, originally a saloon, converted and restored 1989–90 at a cost of over £40,000, engine rebuilt, new braking system, new wire wheels, brightwork rechromed, resprayed in red, retrimmed in black leather, mohair hood, very good condition.
£25,000–30,000 / $36,250–43,500 ⚒ H&H

II. 1968 Aston Martin DB6 Mk I Volante, 3995cc engine, triple SU carburettors, 282bhp, ZF 5-speed manual gearbox, engine rebuilt, blue Connolly leather interior, very good condition throughout.
£70,000–80,000 / $101,500–116,000 ⚒ BKS
In all, 1,575 DB6s were made between 1965 and 1970, but of these only 140 were Volantes.

Item I is aptly described as a DB6 drophead, rather than a Volante, the correct factory designation for convertible. This is because it started life as a coupé and subsequently was converted. Undertaking the conversion is understandable when you consider the rarity of the true Volantes; around 140 were built. Even so, as our valuations show, a conversion will rarely come anywhere near the value of a true original. This is also true of other conversions, including those on Ferrari Daytonas and Maseratis.

◀ **1969 Aston Martin DB6 Mk II,** 3995cc engine, manual gearbox, finished in gold, interior trimmed in navy blue.
£28,000–34,000 / $40,500–48,500 ⚒ H&H

1970 Aston Martin DB6 Mk II, 3995cc engine, DBS-type wire wheels, power steering, finished in olive green, beige interior, 35,000 miles from new, excellent original condition throughout.
£40,000–45,000 / $58,000–65,250 ⚒ COYS

◀ **1970 Aston Martin DB6 Mk I,** 5-speed manual gearbox, power steering, air conditioning, finished in metallic light blue, black leather interior, 96,000 miles from new.
£18,000–22,000 / $26,000–32,000 ⊞ VIC

1970 Aston Martin DB6 Mk II Vantage, 3995cc double-overhead-camshaft 6-cylinder engine, 325bhp, completely restored at a cost of over £45,000, all mechanical systems overhauled or replaced as necessary, engine converted to unleaded fuel, stainless-steel exhaust system, bare-metal respray, original Connolly leather interior.
£45,000–50,000 / $65,250–72,500 ⚒ COYS

1973 Aston Martin AM Vantage, 3995cc 6-cylinder engine, 325bhp, 148mph top speed, automatic transmission, chrome wheels, finished in grey, cream leather interior, 41,500 miles from new, original specification in all major respects, good condition overall.
£13,000–16,000 / $18,850–23,200 ⚒ BKS
The AM Vantage was introduced as a so-called 'economy' model. Styling changes from the DBS included the redesigned grille, which reverted to two 7in headlights, and a nose profile more reminiscent of the DB Mk II and DB4 models. Approximately 70 AM Vantages were built.

1971 Aston Martin DBS, 3995cc double-overhead-camshaft 6-cylinder engine, manual gearbox, chrome wire wheels, stainless-steel exhaust, £18,000 spent on engine and bodywork, finished in red, red leather interior, 71,000 miles from new.
£16,000–19,000 / $23,200–27,500 ⊞ TSG

1971 Aston Martin DBS, 3995cc 6-cylinder engine, manual gearbox, restored at a cost of £18,000, finished in red, red leather interior, new carpets, engine and gearbox in excellent condition.
£10,000–12,000 / $14,500–17,500 ⚒ BRIT
The DBS was the first Aston Martin to feature William Towns' striking new design, being produced between 1967 and 1972. The previous live rear axle had been replaced with a De Dion set-up, which gave improved ride and further enhanced handling. Only 860 examples were produced before the DBS was replaced by the 1972/73 Vantage model, making the six-cylinder DBS comparatively rare.

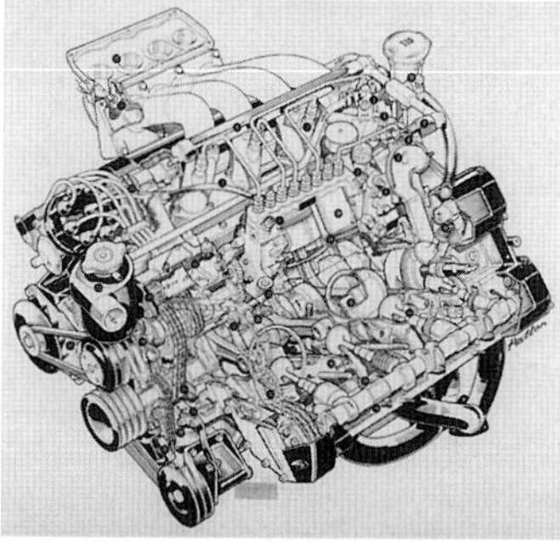

A cut-away of an Aston Martin V8 engine, in pen and Indian ink, heightened with white, signed by Brian Hatton, dated September 1969, 22 x 27in (56 x 68cm).
£1,000–1,500 / $1,450–2,200 ⚒ BKS

Auction prices

Miller's only includes cars declared sold. Our guide prices take into account the buyer's premium, VAT on the premium, and the extent of any published catalogue information relating to condition and provenance. Cars sold at auction are identified by the ⚒ icon; full details of the auction house can be found on page 330.

1973 Aston Martin DBS V8, 5340cc V8 engine, automatic transmission, De Dion rear axle, 4-wheel disc brakes, finished in red, black leather interior.
£13,000–16,000 / $18,850–23,200 ⚒ Pou

1974 Aston Martin V8, 5340cc V8 engine, 3-speed automatic transmission, stainless-steel exhaust, alloy wheels, electric sunroof, resprayed in blue, blue interior, 45,000 miles from new, excellent condition.
£15,000–17,000 / $21,750–24,750 ⚒ H&H

1977 Aston Martin V8, 5340cc V8 engine, Weber carburettors, finished in red, excellent condition throughout.
£16,000–18,000 / $23,200–26,200 BARO
With the departure of David Brown, Aston Martin dropped the DB prefix from the model range, and the DBS V8 became the Aston Martin V8.

1979 Aston Martin V8 Volante, automatic transmission, road test mileage only since full rebuild, finished in royal blue, dark blue hide interior.
£70,000–80,000 / $101,500–116,000 RSW

1979 Aston Martin V8, 5340cc V8 engine, sills and A-frames rebuilt, later-specification BBS alloy wheels, resprayed 1997, engine rebuilt and converted to unleaded fuel 1998, finished in dark green, beige leather interior.
£15,000–18,000 / $21,750–26,000 BRIT
The Series IV Aston Martin V8 was launched late in 1978, and boasted a revised bonnet and restyled tail incorporating a spoiler on the boot lid. Known at the factory as 'Oscar India', the new model also featured a redesigned interior with wood trim, leather headlining and an improved air conditioning system.

1980 Aston Martin V8, Weber 42DCNF carburettors, automatic transmission, finished in red, black leather interior, good condition throughout.
£14,000–17,000 / $20,300–24,600 BKS

1977 Aston Martin V8 Vantage, X-specification engine rebuilt 1997, sports exhaust, polished 16in road wheels, original GKN wheels, factory handling kit, finished in blue, magnolia interior.
£22,000–25,000 / $31,900–36,250 BKS
Continuing the marque's tradition of offering a higher-performance version of the standard car, the 1977 Vantage specification included an engine with revised cams, valves and carburettors, developing close to 400bhp. The extra power together with revisions to the suspension geometry, springs, dampers, wheels and tyres, as well as subtle body modifications following wind-tunnel testing, led *Motor* magazine to describe it as 'startlingly impressive'. Contemporary issues of *The Guinness Book of Records* confirmed the Vantage as the fastest accelerating production car.

1979 Aston Martin V8 Volante, 5340cc double-overhead-camshaft V8 engine, upper and lower wishbone independent front suspension, de Dion rear suspension, 4-wheel disc brakes, 42,000 miles from new, original condition.
£25,000–30,000 / $36,250–43,500 RM

1979 Aston Martin V8, automatic transmission, restored at a cost of £30,000, engine upgraded to Vantage specification, converted to unleaded fuel, finished in silver, red leather interior, excellent condition.
£21,000–24,000 / $30,500–34,800 BKS
A heavier car than its six-cylinder predecessor, the V8 suffered as emissions legislation became ever more strangulating, leading to concern that Aston Martin's traditional performance image might be lost. The arrival of the Vantage dispelled any such worries. Propelling Aston's V8 back into the supercar league was a tuned version of the existing 5340cc engine, breathing through a quartet of 48mm Weber carburettors rather than the standard 42mm units. Valves and ports were enlarged and the camshafts changed, the result being an estimated maximum output of around 375bhp. Chassis changes were minimal, apart from the adoption of larger ventilated discs all-round, revised springing and damping, and low-profile Pirelli tyres. Nevertheless, the Vantage was readily distinguishable from the standard product by virtue of its blocked-off bonnet scoop, blanked air intake, front chin spoiler and lip on the boot lid.

1985 Aston Martin V8 Vantage, manual gearbox, finished in dark grey, parchment hide interior, 48,000 miles from new.
£50,000–55,000 / $72,500–79,750 ⊞ RSW

1987 Aston Martin Vantage Volante, automatic transmission, finished in metallic grey, black hide interior, 10,000 miles from new.
£85,000–95,000 / $123,250–137,750 ⊞ RSW

1988 Aston Martin V8 Volante, 5340cc double-overhead-camshaft V8 engine, 397bhp, upper-and-lower-wishbone independent front suspension, De Dion rear suspension, 4-wheel disc brakes, finished in magnolia, magnolia interior with red piping, 1 owner and 7,800 miles from new, original condition.
£50,000–60,000 / $72,500–87,000 ⚒ RM

1989 Aston Martin V8 Vantage Volante 'Prince of Wales', finished in graphite grey, black hood, burgundy hide interior, 1 owner and 12,500 miles from new.
£95,000–105,000 / $137,750–152,750 ⚒ BKS
Produced to satisfy demands from the USA, the Volante convertible debuted in 1978, but did not become available to Vantage specification until 1986. Along with the Vantage engine came flared wheel arches, a boot spoiler and an extended front spoiler, while sill extensions replaced the model's hitherto characteristic stainless steel sill covers. The result was a muscular, aggressive-looking car that could justifiably claim to be the world's fastest convertible. Not all Aston Martin customers found the look to their liking, however, preferring the more restrained appearance of the earlier model. Foremost among these was HRH The Prince of Wales, whose Volante was built with Vantage engine and chassis, but otherwise effectively to standard specification. The factory went on to build 25 examples to the 'Prince of Wales' specification before production finally ceased in December 1989.

◀ **1979 Aston Martin Lagonda,** 5340cc V8 engine, electronic fuel injection, 375bhp, automatic transmission, 4-wheel independent suspension, 4-wheel disc brakes, finished in black.
£15,000–17,000
$21,750–24,750 ⚒ Pou

▶ **1991 Aston Martin Virage,** 5.3 litre V8 engine, 4 valves per cylinder, electronic fuel injection and engine management system, automatic transmission, 0–60mph in 6 seconds, 155mph top speed, finished in black, mushroom hide upholstery piped in black, walnut veneer interior trims, slight transmission bearing noise, otherwise good general condition.
£38,000–44,000
$55,000–64,000 ⚒ BKS

Auburn

An American Auburn showroom poster, linen backed, fold marks, 1930, 38 x 28in (96.5 x 71cm).
£275–325 / $400–470 ⚒ RM

1933 Auburn Rumble Seat Roadster, 8-cylinder Lycoming engine, folding top, wind-up windows, completely restored, finished in red and cream, excellent condition.
£70,000–80,000 / $101,500–116,000 ⚒ BJ

► 1935 Auburn 851 Speedster, Lycoming 8-cylinder inline engine, supercharger, restored, finished in red, excellent condition.
£60,000–70,000
$87,000–101,500 ⚒ BJ
Each Auburn 851 Speedster was driven at 100mph prior to delivery to the customer.

Audi

1986 Audi 200 Quattro Treser, 2144cc 5-cylinder engine, turbocharger, full Treser conversion, lowered suspension, Bilstein shock absorbers, alloy wheels, believed to have been converted from new, finished in blue, leather Recaro interior, 67,000 miles from new.
£2,250–2,750 / $3,200–4,000 ⚒ H&H
This Quattro features a conversion developed by former Audi rally team manager, Walter Treser.

1986 Audi Quattro, 2.1 litre 5-cylinder engine, KKK turbocharger, 200bhp, 4-wheel drive, finished in metallic dark blue, black leather interior.
£5,000–6,000 / $7,250–8,750 ⚒ BKS

1987 Audi Quattro Treser Turbo Coupé, 2144cc, stainless-steel exhaust system, 4-wheel drive, 17in alloy wheels, restored, finished in pearl white, red leather interior, 79,000 miles from new.
£7,500–8,500 / $10,800–12,350 ⚒ H&H

Austin

The Austin marque finally disappeared in 1987, yet throughout the company's life, from its foundation in 1905, the name ran through the mainstream of the British motor industry. Rarely were Austins glamorous, but generally they possessed the stout virtues of solid dependability based on sensible engineering rather than fanciful technical wizardry. At various times in its history, Austin was the largest British car maker. As for the cars, Austin's greatest legacy must surely be the two modest machines that transformed British motoring on each side of a world war. The Austin 7 of 1922 brought motoring en masse to the middle classes, and in 1959 the new Austin Se7en, as it was originally badged, brought motoring to millions in a pocket-sized world beater better known as the Mini. Today, only a few early Austins are beyond the pocket of the ordinary enthusiast, and virtually every post-war model can be maintained with relative ease by a competent home mechanic. From the 1950s into the 1970s, many Austin models were offered with only slight variations in trim, decoration and specification as Morris, MG, Wolseley, Riley and Vanden Plas.

Two original Austin Motor Company Ltd photograph albums, covering the period 1906–08, Album 1 containing 81 monochrome images, Album 2 14 images, each image approximately 11 x 9in (28 x 23cm) depicting the works, vehicles, machining and 100hp racing car, hard covers.
£1,400–1,600 / $2,000–2,300 ⚒ BKS

The Austin 7 was made under licence in several countries: France (as the Rosengart), the USA (as the Bantam), in Japan (by Nissan) and in Germany (as the Dixi). The Dixi was the first motor car assembled by BMW.

1928/48 Austin Tractor, 747cc, converted from a 1928 Austin 7 in 1948, restored, finished in blue and black, black interior, very good condition.
£3,000–3,500 / $4,300–5,000 ⚒ H&H
This vehicle was built by William Richard Gill of Ely, Cambridgeshire, as a ploughing tractor. He fitted two gate-change gearboxes to enable it to travel slowly at high revs, and to give it the power needed to perform its job.

1929 Austin 7 Two-Seat Boat-Tail Tourer, restored, finished in red with black wings, folding hood, maroon interior, good condition throughout.
£5,250–6,500 / $7,600–9,500 ⚒ BKS
A huge success from the moment deliveries began in January 1923, the Austin 7 remained in production until 1939. At first, the sole version available was the Chummy tourer, but by 1927, saloon, fabric saloon and coupé versions were on offer. The two-seat tourer of 1929 was the first production 7 made with this type of coachwork since the 1925 Sports model; only six are believed to have survived, this car being the oldest.

1932 Austin 7 Swallow Saloon Mk II, 747cc sidevalve 4-cylinder engine, 3-speed gearbox, mechanical brakes, wire wheels, twin chromed scuttle ventilators, hinged windscreen, ash-framed bodywork, silvered 'houbigant' ladies companion set, rear window shade, smoker's vent, Wilton carpets, mahogany dashboard and door trims, completely restored, finished in red and cream, interior in Connolly hide, believed to be the last Swallow Saloon built.
£20,000–23,000 / $29,000–33,350 ⚒ RM
Capitalising on the success of the Austin 7, many independent coachbuilders produced special-bodied variants of the diminutive car. Among them was the Swallow Sidecar Company, which would go on to develop the legendary Jaguar SS models of the 1930s.

AUSTIN Model	ENGINE cc/cyl	DATES	CONDITION 1	2	3
7 Swallow 2 Seater Sports	747/4	1927–32	£11,000	£8,500	£7,000
7 Swallow 4 Seater Saloon	747/7	1929–32	£10,000	£7,500	£6,000

AUSTIN Model	ENGINE cc/cyl	DATES	CONDITION 1	2	3
25/30	4900/4	1906	£35,000	£25,000	£20,000
20/4	3600/4	1919–29	£20,000	£12,000	£6,000
12	1661/4	1922–26	£8,000	£5,000	£2,000
7/Chummy	747/4	1924–39	£7,000	£5,000	£2,500
7 Coachbuilt/Nippy/Opal etc	747/4	1924–39	£10,000	£9,000	£7,000
12/4	1861/4	1927–35	£5,500	£5,000	£2,000
16	2249/6	1928–36	£9,000	£7,000	£4,000
20/6	3400/6	1928–38	£12,500	£10,000	£8,000
12/6	1496/6	1932–37	£6,000	£4,000	£1,500
12/4	1535/4	1933–39	£5,000	£3,500	£1,500
10 and 10/4	1125/4	1932–47	£4,000	£3,000	£1,000
10 and 10/4 Conv	1125/4	1933–47	£5,000+	£3,500	£1,000
18	2510/6	1934–39	£8,000	£5,000	£3,000
14	1711/6	1937–39	£6,000	£4,000	£2,000
Big Seven	900/4	1938–39	£4,000	£2,500	£1,500
8	900/4	1939–47	£3,000	£2,000	£1,000
28	4016/6	1939	£6,000	£4,000	£2,000

Prices for early Austin models are dependent on body style: landaulette, tourer, etc. eg. Austin Heavy 12/4 Tourer will command a higher price.

Miller's Starter Marque

- **Post-war Starter Austins:** *A55/60 Cambridge; A90/95/99/105/110 Westminster; Nash Metropolitan; A30/35/40; 1100 and 1300.*
- Although post-war Austin models were pretty populous, not all are in plentiful supply. Those we have chosen above are blessed with a good survival rate, spares and club support, and generally possess those Austin virtues of sturdy and sensible dependability.
- One of the most engaging Austins of the post-war era is the Austin/Nash Metropolitan. They should really have called it the Neopolitan, for this quaint little dolly-mixture of a car came in a choice of dazzling ice-cream colours – red, yellow and turquoise over white. The hardtop versions all had white roofs and lower bodies, making them resemble a white-sliced sandwich with a variety of sickly fillings. The Metropolitan was initially built by Austin for the American Nash company as a 'sub-compact' or two-thirds-scale Yank tank, available over here from 1957.

1932 Austin 7 Saloon, completely restored, finished in blue and black, good condition.
£6,000–7,000 / $8,700–10,200 ⊞ WILM

1935 Austin 7 Two-Seater Sports, 750cc, twin aero screens, polished aluminium body, black bonnet, black interior, dry stored since 1993.
£3,750–4,500 / $5,500–6,500 ⚒ H&H

◄ **1934 Austin 7 Saloon,** original specification, finished in dark blue with black wings, blue leather interior, excellent condition.
£4,500–5,000 / $6,500–7,250 ⊞ AS

Austin 7 (1922–39)

Price in 1923: £165 (about the annual salary of a well-paid engineer).
Engine: Water-cooled 4-cylinder of 747.5cc.
Transmission: 3-speed manual; 4-speed from 1933.
Power: 13–23bhp.
Top Speed: 45+mph.
The diminutive Austin 7 introduced real motoring in miniature to first-time car owners all over the world. From its launch in 1922, it was acclaimed as a 'scaled-down motor car, rather than scaled-up motorcycling', and eventually it sold more than 375,000. Today, its cheeky charm will still raise a chuckle, even if you are stuck behind one teetering along a country lane with the meandering gate of a drunk pushing a supermarket trolley. Today, the Austin 7 offers an affordable introduction to vintage-style motoring and the friendly competition of the Vintage Sportscar Club.

1937 Austin 7 Ruby Deluxe, 4-cylinder sidevalve engine, finished in blue and black, navy blue interior, original.
£3,500–4,250 / $5,000–6,000 ⊞ UMC

Here is something you can try at home: the Austin 7 will fit on a full-size billiard table – that is because the original plans for the Austin 7 were drawn up on a billiard table at Herbert Austin's home, Lickey Grange.

1933 Austin 10/4 Saloon, 1125cc 4-cylinder engine, new exhaust front pipe, new track rod ends, pre-focused headlamp units (original headlamp rims and lenses included), finished in correct blue and black, original dark blue leather interior, good condition throughout.
£3,750–4,500 / $5,500–6,500 ⚒ BRIT
At its introduction in April 1932, the Austin 10/4 filled the gap between the 7hp range and the recently introduced Light 12/6. Well received, it went on to become a bestseller and was developed progressively, a 10hp model remaining in Austin catalogues until 1947. Today, the earlier chrome-radiator models, produced between 1932 and 1934, are the most sought-after.

1930 Austin 12 Two-Seater and Dickey, original specification in every major respect, full weather equipment including sidescreens and hood, running-board foot mats, finished in maroon and black, black leather upholstery, concours winner.
£10,500–12,000 / $15,250–17,500 ⚒ BKS
The 1922 season was a landmark year for Austin, seeing the introduction of the 7hp and 12hp models, which would put the company on a sound financial footing. The 12hp model was powered by a conventional four-cylinder, sidevalve engine and, like its 20hp big brother, reflected just a hint of American influence. Its lazy, long-stroke engine proved very reliable, so much so that many vintage Austins continued to give service as farm vehicles, long after their passenger carrying duties had ended. Coachwork on the Austin 12 was quintessentially British, and it was offered in saloon, tourer and two-seater-with-dickey guises.

1938 Austin 7 Opal Two-Seater Tourer, older restoration, finished in dark blue, blue interior trim, excellent condition.
£7,000–8,000 / $10,150–11,600 ⊞ TSG

1936 Austin 10 Four-Door Saloon, 1125cc 4-cylinder engine, finished in green and black, 53,878 miles from new, in need of restoration.
£1,700–2,200 / $2,500–3,200 ⚒ RBB

1952 Austin Sheerline Shooting Brake, coachwork by Harold Radford, 3995cc 6-cylinder engine, leather upholstery, thought to be the only example built on a Sheerline chassis, original, good condition.
£12,000–14,000 / $17,400–20,300 COYS
Harold Radford conceived the idea for this shooting brake style, a derivative of the Radford Countryman, in his bath, having been inspired by multi-role wartime military personnel cars. It was designed to appeal to the sporting gentleman, and the concept was referred to in promotional literature as 'a saloon car with exceptional smartness and unusually commodious luggage accommodation.' A significant advantage of the early Countryman and shooting-brake models was that they were classed as commercial vehicles for taxation purposes, and therefore were exempt from the 66.6 per cent purchase tax – but this also meant that technically they were restricted to a 30mph speed limit.

1953 Austin A40 Somerset, 1500cc 4-cylinder Riley engine, finished in grey, good original tan interior, last used 1990, in need of recommissioning.
£700–900 / $1,000–1,300 CGC

1950 Austin A90 Atlantic Convertible, 2660cc 4-cylinder engine, original home-market model, correct specification, recently restored, finished in metallic green, tan leather interior, matching vinyl hood.
£10,500–12,500 / $15,250–18,000 BRIT
Due to the adverse economic conditions immediately after WWII, the British motor industry was under government pressure to 'export or die'. Efforts were largely directed toward the North American market with its vast potential, although it quickly became apparent that the average British car was largely unsuitable for the road conditions of the USA. Austin addressed this situation with the striking A90 Atlantic. The shape was quite daring, and far more in the modern idiom than other export-orientated cars of the period, like the Riley and Triumph Roadsters. A bench front seat was fitted, together with a column gear change, while the hood and windows were power operated (optional on home-market models). The 2660cc engine, with twin SU carburettors, delivered 88bhp at 4,000rpm. When road tested by the motoring press, the top speed was found to be around 90mph – no mean feat considering the Atlantic's kerb weight of 2,800lb. Despite a substantial cut in price and an impressive publicity campaign in 1949, the envisaged export success was not to be, the Atlantic struggling against rapidly developing and keenly priced indigenous products. The campaign involved two cars being taken to Indianapolis and culminated in a run covering some 11,870 miles over seven days and nights at an average speed of 70.68mph, beating the previous record set by a Studebaker. During this exercise, 63 other records were broken, but US sales were disappointing, which resulted in the burgeoning Australian and South African markets being targeted. By early 1950, the car was available in the UK, a two-door saloon having been announced in 1949. It featured a fabric-covered roof and three-piece rear window with opening centre section. This model sold alongside the convertible until production ceased in 1952.

A known continuous history can add value to and enhance the enjoyment of a car.

Austin A30/A35 (1951–59)

Body styles: Two- and four-door saloon, Countryman estate, van and pick-up (very rare, only 947 produced).
Engine: 803cc (A30) and 948cc (A35), overhead-valve four-cylinder.
Transmission: Four-speed manual.
Brakes: Hydro-mechanical drums.
Power output: 28bhp @ 4,500rpm (A30); 34bhp @ 5,100rpm (A35).
0–60mph: 38 seconds (A30); 29 seconds (A35).
Maximum speed: 65mph (A30); 75mph (A35).
Fuel consumption: 35–45mpg.
Price in 1951: £529.
Production: 576,672.
When the baby Austin A30 appeared in 1951, this peanut-shaped and sized four-seater was intended to rival the Morris Minor, launched in 1948, but shortly after the baby Austin appeared, the two rivals merged under the BMC banner. Even though it was a moderate success the Austin was rather overshadowed by the million-selling Minor. Nevertheless, the A30 was a pert and capable economy package. It was the first Austin to feature unitary construction and initially was powered by a peppy little 803cc overhead-valve engine, the first of the famous A-series engines that went on to power the Mini and the Metro. In 1956, the A30 was updated to become the A35. Externally it featured a larger rear window and other detail changes, but underneath had a 948cc engine that considerably improved performance. Saloon production ended in 1959 with the arrival of the Mini, but A35 vans continued through to 1968.
Pick of the bunch: The bigger-engined A35. If the conditions are right, with a following gale, you might even contemplate overtaking.

AUSTIN Model	ENGINE cc/cyl	DATES	CONDITION 1	2	3
16	2199/4	1945–49	£3,000	£2,000	£1,000
A40 Devon	1200/4	1947–52	£2,000	£1,200	£750
A40 Sports	1200/4	1950–53	£6,000	£4,000	£2,000
A40 Somerset	1200/4	1952–54	£2,000	£1,500	£750
A40 Somerset DHC	1200/4	1954	£5,000	£4,000	£2,500
A40 Dorset 2-door	1200/4	1947–48	£2,000	£1,500	£1,000
A70 Hampshire	2199/4	1948–50	£3,000	£1,500	£1,000
A70 Hereford	2199/4	1950–54	£3,000	£1,500	£1,000
A90 Atlantic DHC	2660/4	1949–52	£10,000	£6,000	£4,000
A90 Atlantic	2660/4	1949–52	£6,000	£4,000	£3,000
A40/A50 Cambridge	1200/4	1954–57	£1,200	£750	£500
A55 Mk I Cambridge	1489/4	1957–59	£1,000	£750	£500
A55 Mk II	1489/4	1959–61	£1,000	£750	£500
A60 Cambridge	1622/4	1961–69	£1,000	£750	£500
A90/95 Westminster	2639/6	1954–59	£2,000	£1,500	£750
A99 Westminster	2912/6	1959–61	£1,500	£1,000	£500
A105 Westminster	2639/6	1956–59	£3,000	£1,500	£750
A110 Mk I/II	2912/6	1961–68	£2,000	£1,500	£750
Nash Metropolitan	1489/4	1957–61	£3,500	£2,000	£750
Nash Metropolitan DHC	1489/4	1957–61	£6,000	£3,000	£1,500
A30	803/4	1952–56	£1,500	£800	-
A30 Countryman	803/4	1954–56	£1,500	£1,000	-
A35	948/4	1956–59	£1,000	£500	-
A35 Countryman	948/4	1956–62	£1,500	£1,000	-
A40 Farina Mk I	948/4	1958–62	£1,250	£750	£200
A40 Mk I Countryman	948/4	1959–62	£1,500	£1,000	£400
A40 Farina Mk II	1098/4	1962–67	£1,000	£750	-
A40 Mk II Countryman	1098/4	1962–67	£1,200	£750	£300
1100	1098/4	1963–73	£1,000	£750	-
1300 Mk I/II	1275/4	1967–74	£750	£500	-
1300GT	1275/4	1969–74	£1,800	£1,000	£750
1800/2200	1800/2200/4	1964–75	£1,500	£900	£600
3 Litre	2912/6	1968–71	£3,000	£1,500	£500

1963 Austin 1100 Four-Door Saloon, finished in cream, original boxed tool kit, same family ownership from new, excellent original condition.
£1,200–1,500 / $1,750–2,200 ⚒ BARO

1981 Austin Allegro 1500 Vanden Plas, 1485cc, finished in blue, full leather interior trim, wooden picnic tables, 1 owner from new, very good condition.
£400–500 / $580–720 ⚒ H&H

1969 Austin Ant Prototype, 2- or 4-wheel drive, high/low-ratio gearbox, restored 1991, finished in green.
£4,000–5,000 / $5,800–7,250 ⚒ BKS
Too far ahead of its time to exploit the current off-roader vogue, the Alec Issigonis-designed Ant was a four-wheel-drive vehicle based on the Austin-Morris 1100/1300 platform. The project was discontinued after BMC's merger with Leyland. Approximately 20 prototypes were made, 12 being sent overseas for testing, while the remainder were used as factory runabouts. Subsequently, four of the latter were sold privately.

1965 Austin Gipsy, 2286cc, finished in green, soft top, rear seats with original plastic covering, always garaged, 1,500 miles from new, completely original.
£3,250–3,750 / $4,700–5,500 ⚒ H&H

Austin-Healey

Donald Mitchell Healey, born in Cornwall in 1898, could well have become a motor-racing hero in his own right. From 1930 to 1934, he raced for the small British firm of Invicta, winning the Monte Carlo outright in an S-Type Invicta in 1931. Yet instead of chasing racing laurels as a driver, he chose to pursue a career as an automotive engineer, working prior to WWII for Riley and Triumph, then, from 1946 to 1954, producing his own sporting Healey motor cars, always in limited numbers. In 1952, his career took a dramatic turn when he unveiled his latest design, the Healey 100, at the Earls Court Motor Show in London. He had already contracted to use an Austin engine in this new sports car, but such was the public response that Austin agreed to manufacture the whole car to give birth to the Austin-Healey marque. Although continually updated, the basic design lasted until 1968. It became increasingly refined with front disc brakes, then wind-up windows, and ever higher top speeds. At the other end of the scale is the much loved Austin-Healey 'Frog-eye' Sprite, which ran from 1958 to 1961. Sprites thereafter were rebadged MG Midgets.

Miller's Compares

I. 1955 Austin-Healey 100/4, 2660cc 4-cylinder engine, restored 1994–96, engine rebuilt and converted to unleaded fuel, 100M manifold and SU HD carburettors, stainless steel exhaust, gearbox overhauled, new wire wheels, rewired, aluminium front wings, new interior trim, excellent condition.
£14,500–17,000 / $21,000–24,650 ⚒ BRIT

II. 1954 Austin-Healey 100, completely restored at a cost of over £25,000, engine, overdrive gearbox, rear axle and suspension rebuilt, new seats, carpets, door trims, hood and side screens, 22 miles covered since restoration, concours condition.
£20,000–23,000 / $29,000–33,350 ⚒ COYS

The price range between these two cars is not as wide as can be found, with the best 100/4 commanding over £20,000 and lesser cars sometimes available in the low teens. Both of the cars above had been the subject of recent restorations; the difference is that item II had undergone a well-documented and complete restoration, reportedly to concours standard and supported by bills exceeding £25,000. The restoration of the lower-priced car was less well documented and not followed through to ultimate completion – it had no hood. Additionally, this car also incorporated several modifications to 100M specification which, while in period with the car, means that some enthusiasts will regard it as less original. This reduces its appeal.

1955 Austin-Healey 100/4 BN1, 2660cc, 4-cylinder engine, upgraded to M-specification 1994–96, 3-speed manual gearbox with overdrive, original right-hand drive, finished in Old English white, black interior trim, 72,000 miles from new, excellent condition throughout.
£16,500–18,000 / $24,000–26,000 ⚒ H&H
In 1951, when the established range of Healey cars was selling steadily, but beyond the price range of most enthusiasts, Donald Healey realised that there was a market for a relatively low-priced, yet high-performance, sports car. A readily available, reliable and tunable engine was required, and BMC agreed to supply the 2660cc four-cylinder unit from its Austin A90, together with Austin's three-speed overdrive gearbox. The new car had a simple, but torsionally strong, ladder frame, which was clothed in an attractive, open two-seat body. The result, launched in 1952, caused a sensation and met with immediate approval from press and enthusiasts alike. It looked superb and had performance to match: developing 94bhp at 4,000rpm, it could achieve 111mph with the windscreen folded flat and 0–60mph acceleration in 10.3 seconds.

AUSTIN-HEALEY Model	ENGINE cc/cyl	DATES	CONDITION 1	2	3
100 BN 1/2	2660/4	1953–56	£20,000	£14,000	£8,000
100/6, BN4/BN6	2639/6	1956–59	£18,000	£13,500	£8,000
3000 Mk I	2912/6	1959–61	£20,000	£13,000	£8,500
3000 Mk II	2912/6	1961–62	£22,000	£15,000	£9,000
3000 Mk IIA	2912/6	1962–64	£23,000	£15,000	£11,000
3000 Mk III	2912/6	1964–68	£24,000	£17,000	£11,000
Sprite Mk I	948/4	1958–61	£10,000	£6,000	£3,000
Sprite Mk II	948/4	1961–64	£5,000	£3,000	£2,000
Sprite Mk III	1098/4	1964–66	£4,500	£3,000	£1,500
Sprite Mk IV	1275/4	1966–71	£5,000	£3,000	£1,500

1955 Austin-Healey 100, restored, upgraded to M-specification, chromed wire wheels, finished in Old English white and black, black leather interior, 1,167 miles in last seven years, excellent condition throughout.
£16,000–19,000 / $23,200–27,500 BKS
Following the Austin-Healey 100's sensational debut in 1952, the works entered two mildly modified cars in the 1953 Le Mans 24-hour race. They finished 12th and 14th, a notable achievement for what were recognisably production sports cars. Accordingly, the name 'Le mans' was chosen for a bolt-on tuning kit offered through Austin-Healey dealers, by means of which private owners could bring their cars up to a specification approaching that of the works entries. The kit included a pair of SU HD6 carburettors, a special inlet manifold and cold air box, a high-lift camshaft, stronger valve springs and a distributor with an alternative ignition advance curve. The kit increased power from the standard 90 to 100bhp. From 1952, the conversion was available factory fitted on the BN2 model as the 100M. In addition to the Le Mans kit, the latter boasted high-compression pistons, a stiffer front anti-roll bar and special front dampers. Power increased to 110bhp and top speed, with windscreen folded, to almost 120mph.

1957 Austin-Healey 100/6 3000cc, overdrive gearbox, alloy wheels, hardtop, original right-hand drive, finished in red and white, black interior trim, good condition throughout.
£11,000–14,000 / $16,000–20,300 H&H

1959 Austin-Healey 3000 Mk I BT7, 2996cc, completely restored, triple Weber carburettors, oil cooler, rear disc brakes, 72-spoke wire wheels, full weather gear, tonneau cover and works hardtop, finished in metallic light blue, blue interior trim, BMI Heritage Trust Certificate.
£28,000–33,000 / $40,600–48,000 H&H

Restored values

The cost of a professional restoration will have an influence on, but no direct relation to, a car's market value. A restored car can have a market value lower than the cost of its restoration.

◀ **1959 Austin-Healey 3000 Mk I,** 2912cc 6-cylinder engine, 4-speed gearbox with overdrive.
£23,000–26,000 / $33,300–37,700 BC

1961 Austin-Healey 3000 Mk I BN7, overdrive gearbox, completely restored, 4,000 miles covered since, new suspension, steering joints and brakes, 5 new 60-spoke chrome wire wheels, factory hardtop, hood, sidescreens and tonneau cover, 3 owners from new, concours winner.
£22,000–25,000 / $31,900–36,250 ⚒ BKS
The 3000 Mk I was produced between 1959 and 1961, during which time small changes included a new '3000' badge on the grille and the fitting of Girling front disc brakes. With twin SU carburettors and 124bhp at 4,600rpm, top speed was in the region of 114mph, while 60mph came up in around 11 seconds. This particular example is one of only 2,825 two-seat BN7 models built.

1966 Austin-Healey 3000 Mk II, 2912cc 6-cylinder engine, twin SU carburettors, 148bhp, 4-speed manual gearbox with overdrive, servo-assisted front disc/rear drum brakes, left-hand drive, finished in metallic grey and blue.
£14,000–16,000 / $20,300–23,200 ⚒ Pou

1959 Austin-Healey Sprite Mk I, restored, fewer than 1,000 miles a year since completion, hood and side screens, finished in Iris blue, dark blue leathercloth interior, very original.
£11,000–13,000 / $16,000–18,850 ⚒ BKS
The Donald Healey-designed Sprite entered production in March 1958. Its distinctive bonnet, topped by two 'frog-eye' headlamps, ensured the model's instant recognition. Healey made use of existing BMC parts, including a very tunable 43bhp version of the overhead-valve, 948cc A-series engine, sporting twin SU carburettors, and the shared A35 gearbox and axles. In a class of its own for price and performance, the Sprite was a huge success during its three-year production life.

1966 Austin-Healey 3000 BJ8, 2912cc 6-cylinder engine, twin 2in SU HD8 carburettors, 4-speed manual gearbox, servo-assisted front disc/rear drum brakes, engine and gearbox rebuilt, finished in blue and white, interior retrimmed to correct specification, wood veneer dashboard.
£20,000–23,000 / $29,000–33,350 ⚒ RM

1966 Austin-Healey 3000 Mk III Phase II, restored, engine overhauled, new sill panels, black-painted stainless-steel exhaust, excellent condition throughout.
£26,000–28,000 / $37,700–40,600 ⚒ BKS
The 3000 Mk III, with 148bhp engine, appeared early in 1964, to be followed later in the year by the Phase II version, which had revised rear suspension. Top speed was 121mph, and the 0–60mph time dipped below ten seconds. Despite the antiquity of the basic design, the big Healey remained as popular as ever, although increasingly stringent safety and emissions legislation meant that its days were numbered. By the time production ended in December 1967, over 16,000 Phase IIs – by far the most popular variant – had been built.

Miller's Starter Marque

Starter Austin-Healeys: *Sprite Mk I 'Frog-eye'; Sprite Mk II–V.*

- Few cars have a cuter face than the cheeky little Austin-Healey Sprite Mk I, which everyone knows as the 'Frog-eye'. Truth to tell, it's not very fast. A contemporary road test in *The Motor* quoted a leisurely 0–60mph time of 20.5 seconds. Acceleration petered out altogether at 84mph but what it lacked in outright pace, it more than made up for with true agility and genuine sporting feel. It's a viable restore-while-you-drive car, with basic readily-available mechanicals – mostly Austin A35 with a bit of Morris Minor thrown in. Many of the same virtues apply to the Sprite Mk II–V, which is identical to the MG Midget in all but minor detail. With both makes to choose from, the 'Spridget' was made in far larger numbers than the 'Frog-eye', and is that much more affordable and readily available.
- The 'Frog-eye' Sprite gets its nickname from the headlamp pods on the bonnet, but Donald Healey originally wanted to use retractable lamps, like those on the later Lotus Elan. Cost ruled these out, however, and helped create a car of great character.

◄ **1959 Austin-Healey Sprite Mk I,** finished in pale yellow, good condition throughout.
£5,000–6,000 / $7,250–8,700 ⚒ BARO

Autobianchi

◄ **1965 Autobianchi Bianchina Cabriolet,** 594cc rear-mounted twin-cylinder engine, 4-speed manual gearbox, 4-wheel drum brakes, wire wheels, left-hand drive, finished in yellow and black.
£5,500–7,000
$8,000–10,150 ⚒ Pou

Autocar

► **1904 Autocar Type X 10/12hp Rear-Entrance Tonneau,** horizontally-opposed twin-cylinder water-cooled engine, 10hp, brass oil lighting, removable canopy and windscreen, side curtains, finished in burgundy with black wings and gold coachlining, deep-buttoned tan upholstery.
£25,000–28,000 / $36,250–40,600 ⚒ BKS

The Clark family – brothers Lewis, John and James – had dabbled with motor car production as early as 1897, forming the Pittsburgh Motor Vehicle Company that year with financial support from Charles Clark, their father, and William Morgan. Their first vehicle was a lightweight petrol-engined tandem tricycle of just 2hp, and in 1898 they built a wicker-bodied four-wheeler, which weighed a very modest 160lb. Production ceased in Pittsburgh in 1900, when the brothers moved to nearby Ardmore and set up as The Autocar Company. By 1902, Autocar was offering a quite sophisticated twin-cylinder 8½hp car, with a front-mounted engine and shaft drive – a major step forward in American motor car technology.

Auto-Union

Formed during 1932, Auto-Union was the combine of DKW, Audi, Horch and Wanderer. From 1946 onward, the branches of the combine in West Germany were merged into one enterprise to produce versions of the DKW. This was followed by twin- and triple-cylinder vehicles, which were largely pre-war designs, and a forward-control van. A more familiar product was the DKW 1000, available as a four-door saloon or two-door pillarless coupé. This was badged as an Auto-Union until 1962. A small number found their way to Britain in right-hand drive form.

◄ **1959 Auto-Union 1000S,** 980cc 3-cylinder two-stroke engine, 4-speed manual gearbox with column change, front-wheel drive, stored for over 25 years, resprayed in blue and white, cream vinyl interior trim with blue piping, good original condition.
£3,000–3,500
$4,350–5,000 ⚒ BRIT

Bentley

Walter Owen Bentley founded Bentley Motors in 1919 and over the following 12 years produced only 3,024 cars. The first production Bentley, the four-cylinder 3 Litre, appeared in 1922; two years later a 3 Litre won the Le Mans 24-hour race, and Bentleys won again in 1927, 1928, 1929 and 1930. Despite racetrack glory, the company's finances were always precarious, and Bentley launched its luxury 8 Litre model in 1931, on the eve of a UK depression. That move brought the company into the hands of Rolls-Royce. The subsequent generation of Bentleys, produced at Rolls-Royce's Derby plant, are now known as the 'Derby Bentleys'. The first new car under RR's ownership was the 3½ Litre, which essentially employed a tuned version of the Rolls-Royce 20/25 six-cylinder, 3669cc engine, gave a lusty 105bhp and powered Bentleys to 90mph, sometimes more. Later the engine was boosted to 4257cc to become the 4¼ Litre, with lighter-bodied cars edging 100mph. It was during this era that Bentleys became dubbed 'The Silent Sportscar', while British coachbuilders graced them with some enduringly elegant and stylish bodies. Today, the quality, styling and originality of coachwork has a significant bearing on the overall value of these cars.

After 1945, Bentley and Rolls-Royce models began to converge, initially with the R-Type Bentley. The standard factory-bodied R-Type was really only a slightly more sporting version of the Rolls-Royce Silver Dawn. However, while the standard-bodied Rolls-Royces and Bentleys were close kin, one Bentley of this period stood alone with no Rolls-Royce counterpart – that was the beautiful R-Type Continental, which had an exquisite coachbuilt fastback body developed in the wind-tunnel and crafted in aluminium by H. J. Mulliner. With the advent of monocoque construction, the era of the great coachbuilt Bentleys came to an end, and the S- and T-Series Bentleys were little more than alternatively badged versions of the Rolls-Royce Silver Cloud and Silver Shadow. In recent years, though, Bentleys have once again forged a distinct identity of sporting luxury with models that are increasingly separate from Rolls-Royce offerings.

1923 Bentley 3 Litre Four-Seat Tourer, 2990cc, gearbox rebuilt, electric fan, bodywork refurbished, finished in green, green interior trim.
£60,000–70,000 / $87,000–101,500 ⚒ H&H
This car was built originally on a 10ft 10in-wheelbase chassis, but it was shortened and raced extensively during the 1920s and early 1930s. Modifications include the fitment of twin 'sloper' carburettors, a steering box from a 4½ Litre and front wheel brakes.

1924 Bentley 3 Litre Four-Seat Tourer, 2990cc, 6½ Litre back axle, weather equipment including side screens, tonneau and hood bag, finished in ivory and black, red interior trim.
£60,000–70,000 / $87,000–101,500 ⚒ H&H

1929 Bentley Speed Six 6½ Litre Tourer, 6597cc overhead camshaft 6-cylinder engine, four valves per cylinder, matching engine/chassis numbers, original period tourer body.
£165,000–180,000 / $240–26,000 ⚒ COYS
The 6½ Litre, recorded as W. O. Bentley's favourite of all his models, was introduced in the mid-1920s to cater for the increasing trend to fit larger and more luxurious coachwork to the then current production chassis, the 3 Litre. He adapted his initial 4½ Litre six-cylinder design, enlarging the capacity to 6597cc, and the 6½ Litre was born. It would become one of the company's most famous and successful models. The 6½ Litre was supplemented in 1928 by the Speed Six, identifiable by its parallel-sided radiator and higher-compression engine with twin carburettors. Originally bodied by Mulliner as a saloon, this car was fitted with tourer coachwork by Windovers during the late 1930s.

BENTLEY Model	ENGINE cc/cyl	DATES	CONDITION 1	2	3
3 Litre	2996/4	1920–27	£100,000	£75,000	£40,000
Speed Six	6597/6	1926–32	£300,000	£250,000	£160,000
4½ Litre	4398/4	1927–31	£175,000	£125,000	£80,000
4½ Litre Supercharged	4398/4	1929–32	£600,000+	£300,000	£200,000
8 litre	7983/6	1930–32	£350,000	£250,000	£100,000
3½ Litre Saloon & DHC	3699/6	1934–37	£70,000	£30,000	£15,000
4¼ Litre Saloon & DHC	4257/6	1937–39	£70,000	£35,000	£20,000
Mk V	4257/6	1939–41	£45,000	£25,000	£20,000

Prices are dependent on engine type, chassis length, matching chassis and engine nos, body style and coachbuilder, and original extras like supercharger, gearbox ratio, racing history and originality. Many Specials built upon the 'Derby' Bentley chassis and Mk VI.

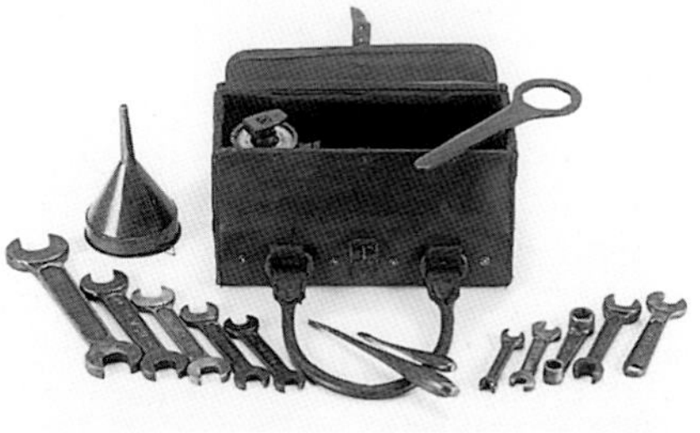

A set of hand tools, of the period and type supplied with vintage Bentley cars, comprising Tecalamit large and small grease guns, Enotes grease gun, tyre levers, BSA open-ended spanners, large and small adjustable wrenches, large and small pliers, feeler gauge, various other spanners, box spanners, tommy bar, bottle jack, screwdrivers and various other tools, all contained in a leather tool bag.
£1,500–2,000 / $2,200–2,900 ⚒ BKS

Bryan De Grineau, Obstructionist, a cartoon depicting a startled Bentley driver being booked by a policeman, inscribed in the artist's hand 'obstructionist' – well - what are you going to charge me with – public danger? – cop – 'loitering!', signed and dated 1932, 14½ x 18½in (37 x 47cm).
£600–700 / $870–1,000 ⚒ BKS

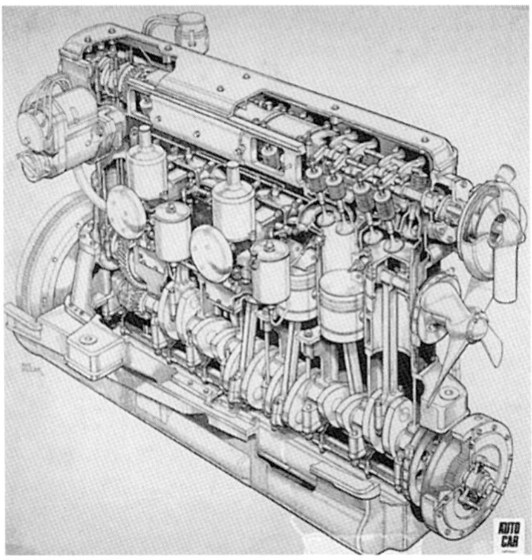

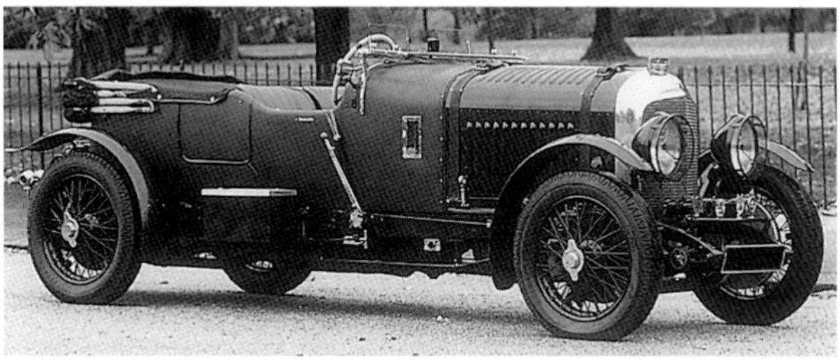

1929 Bentley 4½ Litre Le Mans Replica, originally fitted with saloon coachwork by Mulliner, rebodied as a Le Mans replica in early 1980s, converted to external gear change, finished in British racing green, green leather interior.
£140,000–160,000 / $203,000–232,000 ⚒ COYS
With a design that was basically two-thirds of the existing 6½ Litre six-cylinder engine, the overhead-camshaft 4½ Litre prototype engine boasted four valves and two spark plugs per cylinder. Fitted to the first 4½ Litre chassis, it was used by Frank Clement to set the fastest lap in the 1927 Le Mans race, before he retired following the famous White House crash. It was this car, christened 'Old Mother Gun', that won Le Mans in 1928, driven by Barnato and Rubin. The first 4½ Litre road cars, which produced around 105bhp at 3,500rpm and could accelerate from 0 to 60mph in an impressive 15 seconds and on to a 92mph maximum, became available in September 1927. During a four-year production life, they underwent a multitude of detail changes, but all, bar nine built to special order, had the 10ft 10in chassis of the 3 Litre with all-round semi-elliptic leaf springing, friction dampers and four-wheel brakes with servo. When production ended in 1931, 713 4½ Litres had been built.

1935 Bentley 3½ Litre Three-Position Drophead Coupé, coachwork by Thrupp & Maberly, louvred bonnet, rear-mounted spare with cover, correct lamps, new overdrive unit, beige hood and polished aluminium wheel discs, finished in red, red leather interior.
£52,000–58,000 / $75,500–84,000 ⊞ RCC
One of the previous owners of this car was the actor Albert Finney.

◀ **Max Millar, Bentley 8 Litre engine cut-away drawing,** applied *The Autocar* copyright label, signed, pen and ink, redrawn at the lower right central, repaired tear, 23in (58.5cm) square.
£550–650 / $800–950 ⚒ BKS
Max Millar was probably the best known of the pre-war technical artists. He continued working for *The Autocar* into the 1950s.

1935 Bentley 3½ Litre Two-Door Coupé, coachwork by Mann Egerton, subject of body-off restoration 1980s, flashing indicators, 2 owners since WWII, finished in green over black, tan leather interior, good condition.
£28,000–32,000 / $40,600–46,400 BKS
Although Rolls-Royce's acquisition of Bentley Motors in 1931 robbed the latter of its independence, it did at least ensure the survival of the Bentley name. Launched in 1933, the first of the Derby Bentleys continued the marque's sporting associations but in a more refined manner than before. As befitted its sporting nature, the Derby Bentley was almost always fitted with owner/driver saloon or drophead coupé coachwork (most often by Park Ward), so this fixed-head coupé by Mann Egerton is something of a rarity.

1935 Bentley 3½ Litre Two-Door Coupé de Ville, coachwork by Park Ward, 3669cc overhead-valve 6-cylinder engine, twin SU carburettors, 115bhp, exhibited by Park Ward at the 1935 London Motor Show, restored 1999, finished in grey, blue-grey leather interior, very good condition throughout.
£35,000–40,000 / $50,750–58,000 BKS

1936 Bentley 4¼ Litre Vanden Plas-style Tourer, extensively restored, cutaway rear wheel spats, polished Ace wheel discs, finished in dark green, black weather equipment, polished aluminium dashboard, green interior.
£55,000–60,000 / $79,750–87,000 COYS
The 4¼ Litre Bentley was the last of the Rolls-Bentley sporting cars built in the 1930s. It was introduced in 1936 and offered more power while retaining the integrity of the earlier cars with their superb gear change and servo brakes. This example has been clothed with a tourer body based on the rare and desirable Malcolm Campbell-style tourer by Vanden Plas.

▶ **1937 Bentley 4¼ Litre Saloon,** coachwork by Mann Egerton, 4257cc 6-cylinder engine, crossflow cylinder head, twin SU carburettors, twin fuel pumps, single coil ignition, 4-speed gearbox, centralised lubrication system, leaf-spring suspension, adjustable hydraulic shock absorbers, power-assisted brakes, original burgundy leather upholstery, good overall condition.
£12,000–15,000 / $17,500–21,750 COYS

1936 Bentley 4¼ Litre Drophead Coupé, coachwork by Park Ward, recently refurbished, engine overhauled, new exhaust, resprayed in black, original blue upholstery, in need of minor finishing work.
£44,000–48,000 / $64,000–69,500 RCC

1937 Bentley 4¼ Litre Coupé, coachwork by Gurney Nutting, finished in black, black leather interior, original condition.
£45,000–50,000 / $65,250–72,500 COYS
At a time when most British coachbuilders were more restrained in their styling, Gurney Nutting took a bolder approach and, being increasingly influenced by the more stylish European houses, produced a number of superb, flamboyant designs.

1938 Bentley 4¼ Litre 'High Vision' Saloon coachwork by H. J. Mulliner, Plexiglas roof windows, 1 of the 1st overdrive models, exhibited at the 1938 Earls Court Motor Show.
£25,000–28,000 / $36,250–40,600 ⊞ RCC

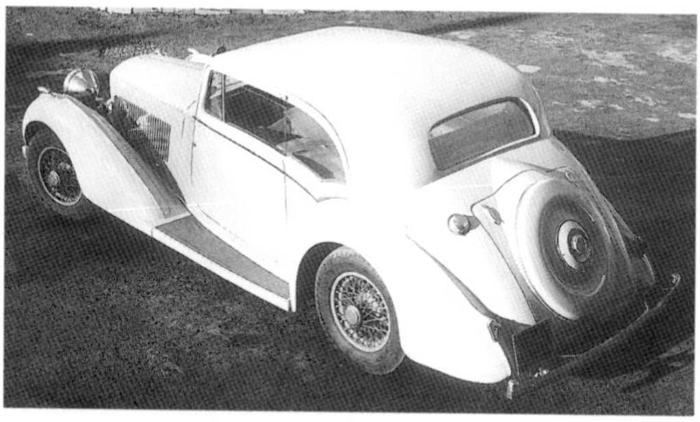

1938 Bentley 4¼ Litre Two-Door Coupé, coachwork by James Young, subject of considerable restoration work, in need of finishing and installation of rebuilt engine, finished in grey, red leather interior trim, sound body.
£24,000–26,000 / $34,800–37,700 ⊞ RCC

1949 Bentley Mk VI Saloon, coachwork by James Young, restored, excellent condition, concours winner.
£40,000–45,000 / $58,000–65,250 ⚒ BJ

1938 Bentley 4¼ Litre Close-Coupled Sports Saloon, coachwork by Thrupp & Maberly, engine rebuilt, original.
£28,000–30,000 / $40,600–43,500 ⊞ BLE

1947 Bentley Mk VI Sedanca Coupé, coachwork by Gurney Nutting, older restoration, finished in black, red leather upholstery and red carpets, first recorded Bentley Sedanca Coupé.
£35,000–38,000 / $50,750–55,000 ⚒ BKS
This car is said to have been chosen by Rolls-Royce and Bentley for a four-month coast-to-coast promotional tour of the United States, arriving in New York on 20 October, 1947, aboard the *Mauritania* and later being displayed in the Waldorf Astoria Hotel.

◀ 1949 Bentley Mk VI Drophead Coupé, coachwork by Park Ward, 4250cc, full oil filter system, finished in maroon, power-operated burgundy hood, radio, beige hide interior, burgundy Wilton carpets, 1 of 45 Drophead Coupés built to Park Ward's design No. 100.
£27,000–32,000
$39,000–46,500 ⚒ BKS
The policy of rationalisation that had begun in the late 1930s continued at Rolls-Royce after the war, leading to the introduction of factory bodywork. The Standard Steel body was available at first only on the Mk VI Bentley, although customers could still opt for a coachbuilt alternative.

BENTLEY Model	ENGINE cc/cyl	DATES	CONDITION 1	2	3
Abbreviations: HJM = H. J. Mulliner; PW = Park Ward; M/PW = Mulliner/Park Ward					
Mk VI Standard Steel	4257/ 4566/6	1946–52	£16,000	£10,000	£5,000
Mk VI Coachbuilt	4257/ 4566/6	1946–52	£25,000	£20,000	£12,000
Mk VI Coachbuilt DHC	4566/6	1946–52	£40,000+	£30,000	£20,000
R-Type Standard Steel	4566/6	1952–55	£12,000	£10,000	£7,000
R-Type Coachbuilt	4566/6	1952–55	£25,000	£20,000	£15,000
R-Type Coachbuilt DHC	4566/ 4887/6	1952–55	£50,000	£35,000	£25,000
R-Type Cont (HJM)	4887/6	1952–55	£80,000+	£40,000	£29,000
S1 Standard Steel	4887/6	1955–59	£15,000	£10,000	£7,000
S1 Cont 2-door (PW)	4877/6	1955–59	£30,000	£25,000	£20,000
S1 Cont Drophead	4877/6	1955–59	£80,000+	£75,000	£50,000
S1 Cont F'back (HJM)	4877/6	1955–58	£50,000	£35,000	£25,000
S2 Standard Steel	6230/8	1959–62	£15,000	£9,000	£6,000
S2 Cont 2-door (HJM)	6230/8	1959–62	£60,000	£40,000	£30,000
S2 Flying Spur (HJM)	6230/8	1959–62	£45,000	£33,000	£22,000
S2 Conv (PW)	6230/8	1959–62	£60,000+	£50,000	£35,000
S3 Standard Steel	6230/8	1962–65	£16,000	£11,000	£9,000
S3 Cont/Flying Spur	6230/8	1962–65	£45,000	£30,000	£25,000
S3 2-door (M/PW)	6230/8	1962–65	£30,000	£25,000	£10,000
S3 Conv (modern conversion – only made one original)	6230/8	1962–65	£40,000	£28,000	£20,000
T1	6230/6, 6750/8	1965–77	£10,000	£8,000	£4,000
T1 2-door (M/PW)	6230/6, 6750/8	1965–70	£15,000	£12,000	£9,000
T1 Drophead (M/PW)	6230/6, 6750/8	1965–70	£30,000	£20,000	£12,000

1951 Bentley Mk VI Landaulette, 4250cc, converted from Standard Steel saloon, new hood, finished in red and silver, red interior trim, good condition throughout.
£5,000–7,000 / $7,250–10,250 H&H

1954 Bentley R-Type Continental, coachwork by H. J. Mulliner, 4566cc 6-cylinder engine, 153bhp, 4-speed automatic transmission, original left-hand drive, professionally restored, 'as-new' condition.
£100,000–120,000
$145,000–174,000 RM

1953 Bentley R-Type Drophead Coupé, coachwork by H. J. Mulliner, overhauled, invoices totalling £40,000, finished in royal blue, magnolia interior.
£55,000–65,000 / $79,750–94,250 COYS
Announced in 1946, the Bentley Mk VI featured a strong channel-section chassis with independent wishbone/coil-spring front suspension and a live, leaf-sprung rear axle. Drum brakes were fitted all-round, with Rolls-Royce's mechanical servo assistance, the front brakes operated hydraulically for the first time on a Bentley. Power was provided by the pre-war B60 4257cc six-cylinder engine – with overhead inlet/side exhaust valves – sufficient to propel the Bentley to 90mph. The only major mechanical change came in May 1951, when engine capacity was increased to 4566cc. The same year, the Mk VI was joined by the R-Type, basically the same vehicle but with a longer and more commodious boot. In total, 5,201 Mk VIs were produced, 4,000 with the 4.5 litre engine, and 2,320 R-Types. Production ceased in 1955.

► **1953 Bentley R-Type saloon,** 4566cc engine, Standard Steel coachwork, finished in dark blue.
£11,000–12,500
$16,000–18,000 BLE

1959 Bentley S1 Saloon, S2 type wings, finished in dark blue over silver, original radio and grey leather interior, 3 owners from new, very good condition.
£12,000–15,000 / $17,400–21,750 ⚒ BKS

1961 Bentley S2 Saloon, basically original, stainless exhaust system, in need of some renovation and recommissioning, sills in need of attention, finished in dark blue, blue-grey leather interior.
£8,500–9,500 / $12,350–13,750 ⊞ RCC

1964 Bentley S3 Saloon, 6320cc overhead-valve V8 engine, 200bhp, 4-speed automatic transmission, hydraulic front brakes, mechanical rear brakes, factory-fitted Webasto sunroof, aftermarket air conditioning unit, period radio, restored, little use since, finished in black with biscuit leather interior.
£9,000–11,000 / $13,000–16,000 ⚒ RM

1979 Bentley T2 Saloon, 6750cc V8 engine, finished in dark green over pewter, original black leather interior trim in very good condition.
£9,500–11,000 / $13,750–16,000 ⚒ BRIT
With only 558 examples produced between 1977 and 1980, the T2 is a rare motor car. It boasted several improvements over its predecessor, including rack-and-pinion steering, a front air-dam and a split-level air conditioning system. The last was deemed necessary because a large proportion of this model was destined for export.

1960 Bentley S2 Saloon, recently recommissioned after a period of storage, finished in deep red and pinkish grey, new red leather interior.
£15,000–17,500 / $21,750–25,375 ⊞ RCC

1961 Bentley S2 Continental Drophead Coupé, 6230cc overhead-valve V8 engine, 200bhp, 4-speed automatic transmission, independent front suspension by coil springs and wishbones, rear semi-elliptic leaf springs, hydraulic front brakes, mechanical rear brakes with servo, power operated hood, electric windows, built to Swiss specification with a heavy-gauge frame, left-hand drive, older restoration, recently recommissioned after period of storage.
£38,000–44,000 / $54,500–64,000 ⚒ C
In all, 388 Continentals were built between 1959 and 1962, selling for up to £8,700 depending on the bodywork. Only 61 of the Drophead Coupé variant were to left-hand-drive specification.

1968 Bentley T1 Saloon, 6230cc, finished in green, green interior trim, 61,000 miles from new, excellent condition throughout.
£6,000–7,000 / $8,700–10,200 ⚒ H&H

1988 Bentley Turbo R Saloon, finished in metallic blue, parchment interior, 74,000 miles from new, excellent condition throughout.
£14,000–16,000 / $20,300–23,200 ⚒ COYS
The Bentley Mulsanne shared an identical specification with the Rolls-Royce Silver Spirit. In 1982, however, it was joined by the more powerful Mulsanne Turbo, which evolved into the Turbo R with alloy wheels, more power, and stiffer and lower suspension. So good were the latter's chassis improvements that they were adopted for a new model, the Mulsanne S, in 1987.

Benz

Karl Benz was a prime mover in the early development of the automobile. In 1894, his Velo became the world's first true production automobile, and he was an early pace-setter in volume production. In 1926, Benz's company merged with that of fellow pioneer Gottlieb Daimler to form Daimler-Benz, the cars being called Mercedes-Benz. Today, the company is Germany's largest industrial concern, but with the recent merger of Daimler-Benz and Chrysler – to form DaimlerChrysler – the Benz name has finally disappeared from the company's masthead.

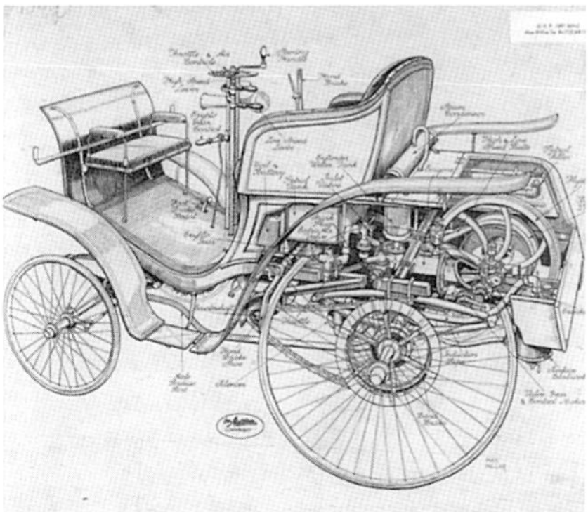

Max Millar, 1897 Benz 3.5hp cut-away drawing, signed and applied with *The Autocar* copyright stamp, pen and Indian ink, 1932, 17 x 21in (43.5 x 53.5cm).
£1,000–1,300 / $1,450–1,900 ⚒ BKS

c1900 Benz 3hp Comfortable, spray carburettor in place of original 'coffee-pot' surface carburettor, period bolt-on accessory crankshaft cover, Crypto hill-climbing gear, starting handle, hood mountings, not run for many years, engine turns freely.
£45,000–55,000 / $65,250–79,750 ⚒ BKS
Benz called the body style with a fully enclosed seat a Comfortable, and the works records show that the first example to this pattern left Mannheim in March 1898. Cars of this type sold in Britain as the Ideal No 2, at a price of 180 guineas.

Restored values

The cost of a professional restoration will have an influence on, but no direct relation to, a car's market value. A restored car can have a market value lower than the cost of its restoration.

1900 Benz Ideal Spindle Seat Dos-à-Dos, trembler coil ignition, vertical tiller steering, full-elliptic end-to-end front suspension, full-elliptic transverse front spring, solid tyres, finished in dark blue with red chassis detail.
£37,000–43,000 / $53,500–62,500 ⚒ BKS
The first car powered by an internal-combustion engine that performed with any degree of success is generally attributed to Carl Benz. It was a spindly three-wheeler with a massive horizontally-mounted engine. By 1892, Benz production centred around a more conventional four-wheeled car, and by the turn of the century Benz was producing the popular Velo, among other models, the sales of which outstripped its major European competitors. The Benz engine design, both in twin- and single-cylinder form, was licensed to other manufacturers, notably Georges Richard, Marshall and Star, and Emile Roger. The basic Benz design was to influence car production from 1885 to 1900, but the arrival of the new *système Panhard* and De Dion Bouton's fast-revving vertical engines sounded its death knell.

c1911 Benz 18hp Two-Seater with Dickey, 4-cylinder sidevalve engine, Zenith carburettor, Stewart Vacuum Gasoline System, Eissemann ignition, 3-speed gearbox, semi-elliptic front leaf springs, three-quarter-elliptic rear leaf springs, rebodied in 1920s fashion with two-seater-and-dickey coachwork, Hall electric lighting, finished in cream, deep red leather interior.
£10,000–13,000 / $14,500–18,850 ⚒ BKS
By 1910, Benz was marketing a wide range of fairly conventional cars, switching from chain drive to shaft drive, and adopting sidevalve engines.

Bitter

◄ **1986 Bitter 3.9 SC Coupé,** 3848cc, finished in blue, correct instrumentation, magnolia interior trim, 82,000 miles from new, good overall condition.
£3,500–5,000
$5,000–7,250 ⚒ H&H
Erich Bitter launched the SC Coupé in 1981, with the objective of producing an exotic and stylish motor car using tried and proven mechanical components, mostly from Opel.

Bizzarrini

After spells at Alfa Romeo and Ferrari, where he was the prime mover behind the 250 GTO, Giotto Bizzarrini turned freelance in 1962. He soon won commissions from Lamborghini, for whom he designed the formidable V12, and from the motorcycle company Iso, before returning to automobile manufacturing with the Rivolta. A four-seater coupé, the Rivolta combined Bertone styling with Chevrolet V8 power, and provided Bizzarrini with the basis for his next project – the Grifo. Also styled by Bertone, the two-seater Iso Grifo Coupé employed a shortened version of the Rivolta's platform chassis together with the larger car's independent front suspension, De Dion rear axle and all-round disc brakes. Performance depended on the engine installed, with up to 180mph claimed for the 7 litre model. Convinced that the car had competition potential, Bizzarrini obtained permission to market a hotter version under his own name. Introduced in 1965, the Bizzarrini Strada featured lightweight aluminium bodywork (which shed 400lb), lowered suspension and a 5.3 litre, 365bhp Chevrolet V8.

1968 Bizzarrini 5300 GT Strada Berlinetta, 5.3 litre Chevrolet V8 engine, 365bhp, manual gearbox, completely restored, converted to unleaded fuel, Dunlop front brake calipers in place of original Campagnolo magnesium items, finished in red, black interior, museum displayed for several years, 28,000 miles from new, 2 miles covered in last 12 years.
£60,000–70,000 / $87,000–101,500 ⚒ BKS

BMW

The first BMW car, built in 1928, was the Dixi, an Austin 7 produced under licence and from those modest beginnings Bayerische Motoren Werke went on to make some fine pre-war touring cars. In 1940 a streamlined BMW 328 won Italy's Mille Miglia. After the end of WWII, the company came close to oblivion on a number of occasions. The beautiful and excrutiatingly expensive 507 of 1956 nearly brought BMW to its knees, while the Isetta microcars (see page 287), built from 1955 to 1965, created another crisis in the late 1950s. In the early 1960s the company got back on course and began to build its modern reputation as a producer of fine executive, luxury sporting machines.

1939 BMW 327/28 Sports Cabriolet, coachwork by Reutter, recently restored, wooden body framework replaced, original specification in all major respects, original Phillips radio and auxiliary lamps, finished in grey and blue, new hood, interior retrimmed in blue leather, 3 owners from new.
£43,000–48,000 / $62,500–69,500 BKS
BMW launched the six-cylinder, 2 litre 327 in late 1937, in Sports Cabriolet and Sports Coupé guises. Some five months after its launch, the new 327/28 was added to the range, a significantly more sporting car derived from the 328, which had been in production since early 1937. The 327/28 adopted the Fritz Feidler designed, six-cylinder engine of the 328. This engine, with its aluminium cylinder head, overhead-valve arrangement and triple Solex downdraught carburettors, developed some 80bhp at 5,000rpm, 25bhp more than the standard 327 engine. Power was transmitted via a four-speed ZF all-synchromesh gearbox, otherwise the chassis specification was similar to the 327. This allowed seating for four in what was one of the quickest touring cars of its era. The 327/28 had a top speed of 87mph with superb handling enhanced by independent front suspension based on a transverse spring and wishbones. During the production run from 1938 to 1941, only 569 327/28s were built, no fewer than 482 of these being in the Cabriolet form.

c1972 BMW 2002 Cabriolet, left-hand drive, fabric-covered targa roof and hood in good condition, original.
£2,700–3,200 / $4,000–4,600 COYS
It was BMW's 1600 saloon of 1966, with new two-door, medium-sized bodywork, that really set the German manufacturer on the road to success. Already the company's four-cylinder overhead-camshaft engine, and MacPherson-strut front and coil spring/trailing arm rear suspension had been proved in its larger four-door saloons. When allied to the new '02-series 1600, the result was a recipe well received. Faster derivatives soon joined the 85bhp 1600: first came the twin-carburettor, 105bhp 1600 Ti of 1967, then the popular 2002 in January 1968. In basic form, the latter's 1998cc engine produced 100bhp, but in the 2002 Ti, with twin carburettors, it gave 120bhp and a top speed of 115mph.

1974 BMW 2000 Tii, 130bhp, fuel injection, undersealed from new, 67,000 miles from new.
£3,500–4,000 / $5,000–5,800 SiC

◀ **1973 BMW 2002 Baur Cabriolet,** 1990cc, 5-speed overdrive gearbox, restored at a cost of over £7,000, alloy wheels, all new chromework, finished in turquoise and black, all new cream leather interior trim, original Motalita steering wheel, excellent condition.
£4,500–5,550 / $6,500–8,000 H&H

BMW Model	ENGINE cc/cyl	DATES	CONDITION 1	2	3
Dixi	747/4	1927–32	£7,000	£3,000	£2,000
303	1175/6	1934–36	£11,000	£8,000	£5,000
309	843/4	1933–34	£6,000	£4,000	£2,000
315	1490/6	1935–36	£9,000	£7,000	£5,000
319	1911/6	1935–37	£10,000	£9,000	£6,000
326	1971/6	1936–37	£12,000	£10,000	£8,000
320 series	1971/6	1937–38	£12,000	£10,000	£8,000
327/328	1971/6	1937–40	£30,000+	£18,000	£10,000
328	1971/6	1937–40	£60,000+	-	-

1972 BMW 2500 Saloon, inclined 6-cylinder engine, 150bhp, manual gearbox, 0–60mph in 11 seconds, 118mph top speed, finished in green, roof and bonnet in need of a respray, brown upholstery, 3 owners, 61,000 miles from new.
£400–600 / $580–870 ⚒ BKS

1972 BMW 3.0 CSL Lightweight, luxury CS specification, 1 of 1,000 built for homologation purposes, excellent condition.
£7,000–8,000 / $10,200–11,600 ⊞ SiC

c1972 BMW 3.0 CS, 4-speed manual gearbox, power steering, electric windows, resprayed in metallic blue 1998, beige interior, 2 owners and 57,000 miles from new, generally good condition.
£3,750–4,500 / $5,500–6,500 ⚒ BKS

Introduced in 1971 and in production until 1975, the BMW 3.0 CS had the same wheelbase and style as the 2800 CS with an improved Karmann-built bodyshell, a full 3 litre engine (overhead-cam straight-six) and four-wheel disc brakes. It provided more power and improved torque, 180bhp being recorded on this model, while even more was available when Bosch fuel injection was fitted.

1979 BMW 3.0 CS, 3 litre overhead-camshaft 6-cylinder engine, 180bhp, left-hand drive, finished in metallic light blue, dark blue leather interior, 2 owners from new, excellent general condition.
£2,000–3,000 / $2,900–4,400 ⚒ COYS

During the 1970s, one of the most exciting categories of racing was the European Touring Car Championship, and the two principal contestants were Ford (Cologne) and BMW. The latter's main weapon was the CSL (Coupé Sport Leichtmetal), a lightweight version of the 3.0 CS with alloy doors, boot lid and bonnet, and more spartan trim.

Miller's Starter Marque

Starter BMWs: *1502, 1602, 2002, 2002 Touring.*

- The '02-series two-door saloons made BMW's fortune in the 1960s and established the marque's modern reputation for sporty stylish saloons. Today, these spirited machines make good sense as usable everyday classics. In general, all are reassuringly solid and robust, and all, except the 1502 'oil-crisis' model, are good for 100mph; the fuel-injected 2002 Tii offered a class-leading 0–60mph time of 8.2 seconds in 1971. This and the twin-carb 2002 Ti are probably the best buys, while the 1602, plain 2002 and 1502 make sensible down-market alternatives.
- Rust problems are no worse than any other steel monocoque saloon, although particular points to watch include the jacking points, which can eventually fall out and leave the sills prone to rotting from the inside out.
- The overhead-cam engine has an alloy cylinder head on a cast-iron block. It's generally long-lived, but the more you know about the car's history the better. Regular oil changes will promote long life, and all-year-round anti-freeze will help prevent corrosion inside the alloy head and reduce the chance of it warping through overheating.
- The Cabriolet versions of the '02 saloons are a little more exotic, but still eminently affordable. However, the rare 2002 Turbo is an enthusiast's car rather than an everyday user. For a start, only 51 were sold in the UK. If you can find one, you'll get performance – and, quite possibly, shattering bills to match.

BMW Model	ENGINE cc/cyl	DATES	CONDITION 1	2	3
501	2077/6	1952–56	£9,000	£7,000	£3,500
501 V8/502	2580, 3168/8	1955–63	£10,000+	£5,000	£3,000
503 FHC/DHC	3168/8	1956–59	£25,000+	£20,000	£15,000
507	3168/8	1956–59	£100,000+	£70,000	£50,000
Isetta (4 wheels)	247/1	1955–62	£7,000	£3,000	£1,200
Isetta (3 wheels)	298/1	1958–64	£8,000	£2,500	£1,500
Isetta 600	585/2	1958–59	£3,000+	£1,800	£500
1500/1800/2000	var/4	1962–68	£1,800	£800	£500
2000CS	1990/4	1966–69	£5,500	£4,000	£1,500
1500/1600/1602	1499/ 1573/4	1966–75	£3,000+	£1,500	£800
1600 Cabriolet	1573/4	1967–71	£6,000	£4,500	£2,000
2800CS	2788/6	1968–71	£5,000	£4,000	£1,500
1602	1990/4	1968–74	£3,000	£1,500	£1,000
2002	1990/4	1968–74	£3,000	£2,000	£1,000
2002 Tii	1990/4	1971–75	£4,500	£2,500	£1,200
2002 Touring	1990/4	1971–74	£3,500	£2,000	£1,000
2002 Cabriolet	1990/4	1971–75	£5,000+	£3,000	£2,500
2002 Turbo	1990/4	1973–74	£10,000	£6,000	£4,000
3.0 CSa/CSi	2986/6	1972–75	£8,000	£6,000	£4,000
3.0 CSL	3003/ 3153/6	1972–75	£16,000	£10,000	£7,500
MI	3500/6	1978–85	£50,000	£40,000	£30,000
633/635 CS/CSI	3210/3453/6	1976–85	£7,000	£3,000	£2,000
M535i	3453/6	1979–81	£4,500	£3,000	£2,500

1986 BMW M535i, 3.5 litre 6-cylinder engine, 4-speed switchable automatic transmission, finished in blue, 3 owners from new, good to excellent condition.
£1,500–2,000 / $2,200–2,900 ⚒ BARO

1985 BMW M635 CSi, finished in dark blue, excellent condition.
£9,000–14,000 / $13,000–20,500 ⊞ MUN

1980 BMW M1 Art Car, 3500cc double-overhead-camshaft 6-cylinder engine, 470bhp, 5-speed manual gearbox, 4-wheel independent suspension, 4-wheel disc brakes, finished in blue and silver, not intended for road use, excellent mechanical condition.
£60,000–70,000 / $87,000–101,500 ⚒ RM
Three kevlar-bodied M1s were constructed by BMW Motorsport with special tuning and refining by AMG, a German tuner, to determine whether building a car with kevlar bodywork would be possible on a production basis. The cars were more than just test mules, however. Special care was taken to ensure that they were presentable inside and out. Rear spoilers, wheel-arch flares and side skirts were fabricated, while the interiors were fitted with show-quality leather upholstery. Wide, low-profile tyres were mounted on three-piece lightweight BBS rims, and the engines were tuned to produce 470bhp. But what made these cars especially significant was their unique custom paintwork, commissioned by BMW and executed in this case by Viennese artist Ernst Fuchs.

► **1990 BMW M3 Evo 2,** finished in red, full Recaro Sports interior.
£4,750–5,750 / $6,750–8,400 ⚒ BARO
The M3 was BMWs answer to the Sierra Cosworth and was yet another homologation special, which gave the man in the street the opportunity to own a real road-racer. All M3s were produced in left-hand drive form.

Bosley

1953 Bosley Mk I G/T Coupé, 331cu.in Chrysler 'Hemi' V8 engine, 4-carburettor inlet manifold, manual gearbox, 1950 Ford front suspension, 1948 Mercury rear axle, rear suspension modelled on Jaguar C-Type, 12in drum brakes, Halibrand magnesium wheels, tubular chassis, 55 gallon fuel tank, fibreglass body, c160mph top speed, restored 1988–94, finished in red, black leather upholstery, concours winner.
£160,000–180,000 / $232,000–260,000 ⚒ BKS
Richard Bosley, from Ohio, loved cars, and when he saw his first pictures of the GT cars that were coming out of Italy in the late 1940s, he decided that he wanted to make one for himself. The body was made in fibreglass over a male mould, while mechanical components came from a variety of contemporary production cars.

Bristol

In 1947, as wartime aviation contracts came to an end, the Bristol Aeroplane Company branched out into car manufacture with an anglicised version of the pre-war BMW 327. The first model, the 400, clearly owed plenty to aircraft construction and design techniques, having a light-alloy outer skin and a streamlined shape developed in the wind-tunnel. The six-cylinder engine was derived from the pre-war BMW's unit. Only 700 of the 400 models were produced up to 1950, and ever since Bristols have continued to be made in small numbers, providing exclusive, handcrafted luxury for those who could afford them. In 1962, the company switched from six-cylinder engines and adopted Chrysler V8s in the quest for refined power. Bristol enthusiasts tend to fall into two camps: some favour the leaner six-cylinder models, while others prefer the easy power of the V8-engined cars.

1951 Bristol 401 Coupé, finished in metallic green, cream leather interior.
£12,000–14,000 / $17,400–20,300 ⊞ TIHO

1955 Bristol 405 Saloon, resprayed in blue 1998, engine in need of minor attention, interior in original condition.
£5,500–7,000 / $8,000–10,000 ⚒ BKS
In 1955, the four-door 405 saloon was introduced with overdrive as standard equipment. An unusual feature was the mounting of the battery and spare wheel in the front wings.

BRISTOL Model	ENGINE cc/cyl	DATES	CONDITION 1	2	3
400	1971/6	1947–50	£16,000	£14,000	£8,000
401 FHC/DHC	1971/6	1949–53	£28,000	£14,000	£8,000
402	1971/6	1949–50	£22,000	£19,000	£12,000
403	1971/6	1953–55	£20,000	£14,000	£10,000
404 Coupé	1971/6	1953–57	£22,000	£15,000	£12,000
405	1971/6	1954–58	£15,000	£12,000	£10,000
405 Drophead	1971/6	1954–56	£22,000	£19,000	£16,000
406	2216/6	1958–61	£12,000	£8,000	£6,000
407	5130/8	1962–63	£15,000	£8,000	£6,000
408	5130/8	1964–65	£14,000	£10,000	£8,000
409	5211/8	1966–67	£14,000	£11,000	£7,000
410	5211/8	1969	£14,000	£10,000	£6,000
411 Mk I–III	6277/8	1970–73	£16,000	£11,000	£8,000
411 Mk IV–V	6556/8	1974–76	£12,500	£9,500	£7,000
412	5900/ 6556/8	1975–82	£15,000	£9,000	£6,000
603	5211/ 5900/8	1976–82	£10,000	£7,000	£5,000

BSA

1930 BSA Three-Wheeler, 1000cc air-cooled V-twin engine, front-wheel drive, hood and tonneau cover, fabric-covered body, finished in dark red with black wings, retains all original fittings, very good condition.
£4,250–5,000 / $6,000–7,250 ⚒ CGC

1936 BSA Scout SIII Coupé, 1141cc, new starter motor, finished in black, red interior trim, 1 of 3 1936 models known to survive, well maintained, good condition, very original.
£4,000–5,000 / $5,800–7,250 ⚒ H&H

Bugatti

1939 Bugatti Type 57C Sport Roadster, coachwork by Van Vooren, 3300cc, double-overhead-camshaft 8-cylinder engine, super-charger, 160bhp, 4-wheel hydraulic drum brakes, red leather interior.
£1,225,000+ / $1,750,000 ⚒ RM

Clearly inspired by the work of noted coachbuilders Figoni and Falaschi, this Type 57 Bugatti was, in fact, created by the French firm of Van Vooren. It was commissioned by the French government as a wedding gift for Prince Mohammed Reza Pahlevi – the future Shah of Persia – who married the sister of Egypt's King Farouk in 1939. It was not seen by the outside world until the early 1960s.

BUGATTI Model	ENGINE cc/cyl	DATES	CONDITION 1	2	3
13/22/23	1496/4	1919–26	£40,000	£32,000	£25,000
30	1991/8	1922–36	£45,000	£35,000	£30,000
32	1992/8	1923	£45,000	£35,000	£30,000
35A	1991/8	1924–30	£110,000+	£90,000	£80,500
38 (30 update)	1991/8	1926–28	£44,500	£34,000	£28,000
39	1493/8	1926–29	£120,000	£90,000	£80,000
39A Supercharged	1496/8	1926–29	£140,000+	-	-
35T	2262/8	1926–30	£140,000+	-	-
37 GP Car	1496/4	1926–30	£110,000+	£90,000	£75,000
40	1496/4	1926–30	£50,000	£42,000	£35,000
38A	1991/8	1927–28	£48,000	£40,000	£35,000
35B Supercharged	2262/8	1927–30	£300,000+	£170,000+	-
35C	1991/8	1927–30	£170,000+	-	-
37A	1496/4	1927–30	£125,000+	-	-
44	2991/8	1927–30	£60,000+	£40,000	£35,000
45	3801/16	1927–30	£150,000+	-	-
43/43A Tourer	2262/8	1927–31	£180,000+	-	-
35A	1991/8	1928–30	£140,000	£110,000	£90,000
46	5359/8	1929–36	£140,000	£110,000	£90,000
40A	1627/4	1930	£55,000	£45,000	£35,500
49	3257/8	1930–34	£60,000+	£45,000	£35,500
57 Closed	3257/8	1934–40	£60,000+	£35,000	£30,000
57 Open	3257/8	1936–38	£90,000+	£60,000	£55,000
57S	3257/8	1936–38	£250,000+	-	-
57SC Supercharged	3257/8	1936–39	£250,000+	-	-
57G	3257/8	1937–40	£250,000+	-	-
57C	3257/8	1939–40	£140,000+	-	-

Racing history is an important factor with the GP cars.

Colour Review

1959 AC Ace, 1991cc overhead-camshaft 6-cylinder engine, 4-speed manual gearbox with overdrive, front disc/rear drum brakes, wood-rim steering wheel, largely original paintwork, original black leather interior, 1 of the last 50 produced.
£27,000–32,000 / $39,000–46,500 ⚒ RM
Lightweight and nimble on its four-wheel independent suspension, the Ace was graced with a simple, yet attractive, body recalling a touring-bodied Ferrari Barchetta. The body was built using *superleggera* techniques, a framework of ¾in tubes supporting a hand-formed aluminium skin. With the aluminium-block AC engine, the Ace weighed well under 2,000lb, giving the much-developed six-cylinder engine little opposition.

1930 Alfa Romeo 6C 1750 Drophead Coupé, coachwork by James Young, 1750cc double-overhead-camshaft engine, 4-speed gearbox, complete and serviceable Autovac, 12 volt SU fuel pump, finished in red, good condition throughout.
£50,000–60,000 / $72,500–87,000 ⚒ BKS

1961 Alfa Romeo Giulietta Sprint Zagato Berlinetta, coachwork by Zagato, 1.3 litre double-overhead-camshaft 4-cylinder engine, 116bhp, completely restored.
£40,000–44,000 / $58,000–63,000 ⚒ BKS

1929 Alvis Silver Eagle Sports Tourer, coachwork by Cross & Ellis, 1991cc, twin carburettors, 100mph speedometer, Bluemels sprung steering wheel, restored at a cost of £25,000 in 1989, 1 owner for 51 years.
£28,000–32,000 / $40,500–46,500 ⚒ BKS

1939 Alfa Romeo 6C 2500 Cabriolet, coachwork by Gebruder Tüscher, 2443cc double-overhead-camshaft 6-cylinder engine, 4-speed gearbox, 4-wheel independent suspension and drum brakes, original engine and chassis, restored over 8 years.
£80,000–90,000 / $116,000–130,500 ⚒ RM

1950 Allard J2, 5.4 litre Cadillac V8 engine, performance camshaft, three 2-barrel carburettors, 300bhp, 4-speed manual gearbox, semi-independent split front axle, De Dion rear suspension, Lockheed 4-wheel hydraulic drum brakes, polished stainless steel side pipes, completely restored, 1 of only 97 built.
£70,000–80,000 / $101,500–116,000 ⚒ RM
The first production models of the Allard Motor Company, founded in 1946, featured American Ford sidevalve V8 engines, more often than not fitted with Sydney's own aluminium inlet manifolds and cylinder heads. By the early 1950s, larger American overhead-valve V8s, like Cadillacs and Chrysler 'hemis', became available. In true hot rod fashion, Sydney wasted no time in shoehorning these into his J2 and J2X sports racing models. The first Cadillac engine was installed in Allard's own J2 racing car, which was entered in the 1950 Tour of Sicily and, in the same year, the Le Mans 24-hour endurance race, where Allard finished third overall. The J2 and J2X models were also raced extensively in the USA during the early 1950s, scoring convincing road-race victories over the latest Ferraris and Jaguars.

1953 Aston Martin DB2 Vantage, 2.6 litre straight-6 engine, 125bhp, left-hand drive, restored, finished in metallic burgundy, tan leather interior.
£32,000–36,000 / $46,000–52,000 ⚒ BKS

1959 Aston Martin DB Mk III, 3 litre double-overhead-camshaft 6-cylinder DBD engine, 180bhp, 4-speed manual gearbox, Girling front disc brakes, rear 'Alfin' drums, Borrani alloy wire wheels, original black Connolly leather interior, wood-rim steering wheel, DB4-style instrument cluster, 29,000 miles recorded.
£30,000–34,000 / $43,000–48,000 ⚒ RM

1954 Aston Martin DB2/4 Drophead Coupé, 2.9 litres, engine overhauled, original condition, 1 of approximately 70 examples built.
£45,000–50,000 / $65,500–72,500 ⚒ BKS
The need to widen the appeal of the already successful DB2 resulted in the October 1953 introduction of the 2+2 DB2/4. Extensive revisions to the rear end made room for two occasional seats and more luggage, the latter being reached through a hatchback rear door.

1962 Austin-Healey 3000 Mk II, 2912cc overhead-valve straight-6 engine, triple carburettors, 4-speed gearbox, disc front/drum rear brakes, recently restored.
£20,000–23,000 / $29,000–33,000 ⚒ RM

1958 Austin-Healey Sprite Mk I, 948cc, recently restored, reconditioned engine, gas-flowed Cooper crossflow cylinder head and exhaust system, resprayed British racing green, pale green interior, very good condition.
£9,000–10,000 / $13,000–14,500 ⚒ BKS

1939 Bentley 4¼ Litre Tourer, 4257cc, crossflow cylinder head, twin SU carburettors, twin fuel pumps, single coil ignition, 126bhp, central lubrication system, leaf-spring suspension, adjustable front and rear hydraulic shock absorbers, power-assisted brakes, stainless-steel exhaust, full-flow engine oil filter system, lightweight Vanden Plas-style tourer body, finished in red, red leather trim and carpets, 1 of the last Derby Bentleys built, very good condition.
£50,000–55,000 / $72,500–79,500 ⚒ COYS
These cars, with their overdrive gearboxes, were capable of sustained cruising speeds of 90mph (a figure impressive even by today's standards), which represented 3,000rpm. The more effective 17in wheels and tyres, and much lighter steering of the later chassis ensured that this produced the ultimate mechanical package for touring abroad.

1947 Bentley Mk VI Convertible, coachwork by Franay, overhead inlet and side exhaust valves, independent front suspension, vanity unit, fitted luggage in boot, completely restored, 1 of only 2 cabriolet bodies built by Franay on the Bentley Mk VI.
£145,000–160,000 / $210,000–232,000 ⚒ BKS

► **1948 Bristol 400,** 1971cc 6-cylinder engine, 80bhp at 4,200rpm, independent front suspension, rack-and-pinion steering, cream leather upholstery, engine rebuilt, uprated oil pump, 1,500 miles covered since, good mechanical condition, sound coachwork and chassis.
£14,000–16,000 / $20,300–23,300 ⚒ BRIT

1939 Bugatti Type 57 Aravis Cabriolet, coachwork by Letourneur et Marchand, chassis no. 57732, straight-8 engine, Stromberg carburettors,140bhp, 4-speed gearbox, semi-elliptic front springs, quarter-elliptic rear springs, hydraulic shock absorbers, 4-wheel hydraulic brakes.
£500,000+ / $725,000 ⚒ Pou

► **1923 Buick Model 48 Coupé,** 242cu.in overhead-valve 6-cylinder engine, 60bhp, 3-speed manual gearbox, semi-elliptic leaf springs all-round, Westinghouse shock absorbers, 2-wheel mechanical brakes, left-hand drive, restored, stored since 1991, good running order.
£6,500–8,000 / $9,500–11,500 ⚒ C
For 1923, Buick substantially improved its models' styling, with domed front and rear wings, more rounded coachwork, scuttle-mounted sidelights and drum headlights; a new radiator grille also appeared. In this year, Buick built its millionth car. The Model 48, was one of the most expensive of the 15 variants offered, at $1,895.

1930 Cadillac Series 353 Roadster, 353cu.in V8 engine, 95bhp, 3-speed synchromesh gearbox, 4-wheel drum brakes, Fleetwood-style coachwork, completely restored.
£40,000–45,000 / $58,000–65,250 ⚒ RM

1947 Cadillac Series 62 Convertible, 346cu.in V8 engine, 150bhp, automatic transmission, tan leather interior, tan top, completely restored, excellent condition.
£25,000–28,000 / $36,250–40,600 ⚒ RM

1957 Chevrolet Corvette, 283cu.in overhead-valve V8 engine, Rochester mechanical fuel injection, 283bhp, 3-speed manual gearbox, heater, Wonderbar radio, white interior, older restoration.
£35,000–40,000 / $50,750–58,000 ⚒ RM
With the advent of the 283cu.in version of Chevrolet's lightweight and durable V8 engine in 1957, the Corvette finally fulfilled its promise as a true American sports car. To complement the 283 Corvette, competition options proliferated, including wide wheels, Positraction rear axles in three ratios, and a racing suspension package with high-performance sintered metallic brake linings.

1969 Chevrolet Corvette L88, 427cu.in V8 engine, aluminium heads, 430bhp, 4-speed manual gearbox, power-assisted 4-wheel disc brakes, 4-wheel independent suspension, restored to original condition.
£50,000–55,000 / $72,500–79,750 ⚒ RM
When launched in 1967, Chevrolet's 427 L88 engine was rated at an almost arbitrary 430bhp. In fact, output was estimated to be 550+bhp. Most performance buyers, however, chose the tri-power L71 engine option, probably because it was rated at 435bhp. What they did not know was that Chevrolet had created a more potent engine in the L88. Although on paper it appeared to offer less power for more money (the L88 was a $950 option, twice the price of the L71 engine), in reality it was the most powerful of the Corvette engine offerings. So powerful was the car, that Chevrolet had to declare it an off-road vehicle in company documentation. Between 1967 and 1969, only 216 L88 Corvettes were built.

1931 Chrysler CG Imperial Dual-Cowl Phaeton, 385cu.in straight-8 engine, 125bhp, 4-speed manual gearbox, 4-wheel hydraulic drum brakes, dual windscreens with wind wings, chrome grille guard, Apcor dual taillights, chrome wire wheels, light tan interior, leather-covered trunk with fitted luggage, originally built as a saloon, new coachwork fitted 1980s.
£85,000–95,000 / $123,250–137,750 ⚒ RM

► **1969 Daimler 250 V8 Saloon,** 2500cc V8 engine, grey trim, 55,000 miles recorded, excellent condition.
£10,500–12,000 / $15,250–17,400 ⚒ H&H

1937 Delahaye Type 135M Drophead Coupé, coachwork in the style of Figoni et Falaschi, 3557cc 6-cylinder engine, triple Solex carburettors, competition camshafts, Cotal electric gearbox, GP brake drums, Borrani 17in wire wheels, fold-down windscreen, Aerolux Marchal lamps and spotlights, restored 1990s, engine rebuilt, resprayed, newly upholstered in pigskin.
£120,000–132,000 / $174,000–190,000 ⚒ BKS

◄ **1926 Dodge Woody Wagon,** 212cu.in L-head 4-cylinder engine, 35bhp, 3-speed gearbox, 2-wheel mechanical brakes, left-hand drive, restored, excellent condition.
£15,000–18,000 / $21,750–26,000 ⚒ RM
Originally known as Depot Hacks, these wood-panelled trucks often seated up to two dozen passengers (with plenty of room for luggage) and were used to ferry people from railway stations to the nearest town. Woodies underwent a transformation in the 1930s from practical workhorses to luxury cars, frequently being the most expensive car in a manufacturer's range.

1929 Duesenberg Model J Convertible Coupé, coachwork by Murphy, 420cu.in double-overhead-camshaft straight-8 engine, 260bhp, 3-speed manual gearbox, 4-wheel vacuum-assisted brakes, original chassis, older restoration, recent full mechanical rebuild, excellent condition.
£350,000+ / $507,500+ ⚒ RM
The trademark of Murphy body design was the 'clear vision' pillar. On the convertible coupé, the windscreen pillars were designed to be as slim as possible, creating a sportier, more open appearance while improving driver vision. In fact, Murphy advertised that its windscreen pillars were 'narrower than the space between a man's eyes', a design it claimed eliminated blind spots.

1931 Duesenberg Mudd Coupé, 420cu.in double-overhead-camshaft straight-8 engine, 8-port chromed exhaust header, 3-speed manual gearbox, semi-elliptic leaf springs and drum brakes all-round, engine-turned dashboard, aircraft-style instruments, including altimeter, sliding sunroof.
£800,000+ / $1,160,000+ ⚒ RM
When it was just a year old, Dr. Seeley G. Mudd purchased a Derham-bodied Duesenberg from his friend, E. F. Fisher. Wanting to improve the performance of the car, he contacted Duesenberg in California. As a result, high-compression pistons, heavier con-rods, Lovejoy shock absorbers, 17in wheels and a supercharger were installed. Mudd also commissioned Bohman and Schwartz (formerly Murphy) to install a fabric-covered body of his own specification on the Duesenberg chassis. The design employed aerodynamic principles that were only experimental in the early 1930s. The swept-back roofline featured a tapered rear deck, integral boot and split rear window.

1963 Ferrari 250 GT SWB Spyder California, Ansa exhausts, Marchal spotlights, carpets and leather seats in Bordeaux red, black soft top, left-hand drive, 8,200 miles recorded, excellent condition.
£750,000+ / $1,087,500 ⚒ Pou

1965 Ferrari 275 GTB/6C Aluminium Berlinetta, coachwork by Pininfarina, chassis no. 8051, dry-sump lubrication, 5-speed transaxle, tubular chassis, 4-wheel independent suspension by parallel A-arms with coil-spring/damper units, anti-roll bars, 4-wheel disc brakes, Borrani wire wheels, aluminium bodywork, original pleated black leather seats and carpets.
£160,000–180,000 / $230,000–260,000 ⚒ BKS
Styled by Pininfarina and built by Scaglietti, the 275 GTB was powered by the 3.3 litre twin-cam 275 engine created for the company's sports-racers, which had already been race proven. The engine developed a claimed 280bhp at 7,500rpm with the standard triple Weber carburettors; when fitted with the optional six-Weber installation, as on this car, output was in the region of 300bhp.

1974 Ferrari 246 GTS Dino Spyder, coachwork by Pininfarina, wheel arches flared for 7½ x 14in alloy wheels, air conditioning, electric windows, 'Daytona' black-ribbed squab panels set in brown leather upholstery, left-hand drive, 55,500 miles recorded, excellent mechanical condition.
£50,000–60,000 / $72,500–87,000 ⚒ BKS

1978 Ferrari 308 GTS, 3 litre double-overhead-camshaft V8 engine, 4 Weber carburettors, 5-speed gearbox, 4-wheel independent front suspension, 4-wheel disc brakes
£25,000–30,000 / $35,250–43,500 ⚒ Pou

◀ **1989 Ferrari F40,** coachwork by Pininfarina, V8 engine, twin IHI turbochargers, Weber-Marelli electronic fuel injection, 478bhp, 5-speed transaxle, 4-wheel independent suspension, 1,500 miles recorded.
£140,000–160,000 / $203,000–232,000 ⚒ BKS

1952 Fiat 8V Berlinetta, 2 litre V8 engine, 105bhp, 4-speed synchromesh gearbox, 4-wheel drum brakes, black upholstery, restored, converted to right-hand drive, 1 of 70 believed to exist, good condition.
£60,000–70,000 / $87,000–101,500 ⚒ BKS
The 1952 Geneva Salon saw Fiat present its most ambitious model ever, the 8V or 'Ottovu'. Designer Fabio Luigi Rapi's brief was that it should be aerodynamically efficient enough to exceed 200km/h. The resulting body was based on a double steel shell, each layer wafer thin. The inner layer provided structural rigidity, while the outer gave the car its aerodynamically clean profile, which had a Cd of 0.17. Between 1952 and 1954, 114 8Vs were made, and they were offered for sale at 2.8 million lire, comparable to a contemporary Ferrari or Maserati. From 1952 to 1958, the 8V achieved no less than 43 class victories.

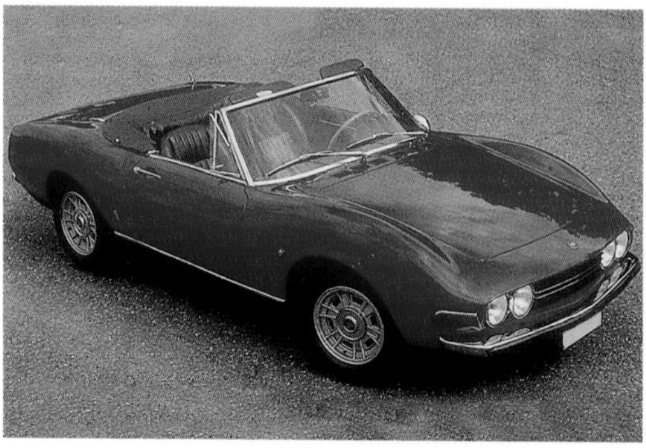

1967 Fiat Dino Spyder, 2 litre double-overhead-camshaft V6 engine, largely original, good condition.
£12,000–15,000 / $17,400–21,750 ⚒ COYS

1970 Fiat 850 Sport, coachwork by Bertone, 903cc, 4-wheel independent suspension, front disc brakes, cosmetic restoration 1992–94, resprayed in original yellow-green, replated bumpers, new headlining and carpets, excellent condition.
£4,000–5,000 / $5,800–7,250 ⚒ BKS

1916 Ford Model T Five-Seat Tourer, 2890cc 4-cylinder sidevalve engine, 22bhp, 2-speed and reverse epicyclic gearbox, beam front axle, semi-elliptic transverse leaf springs front and rear, braking by contracting band on transmission, brass radiator, extensively restored.
£13,000–15,000 / $18,750–21,750 ⚒ C

1934 Ford DeLuxe Roadster, 221cu.in V8 engine, 3-speed gearbox, beam front axle, transverse leaf springs front and rear, 4-wheel drum brakes, 16in accessory wheels, bumper guards, wind wings, radiator temperature indicator, glovebox radio, leather upholstery, body-off restoration 1990, fewer than 100 miles since, engine, gearbox and driveline rebuilt 1999.
£32,000–37,000 / $46,500–54,500 ⚒ RM
The 1934 Ford featured refined styling cues based on the shield-shaped grille that had appeared in 1933. By 1934, all-weather convertibles had made serious inroads into the market for roadsters, but the sporty roadster held on to its position as the vehicle of choice for young men. It cost less than the convertible, making it accessible to young buyers. It weighed 85lb less than the convertible too, giving it the best 'performance per dollar' value in the Ford line-up.

1957 Ford Thunderbird Convertible, 312cu.in V8 engine, 3-speed gearbox, 4-wheel power-assisted drum brakes, power steering, Kelsey Hayes chrome wire wheels, air conditioning, hard and soft tops, completely restored.
£22,000–26,000 / $31,900–37,700 ⚒ RM
Only three per cent of Thunderbirds that rolled off the production line in 1957 were finished in this Dusk Rose colour.

▶ 1967 Ford Shelby GT 500, 7016cc V8 engine, 4-barrel Holley carburettor, 3-speed automatic transmission, disc front/drum rear brakes.
£20,000–25,000 / $29,000–36,000 ⚒ Pou

◀ 1967 Ghia 450SS Convertible, 273cu.in V8 engine, 235bhp, automatic transmission, front disc/rear drum brakes, restored 1999.
£22,000–25,000
$31,900–36,250 ⚒ RM
This Ghia was transformed in 1968 by famed custom coachbuilder George Barris. Among the changes Barris made was the deletion of the front bumper and remodelling of the nose.

▶ 1911 Hupmobile Model 20 Runabout, 4-cylinder engine, Rushmore searchlights, running-board-mounted Phare Universal acetylene canister, lightweight bucket-seat coachwork.
£10,500–12,000 /$15,250–17,400 ⚒ BKS
Following a distinguished career with Oldsmobile, Ford and Regal, Robert Craig Hupp began manufacturing cars bearing his name in 1909 in Detroit, Michigan. The first Hupmobile was a four-cylinder, 16.9hp Runabout with sliding-gear transmission. Designated the Model 20, it found 1,618 customers in the first year. Hupp left the company in 1911 following a disagreement with the board, but Hupmobile continued, the Model 32 of 1912 onwards, an all-steel bodied car, proving extremely popular and being the mainstay of pre-WWI production.

◀ 1967 Iso Grifo, 327cu.in. V8 engine, 340bhp, 4-speed manual gearbox, 4-wheel disc brakes, 1 of 412 Grifos built, restored mechanically, original.
£22,000–25,000
$31,900–36,250 ⚒ RM

1939 Jaguar SS100 Sports Roadster, 3485cc overhead-valve 6-cylinder engine, restored 1980s, new steering box, direction indicators, burgundy leather upholstery, little use since 1966, 1 of 116 built.
£100,000–115,000 / $145,000–166,750 ⚒ BKS
To many people, the SS100 is the archetypal late-1930s sports car. Its long louvred bonnet, slab-tank tail, folding screen, flowing wings, sculpted doors and fine performance added up to an amazing car. It was priced at £395 with a 2½ litre engine and £445 with the 3½ litre unit. The latter propelled the SS100 to 60mph in under 11 seconds.

◀ **1948 Jaguar Mk IV Drophead Coupé,** 3485cc overhead-valve 6-cylinder engine, twin SU carburettors, 125bhp, 4-speed gearbox, Girling mechanical brakes, Lucas headlights, bookmatched walnut veneer woodwork, rear-seat picnic tables, body-off restoration, 1 of 376 left-hand drive examples built.
£40,000–45,000 / $58,000–65,250 ⚒ RM

1950 Jaguar XK120 Lightweight Roadster, 3442cc double-overhead-camshaft 6-cylinder engine, 1 of 240 aluminium-bodied examples built.
£55,000–65,000 / $79,750–94,250 ⚒ BKS
Intended as a low-volume sporting model, the XK120 proved to be immensely more popular than had ever been thought possible, demand for what was then the world's fastest production car taking Jaguar's hierarchy completely by surprise. It immediately became obvious that the new model's ash-framed, aluminium-skinned coachwork – which was hand-built in the best vintage tradition – would have to go, so, after only 240 'aluminium' cars had been completed, the XK120 was re-engineered, enabling it to be speedily assembled using pressed-steel body sections and panels.

▶ **1967 Jaguar 340 Saloon,** 3.4 litre double-overhead-camshaft 6-cylinder engine, manual gearbox with overdrive, chrome wire wheels, tan leather interior, built originally to export specification, restored, fewer than 2,500 miles since 1993.
£16,000–18,000 / $23,200–26,200 ⚒ BKS

1952 Jaguar XK120 SE Coupé, 3442cc double-overhead-camshaft 6-cylinder engine, 4-speed manual gearbox, 4-wheel drum brakes, left-hand drive, completely restored at a cost of over £45,000, only 600 miles recorded since.
£30,000–35,000 / $43,500–50,750 ⚒ RM

▶ **1961 Jaguar E-Type Coupé,** 3781cc double-overhead-camshaft 6-cylinder engine, triple carburettors, 265bhp, 4-speed manual gearbox with synchromesh, anti-dive independent front suspension, 4-wheel servo-assisted disc brakes, restored.
£17,000–20,000 / $24,650–29,000 ⚒ C

Buick

Buick is one of those names that has steered a steady course through the mainstream of the American automobile industry, yet the man who founded the marque was actually a Scot. David Dunbar Buick moved to the USA at an early age, and by 1903 had built and tested his own car. By 1908 Buick had left the company and the dynamic William Crapo Durant was in control, using Buick as the foundation for General Motors. The millionth Buick was built in 1923, and throughout most of its life since Buick has provided stout service as a General Motors middle-market brand.

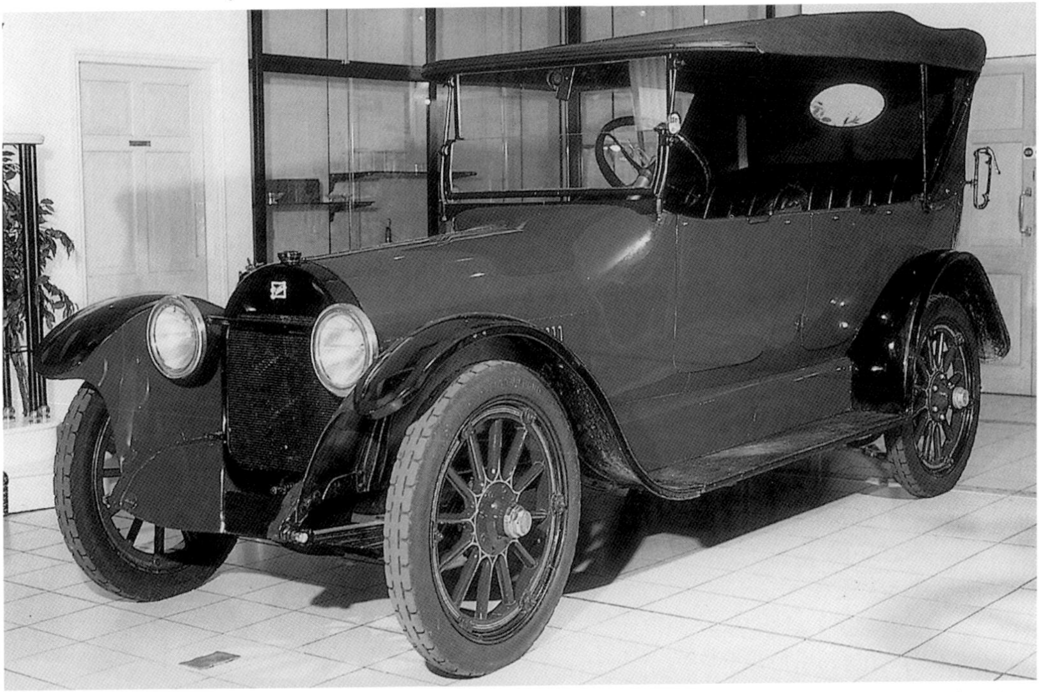

1919 Buick Model 45K Tourer, 4 litre 6-cylinder engine, fitted with modern carburettor, original Marvel Series F carburettor, Autovac and pipework included, new radiator, resprayed in original blue, new hood, hood bag and tonneau cover, reupholstered and carpeted.
£10,500–13,000 / $15,200–19,500 ⚒ TEN

1923 Buick Model 65 Five-Seater Tourer, 4.2 litre overhead-valve 6-cylinder engine, 55bhp, 3-speed manual gearbox, beam front axle, leaf-spring suspension, mechanical drum brakes, left-hand drive, completely restored, finished in burgundy with black wings, black interior trim, good original order.
£15,000–17,000 / $22,475–24,650 ⚒ C
At the heart of Buick's early success were its finely engineered, overhead-valve, six-cylinder power units, the first of which was introduced in 1915, as a reliable 5.4 litre motor providing an abundance of power. With manufacturing policy controlled by GM, the range was simplified, the six being fitted into just two sizes of chassis. But with seven Fisher body styles available, together with many paint and trim options, the possibilities were endless. Given an engine so flexible that, once moving, gear changing was unnecessary under most driving conditions, the Buick was one automobile that lived up to the salesman's promise of easy driving.

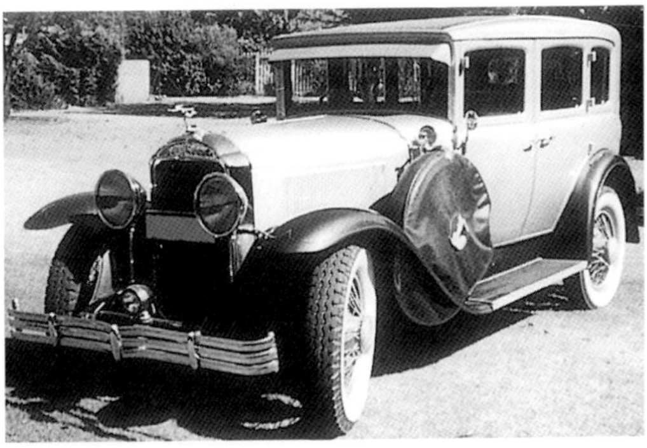

1929 Buick Series 121 Saloon, 5073cc 6-cylinder engine, finished in silver-grey with dark grey wings, dark red leather interior trim, 1 of 355 export models built, of which only 169 in right-hand drive, coachwork sound and rust-free, good mechanical condition, stored for some time, in need of recommissioning.
£9,500–11,500 / $13,775–16,675 ⚒ BRIT
For 1929, the Buick range underwent a substantial redesign, with styling carried out by General Motors' Art and Colour Department. Three new series were available – the 116, 121 and 129 (these numbers representing the wheelbase dimensions). New features were a slightly slanted windscreen on closed models and a new, distinctive radiator shell. Buick was celebrating its silver anniversary that year, and no fewer than 43 exterior colour schemes were offered. An impressive range of coachwork styles was listed on all three chassis, ranging from sporting roadsters to seven-passenger limousines.

BUICK Model	ENGINE cc/cyl	DATES	CONDITION 1	2	3
Veteran	various	1903–09	£18,500	£12,000	£8,000
18/20	3881/6	1918–22	£12,000	£5,000	£2,000
Series 22	2587/4	1922–24	£9,000	£5,000	£3,000
Series 24/6	3393/6	1923–30	£9,000	£5,000	£3,000
Light 8	3616/8	1931	£18,000	£14,500	£11,000
Straight 8	4467/8	1931	£22,000	£18,000	£10,000
50 Series	3857/8	1931–39	£18,500	£15,000	£8,000
60 Series	5247/8	1936–39	£19,000	£15,000	£8,000
90 Series	5648/8	1934–35	£20,000	£15,500	£9,000
40 Series	4064/8	1936–39	£19,000	£14,000	£10,000
80/90	5247/8	1936–39	£25,000	£20,000	£15,000
McLaughlin	5247/8	1937–40	£22,000	£15,000	£10,000

Various chassis lengths and bodies will affect value. Buick chassis fitted with British bodies prior to 1916 were called Bedford-Buicks. Right-hand drive can have an added premium of 25%.

A known continuous history can add value to and enhance the enjoyment of a car.

► **1956 Buick Roadmaster Convertible,** power steering, brakes, top, windows and seats, air conditioning, subject of cosmetic restoration, original rust-free car.
£18,000–22,000
$26,000–32,000 ⚒ BJ

1987 Buick GNX Coupé, 231cu.in turbocharged and intercooled V6 engine, 275bhp, 4-speed automatic transmission, front disc/rear drum brakes, independent front suspension, original alloy wheels, air conditioning, power windows, door locks and seats, tilt steering, cruise control, 533 miles from new.
£17,000–22,000 / $24,500–32,000 ⚒ RM
In the 1980s, Buick continued its long, but erratic, performance history with the Regal Grand National. Based on a front-engine, rear-drive Regal/Malibu platform, it was an attempt to meet the demands of performance-starved enthusiasts with its turbocharged V6. Mid-way through the Grand National's production run, Buick authorised 547 specials, designated GNX. Built by ASC/McLaren, the GNX employed a high-performance Garrett turbocharger, improved intercooler, revised engine management calibration, high-performance transmission valving and free-flow exhaust. Performance was boosted to over 275bhp. Larger tyres, special alloy wheels, a rear axle torque arm and panhard rod, plus added frame stiffening were standard on the GNX. Front wing vents helped engine cooling.

BUICK Model	ENGINE cu. in/cyl	DATES	CONDITION 1	2	3
Special/Super 4-Door	248/364/8	1950–59	£6,000	£4,000	£2,000
Special/Super Riviera	263/332/8	1050–56	£8,000	£6,000	£3,000
Special/Super Convertible	263/332/8	1950–56	£8,500	£5,500	£3,000
Roadmaster 4-door	320/365/8	1950–58	£11,000	£8,000	£6,000
Roadmaster Riviera	320/364/8	1950–58	£9,000	£7,000	£5,000
Roadmaster Convertible	320/364/8	1950–58	£16,000	£11,000	£7,000
Special/Super Riviera	364/8	1957–59	£10,750	£7,500	£5,000
Special/Super Convertible	364/8	1957–58	£13,500	£11,000	£6,000

Cadillac

The very first Cadillac, known retrospectively as the Model A, was completed on 17 October, 1902. That first product of the company founded by Henry Martin Leland was distinguished by its considerable refinement compared with other offerings of the time, and ever since then the Cadillac name has been a byword for prestige motoring. In 1909 the young company was acquired by General Motors, where it has remained pre-eminent ever since as the flagship marque. But Cadillacs were not merely luxurious; in many stages throughout its history, the company has been at the forefront in the practical application of innovation and technology. In 1912 Cadillac became 'the car that has no crank', with the introduction of the electric self-starter; electric lights also appeared that year. In 1914 it introduced its first V8, and that engine layout has remained a feature of the marque ever since. In 1929 Cadillac introduced safety glass and a synchromesh gearbox, and the following year the extravagant V16 arrived, followed closely by the V12 models. Naturally, sales plummeted during the depression following the Wall Street Crash, and the extravagant excess was reined in to match the slimmer wallets of the day. Even so, Cadillac suffered less than many other luxury car manufacturers, and in the years after 1935 nearly half of all cars sold in the USA costing more than $1,500 (£1,000) were Cadillacs. One name that cannot be omitted in any mention is that of GM stylist Harley J. Earl. He drafted his first Cadillacs in 1928, and after WWII went on to create the ultimate automotive expression of the American dream – fins, chrome and bullet-shaped bumpers. Of his creations none is more iconic than the 1959 Cadillac.

◄ **1911 Cadillac Model 30 Open Drive Limousine,** 4.7 litre engine, 3-speed gearbox, twin coil and magneto ignition, oil side lamps, acetylene headlamps, finished in black with red coachlining, 7-passenger, rear compartment features cloth upholstery, fold-away occasional seats, roller blinds to rear windows, drop-down bevelled glass windows, courtesy lights, vase holders with glass vases, individual companion sets, speaking tube, driver's compartment upholstered in black leather, VCC dated.
£15,000–17,000 / $21,750–24,650 ⚒ BKS

► **1931 Cadillac V16 Saoutchik Sunroof Sedan,** full-length sunroof, finished in pale blue, restored, excellent condition.
£85,000–95,000 / $123,000–138,000 ⚒ BJ
The sunroof of this car incorporates a small window that aligns with the rear window when the roof is open.

1938 Cadillac Convertible Victoria, coachwork by Brunn, 346cu.in sidevalve V8 engine, 135bhp, 3-speed synchromesh gearbox with column change, independent front suspension, 4-wheel hydraulic drum brakes, completely restored, excellent mechanical condition.
£90,000–100,000 / $131,000–145,000 ⚒ RM

CADILLAC (pre-war) Model	ENGINE cc/cyl	DATES	CONDITION 1	2	3
Type 57–61	5153/8	1915–23	£20,000+	£14,000	£6,000
Series 314	5153/8	1926–27	£22,000	£15,000	£6,000
Type V63	5153/8	1924–27	£20,000	£13,000	£5,000
Series 341	5578/8	1928–29	£22,000+	£15,000+	£6,000
Series 353–5	5289/8	1930–31	£50,000+	£30,000	£18,000
V16	7406/16	1931–32	£80,000+	£50,000+	£20,000
V12	6030/12	1932–37	£42,000+	£25,000	£15,000
V8	5790/8	1935–36	£30,000+	£15,000	£6,000
V16	7034/16	1937–40	£50,000+	£30,000	£18,000

▶ **1947 Cadillac Series 62 Fastback,** rebuilt at a cost of over £50,000, fitted with later Cadillac 500cu.in V8 engine, automatic transmission, Chevrolet Camaro front subframe, front disc brakes, finished in pale pink, air conditioning, heater.
£40,000–45,000 / $58,000–62,250 ⚒ BJ

1959 Cadillac Coupé de Ville, 6.4 litre V8 engine, automatic transmission, bare-metal respray in metallic dark green 1998, very good condition throughout.
£7,000–10,000 / $10,000–14,500 ⚒ BARO

1959 Cadillac Eldorado Convertible, 390cu.in overhead-valve V8 engine, automatic transmission, power steering and brakes, original Eldorado-only hard parade top cover, factory air conditioning, 42,000 miles from new, restored to concours condition.
£40,000–45,000 / $58,000–62,000 ⚒ RM

Although Cadillac had invented the tailfin in 1948, by the late 1950s, other manufacturers were offering their own versions. In fact, the 1959 Cadillac fins were a response by Cadillac to the 1957 Chrysler line, which had borrowed Cadillac's idea and taken it one step further. According to the late David Holls, former design director at GM, the famous 1959 fins were the result of a directive from management that Cadillac could not be outdone by anyone.

1961 Cadillac Coupé de Ville, V8 engine, automatic transmission, restored at a cost of £12,000, very good condition throughout.
£6,000–8,000 / $8,700–11,600 ⚒ H&H

1961 Cadillac Eldorado Biarritz Convertible, 390cu.in V8 engine, 325bhp, automatic transmission, power quarterlights, 6-way seats, completely restored, finished in Persian Sand.
£18,000–21,000 / $21,000–30,500 ⚒ RM

CADILLAC Model	ENGINE cu. in/cyl	DATES	CONDITION 1	2	3
4-door sedan	331/8	1949	£8,000	£4,500	£3,000
2-door fastback	331/8	1949	£10,000	£8,000	£5,000
Convertible coupé	331/8	1949	£22,000	£12,000	£10,000
Series 62 4-door	331/ 365/8	1950–55	£7,000	£5,500	£3,000
Sedan de Ville	365/8	1956–58	£8,000	£6,000	£4,000
Coupé de Ville	331/ 365/8	1950–58	£12,500	£9,500	£3,500
Convertible coupé	331/ 365/8	1950–58	£25,000	£20,000	£10,000
Eldorado	331/8	1953–55	£35,000	£30,000	£18,000
Eldorado Seville	365/8	1956–58	£11,500	£9,000	£5,500
Eldorado Biarritz	365/8	1956–58	£30,000	£20,000	£15,000
Sedan de Ville	390/8	1959	£12,000	£9,500	£5,000
Coupé de Ville	390/8	1959	£15,000	£9,000	£5,500
Convertible coupé	390/8	1959	£28,000	£20,000	£10,000
Eldorado Seville	390/8	1959	£13,000	£10,000	£6,000
Eldorado Biarritz	390/8	1959	£30,000	£20,000	£14,000
Sedan de Ville	390/8	1960	£10,000	£8,000	£4,500
Convertible coupé	390/8	1960	£27,000+	£14,000	£7,500
Eldorado Biarritz	390/8	1960	£25,000+	£17,000	£10,000
Sedan de Ville	390/ 429/8	1961–64	£7,000	£5,000	£3,000
Coupé de Ville	390/ 429/8	1961–64	£8,000	£6,000	£4,000
Convertible coupé	390/ 429/8	1961–64	£20,000	£9,000	£7,000
Eldorado Biarritz	390/ 429/8	1961–64	£19,500	£14,000	£9,000

Miller's is a price GUIDE not a price LIST

► **1984 Cadillac Eldorado Convertible,** 4.1 litre V8 engine, digital fuel injection, front-wheel drive, finished in gold, brown interior, 59,000 miles from new, very good condition.
£5,500–7,000
$7,975–10,150 ⚒ BKS

Caterham

◄ **1984 Caterham 7 Supersprint,** 1700cc crossflow 4-cylinder engine to Sprint specification, 135bhp, 'long-cockpit' model, finished in red, original, never raced, excellent mechanical condition.
£6,250–7,500
$9,100–10,800 ⚒ BRIT
Caterham Cars acquired the design rights to the Lotus 7 in 1973, since when the car has been progressively developed and improved in detail.

Chandler

1923 Chandler 45hp Seven-Passenger Touring Car, older restoration, excellent condition.
£8,000–9,500 / $11,600–13,800 ⚒ BKS
Chandler was founded in Cleveland, Ohio, by former executives of the Lozier Motor Company, of Detroit, in 1913. Taking its name from Lozier's former sales manager, Fred C. Chandler, the new firm began production in 1914 with a medium-priced six that soon established a reputation for quality and performance. A Chandler was victorious at the prestigious Pikes Peak hillclimb in 1925 – leading to the engine being marketed as the 'Pikes Peak' unit – and the following year another sped through 1,000 miles in 689 minutes. Despite achieving its best sales in 1927, Chandler lost money that year, almost certainly because of the costs incurred in developing its new Eight. The following year it was acquired by the Hupp Motor Corporation, which closed Chandler almost immediately.

Chevrolet

In 1910, when William C. Durant lost control of General Motors, the firm he had founded in 1908, he immediately began making his comeback, and in 1911 set up a new company, naming it after Swiss-born racing driver Louis Chevrolet, who helped design their first car. By 1916 Durant's fortunes had soared so dramatically that his company actually bought General Motors. However, by 1920, as the post-war depression took hold, Durant lost both Chevrolet and General Motors. Durant's legacy, however, is a marque that ever since has steered a steady course through the mainstream of American motoring, running head to head with Ford in the competition for the affections and wallets of working Americans.

1932 Chevrolet Independent Four-Door Sedan, 3000cc 6-cylinder engine, 3-speed manual gearbox, wire wheels, single driver's side windscreen wiper, side-mounted spare, bench front seat, left-hand drive, completely restored, finished in maroon with gold coachlines, black wings, grey buttoned upholstery, excellent condition.
£7,500–9,000 / $10,800–13,000 H&H

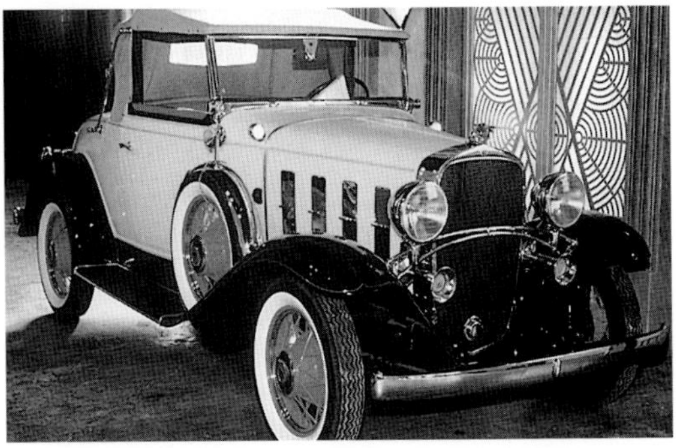

1932 Chevrolet Confederate BA Deluxe Cabriolet, 194cu.in 6-cylinder engine, 60bhp, 3-speed manual gearbox, leaf-spring suspension, 4-wheel drum brakes, older restoration, good condition.
£18,000–20,000 / $26,000–29,000 RM

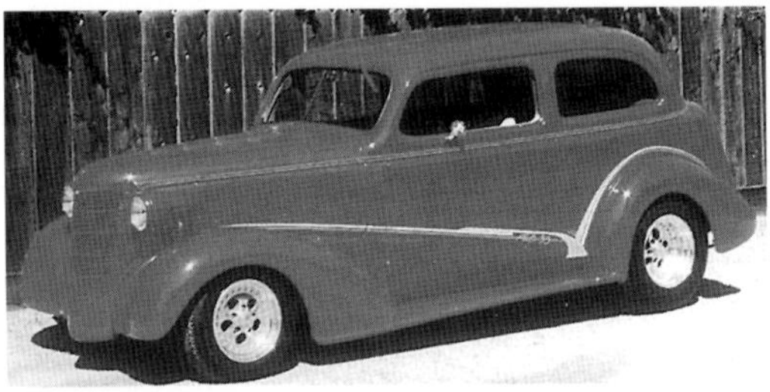

1938 Chevrolet Street Rod, completely rebuilt, auxiliary electric fan, Centerline aluminium wheels, tilt steering, air conditioning, power aerial.
£24,000–27,000 / $34,800–39,000 BJ

1955 Chevrolet Belair Two-Door Hardtop, 265cu.in V8 engine, automatic transmission, restored, very good condition.
£11,000–13,000 / $16,000–18,850 HMM

1956 Chevrolet 150 Two-Door Saloon, V8 engine, twin 4-barrel carburettors, body-off restoration, original, concours winner.
£20,000–22,000 / $29,000–32,000 BJ

1957 Chevrolet Bel Air Two-Door Hardtop, 4350cc V8 engine, twin 4-barrel carburettors, heater, air conditioning, rebuilt at a cost of over £68,000.
£28,000–32,000 / $40,600–46,400 BJ

CHEVROLET Model	ENGINE cc/cyl	DATES	CONDITION 1	2	3
H4/H490 K Series	2801/4	1914–29	£9,000	£5,000	£2,000
FA5	2699/4	1918	£8,000	£5,000	£2,000
D5	5792/8	1918–19	£10,000	£6,000	£3,000
FB50	3660/4	1919–21	£7,000	£4,000	£2,000
AA	2801/4	1928–32	£5,000	£3,000	£1,000
AB/C	3180/6	1929–36	£6,000	£4,000	£2,000
Master	3358/6	1934–37	£9,000	£5,000	£2,000
Master De Luxe	3548/6	1938–41	£9,000	£6,000	£4,000

Chevrolet 150, 210, Bel Air, (1955–57)

Engines: 3862cc straight-six; 4350cc V8; 4674cc V8 (1957 only).
Power output: 123–136bhp for six-cylinder models; 162–225bhp for 4350cc V8; 185–283bhp for 4674cc V8.
Transmission: Three-speed manual, optional overdrive; two- and three-speed automatic.
Maximum speed: 108mph (1956 Turbo-Fire 4350cc V8).
0–60mph: 10.7 seconds (1956 Turbo-Fire 4350cc V8).
'Go all the way, then back off': that was what General Motors' styling chief Harley Earl told his design team to do for the 1955 Chevrolet range. At a stroke, Chevrolet shed its one-time image as a maker of dull, reliable granny-mobiles and assaulted an affluent younger generation with a three-year model range so mythic that enthusiasts have coined their own name for the 1955–57 models – Tri-Chevies. Gone was the paunchy rotundity; in its place crisp, clean lines that inclined forward and made the car look ever so eager. And it was. For the first time in its history, Chevrolet offered a V8 engine option. The injection of potent V8 power was as rejuvenating as Viagra, and now Chevrolet could justifiably advertise itself as 'the hot one'. The line kicked off with the plain-Jane 150; the mid-range 210 added a little more equipment and extra chrome garnish; and at the top, complete with gold name script, was the luxury Bel Air, the model that earned the nickname 'baby Cadillac'. Of the three model years, 1957 is considered the ultimate classic, none more so than the awesome V8 Ramjet fuel-injected 4.7 litre model. In American, that is 283cu.in, and with a power output of 283bhp, Chevrolet claimed it was the first production engine to offer the magic 1bhp/cu.in.

1957 Chevrolet Bel Air Convertible, 283cu.in overhead-valve V8 engine, fuel injection, 283bhp, servo-assisted 4-wheel drum brakes, restored at a cost of over £95,000, concours winner.
£50,000–60,000 / $72,500–87,000 ⚒ RM

1959 Chevrolet Impala SS F1 Coupé, original red paint, original interior, 32,800 miles from new, 1 of 27 fuel-injected cars built in 1959.
£30,000–33,000 / $43,500–48,000 ⚒ BJ

1962 Chevrolet Impala SS409 Sport Coupé, 409cu.in V8 engine, 409bhp, twin Rochester 4-barrel carburettors, Muncie 4-speed manual gearbox, heavy-duty suspension, 4-wheel hydraulic drum brakes, restored, finished in black, red vinyl and cloth interior, original, excellent overall condition.
£16,000–18,000 / $23,000–26,000 ⚒ RM

1970 Chevrolet Nova SS, 402cu.in V8 engine, 375bhp, 4-speed manual gearbox, servo-assisted front disc/rear drum brakes, power steering, subject of no-expense-spared restoration, finished in metallic light blue, black interior, 44,000 miles from new.
£26,000–29,000 / $38,000–42,000 ⚒ RM
When the Nova SS debuted in 1964, it was intended for a very specific market. The model upon which it was based – The Chevy II – was a rather staid, relatively cheap, entry-level car. The Nova SS was available with the 283cu.in V8, which produced 195bhp. Thanks in large part to its low overall weight, it became a contender on the street and on the dragstrip. In fact, the success of the Nova led Chevrolet to adopt all of the engines available in the Camaro line-up, including the 375bhp 396cu.in V8. With this, Chevy created the ultimate 'sleeper', a true wolf in sheep's clothing that could match the performance of cars costing thousands of dollars more. Throughout the 1960s, the Nova SS continued to enjoy horsepower options. A notable change came in 1970, when Chevrolet made a decision to modify the venerable 396 to meet new emissions regulations. The engine was enlarged to 402cu.in, although Chevrolet still referred to it as the 396 or Turbo Jet 400.

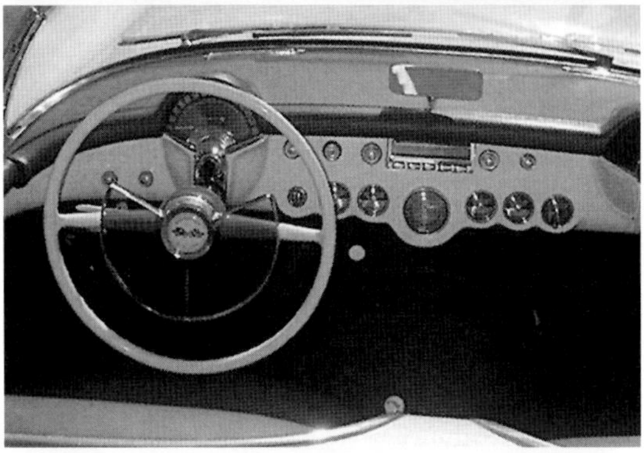

1953 Chevrolet Corvette, 235cu.in 6-cylinder engine, 190bhp, 2-speed Powerglide automatic transmission, 4-wheel hydraulic drum brakes, recently restored, 1 of only 300 produced in 1953.
£52,000–58,000 / $75,000–85,000 ⚒ RM

When General Motors announced the Chevrolet Corvette concept car in January 1953, it immediately captured the imagination of a public ravenous for fast, sporty two-seaters. Dubbed the Corvette Dream Car, it debuted at the Motorama show at the Waldorf-Astoria Hotel in New York. Production of the two-seat roadster began in June 1953, and by the year's end, a total of 300 Corvettes had rolled off the line. The cars featured GM's Blue Flame 235cu.in straight-six engine, with triple carburettors and twin exhaust. However, the engine's respectable 190bhp was transmitted to the road through a two-speed automatic transmission. Corvette production signified an important technical milestone: GM was the first American car manufacturer to successfully mass-produce a vehicle with a bodyshell and floorpan made entirely of fibreglass.

◄ **1959 Chevrolet Corvette,** completely restored, finished in red and white, original.
£28,000–33,000 / $40,000–45,000 ⚒ PALM

1960 Chevrolet Corvette, 283cu.in V8 engine, fuel injection, 290bhp, 4-speed manual gearbox, engine and fuel injection rebuilt, hard and soft tops, finished in blue, black interior, matching numbers, original.
£32,000–35,000 / $46,500–51,000 ⊞ COR

Restored values

The cost of a professional restoration will have an influence on, but no direct relation to, a car's market value. A restored car can have a market value lower than the cost of its restoration.

CHEVROLET Model	ENGINE cu.in/cyl	DATES	CONDITION 1	2	3
Stylemaster	216/6	1942–48	£8,000	£4,000	£1,000
Fleetmaster	216/6	1942–48	£8,000	£4,000	£1,000
Fleetline	216/6	1942–51	£8,000	£5,000	£2,000
Styleline	216/6	1949–52	£8,000	£6,000	£2,000
Bel Air 4-door	235/6	1953–54	£6,000	£4,000	£3,000
Bel Air Sport Coupé	235/6	1953–54	£7,000	£4,500	£3,500
Bel Air convertible	235/6	1953–54	£12,500	£9,500	£6,000
Bel Air 4-door	283/8	1955–57	£8,000	£4,000	£3,000
Bel Air Sport Coupé	283/8	1955–56	£11,000	£7,000	£4,000
Bel Air convertible	283/8	1955–56	£16,000	£11,000	£7,000
Bel Air Sport Coupé	283/8	1957	£11,000	£7,500	£4,500
Bel Air convertible	283/8	1957	£22,000+	£15,000+	£8,000
Impala Sport Sedan	235/6, 348/8	1958	£12,500	£9,000	£5,500
Impala convertible	235/6, 348/8	1958	£14,500	£11,000	£7,500
Impala Sport Sedan	235/6, 348/8	1959	£8,000	£5,000	£4,000
Impala convertible	235/6, 348/8	1959	£14,000	£10,000	£5,000
Corvette	235/6	1953	£25,000+	£18,000	£10,000
Corvetter	235/6, 283/8	1954–57	£20,000+	£13,000	£9,000
Corvette	283, 327/8	1958–62	£24,000+	£16,000	£9,000
Corvette Sting Ray	327, 427/8	1963–67	£19,000+	£15,000+	£10,000
Corvette Sting Ray Roadster	327, 427/8	1963–66	£22,000+	£15,000	£8,000
Corvette Sting Ray Roadster	427/8	1967	£20,000+	£13,000	£10,000

Value will also be regulated by build options, rare coachbuilding options, and de luxe engine specifications' etc.

◀ **1963 Chevrolet Corvette Sting Ray Roadster,** automatic transmission, hardtop, finished in red, factory air conditioning, concours winner.
£35,000–40,000
$51,000–58,000 BJ

▶ **1965 Chevrolet Corvette Sting Ray Coupé,** 396cu.in V8 engine, transistorised ignition, 425bhp, 4-speed manual gearbox, knock-off aluminium wheels, subject of body-off restoration, finished in metallic blue, wood-rim steering wheel, telescopic column.
£38,000–42,000
$55,000–61,000 BJ

◀ **1967 Chevrolet Corvette Sting Ray Coupé,** 427cu.in V8 engine, off-road exhaust, 435bhp, 4-speed manual gearbox, 4-wheel disc brakes, heavy-duty 4-wheel independent suspension, professionally restored, engine rebuilt to manufacturer's specifications, new transistorised ignition and wiring, bumpers rechromed, new emblems, finished in silver pearl with black stripes, new black interior, matching numbers, 43,080 miles from new, concours condition.
£38,000–43,000 / $55,000–62,000 RM
In 1967, Chevrolet offered several new options for the Corvette, the most important of which was a new, more powerful engine. In fact, it was the most powerful engine in the history of the Corvette. On the street, the best of the best was the potent L71 – the triple-carbureted big-block 427, conservatively rated at 435bhp.

1968 Chevrolet Corvette Coupé, 427cu.in V8 engine, L89 aluminium heads, transistorised ignition, 435bhp, 4-speed manual gearbox, heavy-duty suspension, posi-traction rear axle, tinted glass, power windows, telescopic column, speed warning indicator, restored, matching numbers, 1 of 624 built.
£28,000–32,000 / $40,500–46,500 BJ

1969 Corvette Stingray Coupé, 427cu.in V8 engine, factory sidepipes, 4-speed manual gearbox, T-roof, subject of body-off restoration, finished in green, green leather interior, concours winner.
£32,000–35,000 / $46,500–46,500 COR

1978 Chevrolet Corvette Pace Car, 5.7 litre V8 engine, automatic transmission, T-roof, finished in silver and black, air conditioning, new silver leather interior, low mileage.
£13,000–15,000
$18,850–21,750 ⊞ COR

► **1978 Chevrolet Corvette Silver Anniversary,** 350cu.in V8 engine, automatic transmission, T-roof, finished in red, good condition.
£5,000–7,000
$7,250–10,150 ⚒ BRIT

◄ **1982 Chevrolet Corvette Collector Edition,** 350cu.in V8 engine, automatic transmission, glass T-roof, hatchback, engine rebuilt, finished in silver beige, silver beige leather interior.
£10,000–12,000
$14,500–17,500 ⊞ COR

► **1984 Chevrolet Corvette Coupé,** 5.7 litre V8, manual gearbox, tinted acrylic roof, finished in white, leather upholstery, excellent condition.
£8,000–9,000
$11,600–13,000 ⊞ COR

◄ **1988 Chevrolet Callaway Twin-Turbo Corvette Convertible,** 5.7 litre V8 engine, 400+bhp, 6-speed manual gearbox, finished in metallic dark blue, bright blue leather interior, serial number 181.
£17,000–20,000
$24,500–29,000 ⊞ COR

► **1991 Chevrolet Corvette ZRI Coupé,** Jeal conversion, 460bhp, Brembo brakes, full coil-over suspension.
£23,000–25,000
$33,500–36,500 ⊞ COR

Chrysler

1928 Chrysler Sport Roadster, 249cu.in sidevalve 6-cylinder engine, 85bhp, 3-speed gearbox, modified to resemble period Le Mans racer cosmetically and mechanically, electric fuel pump, high-speed limited-slip rear axle, 4-wheel Le Mans-specification drum brakes, Rudge wheels, racing lamps, bodywork restored, competition wings and running boards, bare-metal respray, Connolly leather interior, correctly woodgrained dash.
£18,000–20,000 / $26,000–29,000 ⚒ RM
In 1928 Chrysler introduced the new Series 72, which included in its line-up the raciest model of all – the Sport Roadster. A higher radiator and cowl gave the Series 72 cars a more imposing front view than earlier models, while a more powerful inline six-cylinder engine could be found beneath the revised sheet metal. At the same time, new standard equipment was added, such as hydraulic brakes, a tubular front axle and rubber shock insulators on the springs.

1958 Chrysler 300D Coupé, 392cu.in 'Hemi' V8 engine, 380bhp, automatic transmission, 4-wheel hydraulic drum brakes, subject of body-off restoration, 3 owners, 1 of only 618 coupés produced in 1958.
£14,000–17,000 / $20,500–24,500 ⚒ RM
As a veteran of Raymond Loewy's design team, Virgil Exner was responsible for a number of significant post-WWII automotive designs. One of those was Chrysler's Forward Look design philosophy, which made its debut on the 1955 Chrysler 300C. The 300 had Exner's distinctive styling and a powerful 331cu.in hemi-head engine. Standard performance features included Carter four-barrel carburettors, a solid-lifter camshaft and a big-bore exhaust system. All told, the engine generated 300bhp, an impressive figure for the time. Furthermore, the firm suspension allowed the 300 to be lower and to corner better than most contemporary cars. Continuous improvement throughout the 1950s included upgrading the size and output of the engine. By 1958, displacement was up to 392cu.in, while power exceeded 300bhp.

Citroën

1925 Citroën C3 Cloverleaf Tourer, Cibié headlamps, rear-mounted spare wheel, older restoration, finished in yellow, black canvas hood, black leather interior.
£5,000–6,000 / $7,250–8,700 ⚒ BKS
Citroën's Type C was introduced in 1922 and brought motoring to the masses French-style. Also known as the Cloverleaf because of its two-plus-one seating, or 5CV after its tax rating, the Type C was powered by a four-cylinder sidevalve engine displacing 856cc. Despite its success, the Type C was discontinued at the end of 1925.

1949 Citroën 15/6 Saloon, restored 1999, engine overhauled, finished in black, grey cloth interior, excellent condition.
£12,000–14,000 / $17,500–20,500 ⚒ COYS
Citroën's intention when designing the Six was to build a car suitable for long-distance touring. The engine developed its power low down in the rev range, while the advanced monocoque construction provided a capacious interior and a low centre of gravity.

CITROËN Model	ENGINE cc/cyl	DATES	CONDITION 1	2	3
A	1300/4	1919	£4,000	£2,000	£1,000
5CV	856/4	1922–26	£7,000	£4,000	£2,000
11	1453/4	1922–28	£4,000	£2,000	£1,000
12/24	1538/4	1927–29	£5,000	£3,000	£1,000
2½ Litre	2442/6	1929–31	£5,000	£3,000	£1,500
13/30	1628/4	1929–31	£5,000	£3,000	£1,000
Big 12	1767/4	1932–35	£7,000	£5,000	£2,000
Twenty	2650/6	1932–35	£10,000	£5,000	£3,000
Ten CV	1452/4	1933–34	£5,000	£3,000	£1,000
Ten CV	1495/4	1935–36	£6,000	£3,000	£1,000
11B/Light 15/Big 15/7CV	1911/4	1934–57	£9,000	£5,000	£2,000
Twelve	1628/4	1936–39	£5,000	£3,000	£1,000
F	1766/4	1937–38	£4,000	£2,000	£1,000
15/6 and Big Six	2866/6	1938–56	£7,000	£4,000	£2,000

Miller's Starter Marque

- **Starter Citroën:** *2CV 1948–91.*
- In 1935 Citroën managing director Pierre-Joules Boulanger visited the French market town where he was born, and returned to Paris with an attack of conscience and a great idea. He decreed: 'Design me a car to carry two people and 50 kilos of potatoes at 60km/h, using no more than three litres of fuel per 100km. It must be capable of running on the worst roads, of being driven by a debutante and must be totally comfortable.' The project Toute Petite Voiture also had to be like 'a settee under an umbrella', and capable of 'crossing a field carrying a basket of eggs without breaking any'.
- The rest, as they say, is history. From its Paris launch in 1948 to the end of production in 1991, over seven million 2CVs and its various derivatives have hit the road, making it France's very own people's car.
- It's an undeniable classic yet a frugal utility vehicle at the same time; fun too. The fabric roof rolls right back like the lid of a sardine can, and you can take the seats out for a family picnic.
- A rare wonder these days is that all the body panels simply unbolt. In fact, even the main bodyshell is only held in place by a mere 16 bolts. That means it's easy to repair rust – or crash-damaged panels – but it also means that fresh panels can hide serious rot on the old-style separate chassis.
- Inspect sills – especially at the base of the B-posts – front floorpan, chassis members and chassis rails running to the rear of car. One indicator of chassis trouble is wide gaps around the triangular body section in front of the doors.
- As for that legendary twin-pot, air-cooled engine, it's a remarkably robust unit. Citroën designed it in the knowledge that it was likely to be hammered pretty much all the time and given no more routine maintenance than a farmyard pitchfork.
- In most cases, you'll be looking at a car with the 602cc engine, and the one thing these need is regular oil changes at every 3,000 miles or so. Neglect here will be revealed by big-end knocking.
- There are two types of gearbox: one for drum-brake cars up to 1982, and one for later disc-braked models. The 'drum' box is very robust, and only if it sounds like a lorry will there be any trouble with the bearings. The 'disc' box is a little more fragile, with a tendency to unwind the second-gear selector ring – and that may mean a new unit. Again, listen for excessive noise.
- Brakes are usually trouble free, but on disc-braked cars open up the reservoir to see if it's filled with the correct Citroën LHM clear green fluid. If not, the master cylinder rubbers will soon go, if they haven't dissolved already, and that's £300–400 to rectify.
- Naturally, for a car that's been in production until so recently, parts and spares are plentiful, with supply aided by a number of 2CV specialists and a healthy club network.

1967 Citroën ID, left-hand drive, Cibié spotlamps, finished in black, brown leather upholstery, very original.
£6,000–7,000 / $8,700–10,000 ⊞ UMC

1969 Citroën DS, left-hand drive, finished in cream over light olive, black interior, 2 owners and 63,000km from new, original, excellent condition.
£5,000–6,000 / $7,250–8,700 ⊞ TSG

1973 Citroën SM Maserati, 2670cc, fuel injection, left-hand drive, finished in dark blue, black interior, 3 owners and 51,263 miles from new, very good condition throughout.
£6,000–7,500 / $8,700–11,000 H&H
The marriage of Citroën and Maserati in 1970 produced the SM, which almost revolutionised the motor industry. The engine was an Italian V6 with four overhead camshafts and was mated to a chassis that was pure Citroën, hydraulics and all. The SM was capable of at least 135mph, but it was killed off in 1975, due in part to the fuel crisis. Only 12,920 were built.

CITROËN Model	ENGINE cc/cyl	DATES	CONDITION 1	2	3
2CV	375/2	1948–54	£1,000	£500	£250
2CV/Dyane/Bijou	425/2	1954–82	£1,000	£800	£500
DS19/ID19	1911/4	1955–69	£5,000	£3,000	£800
Sahara	900/4	1958–67	£5,000	£4,000	£3,000
2CV6	602/2	1963 on	£750	£500	£250
DS Safari	1985/4	1968–75	£6,000	£3,000	£1,000
DS21	1985/4	1969–75	£6,000	£3,000	£1,000
DS23	2347/4	1972–75	£6,000	£4,000	£1,500
SM	2670/ 2974/6	1970–75	£9,000	£6,000	£4,500

Citroën DS (1955–75)

Price in 1956: £1726.7s (including purchase tax).
Total production: 1,415,719.
Engines: 4-cylinder, 1911, 1985, 2175 and 2347cc.
Brakes: Front discs, rear drums, self-apportioning power assistance.
Power output: 75bhp @ 4,500rpm (1911cc); 109bhp @ 5,500rpm (2175cc).
0–60mph: 20.6 seconds (1911cc), 12.5 seconds (2175cc).
Maximum speed: 87mph (1911cc), 110mph (2175cc).
At the October 1955 Paris motor show, slack-jawed onlookers gawped in wonder at Citroën's revolutionary new DS. Aptly named to sound like *déesse* – the French for goddess – this futuristic Flash Gordon rocket ship not only looked like it would take you to the moon and back, but it felt like it would too, for it rode on spheres of nitrogen gas that served as the springs of the self-levelling hydro-pneumatic suspension. Indeed, virtually everything was operated by complex hydraulics – steering, semi-automatic transmission, adjustable ride height, brakes and, on later cars, the inner swivelling spotlamps. Then there are little details like front-wheel drive and the first mass-production application of front disc brakes. One thing that wasn't a little detail, though, was the price – the equivalent of nearly two P6 Rover 2000s – and that's why most of the near 1.5 million built stayed in France, even though from 1958 to 1966 Citroën also made DS and the more spartan ID models in Slough. Today's DS devotees assert, with missionary ardour, that this admittedly complex motoring icon still stacks up. They've got a point too. Just lower the suspension fully when you park up, and you'll render your DS unclampable.
Pick of the bunch: Unless you dote on first-of-breed purity, post-1966 cars with modified hydraulic system, known as 'green fluid', are more practical and dependable. Cowled headlights with swivelling spotlamps from 1967 are another favourite.

Clément

◄ **1912 Clément-Bayard 10hp 4M3,** 1357cc 4-cylinder engine, oil headlamps, all mechanical items overhauled, coachwork restored several years ago, new hood, finished in maroon with black wings, grey upholstery, stored for several years, in need of recommissioning.
£6,000–7,500 / $8,700–11,000 ⚒ BRIT
Adolfe Clément opened a cycle shop in Paris in 1878, and before long he began to manufacture his own machines. Automobiles followed after he became involved with Gladiator motor cars, and vehicles were marketed under the name Clément-Gladiator until late 1903, when Clément left to found Clément-Bayard. Five models were listed by 1905, all shaft driven. By 1908, an impressive range was available, from an 8/10hp twin-cylinder car to an imposing 50/60hp four-cylinder machine. The continuing popularity of light cars ensured a ready market for the 4M series, introduced in 1911 with a four-cylinder engine rated at 8.9hp. The 4M was available in Britain as the 8hp two-seater and cost £192 fully equipped. The following year, the designation 4M3 was used.

Cole

The Indianapolis based Cole Motor Car Company was one of the more successful of the smaller independents, producing high-quality cars between 1909 and 1925. Like many early manufacturers eager to prove their cars' speed and reliability, Cole went racing, and in 1910, a Cole 30 Flyer captured the Massapequa Trophy in the Vanderbilt Cup Race, and also competed in the gruelling 24-hour races at Brighton Beach in Brooklyn, New York.

A known continuous history can add value to and enhance the enjoyment of a car.

► **1914 Cole 40 Touring,** 300cu.in sidevalve 4-cylinder engine, 40bhp, 3-speed manual gearbox, older restoration.
£30,000–35,000
$43,500–51,000 ⚒ RM

Cord

Cord's car making career was brief, but glorious. The first car to bear Errett Lobban Cord's name, the luxurious L-29, appeared two months before the Wall Street Crash of 1929 and ceased production in December 1931. Cord resumed car manufacture in 1935, when it announced the dramatic 'coffin-nosed' 810, a high-priced, wildly styled stunner that bristled with innovation. Front-wheel drive helped to keep it low and lean looking, with an overall height of only 4ft 10in; the monocoque construction was also leading edge; and the gear change was by what Cord called an 'electric hand', a small steering-column-mounted handle not dissimilar to a can ring-pull that pre-selected gears by an electro-vacuum mechanism – when you were ready to engage the gear you'd pre-selected, you simply depressed the clutch. In 1936, the very similar 812 appeared, distinguishable by chrome external exhausts. The final and most exuberant flourish before Cord abandoned car manufacture was the 112mph supercharged version of the 812 of 1937 – a fitting epitaph for one of the most dramatic automobiles ever made.

1937 Cord 812SC Convertible Coupé, 269cu.in sidevalve V8 engine, centrifugal supercharger, 190bhp, 4-speed pre-selector gearbox, front-wheel drive, 4-wheel hydraulic drum brakes, engine-turned instrument panel with ivory trim, twin spotlamps, older restoration.
£100,000–120,00 / $145,000–174,000 ⚒ RM
The 1937 Cords, designated 812, were little changed from the 1936 models, apart from the supercharged engine option. Cord's experience with Duesenberg, another of the Cord companies, made it relatively simple to add a Schwitzer-Cummins centrifugal supercharger that provided a maximum of 6psi boost and increased the Lycoming V8's power to between 185 and 195bhp. In September 1937, a team headed by Ab Jenkins used an 812SC to set 35 American speed records on the Bonneville Salt Flats, including 24 hours at an average speed of 101.72mph.

Daimler

Although part of Jaguar since 1960, Daimler has one distinction that no other British car manufacturer can claim: it is the oldest surviving British marque. Formally established in 1896, the company's name and roots derived from the acquisition in 1890 of UK patents and rights for Gottlieb Daimler's pioneering petrol engines. The first British Daimler motor car appeared in March 1897, and through the company's early decades Daimler's bespoke luxury motor basked in the reflected glory of Royal patronage. After WWII, Daimler began to lose direction in a changing world, and the failure of the dramatic fibreglass-bodied SP250 sports car to earn the US export dollars the company hoped for, propelled Daimler into Jaguar's hands. In the 1960s, Daimler and Jaguar products converged, and in today's market the Daimler variants can often be significantly cheaper than their Jaguar counter-parts. Instead of a Mk II Jaguar, you might consider a Daimler 250 V8 saloon, or a Daimler Sovereign as an alternative to a Jaguar 420. The last distinct true Daimler model was the DS420 limousine (1968–92), but Daimler's fluted radiator surround still stands out as a badge of distinction, the luxury flagship of the Jaguar marque.

◄ **1929 Daimler Type P3 35/120 Seven-Seater Limousine,** coachwork by Mulliner, 5.8 litre engine, occasional seats to the rear, wind-down division, hat nets, blinds, opening roof vent to the rear compartment, smoker's companion, walnut veneer dashboard, stored for 5 years, in need of overhaul.
£9,000–11,000 / $13,000–16,000 ⚒ BKS
From as early as 1908, Daimler had adopted the Knight double-sleeve-valve engine, noted for its silence in operation and the whisps of exhaust smoke emitted when properly maintained and lubricated. In 1929, Daimler offered six- and 12-cylinder motor cars; the six-cylinder 35/120 model was the second largest car in the range.

DAIMLER Model	ENGINE cc/cyl	DATES	CONDITION 1	2	3
Veteran (Coventry built)	var/4	1897–1904	£75,000	£60,000	£30,000
Veteran	var/4	1905–19	£35,000	£25,000	£15,000
30hp	4962/6	1919–25	£40,000	£25,000	£18,000
45hp	7413/6	1919–25	£45,000+	£30,000	£20,000
Double Six 50	7136/12	1927–34	£40,000	£30,000	£20,000
20	2687/6	1934–35	£18,000	£14,000	£12,000
Straight 8	3421/8	1936–38	£20,000	£15,000	£12,000

Value is dependent on body style, coachbuilder and condition of the sleeve valve engine.

1937 Daimler 17, engine rebuilt, converted to unleaded fuel, finished in burgundy with black wings, red leather interior, walnut trim.
£7,000–8,000 / $10,000–11,500 SiC

1939 Daimler 2½ Litre Dolphin Tourer, 2522cc overhead-valve 6-cylinder engine, 90bhp, fluid-flywheel pre-selector 3-speed gearbox with overdrive, 4-wheel drum brakes, independent front suspension by coil springs, semi-elliptic leaf-spring rear suspension, original specification apart from single SU carburettor in place of correct twin-carburettor set-up, older restoration, 1 of only 25 believed built.
£20,000–22,000 / $29,000–32,000 C

1951 Daimler DB18 Special Sports Three-Seater Drophead Coupé, coachwork by Barker, 2.5 litre overhead-valve 6-cylinder engine, twin carburettors, 85bhp, fluid-flywheel pre-selector gearbox, independent front suspension by wishbones and torsion bars, semi-elliptic rear leaf springs, 4-wheel hydro-mechanical drum brakes, original upholstery, completely restored.
£12,000–14,000 / $17,500–20,500 C
The close-coupled three-seater drophead coupé was more of a luxurious fast tourer than an outright sports model, cossetting its occupants with deep leather seats, figured-walnut instrument panel and a full complement of clearly marked sports-type instruments. The Daimler abounded with detail to delight the keen owner: a hood with intermediate 'sedanca' position, automatic chassis lubrication and slender screen pillars. Only 608 Special Sports models were built. This example has the rare three-seater coachwork, the rear passenger being afforded extra legroom by being seated transversally.

1952 Daimler DB18 Special Sports Drophead Coupé, coachwork by Barker, 2.5 litre overhead-valve 6-cylinder engine, pre-selector gearbox, finished in black and silver, black and brown interior, original apart from flashing indicators.
£8,500–10,000 / $12,500–14,500 CGC

► **1958 Daimler Conquest Century Saloon,** automatic transmission, 18,000 miles from new.
£6,000–7,000 / $8,700–10,000 GrM

DAIMLER Model	ENGINE cc/cyl	DATES	CONDITION 1	2	3
DB18	2522/6	1946–49	£6,000	£3,000	£1,000
DB18 Conv S/S	2522/6	1948–53	£14,000	£7,000	£2,000
Consort	2522/6	1949–53	£5,000	£3,000	£1,000
Conquest/Con.Century	2433/6	1953–58	£4,000	£2,000	£1,000
Conquest Roadster	2433/6	1953–56	£12,000	£7,000	£4,000
Majestic 3.8	3794/6	1958–62	£5,000	£2,000	£1,000
SP250	2547/8	1959–64	£12,000	£10,000	£4,500
Majestic Major	4561/8	1961–64	£6,000	£4,000	£1,000
2.5 V8	2547/8	1962–67	£8,000	£5,250	£2,500
V8 250	2547/8	1968–69	£8,000+	£4,000	£2,000
Sovereign 420	4235/6	1966–69	£6,500	£3,500	£1,500

Daimler V8 250 (1962–69)

Production: 17,620.
Price in 1962: £1,568.19s.6d.
Engine: 2548cc V8.
Power output: 140bhp @ 5,800rpm.
Transmission: Three-speed automatic; four-speed manual with optional overdrive available from 1967.
Brakes: Discs all-round.
Maximum speed: 112mph.
0–60mph: 12–14 seconds.

The fancy fluted grille that distinguishes the Daimler V8 250 from the Mk II Jaguar might seem nothing more than a pointless flourish or meaningless nuance, but there's a lot more to this car than that. It's a virtual four-wheeled treatise on the British class system. For how else could you explain why a 2½ litre Daimler in a Jaguar bodyshell should cost more than a faster 3.4 litre Mk II and pitch in pretty much on a par with the ultimate 125mph, 3.8 litre Mk II tyre-squealer. It's all to do with class. When Jaguar acquired Daimler in 1960, Sir Williams Lyons got the extra capacity he needed, along with an ugly sports car he didn't want, the Daimler Dart SP250. But something he did appreciate was the Dart's fabulous 2.5 litre V8, designed by Triumph motorcycle legend Edward Turner. When Lyons mated the Daimler V8 with a Mk II bodyshell and topped it off with a fluted Daimler radiator grille, he neatly overcame a social obstacle. You see, not to put too fine a point on it, Jaguars had a certain reputation as – well – cads' cars. Daimlers though, were driven by people with drawing rooms, not dens, lounges or living-rooms, Homburg-hatted gents who'd twitch at a fast fellow in a trilby titfer. It's more than a little telling that the Daimler version was, until 1967, only offered with an automatic transmission to provide sedate, unflustered progress. But there was more to the V8 250 than that. The engine was an absolute jewel, and with less weight over the front wheels, it understeered less than its Jaguar stablemates, not that your average Daimler driver would be likely to encounter the extremes of handling on the way to a Round Table meeting. Today, of course, it's different, and without those obvious colourful associations with cheery, cockney tonic-suited twins, these sterling Daimlers can often be picked up for considerably less than a comparable Mk II.

Miller's Compares

I. **1968 Daimler V8 250 Saloon,** finished in Golden Sand, red leather interior, 2 owners and 25,000 miles from new, excellent original condition.
£9,000–11,000 / $13,000–16,000 ⚒ COYS

II. 1965 Daimler V8 250 Saloon, 2.5 litre V8, automatic transmission, chrome wire wheels, completely restored, £20,000 spent on engine rebuild and spares, £8,500 spent on paint and bodywork, finished in British racing green, interior woodwork and veneers refurbished, Pye radio, light tan leather interior, beige carpets, formerly owned by King Hussein of Jordan, excellent condition throughout.
£21,000–24,000 / $30,500–35,000 ⚒ BKS

Item II commanded an exceptional price for this model, but its market value does not come anywhere close to the cost of its very exacting restoration. In the main, the middle ground for Daimler 250 V8s sold at auction is between £6,000 and £14,000, with only the most outstanding cars commanding more.

1964 Daimler SP250, 2500cc, automatic transmission, factory hardtop, finished in metallic blue, dark blue interior, 3 owners and 44,000 miles from new, very good condition.
£10,000–12,000 / $14,500–17,500 ⚒ H&H

Cross Reference
See Colour Review (page 68)

1968 Daimler V8 250 Saloon, 2548cc V8 engine, refurbished at a cost of £5,000, finished in silver-grey, fewer than 53,000 miles from new.
£9,000–11,000 / $13,000–16,000 ⚒ BRIT

1968 Daimler Sovereign Saloon, automatic transmission, bodywork refurbished 1999, finished in grey, red leather interior, engine and interior in need of attention, 60,962 miles from new.
£2,000–3,000 / $2,900–4,350 BKS
Launched in October 1961, the Jaguar Mk X was technically more advanced than preceding Jaguar saloons and featured independent rear suspension similar to that of the E-Type sports car, together with a well appointed and comfortable interior. By the time the facelifted 420G version came along in 1966, the Mk X was being produced with the 4.2 litre engine and all-synchromesh gearbox, and incorporated numerous other improvements. Introduced at the same time, the Daimler Sovereign version was identical apart from its traditional fluted radiator grille and minor interior trim changes.

1971 Daimler Sovereign, 4235cc 6-cylinder engine, stainless-steel exhaust system, resprayed in maroon mid-1980s, original beige leather interior, excellent bodywork and structure.
£4,500–6,000 / $6,500–8,700 BRIT

1987 Daimler DS420 Limousine, 4235cc 6-cylinder engine, finished in two-tone blue, blue interior, leather to front compartment, velour to rear, 41,000 miles from new.
£6,000–7,000 / $8,500–10,000 BRIT
Following the integration of the Jaguar Group into British Motor Holdings during 1966, the Daimler DS420 limousine was developed effectively to replace the DR450 Series and Princess limousines. The new Daimler made its appearance early in 1968, and was a tasteful blend of old and new, the traditional coachwork being based on a stretched Jaguar 420G floorpan. The 4.2 litre XK-series engine was employed. Varying specifications were available, many examples being tailored specifically to suit individual requirements.

► **1988 Daimler DS420 Limousine,** 4.2 litre 6-cylinder engine, leather to front compartment, cloth to rear, 3 owners from new, good overall condition.
£4,000–5,000 / $5,800–7,200 BARO

1969 Daimler Sovereign Saloon, 4.2 litre 6-cylinder engine, subject of full body restoration, transmission and engine overhauled, stainless steel exhaust system, over £9,000 spent, 62,755 miles from new.
£7,000–8,000 / $10,000–11,500 BKS
Essentially derived from the Jaguar XJ6, the Sovereign was readily identified by the traditional Daimler fluted radiator surround, while the interior was furnished in best Daimler traditions with high-quality leather upholstery, polished figured walnut instrument panel and deep-pile wool carpets.

1971 Daimler Sovereign Saloon, 4235cc 6-cylinder engine, 3-speed automatic transmission, finished in red, biscuit interior, upholstery and interior trim in need of attention, otherwise good condition.
£1,000–1,200 / $1,500–1,700 H&H

1978 Daimler Double Six, V12 engine, finished in blue with black vinyl roof, 2 owners and 78,000 miles from new.
£3,500–4,000 / $5,000–5,800 SiC

Datsun

1970 Datsun 240Z, imported from Canada, finished in silver, new Nissan interior, excellent condition.
£4,000–5,000 / $5,800–7,250 ⚒ COYS
To many, the 240Z-series Datsuns took over the slot left by the demise of the Austin-Healey 3000. The powerful and smooth six-cylinder engine combined with the striking styling to make an attractive and appealing motor car. Nissan in the United States recently began purchasing neglected 240Zs, restoring them and offering them in 'as-new' condition, alongside new models. It was calculated that on each car Nissan made a substantial loss. The reasoning was sound, however, as it was a hugely beneficial brand-management exercise. The public recollection of the Samurai Datsuns led to a rise in the overall sale of new cars, justifying the expense and making the whole venture a great success.

1972 Datsun 240Z, triple carburettors, Wolfrace wheels, restored, finished in red, black interior trim and red carpets, excellent condition.
£7,000–8,500 / $10,000–12,000 ⊞ TSG

▶ **1979 Datsun 280ZX,** finished in metallic red, brown interior, 58,000 miles from new, near concours condition.
£3,500–4,000 / $5,000–5,800 ⊞ SiC

De Dion Bouton

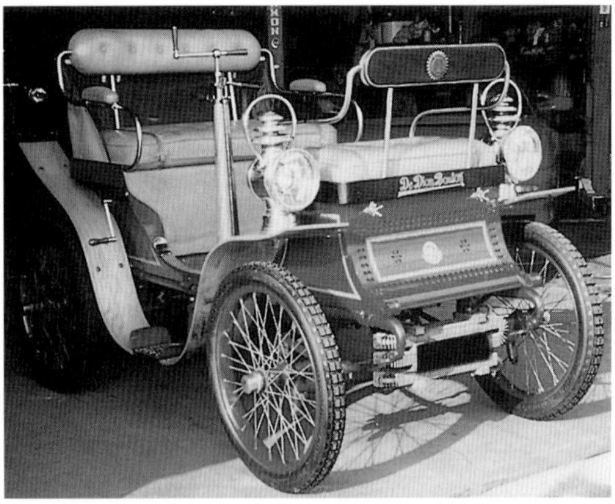

1901 De Dion Bouton 4½hp Vis-à-Vis, 4-seater, vertical tiller, brass paraffin lamps, nickel brightwork, finished in red with gold coachlines, tan upholstery.
£22,000–25,000 / $32,000–36,000 ⚒ BKS
Count Albert De Dion commissioned Messrs Bouton and Trepardoux, brothers-in-law and jobbing engineers, to build light steam carriages for him as early as 1882. In 1895, attention was switched to the fashionable new internal-combustion engine, and De Dion Bouton et Cie began marketing a diminutive petrol-engined tricycle. These early tricycles were powered by Bouton's new, high-speed, single-cylinder vertical engine, which revved at almost twice the speed of the contemporary Daimlers. By 1899, the company was marketing a 3½hp Voiturette, an all-new generation of four-wheel motor car with rear-mounted engine driving through a system of gears to the rear wheels. With the new car came the renowned De Dion rear axle – then years ahead of its time. A larger 4½hp engine was offered in the Vis-à-Vis models from 1900, and with this power unit the car had a comfortable running speed of 25mph.

1911 De Dion Bouton 6hp Model DE1 Two-Seater, Lucifer headlamps and scuttle-mounted side lamps, hinged brass windscreen, finished in brown with black wings, beige canvas hood.
£9,000–10,000 / $13,000–14,500 ⚒ BKS
in 1911, the 6hp DE1 was the smallest offering from De Dion Bouton, and the company's only single-cylinder model. The chassis featured three-quarter-elliptic rear springs, ignition was by magneto, and De Dion Bouton forced lubrication was adopted. The engine, clutch, gearbox and shaft brake were in unit and three-point suspended from the main frame. Power was transmitted via a leather-to-metal three-plate clutch, and final drive was by shaft.

Auction prices

Miller's only includes cars declared sold. Our guide prices take into account the buyer's premium, VAT on the premium, and the extent of any published catalogue information relating to condition and provenance. Cars sold at auction are identified by the ⚒ icon; full details of the auction house can be found on page 330.

Delage

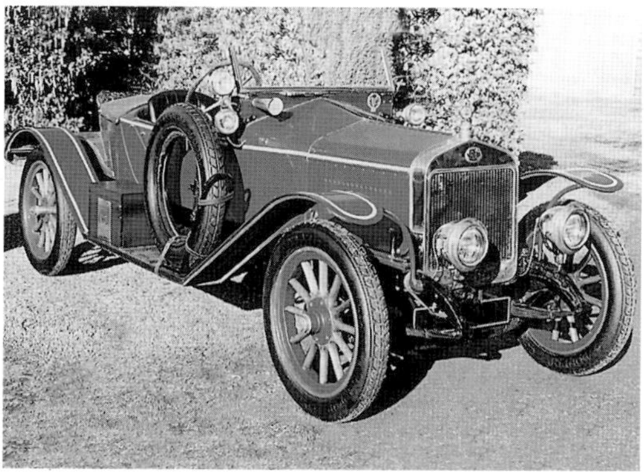

◀ **1913 Delage Model A1 Three-Seater,** 2.3 litre sidevalve engine, copper exhaust pipe, 4-speed manual gearbox, electric starter and lights, bolster fuel tank, mahogany toolbox, varnished wood-spoke wheels, combined spotlamp, motometer, fitted with skiff-type coachwork 1980s, finished in French blue with pale blue coachlines, fully equipped instrument and switch panel with all brass fittings.
£10,500–13,000 / $15,000–18,500 ⚒ BKS
Louis Delage began motor car production in 1906, adopting the ubiquitous De Dion engines for power, and before long his products were a familiar sight in voiturette racing, success in this field promoting the sales of standard production cars. Notable among Delage successes was the outright victory in the 1911 Coupe de l'Auto. By that time, four-cylinder sidevalve engines were the norm in the standard production models.

Delahaye

1947 Delahaye 178 Drophead Coupé, coachwork by Chapron, 4453cc 6-cylinder engine, triple carburettors, 140bhp, 4-speed Cotal electro-mechanical gearbox, 4-wheel hydraulic drum brakes, subject of no-expense-spared restoration, fewer than 750 miles since, concours winner.
£140,000–160,000 / $205,000–220,000 ⚒ RM
In 1947, Delahaye introduced its first real post-war model. In three wheelbases (116, 123 and 131in), the 175/178/180 series featured independent front suspension, hydraulic brakes and a De Dion rear suspension. Like its pre-war predecessors, the Delahaye 175/178/180 was a sophisticated and fast base for bespoke coachwork, and was a substantial improvement on those earlier automobiles. Some of the coachbuilders who had met the needs of 1930s society resumed operations after the war, hoping to recapture their old clientele or establish a new one among post-war businessmen. Among them was the firm of Henri Chapron. In the years following WWII, Chapron would be one of the few coachbuilders to adapt to the new markets. Prominent among Chapron's early successes were the three-position drophead coupés executed on mid-wheelbase Delahaye 178 chassis. Chapron incorporated cosmopolitan aerodynamic shapes while providing traditional comfort and complete weather protection.

1948 Delahaye 135M Three-Position Cabriolet, coachwork by Pennock, 3557cc 6-cylinder engine, 4-speed Cotal electro-mechanical gearbox, 4-wheel hydraulic brakes, restored, resprayed dark green, new tan leather interior, fewer than 17,000 miles from new, excellent condition.
£90,000–100,000 / $130,000–145,000 ⚒ RM

1948 135M Coupé, coachwork by Dubos, 3557cc 6-cylinder engine, triple carburettors, 120bhp, 4-speed Cotal electro-mechanical gearbox, 4-wheel drum brakes, finished in black, leather upholstery.
£20,000–25,000 / $29,000–36,000 ⚒ Pou

1949 Delahaye 135MS Cabriolet, coachwork by Chapron, Cotal electro-mechanical gearbox with column change, Art Deco-style instrumentation, early built in radio, leather bench seat, very original condition.
£85,000–100,000 / $123,000–145,000 ⚒ COYS
The 135 had a very successful competition career, which included second, third, fourth and fifth in the 1936 French Sportscar Grand Prix, wins in the Alpine Trial, first at Monte Carlo in 1937 and 1939, and at Le Mans in 1938, plus second and fourth places, followed by sixth and eighth places and a new lap record in 1939. A one-off challenge race was held at Brooklands in 1939 to find the fastest road car in Britain; this was won by Rob Walker's 135, defeating, among others, a 2.9 litre supercharged Alfa Romeo and a 4 litre Talbot-Lago.

DeLorean

Miller's is a price GUIDE not a price LIST

◀ **1983 DeLorean DMC-12,** 2849cc V6 engine, fuel injection, 130bhp, 5-speed manual gearbox, 4-wheel independent suspension by wishbones and coil springs, 4-wheel disc brakes, 111 miles from new, excellent condition.
£11,000–13,000 / $16,000–19,000 ⚒ COYS

De Tomaso

▶ **1969 De Tomaso Mangusta,** 302cu.in Ford V8 engine, 230bhp, 5-speed manual gearbox, 4-wheel independent suspension, servo-assisted 4-wheel disc brakes, air conditioning, power windows, mechanics overhauled by De Tomaso 1990, 46,500 miles from new, good original condition.
£22,000–25,000 / $32,000–36,000 ⚒ RM
The Mangusta was De Tomaso's first V8 production Grand Touring car. It employed the central-spine chassis design from De Tomaso's previous Vallelunga model. Between 1967 and 1970, just under 410 were produced.

1971 De Tomaso Pantera, 351cu.in V8 engine, 310bhp, 5-speed manual gearbox, 4-wheel disc brakes, recent engine top overhaul, new fuel tank, resprayed white , black interior, 24,000 miles from new, correct and original.
£17,000–20,000 / $25,000–29,000 ⚒ RM

De Tomaso Pantera (1971–93)

Body style: Two-seater sports coupé.
Construction: Unitary with pressed-steel chassis, aluminium and steel body panels.
Engine: Mid-mounted 5763cc cast-iron V8 (Ford).
Transmission: ZF five-speed manual.
Power output: 350bhp @ 6,000rpm.
Suspension: Independent all-round: front and rear upper and lower unequal-length wishbones, coil springs, anti-roll bar.
Brakes: All-round vacuum-assisted discs.
Maximum speed: 159mph.
0–60mph: 5.5 seconds.
Average fuel consumption: 14mpg.

Few cars descend from more mixed parentage than the De Tomaso Pantera. It's not just the Ford V8 and the Italian styling, courtesy of Ghia; the company's founder Alejandro de Tomaso was an Argentinian racing driver turned supercar builder. His first serious effort at series supercar production was the mid-engined Ford powered Mangusta of 1967, and in 1971 the Pantera developed the theme into an awesome supercar. The project was strongly supported by Ford in the USA. Ford's Lincoln-Mercury division was pushing its performance image hard, and the Pantera gave glamour to the showrooms as a plausible Ford GT40 successor. Somewhere between 5,000 and 6,000 were sold in the USA from 1971 to 1974 – no one knows for sure, but after that Ford withdrew showroom support, and production continued at a trickle until 1993. Nevertheless, the gloriously brawny Pantera continued to evolve into GTS and GT5 versions, sprouting wings, spoilers, flared wheel arches and other appendages like a bodybuilder on steroids. The Pantera is a flawed supercar certainly, with annoying little foibles like the tendency for the front end to lift and the steering to lighten alarmingly above 120mph, although the later spoilers and wings helped keep it down. But forget the flaws, and just look at and listen to this primal expression of unleashed power. It's evil, beautifully evil.

Dodge

1929 Dodge Senior Six, 6-cylinder engine, twin side-mounted spares, original dealer plaque, older restoration, museum displayed for many years, recently recommissioned, 1 of only 3 right-hand drive examples imported into Europe in 1929.
£11,000–12,000
$16,000–17,500 ⊞ GrM

1970 Dodge Challenger R/T Convertible, 440cu.in V8 engine, 4-barrel carburettor, power brakes, restored cosmetically, finished in red, white power hood, red interior, power windows, factory air conditioning, woodgrain console, factory tachometer, rally instrument cluster, 1 of 163 440 R/T convertibles built.
£35,000–40,000 / $51,000–58,000 ⚒ BJ

► 1984 Dodge 600 Convertible, 2599cc 4-cylinder engine, converted to LPG, finished in metallic gold, white hood.
£1,000–2,000
$1,500–2,900 ⚒ BRIT

◄ 1996 Dodge Viper GTS Coupé, 488cu.in V10 engine, fuel injection, 450bhp, 6-speed manual gearbox, 4-wheel independent suspension, 4-wheel disc brakes, 0–60mph in 4.25 seconds, 1 owner and 4,500 miles from new.
£35,000–40,000 / $50,500–58,000 ⚒ RM
Introduced to critical acclaim as a concept car at the 1989 North American International Auto Show in Detroit, the first-generation Dodge Viper Roadster – produced between 1992 and 1996 – marked the start of a new chapter for Dodge. The K-car image was finally shed, and first-year demand far exceeded production. By 1996, the GTS Coupé was the next dramatic chapter in the Viper's evolution. While it retained the look of the original Roadster, more than 90 per cent of the car was new, including the body, interior and all-aluminium V10 engine.

Dual-Ghia

1961 Dual-Ghia L6.4 Coupé, coachwork by Ghia, finished in burgundy, brown leather interior, 2 owners, good condition throughout.
£15,000–20,000 / $22,000–29,000 ⚒ BKS
Brainchild of Eugene Cassaroll, proprietor of Automobile Shippers Incorporated, the Dual-Ghia was inspired by Virgil Exner's Dodge Firebomb/Firearrow show cars. The Chrysler chassis were shipped to Turin for bodying by Ghia, before returning to Detroit where Dual Motors installed the drivetrain and interior trim. First-series production lasted from 1956 to 1958, by which time 117 cars had been built, all but two being convertibles. Built entirely in Italy, the second-series L6.4 employed its own bespoke chassis and Chrysler's 6.4 litre V8 engine, and was offered only in coupé form. Just 26 of these cars were made before production ceased in 1963.

Duesenberg

1929 Duesenberg Model J Convertible Coupé, coachwork by Murphy, 420cu.in double-overhead-camshaft 8-cylinder engine, 4 valves per cylinder, 265bhp, 3-speed manual gearbox, front beam axle, servo-assisted 4-wheel hydraulic brakes, original TwiLite headlights, Pilot Ray driving lights, chrome wire wheels, rear-mounted trunk, finished in green, complete and correct, matching numbers, concours winner.

£400,000+ / $580,000+ RM

When the Model J Duesenberg was introduced in 1929, trading was halted on the New York Stock Exchange for the announcement, the chassis alone costing $8,500. It was by far the most expensive car in America. With coachwork, the delivered price of many Duesenbergs approached $20,000, a staggering sum at a time when a typical new family car cost around $500. The Murphy body company of Pasadena, California, is generally recognised as the most successful coachbuilder on the Duesenberg Model J chassis. Murphy bodies were simple and elegant, with trim lines and an undeniable sporting character. They seemed all the more revolutionary when compared to their contemporaries from the east coast, which tended to be heavier, more ornate designs. The trademark of Murphy body design was the 'clear vision' pillar. On the convertible coupé, the windscreen pillars were designed to be as slim as possible, creating a sportier, more open appearance, while improving vision for the driver. The convertible coupé became one of the most popular bodies for the Model J.

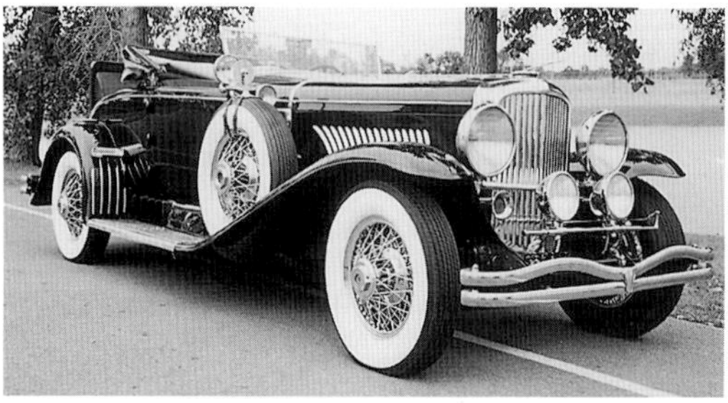

1929 Duesenberg Model J Convertible Roadster, coachwork by Murphy, 420cu.in double-overhead-camshaft 8-cylinder engine, 4 valves per cylinder, 265bhp, finished in black, beige upholstery, 67,526 miles from new, 1 of 60 built, excellent overall condition.

£250,000+ / $365,000+ BKS

This particular convertible roadster is, like the majority of this body style, built on the 'short' 142½in chassis. It was originally delivered with LeBaron sweep-panel phaeton coachwork, but around 1931 Philip K. Wrigley, of the Chicago chewing-gum family and one of the keenest of all Duesenberg owners, took a shine to the LeBaron body and traded the Murphy convertible roadster coachwork from his first Model J with this car's original owner, who fitted it to his own Model J.

1929 Duesenberg Model J Sports Sedan, coachwork by Murphy, 420cu.in double-overhead-camshaft 8-cylinder engine, 265bhp, 3-speed manual gearbox, Bijur chassis lubrication, 4-wheel vacuum-assisted brakes, professionally restored, finished in dark blue, early-style intruments, grey upholstery, 1st of 2 bodied by Murphy, concours condition.

£360,000+ / $522,000+ RM

A known continuous history can add value to and enhance the enjoyment of a car.

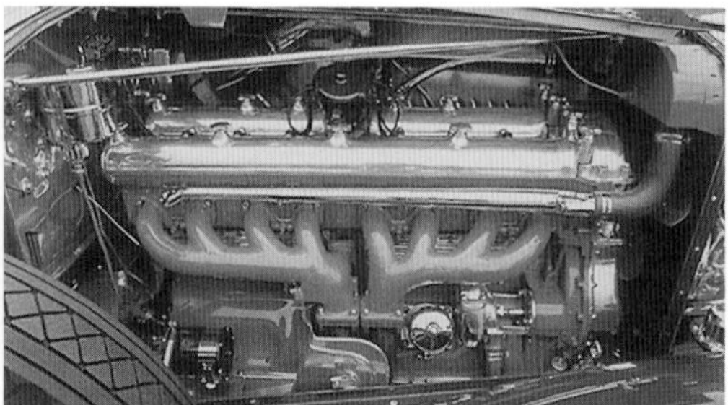

1931 Duesenberg Model J Tourster, coachwork by Derham, 420cu.in. double-overhead-camshaft 8-cylinder engine, 265bhp, 3-speed manual gearbox, Bijur chassis lubrication, 4-wheel vacuum-assisted brakes.

£500,000+ / $725,000 RM

Known for its formal bodies – town cars and limousines, primarily – Derham built relatively few open cars. Among them, however, was the body that many consider to be the firm's *pièce de résistance*, the Derham Tourster. The Tourster was penned by Gordon Buehrig, who designed many of the coachbuilt Duesenberg bodies. Buehrig actually worked for E. L. Cord as chief stylist at Auburn, Cord and Duesenberg. His designs were offered to Model J clients, then the chosen style was built by a selected coachbuilder. Derham was the only builder of Toursters, producing eight examples. The first went to Gary Cooper.

1935 Duesenberg SJN Convertible Coupé, coachwork by Rollston, 420cu.in double-overhead-camshaft 8-cylinder engine, supercharger, 320bhp, 3-speed manual gearbox, 4-wheel hydraulic drum brakes, wire wheels with Duesenberg solid discs, resprayed in cream, front seats reupholstered, full complement of instruments including altimeter, Bakelite cigar lighter, unrestored, 2 owners and fewer than 15,150 miles from new, fewer than 475 miles since 1954.
£650,000+ / $942,000 ⚒ RM
In the mid-1930s, a contemporary series of Duesenberg coachwork was offered that featured a wider body dropped over the chassis rails for a lower profile. Skirted front wings were complemented by an extended rear deck that fully enclosed the fuel tank. Designated the JN series, they were designed by Herb Newport and executed as a group by Rollston, New York. Only ten JNs were built: three convertible sedans, three berlines and four cabriolets. One of the cabriolets was delivered new as an SJ, this example being the only factory-built SJN.

Edwards

1954 Edwards America Convertible, Lincoln V8 engine, 205bhp, GM Hydramatic automatic transmission, 4-wheel drum brakes, removable hardtop, completely restored, finished in metallic green, brown leather interior, 2nd America produced.
£30,000–40,000 / $43,500–58,000 ⚒ RM
Sterling Edwards, a wealthy Californian, was smitten by the style and performance of the Continental sports cars of the 1940s and knew that in the USA there would be strong demand for an American product that combined European inspired styling with powerful American running gear. The first Edwards appeared in 1949 and was built on a tubular chassis with independent front and rear suspension, disc brakes and a highly modified Ford V8 engine. It was a four-seat roadster with a removable hardtop and windscreen. Edwards' aim was to produce a dual-purpose sports/racing car, and it soon became the car to beat. Despite the success of his first car, Edwards realised that there was a larger market for a more refined sports/road car. As a result, the America was announced in 1953. Edwards had added more chrome to give the car a more civilised look. The body was fibreglass. Underneath, the America utilised a combination of Detroit components: a Mercury chassis, Lincoln or Cadillac V8 engine and GM Hydramatic transmission, set off by sporty Kelsey-Hayes wire wheels. Interiors were finished in leather with a full complement of instruments.

Facel Vega

1957 Facel Vega HK500 Coupé, 383cu.in Chrysler V8 engine, 360bhp, older restoration, some wear to paintwork, brightwork in good condition.
£30,000–33,000 / $43,000–47,000 ⚒ RM

1958 Facel Vega Type FV3B Coupé, 4940cc Chrysler V8 engine, 260bhp, 4-speed manual gearbox, 4-wheel hydraulic drum brakes, left-hand drive, finished in green, maroon and beige leather interior.
£20,000–25,000 / $29,000–36,000 ⚒ Pou

Ferrari

Enzo Ferrari had been involved in racing at the highest levels long before there were any road cars bearing his name. Born in 1898, and already driving in his early teens, he went on to race Alfa Romeos with considerable success throughout the 1920s, setting up Scuderia Ferrari in 1929, which became in effect the Alfa Romeo factory team. The decisive moment in Enzo's career came in 1938, when Alfa took back control of its racing activities. In 1940, Ferrari built a Fiat-based racer of his own; even though it did not bear his name, it was surely the first Ferrari car. In late 1946, he began a series of road racers, this time bearing his name, which led to the first true Ferrari production road car, the 166 of 1948. Like the road racers on which it was based, the 166 employed a V12 engine, a configuration that would become a hallmark of the Maranello make. Throughout the 1950s and into the 1960s Ferrari road cars were essentially handmade and dressed with beautiful bodies by the finest Italian stylists. In 1969, Fiat took a 50 per cent interest in Ferrari, and the model range broadened throughout the 1970s, with a corresponding increase in volume; production had reached almost 3,000 cars a year by 1980. When Enzo Ferrari died, in 1988, Fiat took complete control, but to this day cars bearing the Prancing Horse still set pulses racing, even when they're sitting at the kerb.

1949 Ferrari Tipo 166 Inter Coupé, coachwork by Stabilimenti Farina, chassis no. 037S, engine no. 037S, restored over 8 years, over £165,000 recently spent, engine rebuilt and uprated from 2 to 2.5 litres, original single carburettor replaced by triple DFC35 Webers, gearbox rebuilt, shock absorbers and brakes rebuilt, rewired, new aluminium wire wheels, finished in metallic silver-grey over dark blue, grey leather interior, original instruments, 29th Ferrari built, thought to be 1 of only 4 Farina-bodied coupés.
£230,000+ / $350,000 ⚒ BKS
The Tipo 166 is the cornerstone of the Ferrari story. It was capable of winning Le Mans and the Mille Miglia, yet a few were sold as road cars. All 166s shared the same V12 engine, the same five-speed gearbox and the same chassis design, although states of tune and length of wheelbase varied according to the requirements of the customer. Touring, Vignale, Allemano, Stabilimenti Farina, Campana, Pinin Farina and Ghia all executed bodies for the car.

1951 Ferrari 212 Inter Coupé, coachwork by Vignale, chassis No. 0175E, 2562cc V12 engine, triple Weber 36DCF carburettors, 150bhp, 5-speed manual gearbox, 4-wheel hydraulic drum brakes, restored, engine updated with coil valve springs, period US-built rear axle centre section, new interior, concours condition.
£180,000–200,000 / $260,000–290,000 ⚒ RM
The 212's chassis was typically Ferrari, two oval longerons being cross-braced by more oval tubing. The front suspension was by unequal-length wishbones, an anti-roll bar and a transverse spring. At the rear, semi-elliptic springs supported a live rear axle, which was well located by pairs of upper and lower radius arms. Braking was taken care of by huge 12in, hydraulically-operated aluminium drums with steel liners. Borrani wire wheels were standard. The wheelbase was 102.44in, and most Inters weighed around 2,100lb. Contemporary performance tests of the 212 Inter gave a 0–60 mph time of around 9 seconds.

1953 Ferrari 212 Coupé, coachwork by Vignale, chassis no. 0217 EL, V12 engine, mechanics overhauled, finished in metallic brown, green interior, original condition.
£225,000+ / $320,000+ ⚒ COYS

1958 Ferrari 250 GT Series I Cabriolet, coachwork by Pininfarina, chassis no. 0801 GT, engine no. 0801 GT, older restoration, correct inside-plug engine, finished in red, tan leather interior, very good mechanical condition.
£250,000+ / $360,000+ ⚒ BKS

FERRARI Model	ENGINE cc/cyl	DATES	CONDITION 1	2	3
250 GTE	2953/12	1959–63	£32,000	£22,000	£20,000
250 GT SWB (steel)	2953/12	1959–62	£400,000+	£200,000+	-
250 GT Lusso	2953/12	1962–64	£85,000+	£65,000+	£50,000
250 GT 2+2	2953/12	1961–64	£32,000	£24,000	£18,000
275 GTB	3286/12	1964–66	£120,000+	£80,000	£70,000
275 GTS	3286/12	1965–67	£90,000	£70,000	£50,000
275 GTB 4–cam	3286/12	1966–68	£190,000+	£150,000	£100,000
330 GT 2+2	3967/12	1964–67	£27,000+	£18,000	£11,000
330 GTC	3967/12	1966–68	£55,000+	£40,000+	£25,000
330 GTS	3967/12	1966–68	£80,000+	£70,000+	£60,000
365 GT 2+2	4390/12	1967–71	£30,000+	£20,000	£15,000
365 GTC	4390/12	1967–70	£40,000+	£35,000	£30,000
365 GTS	4390/12	1968–69	£150,000+	£100,000+	£80,000
365 GTB (Daytona)	4390/12	1968–74	£80,000	£60,000	£50,000
365 GTC4	4390/12	1971–74	£45,000+	£38,000	£30,000
365 GT4 2+2/400GT	4390/ 4823/12	1972–79	£25,000	£20,000	£10,000
365 BB	4390/12	1974–76	£45,000	£35,000	£25,000
512 BB/BBi	4942/12	1976–81	£50,000+	£40,000	£28,000
246 GT Dino	2418/6	1969–74	£40,000	£30,000	£20,000
246 GTS Dino	2418/6	1972–74	£50,000	£32,000	£20,000
308 GT4 2+2	2926/8	1973–80	£15,000	£10,000	£8,000
308 GTB (fibreglass)	2926/8	1975–76	£25,000	£18,000	£12,000
308 GTB	2926/8	1977–81	£22,000	£16,000	£10,000
308 GTS	2926/8	1978–81	£22,000	£18,000	£11,000
308 GTBi/GTSi	2926/8	1981–82	£24,000	£17,000	£10,000
308 GTB/GTS QV	2926/6	1983–85	£21,500	£16,500	£9,500
400i manual	4823/12	1981–85	£14,000	£11,000	£10,000
400i auto	4823/12	1981–85	£14,000	£11,000	£8,000

1958 Ferrari 250 GT Coupé, coachwork by Pininfarina, chassis no. 1221 GT, 2953cc inside-plug V12 engine, 240bhp, older restoration, finished in silver, burgundy interior, original condition.
£44,000–52,000 / $64,000–75,500 COYS
By the late 1950s, Enzo Ferrari had been producing limited-edition road cars for nearly ten years, but was still concentrating mainly on competition models of various types. What he needed, especially since Maserati had just introduced its first road car destined for full-scale production, was a car that could be built in larger numbers and to a more uniform design. The 250 series, which had begun with the 250 Europa GT in 1954, provided the basis for this new model. Thus the 250 GT coupé was born in mid-1958. Its body was designed by Pininfarina and was very similar in appearance to the 250 GT convertible introduced the year before. It was a great success for Ferrari, and 350 were built before production ceased in late 1960. From then on, Ferrari concentrated on the 250 GT SWB as its mainstay fixed-head two-seater.

◀ **1959 Ferrari 250 GT LWB California Spyder,** coachwork by Scaglietti/Pininfarina, chassis no. 1411 GT, engine no. 0939 GT, inside-plug V12 engine, completely restored, engine rebuilt and converted to unleaded fuel, Koni telescopic shock absorbers all-round, new aluminium body, original hardtop, finished in dark blue, dark red Connolly leather interior.
£300,000+ / $435,000+ BKS
This Ferrari 250 GT California Spyder was discovered in 1986 in a scrapyard in the southern United States. It had been crashed and abandoned. Its first owner was Luigi Innocenti, whose money came from motor scooters. As Innocenti had high standards, he had the car fitted with servo-assisted disc brakes all-round, electric windows and a removable hardtop. He also had the instruments and all the trim changed from the standard chrome items to stainless-steel fittings.

1960 Ferrari 250 GT Series II Cabriolet, coachwork by Pininfarina, chassis no. 3645, engine no. 3645, 3 litre overhead-camshaft all-aluminium V12 engine, 220bhp, 4-speed all-synchromesh gearbox, multi-tubular chassis, independent front suspension, 4-wheel disc brakes, polished Borrani wire wheels, Marchal headlamps, restored, finished in red, black canvas hood, new tan leather interior, complete with unrestored hardtop.
£110,000–130,000 / $159,500–188,500 BKS
Effectively an open-top version of the Pininfarina-built 250 GT Coupé, the chassis and mechanics of which it shared, the Series II Cabriolet was built alongside its closed cousin until 1962 and offered a plusher, more refined alternative to Ferrari's contemporary California Spyder (which cost 10 per cent less than the Series II Cabriolet). Overall design followed that of the Coupé, with short nose and long rear overhang, while a more-vertical windscreen provided greater headroom in the generously sized cockpit. Series II cars benefited from the latest, 240bhp V12 with outside spark plugs, coil valve springs and 12-port cylinder heads. The 250 GT was the most successful Ferrari of its time, production of all types exceeding 900 units, of which 200 were Series II Cabriolets.

1962 Ferrari 250 GT Spyder California, chassis no. 3119 GT, engine no. 168, 3000cc overhead-camshaft V12 engine, triple Weber carburettors, 260bhp, 4-speed manual gearbox, 4-wheel disc brakes, restored, 1 of only 37 covered-headlight cars built.
£800,000+ / $1,150,000+ RM
By 1957, the 250 GT Tour de France lightweight Berlinetta was winning GT races wherever it appeared and was equally at home on the street as a very fast Grand Touring car. Luigi Chinetti, Ferrari's North American agent, foresaw a demand for a convertible version of the Tour de France and pressed Enzo Ferrari to build such a car. The result, completed by December 1957 and called the Spyder California, proved an instant success. Ferrari had Pininfarina design the car and build the bodywork of the first example, but after this, Scaglietti built all production bodies – usually in steel, but with aluminium bonnet, boot lid and doors. A few competition cars, with more powerful engines and all-aluminium bodies, were manufactured and raced. When the long-wheelbase 250 GT Tour de France Berlinetta was phased out in 1959, it was replaced by the SWB (short-wheelbase) Berlinetta fitted with disc brakes, and California Spyders were based on that model.

▶ **1963 Ferrari 250 GTE,** chassis no 4395, engine no. 4395, 2953cc V12 engine, left-hand drive, finished in red, black leather interior, electrical system in need of attention.
£18,000–22,000 / $26,000–32,000 BRIT

1961 Ferrari 250 GT, coachwork by Drogo, chassis no. 1717 GT, V12 engine, tubular chassis, coil-spring/double-wishbone front suspension, rear suspension by semi-elliptic leaf springs and twin trailing arms, finished in red, tan interior, excellent condition.
£190,000–220,000 / $275,000–320,000 COYS
This car is one of a handful bodied by Drogo, a company that was responsible for some of the most exotic and stylish coachwork on such important models as the 206 Dino and the immortal 250 GTO. It is believed that this is one of only three such cars to have survived.

1962 Ferrari 250 GT/L Lusso, engine rebuilt, 7,000 miles covered since, finished in red, black interior, 3rd Lusso built, ex Jo Siffert, original condition.
£75,000–88,500 / $108,750–128,500 HCL

1962 Ferrari 250 GT SWB California Spyder, coachwork by Pininfarina/Scaglietti, chassis no. 03007 GT, engine no. 03007 GT, 2956cc V12 engine, 4-speed manual ribbed competition-type gearbox, tubular frame, 4-wheel disc brakes, coil-spring/double-wishbone front suspension, rear suspension by semi-elliptic leaf springs and twin trailing arms, telescopic shock absorbers, completely restored, engine and gearbox completely rebuilt, exhaust Snaps, bare-metal respray in red, new black interior, 14,000km covered since restoration.
£900,000+ / $1,300,000+ BKS

1963 Ferrari 250 GT Lusso Berlinetta, coachwork by Pininfarina, chassis no. 5251, restored, finished in red, black interior, 1 of only 350 250 GT Lussos made, excellent condition.
£95,000–110,000 / $137,750–159,500 ⚒ BKS
The 250 GT Lusso Berlinetta debuted in October 1961. Styled by Pininfarina and built by Scaglietti, the Lusso (luxury) combined race-track looks with high standards of passenger comfort. Beautifully proportioned, it had a low-slung nose, reminiscent of that of the 400 Superamerica, and a Kamm tail. Slim pillars and wide expanses of glass not only enhanced the car's outward appearance, but also made for excellent vision, and a pleasantly light and airy interior.

1963 Ferrari 250 GT/L Berlinetta Lusso, 2953cc overhead-camshaft aluminium V12 engine, triple twin-choke carburettors, 240bhp, 4-speed manual gearbox with overdrive, 4-wheel disc brakes, Borrani wheels, restored, over £13,500 spent on engine, clutch, gearbox and rear axle, finished in silver, black leather interior.
£80,000–90,000 / $116,000–130,500 ⚒ RM

1963 Ferrari 250 GTE 2+2, coachwork by Pininfarina, chassis no. 3061, engine no. 128/F, 2953cc overhead-camshaft V12 engine, triple Weber carburettors, 235bhp, 4-speed manual gearbox, independent front suspension by coil-springs and wishbones, semi-elliptic rear leaf springs, telescopic shock absorbers all-round, 4-wheel disc brakes, polished alloy Borrani wire wheels, left-hand drive, finished in Italian racing red, new tan leather interior with matching trim and carpets, little use in last 15 years, 89,000 miles from new, original, excellent condition.
£30,000–35,000 / $43,500–50,750 ⚒ C
The GTE coupé was built on the standard 2.6m wheelbase, but by repositioning the engine and transmission, Ferrari was able to accommodate enlarged coachwork with 2+2 seating, which widened the car's appeal. In all, some 950 examples were produced between 1960 and 1963. The engine was an uprated development of Colombo's well-proven V12, which by then was capable of delivering 235bhp at 7,000rpm.

1963 Ferrari 250 GT Lusso Berlinetta, chassis no. 4519, engine no. 6555, completely rebuilt, fitted with 3967cc 330 GTC overhead-camshaft V12 engine, 300bhp, gearbox overhauled, dual rear Watts linkage, resprayed in red, only 1 other known example to this specification.
£90,000–100,000 / $130,000–145,000 ⚒ BKS

1965 Ferrari 500 Superfast Coupé, coachwork by Pininfarina, chassis no. 6043, engine no. 6043, left-hand drive, lowered and lengthened driver's seat, Blaupunkt Koln radio, electric aerial, finished in dark green, black leather upholstery and matching carpets, veneered cappings, never restored, 1 of 37 built.
£180,000–200,000 / $260,000–290,000 ⚒ BKS
Introduced in 1964 and produced for only two years, the opulent 500 Superfast was, at that time, Ferrari's fastest, most powerful, most expensive and most exclusive road car. The Superfast chassis was multi-tubular and initially was fitted with a four-speed overdrive gearbox. Ferrari's racing heritage manifested itself in the Lampredi-designed, 5 litre 'long block' V12 engine, the largest to power a Ferrari up to that point. The Competition-derived Tipo 208's 400bhp made it the most powerful production engine of its day, and it could propel the aerodynamically efficient Superfast to 175mph. After only a few examples had been built, a revised Superfast was made available, the most significant change being the adoption of a five-speed all-synchromesh gearbox. Twelve such cars appear to have been made, outwardly distinguishable by their three-vent engine bay louvres instead of the earlier 11-vent style.

1965 Ferrari 275 GTB, chassis no. 06895, 3286cc overhead-camshaft V12 engine, 260bhp, 5-speed manual gearbox, 4-wheel independent suspension, 4-wheel disc brakes, tubular steel chassis, finished in red, saddle leather interior, fewer than 59,000 miles from new, excellent overall condition.
£125,000–140,000 / $180,000–200,000 ⚒ RM
The 275 GTB Berlinetta was introduced in 1964 as the replacement for Ferrari's 250 GT SWB Berlinetta. Model nomenclature stemmed from engine and cylinder displacement; a key element that helped to differentiate the new from the old. The size of the 12-cylinder engine was increased to 3286cc from 3 litres, which made the capacity of each cylinder roughly 275cc. Covered headlamps, sloping back, slotted front wings and slotted rear sail panels were trademark styling cues, intended to evoke the legendary GTO. The engine, driveshaft and rear-mounted transaxle were combined in a rigid sub-assembly, then bolted to the chassis at four points. These traits helped to give the 275 GTB formidable handling on the road and on the track.

1966 Ferrari 275 GTB/6C Berlinetta, coachwork by Pininfarina/Scaglietti, chassis no. 07995, 3.3 litre V12 engine, 6 Weber carburettors, rear-mounted 5-speed transaxle, 4-wheel independent suspension, Campagnolo alloy wheels, aluminium body, air conditioning, engine rebuilt 1988, finished in red, black seats with grey cloth inserts, 3 owners and 32,000 miles from new, excellent condition.
£195,000–220,000 / $280,000–310,000 ⚒ BKS

1967 Ferrari 275 GTS/4 N.A.R.T. Spyder Replica, converted by Richard Straman, chassis no. 10743, 3286cc V12 engine, 300bhp, rear-mounted 5-speed transaxle, 4-wheel independent suspension, 4-wheel disc brakes, restored at a cost of over £103,000.
£325,000+ / $500,000+ ⚒ RM
When Enzo Ferrari refused to build a convertible version of the GTB/4, Luigi Chinetti pushed the idea for an open version of the car, known as the N.A.R.T. Spyder and named for Chinetti's North American Racing Team. Ten such cars were built for Chinetti by Sergio Scaglietti, all of which were sold in the USA. To promote the car's introduction, Chinetti entered the first N.A.R.T. Spyder in the Sebring 12-hour endurance race with automotive journalist and racer Denise McCluggage behind the wheel. She finished 17th overall, the single Ferrari survivor among a field that included seven cars at the start. Because so few original N.A.R.T. Spyders were built, a handful of Berlinettas were converted into Spyders by noted customiser Richard Straman.

1967 Ferrari 275 GTB/4, chassis no. 09463GT, double-overhead-camshaft V12 engine, dry-sump lubrication, 6 twin-choke Weber carburettors, 300bhp restored, extra servo, Borrani wire wheels, set of original alloy wheels, finished in light metallic green, 1 of only 27 right-hand-drive 275 GTB/4s built.
£215,000–240,000 / $300,000–350,000 ⚒ COYS
The 275 GTB/4 was introduced to the public at the Paris Salon in October 1966, almost two years to the day after the 275 GTB had appeared there. Production of the 275 GTB/4 was short-lived, however. It ended after a year, in mid-1968, by which time only 350 cars had left the factory.

1965 Ferrari 275 GTS Spyder, coachwork by Pininfarina, chassis no. 6809, engine no. 6809, V12 engine, rear-mounted 5-speed transaxle, multi-tubular chassis, 4-wheel independent suspension, Borrani wire wheels, left-hand drive, finished in red, original black leather interior, 64,000km from new, 1 of only 200 275 GTS models built, very good condition.
£110,000–125,000 / $160,000–180,000 ⚒ BKS

1965 Ferrari 330 GT 2+2, chassis no. 8373GT, 3967cc overhead-camshaft V12 engine, 300bhp, 5-speed gearbox, 4-wheel independent suspension and disc brakes, completely restored, finished in dark blue, tan leather interior, concours winner.
£30,000–40,000 / $43,500–58,000 ⚒ RM
Introduced in January 1964, the 330 GT 2+2 was the successor to the 250 GTE. It featured increased engine displacement – from 3 to 4 litres – as well as a longer wheelbase, updated styling and improved brakes. In an attempt to 'Americanise' the car, Ferrari's initial design featured a four-headlight layout. Swift reaction came from *Ferraristi*, and it wasn't positive. The traditional two-headlight styling was quick to return.

1966 Ferrari 330 GTC Coupé, coachwork by Pininfarina, chassis no 09239GT, engine no. 90239GT, new Borrani wire wheels, electric windows, finished in red, beige leather interior, excellent condition throughout.
£50,000–55,000 / $72,500–79,750 ⚒ BKS
Intended to fill a gap between the four-seat 330 GT 2+2 and the racer-on-the-road 275 GTB, the two-seat 330 GTC appeared in March 1966, and in essence was a closed version of the 275 GTS. Pininfarina's understated coachwork combined elements of the latter at the rear, with touches of the 500 Superfast at the front. Beneath the 330 GTC's bonnet resided the 4 litre, 300bhp version of Ferrari's familiar, two-cam, 60-degree V12, as used in the 330 GT 2+2. The chassis followed Ferrari's established practice of tying together sturdy oval-section main tubes in a steel spaceframe, while the suspension was independent all-round by wishbones and coil springs. The rear suspension incorporated the five-speed gearbox in the form of a transaxle. Around 600 cars had been produced before the model was superseded by the short-lived 365 GTC in 1968.

1967 Ferrari 330 GTS Spyder, coachwork by Pininfarina, 3967cc, V12 engine, 300bhp, rear-mounted 5-speed transaxle, 4-wheel independent suspension, tubular steel chassis, mechanics completely restored, subject of partial cosmetic restoration, finished in red, black interior, 3 owners and 40,850 miles from new, matching numbers, 1 of only 100 examples built.
£160,000–180,000 / $230,000–260,000 ⚒ RM

1967 Ferrari 365 GT 2+2, chassis no. 11133, 4380cc, double-overhead-camshaft aluminium V12 engine, triple Weber carburettors, 320bhp, 5-speed transaxle, 4-wheel independent suspension, 4-wheel disc brakes, Borrani wire wheels, air conditioning, restored.
£35,000–40,000 / $50,000–58,000 ⚒ RM

◄ **1969 Ferrari 365 GT 2+2,** completely restored, engine rebuilt and converted to unleaded fuel, finished in red, tan leather interior, bills for £30,000, 56,000 miles from new.
£29,000–34,000 / $42,000–50,000 ⊞ TIHO

1971 Ferrari 365 GTC, coachwork by Pininfarina, chassis no 12437, finished in blue, magnolia leather upholstery, some shrinkage to paintwork, 53,700 miles recorded, 1 of 22 right-hand drive examples built.
£48,000–53,000 / $69,500–77,000 ⚒ BKS
Introduced late in 1968 as a replacement for the 330 GTC, the 365 GTC was identical in appearance apart from engine cooling vents relocated in the bonnet, although this had also been a feature of the last of the 330s. Installing an enlarged 4.4 litre V12 boosted acceleration and increased the luxury coupé's top speed to over 150mph. Like so many European sports cars, the 365 GTC (and convertible 365 GTS) would fall victim to increasingly stringent US safety and emissions legislation, production ceasing after less than a year, during which time fewer than 200 GTC and around 20 GTS models left the factory.

Ferrari 365 GTB/4 Daytona (1968–74)

Engine: Four-camshaft V12, six Weber carburettors, 4390cc.
Power output: 325bhp @ 7,500rpm.
Transmission: Five-speed manual.
Brakes: Four-wheel discs.
Top speed: 174mph.
0–60mph: 5.4 seconds.
Production: 1,412 (including 165 in right-hand drive and 127 spyders).

There's no doubt about it, the Ferrari Daytona's a beautiful dinosaur, for even at its debut at the Paris Salon of 1968, the tide of supercar design was shifting toward mid-engined machinery, yet with the 365 GTB/4 Ferrari persisted with the good old reliable front-engined layout. However, with its fearsome 4.4 litre V12 pushing 325bhp through its fat rear tyres, the Daytona was, quite simply, the world's fastest production car. Its chisel-nosed Pininfarina styling was also luxuriantly extravagant, without crossing the boundary into the dubious automotive netherworld of brutal machismo, chest wigs and medallions. Who cared if the Daytona guzzled fossil fuel at the rate of 14mpg – certainly not your average mature super-rich Daytona driver with a hectic breakfast-in-Paris, dinner-in-Monte Carlo social timetable. Of course, that was until the fuel crisis of October 1973. After that, the Daytona wasn't quite so *de rigueur* among diamond-studded jetsetters with gnawing social consciences, and one of the most beautiful Ferraris ever faded away the following year. But the Daytona theme just won't lie down and die. Witness the 1994 launch of the Ferrari 455 – front-engined, V12, 5.4 litres, 13mpg in town. Maybe when we run out of fossil fuels some people will still buy voluptuous V12 Ferraris – just to look at them.

Daytona Data: Ferrari never officially called the car 'Daytona'. The name was adopted by the press following Ferrari's outright victory in the 1967 24-hour Daytona race. Mel Blanc, creator of cartoon voices for Bugs Bunny, Daffy Duck and the stammering Porky Pig, owned two Ferrari Daytona spyders, one of which sold at auction recently for £304,000.

Daytona spotting: from 1971, retractable headlights replaced earlier Perspex-covered items.

1970 Ferrari 365 GTB/4 Daytona, coachwork by Pininfarina, chassis no. 13213, engine no. 13213, converted to Group 4 specification for historic racing 1983, finished in red with tri-colour stripe, blue cloth upholstery, very good condition.
£75,000–85,000 / $121,000–135,000 ⚒ BKS
When first shown to the public, the GTB created a stir on two counts. The first was that the 365 GTB/4 was front-engined, whereas Ferrari's main rival was the mid-engined Lamborghini Miura. The other thing that raised eyebrows was the claimed top speed of 174 mph, which, if true, made the Daytona the fastest production car ever built. The claim was doubted by many until *Road & Track* tested one and not only verified the headline claim, but also covered the 0-60mph sprint in well under six seconds. The Daytona had independent suspension all-round by coil springs and wishbones and, to achieve perfect balance, a 5-speed transaxle. The engine was the quad-cam V12 bored and stroked to 4390cc. Maximum power was 352bhp at 7,500 rpm, but even more impressive was the 365lb/ft torque at 5,500rpm. Ferrari made 20 Group 4 Daytonas and they became legendary in classic endurance races.

1971 Ferrari 365 GTB/4 Daytona Spyder, coachwork by Pininfarina/Scaglietti, chassis no. 14565, 4390cc V12 engine, 355bhp, 5-speed transaxle, 4-wheel independent suspension, tubular-steel chassis, finished in yellow, black leather interior, 12,798 miles from new.
£250,000–275,000 / $360,000–400,000 ⚒ RM
The first production examples of the GTB/4 reached the USA in 1970 and featured a slightly different nose treatment to their European counterparts. The latter had their headlamps behind a transparent, full-width plastic cover, whereas US versions featured retractable lamps under two flush-fitting panels. Other differences included hexagonal-type wheel nuts on the US version, instead of three-eared knock-off wheel nuts on European models. A Spyder version of the Daytona was introduced in late 1969. Known outside the USA as the 365 GTS/4, the Spyder was an instant success with motoring press and public alike. Despite this popularity, only 121 Spyder Daytonas were built, 96 of them finding their way into the hands of US customers.

Most Ferrari model numbers represented the approximate cubic capacity in cc of one cylinder of the engine. Thus the Ferrari 365 GTB/4 was so called because the capacity of each of its 12 cylinders was approximately 365cc. Overall capacity was 4390cc. One obvious exception is the Ferrari F40 of 1987, so named to celebrate 40 years of the famous prancing horse marque from Maranello.

◀ **1971 Ferrari 365 GTB/4 Daytona,** coachwork by Pininfarina, chassis no. 16357, engine no. 16357, finished in red, racing seat belts, period Blaupunkt radio, black leather upholstery, 65,000km from new, very good condition.
£67,000–74,000 / $97,000–106,000 ⚒ BKS
In 1970, Jacky Ickx was runner-up in the World Championship, winner of three Grands Prix, and the main reason why Ferrari came a close second in the Constructors' Cup after several lean years. Enzo Ferrari was so delighted that he presented his young driver with this car. Ickx used it to drive to races then subsequently sold it. The next owner was Nick Mason, racing driver, Ferrari collector and drummer with Pink Floyd.

1973 Ferrari 365 GTB/4 Daytona, 4390cc V12 engine, 32,163 miles from new, concours condition.
£75,000–85,000 / $110,000–123,000 ⊞ KHP

1972 Ferrari 365 GTC/4, coachwork by Pininfarina, 4390cc V12 engine, 6 Weber 38DCOE carburettors, 340bhp, 5-speed manual gearbox, 4-wheel independent suspension, 4-wheel disc brakes, 260km/h top speed.
£27,000–32,000 / $39,200–46,400 Pou

1974 Ferrari 365 GT/4 Berlinetta Boxer, chassis no. 18291, double-overhead-camshaft flat-12 engine, 5-speed transmission, finished in red, black interior, 30,000 miles from new, very good condition.
£44,000–49,000 / $64,000–70,500 COYS

1977 Ferrari 512 BB, chassis no. 22803, 4942cc light-alloy flat-12 engine, 4 triple-choke Weber carburettors, 360bhp, 5-speed manual transmission, 4-wheel disc brakes, 4-wheel independent suspension, finished in black, tan leather seats and black inserts, 17,000 miles from new.
£42,000–46,500 / $61,000–67,500 RM

1974 Ferrari 365 GT/4 Berlinetta Boxer, coachwork by Pininfarina, chassis no. 17641, mid-mounted engine, 5-speed transaxle, combination tubular/monocoque chassis, stored for many years, mechanically refurbished, cosmetic renovation, 1,500km covered since completion, finished in metallic blue, original black leather interior, very good condition.
£35,000–40,000 / $50,000–58,000 BKS
Faced with having to pitch its top-of-the-range Daytona front-engined model against the mid-engined Lamborghini Miura and Maserati Bora coupés, Ferrari responded boldly with the 365 GT/4 Berlinetta Boxer. It debuted at the 1971 Turin show in prototype form and entered production in 1973 almost unaltered. An entirely new model and the first road-going Ferrari not to have a V-configuration engine, the 365 GT/4 BB reflected Ferrari's motor racing heritage. Its 4.4 litre, four-cam boxer engine drew on experience gained from the Maranello firm's World Championship winning, flat-12 Formula One and sports-racing units, and developed no less than 360bhp at 7,700rpm. The mid-mounted engine gave near-perfect balance and ensured that the Boxer's handling matched its stupendous straight-line speed. Only 367 Ferrari 365 GT4/BBs were constructed before the model was superseded by the 512 BB in 1976.

1979 Ferrari 512 BB Boxer, 4942cc flat-12 engine, 5-speed manual transmission, 4-wheel disc brakes, 4-wheel independent suspension.
£45,000–50,000 / $65,250–72,500 ⊞ FOS

◄ **1982 Ferrari 512 BBi,** 4.9 litre flat-12 engine, Bosch fuel injection, finished in red, tan leather upholstery, 20,000km from new, 'as-new' condition.
£34,000–38,000 / $48,000–54,000 COYS
This car was formerly owned by Formula One racing driver Eddie Irvine.

1968 Ferrari 206 GT Dino, coachwork by Pininfarina, engine replaced 1988, little use since, gearbox, final drive and all other mechanical components completely overhauled, bare-metal respray in original red, interior retrimmed to original specification in black imitation leather.
£37,500–41,500 / $54,000–60,000 ⚒ BKS
The Dino 206 GT was the first production mid-engined Ferrari and is the rarest. A mere 150 or so examples were made. It was intended to be the first of a separate marque established in memory of Alfredino, Enzo Ferrari's only legitimate son, who died at an early age. The name 'Dino' had long been applied to Ferrari's V6 engines, since Dino himself, a gifted engineer, had worked on the prototypes. The car's 2 litre quad-cam V6 engine was mounted transversely and delivered its 180bhp through a 5-speed transaxle. Suspension was independent all-round and, thanks to light weight and low drag, 142mph was possible (0–60 mph in 7.1 seconds).

1972 Ferrari 246 GT Dino, double-overhead-camshaft V6 engine, 190bhp, 5-speed transaxle, 4-wheel independent suspension, right-hand drive, bare-metal respray in red 1995, black leather interior refurbished, 38,000 miles from new.
£41,000–45,000 / $59,500–65,250 ⚒ COYS

1975 Ferrari Dino 208 GT4 Berlinetta, coachwork by Bertone, restored, updated wheels and seatbelts, otherwise to factory specification, finished in silver, red leather upholstery, very good condition.
£9,000–11,000 / $13,000–16,000 ⚒ BKS
Ferrari's continuing family of highly successful V8-engined road cars began with the 308 GT4 of 1973. Badged until 1977 as a Dino, thereafter as a Ferrari, the 308 replaced the preceding Dino 246. The Maranello factory's first mid-engined 2+2, the 308 GT4 was the work of Bertone rather than the customary Pininfarina. By placing the front seats well forward, Bertone made room within the 100in wheelbase for two seats in the rear, while the compact engine/transaxle package left space behind the engine bay for a useful luggage compartment. In 1975, Ferrari introduced a 2 litre version – the 208 GT4 – to take advantage of the Italian vehicle taxation system. The V8 engine was reduced in bore size for a capacity of 1990cc and produced 180bhp at 7,700rpm. Despite the reduction in horsepower, the Dino 208 GT4's all-round performance and 137 mph top speed placed it in the front rank of contemporary 2 litre sports cars.

1974 Ferrari 246 GTS Dino Spyder, coachwork by Pininfarina, left-hand drive, restored, resprayed yellow, tan leather interior.
£46,000–51,000 / $74,000–82,000 ⚒ BKS
A 2.4 litre version on a longer wheelbase, the 246 GT replaced the Dino 206 in late 1969. The body was steel and the cylinder block cast-iron rather than aluminium, but the bigger engine's increased power – 195bhp at 7,600rpm – was adequate compensation for the weight gain. A targa-top version, the 246 GTS, followed in 1972 and accounted for no more than a third of total Dino production. While not as fast in a straight line as its larger V12-engined stablemates, the nimble Dino was capable of showing almost anything a clean pair of heels over twisty going.

1974 Ferrari Dino 246 GTS, 2.4 litre V6 engine, 5-speed transaxle, finished in red, good condition.
£50,000–55,000 / $72,500–79,750 ⊞ WCL

1976 Ferrari 308 GT4, V8 engine, 250bhp, finished in Ferrari red, upholstered in black, good condition.
£10,500–12,000 / $15,250–17,500 ⚒ COYS

> A known continuous history can add value to and enhance the enjoyment of a car.

1978 Ferrari 308 GTB, air conditioning, finished in red, magnolia interior, 60,000 miles from new, in need of minor cosmetic tidying.
£18,000–20,000 / $26,000–29,000 ⊞ VIC

1979 Ferrari 308 GTB Berlinetta, coachwork by Pininfarina, stainless-steel exhaust system, finished in silver, red leather interior, 2 owners and 45,000 miles from new, very good condition.
£13,000–16,000 / $18,750–23,200 ⚒ BKS

1988 Ferrari Mondial 3.2, coachwork by Pininfarina, 3.2 litre engine, 5-speed manual gearbox, sunroof, air conditioning, wheels refurbished, finished in metallic grey, grey leather interior, 60,000km from new, very good condition.
£11,500–13,000 / $16,750–18,750 ⚒ BKS
Ferrari's first effort at building a 'world car', the Mondial 8, deployed the 308 GT4's 3 litre quad-cam V8 engine in a lengthened version of the latter's chassis. Transmission and running gear remained much the same, with a five-speed transaxle and independent suspension all round. Although reckoned less sporting than other Ferraris, the Mondial was still good for 225+km/h, and its ride quality and comfort scored over long distances. Considerably roomier than previous Ferrari 2+2s, the Pininfarina-styled Mondial was described by *Car* magazine as 'The closest you'll get to supercar family transport.' Developments included a Cabriolet version, the introduction of a more-powerful 260bhp, four-valve-per-cylinder engine in 1982, and enlargement to 3.2 litres for 1985.

1990 Ferrari 328 GTS, ABS, air conditioning, finished in red, magnolia hide interior, 16,000 miles from new.
£36,000–40,000 / $52,000–58,000 ⊞ VIC

1977 Ferrari 400 GT, 4823cc V12 engine, 1 of 21 right-hand drive models built with 5-speed manual gearbox, engine rebuilt at a cost of £10,000, 7,000 miles covered since, new brake discs, finished in blue, original tan and black leather interior.
£8,000–10,000 / $11,500–14,500 ⚒ BRIT
At its unveiling at the Paris Salon in October 1976, the 400 GT was hailed by the press as the ultimate 2+2. The 4.8 litre V12 engine, breathing through six 38DCOE Weber carburettors, produced 304bhp at 6,500rpm, giving sensational acceleration and a maximum speed of around 150mph. Only 501 manual five-speed versions were produced.

1989 Ferrari 348 ts, finished in red, black interior, 1 owner and 40,000 miles from new.
£33,000–39,000 / $48,000–56,500 ⊞ HCL

1978 Ferrari 400 GT, 4823cc V12 engine, 6 twin-choke Weber carburettors, automatic transmission, restored 1991–98 at a cost of £52,000, finished in silver-blue, cream interior.
£12,000–14,000 / $17,500–20,300 ⚒ H&H

1978 Ferrari 400 Cabriolet, 4823cc V12 engine, 6 Weber carburettors, 310bhp, 3-speed automatic transmission, 4-wheel ventilated disc brakes, 4-wheel independent suspension.
£22,000–24,000 / $32,000–35,000 ⚒ Pou

1980 Ferrari 400i, automatic transmission, new stainless steel exhaust, new alloy wheels, air conditioning, resprayed in metallic grey, new magnolia leather interior, wood veneer centre console, 50,000 miles from new.
£14,000–16,000 / $20,300–23,200 ⚒ BKS
The original Daytona 4.4 litre V12 engine was enlarged for the 400 model to 4.8 litres, when GM automatic transmission was also offered as an option to the five-speed manual gearbox. The GT with newly introduced fuel injection became the 400i in 1979.

Condition Guide

1. A vehicle in top class condition but not 'concours d'elegance standard, either fully restored or in very good original condition.
2. A good, clean, roadworthy vehicle, both mechanically and bodily sound.
3. A runner, but in need of attention, probably both to bodywork and mechanics. Must have current MoT.

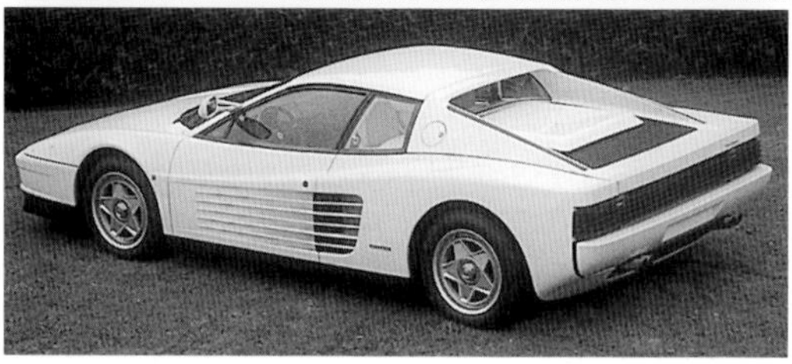

1986 Ferrari Testarossa, coachwork by Pininfarina, finished in white, beige leather upholstery, 1 owner and 2,597km from new.
£32,000–36,000 / $46,500–52,000 ⚒ BKS
Ferrari's flagship model well into the 1990s, the Testarossa revived a famous name from the Italian company's past when it arrived in 1984. A 'next generation' Berlinetta Boxer, the Testarossa retained its predecessor's 5 litre flat-12 engine, which now gave 390bhp courtesy of four-valve cylinder heads. Despite the power increase, smoothness and drivability were enhanced, the car possessing excellent flexibility allied to a maximum speed of 290km/h. Luxury touches included air conditioning, electrically adjustable seats and a tilting steering wheel.

1990 Ferrari F40, coachwork by Pininfarina, 335 miles from new.
£160,000–180,000 / $232,000–260,000 ⚒ BKS
Introduced in 1988 to celebrate Enzo Ferrari's 40 years as a car maker, the F40 represented the ultimate supercar. A mid-engined two-seat Berlinetta, the F40 was a development of the limited-production 288 GTO, and like the latter – but unlike the preceding 308 series – had its power unit mounted longitudinally rather than transversely. A four-cam 3 litre V8 with four valves per cylinder, the F40 engine employed twin turbochargers to liberate 478bhp at 7,000rpm. The F40 combined steel and composite structural materials, a lightweight moulded plastic and composite bodyshell, the latest in aerodynamic aids, dam-shaped nose, fenced rear aerofoil, etc, and Pininfarina claimed a Cd drag factor of only 0.34, generating virtually zero lift at speed. This was considered to be an exceptional achievement without recourse to movable aerodynamic devices, extra spoilers and flippers.

Ferves

Restored values

The cost of a professional restoration will have an influence on, but no direct relation to, a car's market value. A restored car can have a market value lower than the cost of its restoration.

◀ **1969 Ferves Ranger 500,** 499cc Fiat 500 2-cylinder engine, 4-speed manual gearbox, drum brakes, finished in green, 30,000km from new.
£5,000–6,000 / $7,250–8,750 ⚒ Pou

Fiat

The name of Fiat may not set the pulse racing, but the company's signifigance goes far beyond the cars that carry the name. Fiat controls Ferrari, Lancia and Alfa Romeo, and one can only speculate on the fate of those great names had Fiat not stepped in. As for the cars bearing the Fiat badge, there is no doubt that the company's contribution to motoring is on a global scale, with mass-market milestones including the brilliantly packaged 500 Nuova; the 600 Multipla, which served as an early blueprint of the modern people carrier; desirable mainstream sports cars like the 124 Spyder; and the occasional exotic such as the beautiful Dino Spyder. Remarkably, the company that was founded in 1899 by Giovanni Agnelli is still in family control.

1924 Fiat 505 Five-Seat Tourer, full weather equipment, original right-hand drive.
£13,000–15,000 / $18,750–21,750 ⊞ GrM

1931 Fiat 521 Coupe des Alpes, 2516cc sidevalve 6-cylinder engine, 51bhp, manual gearbox, 4-wheel drum brakes, finished in red, restored to 'as-new' condition.
£30,000–33,000 / $43,500–46,500 ⚒ RM
This 521 Coupe des Alpes has a very rare Viotti-designed body. Sold new in Madrid in 1931, the body style is named after the famed Alpine Trial, the Coupe des Alpes.

▶ **1957 Fiat 500 Jolly,** coachwork by Ghia, 479cc overhead-valve 2-cylinder engine, 16.5bhp, 4-speed gearbox, 4-wheel drum brakes, left-hand drive, surrey top and fringing, finished in coral, wicker seats, 1,370 miles from new, original condition.
£14,000–16,000 / $20,300–23,200 ⚒ RM

1937 Fiat 500 Topolino, 570cc sidevalve 4-cylinder engine, right-hand drive, finished in blue and black, blue leather upholstery, restored, good condition.
£4,250–5,000 / $6,250–7,250 ⚒ BKS
Better equipped than many cars twice its size, the Fiat 500 – soon named Topolino (mouse) – brought a degree of refinement hitherto unknown to small cars when launched in 1936. Lockheed hydraulic brakes, independent front suspension and 12 volt electrics were all part of the package, while an engine mounted ahead of the front axle line helped maximise cabin space. Built only in two-seat form at first, the Topolino became available as a four-seater in 1939.

FIAT Model	ENGINE cc/cyl	DATES	CONDITION 1	2	3
501	1460/4	1920–26	£6,000	£3,500	£1,500
519	4767/6	1923–29	£9,000	£7,000	£3,000
503	1473/4	1927–29	£10,000	£4,000	£2,000
507	2297/4	1927–28	£9,000	£5,500	£3,500
522/4	2516/6	1932–34	£10,000	£8,000	£3,500
508	994/4	1934–37	£5,000	£2,500	£1,500
527 Sports	2516/6	1935–36	£14,000	£8,000	£3,500
1.5 litre Balilla	1498/6	1936–39	£10,000	£7,000	£3,000
500	570/4	1937–55	£6,000	£2,500	£1,000
1100 Balilla	1089/4	1938–40	£4,500	£2,000	£1,000

◄ **1970 Fiat Abarth 695 SS,** 2-cylinder engine, Weber carburettors, 4-speed manual gearbox, front disc/rear drum brakes, alloy wheels, finished in red with white stripes.
£5,000–6,000 / $7,250–8,750 Pou

1971 Fiat 500F, enlarged and tuned 650cc engine, alloy wheels, flared wheel arches, finished in metallic navy blue, crackle-finish aluminium dashboard, Ferrari instruments, wood-rim steering wheel, leather upholstery.
£5,000–6,000 / $7,250–8,750 BKS

◄ **1968 Fiat Gamine,** limited-production convertible based on Fiat 500, excellent condition.
£3,500–4,000 / $4,250–5,800 FIA

1962 Fiat 1200 Cabriolet, 1221cc 4-cylinder engine, 4-speed manual gearbox, independent front suspension, 4-wheel hydraulic drum brakes, left-hand drive, restored, finished in red, black interior, 45,612 miles from new, excellent condition.
£4,500–5,000 / $6,500–7,250 RM

Introduced in 1957, the 1200 was offered as a saloon and a cabriolet. The latter was intended to replace the 1100 TV two-seater, while the former was essentially a facelifted 1100. The cabriolet would be restyled by Pininfarina in 1959, with a sleeker body that resembled a 1500. Wind-up windows remained standard, while a mesh-patterned grille with angled sides was added. Standard revolving seats made access easier on the two-seater cabriolet. Production of the 1200 remained little changed until the new 1300/1500 family was introduced. Released at the end of April 1961, the 1300/1500 was designed to replace the 1200, although the latter remained in production until 1963.

Fiat 500D (1957–77)

Production: 4,000,000+ (all models).
Body styles: Saloon, cabriolet.
Construction: Unitary body/chassis.
Engine: Twin-cylinder, air-cooled, 499.5cc.
Power output: 17.5bhp @ 4,400rpm.
Transmission: Four-speed non-synchromesh.
Suspension: Front: independent, transverse leaf, wishbones.
Rear: independent, semi-trailing arms, coil springs.
Brakes: Hydraulic drums.
Maximum speed: 59mph.

Miller's Starter Marque

- **Starter Fiats:** *500, 1957 onward; 600; X1/9; 124 Coupé and Spyder.*
- Four-wheeled fun does not come in a much smaller package than the Fiat 500 – 9ft 9in to be precise. But forget this baby Fiat if you want to hack down to the country for the weekend. In 1957 *The Motor* magazine tested an early 479cc-engined 500 and could only eke out 53mph. Mind you, the fuel consumption was a fantastic 55mpg.
- The best 500 to go for is probably the later and slightly peppier 499cc-engined car. In both cases, you will be served by a crash gearbox, which means you will have to double declutch on the way down through the gears. The buzzing, high-revving, air-cooled twin-cylinder engine in the back of the car has a good reputation though, and if anything should go wrong, it can be removed in under an hour.
- These Fiat's do fray though, and the relatively simple monocoque of the 500 is no exception. You will want to prod any places on the underside and wheel arches where road muck can collect, in particular the structural steel member that runs across the car beneath the front seats. The floors can rust from the inside and outside too; also inspect the welded-on front wings closely and door bottoms.
- But with over four million 500s having been built up to 1975, these baby Fiats have a strong network of parts, spares and club support, making them a viable starter classic that is more distinctive – on British roads at least – than a Mini.
- If the 500's too tight a squeeze, you could always move up – by exactly a foot – to the slightly more commodious 600. It is a fine, well-handling little car, and it will even top 60mph. They do not have quite the cult following of the 500, which means that in general they are slightly cheaper, but harder to find too.
- The Fiat X1/9 offers fresh-air, finesse, fine handling, and Italian flare in a pint-sized and affordable sporting package. Top speed is only just over 100mph, but it will get you there with surefooted finesse. The Fiat's greatest feature is its mid-mounted engine, which provides optimum weight distribution for the kind of handling and adhesion normally associated with mega-money sports thoroughbreds. In short, it is just about the only truly affordable and practical, volume produced, mid-engined sports car. Unfortunately, this little Fiat funster tends to reinforce the once-popular notion that when you buy an Italian car of this period, you pay for the engine and get the body thrown in for free.
- The only thing that does not rust on the Fiat X1/9 is the detachable roof, and that is made of moulded plastic. The rule of thumb is to buy the very best you can afford, as body repairs could soon easily outstrip the value of this bargain-basement sports car. The electrics are also fragile, but the engine, either 1300 or 1500cc, is a little gem, reliable and long-lasting, and generally good for 100,000 miles or more.
- A more substantial sporting Fiat is the 124 Coupé and Spyder. It has got the looks, performance and handling – and an invitingly modest price tag. Unfortunately, the 124 Spyder was never officially imported to Britain, and that means the car you will be looking at is likely to be a left-hooker. But that is an advantage too, as it may well have come from a rust-free area of the United States. For an MGB alternative with a touch of Italian flare, the 124 Spyder is definitely worth consideration.

1967 Fiat 1500 L, right-hand drive, finished in grey, red interior, 53,000 miles from new, original condition.
£2,000–3,000 / $2,900–4,300 ⊞ GrM

1966 Fiat 850 S, 850cc, 4-wheel independent suspension, wire wheels, steering, brakes and suspension refurbished, finished in grey, red interior.
£2,000–2,500 / $2,900–3,600 ⚒ COYS
This car was bought new by John Bolster, chief road tester for *Autocar* magazine. It replaced an AC Aceca, Bolster's thinking being that it could help to conserve his driving licence in the light of the new 70mph speed limit. Evidently this aim was soon forgotten, as a special cylinder head was fitted, together with a Weber carburettor. A more sporting camshaft was also added, plus an exhaust with tuned pipes.

1968 Fiat Dino Spyder, finished in red, black interior, good condition throughout.
£16,000–18,000 / $23,200–26,200 ⚒ COYS
The Dino Spyder made its appearance at the 1966 Turin Salon, along with the prototype Dino Berlinetta GT, which was to become the production Ferrari Dino. Both cars used the 2 litre, four-cam light-alloy V6 engine, the lineage of which could be traced back to the Dino 206 Grand Prix engine and the Dino 166P sports-racing unit. Indeed, this V6 was conceived at Maranello for a Formula Two single-seater, but the governing body of the sport then decreed that for 1967 all power units in that formula had to be derived from mass-produced engines. Thus Ferrari and Fiat entered an agreement, in which the former would supply the Dino engines to the latter, which had the capacity to build the necessary 500 cars to meet homologation requirements.

FIAT Model	ENGINE cc/cyl	DATES	CONDITION 1	2	3
500B Topolino	569/4	1945–55	£5,000	£2,000	£750
500C	569/4	1948–54	£4,000	£1,700	£1,000
500 Nuova	479,499/2	1957–75	£3,000	£1,500	£750
600/600D	633, 767/4	1955–70	£3,000	£2,000	£1,000
500F Giardiniera	479, 499/2	1957–75	£3,000	£1,500	£1,000
2300S	2280/6	1961–68	£3,000	£1,700	£1,000
850	843/4	1964–71	£1,000	£750	-
850 Coupé	843, 903/4	1965–73	£1,500	£1,000	-
850 Spyder	843, 903/4	1965–73	£3,000	£2,000	£1,000
128 Sport Coupé 3P	1116/ 1290/4	1971–78	£2,500	£1,800	£1,000
130 Coupé	3235/6	1971–77	£5,500	£4,000	£2,000
131 Mirafiori Sport	1995/4	1974–84	£1,500	£1,000	£500
124 Sport Coupé	1438/ 1608/4	1966–72	£3,000	£2,000	£1,000
124 Sport Spyder	1438/ 1608/4	1966–72	£5,500	£2,500	£1,500
Dino Coupé	1987/ 2418/6	1967–73	£8,000	£5,500	£2,500
Dino Spyder	1987/ 2418/6	1967–73	£15,000	£10,000	£5,000
X1/9	1290/ 1498/4	1972–89	£4,000	£2,000	£1,500

► **1970 Fiat Dino Coupé,** engine rebuilt, stainless-steel exhaust system, bare-metal respray in green, new tan leather upholstery, 5,000 miles since 1995, good to excellent condition.
£7,000–8,000 / $10,000–11,600 COYS

1970 Fiat Dino 2400 Spyder, coachwork by Pininfarina, 2 litre double-overhead-camshaft V6 engine, left-hand drive, completely restored 1995–96, finished in silver.
£26,000–29,000 / $37,700–42,000 BKS
The Fiat Dino was built as a spyder by Pininfarina and a 2+2 coupé by Bertone. The haste with which the 2 litre Dino was put into production, however, meant that in several respects the design was a little crude. All of these shortcomings were cured, and many other improvements made, with the 2.4 litre Dino introduced in 1969. Assembly of these cars was transferred to the Ferrari works in Maranello, improving build quality. They featured independent rear suspension, improved braking, improved cooling, greater power and torque, larger tyres and a new ZF gearbox. Although the 2.4 was a superior car, only 424 spyders were made, compared to 1,133 2 litre spyders.

1981 Fiat 124 Spyder, 1995cc 4-cylinder engine, replacement Abarth 131-type gearbox, new differential, new Koni shock absorbers, bare-metal respray in metallic blue, beige vinyl hood.
£2,500–3,000 / $3,650–4,350 BRIT

1971 Fiat Shellette Beach Car, coachwork by Michelotti, finished in pale blue, wicker dashboard and seats, 8,200km from new.
£13,500–16,000 / $19,500–23,200 BKS

1984 Fiat X1/9, 1498cc, 5-speed manual gearbox, right-hand drive, finished in brown, tan leather interior, 1 owner and 17,000 miles from new, good condition throughout.
£3,250–3,750 / $4,750–5,250 BKS
Conceived by Bertone and introduced in 1972, the X1/9 was the world's first really successful mass-produced, mid-engined sports car, some 180,000 being built before the end of production in 1989. Of pressed-steel unitary construction, the X1/9 boasted all-round independent suspension by MacPherson struts, and four-wheel disc brakes. Mounted transversely, the 1.3 litre power unit was sourced from the Fiat 128 Rally and transmitted its 75bhp through an integral four-speed gearbox. In 1978, with the advent of the second series, the car received the Ritmo Strada's 1498cc engine and five-speed gearbox. With 85bhp available, the later X1/9 could top 110mph and sprint to 60mph in under 11 seconds.

Ford

After serving an apprenticeship to a machinist, Henry Ford built an internal-combustion engine on his kitchen table in 1893. In 1896 his first motorised vehicle took to the streets of Detroit. Other vehicles followed, including racers, and on 16 June, 1903 the Ford Motor Company was incorporated in Detroit. A month later, the first Ford Model A runabout was sold. The legendary Model T appeared in 1908, and shortly after that, in 1911, Ford's UK assembly plant got rolling in Manchester. From those early beginnings, Ford products in Europe and the USA began to forge their own distinct identities, matched to the needs of their markets. That is why we have separated Fords into UK and US products. Although the Model T was, of course, designed and built initially in the USA, we have included it in the UK section because, as it was built in parallel in the UK, it can also be regarded as a British Ford product. It certainly made a very important contribution to the landscape of British motoring into the 1920s, and paved the way for Ford's British designed products. As for Ford's Mercury and Lincoln divisions in the US, we have given each of these their own alphabetical sections, as their product ranges have established true brand images and market segments.

1915 Ford Model T Tourer, 4-cylinder engine, planetary gearbox, 2-speed Ruckstall axle, Rocky Mountain brakes, Hasler front springs, quick-fit wheels, twin spares, flashing indicators, windscreen wiper, tacho/speedometer, finished in black, black interior.
£12,000–14,000 / $17,500–20,500 ⚒ BKS
This car was prepared for the recent Round the World Rally, but never took part due to the owner's illness.

A Cartier sterling silver model of a 1903 Ford Model A, made to commemorate Ford's 75th anniversary, gold plated detail, lamps include diamonds and rubies, on a solid wood base with gold plated plaque.
£1,150–1,400 / $1,700–2,000 ⚒ BKS

1921 Ford Model T Tourer, 2892cc engine, artillery wheels.
£7,500–9,000 / $10, 850–13,000 ⊞ TUC

1924 Ford Model T Doctor's Coupé, 2890cc 4-cylinder sidevalve engine, 22bhp, 2-speed and reverse epicyclic gearbox, beam front axle, semi-elliptic transverse leaf springs front and rear, braking by contracting band on transmission, self-starter, left-hand drive, original, paintwork and interior in need of improvement.
£7,000–8,500 / $10,250–12,350 ⚒ C

FORD Model	ENGINE cc/cyl	DATES	CONDITION 1	2	3
Model T	2892/4	1908–27	£12,000	£7,000	£4,000
Model A	3285/4	1928–32	£8,500	£6,000	£3,500
Model Y and 7Y	933/4	1932–40	£5,000	£3,000	£1,500
Model C, CX & 7W	1172/4	1934–40	£4,000	£2,000	£1,000
Model AB	3285/4	1933–34	£10,000	£8,000	£4,500
Model ABF	2043/4	1933–34	£9,000	£6,000	£4,000
Model V8	3622/8	1932–40	£8,500	£6,000	£4,500
Model V8-60	2227/8	1936–40	£7,000	£5,000	£2,000
Model AF (UK only)	2033/4	1928–32	£9,000	£6,000	£3,500

A right-hand-drive vehicle will always command more interest than a left-hand-drive example in the UK. Coachbuilt vehicles, and in particular tourers, achieve a premium at auction. Veteran cars (i.e. manufactured before 1919) will often achieve a 20% premium.

1926 Ford Model T Tourer, wooden wheels, optional 'Fat Man' steering wheel, left-hand drive, restored, paintwork in need of attention.
£7,000–8,000 / $10,200–11,600 ⊞ GrM

1953 Ford Anglia, 933cc sidevalve 4-cylinder engine, 3-speed manual gearbox, spotlamp, finished in fawn, red interior, 3 owners and 66,000 miles from new.
£1,400–1,600 / $2,000–2,400 ⚒ H&H

► 1956 Ford E83W Utility, 1172cc 4-cylinder engine, finished in black, sound woodwork.
£2,500–3,000 / $3,650–4,350 ⚒ BRIT

1953 Ford Anglia Saloon, finished in black, red upholstery, 3 owners and 80,000 miles from new, original, unrestored, mechanics and bodywork in good condition.
£1,100–1,300 / $1,500–1,800 ⚒ BKS
Introduced in 1948, Ford's E494A Anglia employed its immediate predecessor's well established 933cc sidevalve engine – a unit that had debuted in the 19Y of 1933 – and a three-speed synchromesh gearbox. A separate chassis was retained, along with the familiar mechanical braking and transverse-leaf springing at front and rear. Budget-priced basic transportation, the Anglia offered 60mph performance while returning 35–40mpg. It remained in production until the arrival of the unitary-construction 100E in 1953.

FORD (British built) Model	ENGINE cc/cyl	DATES	CONDITION 1	2	3
Anglia E494A	993/4	1948–53	£2,000	£850	£250
Prefect E93A	1172/4	1940–49	£3,500	£1,250	£900
Prefect E493A	1172/4	1948–53	£2,500	£1,000	£300
Popular 103E	1172/4	1953–59	£1,875	£825	£300
Anglia/Prefect 100E	1172/4	1953–59	£1,350	£625	£250
Prefect 107E	997/4	1959–62	£1,150	£600	£200
Escort/Squire 100E	1172/4	1955–61	£1,000	£850	£275
Popular 100E	1172/4	1959–62	£1,250	£600	£180
Anglia 105E	997/4	1959–67	£1,400	£500	£75
Anglia 123E	1198/4	1962–67	£1,550	£575	£150
V8 Pilot	3622/8	1947–51	£7,500	£5,000	£1,500
Consul Mk I	1508/4	1951–56	£2,250	£950	£400
Consul Mk I DHC	1508/4	1953–56	£6,000	£3,500	£1,250
Zephyr Mk I	2262/6	1951–56	£3,000	£1,250	£600
Zephyr Mk I DHC	2262/6	1953–56	£7,000	£4,000	£1,300
Zodiac Mk I	2262/6	1953–56	£3,300	£1,500	£700
Consul Mk II/Deluxe	1703/4	1956–62	£2,900	£1,500	£650
Consul Mk II DHC	1703/4	1956–62	£5,000	£3,300	£1,250
Zephyr Mk II	2553/6	1956–62	£3,800	£1,800	£750
Zephyr Mk II DHC	2553/6	1956–62	£8,000	£4,000	£1,500
Zodiac Mk II	2553/6	1956–62	£4,000	£2,250	£750
Zodiac Mk II DHC	2553/6	1956–62	£8,500	£4,250	£1,800
Zephyr 4 Mk III	1703/4	1962–66	£2,100	£1,200	£400
Zephyr 6 Mk III	2552/6	1962–66	£2,300	£1,300	£450
Zodiac Mk II	2553/6	1962–66	£2,500	£1,500	£500
Zephyr 4 Mk IV	1994/4	1966–72	£1,750	£600	£300
Zephyr 6 Mk IV	2553/6	1966–72	£1,800	£700	£300
Zodiac Mk IV	2994/6	1966–72	£2,000	£800	£300
Zodiac Mk IV Est.	2994/6	1966–72	£2,800	£1,200	£300
Zodiac Mk IV Exec.	2994/6	1966–72	£2,300	£950	£300
Classic 315	1340/ 1498/4	1961–63	£1,400	£800	£500
Consul Capri	1340/ 1498/4	1961–64	£2,100	£1,350	£400
Consul Capri GT	1498/4	1961–64	£2,600	£1,600	£800

Miller's Starter Marque

- **Starter Fords:** *Anglia, Prefect, Popular from 1948 onward; Mk I, II and III, Consul, Zephyr and Zodiac, Mk IV Zephyr/Zodiac; Consul Classic 315/Consul Capri; Cortina Mk I, II, and III; Corsair, Capri, Escort.*
- Whatever your tastes, there is a Ford you can afford – in fact more than we have space to mention. Their list of virtues as starter classics is almost as long as the list of models to choose from. Importantly, many were made in their millions, which means that generally there is a ready stock of cars and spares, backed by a healthy network of clubs and specialists. Better still, Fords rarely use exotic materials or obscure, hard-to-grasp, technologies and that makes them a joy for the DIY enthusiast.
- **Consul, Zephyr and Zodiac (Mk I–III):** These are what you might term lifestyle Fords – there is one to match your taste in clothes and music. For Mk I models, read early Elvis, rockabilly rather than rock and roll. They are also ideal for post-war swing spivs with Cesar Romero pencil moustaches, double-breasted suits and nylons to sell. The Mk II is mainstream Elvis, structurally reinforced quiffs, pedal pushers, bowling shirts and Levi 501s. As for the Mk III, that is Elvis at Vegas, teddy boy drape coats, long sideboards and a tub of Swarfega in the hair. All models are eminently viable for the DIY enthusiast. While performance is hardly shattering by today's standards, they are fast enough to go with the flow of modern traffic without causing a tail-back.
- **Anglia:** In 1959 the new Anglia represented the shape of fins to come, a pretty, compact little saloon that was an instant hit with buyers who might otherwise have opted for something familiar like an Austin A40, Morris Minor or Triumph Herald. Although overshadowed by the launch of the top-selling Cortina a couple of years later, the Anglia 105E was a stylish little device with a miniature full-width version of the 'dollar-grin' grille up front and voguish US-hand-me-down rear fins. Under the skin there was a little innovation too, with the first overhead-valve engine for a small Ford and – wonder of wonders – four gears for the first time on a British Ford. The Anglia went on to sell more than a million, before making way for the Escort in 1967.
- **Pick of the bunch:** The Anglia Super 123E; this has an 1198cc engine compared with the 997cc of the 105E, so you'll get to 60mph in 22 seconds rather than 29, and eventually you'll nudge 85mph instead of running out of puff at 75mph.
- **Cortina Mk I:** The Cortina appeared late in 1962, and soon you couldn't miss it on Britain's roads as sales soared. With a mean price tag of just £639, it undercut rivals and, in many cases, offered a lot more. Overall, it added up to the anatomy of a bestseller, in fact, the bestselling British car of its time.
- **Pick of the bunch:** 1500 GT and Cortina Lotus: the 1500 GT gave a creditable 13-second 0–60mph dash and 95mph top speed; the Lotus Cortina, with 1558cc, 105bhp Lotus twin-cam and uprated suspension, scorched its way to 108mph. There were only 4,012 genuine Mk I Cortina Lotuses. They're highly prized, so watch out for fakes – there are plenty.

A known continuous history can add value to and enhance the enjoyment of a car.

1954 Ford Comète, coachwork by Facel Metalon, 2355cc sidevalve V8 engine, 78bhp, 3-speed manual gearbox, column change, hydraulic drum brakes, left-hand drive, finished in blue.
£5,000–6,000 / $7,250–8,500 Pou

1961 Ford Zephyr, extensively rebuilt and modified, original 2553cc 6-cylinder engine, triple SU carburettors, 6-branch exhaust manifold, Vauxhall Ventora 4-speed manual gearbox.
£8,500–10,000 / $12,325–14,500 HMM

1969 Ford Zephyr Mk IV, built to police specification, V6 engine, automatic transmission, 4-wheel drive, Dunlop Maxalet anti-lock dual-line braking system, Ford Mustang dual-wishbone front suspension, finished in white, black interior, 79,000 miles from new.
£1,800–2,100 / $2,600–3,100 H&H

1960 Ford Anglia 105E, overhead-valve 4-cylinder engine, 4-speed manual gearbox, finished in period police livery.
£800–1,000 / $1,150–1,450 CGC

1964 Ford Cortina Lotus Mk I, 1558cc 4-cylinder engine, rebuilt with replacement bodyshell late 1970s, finished in white with green flash, Corbeau seats, stored for a number of years, mechanics and bodywork in good condition.
£3,500–4,000 / $5,000–5,800 BRIT

Shortly after its introduction, the sporting potential of the Cortina became evident, and GT versions were soon introduced. For those seeking even more performance, early in 1963 Ford unveiled the Cortina Lotus, a limited-production model fitted with the excellent Lotus twin-cam engine and featuring light-alloy body panels. Early models utilised Colin Chapman's coil-sprung A-frame rear suspension, although this was deleted in 1964. The Cortina Lotus became a familiar sight on the circuits throughout the 1960s and was a good all-rounder – capable of being driven to work on weekdays and on the racetrack at weekends.

1964 Ford Cortina Lotus Mk I, 1558cc 4-cylinder double-overhead-camshaft 4-cylinder engine, light-alloy body panels, period steel sliding roof, new sills, wire wheels.
£6,500–8,000 / $9,500–11,500 BRIT

Ford GT40

Henry Ford's grandson, Henry II, was determined to win Le Mans, and when his offer to buy Ferrari was rebuffed, his resolve strengthened still further. The result was a Le Mans legend, the awesome GT40, a joint Anglo-American project. After a Le Mans 1-2 in 1966, GT40s won the 24-hour classic for the next three years. Henry Ford II had proved his point emphatically with an achievement that perhaps even surpasses Jaguar's string of Le Mans laurels in the mid-1950s.

◀ **1970 Ford Cortina Mk II 1600E,** restored over 8 years, original specification, concours condition.
£4,500–5,500 / $6,500–8,000 FEO

FORD (British built) Model	ENGINE cc/cyl	DATES	CONDITION 1	2	3
Cortina Mk I	1198/4	1963–66	£1,550	£600	£150
Cortina Crayford Mk I DHC	1198/4	1963–66	£3,500	£1,800	£950
Cortina GT	1498/4	1963–66	£1,800	£1,000	£650
Cortina Lotus Mk I	1558/4	1963–66	£10,000	£7,500	£4,500
Cortina Mk II	1599/4	1966–70	£1,000	£500	£100
Cortina GT Mk II	1599/4	1966–70	£1,200	£650	£150
Cortina Crayford Mk II DHC	1599/4	1966–70	£4,000	£2,000	£1,500
Cortina Lotus Mk II	1558/4	1966–70	£6,000	£3,500	£1,800
Cortina 1600E	1599/4	1967–70	£4,000	£2,000	£900
Consul Corsair	1500/4	1963–65	£1,100	£500	£250
Consul Corsair GT	1500/4	1963–65	£1,200	£600	£250
Corsair V4	1664/4	1965–70	£1,150	£600	£250
Corsair V4 Est.	1664/4	1965–70	£1,400	£600	£250
Corsair V4GT	1994/4	1965–67	£1,300	£700	£250
Corsair V4GT Est.	1994/4	1965–67	£1,400	£700	£350
Corsair Convertible	1664/ 1994/4	1965–70	£4,300	£2,500	£1,000
Corsair 2000	1994/4	1967–70	£1,350	£500	£250
Corsair 2000E	1994/4	1967–70	£1,500	£800	£350
Escort 1300E	1298/4	1973–74	£1,900	£1,000	£250
Escort Twin Cam	1558/4	1968–71	£8,000	£5,000	£2,000
Escort GT	1298/4	1968–73	£3,000	£1,500	£350
Escort Sport	1298/4	1971–75	£1,750	£925	£250
Escort Mexico	1601/4	1970–74	£4,000	£2,000	£750
RS1600	1601/4	1970–74	£5,000	£2,500	£1,500
RS2000	1998/4	1973–74	£4,500	£2,200	£1,000
Escort RS Mexico	1593/4	1976–78	£3,500	£2,000	£850
Escort RS2000 Mk II	1993/4	1976–80	£6,000	£3,500	£2,000
Capri Mk I 1300/ 1600	1298/ 1599/4	1969–72	£1,500	£1,000	£550
Capri 2000/ 3000GT	1996/4 2994/6	1969–72	£2,000	£1,000	£500
Capri 3000E	2994/6	1970–72	£4,000	£2,000	£1,000
Capri RS3100	3093/6	1973–74	£6,500	£3,500	£2,000
Cortina 2000E	1993/4	1973–76	£2,500	£550	£225
Granada Ghia	1993/4 2994/6	1974–77	£3,000	£900	£350

Ford Cortina Mk II (1966–70)

Body styles: Two- and four-door saloon, estate, Crayford convertible.
Engine: Four-cylinder, 1297, 1498 and 1599cc (Cortina Lotus, 1558cc).
Power output: 53.5–88bhp (Cortina Lotus, 106bhp).
Transmission: Four-speed manual, optional automatic.
Brakes: Front discs, rear drums.
Maximum speed: 80–98mph (Cortina Lotus, 105mph).
0–60mph: 12.5–24 seconds (Cortina Lotus, 9 seconds).
Production: 1,010, 580.
Prices in 1968: Two-door 1300, £792; 1600GT, £939; 1600E, £1073; Cortina Lotus, £1163.

The Mk I Cortina was a hard act to follow, not just Britain's bestselling car in its day, but the first British car to top a million sales in four years. As fins faded from automotive fashion, Ford remodelled the Mk I into the square-cut Mk II, which continued the company's domination of middle-market family and professional motoring. As with the Mk I before, there was nothing tricksy or revolutionary about either the styling or engineering of the Mk II, yet once more its mean price undercut rivals and made it hard to resist. What's more, the Cortina was not so much a single model, but rather a whole model range, with versions to match your wallet, aspirations and need for speed, from the plain Standard and DeLuxe versions to the sporty 95–100mph two-door GT or, for £130 more, the 1600E. The 'E' stood for Executive and took the 1600 GT specification as its starting point, adding luxury trim, fancy wheels and two extra doors. Fastest and most expensive was the rare Cortina Lotus Mk II.

Cortina Fact: In 1970 the millionth export Cortina was helicoptered from Ford's Dagenham plant to its buyer in Belgium, achieving a record for the fastest million in overseas sales and the fastest delivery to an export customer.

◀ **1971 Ford Escort 1300XL,** restored at a cost of over £5,000, finished in red, black vinyl interior.
£1,100–1,300 / $1,600–1,900 ⚒ CGC

1982 Ford RS2000, completely rebuilt, correct, 82,000 miles from new, 1 of last 10 registered.
£8,000–10,000 ⊞ COR

1979 Ford RS2000, engine enlarged to 2200cc, 10:1 compression ratio, performance camshaft, 38DGAS carburettor, vernier-type timing wheel, electronic ignition, Piper distributor, 5-speed manual gearbox, lightened and balanced flywheel, front ventilated disc brakes with 4-pot callipers, Bilstein suspension units, finished in midnight blue, graphite interior, excellent condition.
£3,500–4,000 / $5,000–5,800 ⚒ COYS

Ford was not slow to cash in on the enormous cachet of its successful rallying Escorts, using the famous AVO production lines to produce road-going versions of the all-conquering machines. There was the Mexico – named in honour of the 1-3-5-6-8 Ford finish in the 1970 World Cup Marathon – the RS1600 and the RS2000. When the Escort was treated to a facelift in 1976, the RS2000 was similarly updated.

1986 Sierra Cosworth, new exhaust system, original, excellent condition.
£8,000–9,000 / $11,600–13,000 ⊞ WbC

Ford – USA

1935 Ford Model 48 Roadster, 3.6 litre sidevalve V8 engine, rumble seat, rear-mounted spare, restored, finished in maroon, excellent weather equipment, grey leather interior.
£16,500–18,500 / $24,000–26,500 BKS

1936 Ford Five-Window Coupé, 3.6 litre sidevalve V8 engine, subject of body-off restoration, fitted with period speed equipment, including twin carburettors and Mallory ignition, 12 volt electrics, rear skirts, radio, concours winner.
£18,000–20,000 / $26,000–29,000 BJ

1939 Ford Deluxe Coupé, 221cu.in sidevalve V8 engine, oil-bath air cleaner, 85bhp, 3-speed manual gearbox, 4-wheel hydraulic drum brakes, Philco Roto-matic radio, finished in dark green, interior in original taupe broadcloth material.
£15,000–17,000 / $21,750–24,750 RM

► **1939 Ford Convertible Street Rod,** 350cu.in Chevrolet V8 engine, fuel injection, automatic transmission, 9in Ford rear axle, rumble seat, air conditioning.
£40,000–45,000
$58,000–65,250 BJ

FORD (American built) Model	ENGINE cu. in/cyl	DATES	CONDITION 1	2	3
Thunderbird	292/312/8	1955–57	£18,500	£13,500	£9,000
Edsel Citation	410/8	1958	£9,000	£4,500	£2,500
Edsel Ranger	223/6-361/8	1959	£6,000	£3,500	£2,000
Edsel Citation convertible	410/8	1958	£12,000	£6,000	£4,000
Edsel Corsair convertible	332/361/8	1959	£10,500	£7,000	£4,500
Fairlane 2-door	223/6-352/8	1957–59	£8,000	£4,500	£3,000
Fairlane 500 Sunliner	223/6-352/8	1957–59	£12,000	£8,000	£6,500
Fairlane 500 Skyliner	223/6-352/8	1957–59	£14,000	£10,000	£8,000
Mustang 4.7 V8 FHC/Conv.		1964–66	£9,000	£4,000	£2,000
Mustang GT 350		1966–67	£15,000	£10,000	£6,000
Mustang hardtop	260/6-428/8	1967–68	£6,000	£4,000	£3,000
Mustang GT 500		1966–67	£20,000	£14,000	£6,000

◄ **1947 Ford Super DeLuxe Sportsman Convertible,** foglights, windscreen-pillar-mounted spotlight, side mirrors, power windows, power Stayfast top, red leather interior, body-off restoration, excellent condition.
£70,000–80,000 / $101,500–116,000 ⚒ RM
During the woody craze of the 1920–40s, Ford was one of the only car companies to build its own wooden bodies. Other manufacturers sent their chassis to body builders like J. T. Cantrell and Hercules. Henry Ford did not see the need, as he owned huge tracts of forested land in northern Michigan.

1950 Ford Convertible, 239cu.in sidevalve V8 engine, 100bhp, 3-speed manual gearbox, 4-wheel hydraulic drum brakes, subject of body-off restoration, finished in red, red and black interior.
£21,000–23,500 / $30,500–33,500 ⚒ RM
With post-war models being largely unchanged from pre-war production, Ford was anxious to update the look of its cars. The new '49s were the result of a series of collaborations between three men: Dick Caleal, Robert Bourke and Bob Koto. The influence of the latter two – designers at Studebaker's Loewy Studios – accounts for the similarities in later Studebaker designs.

1954 Ford Customline Club Coupé, 239cu.in overhead-valve V8 engine, 130bhp, 3-speed manual gearbox, 4-wheel hydraulic drum brakes, finished in original blue, original Magic-Aire heater and defroster, Console Range radio, optional electric clock, colour-keyed fibre-grained fabric interior.
£7,500–8,500 / $10,800–12,350 ⚒ RM
The most notable feature of the 1954 Ford was the all-new overhead-valve Y-block V8 engine. Of 239cu.in, it was the exact displacement of the previous year's proven, but dated, sidevalve V8. The newly developed engine had a power rating that was 30 per cent better than the previous year's, with far more potential. Another improvement for 1954 was the all-new suspension, which did away with antiquated kingpins at the front, replacing them with ball-joints. These were combined with shock absorbing rubber bushings to make the car's ride smoother and quieter. The rear suspension benefited from new variable-rate leaf springs.

1956 Ford Thunderbird, overhead-valve V8 engine, restored, soft top, 'porthole' hardtop, continental kit, original Town and Country radio, well maintained, good condition.
£14,000–16,500/ $20,300–24,000 ⚒ BKS

1955 Ford Thunderbird, 292cu.in V8 engine, new black mohair hood, correct hardtop, finished in black, original black and white vinyl interior trim, engine and chassis numbers match, excellent condition.
£14,500–17,000 / $21,000–24,650 ⚒ BRIT
Introduced in 1955, the Thunderbird was aimed at a similar market to that of the Chevrolet Corvette. Styled by Frank Hershey, it achieved almost instantaneous success, being steadily developed through the years.

1957 Ford Thunderbird, 312cu.in overhead-valve V8 engine, 4-barrel carburettor, 198bhp, 3-speed automatic transmission, servo-assisted hydraulic drum brakes, power steering, 'porthole' hardtop, soft top, refurbished at a cost of over £125,000 1,476 miles covered since, finished in red, engine and chassis numbers match.
£35,000–38,500 / $50,750–56,000 ⚒ RM
For 1957, the Thunderbird sported a restyled front grille, rear end and bumpers. New features included the Volumatic Radio System, which automatically increased the radio volume as the car's speed increased, and the Dial-O-Matic seat, which provided a memory setting for the driver's seat position.

◄ **1957 Ford Thunderbird,** 312cu.in Y-block V8 engine, factory-fitted twin 4-barrel carburettors, 3-speed overdrive gearbox, wire wheels, hardtop, subject of body-off restoration.
£33,000–36,500
$48,000–53,000 BJ

► **1957 Ford Thunderbird,** stainless-steel exhaust, servo-assisted drum brakes, chrome wheels, finished in pink, Town & Country radio, black and white leather interior.
£20,000–23,000
$29,000–33,350 BJ

1959 Ford Thunderbird Convertible, 352cu.in V8 engine, 300bhp, 2-speed automatic transmission, hydraulic drum brakes, black and white interior.
£11,000–13,000 / $16,000–18,850 Pou

◄ **1959 Ford Thunderbird Convertible,** servo-assisted drum brakes, power steering, wire wheels, restored over 5 years, finished in red, power windows, power seat, air conditioning, leather interior, original.
£34,000–38,000
$48,000–55,000 BJ

► **1959 Ford Edsel Estate,** V8 engine, automatic transmission, restored, good condition.
£8,000–9,000 / 11,600–13,000 HMM
Introduced in 1958 as a product of Ford's Lincoln-Mercury-Edsel Division, the Edsel generated considerable controversy. It was designed after a vast amount of market research had been carried out, but it never sold in the numbers expected – only 35,000 during the first six months of production. Two versions were offered, both with overhead-valve V8 engines, giving a choice of 5.9 or 6.7 litres. After an attempt to widen the Edsel's appeal by marketing cheaper six-cylinder versions, production ceased in 1959.

1963 Ford Falcon Sprint Convertible, 260cu.in V8 engine, automatic transmission, chrome wheels, white power hood, finished in red.
£4,500–5,400 / $6,500–7,800 ⚒ COYS

► 1965 Ford Mustang GT Coupé, 289cu.in V8 engine, automatic transmission, front disc brakes, power steering, foglamps, air conditioning, 2 owners and 53,000 miles from new, finished in blue, cream interior.
£12,000–14,000 / $17,400–20,300 ⊞ HCL

◄ 1965 Ford Mustang Coupé, alloy wheels, black vinyl roof, finished in red, good condition.
£3,000–3,500
$4,350–5,000 ⚒ PALM

1965 Ford Shelby GT 350, 289cu.in V8 engine, solid valve lifters, 306bhp, 4-speed manual gearbox, R-type racing front air dam, matching numbers.
£44,000–48,500 / $64,000–70,500 ⚒ RM

The marriage between Carroll Shelby and the Ford Motor Company began early in 1965, when Ford decided to take a shot at the performance market dominated by the Corvette. Unveiled by Shelby in January 1965, the Mustang GT 350 had a few subtle exterior changes: a fibreglass bonnet with functional air scoop and a clean looking grille bearing a tri-coloured running horse emblem. All 1965 Shelbys were white with blue GT 350 side stripes below the doors. The interior was a black-only option and included a roll-bar, three-spoke wood-rim steering wheel and competition seat belts. A special instrument panel in the centre of the dash held a large oil pressure gauge and tachometer. Engine mofifications boosted the 289's power from 271 to 306bhp. As standard, the cars had Borg-Warner T-10 four-speed gearboxes and 9in Detroit 'No-Spin' differentials. The reworked suspension featured a large front anti-roll bar, lowered upper A-frames, Koni dampers and rear traction bars. The front end was stiffened considerably with an export brace and Monte Carlo bar. The battery was located in the boot for improved weight distribution.

► 1966 Ford Mustang Convertible, 4728cc V8 engine, automatic transmission, restored 1989, finished in white, white and red interior, good condition.
£8,500–10,000
$12,350–14,500 ⚒ BKS

1966 Mustang GT Show Car, completely rebuilt, fitted with 1979 Boss 302 4949cc overhead-valve V8 engine, GMC supercharger, nitrous-oxide system, Mustang II front suspension and disc brakes, fully chromed Jaguar independent rear suspension and limited-slip differential, Dodge Colt rack-and-pinion steering, 15 x 10in rear wheels, finished in candy-apple red.
£8,000–10,000 / $11,600–14,500 ⚒ BKS

1967 Ford Shelby GT 500 Mustang, 428cu.in V8 engine, 355bhp, automatic transmission, professionally restored, engine dress-up kit, correct alloy wheels, air conditioning, original, little use since restoration.
£28,000–32,000 / $40,600–46,400 ⚒ RM
The big news for 1967 was the advent of big-block power in the Mustang. Under the bonnet of the new GT 500 was a special edition of Ford's 400bhp 428cu.in Cobra Jet engine. Also new that year were dramatic inboard-mounted headlights. Not all cars were so equipped, as some states banned them, reportedly because they could be confused with an oncoming motorcycle. They were dropped for 1968.

1970 Ford King Cobra Prototype, Boss 429 'Hemi' V8 engine, 4-speed manual gearbox, only example with a convex rear window, original Carlite stamped glass marked 'prototype development tooling not to specification', many other prototype features, 1st of 3 built, only running prototype.
£65,000–75,000 / $94,250–108,750 ⚒ BJ
The King Cobra was designed to compete with the Plymouth Superbird and Dodge Daytona in NASCAR, but $2.2 million in production costs halted further development.

Miller's is a price GUIDE not a price LIST

Frazer Nash

1925 Frazer Nash Three-Seater Sports, 1496cc Anzani engine, 3-speed manual gearbox, restored.
£23,500–27,000 / $34,000–39,000 ⚒ BKS
Archibald Goodman Frazer Nash completed his secondary education at Finsbury Technical School, where he met Ron Godfrey, later to become his partner in the manufacture of the GN Cyclecars. The partnership was short-lived, however, and Archie Frazer Nash broke away to manufacture his own car. Early models had proprietary engines from Plus Power and Anzani.

Gaz

1957 Gaz M20 Pobieda Saloon, left-hand drive, finished in grey, unrestored.
£2,000–2,500 / $2,900–3,600 ⊞ Now

1976 Gaz Chaika Limousine, restored in Moscow, finished in black.
£3,500–4,000 / $5,200–5,800 ⊞ Now

Genestin

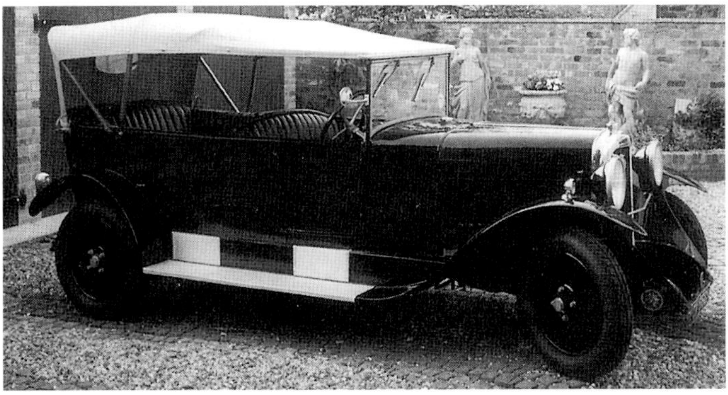

◄ 1926 Genestin G6 Four-Door Tourer, 1200cc 4-cylinder engine, right-hand drive, restored, original engine, double duck hood, finished in blue and black, black leather interior, 1 of only 3 thought to survive.
£7,500–9,000
$10,875–13,000 ⚒ H&H

Ghia

1967 Ghia 450SS Spyder, 273cu.in V8 engine, 235bhp, automatic transmission, front disc/rear drum brakes, wire wheels, completely restored, only occasional use since, new high-output engine, finished in candy-apple red, black leather interior, 1st example built.
£30,000–33,000 / $43,500–48,000 ⚒ RM
The Ghia 450SS Spyder was the result of a collaboration between the Italian design house and Californian entrepreneur Bert Sugarman. Ghia had displayed the body style originally on a six-cylinder Fiat chassis, but Sugarman felt that its 136bhp engine left a lot to be desired and considered Plymouth's 273cu.in, 235bhp V8-engined Barracuda a more suitable basis. The Plymouth package offered an engine that sported restrained muscle-car performance in a competent and economical independent front/solid-axle rear suspension chassis. Moreover, Ghia's stylish steel bodywork easily slipped over the 2in-longer Barracuda wheelbase. Only 52 Ghia 450SS 2+2 Spyders were produced.

◄ **1967 Ghia 450SS Spyder,** 273cu.in Plymouth V8 engine, 235bhp, 3-speed automatic transmission, torsion-bar independent front suspension, front disc/ rear drum brakes, Borrani wire wheels, finished in deep maroon, air conditioning, tan interior, paintwork in need of minor attention, brightwork displaying some blemishing, 1 of approximately 20 examples known to survive.
£19,000–23,000
$27,500–33,500 RM

Gordon Keeble

GORDON KEEBLE	ENGINE	DATES	CONDITION		
Model	cc/cyl		1	2	3
GKI/GKIT	5355/8	1964–67	£20,000	£15,000	£10,000

Haynes

◄ **1917 Haynes Light 12 Four-Seater Tourer,** V12 engine, restored, believed to be the only survivor of its type in the UK, very good condition.
£25,000–30,000 / $36,250–43,500 HMM
This Light 12 was rescued from the jungles of Java, where it had lain hidden for over 30 years in an overgrown wooden warehouse.

Haynes-Apperson

1902 Haynes-Apperson Four/Six-Seater 12hp Surrey, 3900cc, semi-automatic transmission, finished in red, black interior, very good condition.
£23,000–27,000 / $33,350–39,150 H&H
Elwood Haynes was one of the first people to build a motor vehicle. A brilliant metallurgist, he put a Stutz marine engine in a little four-wheel buggy, which made its first run in 1894, just outside his home town of Kokomo, Indiana. Haynes and the Appersons combined in 1898 to form the Haynes-Apperson company, and they produced some of the finest quality American vehicles of their day. The big 12hp, rear-engined twin-cylinder model was built during 1902–03, the $1,800 Surrey being top of the range.

1903 Haynes-Apperson 8hp Runabout, water-cooled horizontally-opposed twin-cylinder engine, make-and-break ignition, magneto, 3 forward gears and reverse, chain final drive, oil sidelamps, centre-mounted acetylene headlamp, folding hood, patent leather-type mudguards, finished in dark green with gold coachlines, 'Fat Man' folding steering column, black buttoned upholstery.
£24,000–27,000 / $34,800–39,150 BKS

Hillman

Hillman is one of many British firms based in the Midlands that made the transition from bicycles to motor cars. The company built its first cars in 1907, and in 1928 came under the control of Humber and the Rootes Group. In the 1930s, the Minx stood out as more refined and luxurious than offerings from rivals. In many ways, these were Hillman's glory days; in 1939, the company was ranked fourth in Britain, and in the last complete model year before the outbreak of war more than 55,000 Minxes were built, amounting to more than a third of all Hillman production up to then. Immediate post-war offerings were equally stylish, but in the 1950s an epidemic of badge engineering saw Hillmans lose their identity, as there was little more than matters of detail and different powerplants to distinguish the Minx range from the Singer Vogue and Sunbeam Rapier. By 1964, Chrysler had taken control of Rootes, and the Hillman name vanished for good in 1976.

1955 Hillman Minx, 1265cc 4-cylinder engine.
£1,500–1,700 / $2,200–2,500 PMo

1969 Hillman Imp De Luxe, 875cc engine, 42bhp, alloy wheels, finished in white, opening rear window, folding rear seats.
£1,100–1,300 / $1,600–1,900 IMP

Miller's Starter Marque

- **Starter Hillmans:** *Californian; Minx models and variants from 1956; Imp; Avenger.*
- One of the most attractive traits of post-war Hillmans is their price. They're affordable and generally reliable, and if you're into budget top-down motoring there's a wide choice from a company that persisted with convertibles when lots of other makers didn't bother. The 1950s Hillman Californian offers a suggestion of transatlantic glamour with straightforward Rootes underpinnings. The problem is going to be finding one, because as with later Hillmans their low values have lured many a salvageable car into the scrapyard. The Super Minx convertible, from 1962 to 1966, makes an interesting four-seat fresh-air alternative to cars like the Triumph Herald. The Super Minx is more substantially bodied and bigger engined. The Imp was a real might-have-been – if only the Mini hadn't appeared three years before, and if only they had been built better. They're redeemed though by a lovely engine, super gearbox and sheer entertainment value when behind the wheel. In the 1970s, the Hillman Avenger tilted against the Morris Marina, Ford Escort and Vauxhall Viva. The GT was surprisingly nimble and offered 100mph performance. The very rare Tiger topped 110mph and enjoyed a successful rallying career.

HILLMAN Model	ENGINE cc/cyl	DATES	CONDITION 1	2	3
Minx Mk I–II	1184/4	1946–48	£1,750	£800	£250
Minx Mk I–II DHC	1184/4	1946–48	£3,500	£1,500	£250
Minx Mk III–VIIIA	1184/4	1948–56	£1,750	£700	£350
Minx Mk III–VIIIA DHC	1184/4	1948–56	£3,750	£1,500	£350
Californian	1390/4	1953–56	£2,000	£750	£200
Minx SI/II	1390/4	1956–58	£1,250	£450	£200
Minx SI/II DHC	1390/4	1956–58	£3,500	£1,500	£500
Minx Ser III	1494/4	1958–59	£1,000	£500	£200
Minx Ser III DHC	1494/4	1958–59	£3,750	£1,500	£400
Minx Ser IIIA/B	1494/4	1959–61	£1,250	£500	£200
Minx Ser IIIA/B DHC	1494/4	1959–61	£3,750	£1,250	£500
Minx Ser IIIC	1592/4	1961–62	£900	£500	£200
Minx Ser IIIC DHC	1592/4	1961–62	£3,000	£1,500	£500
Minx Ser V	1592/4	1962–63	£1,250	£350	£150
Minx Ser VI	1725/4	1964–67	£1,500	£375	£100
Husky Mk I	1265/4	1954–57	£1,000	£600	£200
Husky SI/II/III	1390/4	1958–65	£1,000	£550	£150
Super Minx	1592/4	1961–66	£1,500	£500	£100
Super Minx DHC	1592/4	1962–64	£3,500	£1,250	£450
Imp	875/4	1963–73	£800	£300	£70
Husky	875/4	1966–71	£800	£450	£100
Avenger	var/4	1970–76	£550	£250	£60
Avenger GT	1500/4	1971–76	£950	£500	£100
Avenger Tiger	1600/4	1972–73	£2,000	£1,000	£500

Honda

◄ **1967 Honda S800,** 791ccc double-overhead-camshaft 4-cylinder engine, 4 carburettors, 4-speed gearbox, front disc/rear drum brakes, finished in white with blue stripes, very good condition.
£6,000–7,000 / $8,700–10,200 ⚒ Pou

► **1969 Honda S800,** 791cc double-overhead-camshaft 4-cylinder engine, 4-speed manual gearbox, front disc/rear drum brakes, resprayed in red, 40,000 miles from new, excellent condition.
£4,000–5,000 / $5,800–7,250 ⚒ RM
The Honda S800 began life as a small 360cc car intended for the Japanese market. The programme developed from the early S360 through the S600, with power rising from 33bhp to 57bhp, and culminated in the S800 with 70bhp on tap. All cars featured the famous free-revving Honda four-cylinder engine with needle rollers for the crankshaft. The S800 was unique in that it abandoned the use of twin chain drive (as found on previous models) for a more orthodox live rear axle set-up.

HONDA Model	ENGINE cc/cyl	DATES	CONDITION 1	2	3
S800 Mk I Convertible	791/4	1966–69	£7,000	£4,000	£2,500
S800 Mk I Coupé	791/4	1966–69	£5,000	£3,500	£1,000
S800 Mk II Convertible	791/4	1968–69	£7,000	£5,000	£3,000
S800 Mk II Coupé	791/4	1968–69	£6,500	£4,000	£1,200

Hudson

◄ **1938 Hudson 112 Opera Coupé,** 2868cc 6-cylinder engine, completely restored 1988–89, engine rebuilt, electrical system converted to 12 volts, fitted with alternator, finished in green, beige leather interior.
£6,500–7,500 / $9,500–10,900 ⚒ BRIT
The Hudson Motor Company was founded in 1908 and went on to produce some of America's finest automobiles throughout its long history. During the 1920s and 1930s an excellent range was offered. Especially notable were the Super and Special Sixes which were exceptionally well engineered and offered a combination of good performance and value for money.

► **1954 Hudson Hornet 7D Four-Door Saloon,** 4500cc 6-cylinder engine, 140bhp, 4-speed automatic transmission, finished in pink, cream and white, brown interior, good condition.
£4,500–5,500
$6,500–8,000 ⚒ H&H

Humber

From the manufacture of bicycles, through motorcycles, cyclecars, motor cars, to aeroplanes, the early decades of the Midlands company founded by Thomas Humber were extremely diverse. In 1928 Humber took over nearby Hillman and then, in turn, came under control of the Rootes Group in the early 1930s, a decade in which the imposing six-cylinder Humber Pullmans and Super Snipes enjoyed official patronage. In the late 1940s and into the 1950s, the Super Snipe and gargantuan Pullman and Imperial limousines were impressive machines with considerable kerb presence, if a little funereal. Design was reinvigorated in 1957 with the transatlantic influenced four-cylinder Hawk, which was soon joined by the plusher and more glittery six-cylinder Super Snipe. For many fans, these fine cars rate as the last true Humbers. In 1964 Chrysler took over the Rootes Group, and the Humber's distinction as a marque was speedily devalued, models becoming nothing more than upmarket Hillmans with a little extra garnish. In 1976, the Humber name disappeared for ever.

1904 Humber 8½hp Twin-Cylinder Two-Seater, cape cart hood, brass carriage lamps, two brass bulb horns, brass fire extinguisher, finished in red with yellow coachlines, 1 owner since c1950, unused since 1971.
£60,000–70,000 / $87,000–101,500 BKS
Louis Coatalean joined Humber in 1901 to head the design team, and his particular genius was later spotted by both Hillman and Sunbeam for whom he would work. The 8½hp Humber came from his drawing board and was produced alongside cars of 5hp, 6½hp, 14hp and 25hp in 1904. Humber production was carried on at both Coventry and Beeston, there being some considerable rivalry between the two operations, with informed sources considering Beeston cars to be superior.

Miller's Starter Marque

- **Starter Humbers:** *Hawk and Super Snipe from 1957 onward; Imperial, 1965–67; Sceptre, 1963–76.*
- The Hawk and Super Snipe make interesting alternatives to P4 and P5 Rovers. In 1957, the styling was considered thoroughly voguish, with American overtones, but by the 1960s the shape had more the ambience of sturdy British gentility. The Super Snipe and Imperial, in particular, vied with the P5 Rover for ministerial duties outside 10 Downing Street. Both Hawk and Super Snipe were of unitary construction, the latter being the upmarket model and preferred choice, with a larger engine and all the drawing-room appointments you could ask for. For performance, go for the 3 litre Super Snipes from 1960 on, which offer a quiet 95–100mph.
- The Sceptre of 1963–67 is an elegant mix of Hillman Super Minx and Sunbeam Rapier, with the typical Humber 'garnish'. From 1968, Sceptres were simply jazzed-up versions of the square-cut 'three-box' Hillman Hunter.

Restored values

The cost of a professional restoration will have an influence on, but no direct relation to, a car's market value. A restored car can have a market value lower than the cost of its restoration.

◀ **1959 Humber Hawk,** 2267cc 4-cylinder engine.
£2,500–3,000 / $3,600–4,300 PMo

HUMBER Model	ENGINE cc/cyl	DATES	CONDITION 1	2	3
Veteran	var	1898			
		1918	£30,000+	£20,000+	£14,000
10	1592/4	1919	£7,000	£5,000	£3,000
14	2474/4	1919	£8,000	£6,000	£4,000
15.9–5/40	2815/4	1920–27	£9,500	£7,000	£4,000
8	985/4	1923–25	£7,000	£5,000	£2,500
9/20–9/28	1057/4	1926	£7,000	£5,000	£4,000
14/40	2050/4	1927–28	£10,000	£8,000	£5,000
Snipe	3498/6	1930–35	£8,000	£6,000	£4,000
Pullman	3498/6	1930–35	£8,000	£6,000	£4,000
16/50	2110/6	1930–32	£9,000	£7,000	£5,000
12	1669/4	1933–37	£7,000	£5,000	£3,000
Snipe/Pullman	4086/6	1936–40	£7,000	£5,000	£3,000
16	2576/6	1938–40	£7,000	£5,000	£3,000

Pre-1905 or Brighton Run cars are very popular.

HUMBER Model	ENGINE cc/cyl	DATES	CONDITION 1	2	3
Hawk Mk I–IV	1944/4	1945–52	£3,700	£1,500	£600
Hawk Mk V–VII	2267/4	1952–57	£3,000	£1,500	£400
Hawk Ser I–IVA	2267/4	1957–67	£3,000	£850	£325
Snipe	2731/6	1945–48	£5,000	£2,600	£850
Super Snipe Mk I–III	4086/6	1948–52	£4,700	£2,400	£600
Super Snipe Mk IV–IVA	4138/6	1952–56	£5,500	£2,300	£550
Super Snipe Ser I–II	2651/6	1958–60	£3,800	£1,800	£475
Super Snipe SIII VA	2965/6	1961–67	£3,500	£1,800	£400
Super Snipe S.III–VA Est.	2965/6	1961–67	£3,950	£1,850	£525
Pullman	4086/6	1946–51	£4,500	£2,350	£800
Pullman Mk IV	4086/6	1952–54	£6,000	£2,850	£1,200
Imperial	2965/6	1965–67	£3,900	£1,600	£450
Sceptre Mk I–II	1592/4	1963–67	£2,200	£1,000	£300
Sceptre Mk III	1725/4	1967–76	£2,000	£900	£200

1959 Humber Super Snipe Estate, 2965cc 6-cylinder engine, finished in grey and blue, red interior, 76,000 miles from new, excellent condition.
£7,000–8,000 / $10,000–11,600 ⚒ H&H

1963 Humber Super Snipe, 2965cc overhead-valve 6-cylinder engine, 132bhp, 3-speed manual gearbox with overdrive, automatic transmission, independent front suspension, semi-elliptic rear leaf springs, servo-assisted front disc/rear drum brakes, power steering, finished in midnight blue, chauffeur division, grey leather upholstery, veneered wood trim interior, 2 owners from new.
£4,250–5,000 / $6,000–7,250 ⚒ C

Hupmobile

◀ **1922 Hupmobile Series R 35hp Tourer,** sidevalve 4-cylinder engine, restored, all mechanical components to original specifications, including period Autovac, Splitdorf magneto and Stromberg carburettor, electric lighting/starting, wire wheels, two-piece opening windscreen, weather equipment, sound bodywork.
£7,800–8,600 / $11,300–12,200 ⚒ BKS

The first Hupmobile was a racy-looking two-seater runabout – the Model 20 – powered by a 2 litre four-cylinder engine and priced at $750. Production began in Robert Hupp's hometown of Detroit, Michigan, in March 1909. Output totalled a little over 1,600 by the year's end and more than trebled the following year. For many years, Hupmobile, like Dodge and Chevrolet, built nothing but four-cylinder cars, the last of the line being the Series R manufactured from late 1917 through to 1925.

Innocenti

Dealer prices

Miller's guide prices for dealer cars take into account the value of any guarantees or warranties that may be included in the purchase. Dealers must also observe additional statutory consumer regulations, which do not apply to private sellers. This is factored into our dealer guide prices. Dealer cars are identified by the ⊞ icon; full details of the dealer can be found on page 330.

◀ **1962 Innocenti Spyder S,** MG running gear, rebuilt, finished in pale yellow, red leather interior, 37,000 miles from new.
£9,000–11,000 / $13,000–16,000 ⊞ TSG

Intermeccanica

◀ **1967 Intermeccanica Indra 2+2 Coupé,** 351cu.in V8 engine, 230bhp, 3-speed automatic transmission, servo-assisted 4-wheel disc brakes, power steering, alloy wheels, power windows, power locks, air conditioning, completely restored, finished in red.
£14,000–17,000 / $20,300–24,650 ⚒ RM
Based on a shortened Opel Admiral/Diplomat floorpan, the Indra's bodywork was fabricated of steel, which was unusual for a low-production performance car.

Invicta

The Invicta company was founded in Cobham, Surrey, in 1925, but was effectively killed off by the late 1930s, despite abortive efforts to revive the marque both before and after the war. What was left was a legacy of a mere 1,000 cars, most of them exquisite and none more revered than the rare 4 litre S-Type low-chassis tourer – dubbed 'the 100mph Invicta'. In fact, the S-Type is so fabled that it's surrounded by its own mythology, for even today there's lively debate in vintage circles about just how many were made: some suggest 77; others say around 50. Either way, the rumbustious S-Type was a quintessentially British device – spare, unfussy and unadorned. On the road, the glorious S-Type was a car of prodigious flexibility, able to accelerate from 10mph to its maximum in fourth gear. Neither was its quality nor engineering in any doubt, but with a near-Rolls-Royce price tag that was expected. Those qualities that make Invictas so prized today were also factors in the company's downfall, producing an extravagant, expensive machine as Britain plunged into depression in the early 1930s.

◀ **1931 Invicta 4½ Litre S-Type Low Chassis Tourer,** coachwork by Vanden Plas, completely restored, finished in red.
£180,000–200,000 / $260,000–290,000 ⚒ COYS
Invicta's guiding philosophy was like that of motorcycle manufacturer Brough-Superior, in that it gathered together the very best proprietary components and assembled them into high-quality machines. Thus, at the heart of the S-Type was a 4.5 litre straight-six Meadows engine that produced 115bhp, but was more notable for its low-speed torque and flexibility. The chassis, underslung at the rear, incorporated numerous phospor-bronze and gunmetal castings, and was built without comromise. Suspension was by semi-elliptic springs and hydraulic dampers front and rear, in the classic vintage style, but the car's exceptionally low centre of gravity endowed it with far from ordinary road-holding.

Iso

1968 Iso Grifo GL 350, coachwork by Bertone, 5359cc Chevrolet V8 engine, 4-speed manual gearbox, left-hand drive, completely restored 1994, little use since, finished in dark green, original black leather upholstery, 1 of just 29 built in 1968, excellent condition throughout.
£28,000–32,000 / $40,600–46,400 ⚒ BKS

Iso Grifo

Iso joined the ranks of supercar constructors in 1962 with the launch of the Rivolta Coupé. Powered by a 5.4 litre Chevrolet V8, the Rivolta employed a platform chassis featuring independent front suspension, De Dion rear axle and disc brakes all-round. Developments included the Fidia four-door saloon, the Rivolta's replacement, the Lele, and the short-wheelbase Grifo. Produced between 1963 and 1974, the Grifo used the small-block Chevrolet V8 in all but its final Ford-powered incarnation. There was also a 7 litre model, but even the tamest Grifo was good for 160mph.

ISO Model	ENGINE cc/cyl	DATES	CONDITION 1	2	3
Rivolta V8	5359cc	1962–70	£15,000	£10,000	£3,500
Grifo V8	5359/6899		£28,000	£16,000	£12,000
Lele 2-door fastback coupé	5359	1967–74	£12,000	£8,000	£5,000
Fidia V8 4-door exec. saloon	5359	1967–74	£10,000	£7,000	£5,000

Jaguar

If ever one man's vision steered the fortunes of a motor company, it must surely be that of William Lyons. For as the marque of the leaping cat forges ahead in a new century, the guiding spirit of Jaguar's creator lives on in the lithe athletic shapes that have characterised these Coventry cats for 70 years. The first 'Jaguar' – although it was many years before the company would adopt the name – was not a car at all, but a motorcycle sidecar produced in 1922. Yet the aluminium-bodied sidecar already showed the traits that would later become hallmarks of Jaguar and the company's founder, William Lyons. Born in Blackpool in 1901, William Lyons became an enthusiastic motorcyclist and, on his 21st birthday, he formed the Swallow Sidecar Company with partner William Walmsley. In 1927, the company made the transition to four wheels, clothing a strengthened Austin 7 chassis with a stylish two-toned sports body (see page 43). In 1931, the rakish SS1 appeared, and in 1935, by then with William Lyons as sole proprietor of the company, the Jaguar name was used for the first time. Most prized among the pre-war models is the beautifully rakish and fast SS100. Yet Jaguar's glory years really began after the war with the 1948 launch of the XK120. Since then, virtually every Jaguar produced – both saloon and sporting – has been an enthusiast's motor car, enjoyed by those lucky enough to own them and coveted by those who can only admire them. The best news is that in today's market, all manner of classic Jaguars are at their most affordable for years, in particular Mk II models and E-Types, which have both fallen dramatically from their over-inflated peak values of the late 1980s and early 1990s.

1937 Jaguar SS100 Roadster, 2663cc overhead-valve 6-cylinder engine, 102bhp, 4-speed manual gearbox, beam front axle, 4-wheel finned drum brakes, restored, original engine, finished in red, black upholstery.
£90,000–100,000 / $130,500–145,000 ⚒ RM
Jaguar's marketing literature for the SS100 explained: 'Designed primarily for competition work, this model is equally suitable for ordinary road use, for despite the virility of its performance it is sufficiently tractable for use as a fast touring car without modification.' Enthusiasts quickly recognised the car's performance capabilities, campaigning them successfully in hill climbs, rallies and road races throughout Britain and Europe.

◀ **1947 Jaguar Mk IV Drophead Coupé,** 3485cc overhead-valve 6-cylinder engine, twin SU carburettors, 125bhp, 4-speed manual gearbox, 4-wheel mechanical drum brakes, Lucas headlights, completely restored, bookmatched walnut veneer woodwork, rear seat picnic tables, 1 of only 376 left-hand drive examples built.
£40,000–45,000 / $58,000–65,250 ⚒ RM

SS100 Jaguar (1936–40)

Price new: £395.
Engines: Six-cylinder, 2663cc, 103bhp; 3485cc, 125bhp.
At the 1935 Olympia Motor Show, William Lyons' Swallow Sidecar and Coachbuilding Company debuted the first true Jaguars, for that was the model name he had chosen for his new range. Most stunning of all was the 2 litre Jaguar SS100 open two-seater. These days, the glorious SS100 stands out as the quintessential traditional pre-war sports car. Back then, there was nothing traditional about it at all. In a word, it was flash, and these early Jaguars were often dismissed by the old guard of the Bentley, Lagonda and Invicta brigade as 'Wardour Street Bentleys'; in other words, the kind of car to appeal to cigar-chomping theatrical agents with a penchant for astrakhan coats topped off with a garnish of fur. Nevertheless, the new SS100 was a sparkling performer. The '100' in the name was barely an exaggeration, for the SS100 could reach 96mph and sprint to 60mph in 12.8 seconds. In 1938, a 3 litre version of the SS100 appeared, and that took top speed to just over the ton, with 0–60mph in just over ten seconds. By the outbreak of hostilities, only 309 SS100s had been built.
Pick of the bunch: 3 litre models from 1938; they can make the magic ton, but are rarer (just 116 built) and more expensive.
What to watch: Many an SS saloon has been cut down and passed off as an SS100 sports two-seater.
SS associations: With the onset of hostilities, 'SS' gained rather unfortunate connotations, and at the end of the war William Lyons' company became Jaguar Cars Ltd. The SS100 name had earlier been used as a model name for Brough-Superior, then the Rolls-Royce of motorcycles and with a rather more positive association.

JAGUAR Model	ENGINE cc/cyl	DATES	CONDITION 1	2	3
SSI	2054/6	1932–33	£26,000	£18,000	£12,000
SSI	2252/6	1932–33	£22,000	£17,000	£13,500
SSII	1052/4	1932–33	£18,000	£15,000	£11,000
SSI	2663/6	1934	£26,000	£22,000	£15,000
SSII	1608/4	1934	£18,000	£15,000	£12,000
SS90	2663/6	1935	£60,000+	-	-
SS100 (3.4)	3485/6	1938–39	£90,000+	-	-
SS100 (2.6)	2663/6	1936–39	£90,000+	-	-

Very dependent on body styles, completeness and originality, particularly original chassis to body.

◀ **1949 Jaguar Mk V 2½ Litre Saloon,** 2663cc 6-cylinder engine, 4-speed manual gearbox, finished in maroon, beige interior trim, 89,263 miles from new, very good condition throughout.
£11,000–13,000 / $15,850–18,850 ⚒ H&H
Jaguar introduced the Mk V in 1948 as a transitional model with the old pushrod engine, the XK-type torsion-bar suspension and hydraulic brakes. It remained in production until 1951. Compared to the Mk IV, the body styling gave better all-round vision.

► **1950 Jaguar Mk V 2½ Litre Saloon,** overhead-valve 6-cylinder engine, torsion-bar independent front suspension, 4-wheel hydraulic drum brakes, completely restored 1996–99, finished in dark blue over silver-blue, blue-grey leather interior.
£20,000–23,000 / $29,000–33,300 ⚒ BKS

◀ **1956 Jaguar Mk VIII Saloon,** 3442cc 6-cylinder engine, manual gearbox, factory steel sliding sunroof, refurbished, resprayed in silver over grey, new blue leather interior.
£7,000–9,000 / $10,000–13,000 ⚒ BRIT
The Mk VIII appeared in 1956 and enjoyed a two-year production run before being superseded by the last of the line – the Mk IX.

JAGUAR Model	ENGINE cc/cyl	DATES	CONDITION 1	2	3
1½ Litre	1775/4	1945–49	£8,500	£5,500	£2,000
2½ Litre	2663/6	1946–49	£10,000	£7,500	£2,000
2½ Litre DHC	2663/6	1947–48	£17,000	£11,000	£8,000
3½ Litre	3485/6	1947–49	£12,000+	£6,000	£4,000
3½ Litre DHC	3485/6	1947–49	£19,000+	£13,500	£5,500
Mk V 2½ Litre	2663/6	1949–51	£14,000+	£8,000+	£1,500
Mk V 3½ Litre	3485/6	1949–51	£13,000	£8,000	£3,000
Mk V 3½ Litre DHC	3485/6	1949–51	£22,000+	£17,000+	£8,500
Mk VII	3442/6	1951–57	£10,000	£7,500	£2,500
Mk VIIM	3442/6	1951–57	£12,000	£8,500	£2,500
Mk VIII	3442/6	1956–59	£8,500	£5,500	£2,000
Mk IX	3781/6	1958–61	£9,000	£7,000	£2,500
Mk X 3.8/4.2	3781/6	1961–64	£7,500	£3,500	£1,500
Mk X 420G	4235/6	1964–70	£6,000	£3,000	£1,200
Mk I 2.4	2438/6	1955–59	£7,000+	£5,500	£2,000
Mk I 3.4	3442/6	1957–59	£10,000	£6,000	£2,500
Mk II 2.4	2483/6	1959–67	£9,000+	£6,000	£3,000
Mk II 3.4	3442/6	1959–67	£12,000	£8,000	£4,000
Mk II 3.8	3781/6	1959–67	£18,000+	£11,000	£5,000
S-Type 3.4	3442/6	1963–68	£9,000+	£6,500+	£2,000
S-Type 3.8	3781/6	1963–68	£10,000	£6,500	£2,000
240	2438/6	1967–68	£9,000	£6,000	£2,500
340	3442/6	1967–68	£8,000	£7,000	£3,000
420	4235/6	1966–68	£6,000	£3,000	£2,000

Manual gearboxes with overdrive are at a premium.
Some concours examples make as much as 50% over Condition I.

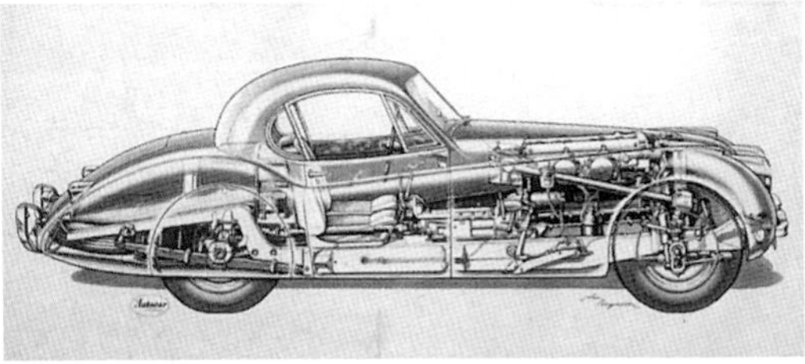

John Ferguson, 1951 Jaguar XK120 fixed-head coupé, signed, pen and Indian ink, applied with *The Autocar* copyright stamp, the reverse dated '2/3/1951', 14½ x 27¼in (37 x 69cm).
£1,250–1,500 / $1,800–2,200 BKS

1951 Jaguar XK120 Roadster, original right-hand drive, finished in correct shade of Suede green.
£25,000–30,000 / $36,250–43,500 COYS

1955 Jaguar XK140MC Roadster, overdrive, chrome wire wheels, older restoration, finished in red, tan interior.
£30,000–35,000 / $43,500–50,750 HCL

1954 Jaguar XK140 Drophead Coupé, completely restored 1992–97, cylinder head overhauled, stainless-steel exhaust system, wire wheels, refinished in original dark blue, km/h speedometer, new beige leather upholstery, polished walnut veneer dashboard and door cappings, excellent condition throughout.
£38,000–44,000 / $55,250–64,000 BKS
Launched in 1954, the XK140 was broadly similar to, although more refined than, the XK120, major engineering changes being confined to moving the engine 3in further forward and adopting rack-and-pinion steering, as used on the racing C-Type. The suspension and brakes remained much as before, although with stiffer torsion bars at the front and telescopic shock absorbers replacing the previous lever type at the rear. Like its forebear, the XK140 was built in three model types: roadster, coupé and drophead coupé, the latter offering the best of both worlds. Outwardly, the newcomer was distinguishable by its revised radiator grille, rear lights incorporating flashing indicators and larger bumpers. The power unit remained Jaguar's well-tried, 3.4 litre twin-cam six, which produced 190bhp in standard trim thanks to higher-lift camshafts and revised porting. A close-ratio gearbox enabled better use to be made of the increased performance.

JAGUAR Model	ENGINE cc/cyl	DATES	CONDITION 1	2	3
XK120 roadster aluminium	3442/6	1948–49	£65,000	£30,000	£20,000
XK120 roadster	3442/6	1949–54	£30,000+	£20,000+	£15,000
XK120 DHC	3442/6	1953–54	£25,000+	£17,000+	£12,000
XK120 Coupé	3442/6	1951–55	£16,000+	£12,000+	£10,000
C-Type	3442/6	1951	£150,000+	-	-
D-Type	3442/6	1955–56	£500,000+	-	-
XKSS (original)	3442/6	1955–57	£400,000+	-	-
XK140 roadster	3442/6	1955–58	£32,000+	£23,000	£16,000
XK140 DHC	3442/6	1955–58	£28,000	£22,000	£15,000
XK140 Coupé	3442/6	1955–58	£18,000	£12,000	£7,500
XK150 roadster	3442/6	1958–60	£35,000	£22,000	£15,000
XK150 DHC	3442/6	1957–61	£28,000	£18,000	£10,000
XK150 Coupé	3442/6	1957–60	£16,000	£10,000	£6,000
XK150S roadster	3442/ 3781/6	1958–60	£40,000+	£26,000	£20,000
XK150S DHC	3442/ 3781/6	1958–60	£36,000+	£22,000	£18,000
XK150S Coupé	3442/ 3781/6	1958–61	£22,000	£18,000	£10,000

D-Type with competition history considerably more.
Watch out for left- to right-hand-drive conversions in the XK series.

1956 Jaguar XK140 Coupé, factory-fitted Borg-Warner automatic transmission, wire wheels, Radiomobile radio, restored, overhauled mechanically, bare-metal respray.
£40,000–45,000 / $58,000–65,250 BKS
This XK140 was styled and autographed by the legendary American hot-rod icon Von Dutch for a Hollywood screenwriter in the 1950s. While many recognise Von Dutch as father of the post-war California car art movement, few realise that the man was a gifted mechanic and machinist. In addition to the obvious cosmetic touches, Von Dutch was responsible for numerous mechanical modifications to the vehicle. The engine was balanced and blueprinted, uprated to C-specification, and fitted with a Mallory dual-point distributor, Mallory ignition coil and twin SU 2in HD8 carburettors.

► **1957 Jaguar XK140MC Drophead Coupé,** overdrive, wire wheels, completely restored, finished in pastel blue, navy leather interior, excellent condition.
£35,000–40,000 / $50,750–58,000 HCL

1958 Jaguar XK150 Fixed-Head Coupé, 3800cc 6-cylinder engine, chrome wire wheels, finished in red, beige interior trim, good condition throughout.
£13,500–16,000 / $19,500–23,250 H&H

► **1958 Jaguar XK150 Fixed-Head Coupé,** 3.8 litre engine, older restoration, engine and gearbox rebuilt, fewer than 5,000 miles since.
£16,500–18,500 / $24,000–26,800 GrM

Jaguar XK150 (1957–61)

Engine: Double-overhead-camshaft, six-cylinder, 3442 or 3781cc.
Power output: 190–265bhp (XK150S 3.8 litre).
Maximum speed: 136mph (XK150S 3.8 litre).
0–60mph: 7.2 seconds (XK150S 3.8 litre).
Take the lithe athleticism and sensational performance of the 1948 Jaguar XK120, add nine years of evolution, a beefier body, technological spin-offs from five Le Mans victories and you end up with the Jaguar XK150. Yet the XK150 remains a slightly overlooked in-betweeny in the Jaguar canon: to some eyes, it looks a little bloated and lacks the primal, pure, raw magnetism of the leaner XK120 and XK140; others prefer the few more mph, and the instant and obvious statement of the later E-Type. Yet the XK150 is a consummate car. At its heart is that fabulous twin-cam six-cylinder engine that first appeared in the XK120, powered the 1950s Le Mans winners and endured until 1986; it will outrun XK120s and XK140s, and in top XK150S spec won't trail too far behind an E-Type. It's also more civilised and luxurious than its XK forebears, and technically superior too, with better steering and all-round disc brakes that were more than man enough to match the sizzling supercar performance.
Pick of the bunch: The XK150S 265bhp, triple-carb 3.8S specification is the most potent and most pricey model in both fixed-head and open versions; best all-round value are the 3.4 and 3.8 drophead coupés, which are slightly cheaper than roadsters, yet have more luxurious furnishings, better weather equipment and rear seats – albeit small ones. One reason they're cheaper is that although the retractable hood gives better weather protection, it makes a considerable bustle when folded; some consider the overall effect slightly inelegant, and of course there's the perverse classic-car mind-set which decrees that anything that adds luxury, comfort and practicality is less sporting and strictly for ninnies and namby-pamby types – you know, those dubious types that actually had hot showers after games lessons.

1958 Jaguar XK150 Roadster, 4-speed manual gearbox, left-hand drive, completely restored over 5 years, 800 miles covered since, £57,000 spent on bodywork, finished in red, black leather interior, matching hood.
£40,000–44,000 / $58,000–64,000 ⚒ BKS

Dunlop disc brakes were the main talking point of Jaguar's XK150 sports car when it arrived in the spring of 1957 – at last the XK had stopping power to match its prodigious straight-line speed. At first available only in fixed-head coupé form, the newcomer sported a restyled, roomier body with a higher front wing line, single-piece wrap-around windscreen and broader radiator grille. The chassis, though, remained much as before, as did the 3.4 litre XK six-cylinder engine and four-speed Moss gearbox. Overdrive and automatic transmission were options, as was the new B-type cylinder head, which boosted maximum power from the standard 190bhp to 210hp. For 1960, the XK150 became available with the 3.8 litre XK engine first seen in the Mk IX saloon. In this form, its increased weight was more than offset by the power of the larger engine, the car regularly recording 130+mph in magazine road tests. XK150 production ceased in 1961 with the arrival of the E-Type.

1961 Jaguar XK150 Drophead Coupé, 1 of 568 3.8 litre drophead coupés built, original, concours condition.
£28,000–34,000 / $40,500–48,500 ⚒ BJ

1960 Jaguar XK150S 3.8 Coupé, 3781cc 6-cylinder engine, manual gearbox with overdrive, wire wheels, original right-hand drive, stored for some years after partial restoration, new stainless-steel exhaust, finished in blue, new red interior trim.
£15,000–18,000 / $21,750–26,000 ⚒ H&H

1959 Jaguar Mk II 3.8 Saloon, chassis No. 7, 3781cc double-overhead-camshaft 6-cylinder engine, manual overdrive gearbox, completely restored, converted to right-hand drive, finished in black, red interior.
£27,500–32,500 / $40,000–47,000 ⚒ H&H

1958 Jaguar Mk I 3.4 Saloon, 3.4 litre 6-cylinder engine, manual gearbox, original right-hand drive, recently restored, stainless-steel exhaust, finished in white, red interior trim.
£10,500–12,000 / $15,500–17,500 ⊞ TSG

Jaguar Mk I (1956–60)

Engine: Double-overhead-camshaft, six-cylinder.
Power output: 112–210bhp.
0–60mph: 9–14.5 seconds.
Maximum speed: 101–120mph.
Production: 36,740.
Price when new: 2.4 litre, £1,344; 3.4 litre, £1,672.

Everybody remembers the tyre-squealing Mk II Jaguar, once beloved of tonic-suited villains and latterly finding favour on the right side of the law as the TV wheels of the opera-loving Inspector Morse. In the late 1980s, the Mk II was virtually standard classic issue for Soho advertising executives along with red-rimmed specs and an expense account at L'Escargot, but the car that paved the way for it is nearly forgotten. In the early 1950s, Jaguar was riding high, winning at Le Mans, and in the home and export markets with the feline XK120 sports car and gargantuan Mk VII saloon. In 1955, the Coventry company added its first unitary-built car, the compact 2.4 litre saloon – known retrospectively as the Mk I – to create its most complete model range ever. On first sight, you'd think someone had customised a Mk II, filling in the rear wheel arches and glass area to create something that looked more menacing than its better-known successor. Even though the engine was a downsized 2483cc version of the famed XK six, the Mk I was still considered sporting with its 100mph performance, while its keen pricing introduced a new group of motorists to Jaguar ownership. In 1957, Jaguar added a 3.4 litre version, followed shortly by optional disc brakes. By the end of production in 1960, the Mk I had become the biggest selling Jaguar ever and contributed to Jaguar's decision to buy neighbouring Daimler for extra production capacity. The Mk II was certainly a more capable car, not least because its widened rear wheel track overcame the Mk I's uncertain handling on the limit, but without the Mk I there would have been no Mk II, although today the near forgotten Mk I is both cheaper and more distinctive.

Jaguar Cat-alogue of Achievement

1901	William Lyons born in Blackpool on 4 September.
1922	On 4 September William Lyons goes into partnership with William Walmsley to form the Swallow Sidecar Company.
1927	Austin 7 Swallow is William Lyons' first car.
1928	Company moves to Coventry, its home ever since.
1933	The Swallow Sidecar and Coachbuilding Company changes its name to SS Cars Ltd.
1935	William Lyons is now sole proprietor of the business. On 24 September, at London's Mayfair Hotel, he introduces the Jaguar name for his new range of cars.
1945	Company changes its name to Jaguar Cars Ltd.
1948	Sensational new XK120 really can do 120mph
1951	C-Type claims Jaguar's first Le Mans 24-hour race victory.
1953	C-Type comes first, second and fourth at Le Mans. Jaguar's secret weapon was disc brakes.
1955	D-Type wins Le Mans.
1956	D-Type wins Le Mans; William Lyons knighted.
1957	D-Type wins Le Mans; fire devastates Jaguar's Browns Lane factory, causing an estimated £3,500,000 worth of damage.
1960	Jaguar buys Daimler.
1961	E-Type is the sensation of the Geneva motor show.
1966	Jaguar merges with British Motor Corporation to form British Motor Holdings.
1968	British Motor Holdings merges with Leyland Group to form British Leyland.
1972	Sir William Lyons retires.
1975	British Leyland, including Jaguar, nationalised.
1984	Jaguar Cars Ltd privatised.
1985	Sir William Lyons dies peacefully at his Warwickshire home on 8 February.
1988	Jaguar wins at Le Mans with XJR-9; XJ220 supercar announced.
1989	Jaguar becomes wholly owned subsidiary of Ford of Great Britain.
1990	Jaguar wins at Le Mans with XJR-9.
1992	First production XJ220s.
1994	XJ220 production ceases at 265.
1995	Geneva launch of XK8 rekindles excitement of E-Type's 1961 launch.
1995	60th anniversary of the Jaguar name.

1960 Jaguar Mk II 3.8 Saloon, rebuilt by Vicarage 1992 at a cost of £74,925, 14,500km covered since, converted to unleaded fuel, automatic transmission, uprated suspension, XJS power steering, chrome wire wheels, electric sunroof, finished in metallic green, heated rear screen, quarterlight-mounted mirrors, remote central locking, air conditioning, Vanden Plas cream leather seating with front headrests, centre console armrest, rear seat belts and leather-bound carpets, leather-trimmed boot, excellent condition.
£32,000–36,000 / $46,500–51,500 ⚒ BKS

Although production ceased in 1967, such is the enduring appeal of Jaguar's classic Mk II saloon that healthy demand still exists – not only for original examples, but also for re-engineered versions. The leader in this field is the Vicarage Classic Car Company, whose reworked Mk II brings Jaguar's original concept up to date. Vicarage cars are not just restored to a high standard, but also extensively modified to produce a classic Jaguar endowed with all the refinements of its modern counterpart.

◀ **1961 Jaguar Mk II 3.8 Saloon,** manual gearbox with overdrive, power steering conversion, chrome wire wheels, finished in red, 66,000 miles from new.
£14,000–16,000 / $20,300–23,200 ⚒ GrM

1962 Jaguar Mk II 2.4 Saloon, manual gearbox with overdrive, finished in red, excellent condition.
£10,000–11,000 / $14,500–16,000 ⊞ UMC

◀ **1964 Jaguar Mk II 3.4 Saloon,** 3442cc 6-cylinder engine, manual gearbox with overdrive, wire wheels, restored 1988, mechanically good, coachwork and structure in excellent condition.
£13,000–15,000 / $18,800–21,800 ⚒ BRIT

1967 Jaguar 240 Saloon, 2483cc, manual gearbox with overdrive, wire wheels, finished in maroon, cream leather upholstery, 78,768 miles from new, chromework and bodywork in very good condition.
£4,500–5,000 / $6,500–7,500 ⚒ H&H

1969 Jaguar 340 Saloon, rebuilt c1988, overdrive, power steering conversion, body-colour wire wheels, finished in Jaguar racing green, upgraded with Mk II wood trim, leather upholstery.
£12,500–14,500 / $18,200–21,000 ⚒ GrM

◄ **1965 Jaguar S-Type Saloon,** bodywork restored 1998, new wire wheels, chromework replated, finished in original metallic silver-blue, original grey leather interior, interior wood repolished, new carpets, 78,000 miles from new.
£13,000–15,000
$18,800–21,800 ⚒ COYS
The S-Type represented a significant advance over the much celebrated Mk II, having E-Type-like independent rear suspension for better handling and a more refined ride.

► **1968 Jaguar 420 Saloon,** manual gearbox with overdrive, unrestored, finished in white, maroon interior in excellent condition, 2 owners from new.
£5,000–6,000 / $7,250–8,500 ⚒ BKS

1966 Jaguar 3.4 S-Type, 3442cc 6-cylinder engine, manual gearbox with overdrive, braking and cooling systems overhauled, finished in dark blue, 9,000 miles covered in last 20 years, original, good condition.
£12,000–14,000 / $17,400–20,400 ⚒ BRIT

1963 Jaguar Mk X Saloon, 4200cc double-overhead-camshaft 6-cylinder engine, 265bhp, 3-speed automatic transmission, 4-wheel independent suspension, 4-wheel disc brakes, power steering, left-hand drive, engine uprated with 8:1 compression head and triple SU carburettors, finished in metallic dark grey, red leather upholstery.
£6,500–8,000 / $9,500–11,500 ⚒ C
Jaguar Cars returned to the large luxury saloon car market in 1961 with the Mk X saloon. Styled by Sir William Lyons, clearly with the needs and preferences of the increasingly important North American market in mind, it was lavishly equipped, surrounding its occupants with deep-pleated leather, thick-pile carpets and highly polished veneers.

1968 Jaguar 420 Saloon, 4235cc 6-cylinder engine, reconditioned gearbox, new chrome wire wheels, finished in red, black interior, excellent condition throughout.
£7,000–8,500 / $10,200–12,300 ⚒ H&H

JAGUAR Model	ENGINE cc/cyl	DATES	CONDITION 1	2	3
E-Type 3.8 flat-floor roadster (RHD)		1961	£40,000	£30,000	£22,000
E-Type SI 3.8 roadster	3781/6	1961–64	£30,000	£19,000	£15,000
E-Type 3.8 FHC	3781/6	1961–64	£20,000	£13,000	£10,000
E-Type SI 4.2 roadster	4235/6	1964–67	£28,000	£18,000	£14,000
E-Type 2+2 manual FHC	4235/6	1966–67	£16,000	£11,000	£9,000
E-Type SI 2+2 auto FHC	4235/6	1966–68	£14,000	£10,000	£9,000
E-Type SII roadster	4235/6	1968–70	£30,000	£21,000	£14,000
E-Type SII FHC	4235/6	1968–70	£18,000	£12,000	£10,000
E-Type SII 2+2 manual FHC	4235/6	1968–70	£15,000	£10,000	£8,000
E-Type SIII roadster	5343/12	1971–75	£30,000+	£26,000	£17,000
E-Type SIII 2+2 manual FHC	5343/12	1971–75	£19,000	£14,000	£10,000
E-Type SIII 2+2 auto FHC	5343/12	1971–75	£17,000	£12,000	£9,000
XJ6 2.8 Ser I	2793/6	1968–73	£3,000	£1,500	£1,000
XJ6 4.2 Ser I	4235/6	1968–73	£3,500	£2,000	£1,000
XJ6 Coupé	4235/6	1974–78	£8,000	£5,000	£3,500
XJ6 Ser II	4235/6	1973–79	£3,500	£2,000	£750
XJ12 Ser I	5343/12	1972–73	£3,500	£2,250	£1,500
XJ12 Coupé	5343/12	1973–77	£9,000	£5,000	£3,000
XJ12 Ser II	5343/12	1973–79	£3,000	£2,000	£1,000
XJS manual	5343/12	1975–78	£5,000	£4,000	£2,500
XJS auto	5343/12	1975–81	£4,000	£3,000	£2,000

Jaguar E-Type Series III Commemorative Roadsters fetch more than SIII Roadster – 50 limited editions only.

1961 Jaguar E-Type 'Flat-Floor' Roadster, 3781cc, 265bhp, all-independent suspension, 4-wheel disc brakes, external bonnet locks, left-hand drive, restored 1996 to concours condition.
£55,000–61,000 / $79,750–88,750 ⚒ BKS
The early 'flat-floor' E-Type proved short-lived, for modifications were quickly made to counter criticism that there was insufficient legroom for tall drivers, while the faired-in headlamps soon fell victim to US legislation.

1963 Jaguar E-Type Roadster, 3781cc double-overhead-camshaft 6-cylinder engine, 265bhp, 4-speed manual gearbox, 4-wheel independent suspension and disc brakes, subject of body-off restoration, finished in white, matching engine and chassis numbers.
£40,000–45,000 / $58,000–65,250 ⚒ RM

1963 Jaguar E-Type Coupé, 3.8 litre engine, restored at a cost of £13,000, chrome wire wheels, finished in mid-green, tan leather interior, matching engine and chassis numbers.
£10,500–12,500 / $15,250–18,250 ⚒ CGC

1965 Jaguar E-Type Coupé, 4200cc, chrome wire wheels, finished in black, red interior, fewer than 71,000 miles from new, very good condition throughout.
£16,000–18,000 / $23,200–26,000 ⚒ H&H

1966 Jaguar E-Type Roadster, restored, finished in red, concours winner.
£30,000–34,000 / $43,500–48,000 COYS

At its Geneva show debut, in March 1961, the E-Type caused a sensation, with all the promise of its looks confirmed by a 150mph top speed and 0–60mph in 6.9 seconds. In October 1964, it was superseded by the 4.2 litre model. Apart from the capacity increase from 3781cc to 4235cc and improved torque, it boasted a new all-synchromesh gearbox, better brake servo and improved seats, an alternator and leather-faced, rather than aluminium, dashboard.

1967 Jaguar E-Type Roadster, 4.2 litre engine, triple carburettors, rust-free body, finished in green, tan interior, in need of cosmetic restoration.
£17,000–20,000 / $24,750–29,000 HCL

► **1968 Jaguar E-Type 2+2 Coupé,** 4.2 litre engine, triple SU carburettors, restored, new bonnet, chrome wire wheels, converted to right-hand drive.
£14,000–16,000 / $20,300–23,200 GrM

Miller's Compares

◄ **I. 1968 Jaguar E-Type Series 1½ Coupé,** manual gearbox, left-hand drive, finished in metallic silver, Bordeaux leather interior, museum displayed for many years, 4,000 miles from new, original condition, minor engine oil leak, otherwise excellent condition throughout.
£38,000–42,000 / $55,000–61,000 BKS

Proposed changes to US legislation would eventually result in the revised Series II E-Type, and from late 1967 Jaguar's sports car began to embody some of the forthcoming modifications – deleted headlight covers and rocker-type dashboard switches among them. These interim cars became known as Series 1½.

► **II. 1971 Jaguar E-Type Roadster,** 5343cc V12 engine, manual gearbox, wire wheels, finished in white, tan interior, 35,500 miles from new, ex-South Africa.
£17,000–20,000
$24,500–29,000 H&H

When conventional wisdom and common sense values open roadsters far more highly than fixed-head coupés, how can it be that item I sold at auction for double the price of item II? In today's markets, with a plentiful supply of decent, but undistinguished, cars, buyers are looking increasingly for some kind of singularity that marks a car out from the masses. Item II, was recently imported from South Africa, as many others have been in recent years, and was in ordinary, middling condition. Item I however, would be a difficult car to duplicate, a time-warp in suspended animation with a mere 4,000 miles on the clock. The point here is that you'd have to look far and wide to find another like it, but on the other hand what do you do with it?

Auction prices

Miller's only includes cars declared sold. Our guide prices take into account the buyer's premium, VAT on the premium, and the extent of any published catalogue information relating to condition and provenance. Cars sold at auction are identified by the icon; full details of the auction house can be found on page 330.

◄ **1969 Jaguar E-Type Series II Roadster,** triple carburettors, finished in burgundy, tan interior, original.
£20,000–23,000 / $29,000–33,350 HCL

1965 Jaguar E-Type Roadster, restored 1990s finished in red, black interior, excellent condition throughout.
£40,000–45,000 / $58,000–65,250 ✗ BKS

▶ **1971 Jaguar E-Type Series III Coupé,** 5300cc V12 engine, automatic transmission, US-specification, left-hand drive, factory air conditioning, restored late 1980s, finished in red, black interior trim, slight blemishes to paintwork, otherwise very good condition.
£9,000–11,000 / $13,000–16,000 ✗ H&H

1972 Jaguar E-Type Series III Roadster, V12 engine, transistorised ignition, manual gearbox, ventilated front disc brakes, power steering, gearbox rebuilt, new top, recently resprayed in original silver-blue, dark blue interior, seats reupholstered, new carpets, 69,000 miles from new, very good condition.
£20,000–23,000 / $29,000–33,300 ✗ BKS

One consequence of the E-Type's long process of development was a gradual increase in weight, but a good measure of the subsequent loss of performance was restored in 1971 with the arrival of the Series III V12. Weighing only 80lb more than the iron-block 4.2 litre XK six, the new all-alloy, 5.3 litre, overhead-camshaft V12 produced 272bhp, an output good enough for a top speed of over 140mph. Further good news was that the 0–100mph time of around 16 seconds made the V12 the fastest-accelerating E-Type ever.

◀ **1972 Jaguar E-Type Coupé,** 5343cc V12 engine, manual gearbox, sunroof, finished in blue, good mechanical condition.
£12,000–14,000 / $17,500–20,300 ✗ BRIT

1972 Jaguar E-Type Roadster, 5354cc double-overhead-camshaft V12 engine, 250bhp, 4-speed manual gearbox, 4-wheel independent suspension, 4-wheel disc brakes, left-hand drive, new brakes and exhaust system, recently resprayed in turquoise, original 'Passport to Service' book, 1 owner from new, very good condition.
£19,000–23,000 / $27,500–33,300 ✗ RM

◀ **1974 Jaguar E-Type Series III Roadster,** automatic transmission, chrome wire wheels, finished in burgundy, factory air conditioning, tan interior.
£21,000–24,000 / $30,500–34,800 ⊞ HCL

Jaguar XJ6 Series I (1968–73)

Engine: Six-cylinder, 2792 or 4235cc.
Transmission: Four-speed manual, optional overdrive; automatic.
Power output: 180bhp (4.2 litre), 140bhp (2.8 litre).
0–60mph: 8.7 seconds (4.2 litre), 12.6 seconds (2.8 litre).
Maximum speed: 120–127mph (4.2 litre), 113mph (2.8 litre).
Production: 78,218.
Price in 1969: £1,797 including purchase tax (2.8 litre); £2,397 (4.2 litre).

Although Sir William Lyons retired as Jaguar boss in 1972, his vision lives on in today's generation of XJ saloons. That original XJ6 of 1968 was the last car on which he exercised his assured styling touch. Into the 1980s, the shape was flat-ironed, folded and creased into a less harmonious fusion of the traditional and merely voguish, but in 1994 the evolution came full circle with the return of the sensuous curves. In fact, so familiar is the essence of the XJ Jag that it's easy to overlook the classic credentials of the original; especially as Series 1 XJ6s spiralled down the food chain, from executive express to become cheap jewellery for sheepskin-coated bookies, until, finally, they were carted off to the breakers when the cost of a new exhaust outstripped the price of a tax ticket. In 1968 though, the XJ6 was a sensation, the press a-gush with praise for the way it blended luxury, refinement, comfort and silence with performance and handling that bettered most sports cars. What's more, like Jags before, although not cheap, it was very keenly priced. It sounded too good to be true, and it was. First, the XJ6 was built down to a price and, second, under the demoralised mess of British Leyland, quality went downhill and tarnished Jaguar's reputation at home and abroad. Now that's all long forgotten and the first-of-breed purity is becoming increasingly admired, with growing numbers being restored, and rare, unabused early XJ6s attracting enthusiasts' devotion.

XJ6 fact: In May 1970, 20 Swiss businessmen were so frustrated after waiting 14 months for new XJ Jags that they demonstrated outside British Leyland's Jaguar showrooms in Berkeley Square.

1974 Jaguar E-Type Roadster, V12 engine, automatic transmission, chrome wire wheels, new hood, finished in signal red, black leather interior, 46,000 miles from new.
£23,000–26,000 / $33,750–37,750 ⊞ TIHO

Cross Reference
See Colour Review (page 72)

1979 Jaguar XJS, V12 engine, manual gearbox, period alloy wheels, sunroof, black leather interior, unused for some years.
£1,800–2,100 / $2,500–3,000 ⚒ COYS
Jaguar's established XJ saloon range received a new GT model in April 1975 with the announcement of the XJS. This had been under development since 1968 and, as a 2+2 fixed-head coupé was intended as a replacement for the E-Type. The design owed much to the requirements of the US regulations in force at the time, even to the extent that most manufacturers had guessed that the Americans would legislate against open-topped cars in the interests of safety, and consequently built coupés. With the 5.3 litre V12 engine from the XJ12 under the bonnet, the XJS was endowed with quite formidable performance.

1972 Jaguar XJ6 SWB Saloon, 4.2 litre engine, converted to unleaded fuel, automatic transmission, full-length Webasto sunroof, finished in red, beige leather interior trim, very good condition.
£2,400–2,600 / $3,500–3,750 ⊞ SiC

1976 Jaguar XJ6C Coupé, 4235cc, vinyl-covered roof, finished in white, red leather interior, 28,700 miles from new, original, excellent condition.
£5,000–6,000 / $7,250–8,750 ⚒ H&H
Although the XJ6 saloon was introduced in 1968, the two-door coupé version, which was only produced for two years, did not appear until 1975. In total, only 6,500 were produced.

1977 Jaguar XJ12C Coupé, 5.3 litre V12 engine, automatic transmission, Ziebart rust-proofed from new, finished in green, brown leather upholstery, c13,000 miles from new, 1 of only 2,244 V12 coupés built, very good condition throughout.
£5,500–6,500 / $8,000–9,500 ⚒ BKS

1985 Jaguar XJS HE, 5.3 litre V12 engine, TWR body kit, finished in red, air conditioning, cruise control, fawn interior, 60,000 miles from new.
£4,500–5,500 / $6,500–8,000 ⊞ UMC

1987 Jaguar XJS Lynx Convertible, electric hood, 56,000 miles from new.
£8,000–10,000 / $11,500–14,500 ⊞ VIC

1990 Lister-Jaguar XJS Mk III Convertible, 7 litre V12 engine, c500bhp, 5-speed manual gearbox, almost 200mph top speed, finished in metallic royal blue, matching hood and tonneau, wood-trimmed interior, magnolia leather interior with dark blue binding, c8,500 miles from new, 1 of only 3 built, 'as-new' condition.
£31,000–35,000 / $44,500–50,000 ⚒ BKS
One of the most illustrious names in sports car racing history, the Lister-Jaguar, designed by Brian Lister, swept almost all before it during its first full racing season in 1957. Today, cars bearing the Lister name are once again a major force in GT racing worldwide. From the early 1980s, the name has also graced some of the world's fastest road cars, after an agreement between engineer Laurence Pearce and Brian Lister saw the former's converted XJS models marketed as Lister-Jaguars.

1987 Jaguar XJS Lynx Eventer Estate, automatic transmission, engine rebuilt, converted to unleaded fuel, bodywork restored and resprayed at a cost of over £22,500, finished in dark green, 3 owners from new.
£11,500–13,000 / $16,600–18,800 ⚒ BKS
This car was converted to an estate by Lynx from new at a cost of around £37,000.

◄ **1989 Jaguar XJS Convertible,** 5.3 litre V12 engine, alloy wheels, finished in blue, air conditioning, cruise control, magnolia leather interior trim, 1 owner from new.
£10,000–11,000 / $14,500–16,000 ⊞ TSG

1989 Jaguar XJS, 3.6 litre engine, converted to unleaded fuel, manual gearbox, finished in red, tan interior.
£3,000–3,500 / $4,400–5,000 ⚒ CGC

1989 Jaguar Sovereign Series III, 5343cc V12 engine, bodywork recently refurbished and resprayed in red, tan interior.
£3,500–4,000 / $5,000–5,800 ⚒ BRIT
The classic XJ6 shape was sharpened and updated by Pininfarina during 1979, the most noticeable changes being the revised front-end treatment and flatter roof. In 1983, the Sovereign title came into use for the V12 model.

Jensen

The recent rebirth of the fabled Jensen marque may be a bold new beginning – we'll have to wait and see. However, one thing's for sure: although total Jensen output (excluding the Jensen-Healey) was less than 10,000 cars, the vehicles possess a powerful mystique. From the 'drastic plastic' fibreglass-bodied 541 and CV8 to the growling, but refined, Interceptor, with its Italian-designed elegance and pioneering four-wheel drive in the FF versions, virtually all Jensens have what you might call 'serious road presence'. Brothers Richard and Allen Jensen started out as coachbuilders before producing their own cars from 1936 onward. The original Interceptor of 1950 to 1957 had an Austin 4 litre engine, which was also employed in the dramatic 541 of 1954. From 1962, with the launch of the CV8, Jensen adopted Chrysler V8 power. The car that really made Jensen a household name was the 1967 Interceptor, which mated the massive American V8 engine with elegant Italian coachwork to create a formidable high-performance GT. Sadly, the gas-guzzling Interceptor's heyday was cut short by two oil crises and a worldwide recession.

◀ **1963 Jensen CV8 Mk I,** 5916cc V8 engine, 4th CV8 built, believed to be the oldest surviving Mk I.
£5,000–6,000 / $7,250–8,500 ⚒ BRIT
The CV8 replaced the 541S in 1962. Built on an entirely new chassis and powered by a Chrysler V8 engine, this sports saloon had distinctive, if somewhat controversial, front-end styling. It was particularly well equipped, the specification including a Salisbury Powr-Lok differential, reclining seats and a radio. Performance was sensational, with a top speed of approximately 140mph. Only 68 examples were produced before the Mk II appeared later in 1963.

1965 Jensen CV8, 6276cc Chrysler V8 engine, converted to LPG, fibreglass body, finished in grey, red and grey interior trim, excellent condition throughout.
£8,000–10,000 / $11,500–14,500 ⚒ H&H

1973 Jensen Interceptor Mk III, completely restored, 56,000 miles from new, excellent condition.
£8,000–10,000 / $11,500–14,500 ⊞ VIC

Miller's is a price GUIDE not a price LIST

▶ **1974 Jensen Interceptor Mk III,** automatic transmission, restored, converted to unleaded fuel, stainless-steel exhaust, new front brake discs, new radiator, new sills and brake pipes, electrical system overhauled, sundry new panels, new windscreen, bumpers rechromed, resprayed in metallic dark blue, tan vinyl roof, tan leather interior, good-to-excellent condition.
£5,500–7,000
$8,000–10,000 ⚒ BKS

JENSEN Model	ENGINE cc/cyl	DATES	CONDITION 1	2	3
541/541R/541S	3993/6	1954–63	£13,000	£7,000	£4,500
CV8 Mk I–III	5916/ 6276/8	1962–66	£14,000	£7,000	£6,000
Interceptor SI–SIII	6276/8	1967–76	£11,000	£8,000	£6,000
Interceptor DHC	6276/8	1973–76	£22,000	£15,000	£10,000
Interceptor SP	7212/8	1971–76	£12,000	£8,000	£5,000
FF	6766/8	1967–71	£15,000	£10,000	£7,000

The Jensen CV8 and 541 are particularly sought after.

1987 Jensen Interceptor Convertible, 5900cc V8 engine, electric exterior mirrors, finished in gold, heated seats, trimmed in magnolia hide, 8,743 miles from new, 1 of only 2 cars built during 1987.
£27,000–30,000 / $39,000–43,500 A BRIT

Jensen-Healey

Restored values

The cost of a professional restoration will have an influence on, but no direct relation to, a car's market value. A restored car can have a market value lower than the cost of its restoration.

◀ **1974 Jensen-Healey GT,** 1973cc 4-cylinder engine, restored 1990, full tonneau, hardtop, finished in red, black interior, excellent condition.
£4,500–5,500 / $6,500–8,000 A CGC

▶ **1976 Jensen-Healey GT,** 1973cc 4-cylinder engine, recently overhauled, new floor panels and sills, finished in maroon, 1 of last built.
£1,500–1,800 / $2,200–2,500 A BRIT
The Jensen-Healey, produced between 1972 and 1976, was powered by a Lotus 16-valve twin-cam engine, which produced 140bhp. The sports two-seater survives in reasonable numbers, but the GT model, with sports hatchback coachwork, is a rarity. Produced for 1975 and 1976, with a run of just 473 examples, the GT had styling that echoed the theme of the Reliant Scimitar GTE and Volvo 1800 ES.

JENSEN-HEALEY Model	ENGINE cc/cyl	DATES	CONDITION 1	2	3
Healey	1973/4	1972–76	£4,500	£3,000	£1,500
Healey GT	1973/4	1975–76	£5,000	£3,000	£2,000

Jowett

◀ **1955 Jowett Jupiter,** 1500cc, engine rebuilt, otherwise unrestored, finished in white, red interior, 86,000 miles from new.
£7,000–8,000 / $10,200–11,600 A H&H
Yorkshire's Benjamin and William Jowett spent some time building experimental flat-twin-engined cars from 1906, and in 1913 their vehicles finally entered production. The power unit was destined for a long life, being used in cars until 1953. The flat-four that went on to power post-war models was introduced in 1936.

Kaiser-Darrin

1954 Kaiser-Darrin Roadster, 161cu.in 6-cylinder engine, 90bhp, 3-speed manual gearbox with overdrive, restored, resprayed, new chrome, new interior, 1 of only 435 made.
£34,000–38,000 / $48,000–54,000 ⚒ RM
Founded during the post-war economic boom, Kaiser-Frazer acquired Willow Run, Ford's huge WWII bomber plant, and set about introducing a line of mid-priced cars. Public acceptance was immediate, and the new company announced a profit of $20 million in 1947, its second year of operation. Kaiser-Frazer's entire line was new for 1951, and the market responded enthusiastically. Striking styling, combined with innovative colour choices, made Kaiser-Frazer's offerings stand out from the crowd. Unfortunately it was not enough and Kaiser's fortunes waned. In 1954, the Darrin, named after its creator, Howard 'Dutch' Darrin, was introduced. With sleek styling, innovative sliding doors, a three-position top and a novel fibreglass body, it could have been the image leader of the line. As it turned out, it was nearly the pall bearer, as Kaiser production ceased in 1955.

Lagonda

In the early 1930s, if you were British, young and fashionably idle, there were three fast and certain ways to lighten the burden of that hefty inheritance burning a hole in your plus-fours. For the mere price of a none-too-pokey working man's house, the sporting automobilist could choose between a Bentley, Invicta and Lagonda, but which one? For those who considered the Bentley a little obvious, the choice was between Invicta and Lagonda, but as Invicta's fortunes waned, Lagonda's short period of full bloom began with the glorious M45, which adopted the powerful six-cylinder Meadows engine used earlier by Invicta. Less dreadnought dour than the Bentley and not as rakish as the Invicta, the M45 Lagonda possessed a rough, tough elegance with a substantial, stiff and sturdy chassis, firm suspension and a series of graceful saloon and open bodies. Even the heaviest-bodied versions could top 90mph, and the tuned short-chassis M45 Rapide versions were good for a ton and more. In 1935, a Lagonda M45 won outright at Le Mans, averaging 77.85mph; but in the same year, the company also foundered and fell briefly into receivership, before being revived with W. O. Bentley as design and technical director. He refined the six-cylinder M45, then produced a magnificent V12, considered by some as his crowning achievement. In 1947, David Brown, who'd just acquired Aston Martin, added Lagonda to his portfolio.

Lagonda M45 (1934–36)
Body styles: Saloon, drophead coupé, tourer.
Engine: 4467cc, six-cylinder.
Power output: 115–130bhp.
Transmission: Four-speed manual, non-synchromesh.
Maximum speed: 95–105+mph.
Production: M45, approximately 410; M45R, approximately 53.

◀ **1928 Lagonda 3 Litre High-Chassis Open Tourer,** coachwork by Brooklands, 3000cc, full hood, finished in black and red, oxblood leather interior, slight damage to driver's seat, otherwise very good condition.
£40,000–45,000 / $58,000–65,000 ⚒ H&H

LAGONDA Model	ENGINE cc/cyl	DATES	CONDITION 1	2	3
12/24	1421/4	1923–26	£14,000	£10,000	£8,000
2 Litre	1954/4	1928–32	£28,000	£25,000	£19,000
3 Litre	2931/6	1928–34	£40,000+	£30,000	£22,000
Rapier	1104/4	1934–35	£15,000	£9,000	£5,000
M45	4429/6	1934–36	£50,000+	£30,000	£20,000
LG45	4429/6	1936–37	£45,000+	£32,000	£20,000
LG6	4453/6	1937–39	£40,000	£28,000	£22,000
V12	4480/V12	1937–39	£75,000+	£50,000	£25,000

Prices are very dependent upon body type, dhc or saloon, originality and competition history.

1934 Lagonda M45 Team Car Replica, Le Mans-type coachwork by G.P. Panelcraft, 4.5 litre engine, racing specification, finished in green, black interior.
£67,000–74,000 / $97,000–107,000 ⚒ COYS
While only in production for two years, the M45 won itself a tremendous following. If other vehicles offered more creature comforts and sophistication, the M45 was aimed at the sporting owner-driver whose idea of transport was not to sit behind a chauffeur, but rather to thunder at speed behind the wheel. Cars prepared by the Fox and Nicholl racing stable not only won Le Mans in 1935, breaking a four-year run by Alfa Romeo, but also in 1936 they took class wins in the French Grand Prix and Spa 24-hour race.

1951 Lagonda 2.6 Litre Saloon, 2580cc double-overhead-camshaft 6-cylinder engine, restored, resprayed in cream, original red leather interior, woodwork repolished, new headlining.
£8,000–9,000 / $11,500–13,000 ⚒ H&H

1954 Lagonda 3 Litre Coupé, finished in silver over blue, light blue leather upholstery.
£15,000–17,000 / $21,750–24,750 ⚒ COYS

1937 Lagonda LG45 Saloon, 4500cc, finished in black, grey interior trim, 49,000 miles from new, unused since 1964, original.
£15,500–17,500 / $22,500–25,000 ⚒ H&H

1939 Lagonda V12 Drophead Coupé, 4.4 litre engine, 4 downdraught SU carburettors, Weslake-inspired cylinder head with smaller valves, 8.5:1 compression ratio, 220bhp, fewer than 1,000 miles since 1992, 1 of last of 189 V12s built, ex-Briggs Cunningham.
£150,000–165,000 / $217,000–239,000 ⚒ BKS
Blessed with a considerable family fortune based on meat packing and banking, Briggs Cunningham was the most dynamic American sportsman of his generation. He spent an estimated $1 million on his attempts on the Le Mans 24-hour race, where his Cunningham sports-racers were strong contenders during the 1950s, their best result being third, fifth and tenth in 1953. His team won the US National Championship four years in succession, between 1956 and 1959. It was just before WWII that Cunningham ordered this V12. Ever the perfectionist, he felt that the standard side-mounted spare wheel and tool kit 'blisters' of the factory-built body spoiled the lines of Frank Feeley's drophead coupé design, so the spare and tool kit were relegated to the boot, 'leaving barely enough room for one's motoring hat and gloves'.

Lagonda Fact

Lagonda may seem quintessentially British, but the company was actually founded by American Wilbur Gunn, an opera singer living in London. He named the company after the Indian name of a river near his birthplace in Ohio.

LAGONDA (post-war) Model	ENGINE cc/cyl	DATES	CONDITION 1	2	3
3 Litre	2922/6	1953–58	£10,500	£7,000	£4,500
3 Litre DHC	2922/6	1953–56	£17,000	£12,000	£9,000
Rapide	3995/6	1961–64	£11,000+	£7,000	£4,500

Lambert

Lambert first came to the attention of the motoring public when the firm of Doué, Lambert et Cie exhibited at the 1901 Paris Salon. In its show report, *The Autocar* referred to the car as economical, reporting that it was shaft driven and could be fitted with either a De Dion or a two-cylinder Abeille engine. By the time of the 1902 Salon, the firm had become the Société Nouvelle d'Automobiles, A. Lambert & Cie. Lambert's 1902 sales brochure lists a range of models: 6 and 9hp De Dion Bouton single-cylinder cars, and single- and twin-cylinder Aster-engined versions, all with tubular chassis, although a wood and flitch-plate version could be specified for an additional 200 francs. Not only did the firm use bought-in engines, but also the running gear of at least the small cars was provided by the well-known components supplier Lacoste et Battmann. This Levallois firm rarely sold complete cars under its own name, yet it was responsible for over 60 makes in both France and Britain during c1901–06.

Miller's is a price GUIDE not a price LIST

◀ **1902 Lambert Type G Two-Seater Voiturette,** coachwork by Botiaux, 942cc De Dion Bouton single-cylinder engine, 3-speed gearbox, semi-elliptic leaf-spring suspension, rear-wheel drum brakes, contracting band on transmission, finished in dark green with yellow chassis, black leather interior, originally built as a rear-entrance tonneau.
£31,000–35,000 / $45,000–50,000 ⚒ C

Lamborghini

In the early 1960s, upstart supercar maker Ferruccio Lamborghini, who'd made his fortune out of tractors and air conditioning, was on a mission, and with the debut of the mesmerisingly beautiful Miura he achieved his goal – to out-Ferrari Ferrari. In fact, the unveiling of the Miura in 1966 did more than that; it set the supercar standard, with technical sophistication, shattering near-180mph performance and race-derived engineering that left rivals floundering in its wake. Not only was the Miura the fastest true road car in its day, but it also made Ferrari's best efforts of the period look old-fashioned and even mundane. Some of the Miura's inspiration came from the looks and the layout of the mid-engined Ford GT40 road-racer that dominated Le Mans. The difference was that the Miura was never meant to go racing, merely to be the supreme road car. So what if early models were plagued by chronic unreliability and an alarming tendency (later sorted with the S version) for the nose to lift at around 125mph, and occasionally for the front wheels to leave the ground completely at 170mph, give or take. Many reckon those exquisitely beautiful lines penned by Bertone make the Miura the most beautiful Lamborghini there's ever been; some say the most beautiful car of all time.

1966 Lamborghini 400GT Coupé, 3929cc double-overhead-camshaft V12 engine, 6 40DCOE twin-choke Weber carburettors, 320bhp, 5-speed manual gearbox, 4-wheel independent suspension, 4-wheel disc brakes, subject of full cosmetic and partial mechanical restoration, 1 of only 23 400GT two-seaters built.
£50,000–55,000 / $72,500–79,500 ⚒ RM

Colour Review

1938 Jensen S-Type Three-Door Tourer, 3.6 litre Ford sidevalve V8 engine, wire wheels, tan upholstery, little recent use, excellent overall condition.
£42,000–48,000 / $60,900–69,600 BKS
Press publicity for Jensen's sports-tourer body on the 1936 Ford V8-68 attracted the attention of a Hollywood entrepreneur named Percy Morgan, who ordered one for himself and one for his friend, Clark Gable, who had recently hit the big time with his Oscar-winning performance in *It Happened One Night*. Although Gable only drove the car for a few days before returning it and asking for his deposit back, he posed for publicity photos with Morgan's Jensen-Ford. Fewer than 50 S-Type tourers and saloons were built.

1935 Lagonda Rapier Two-Seat Tourer, 1104cc 4-cylinder double-overhead-camshaft engine, pre-selector gearbox, grey interior trim, completely rebuilt 1990–95.
£17,000–20,000 / $24,650–29,000 H&H
The Rapier represented an attempt by Lagonda to move into the market for high-quality small cars, and it was launched in 1934. It was made by Lagonda for 12 months, then produced by Rapier Cars in Hammersmith from 1935 to 1937.

◀ **1967 Lamborghini 400 GT 2+2 Coupé,** coachwork by Touring, 3929cc V12 engine, 320bhp, refurbished, approximately 3,000km covered since, resprayed, new grey leather interior, 1 of about 250 examples built.
£60,000–70,000 / $87,000–101,500 BKS

1971 Lamborghini Miura SV Berlinetta, coachwork by Bertone, ex-works prototype, completely restored, 4,500km covered since, resprayed in original colour, very good condition.
£65,000–75,000 / $94,250–108,750 BKS
This historic Miura, chassis no. 4758, was the result of a project overseen by Bob Wallace, the factory's chief development engineer and test driver, to create the definitive Miura: the SV. Wallace – who used the experience gained from his Miura-based Jota – strengthened the existing chassis and redesigned the rear suspension. The V12 engine was uprated, with bigger valves and other tweaks, raising power to 385bhp, and the brakes were ventilated discs. The rear bodywork was flared to accommodate wider tyres, the headlight 'eyelashes' deleted and the cockpit revised.

1925 Lancia Lambda 4th Series Torpedo Tourer, overhead-camshaft V4 engine, 50bhp, 4-speed manual gearbox, 4-wheel mechanical brakes, independent front suspension with sliding pillars, semi-elliptic leaf rear springs, correct instrumentation and engine ancillaries, good original condition.
£28,000–32,000 / $40,600–46,400 C
The Lambda, introduced in 1922, was a technical masterpiece. The combination of stressed-hull frame, sliding-pillar front suspension, V4 engine and four-wheel brakes created a car that was low and spacious, and offered good performance. The Torpedo Tourer went on sale in 1923 and soon became renowned for its performance, handling and safe road holding.

1953 Lancia Aurelia B20 GT 3rd Series Coupé, coachwork by Pinin Farina, 2451cc V6 engine, 118bhp.
£19,000–23,000 / $27,500–33,000 BKS
This B20 GT was owned during the 1950s by works Ferrari driver and Le Mans winner Lorenzo Bandini.

1976 Lancia Stratos, 2418cc 6-cylinder engine, 190bhp, triple Weber 40IDF carburettors, 5-speed manual gearbox, 4-wheel independent suspension, 4-wheel disc brakes.
£35,000–40,000 / $50,750–58,000 Pou

1930 LaSalle 340 Seven-Passenger Tourer, 340cu.in sidevalve V8 engine, 3-speed synchromesh gearbox, 4-wheel mechanical drum brakes, older restoration.
£30,000–35,000 / $43,500–50,750 RM
LaSalle was introduced by General Motors in 1927 as a companion make for Cadillac. It was felt that with a $1,000 gap between Buick and Cadillac, there was room for another car line. Designed by Harley Earl, head of GM's new Art and Colour Department, the new LaSalle borrowed features from the leading marques of Europe and offered a fresh face to a public accustomed to relatively drab domestic US designs. This appeal, combined with the lower price, made LaSalle an instant success.

1933 Lincoln KB Convertible Victoria, coachwork by Brunn, 448cu. in V12 engine, 3-speed manual gearbox, 4-wheel mechanical drum brakes, professionally restored, excellent overall condition.
£100,000–120,000 / $145,000–174,000 RM

1939 Lincoln Zephyr Custom, 350cu.in Chevrolet V8 engine, automatic transmission, chassis and running gear from 1978 Chevrolet station wagon, chassis lowered and stretched to 116in wheelbase, hydraulic suspension, roof lowered 8in, 1940–41 Zephyr nose section, widened front and rear wings, 1939 Ford headlights, Honda Accord windscreen, power windows, steering, brakes and boot lid, Cadillac tilt/telescopic steering column, 6-way Cadillac power seats, black and white leather/vinyl interior.
£150,000–170,000 / $217,500–246,500 RM

1960 Lotus 7 Series I, lightweight tubular spaceframe, alloy panels, fibreglass wings, refurbished, brakes overhauled.
£9,000–11,000 / $13,000–16,000 ⚒ COYS

1967 Maserati Speciale Frua Prototype, 4172cc double-overhead-camshaft V8 engine, 270bhp, 5-speed ZF manual gearbox, 4-wheel disc brakes, body restored late 1980s, complete mechanical overhaul 1999.
£60,000–70,000 / $87,000–101,500 ⚒ RM
In the mid-1960s, Maserati commissioned Bertone, Vignale and Frua each to design a 2+2 prototype coupé based on a shortened Quattroporte V8 chassis. The three prototypes were exhibited at various shows in Europe, the Vignale-bodied version finally becoming the Maserati Mexico. This car is the original, hand-made, one-off prototype from Frua. Its chassis and engine numbers are notable. The chassis number, AM112.001, signifies the first car built on the shortened chassis, while the engine number, 1, shows it to be the very first production unit of Maserati's new race-derived V8.

1951 Maserati A6G Coupé, coachwork by Vignale, original 2 litre overhead-camshaft 6-cylinder engine.
£190,000+ / $275,500+ ⚒ BKS
This is the only single-cam six-cylinder A6G Coupé to have been styled and bodied by Vignale and stylist Giovanni Michelotti. It was commissioned by Roman Maserati concessionaire Guglielmo 'Mimo' Dei – known throughout the motor racing world as the patron and driving force behind the legendary Scuderia Centro-Sud racing team. It was acquired by American racer Bob Estes, who had it shipped to the United States. After enthusiastic use, the car was separated from its engine and transmission, and cobbled together as a runner with a Ford V8 engine, gearbox and back axle. In 1972, the car was rescued from a scrapyard, and over a period of 20 years was restored, being reunited with its original engine and gearbox in the process.

1972 Maserati Ghibli SS 4.9 Spyder, 4930cc double-overhead-camshaft V8 engine, 335bhp, 5-speed manual gearbox, 4-wheel disc brakes, independent front suspension, Borrani wire wheels, power steering, brakes and windows, air conditioning, black leather interior, 1 of only 19 4.9 litre models built, 2 owners, fewer than 19,000 miles from new.
£75,000–85,000 / $108,750–123,250 ⚒ RM

1935 Mercedes-Benz 500K Special Roadster, 5018cc overhead-camshaft engine, supercharger, 4-speed manual gearbox, 4-wheel drum brakes, 10th Special Roadster built, believed to be the last of the sporting 1st series cars, completely restored.
£2,000,000+ / $2,900,000+ ⚒ RM
In 1933 the first of a new generation of Mercedes-Benz cars was announced. The 380 offered full independent suspension, giving unprecedented ride and handling. The car was powered by an overhead-camshaft, supercharged straight-eight engine of 3820cc. These impressive specifications, however, proved less than a match for the elaborate coachwork Mercedes-Benz owners preferred and gave disappointing performance. The 380's successor, however, the W29 160bhp 500K, was completely different. It reintroduced the 'K' (*Kompressor*) designation made famous on the SSK and SSKL. Almost as many 500Ks were built in the changeover year of 1934 (105) as in the 380's two-year run. The 500K was unashamedly luxurious, its standard equipment including two spare wheels, safety glass, electric windscreen wipers, hydraulic brakes, central lubrication, a 12-volt electrical system and a four-speed gearbox, with synchromesh on the top three gears. Approximately 342 500Ks were built, but only 29 had Roadster and Special Roadster coachwork. The first-series Special Roadster was a true sports roadster, without wind-up windows, and with a fully disappearing top and a short tapered tail. The later second-series car was heavier, less sporting, and traded the earlier car's low doors for wind-up windows. It also had a longer tail.

1938 Mercedes-Benz 540K Cabriolet A, 5401cc 8-cylinder engine, supercharger, 180bhp (supercharged), 4-speed manual gearbox, independent front suspension, Lockheed 4-wheel hydraulic drum brakes, older restoration.
£500,000+ / $725,000 ⚒ Pou

1953 Mercedes-Benz 220A Cabriolet, 2195cc 6-cylinder engine, 80bhp, 4-speed manual gearbox, 4-wheel hydraulic drum brakes, resprayed, rechromed, new black Haartz cloth top, interior wood trim refinished, new carpets.
£33,000–38,000 / $48,000–55,000 ⚒ RM

The first post-WWII Mercedes was the 170, rushed into production using what little pre-war tooling could be found. It was powered by a 38bhp, 1697cc, sidevalve four-cylinder engine. In 1951, however, Mercedes installed an overhead-camshaft six of 2195cc, giving 80bhp, in a revised chassis, the 220. This was clothed with attractive bodies from Mercedes' own coachworks, which featured luxury appointments like varnished wood and leather upholstery. Most were saloons, but almost 2,000 were given the more luxurious and attractive open bodywork.

1956 Mercedes-Benz 300SC Roadster, 2996cc 6-cylinder engine, fuel injection, 175bhp, 4-speed synchromesh gearbox, 4-wheel drum brakes, fewer than 14,000 miles from new.
£180,000–200,000 / $260,000–290,000 ⚒ RM

1930 MG M-Type Midget, 847cc 4-cylinder engine, rebodied with beetle-backed fabric coachwork, very good condition.
£7,500–9,000 / $10,900–13,000 ⚒ BRIT

1954 MG TF Midget, 1250cc 4-cylinder engine, twin SU H4 carburettors, 4-speed manual gearbox, independent front suspension, semi-elliptic leaf rear springs, left-hand drive.
£13,500–15,000
$19,500–21,750 ⚒ Pou

◀ **1959 MGA Roadster,** 1600cc 4-cylinder engine, 80bhp, 4-speed manual gearbox, front disc/rear drum brakes, chrome wire wheels, tan interior, left-hand drive, subject of body-off restoration, 'as-new' condition.
£15,000–18,000
$21,750–26,100 ⚒ RM

1913 Morris Oxford Two-Seater, engine rebuilt, correct White & Poppe carburettor, correct P & H acetylene headlamps, oil side and rear lamps, folding windscreen and hood, deep-buttoned red leather upholstery.
£9,500–11,000 / $13,750–15,950 BKS
This car, the fourth oldest on The Register of Morris Cars, was discovered in Lancashire as a rolling chassis. Although generally derelict, it was believed to have covered a low mileage. Restoration work included refabrication of chassis members, refurbishment of all mechanical parts, and the construction of coachwork that followed original designs.

1936 Packard Super Eight Dual-Cowl Sport Phaeton, 384cu. in sidevalve 8-cylinder engine, 150bhp, 3-speed synchromesh gearbox, 4-wheel vacuum-assisted mechanical brakes, accessory Twelve bumpers, twin side-mounted spares, chrome wire wheels, wind wings, spotlights, factory radio, side curtains, professionally restored over 5 years, 1 of 2 known to survive.
£190,000+ / $275,500+ RM

1959 Porsche 356A, 1582cc horizontally-opposed 4-cylinder engine, 90bhp, 4-speed manual gearbox, independent front suspension, rear swing-axles, completely restored, 1 owner, 34,000 miles from new, 'as-new' condition.
£20,000–24,000 / $29,000–34,800 RM

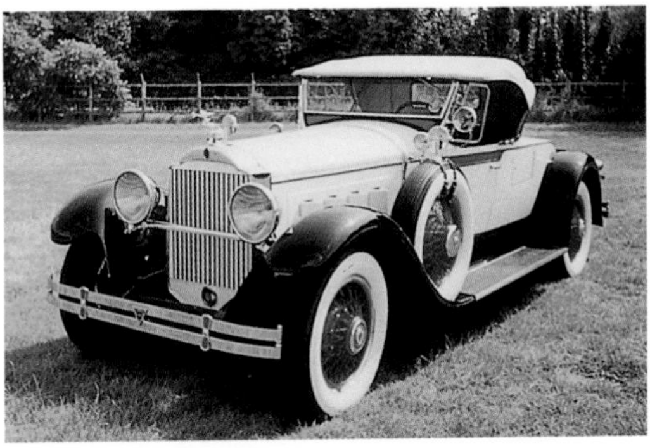

1929 Packard Model 640 Custom Eight 6th Series Roadster, 384cu.in 8-cylinder engine, 105bhp, twin side-mounted spares, lockers behind rear seats, golfer's locker doors on both sides, luggage carrier, headlights with 'tell-tale' lenses, rumble seat, interior trimmed in pleated black leather.
£60,000–70,000 / $87,000–101,500 BKS
In 1916, Packard launched the Twin Six, the world's first production 12-cylinder car which, along with the six- and eight-cylinder cars of the 1920s, put the company high on the list of the world's top manufacturers. The Packard name became synonymous with quality engineering, and the company adopted the attitude that there was no substitute for cubic inches. The unstressed engines offered a combination of smooth performance and reliability. Even in the difficult times of the late 1920s, Packard never sacrificed its ideals.

1921 Peugeot Type 161 Quadrilette Tandem Two-Seater, 668cc 4-cylinder sidevalve engine, 3-speed gearbox, shaft drive to rear wheels, quarter-elliptic leaf springing all-round, brass acetylene headlamps and oil sidelamps, 2-piece opening windscreen, folding hood, restored at a cost of over £8,500, new wings, new mahogany dash panel, blue leather upholstery, excellent condition.
£13,000–15,000 / 18,750–21,750 BKS
Peugeot's Quadrilette, introduced in 1921, followed the pre-war fashion for lightweight, economical cyclecars and was produced in significant numbers.

1968 Porsche 911S Targa, 1991cc horizontally-opposed 6-cylinder engine, 180bhp, 5-speed manual gearbox, 4-wheel disc brakes, matching numbers, completely restored.
£17,000–19,000 / $24,500–27,500 RM

1901 Renault Type D Series E Paris-Berlin, De Dion Bouton single-cylinder engine, Claudel carburettor, 3-speed gearbox.
£27,000–32,000 / $39,200–46,400 Pou

1960 Renault 4CV Jolly Resort Special, coachwork by Ghia, 747cc 4-cylinder engine, 3-speed gearbox, restored, upgraded mechanically, new wicker seats, new Everflex Surrey top, 1 of only 50 4CV Resort Specials built, of which 11 thought to survive, 16,150 miles from new.
£17,000–20,000 / $24,500–29,000 BKS
Ghia's Resort Special, or Beach Car, concept was more commonly based on the Fiat 600, and found favour as courtesy transport for patrons of luxury hotels and for use ashore after one had docked one's yacht on the Italian or French Riviera. Lacking doors, the Jolly was only practical as leisure transport, thus confirming its owner's status as someone who could afford a car 'just for fun'.

◀ **1927 Rolls-Royce Phantom I Phaeton,** major engine rebuild 1985, left-hand drive.
£40,000–45,000 / $58,000–65,250 RCC
One of the first US-built PIs, this car appears to have been modified from a Riviera Town Car, the new bodywork incorporating the original windscreen, scuttle and front doors. It is fitted with a partly opening roof, as opposed to a full convertible.

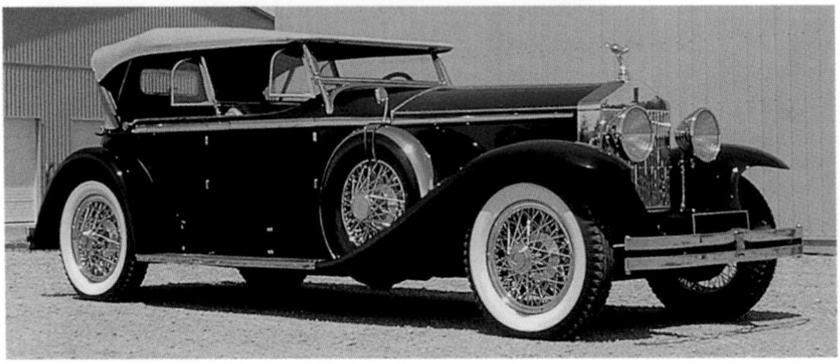

1929 Rolls-Royce Phantom I Ascot Phaeton, 7668cc overhead-valve 6-cylinder engine, 65bhp, 3-speed manual gearbox, 4-wheel drum brakes, 21in wire wheels, left-hand drive, restored, polished aluminium beltlines, biscuit interior, 1 of only 21 Ascot Phaetons built, concours condition.
£100,000–120,000 / $145,000–174,000 RM

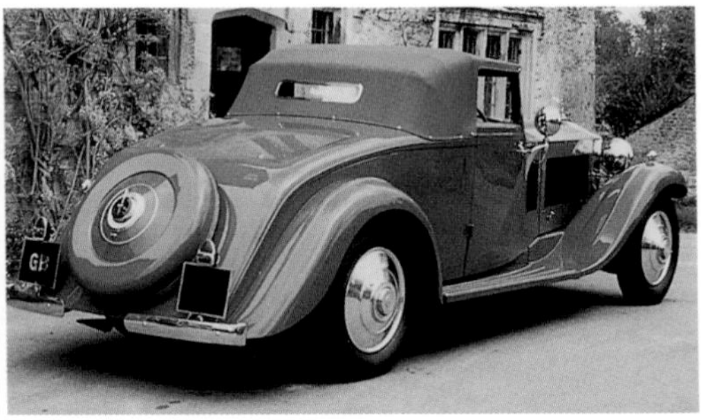

1932 Rolls-Royce Phantom II Continental Drophead Coupé, 7668cc 6-cylinder engine, 120bhp, 4-speed synchromesh gearbox, overdrive, 4-wheel semi-elliptic leaf springs, 4-wheel servo-assisted brakes, restored 1998–2000, excellent condition.
£110,000–130,000 / $159,500–188,500 RM
Sir Henry Royce submitted plans for a special Phantom II with a sports saloon body after inspecting a Riley Nine. The Rolls-Royce sales department disapproved, but Royce proceeded anyway, having designer Ivan Evernden draw up a detailed layout of the chassis and commissioning coachwork by Barker. Royce sent Evernden on a demonstration run to France and Spain. In Biarritz, the car took first place at a Concours d'Elégance, helping to generate interest in the Phantom II and the new body design. It caused further commotion when it arrived in Madrid, and interest followed the car around Europe; customers began to approach Rolls-Royce with orders. By the time Evernden returned, the sales office had already made arrangements for a brochure for the new model, to be known as the Phantom II Continental. Phantom II production spanned only six years, between 1929 and 1935. In all, 1,681 examples were produced, 281 of which were short-wheelbase Continentals.

1965 Shelby Cobra Dragonsnake, 289cu.in V8 engine, 4 Weber 48IDA carburettors, 325bhp, 4-speed manual gearbox, 4-wheel independent suspension, 4-wheel disc brakes, rack-and-pinion steering, completely restored.
£140,000–160,000 / $203,000–232,000 RM
To capitalise on the popularity of drag racing, Shelby American announced the availability of a special model, known as the Dragonsnake, which incorporated 23 different modifications to enhance its performance on the strip. The cars were available in four levels of tune: Stage I-D, 270bhp; Stage II-D, 300bhp; Stage III-D, 325bhp; and Stage IV-D, 380bhp. Stage I and II cars were equipped with conventional carburetion, while the Stage III and IV cars came with four twin-choke Weber 48IDA carburettors. This car was built to III-D specifications, minus only some special head porting from the Stage IV specification. Ultimately, only four Dragonsnakes were built, and they quickly earned a deadly reputation, turning quarter-mile elapsed times in the 11.6–11.9 second range. This car was the last Dragonsnake built.

1955 Studebaker President Speedster, 259cu.in overhead-valve V8 engine, 185bhp, automatic transmission, servo-assisted brakes, subject of body-off restoration, correct tri-colour paint scheme, correct diamond-pleated leather upholstery and engine-turned dashboard, excellent condition.
£16,000–20,000 / $23,000–29,000 RM
The 1955 Studebaker President Speedster featured advanced styling and was produced for one year only. A total of 2,215 were made.

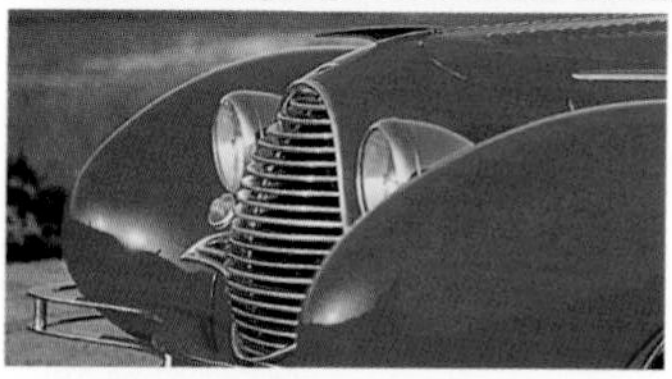

1947 Talbot-Lago T26 Cabriolet, coachwork by Figoni et Falaschi, 5.4 litre Cadillac overhead-valve V8 engine, twin carburettors, 3-speed automatic transmission, 4-wheel drum brakes, complete with original unrestored 4.5 litre 6-cylinder engine and Wilson pre-selector gearbox, tan leather interior.
£150,000–170,000 / $217,500–246,500 RM
This car's first owner was movie director George Sidney, whose credits include *Anchor's Aweigh, The Three Musketeers, Annie Get Your Gun, Show Boat, Pal Joey* and *Viva Las Vegas*.

1967 Triumph Herald Convertible, 1147cc 4-cylinder engine, 61bhp, 4-speed manual gearbox, 4-wheel independent suspension, left-hand drive, professionally restored 1988 at a cost of over £25,000, little use since, excellent condition.
£8,000–9,000 / $11,600–13,000 RM

1930 Vauxhall 20/60 Richmond Four-Door Saloon, 2916cc overhead-valve straight-6 engine, 4-speed manual gearbox, front beam axle, semi-elliptic leaf springs all-round, 4-wheel mechanical drum brakes, restored.
£10,000–12,000 / 14,500–17,500 C

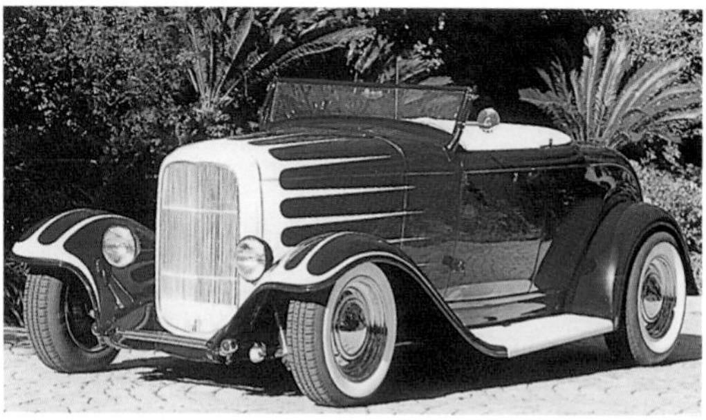

1932 Ford Roadster Hot Rod, built late 1960s, restored 1980, 350cu.in Chevrolet V8 engine, 650cfm Holley 4-barrel carburettor, polished aluminium inlet manifold, stainless-steel exhaust, twin automatic cooling fans, GM Turbo 350 automatic transmission with Hurst Indy shift kit, Camaro front disc brakes, 1957 Chevrolet rear axle and drum brakes, original 1932 Ford chassis rails, Wescott fibreglass body, Stewart Warner instruments, chrome steering column, white vinyl upholstery.
£14,000–16,000 / $20,300–23,300 RM

1989 GTD Ford GT40 Replica, 302cu.in V8 engine, 325bhp, 5-speed Renault Racing transaxle, Halibrand-style wheels, air conditioning, left-hand drive, professionally built.
£40,000–45,000 / $58,000–65,250 RM

► **c1987 Proteus Jaguar C-Type Replica,** 3.8 litre engine, Weber carburettors, overdrive gearbox, approximately 3,000 miles covered since built.
£18,000–22,000 / $26,000–32,000 BKS

1995 Predator Jaguar D-Type Replica, 3.8 litre double-overhead-camshaft 6-cylinder engine, triple Weber carburettors, dry-sump lubrication, 5-speed manual gearbox, XJ6 4-wheel independent suspension and disc brakes, steel tubing chassis, knock-off alloy wheels, fibreglass body, competition instruments, 1 of only 5 built.
£18,000–22,000 / $26,000–32,000 RM

► **1962 Jaguar E-Type Series I 3.8 Roadster,** chassis no. 850342, 342nd right-hand drive roadster built, desirable registration number, generally sound and complete.
£13,000–15,000 / $18,750–21,750 COYS

◄ **1935 Fiat Balilla 508S Two-Seater,** 995cc 4-cylinder engine, 4-speed manual gearbox, 4-wheel hydraulic drum brakes, semi-elliptic leaf springs all-round, original sports wings, British body copied in ash, engine rebuilt, complete with instruments, lights, cycle wings and bulkhead.
£9,000–10,000 / 13,000–14,500 C
'Bert' Westwood was synonymous with these Fiats, having been approached by Fiat England in late 1935, to form and captain a team of works supported private entrants, the Black Diamond Team. The team achieved success in all forms of motorsport. This Balilla was purchased as a spare car, and Westwood retained it together with his No. 1 Black Diamond Team car. Although it never received factory coachwork, it was later fitted with a body so that Westwood could use it for trials, but subsequently this was broken up.

1967 Lamborghini 400GT 2+2, converted under licence by Hooper to right-hand drive, finished in red, black leather upholstery, 1 of only 9 right-hand drive models built.
£19,000–22,500 / $27,500–34,000 COYS
It was at the 1966 Geneva Salon that the Lamborghini 350GT was replaced by the 400GT. The styling was almost identical, but most body panels were in steel, although the bonnet and boot lid remained in alloy. The roof line was higher to accommodate the occasional rear sets, and there were twin, rather than single, headlamps. The V12 engine, now mated to Lamborghini's own five-speed gearbox, boasted 3929cc against the 350GT's 3464cc, while power was up from 280bhp to 320bhp, sufficient to propel the distinctive Italian to 60mph in just 7.5 seconds, and on to a 156mph maximum. The 400GT 2+2 was the the most successful of the 350/400 line, 250 examples being sold.

1969 Lamborghini Miura S, completely restored late 1990s, finished in original white, blue cloth and leather upholstery.
£55,000–65,000 / $80,000–95,000 COYS
The S version of the Miura appeared in 1968 as part of the evolution and improvement of the car. The letter stood for 'Sprinto' (or 'tuned'), and such versions boasted 370bhp, revised tyres, electric windows and a stiffer chassis. Only 140 of these cars were built before the SV version was introduced at the 1971 Geneva Salon; the SV acquired fatter rear wheel arches and an extra 200kg, and lost much of its predecessor's sharpness and purity.

Lamborghini Fact

The Miura was named after a Spanish fighting bull. The charging bull insignia was taken from Ferruccio Lamborghini's star sign, Taurus.

1967 Lamborghini 400GT 2+2, coachwork by Touring, 4 litre V12 engine, 320bhp, finished in original silver, black leather upholstery, 38,000km from new, excellent unrestored condition.
£40,000–45,000 / $58,000–65,250 BKS

A scratchbuilt 1/10-scale model of a 1967 Lamborghini Espada by Michel Conti, opening bonnet and doors, extensive chrome and aluminium brightwork, on a wooden plinth with brass plaque and Michel Conti signature.
£4,250–4,750 / $6,250–6,900 BKS

Lamborghini Miura (1966–72)

Engine: Transverse-mounted V12, 3929cc, double overhead camshafts, four triple-choke Weber carburettors.
Power output: 350–385bhp.
Transmission: Five-speed manual.
0–60mph: 6–6.7 seconds.
Maximum speed: 165–175+mph.
Brakes: Four-wheel ventilated discs.
Production: 763 (some say 764).

1972 Lamborghini Miura P400SV, coachwork by Bertone, 'split-sump' engine, ZF limited-slip differential, completely restored, engine and running gear rebuilt, uprated ignition system, finished in original metallic black with silver sill panels and wheels, air conditioning, black leather interior, many rare factory options, 1,500 miles covered since restoration, 100th Miura constructed, concours winner, excellent condition.
£115,000–130,000 / $166,750–188,500 BKS
Approximately 150 SVs had been made when Miura production ceased in 1972.

LAMBORGHINI Model	ENGINE cc/cyl	DATES	CONDITION 1	2	3
350 GT fhc	3500/12	1964–67	£55,000	£45,000	£25,000
400 GT	4000/12	1966–68	£45,000+	£40,000	£25,000
Miura LP400	4000/12	1966–69	£60,000	£50,000	£30,000
Miura S	4000/12	1969–71	£75,000	£60,000+	£40,000
Miura SV	4000/12	1971–72	£90,000+	£75,000	£60,000
Espada	4000/12	1969–78	£12,000	£10,000	£7,000
Jarama	4000/12	1970–78	£15,000	£13,000	£11,000
Urraco	2500/8	1972–76	£12,000	£10,000	£8,000
Countach	4000/12	1974–82	£60,000+	£40,000	£30,000

Countach limited editions are sought after as well as Miura SV.

1972 Lamborghini Urraco, 2463cc V8 engine, finished in metallic grey, tan interior trim.
£9,500–11,000 / $13,800–16,000 ⚒ BRIT

1972 Lamborghini Urraco P250 Coupé, coachwork by Bertone, 2.5 litre overhead-camshaft transverse-mounted V8 engine, finished in red.
£8,000–10,000 / $11,600–14,500 ⚒ H&H

1980 Lamborghini Countach S, coachwork by Bertone, 4 litre engine, finished in black, white leather interior, 2 owners and 1,428km from new, 'as-new' condition.
£40,000–45,000 / $58,000–65,250 ⚒ BKS

1988 Lamborghini LM 002, 5167cc V12 engine, 420bhp, 5-speed ZF manual gearbox, ventilated disc front brakes, rear drum brakes, 4-wheel independent suspension.
£25,000–30,000 / $36,250–43,500 ⚒ Pou

Lanchester

1935 Lanchester 11 Saloon, 1444cc, pre-selector gearbox, fluid flywheel, dry stored from 1972, restored, original leather seats.
£4,250–5,250 / $6,200–7,600 ⚒ CGC

Dealer prices

Miller's guide prices for dealer cars take into account the value of any guarantees or warranties that may be included in the purchase. Dealers must also observe additional statutory consumer regulations, which do not apply to private sellers. This is factored into our dealer guide prices. Dealer cars are identified by the ⊞ icon; full details of the dealer can be found on page 330.

1935 Lanchester E18, 2504cc 6-cylinder engine, aluminium bodywork, restored over 6 years, stainless-steel exhaust system, new front and rear shock absorbers, recored radiator, rewired, resprayed, new marine-ply floor, original red leather interior, new headlining, good mechanical condition.
£9,500–11,000 / $13,750–16,000 ⚒ BRIT

The Lanchester brothers were innovative pioneers who built their first motor car in 1895. Quality was always the hallmark of Lanchester, the 40hp model of the 1920s being one of the finest cars of its time and frequently the favoured transport of princes and maharajahs. During 1931, the company was acquired by BSA, which also owned Daimler, and throughout the 1930s there were many similarities between the Daimler and Lanchester ranges. A model that enjoyed particular success was the 18, which was powered by a 2.5 litre, seven-bearing engine coupled to a fluid flywheel transmission, which would become a standard feature of all subsequent models. The majority wore coachwork of Daimler manufacture, although a small number received special bodies from a variety of independent coachbuilders.

LANCHESTER Model	ENGINE cc/cyl	DATES	CONDITION 1	2	3
LD10	1287/4	1946–49	£2,500	£1,500	£750
LD10 (Barker bodies)	1287/4	1950–51	£2,800	£1,500	£700

Lancia

Although Lancia never consistently pursued competition glory with the commitment of Maserati, Alfa Romeo and later Ferrari, the character of the marque has always been essentially sporting. Indeed, before setting up his own company late in 1906, Vincenzo Lancia had pursued a racing career from 1900, while working for Fiat. The beginnings of Lancia & Cie were hardly auspicious, as the new company's first automobile was destroyed by fire, but after that hiccough Lancia's cars soon earned a reputation for inspired innovation and technical excellence, often married to stunning shapes. The Lambda of 1922 was tremendously advanced, with a monocoque structure, independent front suspension and a compact, narrow V4 engine with overhead camshaft. At the lower end of the market, in the late 1930s, the Aprilia was a little jewel. In the 1950s, Lancia made some able and beautiful machines, but could never offer a line-up that was comprehensive enough to compete with Alfa Romeo and Fiat. By 1969, long after Lancia family interest in the company had ceased, Fiat had taken control. Shortly after, in 1973, the awesome Lancia Stratos was born and blazed a trail on the international rally circuit.

1955 Lancia Aurelia B20GT 4th Series, coachwork by Pinin Farina, right-hand drive, completely restored 1997, original Nardi modified engine rebuilt, Nardi inlet manifold and airbox, twin Weber carburettors, floor-mounted Nardi gear-change, bare-metal respray in metallic bronze, interior retrimmed in light fawn cloth and correct beige vinyl, 1 of the last 4th Series cars built, excellent condition.
£23,000–27,000 / $33,300–39,000 ⚒ BKS
Lancia's Aurelia, the first car ever to employ a V6 engine, was launched at the 1950 Turin show. The basic saloon was joined the following year by the Pinin Farina-styled B20 Coupé, a fastback 2+2 GT which, with its combination of sports car performance and saloon car practicality, can be said to have introduced the Gran Turismo concept to the world. Lancia had announced an enlarged engine for the 1951 Aurelia saloon, and the B20 made use of this 1991cc unit. Introduced in 1953, the 3rd, and subsequent series, cars were powered by a 2451cc version of the pushrod V6, then in 1954 the original semi-trailing-arm rear suspension was replaced by a De Dion axle. Production ended with the 6th Series in 1958, by which time only 3,871 B20s had been made.

1958 Lancia Aurelia B20GT. coachwork by Pininfarina, 2506cc, right-hand drive, engine rebuilt, chassis and steering overhauled, finished in dark blue, tan interior, 72,000 miles from new.
£17,000–20,000 / $24,650–29,000 ⚒ H&H

1960 Lancia Appia GTE, coachwork by Zagato, 1100cc double-overhead-camshaft V4 engine recently rebuilt, 4-speed manual gearbox, sliding-pillar front suspension.
£14,000–17,000 / $20,300–24,650 ⚒ RM
Built on a 97.6in wheelbase and weighing just 1,800lb, thanks to extensive use of aluminium panels, the Appia had a narrow-angle V4 engine with two camshafts operating inclined valves via pushrods and rocker arms. Eventually it would produce more than 50bhp. Lancia Appias were constructed in a variety of body styles, but the most attractive designs came from Zagato.

Restored values

The cost of a professional restoration will have an influence on, but no direct relation to, a car's market value. A restored car can have a market value lower than the cost of its restoration.

LANCIA Model	ENGINE cc/cyl	DATES	CONDITION 1	2	3
Theta	4940/4	1913–19	£24,000	£16,500	£8,000
Kappa	4940/4	1919–22	£24,000	£16,000	£8,000
Dikappa	4940/4	1921–22	£24,000	£16,000	£8,000
Trikappa	4590/4	1922–26	£25,000	£18,000	£10,000
Lambda	2120/4	1923–28	£40,000	£20,000	£12,000
Dilambda	3960/8	1928–32	£35,000	£16,000	£10,000
Astura	2604/8	1931–39	£30,000	£20,000	£10,000
Artena	1925/4	1931–36	£9,000	£5,000	£2,000
Augusta	1196/4	1933–36	£9,000	£4,000	£2,000
Aprilia 238	1352/4	1937–39	£10,000	£5,000	£3,000

Coachbuilt bodywork is more desirable and can increase prices.

1962 Lancia Flaminia Convertible, coachwork by Touring, 2.5 litre, left-hand drive, resprayed in white, black hood, new red leather upholstery, fewer than 60,000km from new, good condition.
£13,000–15,500 / $18,850–22,600 ⚒ BKS

Lancia's Pininfarina-styled Flaminia saloon debuted at the 1956 Turin show. The Aurelia's replacement, the luxurious Flaminia retained its predecessor's mechanical layout, although the form of unitary construction was changed, and Lancia's traditional sliding-pillar independent front suspension gave way to a more modern double-wishbone-and-coil-spring arrangement. Aurelia carry-overs were the 60-degree, 2458cc, overhead-valve V6 engine and De Dion rear transaxle with inboard brakes. The short-wheelbase Coupé appeared in 1958, followed by the Touring-styled GT and GTL (2+2) coupés, and the Convertible. The latter trio had a further shortened wheelbase shared with the Sport and Super Sport models, and all featured disc brakes and increased power. This was boosted from 119 to 140bhp in 1961, giving the sportier Flaminias a top speed of over 190km/h.

1963 Lancia Flaminia Sport, coachwork by Zagato, 2458cc V6 engine, triple Weber carburettors, 140bhp, 4-speed manual gearbox, independent front suspension, De Dion rear suspension, 4-wheel disc brakes, professionally restored.
£26,000–30,000 / $37,700–43,500 ⚒ Pou

1964 Lancia Flavia Convertible, coachwork by Vignale, 1800cc flat-4 engine, front-wheel drive, 4-wheel disc brakes, factory hardtop, finished in white, oxblood interior, in need of restoration, rust to body.
£1,000–1,200 / $1,500–1,750 ⚒ COYS

1965 Lancia Flavia Coupé, coachwork by Zagato, 1.8 litre flat-4 engine, front-wheel drive, 4-wheel disc brakes, finished in green-grey, light blue interior, good original condition.
£5,000–6,000 / $7,250–8,700 ⚒ BKS

LANCIA Model	ENGINE cc/cyl	DATES	CONDITION 1	2	3
Aprilia 438	1486/4	1939–50	£11,000	£6,000	£3,000
Ardea	903/4	1939–53	£10,000	£5,000	£3,000
Aurelia B10	1754/6	1950–53	£9,000	£6,000	£3,000
Aurelia B15–20–22	1991/6	1951–53	£15,000+	£10,000	£8,000
Aurelia B24–B24 Spyder	2451/6	1955–58	£40,000+	£17,000	£12,000
Aurelia GT	2451/6	1953–59	£18,000+	£11,000	£9,000
Appia C10–C105	1090/4	1953–62	£10,000	£5,000	£2,000
Aurelia Ser II/IV	2266/6	1954–59	£11,000	£6,000	£4,000
Flaminia Zagato	2458/6	1957–63	£18,000+	£10,000	£7,000
Flaminia	2458/6	1957–63	£18,000	£10,000	£5,000
Flavia 1500	1500/4	1960–75	£6,000	£4,000	£2,000
Fulvia	1091/4	1963–70	£3,000	£2,000	£1,000
Fulvia S	1216/4	1964–70	£5,000	£4,000	£1,500
Fulvia 1.3	1298/4	1967–75	£6,000	£4,000	£2,000
Stratos	2418/6	1969–71	£45,000+	£20,000+	£10,000
Flavia 2000	1991/4	1969–75	£3,000	£2,000	£1,000
Fulvia HF/1.6	1584/4	1969–75	£9,000	£5,000	£2,000
Beta HPE	1585/4	1976–82	£3,000	£1,500	£500
Beta Spyder	1995/4	1977–82	£4,000	£1,500	£800
Monte Carlo	1995/4	1976–81	£6,000	£3,000	£1,000
Gamma Coupé	2484/4	1977–84	£2,500	£1,500	£500
Gamma Berlina	2484/4	1977–84	£2,500	£1,200	£300

Competition history and convertible coachwork could cause prices to vary.

1968 Lancia Fulvia Rallye 1.3 Coupé, 1298cc overhead-camshaft V4 engine, 85bhp, front-wheel drive, independent front suspension by double wishbones, 4-wheel disc brakes, finished in metallic light blue, red leather interior, very good condition.
£3,250–4,000 / $4,650–5,800 BKS

Miller's Starter Marque

- **Starter Lancias:** *Fulvia, Beta Coupé and Spyder; Beta HPE; Monte Carlo.*
- Betas and Monte Carlos all rate as highly affordable classics, drivers' cars with interesting engineering, but flawed by a sadly deserved reputation for rusting. The rule of thumb is to buy the best you can, usually a later model if you can find one, and one that's as complete as possible. In some cases, trim and fittings are infuriatingly difficult to track down. Body panels can also be pricey.
- The whole point of buying any Lancia is the styling and performance, and if it's a Beta you're after, the best bets are the two-door coupé, Spyder and HPE – that's the high-performance estate. The four-door saloon has the same Lancia virtues, but it just doesn't look sporting.
- One of the chief virtues is that Fiat-derived double-overhead-camshaft engine, which proved so successful in the Fiat 124. Over the model's lifetime, customers were offered a choice that ran from 1300 to 2000cc, and all of them, even when inserted in the humblest saloon, were good for a genuine 100+mph.
- Then there's the Beta Monte Carlo. A separate car really from the rest of the Beta family, it was an automotive may-be, so right in concept, sadly lacking in execution. The idea was pure Fiat, a mid-engined up-size of the X1/9. In fact, it was even going to be called the X1/20.
- A chunky, tough-looking car with plenty of attitude, the Beta Monte Carlo looked faster than it was, with a top speed of only 120mph or so. The first series cars also had servo-assisted brakes, but only on the front, and that spelled heart-stopping front lock-up in the wet. The Monte Carlo was suspended from 1978, but came back in 1980 as a revised and improved model with better braking. And it's these models that fetch a premium. The trouble is there just aren't many around – some say as few as 200 in the UK — and that means there isn't much choice. Even so, the Monte Carlo does rate highly as an affordable, exclusive and exotically engineered mid-engined sports car.
- From an earlier era, there's the Fulvia, and all but the saloon are as sharp as any Italian suit. Sharpest of all these V4-engined cars is the Zagato coupé. Some think it ugly, but it's definitely striking – and correspondingly pricey. Best mid-price compromise is probably the second-series 1.3 litre Fulvia coupé from 1970 to 1976, or, if you've got the money, the uprated 1.6HF. The Fulvia has a strong following though, because Fulvias simply spell four-wheeled fun in big dollops.

1980 Lancia Beta Spyder Coupé, finished in metallic blue, black interior, rust-free.
£2,800–3,200 / $4,000–4,650 UMC

Cross Reference
See Colour Review (page 145)

1982 Lancia Monte Carlo Series 2, 54,000 miles from new, finished in bright red, black leather interior, completely restored.
£5,000–6,000 / $7,250–8,700 TIHO

◄ **1982 Lancia Monte Carlo Coupé,** coachwork by Pininfarina, engine balanced and uprated with twin Weber carburettors, gas-flowed head, Aquila manifold, high-lift camshafts, Primaflow exhaust and lightened flywheel, lowered suspension, uprated brakes, Compomotive three-piece alloy wheels, quad-headlamp conversion, removable roof panel, finished in gold, brown cloth interior, 46,000 miles from new.
£3,800–4,400 / $5,500–6,250 BKS
Introduced in 1976, the stylish Monte Carlo coupé was a mid-engined road car from the drawing boards of Pininfarina. It adopted an uprated version of the engine used in the more sedate Beta, the 1995cc twin-cam four being mounted transversely behind the seats and developing 120bhp at 6,000rpm.

1974 Lancia Stratos, coachwork by Bertone, finished in pistachio green, beige suede interior, first registered 1998, 1,071km from new, original.
£65,000–72,000 / $94,250–103,500 BKS
In 1973, the FIA instituted a World Rally Championship for manufacturers, and the Stratos was the first car to be designed specifically for rallying. For homologation purposes, at least 400 examples had to be built. It was based on a 1970 Bertone styling exercise on a Lancia Fulvia, which was snapped up by Lancia's competition manager, Cesare Fiorio. A prototype using Lancia running gear was built, but the chassis showed so much potential that a 2.4 litre Ferrari Dino engine and five-speed gearbox were substituted. The chassis had all-independent suspension, while the body was built from fibreglass. In production form, the Stratos had a top speed of 143 mph and could sprint to 60mph in 6.8 seconds – better figures than the Ferrari Dino that had donated the running gear. This performance, allied with superb handling and brakes, elevated the Stratos into the supercar category. That image was reinforced when Lancia took a hat-trick of World Rally Championships from 1974 to 1976.

1976 Lancia Stratos, coachwork by Bertone, 2.4 litre Ferrari Dino V6 engine, 190bhp, adjustable 4-wheel independent suspension, 4-wheel disc brakes, finished in bright orange, black Alcantara interior, fewer than 10,000km from new.
£37,000–42,000 / $53,650–61,000 BKS

1992 Lancia HF Integrale Martini 5, finished in white with Martini stripes, black Alcantara interior, fewer than 5,000km from new, excellent condition.
£17,500–21,000 / $25,400–30,500 BKS
During its production life, the four-wheel-drive Integrale was constantly uprated. The HF offered 165bhp from its 2 litre, turbocharged 'eight-valve' engine, while the last regular '16-valve' cars gave 215bhp. Lancia also made a special run of 400 numbered examples boasting 240bhp to commemorate its fifth rally championship – the Martini 5. Special features of these expensive cars included ABS braking, an alarm, 15in alloy wheels, red seat belts, air conditioning, Michelin MXX tyres, red valve covers, a matt black roof spoiler and Recaro sports seats.

◄ **1989 Lancia Delta HF Integrale,** 2 litre engine uprated with increased turbo boost and engine management chip, correct alloy wheels, converted to right-hand drive, power-assisted steering, sunroof, electric windows, central locking, Recaro seats, good condition.
£4,000–5,000 / $5,800–7,250 CGC

Land Rover

1955 Land Rover Series 1, recently refurbished at a cost of c£2,500, full canvas tilt, period PTO, finished in green, matching interior, formerly owned by Rowan Atkinson.
£4,000–4,500 / $5,800–6,500 ⚒ BKS

A known continuous history can add value to and enhance the enjoyment of a car.

1978 Land Rover Series III County 88, restored and upgraded at a cost of over £18,000, reconditioned 90 Series 2.5 litre petrol engine, SU carburettor, sports exhaust system, new parabolic leaf springs, new shock absorbers and bushes, rebuilt front and rear axles, brakes refurbished, new 16in modular wheels, new heavy-duty galvanised chassis, finished in metallic dark green, new luxury interior, soundproofing.
£5,000–6,000 / $7,250–8,500 ⚒ BKS

LAND ROVER Model	ENGINE cc/cyl	DATES	CONDITION 1	2	3
Ser 1	1595/4	1948–51	£6,000	£3,000	£1,500
Ser 1	1995/4	1951–53	£4,500	£2,500	£1,000
Ser 1	1995/4	1953–58	£4,000	£2,000	£500
Ser 1	1995/4	1953–58	£3,000	£1,800	£800
Ser 2	1995/4	1958–59	£2,000	£950	£500
Ser 2	1995/4	1958–59	£2,800	£1,200	£500
Ser 2	2286/4	1959–71	£2,000	£950	£500
Ser 2	2286/4	1959–71	£2,500	£1,200	£500

Series 1 Land Rovers are very sought after.

La Salle

1940 La Salle Series 52 Convertible, 322cu.in. sidevalve V8 engine, 3-speed manual gearbox, 4-wheel drum brakes, restored at a cost of £69,000, 450 miles covered since, finished in maroon, matching leather interior, all mechanical and electrical components in excellent condition, 1 of only 425 Series 52 convertible coupés built in 1940.
£50,000–55,000 / $72,500–79,750 ⚒ RM
Introduced in 1927 as a junior companion to the upmarket Cadillac marque, La Salle became an almost immediate sales success. Much of the popularity La Salle enjoyed was a result of the design talents of Harley Earl. La Salle was his first project at GM, and during the 14-year life of the marque, Earl kept a close personal eye on his 'baby'. A survivor of the 1930s Depression, La Salle emerged with dynamic styling, helping to bolster Cadillac sales, the division responsible for producing and marketing the brand.

Lea-Francis

In 1895, Richard Henry Lea and Graham Ingoldsby Francis formed a partnership to make bicycles. In 1904, they produced a car design, but it was 1920 before production really got going. During the vintage era, they built some fine small sports cars. After financial setbacks, a new company began producing a range of more modern sporting cars in 1937, and these provided the basis of machines built until 1952. A revival was attempted in 1960 with the unhappy-looking Lynx, but only three prototypes were made.

Restored values

The cost of a professional restoration will have an influence on, but no direct relation to, a car's market value. A restored car can have a market value lower than the cost of its restoration.

◄ **1949 Lea-Francis 14hp Saloon,** 1.8 litre double-overhead-camshaft engine, light alloy coachwork, finished in maroon, red leather interior, original.
£5,000–6,000 / $7,250–8,700 ⊞ GrM

LEA-FRANCIS Model	ENGINE cc/cyl	DATES	CONDITION 1	2	3
12HP	1944/4	1923–24	£10,000	£5,000	£3,000
14HP	2297/4	1923–24	£10,000	£5,000	£3,000
9HP	1074/4	1923–24	£7,000	£4,000	£2,000
10HP	1247/4	1947–54	£10,000	£5,500	£3,000
12HP	1496/4	1926–34	£12,000	£6,000	£4,000
Various 6-cylinder models	1696/6	1927–29	£13,500	£9,500	£5,000
Various 6-cylinder models	1991/6	1928–36	£10,500	£8,750	£5,000
14HP	1767/4	1946–54	£10,000	£6,000	£4,000
1.5 Litre	1499/4	1949–51	£11,000	£6,000	£3,000
2.5 Litre	2496/4	1950–52	£14,000	£8,000	£4,000

Leblond

◄ **1955 Leblond Speciale,** 1971cc 6-cylinder BMW engine, 2 Solex carburettors, 4-speed BMW 327 gearbox, independent front suspension, Bugatti 57 SC hydraulic drum brakes, Rudge wire wheels, tubular-steel chassis, steel coupé bodywork, only example produced.
£10,000–12,000
$14,500–17,400 ⚒ Pou

Le Zebre

◄ **c1912 Le Zebre 5hp Series 13 Two-Seater,** original chassis and running gear, period-style replica coachwork, period accessories, finished in white.
£6,000–7,000 / $8,700–10,200 ⚒ BKS
Le Zebre was just one of the prolific number of early minor French motor car manufacturers. It began production in 1909, being comparatively late on the scene. The diminutive 5hp model was powered by a 600cc vertical single-cylinder engine. Early examples had a two-speed gearbox, but by 1912 a three-speed box was standard, with quadrant change, metal disc clutch and bevel final drive. The car had a 6ft-wheelbase chassis.

Lincoln

The name says it all. When Henry Leland walked out of Cadillac in 1917, he named his new company after the president he had first voted for in 1864. The first Lincolns appeared in 1920, and while Leland was thoroughly committed to engineering excellence, initially the cars were rather dowdy and formal. In 1922, Ford stepped in and bought the company, which produced a car that was at the other end of the motoring spectrum from its own Model T and cost more than ten times as much. Under Ford's ownership, the Lincoln brand grew to fulfill its flagship aspirations, and presidential patronage included Coolidge, Roosevelt, Truman and the tragic John F. Kennedy, whose life ended in the back of one.

1940 Lincoln Continental Convertible, 292cu.in sidevalve V12 engine, 3-speed manual gearbox, 4-wheel hydraulic drum brakes, correct gravel guard, metal spare tyre cover, red leather interior, 1 of only 350 convertibles built in 1940.
£70,000–80,000 / $101,500–116,000 ⚒ RM
Of all his accomplishments, perhaps Edsel Ford's greatest automotive legacy is the first-series Lincoln Continental. Based on the streamlined Lincoln Zephyr, the car's design was the work of E. T. 'Bob' Gregorie, who received from Edsel Ford only the simple brief that he wanted a 'special convertible coupé that was long, low and rakish'. Amazingly, Gregorie had the basic concept of the car roughed out in less than an hour, and was given the go-ahead by Edsel shortly thereafter. Oddly, the trademark continental spare wheel arrangement was not part of the original design, but was born of necessity. The attractive, squared-off short boot of the 'special convertible coupé', as it was then known, originally contained the spare, but this restricted luggage space. Rather than revamp the body, and to keep the project on schedule, Gregorie and Ford decided to mount the spare on the outside. It was only when the car was about to go into production that Edsel Ford named it 'Continental'. This car's first owner was the legendary baseball player Babe Ruth, who was given it on 29 April, 1940 by Yankees baseball club president Joe McCarthy. A small plaque was affixed to the dashboard stating that this Lincoln was 'Presented to George Herman "Babe Ruth" Home Run King, New York Yankees, April 29, 1940.'

1941 Lincoln Continental Convertible, 292cu.in sidevalve V12 engine, 130bhp, 3-speed manual gearbox, overdrive, 4-wheel hydraulic drum brakes, completely restored, engine rebuilt, hot-air heater, working original AM radio, 46,500 miles from new, 1 of only 400 produced in 1941.
£30,000–35,000 / $43,500–50,750 ⚒ RM

LINCOLN Model	ENGINE cu. in/cyl	DATES	CONDITION 1	2	3
Première Coupé	368/8	1956–57	£6,000	£4,000	£2,000
Première Convertible	368/8	1956–57	£14,000	£8,000	£5,000
Continental Mk II	368/8	1956–57	£10,000	£6,000	£4,000
Continental 2-door	430/8	1958–60	£6,000	£4,000	£2,000
Continental Convertible	430/8	1958–60	£18,000+	£10,000+	£7,000+

1948 Lincoln Continental Convertible, 292cu.in. sidevalve V12 engine, 130bhp, 3-speed gearbox, servo-assisted 4-wheel hydraulic drum brakes, power top, power windows, older restoration, resprayed in white, dark red leather interior.
£16,000–19,000 / $23,200–27,500 RM
The 1948 Continental was the last of the classic Continentals, and the final model to offer the much-loved V12 engine.

Lincoln Continental (1961–64)

UK price when new: £4,247 15s 5d.
Engine: Overhead-valve cast-iron-block V8, 7050cc.
Power output: 300–320bhp @ 4,100rpm.
Transmission: Three-speed automatic.
Brakes: Self-adjusting power-assisted drums.
Maximum speed: 115mph.
The American concept of the 'Continental' was the idea of Henry Ford's son, Edsel, who, upon his return from a 1938 trip to Europe, commissioned a one-off custom design that would be 'strictly continental'. Such was the response that the stunning Continental model went into production; the theme was revisited in 1956, then refreshed with the 1961 Lincoln Continental. European critics may think that 'Continental' is merely a description of the turning circle of this near 18-footer, but to American eyes its restrained styling was the last word in sophistication and elegance. And in a way, they were right, for at least compared with the fins and dripping chrome of the drive-in diner-society Cadillacs of the time, the Lincoln has all the café-society class of Cary Grant. It was also substantially more expensive than a Cadillac, and therefore more exclusive. Yet it was also considerably cheaper than a Regency-wardrobe Rolls-Royce and came as standard with a lot that the cars from Crewe didn't offer, including more electrical appliances than British Home Stores. Additionally, it was built to exacting standards, with every engine tested on a dynamometer at 3,500rpm – equivalent to 98mph – for three hours, then stripped and rebuilt; each car was also individually road tested, then subjected to over 200 pre-delivery checks.
Clouseau's Continental: Comic actor Peter Sellers briefly owned a Lincoln Continental saloon from 1963 to 1964. With just 36,000 miles on the clock, it was sold at auction in 1996 for a knock-down £7,600.

Locomobile

1899 Locomobile Type 2 3½hp Spindle-Seat Runabout, 2-cylinder double-acting steam engine with slide valves operated by Stephenson's link motion, chain final drive, contracting brakes on open differential, central-tiller steering, older restoration, VCC dated, partially dismantled, engine rebuilt, in need of completing.
£24,000–27,000 / $34,800–39,000 BKS
The Locomobile Company was formed in 1899, when A.L. Barber and J.B. Walker purchased the rights to manufacture a steam car design from the Stanley Brothers. The Barber/Walker partnership was short-lived, but Barber continued the Locomobile business, building his first car in 1899.

1925 Locomobile Junior 8 66hp Tourer, 8-cylinder engine, 3-speed gearbox, left-hand drive, original mechanical specification in all major respects, coachwork original, hood recovered, resprayed in green and black, original black leather interior, 3 owners and 80,000km from new.
£18,000–22,000 / $26,000–32,000 BKS
William C. Durant put Locomobile on to a stable financial footing in the 1920s, his policy being to establish the marque as a flagship among the clutch of companies that he had acquired. One of the early products following the Durant take-over was the overhead-valve Junior 8, which was developed into the Model 8-70 and remained in production until 1928, the company finally submitting in 1929 following The Wall Street Crash.

Lotus

From the humblest beginnings – an Austin 7-based trials special created in a north London lock-up – Colin Chapman's Lotus has collected a remarkable haul of motor-racing trophies and produced a string of road cars that, at their very least, were always innovative and sometimes quite brilliant. The Lotus Super 7 lives on today as the Caterham. As for the current Elise, it is one of the few modern sports cars that has broken free from the blight of today's obsession with retro-styling and, through its fresh and progressive thinking, is very much a car in the spirit of Colin Chapman.

1954 Lotus 6, 1172cc, completely restored, Aquaplane aluminium cylinder head, 4-branch exhaust, twin SU carburettors, original Bellamy wheels, finished in blue and polished aluminium, original instruments, aluminium competition steering wheel, brown leather interior.
£13,000–14,500 / $18,850–20,300 ⚒ H&H
In 1952, Colin Chapman formed Lotus with Michael Allen, the first model in regular production being the 6. It was offered in kit form with a multi-tubular frame, stressed aluminium panels, coil-spring suspension and Ford running gear.

1972 Lotus 7 Series 4, spaceframe chassis, fibreglass body, finished in British racing green, good condition.
£2,500–3,000 / $3,600–4,300 ⚒ COYS
The 7 was a no-frills, pared-to-the-bone sports car that offered staggering performance and handling. With a lightweight tubular spaceframe, alloy body panels and alloy or fibreglass mudguards, so successful was the car on the race tracks that it was banned from racing. The slogan 'Lotus 7 – too fast to race' was adopted by its enthusiastic followers.

1965 Lotus Super 7, 1500cc, twin 45DCOE carburettors, fully race prepared, finished in green, black interior.
£18,000–22,000 / $26,000–32,000 ⊞ HCL

Cross Reference
See Colour Review (page 147)

1959 Lotus Elite, rebuilt 1981, ZF gearbox, Le Mans headlamps, finished in pale blue, black and grey leather upholstery, hardly used since restoration.
£18,000–21,000 / $26,000–30,500 ⚒ BKS
With the Mk14 of 1959, better known as the Elite, Colin Chapman demonstrated that his skill as a racing-car designer and constructor could just as easily be applied to production road cars. The Elite was nevertheless conceived with competition in mind, as Chapman had his sights set on class wins at Le Mans and in the Monte Carlo Rally.

Lotus Elite (1957–63)

Production: 988 approximately.
Body style: Two-door, two-seater sports coupé.
Construction: Fibreglass monocoque.
Engine: Coventry Climax overhead-camshaft four-cylinder, 1216cc.
Power output: 75–105bhp @ 6,100–6,800rpm.
Transmission: Four-speed MG or ZF manual gearbox.
Suspension: Independent all-round by wishbones and coil springs at front, and MacPherson-type 'Chapman struts' at rear.
Brakes: Discs all-round (inboard at rear).
Maximum speed: 118mph.
0–60mph: 11.1 seconds.
Average fuel consumption: 35mpg.

If ever a car was a marque landmark, this is it. The Elite was the first Lotus designed for road use rather than out-and-out racing, paving the way for a string of stunning sports and GT cars that were always innovative. But the first Elite was much more than that. Its all-fibreglass construction – chassis as well as body – was a bold departure which, coupled with many other unique ideas, marked the Elite as truly exceptional, and all the more so considering the small-scale operation that created it. What's more, its Lotus race-breeding gave it phenomenal handling. When combined with an unparallelled power-to-weight ratio, this brought an almost unbroken run of racing successes. It also happens to be one of the prettiest cars of its era.

Leslie Cresswell, cut-away drawing of a 1960 Lotus Elite, applied *Motor* copyright label, pen and ink with grey wash highlighted with white, dated on the reverse '22 June 1960', signed, slight rub marks, 29 x 21in (73.5 x 53.5cm).
£550–650 / $800–950 ⚒ BKS

1967 Lotus Elan S3, finished in British racing green, well maintained.
£6,000–7,000 / $8,700–10,200 ⚒ BARO

Miller's is a price GUIDE not a price LIST

◄ **1971 Lotus Elan S4,** rebuilt Sprint engine, 130bhp, finished in Sprint colours of red, white and gold, excellent condition.
£10,000–12,000 / $14,500–17,400 ⊞ WbC

1971 Lotus Elan, 1558cc double-overhead-camshaft 4-cylinder engine, twin Weber 40DCE carburettors, 105bhp, close-ratio gearbox, 4-wheel independent suspension, backbone chassis, fibreglass body, left-hand drive, finished in yellow over white, good condition.
£6,000–7,000 / $8,700–10,200 ⚒ COYS

1968 Lotus Elan +2, finished in blue, black interior, 3 owners and 27,000 miles from new, original, good condition.
£3,500–4,000 / $5,000–6,000 ⚒ BKS
Launched in 1966 and based on the successful Elan, the +2 retained the former's independently suspended backbone chassis, but came with a wheelbase lengthened by 12in to accommodate two occasional rear seats. Aimed at the sports car enthusiast with a young family, the Elan +2 represented a move upmarket by Lotus. It featured an improved interior with a walnut-veneered dashboard, electric windows, radio and alarm as standard. The 1558cc twin-cam engine was that of the Elan SE, and with 118bhp on tap, the +2 was good for nearly 120mph.

Lotus Elan (1962–73)

Production: 12,224.
Engine: Ford double-overhead-camshaft four-cylinder, 1588cc.
Power output: 126bhp (Elan Sprint).
Transmission: Four/five-speed manual.
Brakes: Discs all-round.
0–60mph: 6.7 seconds (Elan Sprint).
Top speed: 121mph (Elan Sprint).
Colin Chapman's original Lotus Elite was an exquisite delicacy enjoyed by a very lucky few, but its successor, the Elan, was the small company's first really practical road-going package. Little larger than a half-sucked boiled sweet, and just as sticky when it came to gripping the road, the lithe fibreglass-bodied Elan could embarrass and bait much bigger-engined sports rivals on the road and track, thanks to its superb dynamics and race-breeding. From 1962 to 1973, the little Elan evolved into a very accelerative machine, culminating in the Elan Sprint, a 126bhp banshee. In the 1980s, there was much talk of how the Mazda MX-5 recreated the spirit of the original Elan. Well, the Elan – any Elan, in fact – had stronger acceleration than the latter-day pastiche.
For: Sublime handling finesse; gutsy Ford-based twin-cam that's as lively as many a 16-valve GTi unit; and poise and suppleness that would would make an MGB or TR Triumph feel like a clapped-out tractor.
Against: Build quality was undoubtedly indifferent. Neither does it help that many Elans were home-built from kits. They also appealed to hard-charging, string-backed-glove types who would fiddle with and tune their cars until they broke, crashed or caught fire.
Best buy: The Elan you want is either an unrestored warts-and-all car, or a first-class restoration that's been properly stripped, refurbished and repainted. The key to the engine is careful and regular maintenance, so make sure you study the bills and service history. By now, most cars will have had a replacement backbone chassis – galvanised if it was made after 1980. Even if it hasn't, you can buy a galvanised replacement.

Lotus Europa (1966–75)

Colin Chapman's original intention with the Europa was to produce a mid-engined car that would compete on price with the MG Midget. Well, he didn't quite pull it off. Instead its price pitched it pretty much against the Lotus Elan, but it still bore the hallmarks of Chapman's genius, combining fabled finesse with stunning, almost outrageous looks. The fibreglass-bodied Europa is a delicate beauty, but one that's worth bearing with. A good one's a supreme classic road-racer, and a rough one's still a beautiful sight, even if it's laid up in your garage.

Pick of the bunch: The Europa really came of age when the tad-underpowered Renault engine was replaced in 1971 with the Lotus-Ford twin-cam. Then in 1972 came the Europa Special, fitted with a big-valve version of the Elan's Lotus-Ford twin-cam. Its 0–60mph time of 6.6 seconds and top speed of 123mph make it the number-one performance choice.

For: Handling is simply sensational and the steering, if well-sorted, razor-sharp. That low-profile Kamm-tailed body was honed in the wind tunnel to produce a remarkably low drag co-efficient of 0.29. Best of all, this two-seater's got no room at all for kids or mothers-in-law. It's an uncompromised sports car.

Against: An uncompromised sports car means compromises. The ridiculous ventilation system and sliver of rear windscreen were hardly practical, and the flying buttresses all but obliterated what little rear vision there was. If you travel with more than a squash racket as luggage, you're in trouble. Earlier cars had very restricted headroom, later improved with adjustable seats and longer footwells.

What to watch: The early Renault-engined cars are least favoured performers. On cars produced up to 1969, the body is bonded to the chassis, and that's a nightmare when it comes to major work. Watch also the steel backbone chassis, because if it's damaged or rotten, replacement isn't cheap. Both Renault and Lotus-Ford engines are pretty tough.

◀ **1969 Lotus Elan +2,** double-overhead-camshaft 4-cylinder engine, 4-wheel disc brakes, 4-wheel independent suspension, sliding sunroof, finished in red, black interior.
£4,000–5,000 / $5,800–7,250 ⚒ CGC

1971 Lotus Elan +2S, 1558cc 4-cylinder engine, restored 1995–98, big-valve cylinder head, new chassis, finished in dark blue.
£6,500–8,000 / $9,400–11,600 ⚒ BRIT

1971 Lotus Elan +2S 130, 1558cc 4-cylinder engine, body restored 1985, engine rebuilt 1989, 10,000 miles covered since, finished in red, black interior, excellent condition.
£4,000–5,000 / $5,800–7,250 ⚒ H&H

▶ **1970 Lotus Europa,** 1470cc 4-cylinder engine, largely original, resprayed in white, black interior.
£6,250–7,250 / $9,000–10,500 ⚒ BRIT

Launched in 1966 for the French market only, the original Europa was powered by a 1470cc Renault engine, which produced 78bhp at 6,000rpm. By early 1968, the Europa was available throughout Europe, but was not offered in the UK until 1969. Produced until 1975 (later models being powered by the Lotus-Ford twin-cam unit), the Europa utilised an Elan-type backbone chassis.

◀ **1973 Lotus Elite,** 1973cc, stainless-steel exhaust system, original alloy wheels, finished in red, cream interior, 72,000 miles from new.
£1,600–2,000
$2,300–2,900 ⚒ H&H

◄ **1981 Lotus Eclat,** 2200cc double-overhead-camshaft 4-cylinder engine, 5-speed manual gearbox, finished in gold, cream interior, very good condition.
£2,750–3,250
$3,950–4,750 ⚒ H&H

1981 Lotus Esprit Turbo, alloy wheels, sunroof, finished in white, air conditioning, black leather interior, 55,000 miles from new.
£11,000–12,500 / $16,000–17,600 ⊞ TSG

1981 Lotus Esprit Turbo, 2174cc 4-cylinder engine, brakes overhauled, new turbo wastegate, exhaust system, shock absorbers and steering rack, finished in white.
£8,000–9,500 / $11,600–13,800 ⚒ BRIT

The mid-engined Esprit was introduced during 1976 with striking styling by Guigiaro of Ital Design. The earliest versions were powered by a 2 litre engine, this subsequently being enlarged to 2.2 litres, and both versions utilised the 5-speed Citroën transmission. During 1980, a Turbo version became available with a revised engine fitted with a Garrett T3 turbocharger. Power output was 210bhp, which ensured a sensational performance allied to the legendary Lotus handling.

1988 Lotus Esprit Turbo, 2174cc 4-cylinder engine, 228bhp, 5-speed Citroën transmission, finished in red, magnolia hide interior, 21,950 miles from new, excellent condition.
£11,000–12,500 / $16,000–17,600 ⚒ BRIT

► **1985 Lotus Excel 2.2 SE,** power-assisted steering, alloy wheels, sunroof, finished in blue, air conditioning, blue leather upholstery, 41,000 miles from new.
£5,000–6,000 / $7,250–8,700 ⊞ TSG

LOTUS Model	ENGINE cc/cyl	DATES	CONDITION 1	2	3
Six		1953–56	£13,000+	£7,000+	£5,000+
Elite 1172/4		1957–63	£22,000+	£15,000+	£10,000
7 S1 Sports	1172/4	1957–64	£12,000+	£9,000+	£5,000+
7 S2 Sports	1498/4	1961–66	£10,000+	£8,000+	£5,000+
7 S3 Sports	1558/4	1961–66	£10,000+	£8,000+	£5,000+
7 S4	1598/4	1969–72	£8,000	£5,000	£3,000
Elan S1 Convertible	1558/4	1962–64	£12,000+	£8,000	£4,500
Elan S2 Convertible	1558/4	1964–66	£12,000+	£7,000	£4,000
Elan S3 Convertible	1558/4	1966–69	£12,000+	£8,000	£5,000
Elan S3 FHC	1558/4	1966–69	£13,000	£7,000	£5,000
Elan S4 Convertible	1558/4	1968–71	£14,000+	£9,500	£7,000
Elan S4 FHC	1558/4	1968–71	£10,000+	£7,500	£5,000
Elan Sprint Convertible	1558/4	1971–73	£15,000+	£8,500+	£7,000
Elan Sprint FHC	1558/4	1971–73	£10,000+	£7,000	£6,000
Europa S1 FHC	1470/4	1966–69	£4,000+	£3,500	£2,000
Europa S2 FHC	1470/4	1969–71	£5,500+	£3,000	£2,000
Europa Twin Cam	1558/4	1971–75	£8,000	£6,000	£4,000
Elan +2S 130	1558/4	1971–74	£8,000	£5,000	£4,000
Elite S1 FHC	1261/4	1974–80	£3,500	£2,500	£1,500
Eclat S1	1973/4	1975–82	£3,500	£3,000	£1,500
Esprit 1	1973/4	1977–81	£6,500	£5,000	£3,000
Esprit 2	1973/4	1976–81	£7,000	£4,000	£2,500
Esprit S2.2	2174/4	1980–81	£7,000	£5,500	£3,000
Esprit Turbo	2174/4	1980–88	£10,000	£7,000	£4,000
Excel	2174/4	1983–85	£5,000	£3,000	£2,500

Prices vary with some limited-edition Lotus models and with competition history.

Marcos

◀ **1990 Marcos ST2,** 3050cc V6 engine, 5-speed manual gearbox, steering overhauled, finished in silver, grey and black interior, 10,518 miles from new.
£5,750–6,500 / $8,300–9,400 H&H

MARCOS Model	ENGINE cc/cyl	DATES	CONDITION 1	2	3
1500/1600/1800	1500/1600/ 1800/4	1964–69	£8,000	£5,000	£2,500
Mini-Marcos	848/4	1965–74	£3,500	£2,500	£1,500
Marcos 3 Litre	3000/6	1969–71	£9,000	£6,000	£4,000
Mantis	2498	1970/71	£10,000	£4,500	£1,500

Maserati

Founded by five brothers, Maserati built racing cars that gained an awesome reputation from the 1930s through to the 1950s. A string of world-beating racers was driven by some of the all-time greats, including Stirling Moss, Juan Manuel Fangio and Mike Hawthorn. In the late 1950s, the company withdrew from competition and concentrated on producing stunning luxury GT and sports cars, yet it always struggled to keep abreast of Ferrari. Many reckon the peak of Maserati's art is represented by the gorgeous Ghibli, penned by Giorgetto Giugiaro at Ghia and the car that really tilted at Ferrari's Daytona. Despite producing sensational machines, the company struggled to make money. In 1969, Citroën stepped in with finance, and when Citroën pulled out in 1975, Alejandro de Tomaso came to the rescue. That famous Maserati trident is the symbol of the city of Bologna, where the brothers started production.

1949 Maserati A6 Coupé, coachwork by Pinin Farina, A6G-series 2 litre 6-cylinder engine, left-hand drive, restored, finished in burgundy, blue and grey leather interior.
£65,000–75,000 / $94,250–108,750 BKS
The 1500cc, single-cam six-cylinder A6 model – the 'A' paying homage to Alfieri Maserati, the company's founder – had been launched at the 1947 Geneva Salon as a Pinin Farina-bodied two-seat coupé, while a four-seat variant followed at the 1948 Turin show. The A6G model, with 2 litre cast-iron-block engine – iron being '*ghisa*' in Italian – replaced this pioneering design from 1951. Over the four full years of the model's production, from 1946 to 1950, little more than 60 of these cars were manufactured. Apart from two chassis fitted with Zagato coachwork, all the A6 core production wore bodywork styled and derived from Pinin Farina. While the A6 1500 engine developed 65bhp at 4,700rpm, the 2 litre A6G engine, as fitted to this particular example, delivered a full 100bhp at 5,500rpm.

▶ **1958 Maserati 3500GT,** coachwork by Touring, 3485cc 6-cylinder engine, triple Weber 45DCOE carburettors, 220bhp, 4-speed manual gearbox, independent front suspension, semi-elliptic leaf-spring rear suspension, 4-wheel hydraulic drum brakes, 230km/h top speed,finished in red.
£18,000–22,000
$26,000–32,000 Pou

MASERATI Model	ENGINE cc/cyl	DATES	CONDITION 1	2	3
AG-1500	1488/6	1946–50	£30,000+	£20,000	£10,000
A6G	1954/6	1951–53	£50,000+	£35,000	£22,000
A6G-2000	1985/6	1954–57	£45,000+	£35,000	£20,000
3500GT fhc	3485/6	1957–64	£20,000	£14,000	£10,000
3500GT Spyder	3485/6	1957–64	£35,000+	£22,000	£15,000
5000GT	4935/8	1960–65	£60,000+	£20,000	£15,000
Sebring	3694/6	1962–66	£20,000	£15,000	£10,000
Quattroporte	4136/8	1963–74	£11,000	£9,000	£7,000
Mistral	4014/6	1964–70	£15,000	£11,000	£9,000
Mistral Spyder	4014/6	1964–70	£30,000+	£18,000	£12,000
Mexico	4719/8	1965–68	£15,000	£12,000	£9,000
Ghibli	4719/8	1967–73	£20,000	£15,000	£12,000
Ghibli-Spyder/SS	4136/8	1969–74	£50,000+	£40,000	£25,000
Indy	4136/8	1969–74	£18,000	£13,000	£10,000
Bora	4719/8	1971–80	£25,000	£18,000	£11,000
Merak/SS	2965/6	1972–81	£16,000	£14,000	£9,000
Khamsin	4930/8	1974–81	£16,000	£11,000	£9,000

Early cars with competition/Berlinetta coachwork, eg. Zagato, command a premium.

1965 Maserati Sebring S2 Coupé, 3694cc, chassis, engine and interior restored, original Lucas fuel injection system, original Borrani wire wheels, finished in red, black interior, 1 of only 7 right-hand drive examples built.
£13,000–15,000 / $18,850–21,750 ≯ H&H

1966 Maserati Mistral, 3694cc 6-cylinder engine, Lucas fuel injection, 245bhp, 5-speed manual gearbox, 4-wheel disc brakes, 240km/h top speed, finished in silver.
£18,000–21,500 / $26,000–31,000 ≯ Pou

1968 Maserati Ghibli Coupé, coachwork by Ghia, 4.7 litre engine, left-hand drive, resprayed in black, interior retrimmed in parchment leather, good condition.
£13,000–15,500 / $18,850–22,500 ≯ BKS

1970 Maserati Ghibli SS Coupé, 4930cc V8 engine, 335bhp, 5-speed manual gearbox, 4-wheel disc brakes, finished in yellow, 36,000 miles from new, original.
£25,000–30,000 / $36,250–43,500 ≯ RM

Maserati Ghibli (1967–73)

Production: 1,274.
Body styles: Two-door sports coupé or open Spyder.
Construction: Steel body and tubular chassis.
Engine: Four-camshaft 90-degree V8, 4719cc (4930cc, SS).
Power output: 330bhp @ 5,000 rpm (4719cc); 335bhp @ 5,500rpm (4931cc).
Transmission: ZF five-speed manual or three-speed Borg-Warner automatic.
Suspension: Wishbones and coil springs at front; rigid axle with radius arms and semi-elliptic leaf springs at rear.
Brakes: Girling discs all-round.
Maximum speed: 154mph (168mph, SS).
0–60mph: 6.6 seconds (6.2 seconds, SS).
0–100mph: 15.7 seconds.
Average fuel consumption: 10mpg.

The Ghibli was the sensation of the 1966 Turin show, and 30 years on it is widely regarded as Maserati's ultimate front-engined road car, a supercar blend of luxury, performance and stunning good looks that never again quite came together so sublimely on anything bearing the three-pointed trident. Pitched squarely against the Ferrari Daytona and Lamborghini Miura, the Ghibli outsold both. Its engineering may have been dated, but it had the perfect pedigree, with loads of grunt from its throaty V8 engine, especially low down, and roadholding bred of a long racing heritage. With the flawless Ghia design and five-star interior appointments that were a clear cut above contemporary Lambo and Ferrari interiors in finish, detail and layout, the result was something very special.

◄ **1977 Maserati Merak SS,** 2965cc mid-mounted double-overhead-camshaft V6 engine, Weber 42DCNF carburettors, 5-speed gearbox, 4-wheel independent suspension, 4-wheel disc brakes, finished in yellow, black interior, fewer than 29,500 miles from new, immaculate condition.
£15,000–18,000
$21,750–26,000 RM

1987 Maserati Bi-Turbo Spyder, 2500cc V6 engine, twin turbochargers, 5-speed close-ratio manual gearbox, power steering, alloy wheels, resprayed in black, fully lined mohair hood, air conditioning, electric seats and windows, cream interior, 30,000 miles from new.
£7,500–8,500 / $10,875–12,300 H&H

1988 Maserati Bi-Turbo, air conditioning, magnolia leather interior.
£4,000–4,500 / $5,800–6,500 BARO

1989 Maserati Karif, 2790cc V6 engine, fuel injection, twin turbochargers, 285bhp, 5-speed manual gearbox, 4-wheel independent suspension, 4-wheel disc brakes, 255km/h top speed, finished in red, 362km from new.
£16,000–18,000 / $23,200–26,000 Pou

1989 Maserati 430, 3 litre V6 engine, twin turbochargers, 225bhp, 145mph top speed, turbochargers overhauled, new stainless-steel exhaust, BBS wheels, finished in blue.
£3,000–3,500 / $4,400–5,200 COYS

► **1982 Maserati Quattroporte III Saloon,** 4.9 litre, left-hand drive, finished in metallic dark blue, tan leather interior, 32,200km from new, good condition apart from non-functioning rear door handle.
£4,000–5,000 / $5,800–7,250 BKS
Following the demise of the Citroën V6-powered, four-wheel-drive Quattroporte II, Maserati V8 power was restored in 1978 for the Ital-styled Quattroporte III. The car reverted to rear-wheel drive using a lengthened Kyalami floorpan and all-independent suspension.

Mazda

Condition Guide

1. A vehicle in top class condition but not 'concours d'elegance standard, either fully restored or in very good original condition.
2. A good, clean, roadworthy vehicle, both mechanically and bodily sound.
3. A runner, but in need of attention, probably both to bodywork and mechanics. Must have current MoT.

◄ **1987 Mazda RX7 Mk II,** sunroof, alloy wheels, sports seats, finished in blue, grey interior, 70,000 miles from new.
£4,750–5,750 / $6,900–8,300 TSG

Mercedes-Benz

Mercedes-Benz motor cars have only truly existed since 1926, following the merger of the separate Daimler (Mercedes) and Benz companies. Today, Germany's largest industrial concern is an even bigger global player after recently teaming up with Chrysler. It's all a very long way from 1886, when Karl Benz and Gottlieb Daimler, working independently of each other, both produced petrol-engined road vehicles. In 1894, Benz's Velo became the world's first true production automobile. The name Mercedes was first used on a Daimler in 1899. In 1926, the two concerns merged to form Daimler-Benz, the cars being called Mercedes-Benz. In the 1930s, the range of road cars was thoroughly comprehensive, and from 1934 to the outbreak of WWII, Mercedes-Benz dominated the Grand Prix scene along with its compatriot Auto Union. Following post-war reconstruction, Mercedes-Benz signalled to the world that it was back on top with the gorgeous 300SL Gullwing, the forerunner of modern supercars. Since then, the company has concentrated on producing upmarket executive saloons, sporting coupés and cabriolets, all formidably engineered. And now with the A-class, the Mercedes product range is the broadest it's ever been.

1937 Mercedes-Benz 540K Cabriolet A, 5401cc straight-8 engine, supercharger, 180bhp, later synchromesh gearbox with overdrive, coil-spring/parallel-wishbone independent front suspension, coil-spring swing-axle independent rear suspension, servo-assisted 4-wheel hydraulic drum brakes, left-hand drive, older restoration, museum displayed for 25 years, 75,000km from new, 1 of 83 examples built, excellent mechanical condition.
£400,000+ / $580,000+ ⚒ RM

1949 Mercedes-Benz 170S Cabriolet B, 1767cc 4-cylinder engine, 4-speed manual gearbox, transverse semi-elliptic leaf-spring front suspension, coil-spring rear suspension, 4-wheel hydraulic drum brakes.
£18,000–22,000 / $26,000–32,000 ⚒ Pou

1955 Mercedes-Benz 180 Ponton Saloon, 1767cc sidevalve 4-cylinder engine, 52bhp, 4-speed manual all-synchromesh gearbox, 4-wheel independent suspension by unequal-length wishbones and coil-springs at front, coil-springs and swing-axles at rear, 4-wheel hydraulic drum brakes, original paintwork, interior upholstery and all fittings, 1 owner and 88,000 miles from new, original.
£5,000–6,000 / $7,250–8,700 ⚒ C

The 180 was Mercedes-Benz's first unitary-construction automobile, its bodyshell welded to a rigid platform to form a central passenger cell with crumple zones at each end. The car's front suspension was fitted to a rubber-mounted subframe, from which derives the type's 'ponton' (bridge) nomenclature. Production began during 1953. With 52bhp to propel a car weighing 3,637lb, performance was not sparkling, but the roomy saloon rode comfortably on its independent suspension, had pleasing lines and was built with all Mercedes' traditional precision. Combining outstanding fuel economy with an impressive 78mph maximum speed, it suited the times and was to remain in production until 1962.

▶ **1958 Mercedes-Benz 220S Cabriolet,** 2195cc 6-cylinder engine, 4-speed gearbox, column change, completely restored, finished in burgundy, tan interior.
£30,000–34,000 / $43,500–49,000 ⚒ BJ

1958 Mercedes-Benz 220SE Cabriolet, 2195cc overhead-camshaft 6-cylinder engine, Bosch mechanical fuel injection, 115bhp, 4-speed manual gearbox, 4-wheel independent suspension, recently restored, excellent mechanical condition.
£28,000–32,000 / $40,600–46,400 ⚒ RM

Starting in 1954, Mercedes began offering a host of six-cylinder versions to capitalise on the growing wealth of consumers who wanted more power. The 220 (1954–56), the 219 (1956–59), 220S (1956–59) and 220SE (1958–59) afforded customers the power and torque they were looking for in the smaller body style. Only the 220S and SE were available as coupés and cabriolets, however.

◀ **1958 Mercedes-Benz 220SC Cabriolet,** 2195cc overhead-camshaft 6-cylinder engine, servo-assisted brakes, original right-hand drive, restored over 4 years at a cost of over £25,000, finished in Mercedes racing silver, dark blue weather equipment, red leather upholstery.
£23,000–26,000
$33,300–37,700 ⚒ COYS

▶ **1954 Mercedes-Benz 300B Saloon,** 2996cc, engine rebuilt, finished in green, grey interior trim, 1 of only 96 right-hand drive models imported to the UK, 45,000 miles from new, original, very good condition throughout.
£8,000–10,000 / $11,600–14,500 ⚒ H&H
Mercedes-Benz introduced Germany's first post-war prestige automobile in 1952 with the 300 Model A, and it was available in the UK from late 1953. The model range continued until 1957 with the Models B and C respectively. This six-light saloon, which was good for about 100mph, had a tubular cruciform chassis and seven-bearing engine.

1956 Mercedes-Benz 300C Saloon, 2996cc 6-cylinder engine, 3-speed automatic transmission, right-hand drive, finished in blue, blue interior trim, 64,579 miles from new.
£6,000–7,500 / $8,700–10,800 ⚒ H&H

1959 Mercedes-Benz 300D, 2996cc 6-cylinder engine, Bosch mechanical fuel injection, 160bhp, 3-speed automatic transmission, 4-wheel independent suspension, servo-assisted 4-wheel hydraulic drum brakes.
£9,000–11,000 / $13,000–16,000 ⚒ Pou

1953 Mercedes-Benz 300S Cabriolet, 2996cc 6-cylinder engine, 150bhp, 4-speed synchromesh gearbox, 4-wheel drum brakes, never restored, original interior, c10,000 miles from new, in need of cosmetic attention.
£70,000–80,000 / $101,500–116,000 ⚒ RM

1955 Mercedes-Benz 300S Coupé, 2996cc 6-cylinder engine, 150bhp, 4-speed synchromesh gearbox, 4-wheel hydraulic drum brakes, never restored, 88,000km from new, excellent cosmetic and mechanical condition.
£45,000–55,000 / $65,250–79,750 ⚒ RM

◀ **1955 Mercedes-Benz 300SL Gullwing,** 2996cc 6-cylinder engine, fuel injection, dry-sump lubrication, 215bhp, completely restored early 1990s, matching numbers, original full-length undertrays, finished in grey, red leather interior.
£110,000–125,000
$159,500–180,000 ⚒ COYS
This car was displayed at the 1955 Canadian International Fair.

Mercedes-Benz 300SL Gullwing (1954–57)

Production: 1,400.
Body style: Two-door, two-seat coupé.
Construction: Multi-tubular spaceframe with steel and alloy body panels.
Engine: Inline six-cylinder, overhead-camshaft, 2996cc.
Power output: 240bhp at 6,100rpm.
Transmission: Four-speed, all-synchromesh manual gearbox.
Suspension: Coil springs all-round, with double wishbones at front, swinging half-axles at rear.
Brakes: Finned alloy drums all-round.
Maximum speed: 135–165mph, depending on gearing.
0–60mph: 8.8 seconds.
0–100mph: 21.0 seconds.
Average fuel consumption: 18mpg.
In 1952, Mercedes had stormed back into motor sport with a spaceframe-chassised car that didn't allow for conventional doors. Its engine was a development of the 3 litre unit of the 300-series saloons. This aluminium-bodied car was called the 300SL – 'SL' stood for 'Super Light' – and it was right straight out of the box. In its first race, the 1952 Mille Miglia, the 300SL finished second, then went on to snatch outright victory at the Berne Grand Prix, took a 1-2 at Le Mans, won at the Nürburgring, and finished the year with a 1-2 in the gruelling Carrera Panamericana Mexican road race. Mercedes had proved its point, and in 1954 turned its attention once more to Grand Prix goals. But the 300SL Gullwing was about to enter a new life. New York sports car importer Max Hoffman was instrumental in Mercedes' decision to unleash the 300SL Gullwing as undoubtedly the fastest and most glamorous production car of its era. Hoffman was so convinced of the 300SL's appeal that he was willing to back his word with a large firm order – up to 1,000 – if Mercedes would build them. The road-going 300SL was still clearly based on the racer, although it was kitted out with a host of luxury refinements and its suspension was derived from the Mercedes saloons. Most importantly, it shared the spaceframe chassis of the racer, and that meant it retained its Gullwing doors.
Eyebrows: Mercedes insisted that the `eyebrows' over the wheel arches were aerodynamic aids, to separate upper and lower body airflows; more likely they were styling touches to appeal to US tastes.

1956 Mercedes-Benz 300SL Gullwing, original undertrays, finished in original red, Nardi wood-rim steering wheel, period Blaupunkt radio, black leather interior, excellent condition throughout.
£125,000–140,000 / $180,000–203,000 ⚒ BKS
Initial versions of the 300SL racer were open-topped, but before the 1952 season's end, the distinctive gullwing-doored coupé had appeared. Unusually high sills were a feature of the 300SL's multi-tubular spaceframe chassis, and while access was not a problem with the open car, the adoption of coupé bodywork required innovative thinking – hence the gullwing doors. The production version's 2996cc, overhead-camshaft, dry-sump six was canted over at 45 degrees to achieve a lower, more aerodynamically-efficient bonnet line.

1957 Mercedes-Benz 300SL Roadster, 2996cc overhead-camshaft 6-cylinder engine, fuel injection, stainless-steel exhaust, 225bhp, 4-speed manual gearbox, 4-wheel independent suspension, 4-wheel drum brakes, European headlights, hard and soft tops, Becker Mexico radio, later-style Nardi steering wheel, older cosmetic restoration including respray, original red leather interior.
£80,000–90,000 / $116,000–130,500 ⚒ RM
By 1957, the Gullwing was no longer competitive in sports car racing. As a result, Mercedes' North American distributor Max Hoffman thought that the best way to satisfy the American appetite for open-air motoring was to offer a convertible. Thus, 1957 saw Mercedes-Benz replace the coupé with a well-designed and engineered roadster. Further chassis and engine refinements actually improved performance over the coupé.

1959 Mercedes-Benz 300SL Roadster, fitted with GM V8 engine and automatic transmission late 1970s, finished in Italian racing red, black interior and weather equipment, excellent condition.
£65,000–72,000 / $94,250–103,750 ⚒ COYS

◄ **1960 Mercedes-Benz 300SL Roadster,** hard and soft tops, finished in white, red interior, 69,000 miles from new, original, excellent mechanical condition.
£100,000–115,000 / $145,000–167,000 ⊞ HCL

1960 Mercedes-Benz 190SL, 1897cc overhead-camshaft 4-cylinder engine, twin Solex carburettors, original right-hand drive, restored over 10 years, bare-metal respray in red, burgundy mohair hood, biscuit leather interior trim.
£24,000–27,000 / $34,900–39,000 ≯ BRIT

1964 Mercedes-Benz 220SEB Coupé, 4-speed manual gearbox, completely original, finished in metallic bronze, dark green leather upholstery and carpets, walnut cappings and trim, original mechanical clock, rev-counter, 1 family owner from new.
£6,000–7,000 / $8,700–10,400 ≯ BKS

1965 Mercedes-Benz 190DC Saloon, 1988cc diesel engine, original right-hand drive, new short motor 1990, body restored early 1995, finished in black, dark blue interior trim, 1 of 17 known to survive in UK, very good condition throughout.
£2,000–2,500 / $2,900–3,600 ≯ H&H

1963 Mercedes-Benz 300SE Coupé, optional steel sunroof, recently restored, engine overhauled, finished in metallic green, new tan interior upholstery, good condition throughout.
£8,000–9,500 / $11,600–13,900 ≯ BKS
The 300SE entered production in saloon form in 1961, with coupé and cabriolet models arriving the following year. Although similar in appearance to the contemporary 220, the 500 was mechanically more refined, featuring 600-type self-levelling air suspension, disc brakes on all four wheels and, from August 1963, dual-circuit braking. From 1964, the 1996cc Bosch fuel-injected M189 six produced 170bhp, an output sufficient to propel the luxuriously equipped 300SE to around 120mph.

◀ **1967 Mercedes-Benz 300SE Cabriolet,** 2996cc 6-cylinder engine, Bosch fuel injection, 170bhp, 4-speed manual gearbox, 4-wheel independent suspension, servo-assisted 4-wheel disc brakes.
£20,000–24,000 / $29,000–34,800 ≯ Pou

Mercedes-Benz Fin-Tail Saloons (1959–68)

Production: 1,001,796 saloons.
Body style/construction: Four-door monocoque saloon.
Engines: 1897cc, four-cylinder; 2996cc, six-cylinder.
Power output: 1897cc diesel, 55bhp; 2996cc six-cylinder, 185bhp.
Transmission: Four-speed manual or four-speed automatic; both column change.
Brakes: Drums all-round on early models; front discs/rear drums from late 1963.
Maximum speed: 107mph (220SE, 2195cc six-cylinder).
0–60mph: 12.8 seconds (220SE, 2195cc six-cylinder).

The boffins at Bletchley Park may have broken the Enigma Code, but it's doubtful whether they'd have been able to unravel the key to this most cryptic of Mercedes model ranges. In house at Mercedes, the four-door saloons were known as the W110, W111 and W112; on the road, they were ascribed model numbers from 190 to 300, to which were tagged an alphabet soup of letter suffixes. As a result, and for simplicity, they've become known to their large flock of fans as 'fin-tails'. True, their modest rear wings seem almost guilty and possibly even ashamed that German engineering should be compromised by pandering to an American fad, but those fins are just about the one common element throughout this extended family. Now forget all that and recall the 1960s Austin Cambridge and France's Peugeot 404. There's an undeniable resemblance, and what those models were in Britain and France, the Mercedes fin-tails were in Germany, straightforward and largely unglamorous family saloons. Where BMC's models ran the gamut from humdrum Austin and Morris through MG, Riley and Wolseley, up to the plush Vanden Plas 4 Litre R, the Mercedes range rose from Teutonic taxis chugging on diesel to a bechromed crescendo with a 3 litre autobahn armchair, the 300SE. Any further comparison is unfair, because the Mercedes models were not only far superior, but also correspondingly more expensive. And today, preferably in sinister diplomatic black, these fin-tail Mercs offer an undeniable touch of elegant Cold War chic.

1965 Mercedes-Benz 600, original right-hand drive, completely restored 1987 at a cost of £40,000, 2,000 miles covered since, finished in dark blue, grey leather upholstery, excellent condition throughout.
£16,000–19,000 / $23,200–27,500 COYS
With a 6.3 litre fuel-injected V8 engine producing 300bhp at the wheels, the 600 was capable of over 120mph and 0–60mph in just 9.5 seconds, not bad for a car weighing some 7,000lb. It was equipped with a limited-slip differential, servo steering and all-round disc brakes with vacuum servo. Other amenities included hydraulically operated windows, a sunroof, glass partition and full air conditioning.

1968 Mercedes-Benz 280SL, finished in silver grey, seats recently upholstered in black leather.
£15,500–17,500 / $22,500–25,400 COYS
In March 1963, the new generation of SL sports cars was launched with the debut of the 230SL at the Geneva show. This model replaced the ageing 190 and 300SL models. Mercedes engineering, together with elegance and practicality, made the 'pagoda-top' SL one of the most distinctive designs of its era. In closed form, it offered handsome proportions and coupé-like comfort, while the easy removal of the hardtop turned it into an open sports car for the summer. During the 1960s, Mercedes-Benz refined the model, later fitting the 250 engine and finally arriving at the 280SL. This represented the ultimate evolution of the range, with its 2.8 litre, six-cylinder, fuel-injected engine, complemented by power steering and an automatic transmission.

1965 Mercedes 230SL, fitted with 250 engine, no hardtop, paintwork in need of attention.
£7,500–8,500 / $10,900–12,300 UMC

1967 Mercedes 250SL, automatic transmission, hard and soft tops, finished in silver, black interior in very good original condition with correct black rush matting.
£17,000–20,000 / $24,650–29,000 CGC

1968 Mercedes-Benz 250SL, 2496cc, converted to unleaded fuel, hard and soft tops, finished in silver, black interior trim 1 family owner since 1971, 2,500 miles in last 10 years, very good condition.
£11,000–13,000 / $16,000–18,850 H&H

Mercedes-Benz 230/250/280SL (1963–71)

Production: 230SL, 19,831; 250SL, 5,196; 280SL, 23,885.
Body style: Two-door, two-seat convertible with detachable hardtop.
Construction: Pressed-steel monocoque.
Engines: 2281, 2496 and 2778cc inline six.
Power: 230/250SL, 150bhp; 280SL, 170bhp.
Transmission: Four- or optional five-speed ZF manual, or optional four-speed automatic.
Brakes: 230SL, servo-assisted front discs and rear drums; 250/280SL, discs all-round.
Maximum speed: 115–125mph.
0–60mph: 9.3–11 seconds.
In 1963 the new SLs took over the sporting mantle of the ageing 190SL. In its place, the new 230SL, which evolved through the 250SL to the 280SL, was strikingly modern with uncluttered clean-shaven good looks that endured until 1971 and still look crisp today. In fact, you can still pick out some of the styling motifs on today's sporting Mercs. Underneath the elegant sheet metal, they were based closely on the earlier `fin-tail' saloons, sharing even the decidedly unsporting recirculating-ball steering. Suspension too was on the soft side for string-backed-glove types. Yet it's the looks that really mark this Merc out as something special, and that enduring design, with its distinctive so-called `pagoda roof', is down to Frenchman Paul Bracq. It's certainly not the most hairy-chested sports car, yet this well-manicured Merc is a beautifully built boulevardier that will induce a sense of supreme self-satisfaction on any journey.
Market comment: There's little to choose between the 230 and 250SL, both in price and overall performance – the latter offered no more power, but a little more torque. The 280SL was appreciably more powerful and is, today, the most prized model, commanding a premium of £2,000 or more for better cars.
SL jargon: In Mercedes code speak, the 'S' stood for 'Sport' or 'Super', 'L' for 'Leicht' (light) and sometimes 'Luxus' (luxury), although at well over 3000lb, the 280SL certainly wasn't very light.

◄ **1971 Mercedes-Benz 280SL,** left-hand drive, 5-spoke alloy wheels, finished in red, black top.
£12,000–13,500 / $17,400–19,600 PALM

1969 Mercedes-Benz 280S, original, excellent condition.
£3,500–4,250 / $5,000–6,100 SiC

◄ **1970 Mercedes-Benz 280SE Coupé,** manual gearbox, servo-assisted brakes, power steering, right-hand drive, finished in ivory, burgundy leather upholstery, walnut veneer cappings, good condition throughout.
£6,500–8,000 / $9,400–11,600 BKS

1970 Mercedes-Benz 280SE Cabriolet, 3.5 litre V8 engine, 200bhp, 4-speed automatic transmission, 4-wheel independent self-levelling air suspension, 4-wheel disc brakes, restored, engine and transmission overhauled, electrics refurbished, chassis restored, bare-metal respray in metallic dark green, new dark green hood, new parchment leather upholstery, wood veneers repolished, very good condition.
£45,000–50,000
$65,250–72,500 BKS

► **1970 Mercedes-Benz 280SE Cabriolet,** 3499cc overhead-camshaft V8 engine, fuel injection, transistorised ignition, 200bhp, 3-speed automatic transmission, 4-wheel independent suspension, servo-assisted 4-wheel disc brakes, power steering, electric windows, air conditioning, leather interior, polished wood trim.
£19,000–23,000
$27,500–33,000 RM
Only 4,502 of these cars – in coupé and cabriolet form – were sold between 1969 and 1971.

MERCEDES-BENZ Model	ENGINE cc/cyl	DATES	CONDITION 1	2	3
300ABCD	2996/6	1951–62	£15,000	£10,000	£8,000
300D Cabriolet	2195/6	1951–62	£80,000	£50,000	£30,000
220A/S/SE Ponton	2195/6	1952–60	£10,000	£5,000	£3,000
220S/SEB Coupé	2915/6	1956–59	£11,000	£7,000	£5,000
220S/SEB Cabriolet	2195/6	1958–59	£28,000+	£18,000	£7,000
190SL	1897/4	1955–63	£20,000+	£15,000+	£10,000
300SL Gullwing	2996/6	1954–57	£120,000+	£100,000	£70,000
300SL Roadster	2996/6	1957–63	£110,000+	£90,000	£70,000
230/250SL	2306/ 2496/6	1963–68	£14,000+	£10,000+	£7,000
280SL	2778/6	1961–71	£16,000	£12,000	£9,000
220/250SE	2195/ 2496/6	1960–68	£10,000	£7,000	£4,000
300SE	2996/6	1961–65	£11,000	£8,000	£6,000
280SE Convertible	2778/6	1965–69	£25,000	£18,000	£12,000
280SE V8 Convertible	3499/8	1969–71	£30,000+	£20,000	£15,000
280SE Coupé	2496/6	1965–72	£12,000	£8,000	£5,000
300SEL 6.3	6330/8	1968–72	£12,000	£7,000	£3,500
600 & 600 Pullman	6332/8	1964–81	£40,000+	£15,000	£8,000

1969 Mercedes 230 Saloon, automatic transmission with column change, finished in white, red interior trim, 85,000 miles from new, very original condition.
£3,500–4,000 / $4,700–5,800 ⊞ VIC

Mercedes-Benz 250CE, 2496cc 6-cylinder engine, new front wings, finished in blue, good mechanical condition.
£3,500–4,200 / $5,000–6,000 ⚒ BRIT

1984 Mercedes-Benz 280SL, 2746cc, hard and soft tops, finished in beige, beige interior trim, fewer than 74,000 miles from new, good condition throughout.
£8,500–9,500 / $12,300–13,800 ⚒ H&H

1986 Mercedes-Benz 300SL, 2962cc 6-cylinder engine, cruise control, gearbox with sport mode, hard and soft tops, resprayed in white, burgundy leather upholstery, walnut trim, optional rear seat.
£8,000–9,500 / $11,600–13,800 ⚒ BRIT

1987 Mercedes-Benz 300SL, 2962cc, cruise control, hard and soft tops, finished in signal red, rear seat conversion, air conditioning, grey interior trim, 44,000 miles from new.
£14,500–16,500 / $21,000–24,000 ⚒ H&H

1974 Mercedes-Benz 350SL, hard and soft tops, finished in metallic red, white leather upholstery.
£7,000–8,000 / $10,200–11,600 ⊞ SiC

1977 Mercedes-Benz 350SLC, 3499cc V8 engine, cruise control, correct alloy wheels, electric sunroof and windows, finished in metallic brown, air conditioning, cream leather interior, 35,000 miles from new.
£9,500–11,000 / $13,800–16,000 ⚒ BRIT

1978 Mercedes-Benz 350SL, 3499cc V8 engine, new blue hood, hardtop, finished in metallic blue, good mechanical condition, body excellent.
£5,500–6,500 / $8,000–9,400 ⚒ BRIT

1981 Mercedes-Benz 380SL, automatic transmission, alloy wheels, hard and soft tops, finished in metallic silver-blue, blue interior trim, rear seat, 1 owner and 56,000 miles from new.
£13,500–15,000 / $19,600–21,750 ⊞ TSG

▶ 1987 Mercedes-Benz 420SL, 4196cc V8 engine, cruise control, finished in red, cream leather interior, air conditioning, heated seats, rear seat, 46,600 miles from new.
£16,000–18,000
$23,200–26,000 ⚒ BRIT
The replacement for the 350SL, the 420SL was introduced in 1985, its 4.2 litre engine providing more urge in the mid-range and producing 218bhp.

Miller's is a price GUIDE not a price LIST

◀ 1975 Mercedes-Benz 450SLC, finished in metallic dark green, new leather upholstery.
£6,000–7,000 / $8,700–10,200 ⊞ UMC

1979 Mercedes-Benz 450SL, 4500cc V8 engine, automatic transmission, hard and soft tops, alloy wheels, electric aerial, finished in blue, dark blue interior, rear seats, over £3,500 spent recently, excellent condition throughout.
£4,750–5,500 / $6,800–8,000 ⚒ H&H

1982 Mercedes-Benz 230CE, new engine at a cost of £3,300, new exhaust, very good condition.
£4,000–5,000 / $5,800–7,250 ⊞ SiC

1984 Mercedes-Benz 250 Limousine, seating for 8 including chauffeur, finished in black and pewter, electric windows, mirror and aerial, air conditioning, cylinder head overhauled, new exhaust, new self-levelling dampers and track control arms, brakes overhauled, interior retrimmed.
£3,500–4,200 / $5,000–6,000 ⚒ BARO

1987 Mercedes-Benz 420SE Saloon, 4196cc V8 engine, 4-speed automatic transmission, finished in gold, very good condition throughout.
£2,000–2,400 / $2,900–3,400 ⚒ BARO

1986 Mercedes-Benz 500SEL, cruise control, automatic transmission, ABS brakes, air conditioning, electric sunroof, windows and seats, finished in blue, blue velour interior trim, excellent condition.
£7,000–8,000 / $10,200–11,600 ⊞ TSG

1987 Mercedes-Benz 300SE, finished in maroon, beige fabric interior.
£4,000–5,000 / $5,800–7,250 ⊞ GrM

1979 Mercedes-Benz 450SEL, 4520cc V8 engine, excellent condition throughout.
£3,750–4,500 / $5,200–6,200 ⚒ BRIT
The 450SEL was the long-wheelbase version of the 450SE.

1984 Mercedes-Benz 500SEC, finished in silver-blue, air conditioning, excellent condition.
£5,500–6,250 / $8,000–9,000 ⊞ UMC

1990 Mercedes-Benz 190 Evo II, new engine and gearbox 1995, 30,000km covered since, finished in metallic blue-black, air conditioning, black leather interior, 2 owners from new, 1 of 500 built, good condition throughout.
£11,500–13,500 / $16,700–19,600 ⚒ COYS
The 2.5 litre Evolution II was built in small numbers as a homologation special, since the car was to be Mercedes' weapon in European touring car racing before the DTM series was launched, which Mercedes embraced with enthusiasm. So successful was it that it was banned.

Mercury

◄ **1950 Mercury Convertible,** 250cu.in sidevalve V8 engine, 110bhp, 3-speed manual gearbox with overdrive, 4-wheel hydraulic drum brakes, professionally restored, original engine, finished in deep burgundy, matching leather interior.
£35,000–40,000 / $50,750–58,000 ⚒ RM
Like most American makes, Mercury introduced completely new, modern styling in 1949. Based on the Lincoln bodyshell, it was longer, lower and wider than ever before, with just enough styling cues carried over to maintain the family identity. Mechanically, the car received a new 110bhp version of Ford's sidevalve V8, giving the upmarket Mercury division a solid performance advantage.

1955 Mercury Montclair Convertible, 292cu.in overhead-valve V8 engine, 198bhp, automatic transmission, 4-wheel hydraulic drum brakes, power hood, subject of recent professional body-off restoration, many factory options including 'multi-luber' kit, accessory steering wheel and horn ring, deluxe exhaust ports, continental kit, bumper guards, fog lamps and spinner wheel trims.
£28,000–34,000 / $40,600–50,000 ⚒ RM
For 1955, the all-new Montclair led Mercury's range. A longer, more robust chassis and a more powerful engine were two features that made it a popular choice. With its standard 8.5:1-compression 292cu.in V8 and smooth-shifting push-button Merc-O-Matic transmission, the Montclair convertible was a stylish ride.

Merlin-Aerees

1939 Merlin-Aerees, 3.4 litre double-overhead-camshaft 6-cylinder engine, aircraft-type dashboard with 540 gallon fuel gauge, altimeter and magneto switches, gearlever made from Harrier 'Jump-Jet' control column, tiger lamp, secret trunk for carrying sporting guns, finished in silver-grey, black leather interior, good condition.
£15,000–18,000 / $21,750–26,000 ⚒ COYS
This four-seater sports car was designed by the late Dennis Owen-Rees, racing car builder and pilot, who was known as the Welsh Wizard. It is based on a 1939 Daimler EL24, which was chosen for its beautiful sweeping side elevation, lightness and rigid boxed construction. Powered by a Jaguar 3.4 litre engine with modified camshafts and tensioners, mated to a synchromesh overdrive gearbox, the Merlin-Aerees has large finned brake drums with servo assistance, and retains the original Daimler worm drive rear axle and Rudge Whitworth 17in wire wheels.

MG

As another year passes, there's yet another twist in the saga of MG. Its short tenure in BMW's hands is over, and once more the marque is in British hands as part of Rover. It's been a long road with many a twist since 1923, when Cecil Kimber, general manager of the Morris Garages in Oxford, attached a stylish two-seater sporting body to a Morris chassis and created MG as a sporting marque. Since then, those 'MG' initials have spelled affordable sports car fun for literally millions of enthusiasts. Throughout much of its history, MG has been starved of resources and been close to oblivion. Since 1935, when it became part of the Morris empire, the MG marque has had to endure a succession of owners who, at times, were both apathetic and completely disinterested. Yet somehow, through the good years and the lean times, MG has mostly managed to retain an individual sporting identity. In 2001, MG was due to return to Le Mans, but who knows what further twists there are to come in the tale of this spirited sporting marque.

1930 MG M-Type Midget, restored, finished in dark red, unused for some years, good condition.
£5,500–6,600 / $8,000–9,600 ⚒ COYS
The MG name first appeared in 1923 on a rebodied Morris Cowley, in which founder Cecil Kimber clinched a gold award on the Lands End Trial. The following year, the popular Super Sports appeared, a stylishly rebodied, but also tuned, Oxford model. However, it was not until early 1928 that the MG Car Company was officially formed and the first true production MG, the six-cylinder 18/80, introduced. Some nine months later, the Midget was launched to an enthusiastic public. Based on the 847cc Morris Minor, with its overhead-camshaft, four-cylinder engine producing 20bhp and lowered leaf-spring suspension, the diminutive, fabric-bodied boat-tail two-seater was capable of 65mph and lively acceleration via its three-speed gearbox. As such, the Midget, or M-Type, was to become the first British sports car offering fun, reliability and performance at an affordable price – the first real sports car for the masses. Competition development inevitably followed, and in 1930 M-Type Midgets won the team prize in the Brooklands Twelve Hours.

1935 MG PB Midget, 847cc overhead-camshaft 4-cylinder engine, completely restored, concours winner, excellent condition.
£16,000–18,000 / $23,200–26,000 ⚒ COYS
By the 1930s, the MG Midget, in its various guises, had proved immensely popular thanks to its cheap price and running costs, and its effectiveness in virtually any area of amateur motor sports. The P-Type Midget was launched in March 1934. Compared to earlier models, its leaf-sprung chassis was stronger and had a longer wheelbase, while the drum brakes had been increased in size to 12in diameter. The 75mph P-Type was far more robust and tunable, while the clutch, gearbox and differential were also strengthened.

1932 MG M-Type Midget, 848cc overhead-camshaft engine, Brooklands-style 'fishtail' exhaust, aero screens, fabric-covered body, recently restored, finished in grey and cream, black leather upholstery.
£8,000–10,000 / $11,600–14,500 ⚒ BKS

1933 MG J2 Midget, engine professionally rebuilt 1997, drive-train, brakes and steering in good condition, serviceable weather equipment, in need of some restoration.
£9,500–11,500 / $13,800–16,700 ⚒ BKS

A colour brochure detailing the MG 8/33 Midget, including the Sportsman's Coupé and sports two-seater, images by Connolly, very good condition, 9 x 11in (23 x 28cm).
£40–48 / $60–70 ⚒ BKS

1939 MG TA Drophead Coupé, coachwork by Tickford, 1292cc 4-cylinder engine, Spax adjustable shock absorbers, finished in 2-tone green, tan interior, MotoLita wooden steering wheel, excellent condition.
£14,000–16,000 / $20,300–23,200 H&H

1939 MG TB Midget, 1250cc 4-cylinder engine, full weather equipment, very good condition.
£11,500–13,500 / $16,700–19,600 BRIT
The TB Midget was produced for less than six months, the outbreak of WWII curtailing production.

► **1946 MG TC Midget,** completely restored 1991, 250 miles covered since, finished in black, black hood and tonneau cover, full side screens, green leather upholstery, recently stored, in need of recommissioning.
£16,000–18,000 / $23,200–26,000 BKS
Like its pre-war predecessor, the TC was produced on traditional lines with a coachbuilt body on a box-section frame, underslung at the rear. The renowned XPAG engine was used for the first time, a 1250cc four-cylinder engine with pushrod-operated overhead valves and twin SU carburettors, driving through a four-speed gearbox with synchromesh on second, third and top gears. The model was adopted by several police forces for road patrol and achieved success in various types of competition.

1946 MG TC Midget, 1250cc 4-cylinder engine, finished in red, beige hood, red leather interior trim, good mechanical condition, chassis and structure excellent.
£15,000–17,000 / $21,750–24,650 BRIT

1948 MG TC Midget, finished in blue, green interior, in need of restoration.
£7,000–8,000 / $10,200–11,600 VIC

MG Model	ENGINE cc/cyl	DATES	CONDITION 1	2	3
14/28	1802/4	1924–27	£26,000	£18,000	£10,000
14/40	1802/4	1927–29	£25,000	£18,000	£10,000
18/80 Mk I/Mk II/Mk III	2468/6	1927–33	£40,000	£28,000	£20,000
M-Type Midget	847/4	1928–32	£11,000	£9,000	£7,000
J-Type Midget	847/4	1932–34	£15,000	£12,000	£10,000
J3 Midget	847/4	1932–33	£18,000	£14,000	£12,000
PA Midget	847/4	1934–36	£13,000+	£10,000	£8,000
PB Midget	936/4	1935–36	£15,000	£10,000	£8,000
F-Type Magna	1271/6	1931–33	£22,000	£18,000	£12,000
L-Type Magna	1087/6	1933–34	£26,000	£18,000	£12,000
K1/K2 Magnette	1087/6	1932–33	£35,000	£30,000	£20,000
N Series Magnette	1271/6	1934–36	£30,000	£28,000	£20,000
TA Midget	1292/4	1936–39	£13,000+	£12,000	£9,000
SA 2 Litre	2288/6	1936–39	£22,000+	£18,000	£15,000
VA	1548/4	1936–39	£12,000	£8,000	£5,000
TB Midget	1250/4	1939–40	£15,000	£11,000	£9,000

Value will depend on body style, history, completeness, racing history, the addition of a supercharger and originality.

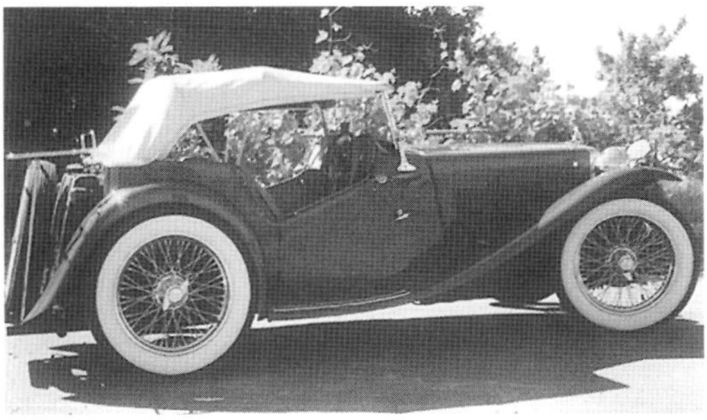

1949 MG TC Midget, 1250cc 4-cylinder engine, 54bhp, 4-speed manual gearbox, 4-wheel hydraulic drum brakes, restored, fewer than 300 miles since.
£16,000–18,000 / $23,200–26,000 RM

1949 MG TC Midget, restored, finished in red, red interior.
£14,000–16,000 / $20,300–23,200 VIC

1950 MG TD Midget, 1250cc 4-cylinder engine, completely restored, converted to unleaded fuel, MGA differential, hood and side screens, finished in red, new red leather upholstery.
£8,500–10,000 / $12,300–14,500 H&H

1951 MG TD Midget, restored, full weather equipment, left-hand drive.
£10,500–12,000 / $15,400–17,400 GrM

1952 MG TD Midget, 1250cc, left-hand drive, full weather equipment, completely restored 1998, finished in ivory, red interior.
£9,000–10,500 / $13,000–15,250 H&H

1952 MG TD Midget, 1250cc 4-cylinder engine, twin SU H4 carburettors, 57bhp, 4-speed manual gearbox, 4-wheel hydraulic drum brakes.
£8,000–10,000 / $11,600–14,500 Pou

c1953 MG TF Midget, 1250cc, 4-speed gearbox, full weather equipment including a tonneau cover, finished in ivory, green interior, very good condition throughout.
£11,000–13,000 / $16,000–18,850 H&H

◀ **1953 MG TF Midget,** 1250cc 4-cylinder engine, wire wheels, refurbished, cylinder head overhauled, new valves, finished in red, grey twill hood and side screens, black leatherette interior trim.
£12,000–14,000 / $17,400–20,300 ⚒ BRIT
Originally conceived as a stop-gap measure while the MGA was under development, the TF was effectively a facelifted TD. Despite a somewhat cool reception at its launch – the TF was seen to be far too old-fashioned in the face of sleek newcomers such as the Triumph TR2 and Austin-Healey 100 – it went on to become one of the most revered of all MG models. In all, 9,600 were produced, most going overseas.

▶ **1953 MG TF Midget,** 1250cc 4-cylinder engine, completely restored at a cost of over £15,000, fewer than 100 miles covered since, engine rebuilt and converted to unleaded fuel, new ash body frame, finished in red, black interior.
£11,000–13,000 / $16,000–18,850 ⚒ BARO

1949 MG YA Saloon, 1250cc 4-cylinder engine, finished in red, red interior trim, 10,000 miles from new, excellent condition throughout.
£8,000–9,000 / $11,600–13,000 ⚒ H&H
Introduced in 1947, the MG YA sports saloon was replaced in 1951 by the YB. Both cars had the 1250cc, four-cylinder overhead-valve engine. The chassis, suspension and steering were based on those of the TD, while the body panels were Morris 8.

▶ **1952 MG YB Saloon,** 1250cc 4-cylinder engine, finished in maroon, good condition.
£2,500–3,000 / $3,600–4,300 ⚒ H&H

1957 MGA 1500 Roadster, left-hand drive, restored, new chrome wire wheels, finished in red, new black leather upholstery, good condition throughout.
£7,000–8,000 / $10,200–11,600 ⚒ BKS
A successful outing for three EX182 pre-production prototypres at the Le Mans 24-hour race in 1955 provided perfect pre-launch publicity for MG's new sports car. Conceived as a replacement for the traditional T-Type MGs, and launched in 1955, the MGA combined a rigid chassis with the Austin-designed 1489cc engine, which had first appeared in the MG ZA Magnette. The overhead-valve B-series unit produced 68bhp (later 72bhp) at 5,500rpm, employing twin SU carburettors. Running gear was based on that of the TF, with independent coil-spring/wishbone front suspension and a leaf-sprung live rear axle. Clad in a stylish aerodynamic body and capable of topping 95mph, the MGA proved a hit, selling 13,000 units in its first full year of production.

◄ **1959 MGA 1600 Coupé,** completely restored, wire wheels, finished in white, black upholstery piped in white, excellent condition.
£9,000–10,000
$13,000–14,500 BKS

Miller's Starter Marque

- **Starter MG:** *MGA.*
  This is the separate-chassis forerunner to the MGB. It wasn't made in anything like the numbers of the MGB: 101,000 MGAs were built between 1956 and 1962, and a staggering 81,000 of those were exported to America. Although that makes it rare compared with the MGB, the MGA is still eminently practical and usable. One good reason is that so many parts – notably the unburstable BMC B-series engine – were shared with other vehicles under the Morris-BMC-Nuffield banner.

1959 MGA Roadster, restored, finished in powder blue, black leather interior.
£8,000–10,000 / $11,600–14,500 VIC

Miller's Compares

◄ **I. 1959 MGA 1600 Roadster,** 1588cc 4-cylinder engine, extensively refurbished, new radiator and track rod ends, wire wheels sandblasted and repainted, many electrical items renewed, new exhaust system, bare-metal respray in red, black mohair hood, all chromework replated or replaced, retrimmed to original specification in black leather with red piping, new carpets.
£8,000–9,500 / $11,600–13,800 BRIT

► **II. 1960 MGA Twin Cam Roadster,** 1588cc double-overhead-camshaft 4-cylinder engine, 4-speed manual gearbox, rack-and-pinion steering, Dunlop knock-off wheels, Tri-Light headlights, completely restored, little use since.
£20,000–22,000 / $29,000–32,000 RM
MG announced the Twin Cam MGA in the spring of 1958. With twice the power of the standard engine, the new double-overhead-camshaft four-cylinder engine featured twin SU carburettors and pumped out an impressive 108bhp. For the most part, the MGA Twin Cam was really road-going racing car. It was equipped with four-wheel disc brakes and was capable of a top speed in excess of 110mph. Total production of Twin Cams ran to 2,111 between 1958 and 1961.

These two cars tell the tale of the 'continental drift' in the classic car market. Over three quarters of MGAs produced were exported to the USA, and many, like item I, have found their way back to the UK. This one was re-imported in 1999 and subsequently was extensively restored. You might have expected it to command more than the price range given above, but in the UK market a left-hand-drive car like this one will always be worth less than an original right-hand-drive UK market car. Item II is a rare Twin Cam roadster, which realised far more than item I at a US auction. A price that any UK Twin Cam owner would be delighted with. In fact, it's probably a fair bit more than the car would command in the UK. There are two factors at play here: first, the car had been subjected to a very exacting restoration, and many American collectors are prepared to pay a premium for such cars; second, over the period of data compilation for this book, some sectors of the US market were particularly buoyant, with prices ahead of the European scene. One of these sectors was for well detailed restorations of British mainstream sporting marques.

An MG advertising poster for the 1.5 litre Magnette saloon, minor creasing to edges, 22 x 30in (56 x 76cm).
£180–220 / $260–320 ⚒ BKS

1973 MG Midget, 1275cc 4-cylinder engine, round-wheel-arch model, completely restored, new engine and gearbox, new body panels, finished in original red, new black interior, excellent condition throughout.
£2,800–3,200 / $4,000–4,650 ⚒ H&H

1973 MG Midget Mk III, finished in gold, black vinyl interior, 1 owner and 61,000 miles from new, good condition throughout.
£2,000–2,500 / $2,900–3,600 ⚒ BARO

Miller's Starter Marque

- **Starter MG:** *Midget 1961 onward.* When it comes to breezy budget motoring, about the only thing that matches the MG Midget is the Austin-Healey Sprite, for apart from badging, trim and instruments, they're the same thing (the earlier Mk I 'Frog-eye' Sprite though, was only produced as an Austin-Healey). The Midget is a compelling classic cocktail for the cost conscious – in fact about the only cheaper way of enjoying fresh air on four wheels is probably to buy a skateboard. Midgets have a massive following, with more than 200,000 having been built up to 1979, and that means there's tremendous club support, a well-established and competitive spares and re-manufacturing industry, and a mature network of established marque specialists and restorers. Better still, the 'Spridget', as the Midget/Sprite models are often called, is a BMC parts-bin special based on the mechanicals and running gear from the likes of the million-selling Morris Minor and Austin A35. If the body's riddled with rust, you can also get a complete new shell from Rover subsidiary British Motor Heritage.
- **What to watch:** Particular points include the inner and outer sills. Be wary of ill-fitted replacement sills and check the closing action of the doors. If they bind or snag, someone may have welded on new sills without supporting the car in the middle to ensure that the frame maintains its correct shape. Another trouble area is the door pillar. You should shake each door firmly in this area to reveal any flexing. The engines are generally reliable and long-lasting, but check for fluid leaks. Gearboxes can be noisy, but are similarly robust, and the rear axle – similar to the Morris Minor's – rarely gives trouble.
- **Pick of the bunch:** For classic credibility, the Sprite Mk IV and Midget Mk III (1966–70) are probably the best bet, with better performance from the 1275cc engines than earlier cars. They are still chrome-era classics, however, with all the visual appeal of the older versions. If performance matters more, the 1500cc Triumph Spitfire-engined Midgets from 1974 will touch 100mph, but they have the vast black plastic bumpers that some people loathe.

◀ **1976 MG Midget,** 1500cc, completely restored, fully rust-proofed, finished in red, black interior, roll-bar, sports steering wheel, fewer than 47,000 miles from new, excellent condition throughout.
£3,000–3,600
$4,400–5,150 ⚒ H&H

▶ **1979 MG Midget 1500,** 1491cc 4-cylinder engine, stored 3 years, recently recommissioned, finished in yellow, fewer than 16,000 miles from new, very good original condition throughout.
£3,500–4,200 / $5,000–6,100 ⚒ BRIT
The last of the Midget line, the 1500 utilised the engine of the final-series Triumph Spitfire. Readily distinguishable from its predecessors by the large urethane bumpers, the car also sat higher to comply with US legislation, while the rear of the body reverted to squared-off wheel arches. The increase in power meant that the Midget could top 100mph, and in this guise it remained in production until late 1979.

1966 MGB Roadster, wire wheels, older restoration, finished in black, red leather upholstery and hood, good condition.
£6,500–7,500 / $9,400–10,875 ⊞ GrM

1967 MGB Roadster, 1798cc, restored, stainless-steel exhaust system, overdrive gearbox, Minilite-style alloy wheels, finished in red, black leather interior trim piped in white, very good condition throughout.
£5,000–6,000 / $7,250–8,700 ⚒ H&H

> A known continuous history can add value to and enhance the enjoyment of a car.

1968 MGB Roadster, chrome wire wheels, finished in red, black hood, black leather seats, good condition.
£6,600–7,500 / $9,500–10,870 ⊞ CARS

► **1970 MGB GT,** 1798cc engine,overdrive gearbox, Rostyle wheels, finished in red, original.
£3,750–4,250 / $5,400–6,200 ⊞ UMC

MG Model	ENGINE cc/cyl	DATES	CONDITION 1	2	3
TC Midget	1250/4	1946–49	£13,000	£11,000	£7,000
TD Midget	1250/4	1950–52	£13,000	£9,000	£5,000
TF Midget	1250/4	1953–55	£15,000	£13,000	£8,000
TF 1500	1466/4	1954–55	£16,000	£14,000	£9,000
YA/YB	1250/4	1947–53	£5,500+	£2,750	£1,500
Magnette ZA/ZB	1489/4	1953–58	£3,500	£2,000	£500
Magnette Mk III/IV	1489/4	1958–68	£3,500	£1,200	£350
MGA 1500 Roadster	1489/4	1955–59	£11,000+	£7,000	£4,000
MGA 1500 FHC	1489/4	1956–59	£8,000	£6,000	£3,000
MGA 1600 Roadster	1588/4	1959–61	£12,000	£9,000	£4,500
MGA 1600 FHC	1588/4	1959–61	£7,000	£5,000	£3,000
MGA Twin Cam Roadster	1588/4	1958–60	£16,000	£12,000	£9,000
MGA Twin Cam FHC	1588/4	1958–60	£13,000	£9,000	£7,000
MGA 1600 Mk II Roadster	1622/4	1961–62	£12,000	£10,000	£4,000
MGA 1600 Mk II FHC	1622/4	1961–62	£9,000	£7,000	£3,000
MGB Mk I	1798/4	1962–67	£7,000	£4,000	£1,200
MGB GT Mk I	1798/4	1965–67	£5,000	£3,500	£1,000
MGB Mk II	1798/4	1967–69	£7,500	£4,000	£1,500
MGB GT Mk II	1798/4	1969	£4,500	£2,500	£850
MGB Mk III	1798/4	1969–74	£6,500	£4,000	£1,100
MGB GT Mk III	1798/4	1969–74	£4,500	£2,500	£1,000
MGB Roadster (rubber bumper)	1798/4	1975–80	£6,000	£4,500	£1,200
MGB GT	1798/4	1975–80	£5,000	£3,000	£1,000
MGB Jubilee	1798/4	1975	£5,000	£3,000	£1,200
MGB LE	1798/4	1980	£8,500	£4,750	£2,250
MGB GT LE	1798/4	1980	£6,000	£3,750	£2,000
MGC	2912/6	1967–69	£8,000	£6,500	£4,000
MGC GT	2912/6	1967–69	£7,000	£5,000	£2,000
MGB GT V8	3528/8	1973–76	£9,000	£6,000	£3,000
Midget Mk I	948/4	1961–62	£4,000	£2,000	£850
Midget Mk II	1098/4	1962–66	£3,000	£2,000	£850
Midget Mk III	1275/4	1966–74	£3,200	£2,000	£850
Midget 1500	1491/4	1975–79	£3,000	£2,000	£850

All prices are for British right-hand-drive cars. For left-hand-drive varieties deduct 10–15% for UK values, even if converted to right-hand drive.

1971 MGB Roadster, 1798cc, stainless-steel exhaust, wire wheels, battery moved to boot, hard and soft tops, tonneau cover, finished in white, black interior, 2 owners from new.
£4,000–5,000 / $5,800–6,500 ⚒ H&H

1972 MGB GT, restored early 1990s at a cost of £18,000, Oselli Stage II tuned 1950cc engine, gearbox rebuilt, front and rear anti-roll bars, Minilite alloy wheels, Britax folding sunroof, finished in white, leather interior trim and upholstery, walnut dashboard, centre console, door cappings and door pulls, wood-rim steering wheel, concours winner.
£4,700–5,500 / $6,850–8,000 ⚒ BKS

1972 MGB Roadster, overdrive, wire wheels, restored, finished in red, black leather interior.
£8,000–9,000 / $11,600–13,000 ⊞ VIC

► **1973 MGB Roadster,** completely restored, Rostyle wheels, finished in British racing green, black interior, excellent condition.
£6,000–7,000 / $8,700–10,200 ⊞ WbC

1977 MGB Roadster, 1798cc engine, 4-speed manual gearbox with overdrive, wire wheels, driving lights, finished in red, very good mechanical condition.
£2,250–2,750 / $3,300–3,900 ⚒ BARO

► **1974 MGB GT,** 1798cc, overdrive gearbox, restored at a cost of over £5,000.
£4,000–5,000 / $5,800–7,250 ⊞ SiC

Miller's Starter Marque

- **Starter MG:** *MGB, MGB GT.*
  The MGB has got to be one of the most practical, affordable and enjoyable classic sporting packages around. For a start, it's the most popular British sports car ever made, a winning formula based on rugged reliability, simple clean lines, fine road manners and adequate performance. For sheer classic credentials, models before the 1974 introduction of rubber-bumper cars with higher ride height are favoured, but later examples can be even more affordable. They're also a great way to make 50,000 friends, for that's how many members there are in the MG Owners' Club, the world's largest one-make car club. There is also a superb parts and specialist network, even down to brand-new bodyshells being made on original tooling. The fixed-head MGB GT is cheaper than the open roadster, yet offers additional practicality and comfort.
- **What to watch:** Few worries with engines and mechanicals, but MGBs can rot, and because of unitary construction pay particular attention to sills and other structural aspects.

1972 MGB Roadster, 1798cc 4-cylinder engine, restored to concours condition, new water pump, engine repainted and fitted with new original-specification labels, new radiator and exhaust system, new trunnion bushes and brake discs, rewired, chrome wire wheels, bare-metal respray, all door locks and bare-metal nuts and bolts re-anodised, new hood, 30,000 miles from new.
£9,500–10,750 / $13,800–15,600 ⚒ BRIT

1978 MGB GT, overdrive gearbox, Rostyle wheels, finished in vermillion, grey and black cloth interior, walnut dashboard, structurally sound, but some blistering on nearside sill.
£1,200–1,500 / $1,750–2,170 ⚒ CGC

1978 MGB Roadster, 1798cc, finished in yellow, original and unrestored.
£5,000–6,000 / $7,250–8,700 ⊞ VIC

◄ **1979 MGB Roadster,** 1798cc engine, Weber carburettor, left-hand drive, subject of major reburbishment in USA before being imported to UK, American-specification pollution controls removed, engine rebuilt, new water pump, new exhaust, luggage rack, finished in green, AM/FM radio/8-track stereo, tan interior, 2 owners and 52,000 miles from new.
£5,000–5,750 / $7,250–8,300 ⚒ BKS

1979 MGB GT, 1798cc 4-cylinder engine, overdrive gearbox, finished in white, orange and black striped fabric interior trim, 2 owners and 74,000 miles from new, original specification.
£2,500–3,000 / $3,600–4,300 ⚒ BRIT

1979 MGB GT, manual gearbox with overdrive, finished in dark green green.
£2,750–3,250 / $3,900–4,700 ⊞ SiC

► **1968 MGC Roadster,** 2912cc 6-cylinder engine, 4-speed manual gearbox with overdrive, wire wheels, finished in black.
£12,000–13,000 / $17,400–18,850 ⊞ PM

1968 MGC Roadster, manual gearbox with overdrive, wire wheels, restored at a cost of over £9,900, stored 1992–2000, recommissioned, further £3,400 spent on mechanical work, finished in tartan red, black leather interior with red piping.
£7,000–8,000 / $10,200–11,600 ⚒ BKS

Cross Reference
See Colour Review (page 148)

► **1968 MGC Roadster,** 2912cc 6-cylinder engine, refurbished 1994, stainless-steel exhaust system and petrol tank, new gearbox, chrome wire wheels, rewired, new mohair hood, finished in white, new carpeting, excellent condition.
£7,000–8,000 / $10,200–11,600 ⚒ BRIT

MGC & MGC GT (1967–69)

Engine: 2912cc overhead-valve six-cylinder.
Power output: 145bhp @ 5,250rpm.
Transmission: Four-speed manual, optional overdrive; three-speed automatic.
Top speed: 120–122mph.
0–60mph: 10 seconds.
Production: MGC, 4,552; MGC GT, 4,457.
Prices in 1968: MGC (roadster), £1,145; MGC GT (fixed-head), £1,299.

Misunderstood, that's the MGC, and some cruel critics might say misbegotten too. In the second half of the 1960s, BMC's no-nonsense MGB was soaring up the sales charts, while time was fast catching up with the characterful Austin-Healey 3000, the oldest sports car in BMC's portfolio. At the time, BMC was also reworking the Austin-Healey's six-cylinder engine for the upcoming Austin 3 Litre saloon, and thus the MGC was born, a parts-bin hybrid that looked like an MGB, but wasn't man enough to carry the mantle of the Austin-Healey. The C was slower than the Austin-Healey 3000, lacked its handling and sports car exuberance, and for the short period of model overlap was more expensive than the butch old Healey. Gone too were many of the MGB's virtues. The six-cylinder engine, all of 200lb heavier than the B's four-pot, was levered in using the crow-bar approach, with a bonnet bulge, higher ride height and revised front suspension. The result? A front-heavy understeerer that lacked the MGB's lively handling. The press panned the unfortunate MGC, and in a little over two years of dismal sales it disappeared into the hole BMC had made between two stools. Certainly, part of the MGC's burden was the weight of unfair comparison, because in reality the it's not so much a true sports car, but rather a pleasant long-legged cruiser, more at home than either the MGB or Austin-Healey on motorways and the *routes nationales.* If not for the dual blight of blending MGB looks with Austin-Healey expectations, the MGC might have carved a more memorable niche for itself.

◀ **1971 MGB GT V8,** restored and converted to V8 power 1992 by Abingdon Car Restoration Company, Rover SD1 engine and 5-speed manual gearbox, aluminium inlet manifold, Holley 4-barrel carburettor, stainless-steel exhaust, electronic ignition, steering, suspension and brakes uprated using genuine MGB V8 components, new body panels including sills, front wings, rear half wings, jacking points and rear valence, Special Tuning chin spoiler, Minotaur alloy wheels, Waxoyled 1992 and 1996, finished in red, black interior, excellent mechanical condition, good bodywork and interior.
£5,000–6,000 / $7,250–8,700 ⚒ BKS

1975 MGB GT V8, 3528cc V8 engine, restored 1991–92 at a cost of over £10,000, 13,000 miles covered since, finished in red, black interior.
£3,250–4,000 / $4,700–5,800 ⚒ H&H

1976 MGB Costello V8 Roadster, manual gearbox with overdrive, completely restored 1991, 66,000 miles from new, finished in red, black leather interior.
£5,500–6,500 / $8,000–9,400 ⚒ BKS

In 1970, Kent-based engineer Ken Costello began selling MGBs fitted with the 3.5 litre Rover V8 engine, their favourable reception prompting British Leyland to follow suit. The aluminium V8 weighed a few pounds less than the cast-iron B-series four it replaced, so little re-engineering of the existing suspension was called for, and the Costello version even kept the standard MGB drivetrain. Whereas the Leyland product was only built in GT form and used the 137bhp Range Rover power unit, Costello employed the Rover saloon's 144bhp engine in both roadsters and GTs. Having 50 per cent more horsepower and twice as much torque as the standard B, the V8 cars possessed blistering performance, reaching 60mph in under eight seconds and being capable of exceeding 130mph flat-out. Although Costello's product was reckoned to be superior to the Leyland version, he could not compete on price and is thought to have made around only 200 cars before ceasing production.

MGB GT V8 (1973–76)

Body style: 2+2 fixed-head coupé.
Construction: Unitary.
Engine: 3528cc alloy V8.
Power output: 137bhp @ 5,000rpm.
Suspension: Front, coil springs and wishbones; rear, semi-elliptic leaf springs.
Brakes: Servo-assisted front discs, rear drums.
Steering: Rack-and-pinion.
Maximum speed: 125mph.
0–60mph: 8.5 seconds.
Average fuel consumption: 20–27mpg.
Production: 2,591.

Minerva

1924 Minerva Model WW Faux Cabriolet, 5355cc 6-cylinder double-sleeve-valve monobloc engine, 30bhp, 4-speed manual gearbox, 4-wheel brakes by Perrot shaft, handbrake on transmission, semi-elliptic front suspension, cantilever rear suspension, right-hand drive, seating for 4 plus dickey, 3-piece opening windscreen, scuttle-mounted side lights, fold-down luggage grid, twin side-mounted spare wheels, partially restored, brown vinyl upholstery.
£14,000–17,000 / $20,300–24,650 C
Starting with bicycles in 1897, Sylvain de Jong progressed to motorcycles, then cars. By 1904, a full production-series voiturette was offered, named the Minervette, but it was not until 1908, when de Jong was granted a licence to produce Knight sleeve-valve engines, that the company developed. The model WW, was one of the earlier, larger-capacity Minervas, of approximately 5.3 litres, and was built only in 1924 and 1925. These models benefited from having four-wheel brakes.

Mini

At long last the new Mini's here, but only time will tell if BMW's 'life-style' Mini will charm the world in the same way as the original.
The intention of the remarkable designer Alec Issigonis was to create a car that would be parked outside the cottage of every working man. In its long life, which began in 1959, the Mini achieved far more than that. On the one hand, it was a no-nonsense family runabout, a miniature van and pick-up workhorse, then a world-beating rally giant killer, the last word in Swinging Sixties chic, a top-billing film star with Michael Caine in *The Italian Job*, and a celebrity accessory adopted by everyone from The Beatles to Twiggy and Peter Sellers. In the hands of customisers, the Mini has also mutated into myriad fanciful and fantastic permutations. In short, the car intended as a modest working hack has become a classless icon. That's quite some act to follow.

1959 Morris Mini Minor, restored, new engine, finished in pale blue, displayed by Rover at various European motor shows.
£4,500–5,000 / $6,500–7,250 MINI

1960 Austin Seven Mini, 848cc 4-cylinder engine, Minilite-type wheels, wheel-arch extensions, bonnet straps, finished in tartan red, rally trip meter, good condition.
£1,000–1,200 / $1,500–1,800 BRIT

1961 Austin Seven Mini, barn stored 12–15 years, non-runner, engine turns over, fuel pump defective, finished in grey, blue-grey interior, 33,739 miles from new.
£1,700–2,200 / $2,450–3,200 BKS

Although there had been many front-wheel-drive designs before the Mini's arrival, the transverse engine layout allowed Issigonis to create a trend-setting masterpiece of automotive packaging. BMC marketed the car as the Austin Seven and Morris Mini Minor before Mini was created as a marque in its own right in 1969. In due course, estate and van versions arrived, larger engines became available, more luxurious Riley and Wolseley models joined the line-up, and the sporting Mini Cooper was introduced. The early Mk I had the 848cc A-series engine, rubber-cone suspension and a floor-mounted starter button, the last two features being replaced by Hydrolastic suspension and key starting respectively in 1964.

1966 Austin Mini Traveller, 848cc, 4-speed manual gearbox, left-hand drive, restored finished in metallic blue, blue interior, excellent condition.
£4,000–5,000 / $5,800–7,250 Pou

1961 Austin Seven Mini, 848cc, finished in red, excellent condition.
£5,500–6,100 / $8,000–8,800 MINI

1965 Morris Mini Cooper, blueprinted 970cc Cooper S engine, unleaded big-valve head, 4-speed synchromesh gearbox with Cooper S output shafts, genuine Minilite wheels, right-hand tank, finished in tartan red, full-length black fabric sunroof, fully refurbished Innocenti interior.
£8,000–9,000 / $11,600–13,000 WbC

1966 Mini Cooper, 998cc 4-cylinder engine, finished in green and white.
£5,000–6,000 / $7,250–8,700 MINI

◄ **1966 Radford Mini Cooper,** completely restored, 998cc engine, Benelite grille with spot and driving lamps, folding sunroof, finished in royal blue, electric windows and quarterlights, De Ville wooden dashboard and instruments, Les Leston-style wood-rim steering wheel, arm rest/console, period radio, reclining seats, black leather upholstery.
£6,000–7,000 / $8,700–10,200 WbC

MINI Model	ENGINE cc/cyl	DATES	CONDITION 1	2	3
Mini	848/4	1959–67	£3,500	£1,200	-
Mini Countryman	848/4	1961–67	£2,500	£1,200	-
Cooper Mk I	997/4	1961–67	£8,000	£5,000	£2,500
Cooper Mk II	998/4	1967–69	£6,000	£4,000	£1,500
Cooper S Mk I	var/4	1963–67	£7,000	£5,000	£2,000
Cooper S Mk II	1275/4	1967–71	£6,000	£5,000	£2,000
Innocenti Mini Cooper	998/4	1966–75	£4,500	£2,000	£1,000

Miller's Starter Marque

- **Starter Minis:** *All models.*
- Whether yours is a 1959 car with sliding windows, cord door pulls and external hinges, or a 2001 model, all Minis are classics. Even though modern Minis are still closely related to the 1959 original, the early cars have an extra, subtle charm. Parts are rarely a problem, but the Mini's major enemy is rust, so here are a few guides to buying a sound older example.
- Before looking underneath, inspect the roof panel, guttering and pillars supporting the roof. If they are rusted or show signs of filler, it suggests that the rest of the structure may be in similar or worse shape.
- Examine floorpans from above and below, joints with the inner sill, front and rear bulkheads, crossmember and jacking points. If the subframe has welded plates, check that they've been attached properly. Look inside the parcel compartment on each side of the rear seat, beneath the rear seat, all corners of the boot, the spare-wheel well and battery container. These are all common rust spots.
- Clicking from beneath the front of the car indicates wear in the driveshaft constant-velocity joints – not easy or cheap to rectify.
- Rear radius-arm support bearings deteriorate rapidly unless regularly lubricated; check the grease points ahead of each rear wheel for signs of recent attention.
- The A-series engine is generally reliable and long-lived. However, expect timing-chain rattle on older units; exhaust-valve burning can be evident on high-mileage examples, as can exhaust smoke under hard acceleration, indicating cylinder/piston wear.
- Mini Coopers can be worth more than double the price of an ordinary classic Mini. Consequently, fakes abound. It's not just a question of checking the uprated specification – twin carbs, disc brakes, badges and the like – but also of unravelling the engine and chassis numbers and subtle tell-tale signs that you'll only learn about from club and professional experts. First join the club, then go shopping (see our clubs guide on pages 336-342).
- **Pick of the bunch:** Of the original generation of Coopers, the best all-round performer is the 1275 S, with 60mph coming up in 10.9 seconds and puff running out just shy of the ton. As usual, the aficionados prefer first-of-breed purity of earlier cars with sliding windows, cord door pulls and external hinges.

1969 Morris Mini Cooper S, 1275cc, restored to original specification 1990s, only 700 miles covered since, original steel wheels, set of period Cosmic alloy wheels, finished in red and white, black interior.
£4,500–5,500 / $6,500–8,000 ⚒ H&H

1967 Austin Mini Cooper, 998cc, completely restored 1994, engine and gearbox rebuilt, mechanics overhauled, bare-metal respray in white and black, new interior, outstanding condition throughout.
£4,000–4,500 / $5,800–6,500 ⚒ BARO
Mini designer Alec Issigonis didn't approve when John Cooper approached him with plans for a hot Mini. The creator of the miniature marvel stuck steadfastly to his vision of a car that would provide 'everyman transport'. But Cooper went over his head, got the go-ahead to breathe magic on the Mini, and created an unlikely sporting legend. The Mini's engine was bored out to 997cc and fitted with twin SU carbs, gear ratios altered, a remote gear change installed in place of the waggly wand, and to stop this pocket rocket Cooper challenged Lockheed to produce 7in front disc brakes. The result was a rallying world-beater, which was so invincible that when Coopers came home 1-2-3 in the infamous 1966 Monte Carlo Rally, the miffed Monagasque organisers disqualified them on trumped-up technicalities.

1968 Austin Mini Cooper, body restored and resprayed, fabric-type sunroof.
£2,600–3,250 / $3,800–4,700 ⊞ GrM
What did John Cooper get from the original Mini Cooper? A £2 royalty for each example built. But he's not complaining. He recalls, 'Harriman [then BMC Chairman George Harriman] said we had to make 1,000 – but we eventually made 150,000.' That translates into £300,000 commission.

1969 Mini Cooper S, 1275cc, original specification, finished in blue and white, black interior, stored for approximately 20 years, 1 owner from new, bodywork in good condition .
£5,000–6,000 / $7,250–8,700 ⚒ BKS

Colour Review

1913 Peugeot Bébé Grand Prix Racer, chain drive, rear brakes, knock-off wire-spoked wheels, white Michelin tyres.
£12,000–14,000 / $17,400–23,200 ⚒ RM
Throughout the early part of the 20th century, Peugeot racers dominated high-profile events. Wins at the French Grand Prix in 1912 and 1913, and first-place finishes at the Indianapolis 500 in 1913 and 1916 did much to cement Peugeot's legacy as one of the most successful firms in racing at the time. The company was renowned for exceptional design and, after 1912, owed much of its achievement to the development of the double-overhead-camshaft engines on their competition cars.

1927 Bugatti Type 35B Grand Prix, chassis no. 4845, engine no. 114T, 2262cc overhead-camshaft 8-cylinder engine, paired cylinder blocks with integral heads, 1 exhaust/2 inlet valves per cylinder, supercharger, 4-speed manual gearbox, 4-wheel drum brakes, reversed quarter-elliptic rear springs, 8-spoke cast-aluminium wheels incorporating integral brake drums, completely restored, all original major mechanical components retained.
£400,000+ / $580,000+ ⚒ RM

◀ 1936 Talbot Lago T150C, restored at a cost of approximately £100,000.
£500,000+ /$725,000+ ⚒ COYS
This car participated in 28 Grands Prix, and it competed at Le Mans no fewer than four times. It has completed the Mille Miglia on five occasions, and has been driven by Gadot, Chiron, Chinetti, Bradley and Levegh.

1952 Ferrari 375 'Indianapolis' Formula 1/AAA Championship Trail Racing Single-Seater, ex-Johnny Parsons 'Grant Piston Ring Special', subject of no-expense-spared restoration, wheels, brake assemblies, suspension and transaxle casing rebuilt, mechanics overhauled, tuned to running order.
£500,000+ / $725,000 ⚒ BKS
This Monoposto Ferrari is one of the limited-edition batch of 4.5 litre, 24-plug, V12-engined cars that Ferrari built specifically to compete in the Indianapolis 500-mile race of 1952 which, at that time, was a qualifying round for the FIA Drivers' World Championship series, contested primarily by national Grand Prix races in Argentina, Great Britain and Continental Europe. These cars drew upon Ferrari's stock of Modello 375 4.5 litre Formula 1 components that had been accumulated during the Grand Prix seasons of 1950 and 1951. But the factory's hard-pressed Formula 1 frames from those seasons could not be used in this 'Indy' guise, since their wheelbase was too short to comply with the minimum specified for Indianapolis-style Championship Trail speedway cars. Consequently new longer-wheelbase chassis were built, primarily for the 1952 Indianapolis customer racing programme. These incorporated a robust superstructure system combining body-supporting tail and scuttle hoops, with additional horizontal longerons above the main oval-section frame tubes, plus long diagonal engine-bay braces.

1952 Ferrari 500/625 Grand Prix Formula 1 Single-Seater, 2.5 litre, 'Argentina' Ferrari 625 body, all necessary FIA historic paperwork, ready to race.
£400,000+ / $580,000 ⚒ BKS
This Grand Prix racing Ferrari not only has a long history of World Championship level competition within two different Formulae over no fewer than four seasons, 1952–55, but it also was the earliest Ferrari to have carried a Maranello works team driver to the World Championship crown. That driver was the legendary Alberto Ascari.

1978 Ferrari 312T3 Grand Prix Formula 1 Racing Single-Seater, ex-Gilles Villeneuve/Carlos Reutemann, United States GP winner, 4th T3 built, excellent condition.
£300,000+ / $435,000+ ⚒ BKS

Miller's is a price GUIDE not a price LIST

1954 Maserati 250F, ex-Baron Emmanuel de Graffenried/ Ottorino Volonterio, 2.5 litre, unrestored, Grand Prix history.
£500,000+ / $725,000+ ⚒ COYS
To many, the Maserati 250F is the ultimate front-engined Grand Prix car. During the halcyon days of the 1950s – the golden era of motor racing – few cars could compete with it in terms of popularity and success. Stirling Moss stated that it 'steered beautifully, and inclined towards stable oversteer, which one could exploit by balancing it against the smooth power delivery and steer in long sustained drifts through the corners.'

1959 Lotus-Climax Type 16 Formula Racing Single-Seater, 2.7 litre Griswold Climax engine, lightweight aluminium bodywork, restored to racing order, thought to be the most original surviving active Lotus 16.
£130,000–150,000 / $188,500–217,500 ⚒ BKS
This particular car was supplied new to Innes Ireland as the 1959 works team Formula 1 driver's privately prepared, but quasi-works entered, Formula 2 mount.

1961 Cooper-Climax T55 'Slimline' Formula 1 and Tasman Racing Single-Seater, ex-works and Sir Jack Brabaham, completely restored, mostly original, excellent condition.
£95,000–110,000 / $137,750–159,500 ⚒ BKS
This 1.5 litre Formula 1 Grand Prix and 2.5/2.7 litre Tasman car marked the end of double World Champion Jack Brabham's race-winning career with the Cooper works team. In its heyday, it was an intermediate design that introduced the Cooper marque to the newly-instituted 1.5 litre Formula 1 class, and which bridged the gap until the latest Coventry Climax V8 engine became available to replace the original Climax four-cylinder unit. Only two of these works cars were built, the other being campaigned by New Zealander Bruce McLaren. These cars had the same coil-and-wishbone suspension as the 1960 T53P 'Lowline'. The engine, however, was slung slightly lower in the frame, and the fuel pump repositioned, to enable an even lower-line and slimmer bodyshell. Cooper had also developed a six-speed version of the Cooper C5S transaxle. It worked well and helped the drivers to balance the T55 on the Formula 2-derived Climax FPF engine's relatively narrow torque band, particularly on wet tracks. In all, the works T55 cars made 19 race starts during the 1961 Formula 1 season, returning 13 finishes and six retirements, the highlight of the year being Brabham's victory first time out at Aintree in this car. Then he took the car to New Zealand and Australia for the Tasman series in the opening months of 1962. Tasman regulations permitted engines of up to 3 litres capacity, and this car was uprated with alternative 2.7 and 2.5 litre Climax FPF engines to suit.

◄ **1969 Ford GT40,** 1 of the last to be built, extensively restored, race ready.
£280,000+ $406,000+ ⚒ BJ

1987 Courage Cougar C20 Porsche, 2160cc 6-cylinder engine, fuel injection, 720bhp, 5-speed manual gearbox, restored, excellent condition.
£75,000–85,000 / $108,750–123,250 ⚒ Pou

1997 McLaren F1 GTR 'Longtail' World GT Championship Racing Coupé, 6 litre McLaren-BMW S70/2 GTR V12 engine, running order.
£275,000–300,000 / $395,000–435,000 ⚒ BKS
The McLaren F1 emerged in 1993 as the world's fastest production car ever – 241mph – and the world's first-ever practical three-seat, central-driving-position high-performance coupé. In 1995, the F1 GTR road-racing variant achieved the most successful new-marque debut in the history of the Le Mans 24-hour race, five of the six F1 GTRs that started reaching the finish, in first, third, fourth, eighth and 13th. The much improved and even more sophisticated F1 GTR 'Longtail' model was produced to defend McLaren's pre-eminence during the 1997 FIA GT Championship, in which the cars faced the strongest ever challenge from the works Mercedes-Benz CLK Coupés, with which they fought a season-long battle for supremacy.

1989 Ferrari F40 LM, 2936cc V8 engine, 720bhp, 4-wheel independent suspension, 4-wheel ventilated disc brakes, carbon-fibre/kevlar bodywork, built as an experimental road car, modified to LM specification.
£300,000+ / $435,000 ⚒ Pou

1997 Ferrari F50 GT1, 4700cc double-overhead-camshaft 8-cylinder engine, 5 valves per cylinder, 6-speed sequential transmission, 4-wheel independent suspension and disc brakes, last of 3 GT1 prototypes to be completed.
£1,000,000+ / $1,450,000 ⚒ RM
The F50 GT1 study was commissioned by Ferrari with a view to winning Le Mans and other GT races in 1995 and 1996. It was powered by a larger-displacement version of the fabled 333 SP powerplant. The transmission was also derived from that of the 333 SP. Ferrari seemed poised to enter the fray in 1996, but three factors dictated otherwise. Budgetary restraints at Maranello and the factory's all-out emphasis on Formula One killed the programme after only three prototypes had been completed. The third and most critical reason for cancelling the programme was simply that Ferrari's design, like the first McLaren, adhered too closely to the spirit of the new rules. The Ferrari qualified as a true road-going GT, while the later McLaren, Porsche and Nissan entries had already escalated into the ACO-accepted version of GT1, which allowed true racing versions of GT coupés. Instead of adhering to the ACO technical committee's original intent, the club officials reversed their original idea of having constructors rebuild road cars for racing. The class had evolved into specially-built race cars detuned to meet road standards. Ferrari was left with one of the most beautiful examples of the era, but which was no longer competitive.

1998 Ferrari F355 Challenge Car, 3496cc V8 engine, 5 valves per cylinder, 375bhp, 6-speed transmission, 4-wheel independent suspension, 4-wheel disc brakes.
£80,000–90,000 / $116,000–130,500 RM

1958 Lotus Seventeen-Climax, 1100cc Coventry Climax engine, twin Weber carburettors, finished in British racing green.
£35,000–40,000 / $50,750–58,000 BKS

1959 Osca Tipo S750 Sports Racing Two-Seater, double-overhead-camshaft 4-cylinder engine, twin Weber carburettors, 4-speed manual gearbox, independent front suspension by double wishbones and coil springs, live rear axle with coil springs and radius arms, 4-wheel hydraulic drum brakes, alloy wheels, left-hand drive, restored, original-type engine rebuilt, original body panels and chassis, racing bucket seats.
£90,000–100,000 / $130,500–145,000 C
This car was purchased new by the New York Ferrari importer Luigi Chinetti for his NART racing team. It was entered in the 1959 Le Mans 24-hour race and driven by the Mexican brothers Pedro and Ricardo Rodriguez. Unfortunately, after a promising start, it retired with mechanical problems.

1953 Ferrari 625 TF Barchetta, ex-works/Mike Hawthorn, 2.5 litre, 4-cylinder engine, restored, finished in Ferrari racing red, only survivor of 3 built, excellent condition.
£500,000+ / $725,000 COYS
This sports-racing Ferrari was first aired in June 1953, at the Gran Premio dell' Autodromo at Monza. The driver that day was British star Mike Hawthorn.

1951 Ferrari 340 America Competition Spyder, 4.1 litre overhead-camshaft V12 engine, triple carburettors, 300bhp, 5-speed manual gearbox, 4-wheel hydraulic drum brakes, restored at a cost of £300,000, replica Vignale body.
£410,000+ / $600,000+ RM
By 1950, Ferrari had enlisted the talents of Ing. Lampredi to develop a new engine for both Formula One and sports racing cars. With the realisation of the 4.5 litre Tipo 375 F1 racers, a slightly smaller engine, with a capacity of 4.1 litres, became available in a range of sports and GT cars. The first of these was the 340 America. Approximately 25 of these were built, the accent being placed on pure competition. Vignale bodied 11 examples, of which six were completed with open coachwork. The other five were Berlinettas. In an infamous incident, this car was completely dismantled and all the major components hidden in oil drums. The chassis was also concealed. A few years later, all of the parts were seized by the police and placed in storage. Eventually, the parts were liberated, and in 1995 a full restoration was begun.

1938 Alfa Romeo 8C 2900B Berlinetta, coachwork by Touring, ex-Romano/Biondetti Mille Miglia winner, completely restored.
£2,000,000+ / $2,890,000 BKS
Romano, the Alfa Romeo agent in Brescia, was looking for a car for the 1947 Mille Miglia, but the organisers had banned superchargers, so his problem was what to race? The answer was to buy this 1938 2.9 and, apparently working with Alfa Romeo, convert it to run unsupercharged with four Weber carburettors on a specially made manifold. The engine was down to 137bhp – compared to 180bhp for a standard road car, and 225bhp for a competition version of the 2.9 – but this was still a lot more power than the best Fiat 1100cc motors. The organisers had offered brand-new Pirelli tyres and a tank of fuel to any entrant, so not surprisingly there were 90 entrants who went through scrutineering, picked up their goodies, and never re-appeared for the race. That left 155 competitors, including a single Ferrari 125 and a team of new Cisitalias. To improve his chances, Romano recruited pre-war star and 1938 Mille Miglia winner, Clemente Biondetti as his co-driver. In fact, Biondetti seems to have done most of the driving – to good effect, as the pair recorded the winning elapsed time.

1955 Jaguar D-Type 'Shortnose' Sports-Racing Two-Seater, 3.4 litre XK-series double-overhead-camshaft 6-cylinder engine, dry-sump lubrication, 4-speed manual gearbox, 4-wheel disc brakes, restored to running order, original, low mileage.
£700,000+ / $1,015,000+ ⚒ BKS

1959 Ferrari 250 GT SWB Competizione, chassis no. 1613GT, completely restored, all major original components retained, finished in red, black leather interior.
£600,000+ ⚒ COYS
Introduced in 1954, the long-wheelbase 250 GT was Ferrari's first road car to sell strongly, although at two or three a week, the numbers were small by most standards. Examples were often raced, and one finished third in the 1957 Mille Miglia. At about the same time, long-distance sports car racing was beginning to undergo a change, which would see the emphasis shift away from the open sports-racer to the GT car. In October 1959, Ferrari unveiled the car that brought together the best qualities of road and race practice in the short-wheelbase 250 GT. Although it had been shortened by only 5¾in, this seemed more because of the compact, muscular body styled by Pininfarina and built by Scaglietti. It came in two versions: standard (steel) and competition (aluminium), but even the steel-bodied cars had aluminium doors, bonnet and boot, since it was expected that most would be raced. The 'short block' overhead-cam V12 had modified cylinder heads with relocated spark plugs and coil valve springs instead of the traditional hairpins. In competition form, it produced 280bhp, and performance depended on which of six rear axle ratios was chosen. The short wheelbase made for a stiffer chassis, so handling was improved, and for the very first time a Ferrari was offered with disc brakes.

1959 MGA Twin Cam Sports-Racer, prepared in the manner of a Le Mans racer, double-overhead-camshaft cylinder head, B-series cylinder block, 4-wheel disc brakes, Dunlop centre-lock wheels, wrap-around windscreen, driver's headrest, passenger-side metal tonneau, finished in British racing green, sports seats, light brown upholstery, very good condition.
£15,000–18,000 / $21,750–26,000 ⚒ BKS

1958 Devin Super Sport, 283cu.in V8 engine, period Offenhauser triple-carburettor inlet manifold, 300bhp (estimated), 4-speed alloy-cased Borg-Warner T-10 gearbox, 4-wheel independent suspension and disc brakes, rack-and-pinion steering, tubular-steel chassis, chrome wire wheels, restored, 5th SS built, 1 of 15 known to survive.
£100,000–115,000 / $145,000–166,750 ⚒ RM
In 1958, chassis engineer Malcolm MacGregor of Devonshire Engineering in Belfast, Northern Ireland, began shipping rolling chassis to Bill Devin of Devin Enterprises in El Monte, California. Devin's workers added a Corvette 283cu.in V8 and Borg-Warner four-speed gearbox prior to mounting the fibreglass body, which was styled after the 1958 Fantuzzi-bodied Ferrari Testa Rossa. The basis of MacGregor's chassis was a pair of 3in steel-tubing chassis rails, tied together with six tubular crossmembers. The front suspension employed equal-length parallel A-arms, coil-spring/damper units, outboard 12in Girling disc brakes and 15in Dunlop knock-off wire wheels. Rack-and-pinion steering was standard, and customers could choose left- or right-hand drive. The rear suspension was independent, with 11in Girling disc brakes mounted inboard on each side of the Salisbury differential. There was a pair of parallel trailing arms on each side, plus a 3in De Dion tube connecting the rear hubs. Like the front, the rear used coil-spring/damper units and knock-off Dunlop wire wheels.

A known continuous history can add value to and enhance the enjoyment of a car.

1965 Austin Mini Cooper S, 1293cc 4-cylinder engine, 126bhp, 4-speed manual gearbox, German-market model, left-hand drive, engine and gearbox recently rebuilt, race ready.
£8,000–10,000 / $11,500–14,500 ⚒ BKS
To many – including its designer Alec Issigonis – the notion that the Mini might have a future as anything other than basic transport was an anathema, and the idea of a high-performance version was laughable. One man, though, saw it quite differently. Racing car manufacturer John Cooper already knew quite a bit about tuning BMC's A-series engine – he was running the company's Formula Junior effort at the time – and a test drive in a prototype Mini convinced him of the car's competition potential. The result, launched in September 1961, was the Mini Cooper. Its prodigious roadholding and excellent power-to-weight ratio enabled the Mini Cooper to compete successfully with larger-capacity rivals, and on tight twisting circuits, the car was often a candidate for outright victory.

H.J. Moser, a scene from the 1934 Grand Prix D'Albi at Les Planques, depicting Featherstonhaugh driving the Maserati 8C 2500 to victory, watercolour, signed and dated 1935, 21 x 24in (53.5 x 61cm).
£1,800–2,200 / $2,600–3,200 ⚒ BKS

Brian Hatton, a cut-away of a 1935 Trossi Radial single-seater racing car, No. 1 in a series of illustrations for *Motor* magazine, entitled 'Non Conformists', black ink and watercolour, dated on the reverse 12 November 1971, signed, 26 x 22in (66 x 56cm).
£230–280 / $330–400 ⚒ BKS
Brian Hatton was one of the masters of cut-away art during the post-war years, and is well-known for his Formula One cars.

Frederick Gordon Crosby, The British Empire Trophy Race at Brooklands 1932, depicting Birkin's red Bentley high on the banking in the lead, with Eystonis' Panhard rising above it, closely followed by Cobb's Delage and Howe's Grand Prix Delage, watercolour with charcoal, signed, inscribed and dated 'Brooklands 1932', 27 x 20in (68.5 x 51cm).
£17,000–20,000 / $24,500–29,000 ⚒ BKS

Tony Upson, Mercedes-Benz W154 at speed, oil on canvas, signed, 48 x 96in (122 x 244cm).
£330–380 / $480–550 ⚒ BKS

Helen Taylor, Louis Chiron in the V8 Lancia D50 at the Monaco Grand Prix 1955, mixed media on Fabriano paper, 26½ x 33½in (67.5 x 85cm).
£220–250 / $320–360 ⚒ BKS

Tony Upson, 'Monaco 6eme Grand Prix Automobile 1934', depicting a Maserati 8CM at speed, acrylic on board, 96 x 36in (244 x 91.5cm).
£800–1,000
$1,150–1,450 ⚒ BKS

Pierre Jacotin, 'Les 12 Heures Reims 1957', original poster for the long-distance event, colour lithograph, unframed, 24 x 18in (61 x 45.5cm).
£120–150 / $175–220 ⚒ C

Miller's is a price GUIDE not a price LIST

J. Ramel, '22e Grand Prix Automobile Monaco 1964', original advertising poster, linen-backed, framed, 23 x 15in (58.5 x 38cm).
£400–450 / $580–720 ⚒ RM

Renzo Iarno Vandi, a bronze sculpture, depicting a Ferrari 250 GTO, 15¾in (40cm) long.
£1,200–1,400 / $1,750–2,000 BKS

A French CIJ clockwork model of an Alfa Romeo P2, smooth balloon tyres, André brake drums, fully operational steering, opening petrol, oil and radiator caps, faux rusted exhaust, working clockwork motor, some minor restoration, original paint, with original box, 1926.
£4,000–4,500 / $5,800–6,500 BKS

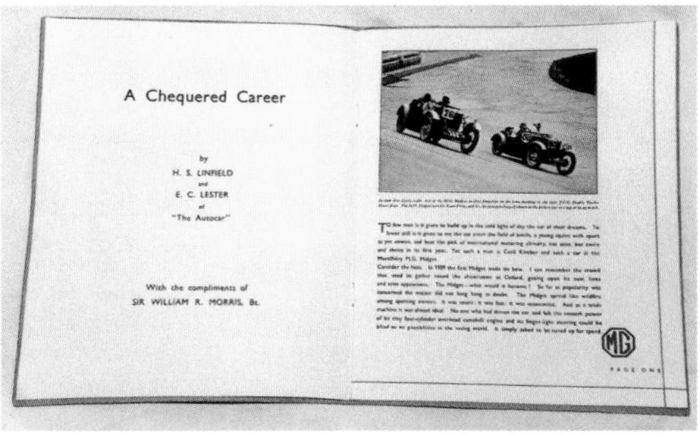

▲ ► *A "Chequered" Career!*, a 14-page publicity brochure, recording the competition successes of MG Midgets at various events, centrefold has double-page reproduction of F. Gordon Crosby's Midget exceeding 100mph at Montlhéry, 2 colour racing images by Connolly on the front cover, very good condition, 1932, 9 x 11in (23 x 28cm).
£80–100 / $115–145 BKS

◄ A Pocher 1/8-scale model of an Alfa Romeo 8C 2300 Monza, opening bonnet, detailed engine, wiring, fully operable steering and suspension, rubber tyres, cockpit with detailed fascia, 1960s.
£370–420 / $540–600 BKS

A painted side profile of an Alfa Romeo racing car, 45in (114.5cm) long.
£500–600 / $720–870 BKS

A scratchbuilt 1/8-scale model of a 1936/37 Auto Union Type C Grand Prix car, made from brass, aluminium, moulded resin, white metal and GRP, spoked wheels, dashboard instruments, on a faux tile base, 23in (58.5cm) long.
£1,300–1,500 / $1,850–2,200 BKS

◄ Two programmes for events at the Nürburgring, 1960 and 1961, 6 x 8in (15 x20.5cm).
£20–30
$30–45 each DT

► A bronze bust of Ayrton Senna, by Livingstone Art Founders, mounted on a solid square base, 1 of only 2 cast, 1998.
£4,000–5,000
$5,800–7,250 BKS

A Berlin Motor Sports Association fanfare trumpet, attached double-sided embroidered banner, 'Berlin Motor Club' and the arms of the city, believed to have been used at the Nürburgring to herald the race victor to the podium, 1930s.
£500–600 / $720–870 ⚒ BKS

A Bell helmet, worn by Emerson Fittipaldi while driving for McLaren throughout the 1974 World Championship winning season.
£3,700–4,200 / $5,250–6,000 ⚒ BKS
Surprisingly, this helmet was sponsored by AGV. After the Monza Grand Prix, the company insisted that Fittipaldi use one of its own products.

An Arai helmet, worn by Eddie Irvine, full radio system, signed on the tinted visor, 1995.
£1,900–2,100 / $2,750–3,000 ⚒ BKS

A Bieffe Formula 1 racing helmet, worn by Luca Badoer while driving for Forti-Ford, blue padded lining, clear visor, chin straps, 1996.
£1,100–1,300 / $1,600–1,900 ⚒ BKS

An Arai GPN helmet, worn by Mike Thackwell during the late 1980s, clear visor.
£500–600 / $725–870 ⚒ BKS

A Sparco race suit, worn by Rubens Barrichello, 1995.
£600–700 / $870–1,000 ⚒ BKS

◄ **An Arai helmet,** worn by Rubens Barrichello while driving for the Jordan team, full radio system, clear visor, signed in black on the visor, 1996.
£2,500–3,000 / $3,600–4,300 ⚒ BKS

A Shoei helmet, worn by Jan Lammers at the Japanese and Australian Grands Prix in 1992 while driving for the Leyton House Team, signed in black on the crown.
£1,200–1,500 / $1,750–2,200 ⚒ BKS

An Arai GP4 helmet, worn by Heinz-Harald Frentzen while driving for Williams Formula 1, full radio system, no visor, 1997.
£2,800–3,200 / $4,000–4,650 ⚒ BKS

An Arai Grand Prix helmet, worn by Ukyo Katayama while driving for Tyrrell, 1995.
£1,800–2,200 / $2,600–3,200 ⚒ BKS
This helmet was Ukyo's 'crew-cut' helmet, having been modified with extra padding to take account of the driver's drastic haircut.

A Stand 21 blue Nomex race suit, worn by Alain Prost in his World Championship winning year with Williams, embroidered name, 1993.
£2,400–2,800 / $3,500–4,000 ⚒ BKS

1970 Mini 1275GT, 1275cc 4-cylinder engine, finished in red, 1 owner and fewer than 7,500 miles from new, original condition.
£4,250–5,000 / 6,200–7,250 ⚒ BRIT
Introduced in late 1969, the 1275GT, with its 59bhp engine, was seen as a replacement for the Mini Cooper. The specification included servo-assisted front disc brakes, and the car shared the restyled bodyshell of the Mini Clubman. Early examples were fitted with rubber-cone suspension and 10in wheels, although by 1974, 12in wheels were standard with the option of Denovo tyres.

1971 Mini Cooper S Mk III, 1275cc engine, finished in red with white roof.
£6,000–7,000 / $8,700–10,200 MINI
A commuter runabout, a racing and rallying giant-killer and a living legend, the Mini is all of these things. Alec Arnold Constantine Issigonis, creator of the Morris Minor and Mini, would have made a great end-of-pier gypsy clairvoyant. For this Greek-born son of an itinerant marine engineer once showed an uncanny prophetic talent when he quipped to Italian automobile couturier Sergio Farina: 'Look at your cars, they're like women's clothes – they're out of date in two years. My cars will still be in fashion after I've gone.'

1974 Mini Sprint, 1275cc 4-cylinder engine, twin SU carburettors, 80bhp, 4-speed manual gearbox, front disc/rear drum brakes, left-hand drive, roof chopped, flared wheel arches, Minilite-type wheels, finished in blue.
£10,000–11,500 / $14,500–16,700 ⚒ Pou

1971 Mini Cooper S Mk III, 1275cc engine, finished in red, good condition.
£6,000–7,000 / $9,000–10,200 MINI

1973 Mini Cooper S Mk III, engine rebuilt by Oselli, enlarged to 1380cc, 100bhp, gearbox and brakes upgraded, full-length Webasto sunroof, finished in metallic grey, bodywork in good condition.
£4,000–5,000 / $5,800–7,250 ⚒ COYS

Miller's is a price GUIDE not a price LIST

1973 Innocenti Mini Cooper 1300, extensively modified from new by Milan coachbuilder Pavesi, rebuilt and uprated engine, 98bhp, quarterlights, electric windows, tinted glass, adjustable seats, 'Louis XV' fabric upholstery, wood interior trims, CD player, very good condition.
£5,000–6,000 / $7,250–8,700 ⚒ BKS
Best-known for its Lambretta scooter, Innocenti began licensed production of the Mini, known in Italy as the Innocenti Mini Minor 850, in 1965, and the following year offered its own version of the Mini Cooper. For the most part, the Italian-built Minis kept in step with developments of the UK product, although Innocenti's Mk III Mini Cooper enjoyed the advantage of a full-width fascia incorporating a plethora of instruments quite unlike anything seen in a British Mini. Innocenti continued to manufacture its Cooper 1275 S equivalent – the Mini Cooper 1300 – until 1973, two years after the end of UK production, and the model's final incarnation – the Mini Cooper 1300 Export – until late 1975.

1975 Innocenti Mini Cooper, 1300cc, left-hand drive, finished in red, black interior, 74,000 miles from new, excellent condition throughout.
£2,750–3,300 / $3,900–4,600 H&H

► **1984 Mini Speciale,** originally a Mini 1000 City, rebuilt by GHM Motorsport 1997, 1293cc 4-cylinder engine, uprated suspension, 12in Minilite-style wheels, Mk I Mini Cooper grille, wheel-arch extensions, finished in green with white roof, good condition throughout.
£2,750–3,500 / $3,900–5,000 BRIT

1984 Mini 25, finished in silver, 300 miles from new, 'as-new' condition.
£5,000–6,000 / $7,250–8,700 MINI

1987 Mini, glass sunroof, finished in red, black interior, good condition.
£2,000–2,500 / $2,900–3,600 MINI

1981 Mini, 850cc, resprayed in original metallic blue, 54,000 miles from new, original, good condition throughout.
£1,250–1,500 / $1,800–2,150 BKS

1985 Mini Cooper Retro Replica, originally a Mini Mayfair, restored, Janspeed tuned 1380cc engine, converted to unleaded fuel, close-ratio gearbox, Mk I grille grille with twin-recessed Lucas spotlights, Mk I rear lamps, finished in metallic dark blue with silver roof, period leather-rim steering wheel, Mk I central speedometer and 'works style' dashboard with Smith's auxiliary gauges, aluminium interior door handles and window winders, Corbeau cloth reclining seats with headrests.
£3,500–4,000 / $5,000–5,800 BRIT

1989 Mini 30, John Cooper conversion from new, finished in cherry red, 300 miles from new, 'as-new' condition.
£7,000–8,000 / $10,200–11,600 MINI

Morgan

Morgan is a small-scale producer whose customers are prepared to wait years for the delivery of a car that is defiantly traditional. At least, that's the way it was until recently. Early in 2000, the Malvern-based company created a sensation with the launch of the blood 'n' thunder Aero 8, a brutal-looking blend of tradition – there's still an ash body frame – and modern technology. For once, we'll have to wait and see if the Aero 8 becomes a classic. As for its other current products, they are, almost by definition, classics from the day they are made, displaying a direct lineage back to the company's original pre-war four-wheeler, the 1935 4/4 model. Until then, from its foundation in 1910 by H.F.S. Morgan, the company's output had been purely three-wheelers. In fact, the three-wheelers soldiered on until 1952. The four-wheeled Morgans have evolved ever so gently over the years, powered by a wide variety of proprietary four-cylinder engines. One of the biggest changes was with the Plus 8 of 1968, for which Morgan adopted the 161bhp Rover 3.5 litre V8 to create a thrilling 125mph charger.

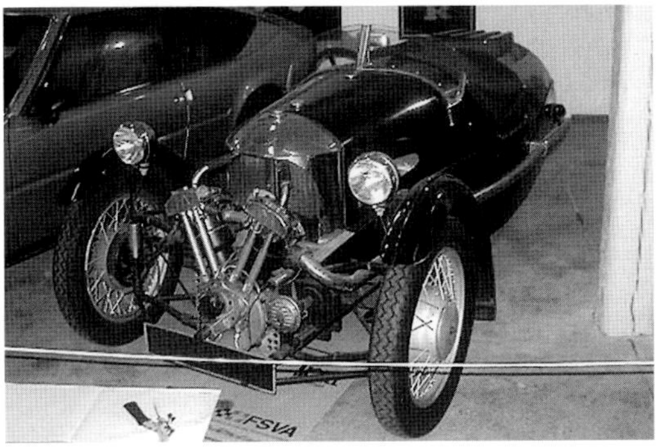

1939 Morgan Supersports Barrel-back, Matchless overhead-valve V-twin engine, high-level twin exhausts, 3-speed and reverse gearbox, rear-mounted spare wheel with aluminium cover, finished in black, green leather upholstery, original condition.
£16,000–18,000 / $23,200–26,000 COYS
The Morgan three-wheeler formula was remarkably successful, either in family runabout configuration, or developed for high-speed motoring, in Aero, Grand Prix and Super Sports form. Blackburne, JAP and Matchless engines were used in the early cars, which achieved excellent results in various types of motorsport.

1952 Morgan Plus 4 Drophead Coupé, 2088cc Standard Vanguard engine, flat-radiator model, rebuilt 1996, finished in British racing green, black leather upholstery.
£15,000–17,000 / $21,750–24,650 FHD

1952 Morgan Plus 4 Drophead Coupé, upgraded with more powerful TR-type engine late 1950s, flat-radiator model, flashing indicators, finished in cream, original green interior, 1 owner from new, unused since 1982.
£7,000–8,000 / $10,200–11,400 BKS

1948 Morgan 4/4 Drophead Coupé, chromed bullnose radiator grille and replacement chassis fitted by Morgan factory 1960, finished in black, navy blue leather interior, 2 owners from new.
£7,500–9,000 / $10,875–13,000 BKS
The first four-seater, four-wheeled Morgan appeared in 1937, and a special Coventry Climax-engined sports model competed at Le Mans in 1938, qualifying for the Biennial Cup. A special Standard 1267cc overhead-valve four-cylinder engine was introduced for the 1939 season, alongside a new 2+2 drophead coupé, and would continue to power the 4/4 up to 1950. By that time, fewer than 50 drophead coupés had been built.

MORGAN Model	ENGINE cc/cyl	DATES	CONDITION 1	2	3
4/4 Series I	1098/4	1936–50	£10,000	£7,000	£6,000
Plus 4	2088/4	1950–53	£15,000	£10,000	£7,000
Plus 4	1991/4	1954–68	£14,000	£11,000	£7,000
4/4 Series II/III/IV	997/4	1954–68	£10,000+	£7,000	£5,000
4/4 1600	1599/4	1960 on	£14,000+	£9,000	£6,000
Plus 8	3528/8	1969 on	£17,000+	£13,500	£10,000

1955 Morgan Plus 4 Drophead Coupé, engine uprated to more powerful TR4 specification, resprayed in red, original chassis/engine numbers.
£9,000–11,000 / $13,000–16,000 BKS

1990 Morgan 4/4, spotlights, luggage carrier, finished in metallic grey, black leather interior, well maintained, 2 owners and 37,000 miles from new, concours winner, excellent condition.
£15,000–16,500 / $21,750–24,000 FHD

► **1991 Morgan Plus 8,** 3.9 litre V8 engine, performance exhaust, spotlights, luggage rack, finished in red, stone leather upholstery, reclining seats, walnut dash, 34,000 miles from new.
£17,000–20,000 / $24,650–29,000 FHD

Morris

Morris, like so many other early British car makers, had its roots in the bicycle boom of the latter half of the 19th century. Born in 1877, the eldest son of an Oxford farm manager, William Morris's only job working for someone else was at an Oxford bicycle shop, where he lasted a year before leaving in a huff when his request for a pay rise was turned down. Using his savings of £4, Morris set up on his own at home. A fine athlete and trophy-winning cyclist, his local fame boosted his business, and as it expanded he tinkered with motorbikes and started selling and servicing cars. The first Morris car was the 1 litre 'bull-nose' Morris Oxford, produced in 1913, and by 1924 Morris was Britain's biggest car manufacturer. In fact, for 70 years, from 1913, the name of Morris was a byword for middle-class motoring; the cars were rarely exciting, but usually deserving of their reputation as no-frills, stoutly dependable machines. However, by the time the Morris name was finally dropped from the Austin-Rover inventory in 1984, it had been sadly devalued and had come to stand for mediocrity. Those ungainly Morris Marinas, Itals, and the short-lived Morris 1800 and 2200 'cheese wedges' of the 1970s serve as an inglorious monument to a remarkable man and a company that once was Britain's largest car maker. A more fitting memento is the wonderful 1948 Morris Minor, which went on to become Britain's first million-selling motor car.

◄ **1925 Morris Cowley Two-Seater with Dickey,** side-mounted spare wheel, modern flashing indicators, black hood, finished in dark blue, red upholstery, original apart from chrome-plated windscreen surround, nickel-plated fittings in good condition.
£9,500–11,000 / $13,800–16,000 CGC

Morris Milestones

1877 William Richard Morris born on October 10 near Oxford.
1905 William Morris buys his first car.
1913 In Morris's first year, 393 cars are produced.
1917 William Morris receives OBE for war work.
1919 WRM Motors Ltd becomes Morris Motors Ltd.
1924 Morris Motors becomes Britain's biggest producer of motor cars.
1926 Morris Motors Ltd becomes a public company.
1927 William Morris personally buys Wolseley with his own money.
1929 Morris Motors employs over 10,000 workers.
1929 William Richard Morris is knighted.
1934 Sir William Morris becomes Baron Nuffield.
1935 Morris Motors takes over MG.
1938 Morris Motors Ltd takes over Riley and becomes the Nuffield Organisation.
1938 William Morris becomes Viscount Nuffield of Nuffield in the County of Oxfordshire.
1939 The millionth Morris rolls off the production line on 22 May.
1948 First Morris Minor built on September 20.
1949 Market share of the Nuffield Organisation, is down to one-sixth of total British production – half the share it had in 1939.
1952 Austin and Morris merge to form British Motor Corporation (BMC) on 1 April.
1954 William Morris retires.
1959 Mini launched on 26 August.
1960 On 10 December, the millionth Morris Minor is made.
1963 William Morris dies on 22 August.
1966 British Motor Corporation becomes British Motor Holdings after merger with Jaguar.
1968 Merger with Leyland results in another name, British Leyland Motor Corporation.
1970 Last Morris Minor built on 12 November.
1975 British Leyland nationalised.
1980 British Leyland reorganises under Austin Rover Group banner.
1984 Morris name disappears from Austin Rover inventory.
1986 Five-millionth Mini produced on 19 February.

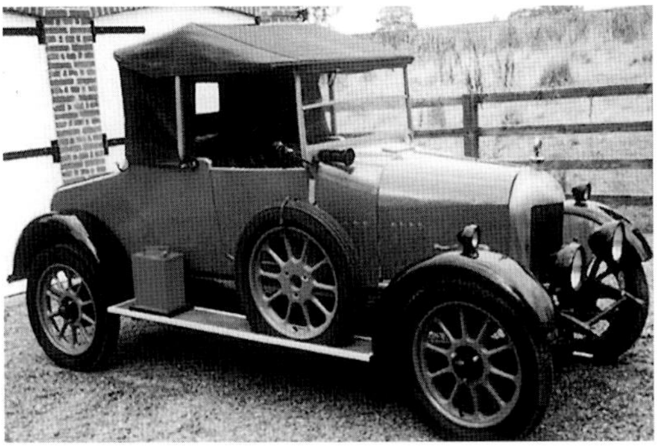

1925 Morris Cowley 11.9hp Two-Seater Tourer with Dickey, restored, finished in grey with black wings, black interior, good condition throughout.
£7,000–8,000 / $10,200–11,600 BKS
Introduced in 1919 as a cheaper alternative to the Oxford, the Morris Cowley employed bought-in American components and running gear to undercut the opposition and score an outstanding sales success. However, the supply of Continental engines did not last long, and William Morris was forced to turn to Hotchkiss's Coventry subsidiary – a firm he would later acquire – for an alternative. A reputation for quality and a drop in price saw the Cowley established as the UK's most popular car by the early 1920s.

1933 Morris Minor Two-Door Saloon, body and interior completely restored.
£4,000–4,500 / $5,800–6,500 GrM

Restored values

The cost of a professional restoration will have an influence on, but no direct relation to, a motorcycle's market value. A restored motorcycle can have a market value lower than the cost of its restoration.

MORRIS Model	ENGINE cc/cyl	DATES	CONDITION 1	2	3
Prices given are for saloons					
Cowley (Bullnose)	1550/4	1913–26	£12,000	£8,000	£6,000
Cowley	1550/4	1927–39	£10,000	£6,000	£4,000
Oxford (Bullnose)	1803/4	1924–27	£14,000	£10,000	£6,000
Oxford	1803/4	1927–33	£10,000	£8,000	£6,000
16/40	2513/4	1928–33	£8,000	£7,000	£6,000
18	2468/6	1928–35	£9,000	£7,000	£5,000
8 Minor	847/4	1929–34	£5,500	£4,000	£2,000
10/4	1292/4	1933–35	£5,000	£3,000	£1,500
25	3485/6	1933–39	£10,000	£8,000	£5,000
Eight	918/4	1935–39	£4,000	£3,000	£1,500
10HP	1140/4	1939–47	£4,500	£3,000	£1,500
16HP	2062/6	1936–38	£5,000	£3,500	£2,000
18HP	2288/6	1935–37	£5,000	£3,500	£2,500
21HP	2916/6	1935–36	£6,000	£4,000	£2,500

A touring version of the above is worth approximately 30% more. Value is very dependent on body type and is greater if coachbuilt.

1946 Morris Eight Series E Saloon, 1 owner for c40 years, 84,000 miles from new, very good condition.
£4,750–5,500 / $6,900–8,000 ⚒ TEN

Introduced in 1939, the Series E was Morris's first attempt to offer a streamlined model for the masses. It had the well-proven power unit, but with the headlamps incorporated in the mudguards, it was well ahead of its time and set the trend for other manufacturers.

1957 Morris Minor 1000 Four-Soor Saloon, 948cc 4-cylinder engine, largely original order, finished in green, original green leather interior, new carpets, largely original, body and mechanics in good condition.
£1,350–1,650 / $1,900–2,375 ⚒ BRIT

In 1950, a Minor even tempted the young Stirling Moss into high-speed cornering antics that lost him his licence for a month.

Miller's Starter Marque

Starter Morrises: *Minor, 1948–71.*

- Designed by Alec Issigonis, the genius who later went on to pen the Mini, the 1948 Morris Minor became Britain's first million-seller, a feat marked in 1960 with a series of 349 livid lilac-hued Morris 'Millions'. The Minor featured the then novel unitary chassis/body construction, and its famed handling finesse and ride comfort more than made up for the lack of power. The combination proved to be just what ordinary people needed from a car, and the Minor soldiered on until 1971.
- Any model is eminently affordable and almost as practical to own now as when in production, owing to ready availability and a blossoming cottage industry that provides everything you need to keep your Minor in fine fettle. The Minor is also generally long-lived and one of the easiest cars for DIY maintenance. Front and rear wings are bolt-on items, and sound examples can conceal horrors underneath. On Travellers, the wood framing is structural and should be checked very carefully.
- **Pick of the bunch:** The first split-screen 'low-light' models, especially convertibles, produced before the headlights were raised to the top of the wings to conform to US regulations.
- **What to watch:** Beware 'rogue rag-tops'. Convertibles are more prized, and although there's a legitimate industry converting saloons to open tops, there are fast-buck cowboys and inept DIY bodgers out there. Bodged convertibles are potential killers – literally.
- **Production:** 1,619,958.
  Body styles: Saloon, convertible Tourer, estate Traveller.
  Engine: Four-cylinder, 803–1098cc.
  Power: 28–48bhp.
  Top speed: 62–75mph.

1966 Morris Minor Traveller, restored 1993, engine and suspension overhauled, new braking system, new woodwork, good condition throughout.
£2,000–2,500 / $2,900–3,600 ⚒ BARO

1966 Morris Minor Convertible, finished in green, green interior, very good condition throughout.
£1,500–1,800 / $2,170–2,900 ⚒ CGC

A Morris double-sided illuminated wall sign, very good original condition.
£300–350 / $440–500 ⚒ BKS

▶ **1968 Morris Minor Two-Door Saloon,** 1098cc engine, finished in blue, blue interior, 49,500 miles from new, interior in need of refurbishment, otherwise very good condition.
£1,000–1,200 / $1,500–1,800 ⚒ H&H

MORRIS Model	ENGINE cc/cyl	DATES	CONDITION 1	2	3
Minor Series MM	918/4	1948–52	£3,000	£1,600	£800
Minor Series MM Conv	918/4	1948–52	£4,500	£2,200	£1,200
Minor Series II	803/4	1953–56	£2,000	£1,000	£500
Minor Series II Conv	803/4	1953–56	£5,500	£3,500	£1,500
Minor Series II Est	803/4	1953–56	£3,000	£1,250	£800
Minor 1000	948/4	1956–63	£1,750	£925	£250
Minor 1000 Conv	948/4	1956–63	£4,000+	£2,000	£750
Minor 1000 Est	948/4	1956–63	£4,000	£2,200	£1,200
Minor 1000	1098/4	1963–71	£2,000	£950	£250
Minor 1000 Conv	1098/4	1963–71	£4,500	£3,000	£1,500
Minor 1000 Est	1098/4	1963–71	£4,000	£3,000	£1,500
Cowley 1200	1200/4	1954–56	£1,675	£1,000	£300
Cowley 1500	1489/4	1956–59	£1,750	£950	£350
Oxford MO	1476/4	1948–54	£2,000	£850	£250
Oxford MO Est	1476/4	1952–54	£3,000	£1,500	£350
Series II/III	1489/4	1954–59	£2,000	£1,200	£300
Series II/III/IV Est	1489/4	1954–60	£2,250	£1,350	£250
Oxford Series V Farina	1489/4	1959–61	£1,800	£800	£250
Oxford Series VI Farina	1622/4	1961–71	£1,750	£750	£200
Six Series MS	2215/6	1948–54	£2,500	£1,500	£500
Isis Series I/II	2639/6	1955–58	£2,500	£1,300	£450
Isis Series I/II Est	2639/6	1956–57	£2,600	£1,350	£500

Moskvich

1960 Moskvich 403 Four-Door Saloon, restored by Moskvich factory, finished in fawn, good condition.
£1,200–1,400 / $1,750–2,000 ⊞ NOW

1972 Moskvich 427 Four-Door Estate, unrestored, resprayed in turquoise, beige interior.
£600–700 / $800–1,000 ⊞ NOW

Nagant

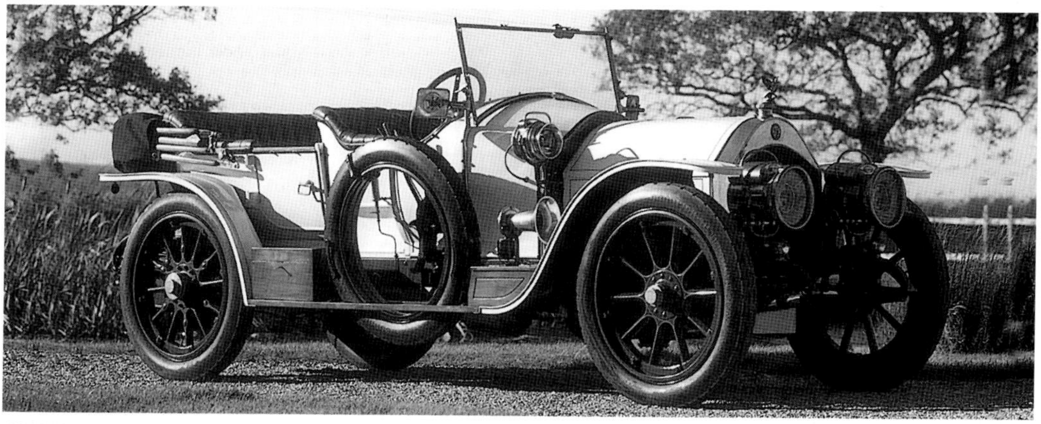

1910 Nagant 24/30hp 5½ litre Toy Tonneau, subject of no-expense-spared restoration, engine rebuilt and balanced, 12 volt electrical system, detachable-rim wheels, 10in brass Ducellier self-generating headlamps, electric klaxon, mahogany toolboxes, brass-framed windscreen, finished in off-white, full weather equipment comprising tonneau covers, hood, side screens and running board spats in chocolate double duck, button-backed tan Connolly hide upholstery, comprehensive dashboard instrumentation, VCC dated.
£70,000–80,000 / $101,500–116,000 BKS

Nagant Frères began motor car production in 1900 in Liège, this new venture being a logical offshoot from existing successful armaments manufacture. Early products were complex, opposed-piston affairs, built under licence from Gobron Brillié in France, but by 1905 or so, the brothers were building conventional-engined cars to their own design. In Britain, these were marketed as Nagant-Hobsons by H.M. Hobson Ltd. Nagant-Hobsons took part in the 1908 2,000 mile Scottish Reliability Trials, and on the Continent the celebrated French aviator Jules Busson campaigned a very sporting, chain-driven 35/40hp Nagant in the arduous Spa-Ostend and Reims-Spa events. By 1910, all Nagants were shaft-driven, enhancing their reliability further.

Nash-Healey

1954 Nash-Healey Le Mans Replica, 252cu in 6-cylinder engine, twin Carter carburettors, 140bhp, 3-speed manual gearbox, Healey trailing-link front suspension, 4-wheel drum brakes, recently restored, finished in silver, 1 of the last to be built, excellent condition.
£28,000–32,000 / $40,600–46,400 ⚒ RM
While sailing on the liner *Queen Elizabeth*, the president of the American Nash-Kelvinator Corporation – George Mason – had a chance encounter with British sports car builder Donald Healey. Mason wanted to boost the image of his Nashes, which had a stodgy reputation. By the end of their voyage, the two had agreed to collaborate on a British-American hybrid sports car with Nash mechanicals. The resulting Nash-Healeys, with styling by Pinin Farina, soon appeared on race tracks around the world. In 1951, an experimental model managed a third in class and a sixth overall at Le Mans. The following year at the same race, a Nash-Healey finished third overall and took second in the Index of Performance. Pinin Farina restyled the roadster body in 1952, giving it a lower, one-piece windscreen and rear wing bulges. Steel replaced aluminium bodywork, and a larger, Carter-carbureted engine, giving an extra 15bhp, rounded out the package. These cars were referred to by the factory as Le Mans Replicas, in recognition of the outstanding performance in that race.

NSU

NSU built its first vehicles in 1905, and went on to produce some successful small cars through to 1930, when it sold its new factory to Fiat. The company resumed car manufacture in 1957 with the Prinz range, and in 1967 stunned the motoring world with the technically advanced rotary-engined Ro80. This visionary machine was acclaimed as 'Car of the Year', but the Felix Wankel-designed power unit proved troublesome and, due to acute rotor tip wear, could expire after 15,000–20,000 miles. The company was amalgamated with Audi under VW in 1969, and NSU died as a marque in 1977 when the once-so-promising Ro80 faded away.

◄ **1971 NSU Prinz 4L Two-Door Saloon,** right-hand drive, finished in blue, brown upholstery, unused since 1984, original interior in good condition.
£200–250 / $290–350 ⚒ BKS
A mini-car constructed along typically Continental lines, the Prinz was rear-engined and equipped with all-independent suspension. The air-cooled, overhead-cam twin-cylinder engine displaced 583cc and developed 23bhp in the Prinz I. Later models had a more powerful, 30bhp 598cc unit. Introduced in 1961, the Prinz 4 was built on a longer wheelbase and featured the distinctive 'bathtub' body style most readily associated with the model. The 30bhp engine and an all-synchromesh gearbox were standard. In this form, the Prinz was good for 70+mph. Production ceased in 1973.

Oldsmobile

OLDSMOBILE Model	ENGINE cc/cyl	DATES	CONDITION 1	2	3
Curved Dash	1600/1	1901–04	£16,000	£14,000	£12,000
30	2771/6	1925–26	£9,000	£7,000	£4,000
Straight Eight	4213/8	1937–38	£14,000	£9,000	£5,000

1935 Oldsmobile Six Four-Door Saloon, 3764cc straight-6 engine, 4-speed manual gearbox, right-hand drive, finished in black, new blue interior, very good condition throughout.
£4,750–5,700 / $6,900–8,250 ⚒ H&H

1962 Oldsmobile Dynamic 88 Convertible, 394cu in V8 engine, bare-metal respray in red late 1980s, white hood, red and white interior, largely original, good mechanical condition.
£6,000–7,000 / $8,700–10,200 ⚒ BRIT

Opel

Opel GT (1968–73)

The Opel Kadett's companion model, the Opel GT, was a little stunner, a cut-down Corvette look-alike that offered suburban Fangios the opportunity for a little harmless supercar role-playing. The Corvette references are obvious; in fact, the GT was designed by a former Chevrolet man. Unfortunately, it didn't quite have the muscle to match, for underneath that slippery skin with its 0.39Cd, the GT was only really a lightly modified Kadett, a German Vauxhall Viva if you like. Even so, it's an MGB GT beater, with a top-speed of 105–115mph.

Of course, rarity in the UK adds to curiosity appeal, but in practical terms you could be in for a long hunt, for out of 103,000 built from 1968 to 1973, a mere 148 were imported into Great Britain – and all of them are left-hookers. Most of the rest, 80,000 in fact, were exported to the USA.

1968 Opel Olympia Coupé, 1078cc 4-cylinder engine, twin carburettors, 67bhp, servo-assisted front disc/rear drum brakes, resprayed in original fawn, red interior, 3 owners and 52,000 miles from new, excellent mechanical condition.
£1,000–1,200 / $1,500–1,750 ⚒ BRIT

Otto

▶ **1910 Otto Type K4 9hp Doctor's Coupé,** 4-cylinder engine, magneto ignition, Zenith carburettor, 3-speed manual gearbox, foot-operated transmission brake, hand-operated rear drum brakes, wooden artillery wheels, acetylene headlamps, right-hand drive, finished in white and black, beige interior, museum displayed for 60 years.
£5,000–6,000 / $7,250–8,700 ⚒ Pou

Packard

Founded by James Ward Packard in Ohio, the company produced its first motor cars in 1899 and went on to build an envied reputation in the luxury-car field. In 1915, Packard introduced the world's first production V12 engine, and in the 1920s built some magnificent cost-no-object machines. In the following decade, faced with a dwindling luxury market, Packard's salvation came with a move into the middle market with the 120-series cars. After WWII, Cadillac made severe inroads into Packard's traditional luxury market, and even though Packard bought Studebaker in 1954, the Packard name disappeared in 1958.

1929 Packard 640 Custom Eight Runabout, 385cu in straight-8 engine, 105bhp, 3-speed manal gearbox, four-wheel drum brakes, completely restored, little use since, 'as-new' condition.
£50,00–60,000 / $72,500–87,000 ⚒ RM
Packard introduced the 640 Custom Eight in 1929. It was designed specifically for the bespoke coachwork of the day. The Sixth-series cars were a cut above the previous year's Packard line-up. The suspension was based on a shock-absorbed, loose-trunnion system remarkably similar to modern designs. Other improvements included moving the coolant temperature gauge from the radiator filler cap to an easy-to-read intrument on the dashboard, and the addition of an automatic cylinder oiler, which helped to prevent unnecessary wear caused by dry start-ups.

1931 Packard 840 Town Car, coachwork by Kellner, 385cu.in straight-8 engine, 120bhp, 4-speed manual gearbox, Bijur chassis lubrication, 4-wheel mechanical drum brakes, older restoration, only example built by Kellner.
£100,000–115,000 / $145,000–166,750 ⚒ RM
Following the tremendous success of the Seventh-series cars, Packard introduced a number of improvements for the Eighth series. The biggest news was a 20-per-cent gain in horsepower, due primarily to improved breathing and changes in carburation; both being lessons learned from experience with the 734 Speedster Eight. Other upgrades included Bijur chassis lubrication and the introduction of a Stewart Warner mechanical fuel pump to replace the more troublesome vacuum-tank set-up found on earlier cars.

1931 Packard 833 Limousine, 319.2cu in straight-8 engine, light alloy crankcase with nine main bearings, finished in cream with maroon wings, new tan Ambla-type upholstery, only known right-hand-drive example, good mechanical condition, stored for some time, in need of some refurbishment and recommissioning.
£15,000–18,000 / $21,750–26,000 ⚒ BRIT

1937 Packard Eight Type 120C Three-Position Drophead Coupé, coachwork by Chapron, 282cu.in straight-8 engine, 120bhp, 3-speed synchromesh gearbox, coil-spring independent front suspension, 4-wheel hydraulic drum brakes, left-hand drive, automatic radiator shutters, finished in pink with grey wings, grey upholstery.
£26,000–30,000 / $37,700–43,500 ⚒ C
At one time, this car's flamboyant colour scheme included a chrome-plated bonnet top, but the subsequent dazzling reflections overpowered both driver and onlooker alike, so it was painted in matching pink. Recent participation in the retrospective Rallye de Monte Carlo led to the car being awarded the Coupe de Dames in the Concours d'Elegance.

▶ **1956 Packard Caribbean Convertible,** restored, finished in 3-tone cream, red and black, matching interior, 1 of only 263 built.
£38,000–44,000 / $55,000–64,000 ⚒ HCL

PACKARD Model	ENGINE cc/cyl	DATES	CONDITION 1	2	3
Twin Six	6946/12	1916–23	£30,000	£20,000	£15,000
6	3973/6	1921–24	£20,000	£15,000	£12,000
6, 7, 8 Series	5231/8	1929–39	£35,000+	£25,000+	£14,000+
12	7300/12	1936–39	£50,000+	£30,000+	£18,000+

Peugeot

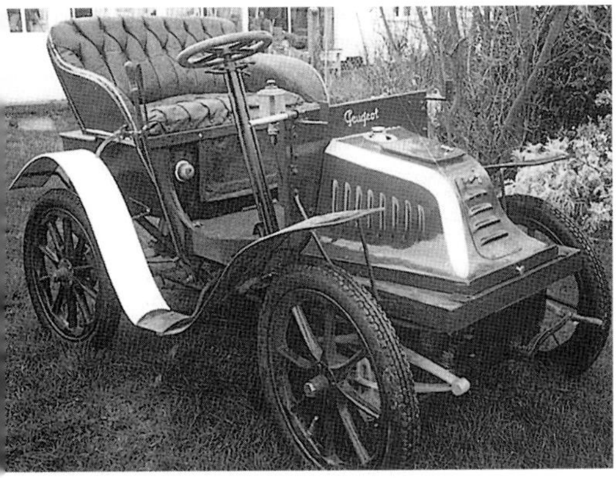

1903 Peugeot Type 54 5hp Two-Seater, older partial restoration, stored for a number of years, in need of completion.
£18,000–22,000 / $26,000–32,000 BKS
Armand Peugeot introduced bicycles to the family ironmongery business in 1885, and soon, in collaboration with Serpollet, he was building his first steam carriage. Rapid developments in the infant motor industry led Peugeot to adopt the internal-combustion engine, initially from Daimler and later Panhard-Levassor. In 1902, the first of the famous 'Baby' Peugeots arrived. Conventional in most respects, they were powered by a vertically-mounted single-cylinder engine and featured shaft drive to the rear axle. This particular car was discovered under the floorboards of a London house in 1961. At that time, the car was substantially complete mechanically, although missing coachwork and wheels. It is thought that the car had been dismantled and stored in this manner, perhaps when its young owner went off to war in 1914.

Miller's is a price GUIDE not a price LIST

1904 Peugeot 5hp Two-Seater, single-cylinder engine, shaft drive to rear axle, oil side and rear lamps, hood, double-twist bulb horn, VCC dating plate, with purpose-built trailer.
£27,000–32,000 / $39,000–46,400 BKS

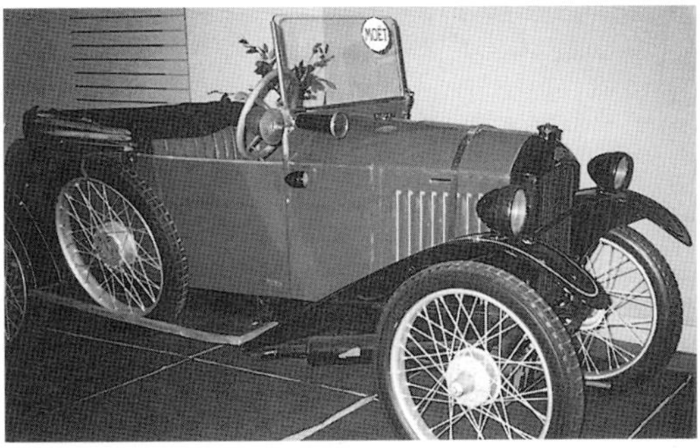

1923 Peugeot 6hp Quadrilette Tourer, 667cc, sidevalve 4-cylinder engine, pressed-steel punt chassis, staggered seating for 2, good condition.
£6,000–7,000 / $8,700–10,400 BKS

1914 Peugeot Bébé 6hp Type BPI Two-Seater, coachwork by James Pearce in the style of Henri Gauthier, acetylene headlamps, oil sidelamps, lion rampant mascot, restored, finished in blue, brown leather upholstery.
£25,000–30,000 / $36,250–43,500 BKS
Ettore Bugatti was responsible for the design of the Bébé Peugeot at a time when production of Bugatti cars at the Molsheim works was slowly getting off the ground. Only five Bugattis were built in 1910, 75 in 1911 and 175 in 1913, so the sale of the T-head lateral-valve engine design to Peugeot generated a useful injection of capital for Bugatti's operation, while also providing Peugeot with a design that put the company at the forefront of French light-car design. The 856cc engine was a neat and efficient unit, and the chassis layout of the new horseshoe-radiatored Bébé featured the reverse-quarter-elliptic leaf-spring rear suspension that would be a feature of Bugatti's later models.

PEUGEOT Model	ENGINE cc/cyl	DATES	CONDITION 1	2	3
Bébé	856/4	1912–14	£18,000	£12,000	£8,000
153	2951/4	1913–26	£9,000	£5,000	£3,000
163	1490/4	1920–24	£5,000	£4,000	£2,000
Bébé	676/4	1920–25	£7,000	£6,000	£3,000
156	5700/6	1922–24	£7,000	£5,000	£3,000
174	3828/4	1922–28	£7,500	£5,000	£2,000
172	714/4	1926–28	£4,000	£3,000	£1,500
183	1990/6	1929–30	£5,000	£3,000	£1,500
201	996/4	1930–36	£6,000	£3,000	£1,500
402	2140/4	1938–40	£4,500	£3,000	£1,000

Right-hand-drive cars and tourers will always achieve more interest than left-hand drive. Good solid cars.

1932 Peugeot 201B, 1122cc 4-cylinder engine, transverse leaf-spring front suspension, quarter-eliptic leaf-spring rear suspension, restored mid-1980s, finished in black, grey cloth interior, red carpeting, very good mechanical condition.
£3,000–3,500
$4,400–5,200 BRIT

Peugeot 504 Coupé (1969–83)

The stylish Peugeot 504 Coupé is one of France's best kept secrets. Production began in 1969 and continued until well into the 1980s, but with its high price, it found few takers in the UK. What they were missing out on was a refined, practical and eye-catching car with a broad-shouldered, on-the-road elegance. Underneath the stylish Pininfarina-built body lies either a 1971cc engine with mechanical fuel injection or, from 1974, the 604's 2.7 litre V6. To confuse matters further, the 1971cc engine became available again from 1977. Production of the 504 Coupé finally ceased in 1983, while the 504 saloon soldiered on until 1984.

► **1975 Peugeot 304 Cabriolet,** 1288cc engine, restored, finished in metallic blue, black and tan upholstery, original seats worn, otherwise good condition.
£2,500–3,000
$3,600–4,400 H&H

Pierce-Arrow

The first Pierce cars appeared in 1902; by 1908, the company had become Pierce-Arrow, and it went on to produce some gorgeous and magnificent luxury machines. Studebaker took over in 1928, and these later Pierce-Arrows were perhaps the best, serious rivals certainly in the USA to Cadillac and Lincoln. The last Pierce-Arrow car was built in 1938.

1924 Pierce-Arrow Series 80 Saloon, 2750cc engine, restored, engine completely overhauled, resprayed in burgundy and black, grey interior, original tool kit, 3 owners from new.
£10,500–12,500 / $15,250–18,250 H&H

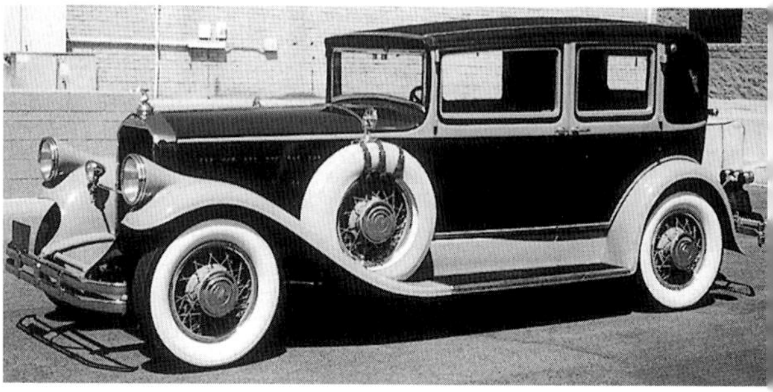

1929 Pierce-Arrow Club Brougham, older restoration, finished in black and green, good condition.
£20,000–24,000 / $29,000–34,800 BJ

Plymouth

◄ **1939 Plymouth Road King P7 Business Coupé,** 201.3cu.in 6-cylinder engine, new radiator, finished in black and silver, red leatherette interior, new carpets, excellent mechanical condition, interior good.
£6,500–7,500 / $9,400–10,875 ⚒ BRIT
The Plymouth marque was created by Chrysler during 1928 for a new low-priced line of models, the name being taken from Plymouth Rock, Massachusetts. The move was to prove particularly timely as, during the Depression years, the only cars to sell in respectable numbers were those that truly represented sound value, and Plymouths did just that. The Road King series was introduced in 1938. It was an impressive range, offering no fewer than ten different body styles.

1969 Plymouth Road Runner, 'Hemi-head' V8 engine, carburettor fresh-air package, factory rev-counter, completely restored, finished in original metallic bronze, white interior.
£25,000–30,000 $36,250–43,500 ⚒ BJ
The 'Hemi' Road Runner was voted 'Car of the Year' in 1969 by *Motor Trend* magazine. Only 421 examples were built, of which 187 had automatic transmission.

Pontiac

◄ **1964 Pontiac Parisienne Four-Door Pillarless Saloon,** 283cu.in overhead-valve V8 engine, right-hand drive, restored 1988 at a cost of over £12,400, finished in silver, original blue and cream fabric/leather interior in good condition, 89,500 miles from new, would benefit from further cosmetic and mechanical refurbishment.
£2,000–2,400 / $2,900–3,400 ⚒ BKS
Manufactured at General Motors' Oshawa plant in Ontario, Canadian Pontiacs were given their own unique model names, 'Parisienne' being adopted for the range marketed as the 'Catalina' in the USA. Restyled for 1963 and facelifted for 1964, the Catalina/Parisienne was manufactured in a variety of body styles, including a conventional four-door saloon, station wagon, a two-door convertible and a two-door pillarless coupé. A wide range of engine sizes and power outputs was available.

► **1970 Pontiac Firebird Concept Car,** rear-wheel skirts, finished in red, beige interior, only example built.
£40,000–45,000 $58,000–65,250 ⚒ BJ
A one-off design by Harry Bentley Bradley, 'Pontiac One' was created to give a vivid glance into the future of the Firebird.

PONTIAC Model	ENGINE cc/cyl	DATES	CONDITION 1	2	3
Six-27	3048/6	1926–29	£9,000	£7,000	£4,000
Silver Streak	3654/8	1935–37	£12,000	£9,000	£5,500
6	3638/6	1937–49	£7,000	£4,000	£3,500
8	4078/8	1937–49	£7,000	£4,000	£3,500

Porsche

Few would argue with the classic credentials of any Porsche model, whether the first-of-breed 356 or today's super-performers and the lovely retro-styled Boxster. One reason is that current models still display an unbroken linear descent from the very first 356 model of 1949, both in styling and concept. Volkswagen Beetle designer Ferdinand Porsche may have given the world the people's car, but it was his son Ferry who, with long-time associate Karl Rabe, created a car that people all over the world would prize from the day the first example rolled off the production line.

1955 Porsche 356 Coupé, 1582cc flat-4 engine, 70bhp, 4-speed manual gearbox, independent front suspension, rear swing-axles, 4-wheel hydraulic drum brakes, factory sunroof, restored, original numbers-matching 1500 Super Motor, fitted with updated carburettors, original carburettors and manifold supplied, finished in red, beige interior.
£17,000–20,000 / $24,650–29,000 RM

1957 Porsche 356A Carrera Speedster, restored, fitted with Weber carburettors, Rudge knock-off wheels, finished in black, red interior, excellent condition.
£110,000–125,000 / $159,500–180,000 BKS
The work of Ferry Porsche, the 356 was based on the Volkswagen designed by his father. It employed a platform-type chassis with rear-mounted, air-cooled engine and all-independent torsion-bar suspension. Constant development saw the 356's engine enlarged first to 1.3, then to 1.5 litres, the original split windscreen being replaced by a one-piece unit, and a synchromesh gearbox adopted. In 1952, a batch of 15 roadsters was constructed, their successful reception in the USA leading to the introduction of the Speedster in 1954. The Speedster was an economy model intended to compete with the cheaper British sports cars. It proved popular, 4,822 being constructed between 1954 and 1958. The Carrera name appeared in 1955. Applied to a 356 powered by a slightly less ferocious version of the 550 Spyder's 1.5 litre, double-overhead-camshaft, roller-bearing engine, it had been adopted to capitalise on Porsche's victories in the Carrera Panamericana in 1952 and 1954. Dry-sumped like the racers, the four-cam Carrera engine produced 100bhp, which was good enough to propel the 356 Carrera to 125mph, making it the fastest 1.5 litre production car of its day.

1957 Porsche 356A 1600 Cabriolet, 1600cc overhead-valve flat-4 engine, 60bhp, 4-speed manual gearbox, 4-wheel independent suspension, 4-wheel hydraulic drum brakes, professionally restored, engine and drivetrain rebuilt, finished in silver, correct German leather interior.
£30,000–35,000 / $43,500–50,750 RMS
The 356A Cabriolet took much of the minimalist edge off the no-frills Speedster, and it proved to be a great sales success. The latter's basic lightweight soft top, for example, was replaced with a civilised hood that was padded and more aesthetically pleasing in design. When combined with wind-up windows, it not only made the Cabriolet much quieter, but also provided excellent protection from the elements.

Porsche 356

The Porsche 356 is the car that started it all, beginning a proud sporting tradition that continues to this day. In many ways too, the 356 is the Beetle's athletic son, its concept, rear-engined layout and design descending directly from the father car. Even its flat-four air-cooled engine – although not a Beetle engine – is Beetle derived. It hardly sounds exotic, but the 356 is much more than a Bug in butterfly's clothes. In the 356, the humble Volkswagen genes are miraculously mutated into a true sporting machine, a peppy, pert piece of precision engineering available in myriad combinations from humble 'cooking' models for modest money to the exotic and very precious Speedsters and quad-cam Carreras.
Pick of the bunch: Ultimate in performance and price is the 356C Carrera II. Some purists favour the earliest split-windscreen jelly-mould shape, but for all-round drivability and affordability, the last-of-the line 1600cc 356C coupes with all-round disc brakes make most sense.

Porsche 356B (1959–63)

Production: 30,963 (all Porsche 356Bs).
Body styles: 2+2 fixed-head coupé, cabriolet and Speedster.
Construction: Unitary – steel body with integral pressed-steel platform chassis.
Engine: Air-cooled, horizontally-opposed flat-four of 1582cc with twin carburettors.
Power output: 90bhp @ 5,500rpm (Super 90).
Transmission: Four-speed manual, all-synchromesh, rear-wheel drive.
Suspension: Front: independent, trailing arms with transverse torsion bars and anti-roll bar.
Rear: independent, swing half-axles, radius arms and transverse torsion bars. Telescopic shock absorbers.
Brakes: Hydraulic drums all-round.
Maximum speed: 110mph.
0–60mph: 10 seconds.
Average fuel consumption: 30–35mpg.

Tony Upson, large mural depicting a 1958 Porsche 356, alongside the Porsche emblem, acrylic on board, 96 x 36in (244 x 91.5cm).
£275–325 / $400–470 BKS

1960 Porsche 356B Roadster, completely restored early 1990s, finished in red, beige interior, excellent condition throught.
£35,000–40,000 / $50,750–58,000 COYS

1962 Porsche 356B Coupé, 1700cc flat-4 engine, 4-speed manual gearbox, subject of complete mechanical overhaul, converted to unleaded fuel, finished in red, new magnolia leather upholstery, very good condition throughout.
£8,000–9,500 / $11,600–13,800 H&H

1964 Porsche 356SC Cabriolet, recently restored, finished in red, tan interior.
£30,000–34,000 / $43,500–49,250 HCL

PORSCHE Model	ENGINE cc/cyl	DATES	CONDITION 1	2	3
356	var/4	1949–53	£15,000+	£8,000	£5,000
356 Cabriolet	var/4	1951–53	£20,000+	£14,000	£10,000
356A	1582/4	1955–59	£13,000	£9,000	£5,000
356A Cabriolet	1582/4	1956–59	£16,000	£10,000	£7,000
356A Speedster	1582/4	1955–58	£25,000+	£19,000	£14,000
356B Carrera	1582/ 1966/4	1960–65	£40,000+	£30,000+	£18,000
356C	1582/4	1963–65	£15,000	£11,000+	£5,000
356C Cabriolet	1582/4	1963–64	£25,000+	£16,000	£10,000
911/911L/T/E	1991/6	1964–68	£12,000	£7,000	£5,000
912	1582/4	1965–68	£6,500	£5,000	£2,000
911S	1991/6	1966–69	£12,000	£8,000	£5,500
911S	2195/6	1969–71	£13,000	£9,000	£6,000
911T	2341/6	1971–73	£13,000	£8,000	£6,000
911E	2341/6	1971–73	£12,000+	£8,000	£6,000
914/4	1679/4	1969–75	£4,000	£3,000	£1,000
914/6	1991/6	1969–71	£6,000	£3,500	£1,500
911S	2341/6	1971–73	£16,000	£10,000	£8,500
Carrera RS lightweight	2687/6	1973	£40,000	£28,000+	£16,000
Carrera RS Touring	2687/6	1973	£30,000	£26,000	£17,000
Carrera 3	2994/6	1976–77	£14,000	£9,000	£7,000
924 Turbo	1984/4	1978–83	£5,000	£4,000	£2,000
928/928S	4474/4664/V8	1977–86	£10,000	£7,000	£4,000
911SC	2993/6	1977–83	£13,000	£8,000	£6,000

Sportomatic cars are less desirable.

1964 Porsche 356C 1600SC Coupé, air-cooled flat-4 engine, 4-wheel torsion-bar independent suspension, restored 1994/5 at a cost of £40,000, engine uprated, sports exhaust, finished in black, tan leather interior, excellent condition throughout.
£17,000–20,000 / $24,650–29,000 ⚒ BKS
Outwardly very similar to the final 356Bs, the ultimate 356C arrived in 1963, sporting four-wheel disc brakes among other improvements. Engines available were the 75bhp 'C' and 95bhp 'SC', the latter replacing the Super 90. Production lasted into the 911 era, coming to an end in April 1965.

1971 Porsche 911 2.2S, 2.2 litre flat-6 engine, mechanical fuel injection, left-hand drive, restored, Recarro lightweight interior in good condition.
£11,500–13,500 / $16,700–19,600 ⚒ COYS

1976 Porsche 911 Lux 2.7i, finished in white, engine rebuilt, 16,000 miles since, factory specification.
£10,500–12,000 / $15,600–17,400 ⊞ UMC

1980 Porsche 911SC Targa Sport, extensively refurbished, engine rebuilt, finished in metallic silver, dark blue half-leather interior.
£11,200–12,500 / $16,300–18,150 ⊞ UMC

1973 Porsche 911S 2.4 Targa, 2.4 litre engine, manual gearbox, restored 1997, finished in silver, black interior, good condition throughout.
£9,000–11,000 / $13,000–16,000 ⚒ BKS
A lengthened wheelbase introduced in 1969 improved the handling of the 911, then in 1970 the engine enjoyed the first of many enlargements – to 2.2 litres. All 911 variants received the 2.4 litre unit for 1972 – that of the 911S producing 190bhp – by which time the latter featured a five-speed gearbox and 6in rims. Two years after the introduction of the 911 coupé, a convertible stablemate – the Targa (named after the Targa Florio) – arrived in 1966. The Targa sported a hefty roll-over bar to protect the occupants in the event of an inversion, plus removable roof and rear hood sections stowable in the boot. For 1969, a quieter and less leak-prone fixed rear window replaced the rear hood, and the ever-popular Targa would continue in this form into the 1990s.

1981 Porsche 911 3.3 Turbo, 3299cc flat-6 engine, electric sunroof, finished in gold, factory air conditioning, black leather interior, 1 owner and c66,000 miles from new, excellent condition throughout.
£20,000–24,000 / $29,000–34,800 ⚒ BRIT

1983 Porsche 911SC, 2993cc 6-cylinder engine, gearbox rebuilt 1998, finished in red, beige interior, good mechanical condition.
£11,000–13,000 / $16,000–18,850 ⚒ BRIT

1989 Porsche 911 Carrera Speedster, 913cu.in overhead-camshaft flat-6 engine, dry-sump lubrication, 231bhp, 5-speed manual gearbox, 4-wheel independent suspension, 4-wheel disc brakes, finished in blue, dark blue convertible top, cruise control, air conditioning, grey leather interior, 1,260 miles from new, 'as-new' condition.
£50,000–55,000 / $72,500–79,750 ⚒ RM
The 1989 911 Carrera Speedster, with its steeply-raked, low-cut windscreen and cockpit cover was inspired by the original 356 Speedsters produced in the 1950s. Only 2,104 examples were built in a single model year.

1986 Porsche 924S, 1984cc, good condition.
£3,750–4,250 / $5,450–6,250 ⊞ GrM

1973 Porsche 911 2.7 RS Carrera, 2695cc, stainless-steel exhaust system, 5-speed manual gearbox, Bilstein suspension, alloy wheels, left-hand drive, lightweight front and rear valances, ducktail rear spoiler, electric sunroof, finished in white, black interior, good condition.
£30,000–35,000 / $43,500–50,750 ⚒ H&H

1991 Porsche 911/993 GT2 Conversion, tuned 6-cylinder engine, turbocharger, twin-coil ignition, c530bhp, 5-speed G50 competition gearbox, internally-vented disc brakes, 4-channel ABS, Fiske 3-piece wheels, bodywork upgraded to 993 specification with fibreglass panels and carbon-fibre doors and rear spoiler, finished in red, black interior, Recaro carbon-fibre bucket seats, 5-point competition seat belts.
£20,000–23,000 / $29,000–33,300 ⚒ COYS

1992 Porsche 944 Cabriolet, power steering, electric hood, finished in red, air conditioning, black half-leather upholstery, 39,000 miles from new.
£14,000–16,000 / $20,200–23,200 ⊞ VIC

1988 Porsche 959, 2849cc flat-6 engine, electronic fuel injection, turbocharger, 450bhp, 6-speed transaxle, permanent 4-wheel drive, 4-wheel independent suspension, 4-wheel ventilated disc brakes, ABS, 310+km/h top speed, 1 of 200 built.
£100,000–115,000 / $145,000–166,750 ⚒ Pou

Range Rover

1983 Range Rover Four-Door Estate, automatic transmission, finished in green, air conditioning, beige interior, in need of cosmetic refurbishment, 1 owner from new.
£3,750–4,250 / $5,500–6,200 BKS

1983 Range Rover Four-Door Estate, lamp protectors, rear window louvre, finished in black and silver, electric windows, air conditioning, head restraints, 1 owner and fewer than 3,100 miles from new.
£6,500–7,200 / $9,400–10,250 BKS

Reliant

Although best-known today for its fibreglass-bodied Scimitar GTE sports car, Reliant started out in 1935 by making three-wheeled utility vehicles. From 1952, the three-wheelers were also produced as passenger cars, and a fourth wheel was added with the launch of the Rebel in 1965. Meanwhile the company had also turned its attention to sporting products, starting off with the quirky Sabre of 1961–63, which grew into the far more harmonious Sabre Six of 1962–64, then the ground-breaking Ogle designed Scimitar. Although there was nothing revolutionary in the production of its fibreglass body, the shape and styling of the Scimitar GTE created a new class of car, the sports estate. This cross-country carry-all with sports appeal appeared three years before Volvo leapt on the sports-wagon bandwagon with the P1800ES. Today, this plastic classic still cuts it as one of that rare breed of sensible sports cars. It's a mark of how enduring the design was that the Scimitar GTE lasted from 1968 to 1986 and still looked fresh even at the end of the 16,000 production run.

A known continuous history can add value to and enhance the enjoyment of a car.

◀ **1966 Reliant Scimitar SE4,** manual gearbox with overdrive, chrome wire wheels, subject of body-off restoration, mechanics rebuilt 1992–97, finished in red, concours winner.
£9,000–10,000 / $13,000–14,500 SiC

1966 Reliant Scimitar SE4, mechanics refurbished at a cost of almost £2,000, finished in red, cream interior, overdrive not functioning, otherwise good condition.
£2,000–2,400 / $2,900–3,300 BKS
Following its first forays into the sports car market – the Sabre and Sabre Six – Reliant began achieving commercial success in 1964 with the introduction of the Scimitar. The newcomer's 2+2 coupé body was the work of the Ogle design studio, while beneath the fibreglass skin there was a new chassis, plus the running gear and Ford 2.5 litre straight-six engine of the Sabre Six. The Scimitar's straight-line performance was excellent right from the start – 116mph and 0–60 in 11.4 seconds – and once the rear suspension had been revised (in 1965), it possessed handling to match. Slightly fewer than 300 were made before the arrival of the improved, Ford V6-engined versions in 1966.

1971 Reliant Scimitar GTE SE5A, 2994cc, manual 4-speed gearbox and overdrive, stainless-steel exhaust and fuel tank, finished in white, black interior, 82,000 miles from new.
£2,000–2,400 / $2,900–3,300 H&H
Best of the GTEs, according to those in the know, is the revised and updated SE5A, produced from 1971 to 1975, particularly models from 1972-on with Ford Granada-spec 135bhp 3 litre V6. The SE6 from 1975 is a wider, heavier, softer 'executive' Scimitar, created by splitting the SE5 moulds to add 4in extra length and 3in more width. It may be a better family formula, but it feels slightly softer in character too.

RELIANT Model	ENGINE cc/cyl	DATES	CONDITION 1	2	3
Sabre 4 Coupé & Drophead	1703/4	1961–63	£5,500	£2,750	£1,000
Sabre 6 Coupé & Drophead	2553/6	1962–64	£6,000	£3,500	£1,500
Scimitar GT Coupé SE4	2553/6, 2994 V6	1964–70	£4,500	£2,500	£1,000
Scimitar GTE Sports Estate SE5/5A	2994/V6	1968–75	£5,000	£3,000	£750
Scimitar GTE Sports Estate SE6/6A	2994/V6	1976–80	£5,000	£3,500+	£1,250
Scimitar GTE Sports Estate SE6B	2792/V6	1980–86	£6,500	£5,000	£2,000
Scimitar GTC Convertible SE8B	2792/V6	1980–86	£8,000	£7,000	£5,500

Renault

Louis Renault's first car design, based on a De Dion tricycle, emerged in 1898. In the company's very earliest years, Louis concentrated on racing until his brother, Marcel, was killed in the 1903 Paris-Madrid race. Thereafter, he devoted his efforts to car production and soon built up a comprehensive model range. By 1913, the company was responsible for around 20 per cent of French automobile production. The company was nationalised in 1945, shortly after Louis Renault's death. Since then, there have been an equal measure of landmark cars – such as the 4CV of 1947, the Dauphine, and Renault 4 and 5 – along with some interesting diversions, such as the pretty Floride and Caravelle small sports cars.

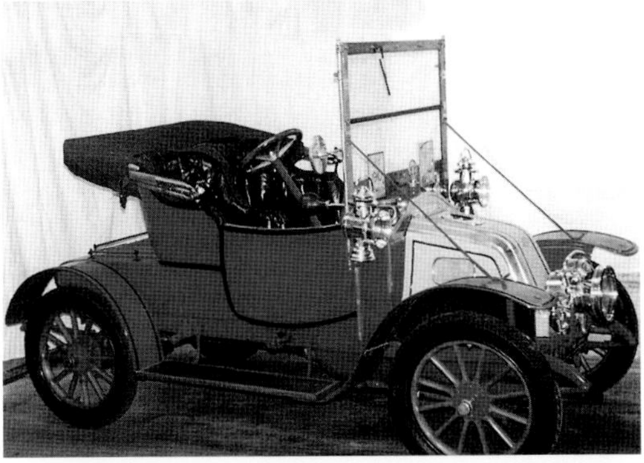

◄ **1910 Renault AX 8hp Two-Seater,** vertical twin-cylinder engine, mechanical valves, 3-speed gearbox, acetylene headlamp, oil side lamps, 2-piece windscreen, hood, finished in red, black buttoned leather interior, VCC dated, unused since 1995, in need of recommissioning.
£17,000–20,000 / $24,650–29,000 ⚒ BKS

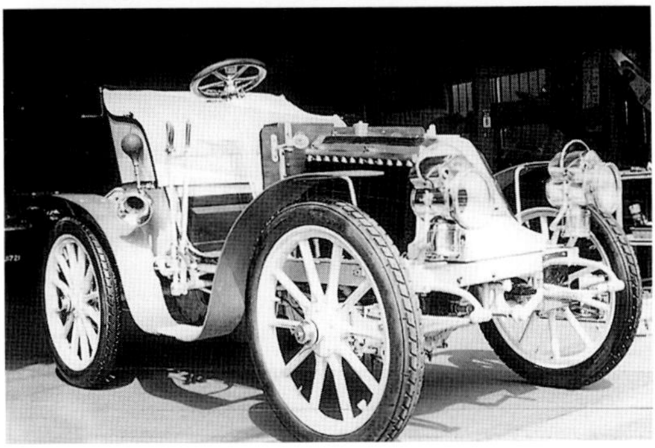

1902 Renault Type G 6hp Two-Seater, single-cylinder engine, mechanical exhaust valve, atmospheric inlet valve, twin side-mounted gilled tube radiators, brass acetylene headlamps, bulb horn, original mechanical specification in all major respects, finished in white, white interior, VCC dating plate.
£32,000–37,000 / $46,400–53,650 ⚒ BKS
Louis Renault was a pioneer in automobile design in the French motor industry, building his first car as early as 1898, mounting a De Dion Bouton engine on the front of a primitive tubular frame. He broke from traditional design by featuring a sprung live rear axle, a feature soon to be copied by his contemporaries. With substantial financial backing production began at Billancourt of 1¾hp and 3hp cars, with 4½hp cars appearing in 1900 and by 1902 the single cylinder cars were built in 6hp and 8hp versions alongside a 10hp twin.

RENAULT Model	ENGINE cc/cyl	DATES	CONDITION 1	2	3
40hp	7540/6	1919–21	£30,000	£20,000	£10,000
SR	4537/4	1919–22	£10,000	£7,000	£5,000
EU-15.8HP	2815/4	1919–23	£8,000+	£5,000	£2,000
GS-IG	2121/4	1920–23	£5,000	£3,000	£2,000
JP	9123/6	1922–29	£25,000	£20,000	£15,000
KJ	951/4	1923–29	£6,000	£4,000	£2,000
Mona Six	1474/6	1928–31	£7,000	£5,000	£3,000
Reinastella	7128/8	1929–32	£25,000	£20,000	£15,000
Viva Six	3181/6	1929–34	£10,000	£7,000	£3,000
14/45	2120/4	1929–35	£7,000	£5,000	£2,000
Nervahuit	4240/8	1931	£12,000	£10,000	£7,000
UY	1300/4	1932–34	£7,000	£5,000	£2,000
ZC/ZD2	4825/8	1934–35	£12,000	£10,000	£7,000
YN2	1463/4	1934–39	£7,000	£5,000	£2,000
Airline Super and Big 6	3620/6	1935	£10,000	£8,000	£5,000
18	2383/4	1936–39	£9,000	£5,000	£3,000
26	4085/6	1936–39	£12,000	£8,000	£5,000

Veteran pre-war models like the 2-cylinder AX, AG and BB are very popular, with values ranging between £6,000 and £15,000. The larger 4-cylinder cars like the AM, AZ, XB and VB are very reliable and coachbuilt examples command £30,000+, with 6-cylinder coachbuilt cars commanding a premium.

1932 Renault Novaquatre Coupé, 1200cc 4-cylinder engine, right-hand drive, finished in cream and blue, new blue and grey upholstery, good condition.
£5,000–6,000 / $7,250–8,700 CGC

1963 Renault Dauphine, 845cc 4-cylinder engine, bare-metal respray, finished in blue, blue vinyl and cloth interior in excellent condition, 41,000 miles from new, original specification throughout.
£4,250–4,750 / $6,200–6,900 BRIT
The Dauphine first appeared in 1956, being effectively an updated version of the highly successful 4CV.

◄ **1985 Renault 5 Turbo 2 Group B,** 1400cc mid-mounted engine, turbocharger, stainless-steel exhaust, 3-point engine immobiliser, Azvec alloy wheels, professionally converted to right-hand drive, finished in pearl white, electric windows, 2-seater, Sparco seats, demountable full-harness belts, Racetech auxiliary gauges, Momo leather steering wheel, 24,000 miles from new, excellent condition.
£6,500–8,000 / $9,400–11,600 BARO
The Turbo 2 was produced to compete against the Group B Peugeot, Audi and Metro 6R4 on the world rally scene. The FIA required manufacturers to produce 500 cars to meet homologation requirements, and this is one of those homologation specials.

Renault Dauphine (1956–67)

Engine: 845cc, four-cylinder.
Power: 32bhp @ 4,500rpm.
Transmission: Three-speed manual, four-speed from 1961; three-speed automatic with electric clutch.
Brakes: Drums all-round, discs all-round from 1964.
0–60mph: 31.6 seconds.
Maximum speed: 71mph.
Average fuel consumption: 35–45mpg.
When introduced in 1956, the Renault Dauphine was a delightfully unorthodox little machine, with a water-cooled, rear-mounted engine, all-round independent suspension and an adventurously streamlined body on a unitary base. With compact four-seater accommodation, it was also better equipped than many rival UK offerings, with a steering lock as standard, automatic choke and courtesy lights in the front luggage compartment and rear engine bay. It even had special concave head-lamp lenses that were supposed to generate a pocket of air and prevent insects from committing suicide. Most daring of all was an optional semi-automatic three-speed transmission. The motor magazines waxed lyrical, and discerning British motorists eventually cottoned on to the revolutionary Renault. Production eventually ran to well over two million.
Pick of the bunch: Amedée Gordini did for the little Renault what John Cooper later did for the Mini. The Dauphine Gordini's 845cc engine produced 37.8bhp and took top speed up to 75.6mph; no road burner, but a bit more fun than the base Dauphine.
Dauphine facts: From 1956 to 1958, right-hand-drive Dauphines were assembled in Britain in west London. In 1958, a basic Dauphine won the Monte Carlo Rally; in that same year, Dauphines took first to fourth in class in the Mille Miglia.

RENAULT Model	ENGINE cc/cyl	DATES	CONDITION 1	2	3
4CV	747/ 760/4	1947–61	£3,500	£2,000	£850
Fregate	1997/4	1952–60	£3,000	£2,000	£1,000
Dauphine	845/4	1956–66	£1,500	£1,000	£350
Dauphine Gordini	845/4	1961–66	£2,000	£1,000	£450
Floride	845/4	1959–62	£3,000	£2,000	£600
Caravelle	956/ 1108/4	1962–68	£4,500	£2,800	£750
R4	747/ 845/4	1961–86	£2,000	£1,500	£350
R8/R10	1108/4	1962–71	£1,800	£750	£200
R8 Gordini	1108/4	1965–66	£8,000	£5,000	£2,000
R8 Gordini	1255/4	1966–70	£8,000	£5,500	£2,500
R8S	1108/4	1968–71	£2,000	£1,200	£400

Renault-Alpine

In France, the Renault-Alpine A110 is a national institution, an icon on four wheels that inspires patriotic fervour. Ask any Frenchman and he'll tell you that the A110 is not only as nimble as a mountain goat, but that it also combines all the best virtues of contemporary Lotuses, Porsches and anything else with sporting pretensions. In the UK, the Alpine is a car for aficionados. It was only built in left-hand drive, and anyone who wants an instantly recognisable pose-mobile would be far better off buying a cooking Porsche 911 for around the same money or less. The Alpine A110 was the brainchild of Jean Redélé, at one time the youngest Renault agent in France. His passion for motorsport led him to modify Renault products, then produce his own, based on Renault running gear and engines. The result was a remarkably nimble sporting package that dominated world rallying for a while and rewarded the road user with limpet-like grip. In short, it was a thinly disguised racer and just about the most fun you could have this side of a Lancia Stratos.

1974 Renault-Alpine A110 1600S, 1605cc 4-cylinder engine, 140bhp, Kugelfischer fuel injection, 5-speed manual gearbox, 4-wheel independent suspension, 4-wheel disc brakes.
£21,000–24,000 / $30,500–34,800 ⚒ Pou

Renault-Alpine A110 (1963–77)

Production: 8,203.
Body style: Two-seater sports coupé.
Construction: Fibreglass body integral with tubular-steel backbone chassis.
Engine: Four-cylinder, 956cc–1796cc.
Brakes: Four-wheel discs.
Maximum speed: 110–132mph.
Alpine fact: The Alpine was most at home in rally conditions and won everything going on the world stage, including a staggering 1-2-3 in one of the snowiest Monte Carlo Rallies ever in 1971.

1975 Renault-Alpine 1600SC, 1605cc 4-cylinder engine, twin Weber 45DCOE carburettors, 5-speed manual gearbox, 4-wheel independent suspension, 4-wheel disc brakes, 215km/h top speed, 35,600km from new, finished in metallic blue.
£20,000–23,000 / $29,000–33,300 ⚒ Pou

Riley

It's a little sad that the once forward-thinking Coventry firm of Riley ended its days as little more than an upmarket badge of dubious distinction on mainstream BMC products. Indeed, when the name died in 1969, some Riley fans who'd remembered the fine, sporting RM Rileys of the immediate post-war period, probably thought it a blessed relief. Like many of the early automobile firms around Coventry and Birmingham, Riley came to car making via bicycle manufacture, producing its first car in 1898. In the 1920s and 1930s, the firm produced some very appealing and highly regarded small sporting cars, before being taken over by Morris in 1938. The immediate post-war products, the RM-series cars, were hallmark Riley sporting saloons that managed to retain a distinct identity before the rot set in with the plague of badge-engineering. For many, the RMs also rate as the last real Rileys.

1929 Riley 9 Mk IV Four-Seater, 1030cc, Lynx-style coachwork, finished in red, black interior.
£6,500–7,500 / $9,400–10,875 ⚒ H&H

1932 Riley 9 Monaco Four-Door Saloon, 1034cc, twin low-set cams operating pushrods and overhead valves, sunroof, restored, finished in black, engine rebuilt, original body panels, original green leather upholstery, folding rear seat, door trims, headlining and all woodwork in excellent condition, concours winner.
£10,000–11,500 / $14,500–16,700 ⚒ BKS
Introduced in 1927, the sporting Monaco saloon proved a bestseller in the Riley range.

1936 Riley 12/4 Special, converted from Special Series Kestrel six-light saloon, chassis shortened to 8ft 1½in wheelbase, Kestrel's rear track retained, 1496cc engine, 4-speed pre-selector gearbox, differential uprated and geared up, aluminium body, restored 1992, finished in British racing green, matching leather interior, good condition.
£16,000–19,000 / $23,200–27,500 ⚒ BKS
Riley's 9hp twin-cam four was an outstanding engine design by any standards, and its high-camshaft layout was retained for the new Hugh Rose-designed 1.5 litre four introduced in 1935. The Falcon saloon debuted on the new 12hp chassis, which was also available with the familiar Kestrel saloon and Lynx tourer coachwork, and in the following year the range was augmented by the short-wheelbase Sprite two-seater sports.

RILEY Model	ENGINE cc/cyl	DATES	CONDITION 1	2	3
9hp	1034/2	1906–07	£9,000	£6,000	£3,000
Speed 10	1390/2	1909–10	£10,000	£6,000	£3,000
11	1498/4	1922–27	£7,000	£4,000	£2,000
9	1075/4	1927–32	£10,000	£7,000	£4,000
9 Gamecock	1098/4	1932–33	£14,000	£10,000	£6,000
Lincock 12hp	1458/6	1933–36	£9,000	£7,000	£5,000
Imp 9hp	1089/4	1934–35	£35,000	£28,000	£20,000
Kestrel 12hp	1496/4	1936–38	£8,000	£5,000	£2,000
Sprite 12hp	1496/4	1936–38	£40,000	£35,000	£20,000

Many Riley 9hp 'Specials' available; ideal for VSCC and club events.

RILEY Model	ENGINE cc/cyl	DATES	CONDITION 1	2	3
1½ Litre RMA	1496/4	1945–52	£6,000	£3,500	£1,500
1½ Litre RME	1496/4	1952–55	£6,000	£3,500	£1,500
2½ Litre RMB/F	2443/4	1946–53	£9,000	£7,000	£3,000
2½ Litre Roadster	2443/4	1948–50	£18,000	£11,000	£9,000
2½ Litre Drophead	2443/4	1948–51	£18,000	£14,000	£10,000
Pathfinder	2443/4	1953–57	£3,500	£2,000	£750
2.6	2639/6	1957–59	£3,000	£1,800	£750
1.5	1489/4	1957–65	£3,000	£2,000	£850
4/68	1489/4	1959–61	£1,500	£700	£300
4/72	1622/4	1961–69	£1,600	£800	£300
Elf I/II/III	848/4	1961–66	£1,500	£850	£400
Kestrel I/II	1098/4	1965–67	£1,500	£850	£400

1937 Riley Kestrel-Sprite, completely restored early 1990s, finished in cream, new red leather interior and carpets, wooden dashboard, temperature gauge faulty, aluminium coachwork and mechanical components in good condition.
£11,000–12,500 / $16,000–18,150 ⚒ BRIT
In 1937, for the discerning driver seeking additional performance, Riley listed the Kestrel-Sprite, powered by the same engine as utilised in the successful Sprite sports model, an example of which had won the 1936 Tourist Trophy Race. Contemporary road tests reported a maximum speed in excess of 85mph with effortless cruising at 70+. The specification included Girling brakes, while the increased power output of the engine necessitated the use of a Scintilla Vertex magneto. As with other Riley models of this period, the Kestrel-Sprite employed a pre-selector transmission.

1950 Riley 2½ Litre RMD Drophead Coupé, barn find, completely restored, finished in white, red interior.
£11,500–14,000 / $16,300–20,300 ⊞ RIL

1954 Riley RME Saloon, 1496cc 4-cylinder engine, 4-speed manual gearbox, finished in black, good condition.
£3,000–3,500 / $4,400–5,200 ⚒ H&H

◀ **1954 Riley 1½ Litre RME Saloon,** 1496cc 4-cylinder engine, brakes overhauled, finished in black, 2 owners and 50,000 miles from new, unrestored, original condition.
£5,250–6,250 / $7,600–9,150 ⚒ BRIT
The RM models were quality vehicles in the best Riley tradition. Their excellent twin-cam engine was available in 1½ litre and 2½ litre versions, and the interior appointments were of the highest standard. With rack-and-pinion steering and 'torsionic' front suspension, the RM cars were blessed with sports car handling.

Riley RM (1946–55)

Engine: Twin-cam 1496 and 2443cc straight-four.
Transmission: Four-speed manual.
Brakes: Drums all-round, hydraulic at front, rod-operated at rear; hydraulic all-round from 1952.
Steering: Rack-and-pinion.
Power output: 90–100bhp for 2443cc; 55bhp for 1496cc engine.
Maximum speed: 75mph for 1496cc; 90–95mph for 2443cc.
0–60mph: 15.2–16.5 seconds for 2443cc; 25–31 seconds 1496cc.
These fine sporting saloons and convertibles, which emerged just after the war, were classically British in an age when Britishness was nothing but shorthand for a whole catalogue of virtues. As one of the very first new post-war British designs, the RM's elegant styling was pleasingly traditional and reassuring, rather than faddishly modern. On the inside, that whiff of Wilton and leather, and the deep lustre of the walnut dash said more about you than cash alone ever could. And on the road, the RM offered brisk performance and confident poise. In short, these Rileys were sporting in the manner of blazers, cravats and slacks rather than Nikes, Lycra and steroids.
Which is which? The RM series had a confusing array of suffixes. The RMA and RME were 1.5 litre saloons; The RMB and RMF were longer-chassis 2.5 litre saloons; The RMC was a three-abreast 2.5 litre roadster; the RMD was a four-seater drophead.
What to watch: Engines have a deservedly high reputation. A greater worry is the ash body frame, which can all but disintegrate to leave a body with only a sentimental attachment to its chassis.
Famous RM Riley owners: Lord Mountbatten owned a succession of 2.5 litre saloons; Clark Cable owned a drophead.

Rolls-Royce

From the beginning of their partnership in 1904, Henry Royce and the Honourable Charles Rolls established Rolls-Royce's credentials as an exclusive producer of very expensive and superb motor cars of the highest quality. Henry Royce was a Manchester electrical engineer who built three experimental 10hp two-cylinder cars in 1903. Charles Rolls was an entrepreneur who sold foreign cars in London. The company's early reputation was founded on the 40/50, now known universally as the Silver Ghost. The model was introduced in 1906 and began the long-established Rolls-Royce practice of evolution rather than revolution, the car being refined and developed through the years until its replacement in 1925 by the New Phantom. Incidentally, although Charles Rolls had died in a flying accident in 1910, the impact on the company was far from disastrous, as by then he had largely lost interest in motor cars. The same could not be said of Sir Henry Royce (made a baronet after the success of Rolls-Royce powered aircraft in the 1931 Schneider Trophy race). He died in 1933, three years before the magnificent V12-engined Phantom III, which he'd inspired, went into production. In 1949, Rolls-Royce entered a new era with the Silver Dawn, the first Rolls-Royce offered complete by the factory rather than as a chassis to be fitted with bespoke coachwork of the owner's choosing. Rolls-Royce continued to offer chassis to coachbuilders alongside its own factory-bodied cars until 1965 with the launch of the Silver Shadow. This new Rolls-Royce was the first to feature monocoque construction with an integral body and chassis which, at a stroke, removed the scope for coachbuilt bodies, although the Phantom V Limousine still retained a separate chassis. In 1971, Rolls-Royce Limited became bankrupt after trouble with the RB211 aircraft engine, and the car division was separated out and floated as a public company. In 1980, Rolls-Royce was acquired by Vickers, and the more modern Silver Spirit replaced the ageing Silver Shadow. Now, the company that produced the Merlin aero engine for Spitire fighters during WWII is owned by BMW.

1912 Rolls-Royce 40/50hp Silver Ghost Tourer, chassis no. 2142, Barker-style coachwork, finished in midnight blue, burgundy leather interior.
£100,000–120,000 / $145,000–174,000 ⚒ COYS
The Rolls-Royce 40/50 was introduced at the 1907 Olympia Motor Show, where it caused a sensation. Its 7036cc, six-cylinder sidevalve engine featured a seven-bearing crankshaft, integral cylinder heads, roller cam followers, full pressure lubrication, twin plugs per cylinder, and dual magneto and coil ignition. It produced 50bhp at a lowly 1,500rpm allied to tremendous torque and unrivalled smoothness; using a four-speed gearbox in unit, with the engine, it was also capable of 55mph. By 1908, the Silver ghost – so renamed after the striking silver plating and paintwork of the 13th 40/50 produced – was Rolls Royce's only model. For 1909, capacity increased to 7428cc, and two years later a torque-tube drive was fitted, while power rose to 58bhp. The latter was instigated for the Scottish Reliability Trial, in which a Silver Ghost ran from the south coast to Scotland entirely in top gear. This car was sent originally to Australia, where at some stage it was converted to a single-seater. Then the running gear and chassis were incorporated into a yacht. Eventually, it was restored with Barker-style touring coachwork.

▶ **1913 Rolls-Royce 40/50hp Silver Ghost Roi de Belges Tourer,** chassis no. 2582, engine no. 90V, 7428cc, restored with Roi-de-Belges coachwork 1970s, engine rebuilt 1996, stainless-steel exhaust system, Hartford rear shock absorbers, leather spring gaiters, electric lighting, starter and dynamo, new wheel rims, extra 7.5 gallon fuel tank, divers-helmet rear lamps, teak running-board toolboxes, electric klaxon, boa-constrictor horn, 2-piece cranked windscreen, resprayed 1987 in dark blue with pale blue coachlines, full hood, front and rear tonneau covers, Elliott speedometer, Hunts 8-day dashboard clock, interior upholstered in deep-buttoned pleated grey leather, tailored waterproof cover.
£160,000–180,000 / $232,000–260,000 ⚒ BKS

ROLLS-ROYCE Model	ENGINE cc/cyl	DATES	CONDITION 1	2	3
Silver Ghost 40/50	7035/6	pre-WWI	£350,000+	£120,000	£80,000
Silver Ghost 40/50	7428/6	post-WWI	£110,000+	£70,000	£40,000
20hp (3 speed)	3127/6	1922–25	£29,000+	£23,000	£15,000
20hp	3127/6	1925–29	£30,000+	£24,000	£15,000
Phantom I	7668/6	1925–29	£50,000+	£28,000	£22,000
20/25	3669/6	1925–26	£30,000+	£18,000	£13,000
Phantom II	7668/6	1929–35	£40,000+	£30,000	£20,000
Phantom II Continental	7668/6	1930–35	£60,000+	£40,000	£28,000
25/30	4257/6	1936–38	£24,000+	£18,000	£12,000
Phantom III	7340/12	1936–39	£38,000	£28,000	£14,000
Wraith	4257/6	1938–39	£38,000	£32,000	£25,000

Prices will vary considerably depending on heritage, originality, coachbuilder, completeness and body style. A poor reproduction body can often mean the value is dependent only upon a rolling chassis and engine.

1914 Rolls-Royce 40/50hp Silver Ghost Tourer, chassis no. 20 RB, engine no. 65Q, supplied originally with Barker cabriolet coachwork, converted to estate-car coachwork 1925, subsequently altered to tourer form late 1950s, 4-speed gearbox, wooden artillery wheels with Warland rims, Colonial chassis, period headlights and sidelights, chassis and running gear to original specification, unused for 13 years.
£90,000–110,000 / $130,000–159,500 ⚒ BKS

1926 Rolls-Royce 20hp Two-Door saloon, chassis no. GOK77, 21in wheels, correct lamps, recently resprayed in black and dark blue, new pale blue leather interior, not totally correct.
£17,000–20,000 / $24,650–29,000 ⊞ RCC

1928 Rolls-Royce 20hp Doctor's Coupé, coachwork by Thrupp & Maberly, chassis no. GUJ48, engine no. H8T, 3.1 litre engine, nickel fittings, spring-loaded side windows, undertrays, dickey seat, twin spare wheels, restored late 1980s, little use since, later full-flow oil system, finished in deep burgundy with black wings.
£34,000–38,000 / $49,250–55,250 ⚒ BKS

1924 Rolls-Royce 20hp Four-Door Tourer, coachwork by Hooper, chassis no. GAK1, 32 x 4½in straight-sided tyres, full set of wet weather gear, rear Auster screen, swivel-mounted mirror-backed pillar lamp, full toolkit, finished in green, black hood, original leather upholstery.
£40,000–45,000 / $58,000–65,250 ⊞ RCC

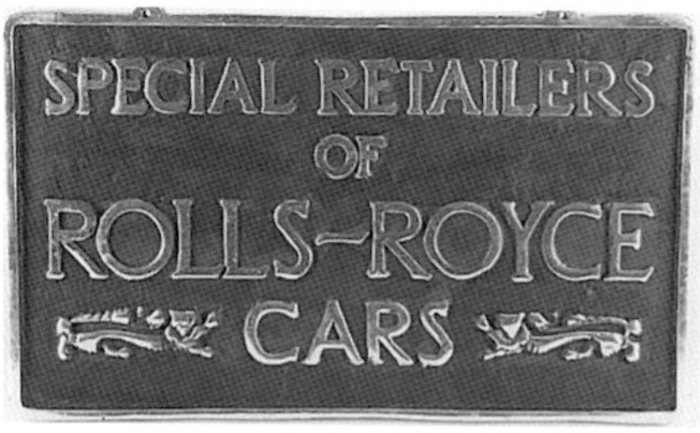

A Rolls-Royce Cars double-sided, cast aluminium dealer sign, reproduced from original mould, late 20thC, 26 x 16in (66 x 40.5cm).
£350–400 / $500–580 ⚒ BKS

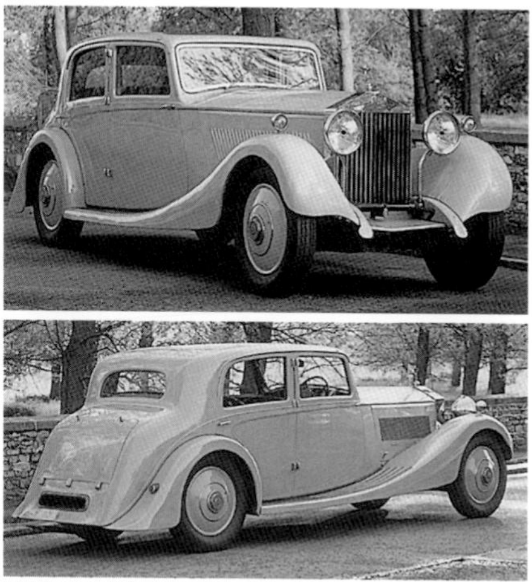

1929 Rolls-Royce Phantom 1 Saloon, coachwork by Southern, chassis no. 116WR, engine no. AE35, 7668cc overhead-valve 6-cylinder engine, 4-speed manual gearbox, front suspension on semi-elliptic leaf springs, rear live axle on cantilever leaf springs, 4-wheel servo-assisted mechanical drum brakes, rebodied late 1930s, restored, finished in dove grey with blue coachlines, dark blue interior.
£21,000–25,000 / $30,500–36,250 ⚒ C

The 40/50hp Phantom 1 of 1925 was only the second new Rolls-Royce type to be offered to the public in the 20 years since the Silver Ghost had been launched in 1906. Deriving directly from the Ghost, its engine being influenced by the overhead-valve 20hp introduced a few years previously, it possessed excellent servo-assisted four-wheel brakes and an engine claimed to offer one third power more than the Ghost's. Even with the elaborate formal coachwork, its maximum was some 80mph, with a lightness in handling and controls that belied its great size. Many Phantom 1s were updated with more fashionable coachwork during the 1930s, and this is one such car.

1932 Rolls-Royce 20/25 Drophead Coupé, coachwork by Mulliner, chassis no. GTZ81, engine no. B7N, disappearing hood mechanism, dickey seat, finished in blue over black, correct instrumentation, original blue leather interior, 1 owner since 1949, little recent use, original.
£50,000–55,000 / $72,500–79,750 ⚒ CGC

1929 Rolls-Royce Phantom 1 St Albans Limousine De Ville, coachwork by Brewster, chassis no. S342LR, left-hand drive, leather-covered sedanca roof, twin spare wheels, finished in primrose yellow and black, division, occasional seats, correct instruments, recently fitted with new pistons and cylinder head.
£43,000–48,000 / $62,400–69,600 ⊞ RCC

1931 Rolls-Royce Phantom I Newmarket Convertible, chassis no. S201PR, left-hand drive, twin side-mounted spare wheels, wind-up windows, removable centre pillars, finished in black and yellow, beige leather interior, good mechanical condition, in need of tidying, 1 of last Phantom Is built in USA.
£45,000–50,000 / $65,250–72,500 ⊞ RCC

1931 Rolls-Royce 40/50hp Phantom 1, 7668cc, left-hand drive, restored, excellent condition.
£48,000–54,000 / $69,600–78,250 ⊞ COHN

1932 Rolls-Royce 20/25hp Sports Saloon, coachwork by Mulliner, chassis no. GBT26, louvred bonnet, recessed rear-mounted spare wheel, finished in 2-tone grey, original brown leather interior, in need of cosmetic attention.
£16,000–19,000 / $23,200–27,500 ⊞ RCC

1933 Rolls-Royce 20/25 Sports Saloon, coachwork by Rippon, chassis no. GHW5, Zeiss headlamps, tubular bumpers, new stainless-steel exhaust system, finished in silver, blue interior, stored for some time, in need of tidying.
£17,500–20,000 / $25,400–29,000 ⊞ RCC

1933 Rolls-Royce 20/25 D-Back Saloon, coachwork by Barker, chassis no. GTZ26, synchromesh on third and fourth gear ratios, centralised lubrication system, thermostatically-controlled radiator shutters, louvred bonnet, P100 headlamps, wire wheels, completely restored, engine rebuilt, finished in white with black wings, chauffeur's compartment upholstered in leather, passenger compartment in Bedford cord, interior in very good condition, excellent mechanical condition.
£20,000–22,000 / $29,000–32,000 ⊞ RCC

Auction prices

Miller's only includes cars declared sold. Our guide prices take into account the buyer's premium, VAT on the premium, and the extent of any published catalogue information relating to condition and provenance. Cars sold at auction are identified by the icon; full details of the auction house can be found on page 330.

1933 Rolls-Royce 20/25 Four-Door Saloon, coachwork by Barker, chassis no GEX29, engine no. K6E, coil ignition, finished in beige and black, brown leather interior, good original condition.
£13,500–16,500 / $19,600–24,000 BKS

A development of the 20hp – the first 'small' Rolls-Royce – the 20/25hp model was launched in 1929. The capacity of the overhead-valve, six-cylinder engine was increased from 3127 to 3699cc, and a crossflow cylinder head adopted. Apart from the revised engine, early 20/25 chassis were identical to those of the last 20s, both models being produced during 1929. Thus the 20/25 inherited the right-hand gear change lever and servo-assisted brakes introduced on its predecessor for 1926, as well as Phantom-style vertical radiator shutters. Produced concurrently with the Phantom II, the 20/25 benefited from many of the features developed for the larger model, such as synchromesh gears and centralised chassis lubrication, becoming the bestselling Rolls-Royce of the inter-war period.

1934 Rolls-Royce 20/25 Drophead Coupé, coachwork by Mulliner, chassis no. GXB45, louvred bonnet, rear-mounted spare wheel, finished in maroon, good mechanical condition.
£39,000–43,000 / $56,500–62,500 ⊞ RCC

1934 Rolls-Royce 20/25 Two-Door Drophead Coupé, coachwork by Park Ward, chassis no. GHA1, engine no G2Z, unused since 1974.
£15,000–18,000 / $21,750–26,000 BKS

1935 Rolls-Royce 20/25 Tourer, coachwork in Vanden Plas style, chassis no. GLJ74, hood, side screens, tonneau cover, rear-mounted spare wheel, finished in white, red interior, in need of cosmetic attention.
£27,000–30,000 / $39,000–43,500 ⊞ RCC

1935 Rolls-Royce 20/25 Sedanca De Ville, coachwork by Gurney Nutting, chassis no. GRF20, engine no. P9H, 3.7 litre engine, louvred bonnet, twin trumpet horns, centre driving lamp, windscreen spotlamp, shortened steering column, restored 1995–97, finished in black over sand, new beige leather upholstery.
£27,000–32,000 / $39,000–46,400 ⚒ BKS

1935 Rolls-Royce 20/25 Sports Saloon, coachwork by Hooper, chassis no. GPG58, P100 headlights, Ace wheel discs, finished in black and white, refurbished brown leather interior, 1 owner for 32 years, correct specification, good condition.
£19,000–22,000 / $27,500–32,000 ⊞ RCC

1931 Rolls-Royce Phantom II Huntington Limousine, chassis no. 209AJS, finished in dark red and maroon, original black leather upholstery to front compartment, beige cloth to rear, 1 of only 125 PIIs built in left-hand-drive form.
£29,000–33,000 / $42,000–47,900 ⊞ RCC

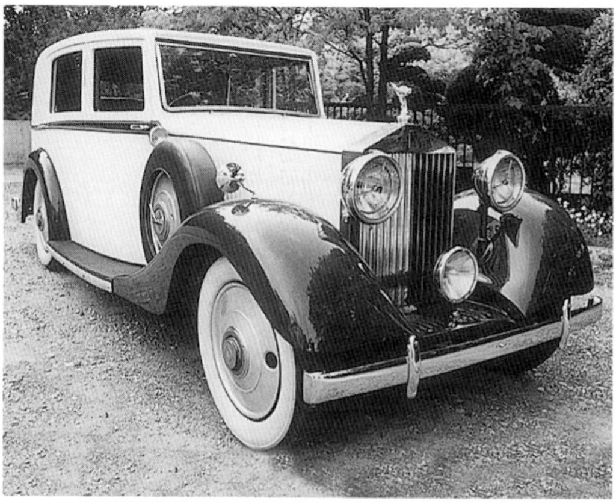

1935 Rolls-Royce 20/25 Limousine, coachwork by Hooper, chassis no. GLG38, engine no. M6K, 3699cc overhead-valve straight-6 engine, 4-speed manual gearbox with side change, synchromesh on top ratios, beam front axle, semi-elliptic leaf-spring suspension, 4-wheel servo-assisted mechanical drum brakes, older restoration, in need of cosmetic attention.
£12,500–15,000 / $18,150–21,750 ⚒ C
This particular car was supplied new to the King of Siam (Thailand).

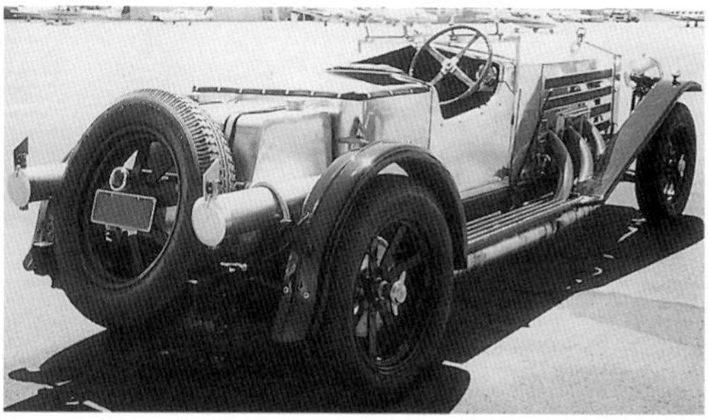

1930 Rolls-Royce Speed Wagon, 1620cu.in Rolls-Royce Merlin V12 engine, 1,000bhp, 2 twin-choke Zenith updraught carburettors, twin magnetos, twin mechanical fuel pumps, Ki Gas pre-start hand primer system, 15 gallon dry-sump oil tank, twin 6in exhaust systems, 4-speed epicyclic manual transmission, hydrokinetic clutch with manual lock-up facility, Lockheed 17in finned drum brakes, 24 x 700 tyres, Bugatti-style steel-blade wheels, 50 gallon alloy fuel tank, fully cantilevered chassis, semi-elliptic leaf-spring suspension, 2-seater polished aluminium coachwork.
£140,000–160,000 / $203,000–232,000 ⚒ RM

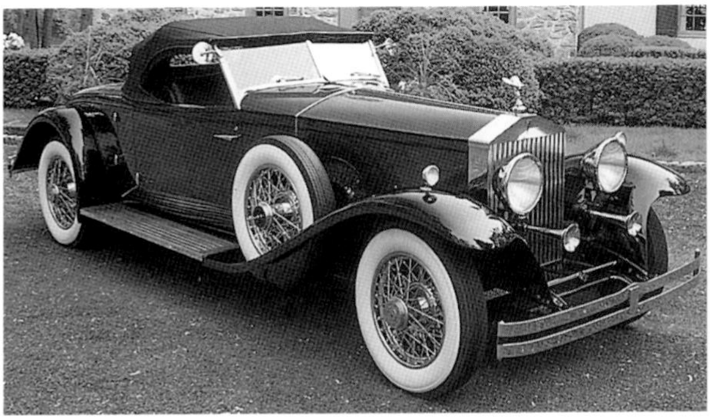
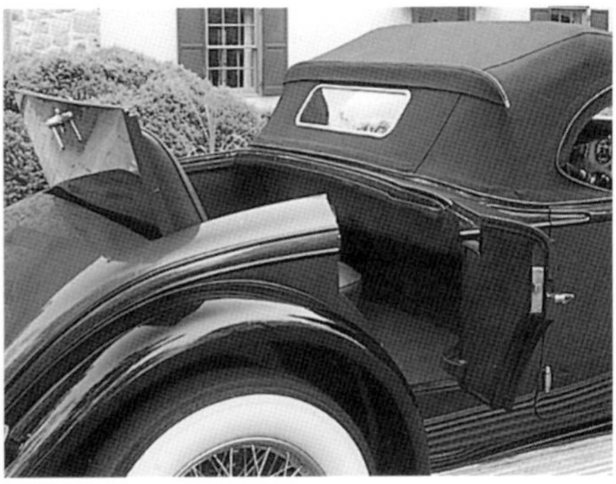

1932 Rolls-Royce Phantom II Henley Roadster, coachwork by Brewster, 7768cc 6-cylinder engine, left-hand drive, older restoration, black interior, 1 of 8 Henley Roadsters built, very good condition.
£300,000+ / $235,000 ⚒ BKS
This car was originally delivered to Tommy Manville, 'one of the most notorious playboys in US history'. Manville is chiefly remembered as a persistent serial monogamist, who was married 13 times to a total of 11 glamorous women. He is said to have given this car to wife number seven as a gift. Born in 1894, Manville inherited his vast fortune from the family firm, Johns-Manville, which had been founded in 1858 to manufacture asbestos-based building materials. He would modestly describe his occupation on wedding certificates as 'retired businessman' or as 'looking after my estate', but his lurid matrimonial antics inspired the 1938 Ernst Lubitsch/Billy Wilder movie *Bluebeard's Eighth Wife*, starring Claudette Colbert, Gary Cooper and David Niven.

1934 Rolls-Royce Phantom II Sedanca De Ville, coachwork by Windovers, chassis no. 11RY, engine no. YO15, restored 1982–99, engine rebuilt with new cylinder blocks, resprayed in red and grey, red and black leather interior, wood trim refurbished, new cocktail cabinet, new grey woollen carpets, concours winner.
£100,000–120,000 / $145,000–174,000 ⚒ BKS
The Phantom I was beginning to look rather dated by 1929, but the Phantom II, unveiled at the Olympia Motor Show in 1929, answered all the critics. It was technically up-to-the-minute in design, while retaining all the features of mechanical excellence shared by its predecessor. The new car featured unit construction of engine and gearbox, improved ride and handling characteristics, and better braking. It was powered by a 7.7 litre, six-cylinder, pushrod overhead-valve engine, which was very quiet, yet provided more than ample power to carry the most flamboyant of coachwork.

1935 Rolls-Royce Phantom II Special Sedanca De Ville, coachwork by Windovers, chassis no. 197TA, engine no. NB35, 7.7 litre 6-cylinder engine, encased side-mounted spare wheel, pram irons to the rear quarter, blade bumpers, centre-mounted spotlight, restored 1989, finished in 2-tone burgundy, red leather interior.
£90,000–110,000 / $130,500–159,500 ⚒ BKS

1938 Rolls-Royce 25/30 Sports Saloon, coachwork by Thrupp & Maberly, chassis no GGR58, engine no. C22G, 4257cc, completely restored at a cost of £48,000, converted to unleaded fuel, finished in black, grey leather upholstery, dark blue carpets.
£28,000–32,000 / $42,000–46,400 ⚒ BKS

◀ 1938 Rolls-Royce Wraith Four-Door Limousine, coachwork by Park Ward, chassis no. WXA-8, engine no W111N09, B60 inlet-over-exhaust engine, sunroof, division, fitted luggage, restored, 500 miles covered since, stainless-steel exhaust system, bare-metal respray in black and blue, new upholstery, very good condition throughout.
£15,000–18,000 / $21,750–26,000 ⚒ BKS
This car was the sixth and final Wraith prototype. Its original engine was replaced by a B60 unit in 1939. During WWII, it was used by the RAF as a staff car for senior officers and carries a dashboard plaque to that effect.

ROLLS-ROYCE Model	ENGINE cc/cyl	DATES	CONDITION 1	2	3
Silver Wraith LWB	4566/ 4887/6	1951–59	£25,000	£17,000	£10,000
Silver Wraith SWB	4257/ 4566/6	1947–59	£20,000	£13,000	£10,000
Silver Wraith Drophead	4257/ 4566/6	1947–59	£50,000	£35,000	£25,000
Silver Dawn St'd Steel	4257/ 4566/6	1949–52	£25,000	£15,000	£10,000
Silver Dawn St'd Steel	4257/ 4566/6	1952–55	£30,000	£20,000	£15,000
Silver Dawn Coachbuilt	4257/ 4566/6	1949–55	£35,000+	£25,000	£18,000
Silver Dawn Drophead	4257/ 4566/6	1949–55	£60,000	£50,000	£30,000
Silver Cloud I	4887/6	1955–59	£18,000	£10,000	£8,000
SCI Coupé Coachbuilt	4887/6	1955–59	£30,000	£20,000	£15,000
SCI Conv (HJM)	4887/6	1955–59	£80,000+	£60,000+	£40,000
Silver Cloud II	6230/8	1959–62	£19,000	£10,000	£8,000
SCII Conv (HJM)	6230/8	1959–62	£80,000	£75,000	£40,000
SCII Conv (MPW)	6230/8	1959–62	£60,000	£40,000	£32,000
Silver Cloud III	6230/8	1962–65	£25,000	£12,000	£10,000
SCIII Conv (MPW)	6230/8	1962–65	£70,000	£45,000	£35,000
Silver Shadow	6230/ 6750/8	1965–76	£14,000	£9,000	£7,000
S Shadow I Coupé (MPW)	6230/ 6750/8	1965–70	£15,000	£10,000	£8,000
SSI Drophead (MPW)	6230/ 6750/8	1965–70	£33,000	£25,000	£18,000
Corniche FHC	6750/8	1971–77	£15,000	£11,000	£8,000
Corniche Convertible	6750/8	1971–77	£28,000	£22,000	£18,000
Camargue	6750/8	1975–85	£30,000	£25,000	£18,000

1949 Rolls-Royce Silver Wraith Touring Limousine, coachwork by Freestone & Webb, 4257cc, restored, finished in black and yellow, brown interior.
£17,000–20,000 / $24,650–29,000 H&H

1952 Rolls-Royce Silver Dawn Saloon, 4566cc 6-cylinder engine, 4-speed gearbox, 4-wheel servo-assisted drum brakes, left-hand drive, finished in dark green, tan leather interior, fewer than 37,000 miles from new.
£26,000–30,000 / $37,700–43,500 Pou

A.F. McNeil, a pen and ink and colour wash profile drawing, depicting the James Young Rolls-Royce Two-Door Fixed-head Coupé, mounted, framed, glazed, 1951, 23 x 15in (58.5 x 38cm).
£500–600 / $720–860 BKS

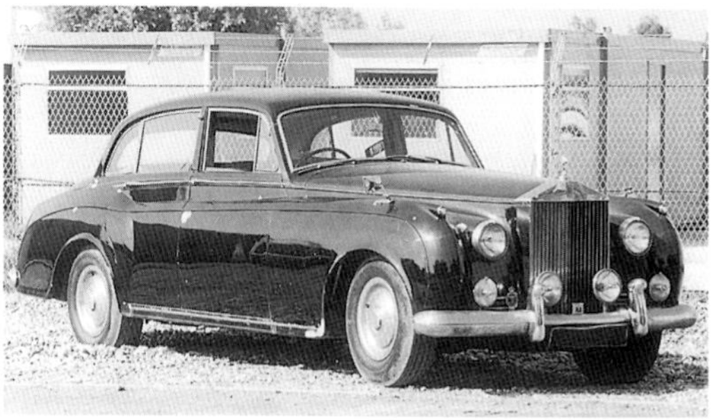

1959 Rolls-Royce Silver Cloud I Saloon, coachwork by James Young, 1 of 3 long-wheelbase cars built, only example without division, headlining, leather upholstery and interior woodwork in good condition, body, chassis and running gear in need of restoration.
£6,000–7,000 / $8,700–10,400 BKS

The S1, S2 and S3 were Bentley's equivalents of the Rolls-Royce Silver Cloud I, II and III. Although virtually identical, apart from the distinctive radiator, Bentley versions can often be cheaper than Rolls-Royce counterparts. This is not a factor of rarity, as with the launch of the Silver Cloud II in 1959, Rolls-Royce versions outnumbered Bentley offerings for the first time.

Miller's Compares

I. 1957 Rolls-Royce Silver Cloud I, power steering, finished in light over dark green, 46,600 miles from new, very good condition throughout.
£15,000–18,000 / $21,750–26,000 ⚒ CGC

II. 1962 Rolls-Royce Silver Cloud II Saloon, coachwork by Mulliner, electrically-controlled dampers, power-assisted steering, brakes overhauled, resprayed in black, new light tan leather interior, 59,680 miles from new, originally owned by Mary Pickford, excellent condition.
£35,000–40,000 / $50,750–58,000 ⚒ BKS

The 1957 Silver Cloud, item I, sold at auction in the UK for half the price that item II commanded in the USA. The difference in value is not so much due to the condition, but the provenance; in fact, a large measure of the more valuable car's worth – possibly as much as half – rests in the fact that it was owned by silent screen star Mary Pickford until her death in 1979. Another example of the high value attached to celebrity ownership was a 1961 Bentley S2 (companion model to the Rolls-Royce Silver Cloud) owned by screen legend James Cagney. In the year 2000, it commanded £37,000 in the US. Without the Cagney connection, it might not have been worth even half that. While these Rolls-Royce and Bentley models are relatively plentiful, only one person can own a Cagney S2 or Pickford Silver Cloud, and some people are prepared to pay a lot extra for these unique distinctions.

Mary Pickford was one of the great stars of the silent movies. When she was just 16, she was cast by the legendary director D.W. Griffith. Before long, her charming screen personality, portrayed in a succession of 'Cinderella' roles, won her the title 'the world's sweetheart'. Despite her winsome looks, however, she had a formidable business brain. She was one of the founders of United Artists Films, and became one of the richest women in America. Pickford was one of the very first of the Hollywood set to own a Rolls-Royce, a 1936 Phantom I, which had a secret compartment to store liquor – Prohibition was in force. The Silver Cloud above was the last car she owned. Introduced in 1959, the Silver Cloud II benefited from a smooth running 6230cc V8, which drove through a four-speed automatic transmission and could propel the car to 115+mph in silence.

1965 Rolls-Royce Silver Cloud III, completely restored, finished in 2-tone metallic grey.
£15,000–18,000 / $21,750–26,000 ⚒ PALM

1965 Rolls-Royce Silver Cloud III Coupé, coachwork by Mulliner Park Ward, 6230cc V8 engine, 220bhp, 4-speed automatic transmission, 4-wheel servo-assisted drum brakes, finished in dark brown, cream interior, well maintained, originally owned by Brigitte Bardot.
£45,000–50,000
$65,250–72,500 ⚒ Pou

Rolls-Royce Silver Cloud (1955–65)

Engines: 4887cc six-cylinder, 1955–59; 6230cc V8.
Power output: Rolls never revealed this, preferring to describe power output as 'adequate'. However, a consensus credits the six-cylinder cars with around 178bhp, about 200–220bhp for the V8s.
Transmission: Four-speed automatic; manual by special order.
Brakes: Servo-assisted drums.
Maximum speed: 100–116mph.
0–60mph: 10.8–14+ seconds.
In 1955, the new Rolls-Royce Silver Cloud and its Bentley sibling straddled a divide between an old world aristocracy clinging to crumbling stately homes and a new world order of emerging entrepreneurs, like Berlin airlift tycoon Freddy Laker. It was the last Rolls-Royce, other than bespoke limousines, to ride on a separate chassis to which the dwindling number of coachbuilders could still tailor bespoke bodywork. Yet it also came 'ready to wear', straight off the peg with so-called Standard Steel factory coachwork. Notwithstanding the Silver Cloud's dreadnought proportions, Rolls-Royce acknowledged that there was a new breed of owner who actually preferred to drive as well, yet initially it seemed a grudging concession, as power steering wasn't even an option for the first two years of production. In 1959, with the Silver Cloud II and S2 Bentley, Rolls gave its leviathan the V8 engine it had intended all along, in place of the six-cylinder unit that was a modified pre-war design. Another sign of the times was the disappearance of the complex pedal operated one-shot chassis and suspension lubrication system – a trusty chauffeur could be relied upon to keep everything oiled, but the owner-driver would probably forget. In 1962, the Silver Cloud III and S3 Bentley, offered a little more power from the V8 and were identified externally by quad head lamps, and a lower radiator and bonnet line.
Prices when new: In 1965, £5,500 bought a seven-bedroomed house, 11 Austin Minis, eight Triumph Heralds – or one Rolls-Royce Silver Cloud III.
Market comment: Dark colours are always easier to sell – beware the porcelain-white wedding hire hack pregnant with filler and a glove box full of confetti. Bentley versions can be slightly cheaper.
Production: Rolls-Royce, approximately 7,000; Bentley, approximately 6,500.

1960 Rolls-Royce Phantom V Sedanca De Ville, coachwork by James Young, 6230cc aluminium overhead-valve V8 engine, sliding De Ville extension to front compartment, electric windows, pushbutton door locks, twin spotlights, pennant holder on mascot, finished in burgundy, figured walnut dashboard, light beige interior, lockers with sliding shutters in front and rear doors for personal papers, picnic set, field glasses, mirror-back companions, reading lights, cocktail cabinet, glass cabinet under each table to the rear, occasional seats, 1 of 7 thought to have been built to this design.
£75,000–85,000 / $108,750–123,250 BKS

1961 Rolls-Royce Phantom V Limousine, coachwork by Park Ward, chassis finished in black and burgundy, black and beige leather interior, in need of some refurbishment.
£25,000–30,000 / $36,250–43,500 RCC

◄ **1969 Rolls-Royce Phantom VI Limousine,** 6230cc V8 engine, stainless-steel exhaust system, finished in silver-grey, blue interior, fewer than 50,000 miles from new, originally owned by Engelbert Humperdink, very good condition.
£29,000–34,000
$49,250 H&H

1968 Rolls-Royce Silver Shadow Convertible, new power hood, finished in red, grey leather interior, new wood trim, excellent condition.
£25,000–30,000 / $36,250–43,500 TIHO

1970 Rolls-Royce Silver Shadow I, 6230cc V8 engine, 4-speed automatic transmission, 4-wheel disc brakes, finished in black, good condition.
£6,500–8,000 / $9,400–11,600 Pou

1970 Rolls-Royce Silver Shadow I, finished in silver, black leather interior, 3 owners and 76,000 miles from new.
£6,500–8,000 / $9,300–11,600 ⊞ VIC

The T1 and T2 were Bentley's equivalents of the Rolls-Royce Silver Shadow I and II. Although virtually identical, apart from the distinctive radiator, Bentley versions can often be cheaper than Rolls-Royce counterparts, despite the fact that Bentley versions are far rarer.

1971 Rolls-Royce Silver Shadow I, 6750cc V8 engine, finished in white, black interior.
£5,000–6,000 / $7,250–8,700 ⊞ VIC

► **1975 Rolls-Royce Silver Shadow LWB,** 6750cc V8 engine, 4-wheel independent self-levelling suspension, 4-wheel disc brakes, new exhaust, brakes overhauled, finished in brown, cream Everflex roof, 6,000 miles covered in past 10 years, good condition throughout.
£5,000–6,000 / $7,250–8,700 COYS

1978 Rolls-Royce Silver Shadow II, finished in peacock blue, magnolia hide interior, 57,000 miles from new.
£10,000–11,000 / $14,500–16,000 ⊞ VIC

A known continuous history can add value to and enhance the enjoyment of a car.

1979 Rolls-Royce Silver Shadow II, 6750cc V8 engine, finished in metallic blue, black Everflex roof, grey interior, ex James pop group promotional car, removable stickers.
£4,000–5,000 / $5,800–7,250 H&H

This particular car was the prize in a competition run by *The Sun* newspaper. Previously, it had been used by James, the pop group, to promote their album and tour in the summer of 1999.

1970 Rolls-Royce Silver Shadow I Two-Door Saloon, 6230cc V8 engine, resprayed in maroon, black Everflex roof, grey hide interior, 1 of 660 built, good condition throughout.
£8,500–10,000 / $12,300–14,500 BRIT

1974 Rolls-Royce Silver Shadow Saloon, 6750cc V8 engine, 4-wheel independent suspension, servo-assisted 4-wheel disc brakes, left-hand drive, finished in black and green, green Connolly leather interior, 2 owners and 51,000km from new, good condition throughout.
£6,500–8,000 / $9,400–11,600 BKS

1979 Rolls-Royce Silver Shadow II, 6750cc V8 engine, power-assisted rack-and-pinion steering, finished in gold, split-level air conditioning, beige hide interior, 47,200 miles from new, excellent mechanical condition.
£12,500–14,000 / $18,150–20,300 ⚒ BRIT

1972 Rolls-Royce Corniche Coupé, finished in navy blue, cream leather interior, lambswool rugs, good condition.
£8,000–10,000 / $11,600–14,500 ⚒ COYS
In 1971, the two-door coupé and drophead models were renamed Corniche, simultaneously receiving a ten-per-cent power increase over the four-door Silver Shadow, which raised top speed to 120mph. In 1972, the suspension was completely redesigned, greatly enhancing the car's handling.

1981 Rolls-Royce Silver Spirit, 6750cc V8 engine, electric sunroof, finished in black, beige leather interior.
£8,500–10,500 / $12,300–15,250 ⚒ BRIT

1983 Rolls-Royce Silver Spirit, finished in dark blue, tan interior, 63,000 miles from new.
£10,000–12,000
$14,500–17,400 ⊞ VIC

1977 Rolls-Royce Silver Wraith II Four-Door Saloon, power-assisted rack-and-pinion steering, finished in dark blue, Everflex roof, split-level air conditioning, division, blue interior with cream piping, over-rugs, full toolkit, c12,000 miles from new.
£16,000–18,000 / $23,200–26,000 ⚒ BKS
To satisfy the market for chauffeur-driven cars, a long-wheelbase version of the Shadow II – available with or without division – was introduced in 1969. This longer Shadow was christened Silver Wraith II on the introduction of the Mk II range.

1980 Rolls-Royce Corniche Cabriolet, updated to Corniche III appearance, finished in white, tan leather interior and roof, 68,000 miles from new.
£30,000–35,000 / $43,500–50,750 ⊞ HCL

1976 Rolls-Royce Camargue, 6750cc V8 engine, finished in metallic light blue, black interior, original velvet front seats, Bakelite radio-telephone with sender unit in boot, woodwork restored at a cost of £1,000, 1 of 531 examples built, very good condition.
£8,500–10,500 / $12,300–15,250 ⚒ H&H
The unique partnership between Rolls-Royce and Pininfarina produced the Camargue, which was built at Mulliner Park Ward, using the Silver Shadow's floorpan and running gear. The styling was controversial and not universally liked. The Camargue was one of the first Rolls-Royce's to have split-level air conditioning.

► **1981 Rolls-Royce Silver Spur Four-Door Saloon,** finished in black, Everflex roof, beige leather interior, 1 family ownership from new, very good condition.
£13,000–15,000
$18,850–21,750 ⚒ BKS

Rover

Although Rover had produced cars in Coventry from 1904, it wasn't until the late 1920s that the recognisable brand qualities of solid, middle class motoring became established. Rover's earlier riposte to the cheap and cheerful Austin 7 had failed, and with losses mounting, Spencer Wilks, formerly of Hillman, was appointed general manager in 1929. He soon established the Rover quality-first credo that positioned the company firmly in the upper middle market, above the likes of Ford, Austin and Morris. By the outbreak of WWII, Rover was building 11,000 cars a year and making an annual profit of over £200,000. After the war, Spencer's brother, Maurice, also working at Rover, was a prime mover behind the Land Rover. Meanwhile, the successive P4, P5 and P6 Rovers earned a loyal following and production climbed steadily. Spencer Wilks retired in 1962; in 1965, Rover took over Alvis, and in 1967 was merged into BMC. Although not the top dog among the myriad marques under the BMC banner, it was the Rover name that survived when the combine became the Rover Group in 1986. After a spell under BMW's ownership, today Rover is back in British hands.

1930 Rover 10/25hp Tourer, restored, navy blue fabric body, red interior.
£6,500–7,500 / $9,400–10,875 ⊞ UMC

1938 Rover 12 Saloon, dry stored 17 years, complete, engine runs.
£1,100–1,300 / $1,600–1,900 ⚒ RBB

1957 Rover 75, recently resprayed, original interior, 3 owners and 47,000 miles from new.
£3,000–3,500 / $4,400–5,000 ⊞ GrM

1937 Rover 10/12 Sports Special, 1496cc 4-cylinder Rover 12 engine, stainless-steel exhaust system, rewired, originally a 10 saloon, rebodied as a sports tourer, fabric-covered coachwork, polished aluminium bonnet, no hood, finished in British racing green, new green leather upholstery, all mechanical components in good condition.
£5,000–6,000 / $7,250–8,700 ⚒ BRIT

1950 Rover 75 Saloon, restored, galvanised chassis, underseat tool kit, finished in white, red leather interior, concours condition.
£5,000–6,000 / $7,250–8,700 ⚒ BKS

Rover enjoyed a well established reputation for solid quality, allied to reasonably affordable prices, appealing decidedly to the upper middle classes. In the late 1940s, stylist Maurice Wilks and body designer Harry Loker produced a new design, the P4 'Cyclops' model first shown at the 1949 London Motor Show. In six-cylinder 75 form and sporting the long awaited full-width enveloping bodywork, the new model broke away from the marque's traditional use of flowing wings and running boards. The 2103cc engine featured an aluminium head and twin SU carburettors. With revised front suspension, the all-new chassis carried a combination body in steel with 'Birmabright' aluminium-alloy doors, bonnet and boot lid.

ROVER Model	ENGINE cc/cyl	DATES	CONDITION 1	2	3
10hp	998/2	1920–25	£5,000	£3,000	£1,500
9/20	1074/4	1925–27	£6,000	£4,000	£2,000
10/25	1185/4	1928–33	£7,000	£4,000	£2,500
14hp	1577/6	1933–39	£6,000	£4,250	£2,000
12	1496/4	1934–37	£7,000	£4,000	£1,500
20 Sports	2512/6	1937–39	£7,000	£4,500	£2,500

Rover P4 (1950–64)

Production: 130,342.
Engines: 1997cc and 2286cc, four-cylinder; 2103–2638cc, six-cylinder.
Power output: 60–77bhp for four-cylinder models; 75–123bhp for six-cylinder models.
0–60mph: 15–23 seconds.
Maximum speed: 78–100+mph.
Rover traditionalists choked in their cravats when the normally conventional car maker introduced the P4 in 1950. Gone were the traditional separate wings and running boards, replaced by a daring and up-to-the minute American-inspired, slab-sided full-width body. If the exterior caused the odd sharp intake of breath, inside everything was reassuringly Rover, a leather, wood and Wilton combination of comfort and sober good taste. There were other Rovers virtue too, a massive separate chassis, high build quality and long-lasting four- and six-cylinder engines. The whole package added up to steady reliable transport for steady professional types. By the mid-1950s, everyone had become used to the once-controversial contours, and since then they've earned the affectionate appellation of 'Auntie' Rovers because of the amiable qualities that made many a P4 a much loved member of the family.
P4 fact: The design was closely based on the American Studebaker Commander, and it was rumoured that a Studebaker body had been dropped onto a Rover chassis to create a prototype. Later destroyed, it was referred to as the 'Roverbaker'.

Miller's Compares

I. 1961 Rover 100, 2625cc 6-cylinder engine, unrestored, finished in green, matching interior, MoT.
£800–950 / $1,150–1,350 BRIT

II. 1961 Rover 100, 2625cc, overdrive gearbox, fog lamps, finished in burgundy, grey leather interior, 1 owner since 1964, documented history, 27,000 miles from new, completely original, excellent condition throughout.
£6,500–7,500 / $9,400–10,875 H&H

These two Rovers are the both 1961 P4 100s, the same model and even the same year, yet they represent different ends of the spectrum. Item I was a slightly tired and battle-scarred old soldier; yet it had an MoT, and was said to drive well. Item II sold for much more than item I, far above the top value for that model, as listed in our price box on page 237. Item II was quite exceptional and possibly unrepeatable, a beautifully preserved time-warp 27,000-miler with unmarked leather and with a wealth of history. To bring item I up to the same condition of item II could well use up most of the difference in purchase price, but still it could not be invested with the other car's originality and history. That can be worth a lot to some people, but in reality neither car is a better or worse bargain. It's a question of taste.

1969 Rover P5B Coupé, 3528cc V8 engine, completely restored, engine rebuilt, full tool kit, finished in white and grey, brown interior, 54,000 miles from new.
£2,750–3,250 / $4,000–4,750 H&H
The Rover 3.5 litre was the first Rover to employ the light-alloy ex-Buick V8. The 144bhp engine delivered 108mph and 0–50mph in under nine seconds, even with the compulsory automatic transmission. Power steering and Rostyle wheels were standard.

► **1973 Rover P5B Saloon,** 3528cc, new front wings and sills, finished in dark red, burgundy interior, fewer than 49,000 miles from new, very good condition.
£2,200–2,700 / $3,200–3,900 H&H

Restored values

The cost of a professional restoration will have an influence on, but no direct relation to, a car's market value. A restored car can have a market value lower than the cost of its restoration.

Miller's Compares

I. 1969 Rover P5B Coupé, finished in grey and silver, in need of attention, ideal as a drivable restoration project.
£1,250–1,750 / $1,800–2,500 ⚒ BARO

II. 1972 Rover P5B Saloon, original tool kit, finished in white, 59,000 miles from new, sound body and chassis, excellent mechanics.
£3,700–4,200 / $5,250–6,100 ⚒ BARO

Item I, the 1969 P5B coupe, a car described as sound, but in need of TLC, sold at auction for less than half the price that item II, the 1972 P5 saloon commanded across the block. It had a warranted 59,000 miles and was said to have a superb interior, with sound body and chassis, and accompanying history and documentation. Although very affordable in today's market, Rover P5s remain luxury cars, with opulent carpeted, leather and wood interiors, and plenty of metalwork to care for. As a result, the reality is that a cheap Rover P5 can often work out more expensive once you start paying out to refurbish the car, the cost of interior renovation alone running into thousands. Something to bear in mind when buying.

◀ **1973 Rover 2000 TC,** 1978cc 4-cylinder engine, new cylinder head with hardened valve seat inserts for unleaded fuel, laminated windscreen, Lucas Square 8 fog lamps, continental spare wheel kit, finished in pale grey, bronze herringbone cloth interior, Radiomobile radio, c20,000 miles from new.
£3,400–4,200 / $4,850–6,100 ⚒ BRIT
From 1966, a TC (twin-carburettor) version of the 2000 was offered, which gave crisper performance with the power output boosted to 124bhp. With its excellent handling, the 2000 TC appealed to a more sporting driver and proved a great success.

ROVER Model	ENGINE cc/cyl	DATES	CONDITION 1	2	3
P2 10	1389/4	1946–47	£3,200	£2,500	£1,000
P2 12	1496/4	1946–47	£3,500	£2,800	£1,200
P2 12 Tour	1496/4	1947	£6,000	£3,500	£1,500
P2 14/16	1901/6	1946–47	£4,200	£3,000	£1,000
P2 14/16 Sal	1901/6	1946–47	£3,000	£2,000	£700
P3 60	1595/4	1948–49	£5,000	£2,500	£1,000
P3 75	2103/6	1948–49	£4,000	£3,000	£800
P4 75	2103/6	1950–51	£4,000	£2,000	£1,200
P4 75	2103/6	1952–64	£3,500	£1,800	£1,200
P4 60	1997/4	1954–59	£3,200	£1,200	£1,200
P4 90	2638/6	1954–59	£4,000	£1,800	£1,200
P4 75	2230/6	1955–59	£3,800	£1,200	£1,000
P4 105R	2638/6	1957–58	£4,000	£2,000	£1,000
P4 105S	2638/6	1957–59	£4,000	£2,000	£1,000
P4 80	2286/4	1960–62	£3,000	£1,200	£800
P4 95	2625/6	1963–64	£3,000	£1,600	£500
P4 100	2625/6	1960–62	£3,800	£2,000	£1,000
P4 110	2625/6	1963–64	£3,800	£2,000	£1,000
P5 3 Litre	2995/6	1959–67	£4,000	£2,500	£1,000
P5 3 Litre Coupé	2995/6	1959–67	£5,500	£3,800	£1,000
P5B (V8)	3528/8	1967–74	£6,250	£4,500	£1,500
P5B (V8) Coupé	3528/8	1967–73	£6,250	£4,500	£1,500
P6 2000 SC Series 1	1980/4	1963–65	£2,200	£800	-
P6 2000 SC Series 1	1980/4	1966–70	£2,000	£800	-
P6 2000 SC Auto Series 1	1980/4	1966–70	£1,500	£600	-
P6 2000 TC Series 1	1980/4	1966–70	£2,000	£900	-
P6 2000 SC Series 2	1980/4	1970–73	£2,000	£900	-
P6 2000 SC Auto Series 2	1980/4	1970–73	£1,500	£800	-
P6 2000 TC Series 2	1980/4	1970–73	£2,000	£900	-
P6 3500 Series 1	3500/8	1968–70	£2,500	£1,400	-
P6 2200 SC	2200/4	1974–77	£1,750	£850	-
P6 2200 SC Auto	2200/4	1974–77	£2,500	£1,000	-
P6 2200 TC	2200/4	1974–77	£2,000	£1,000	-
P6 3500 Series 2	3500/8	1971–77	£3,000	£1,700	-
P6 3500 S Series 2	3500/8	1971–77	£2,000	£1,500	-

Saab

Saab could so easily have come down to earth with a bump when it made its first foray into four-wheeled transport. For Svenska Aeroplan AB was a Swedish aeroplane manufacturer, and to design its first car it employed a sculptor. Well, that's not quite true: Sixten Sason started out as a sculptor, but had since become a talented engineer. Remarkably, that first production Saab 92 formed the basis of a model series that ran from 1950 to 1979. This was complemented in 1968 by the new generation 99 series in 1968 and the 99 Turbo of 1977, which set industry standards.

Saab 95 & 96 (1960–79)

Production: 96 saloons, 547,000; 95 estates, 110,500.
Engine: 841cc, three-cylinder, two-stroke; 1498cc V4.
Power output: 841cc, 38+bhp; 1498cc V4, 65bhp.
Transmission: Column-change manual, three- and four-speed.
Brakes: Drums all-round; front discs on some models from 1962, standard on all V4 Saabs.
Maximum speed: 841cc, 75+mph; V4, 91–95mph.
0–60mph: 841cc, 26.6 seconds; V4, 16.2 seconds.
Saab's aircraft background and clean slate resulted in a car that tossed convention aside. Its teardrop shape was like no other car of the era, slippery and aerodynamic. In fact, the wind-tunnel designed prototype, which looked like a sculpted bar of soap, boasted a remarkably low drag factor of 0.32. Under the skin too, the car was different, offering front-wheel drive in a mainstream car long before the Mini. The Saab also had a two-stroke vertical twin-cylinder engine mounted ahead of the front wheels.

The Saab 92 developed neatly into the 93, but for practical purposes the only teardrop Saabs you're likely to come across are its evolutionary successors, the 95 estate of 1959 and the 96 saloon of 1960, which set the rallying world alight in the hands of Erik Carlsson. Victories by Saab in the 1962 and 1963 Monte Carlo Rallies and RAC Rallies of the 1960s firmly established the wider appeal of the 96 saloon. As for the 95 estate, it's a versatile hold-all that can seat seven in three rows. The 95s and 96s fall into two generations: the early cars with three-cylinder 841cc two-strokes built to around 1968; and the 1498cc-engined cars from 1967 with their German Ford-derived V4. Although the earlier two-stroke cars have a stronger uncompromised period appeal, the V4 cars have it on all-out performance and are practical enough to be used as a hard-working classic hack. They're also a lot more plentiful. Best of all, if your Saab 96 is missing its chrome spherical ashtray, you can simply salvage a replacement from an old Saab plane.

1983 Saab 99GL, refurbished aluminium Inca wheels, finished in red, 3 owners from new.
£800–1,000 / 1,150–1,500 SAAB

SAAB Model	ENGINE cc/cyl	DATES	CONDITION 1	2	3
92	764/2	1950–53	£3,000	£1,500	£1,000
92B	764/2	1953–55	£3,500	£1,500	£1,000
93–93B	748/3	1956–60	£3,000	£1,500	£1,000
95	841/3	1960–68	£3,000	£1,500	£1,000
96	841/3	1960–68	£4,000	£1,800	£1,000
96 Sport	841/3	1962–66	£3,500	£1,500	£1,000
Sonnett II	1698/4	1967–74	£3,500	£1,500	£1,000
95/96	1498/4	1966–80	£3,000	£1,000	£800
99	1709/4	1968–71	£2,000	£1,200	-
99	1854/4	1970–74	£2,000	£1,000	-
99	1985/4	1972–83	£2,000	£1,000	£500
99 Turbo	1985/4	1978–83	£3,000	£1,000	£500

Shelby

1966 Shelby 427 Cobra, 427cu.in overhead-valve V8 engine, 485bhp, oil cooler, 4-speed manual gearbox, 4-wheel disc brakes, Halibrand alloy wheels, driver's roll-bar, bonnet scoop, restored, finished in blue with white racing stripes, black leather interior in very good condition.
£160,000–180,000 / $232,00–262,000 RM

1966 Shelby 427 Cobra, 7 litre V8 engine, alloy wheels, left-hand drive, original body panels, finished in red, original black leather interior, 1 of 260 built.
£180,000–200,000 / $260,000–290,000 BJ

Simca

A known continuous history can add value to and enhance the enjoyment of a car.

◄ **1956 Simca Aronde Grande Large,** restored over 2 years, mechanics and electrics overhauled, bare-metal respray in cream and black, 1 of only 2 examples known in the UK, excellent condition throughout.
£2,000–2,400 / $2,900–3,400 BARO

Singer

For 50 years, from 1905 to 1955, the Coventry firm of Singer managed to remain independent, in the 1920s offering appealing and truly competitive alternatives to Austin and Morris products, and the occasional outstanding model, such as the Singer Nine of 1933. However, by 1937 and thanks in part to a bewildering model range, the company had to be reorganised to stay afloat. In 1955, it was acquired by the Rootes Group and was slowly sapped of identity and distinction, to expire quietly in 1970.

◄ **1934 Singer Nine Four-Seater Tourer,** 972cc, engine rebuilt, little use since, dry stored since 1980, finished in cream, green interior, noisy first gear, otherwise very good condition throughout.
£6,000–7,000 / $8,700–10,200 H&H

SINGER Model	ENGINE cc/cyl	DATES	CONDITION 1	2	3
10	1097/4	1918–24	£5,000	£2,000	£1,000
15	1991/6	1922–25	£6,000	£3,000	£1,500
14/34	1776/6	1926–27	£7,000	£4,000	£2,000
Junior	848/4	1927–32	£6,000	£3,000	£1,500
Senior	1571/4	1928–29	£7,000	£4,000	£2,000
Super 6	1776/6	1928–31	£7,000	£4,000	£2,000
9 Le Mans	972/4	1932–37	£13,000+	£8,000	£5,000
Twelve	1476/6	1932–34	£10,000	£7,000	£6,000
1.5 Litre	1493/6	1934–36	£3,000	£2,000	£1,000
2 Litre	1991/6	1934–37	£4,000	£2,750	£1,000
11	1459/4	1935–36	£3,000	£2,000	£1,000
12	1525/4	1937–39	£3,000	£2,000	£1,000

Singer Gazelle (1956–67)

Engine: Four-cylinder; 1494, 1497, 1592 and 1725cc.
Power output: 49–65bhp.
Transmission: Four-speed manual with optional overdrive; optional automatic.
Maximum speed: 78–85mph.
0–60mph: 15–26.6 seconds.

In 1955, the Rootes Group acquired the old established Singer company to add yet another layer to the fine social distinctions of the suburban driveway. At the top of the Rootes hierarchy was Humber, but lower down the new unit-construction Hillman, Singer and Sunbeam shared a common bodyshell with nuances of styling, comfort and performance to separate them in the pecking order of middle-class motoring. The plain-Jane mass-market Hillman Minx was definitely lower-middle, while the two-door Sunbeam Rapier was 'sporty middle'. Meanwhile, the Singer Gazelle was middle-middle, a cut above the Minx, with fillets of wood, carpet and leather to flatter vanity and aspiration. The result was an overlapping three-tier platform to pitch against the likes of Austin, Morris, Ford and Vauxhall. Initially, as a sop to Singer fans, the Gazelle retained the old Singer 1497cc overhead-camshaft engine, compared with 1390cc units in the Hillman and Sunbeam, but from 1958 the trio shared a common range of engines in different states of tune that eventually grew to 1725cc. Today, any real distinction between these badges of suburban rank may seem slight, but to drivers in the 1950s and 1960s they still had real value, for while the Minx sold around 700,000, the plush Gazelle filled a much smaller niche further up the social scale, scoring just over 83,000 sales. In today's classic-car pecking order, the little touch of class that marked out the Gazelle when new still makes it pricier than a Minx.

1936 Singer Nine Le Mans Four-Seater Tourer, older restoration, fitted with 948cc BMC engine.
£8,000–9,000 / $11,600–13,000 ⊞ GrM

1966 Singer Chamois, finished in original black and white, 53,000 miles from new, interior trim and bodywork in very good condition.
£2,300–2,700 / $3,350–3,900 ⊞ SiC

► 1965 Singer Chamois Saloon, 875cc, 42bhp, completely restored, finished in dark green.
£1,750–2,000 / $2,500–2,900 IMP

Standard

Formed in 1903, by the 1920s, Standard was specialising in medium-range cars, but struggling to compete. In 1929, John Black joined the company and engineered its resurgence, building a reputation for keenly-priced, well-built, reliable and comfortable cars.
In 1945, Standard acquired the defunct Triumph marque as an upmarket badge. Standard-Triumph was merged into Leyland in 1961, and ironically it was the Standard name that was dropped first, in 1963. Of the late-era Standards, the Phase I beetle-backed Vanguard is a favourite accessory among swing-era nostalgics, while the Standard 8 and 10 make interesting and less-common alternatives to the Morris Minor and Austin A30/35.

◄ 1931 Standard Big Nine saloon, 1287cc engine, 4-speed gearbox, bolt-on wire wheels, trafficators, spare engine, unrestored, finished in black, red interior.
£2,750–3,500 / $4,000–5,000 H&H

STANDARD Model	ENGINE cc/cyl	DATES	CONDITION 1	2	3
SLS	1328/4	1919–20	£5,000	£4,000	£1,000
VI	1307/4	1922	£5,000	£4,000	£1,000
SLO/V4	1944/4	1922–28	£5,000	£4,000	£1,000
6V	2230/6	1928	£10,000	£8,000	£5,000
V3	1307/4	1923–26	£4,000	£3,000	£1,000
Little 9	1006/4	1932–33	£4,000	£2,000	£1,000
9	1155/4	1928–29	£5,500	£3,000	£1,000
Big 9	1287/4	1932–33	£4,500	£3,250	£2,000
15	1930/6	1929–30	£6,000	£4,000	£2,000
12	1337/6	1933–34	£4,000	£3,000	£1,500
10hp	1343/4	1933–37	£4,000	£2,500	£1,000
9	1052/4	1934–36	£4,200	£2,500	£1,000
Flying 9	1131/4	1937–39	£3,200	£1,800	£750
Flying 10	1267/4	1937–39	£3,500	£2,200	£1,000
Flying 14	1176/4	1937–48	£4,500	£2,200	£1,000
Flying 8	1021/4	1939–48	£4,500	£2,400	£1,000

1955 Standard Eight Saloon, 803cc 4-cylinder engine, unrestored, running.
£350–400 / $500–600 CGC

1957 Standard Eight Saloon, 803cc 4-cylinder engine, unrestored, running.
£400–450 / $580–640 CGC

STANDARD Model	ENGINE cc/cyl	DATES	CONDITION 1	2	3
12	1609/4	1945–48	£2,000	£950	£250
12 DHC	1509/4	1945–48	£3,200	£2,000	£500
14	1776/4	1945–48	£3,000	£950	£250
Vanguard I/II	2088/4	1948–55	£2,200	£1,000	£250
Vanguard III	2088/4	1955–61	£1,800	£900	£200
Vanguard III Est	2088/4	1955–61	£2,000	£1,000	£250
Vanguard III Sportsman	2088/4	1955–58	£2,500	£1,200	£400
Vanguard Six	1998/6	1961–63	£2,000	£1,000	£500
Eight	803/4	1952–59	£1,250	£500	-
Ten	948/4	1955–59	£1,400	£800	-
Ensign I/II	1670/4	1957–63	£1,000	£800	-
Ensign I/II Est	1670/4	1962–63	£1,000	£850	-
Pennant Companion	948/4	1955–61	£1,800	£850	£300
Pennant	948/4	1955–59	£1,650	£825	£250

Star

◀ **1927 Star 20/60hp Libra Four-Door Saloon,** finished in 2-tone grey, blue Ambla interior, very good condition throughout.
£10,500–12,500
$15,250–18,250 BKS
Although technically unadventurous in its early years, Star gained a reputation for building luxurious and well-constructed cars. Four-wheel brakes on the bigger sixes, and overhead valves on the four-cylinder 12/40 made their appearance in the early 1920s. Then in 1927 came the first overhead-valve six, the 20/50hp PL2. This was soon superseded by the 20/60hp PL3, a fine performer capable of 70mph.

Studebaker

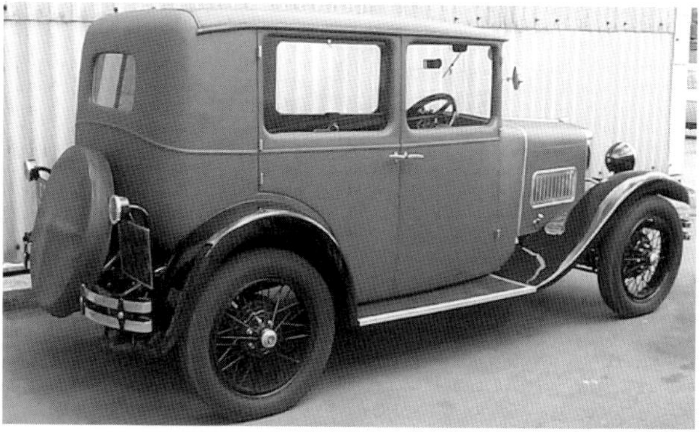

1929 Studebaker (Erskine) 16.5hp Saloon, right-hand drive, original claret fabric coachwork, claret leather interior, only example built with Gordon England coachwork.
£12,500–14,000 / $18,150–20,300 ⊞ UMC

1951 Studebaker Commander Convertible, 233cu.in overhead-valve V8 engine, 120bhp, 3-speed manual gearbox, 4-wheel hydraulic drum brakes, subject of body-off restoration.
£30,000–35,000 / $43,500–50,750 ⚒ RM
Studebaker was the first major American manufacturer to introduce new post-war styling in 1947. Three years later, this styling was updated to feature a 'bullet-nose' and more pronounced rear wings that were capped with vertical taillights. In 1951, the Commander cars received a new overhead-valve V8 engine, in place of the sidevalve six still being used in the Champion model. This particular car was driven by Leslie Nielsen in the film *Mr Magoo*. Its value reflects a US market price.

1963 Studebaker Hawk GT, 4735cc V8 engine, restored early 1990s, factory front disc brake option, finished in gold, red interior, overdrive not functioning, otherwise all mechanical components in good condition.
£2,000–2,500 / $2,900–3,600 ⚒ BRIT
In 1961, when Sherwood Egbert became president of Studebaker, he was conscious that the well-established Hawk and Lark models were in need of restyling. Brooks Stephens of Milwaukee was given the task, and subsequently these models were smartly updated. The large tail fins, which had become extremely dated, were deleted, and the new hardtop styling bore a resemblance to the contemporary Ford Thunderbird. For 1963, further restyling was undertaken, the most obvious changes being the revision of the grille and a new dashboard.

Sunbeam

Sunbeam's light was finally snuffed out for good in 1976, but in the long and often rocky ride from its birth at the dawn of the century, there have been several periods of achievement and distinction. Before WWI, the company notched up considerable competition success, and later went on to become the first British make to win a Grand Prix. In the 1920s, Sunbeam also produced some fine touring and sports cars, rivalling Alvis and Bentley offerings into the 1930s. As part of the unwieldy Sunbeam-Talbot-Darracq combine, the company collapsed in 1935 and was acquired by Rootes. Sunbeams were known as Sunbeam-Talbots from 1935 to 1953, then simply as Sunbeams. Initially, the cars continued in a sporting vein; the 1959 Alpine was a pretty sports car, and the Ford V8-engined Tiger an enjoyable handful. However, in 1964 Chrysler took over, and the last-generation Sunbeams were rarely little more than plain-Jane Hillmans and Humbers in slightly sporting dress.

◄ **1926 Sunbeam 14/40 Tourer,** 2120cc, rear Auster screen, side screens, rear-mounted trunk, engine rebuilt 1993, resprayed in maroon, new hood, hood bag and tonneau covers, new carpets, new black leather upholstery, excellent condition throughout.
£19,000–23,000 / $27,500–33,300 ⚒ H&H
The Sunbeam Motor Car Company began trading in 1905, although it had been formed initially in 1899 in Wolverhampton, under the name John Marston Ltd. Production continued until 1937, the last two years in London. The first really new post-WWI model was the 14hp, introduced for 1922 and later called the 14/40. The engine capacity was increased to 2120cc in 1924.

SUNBEAM Model	ENGINE cc/cyl	DATES	CONDITION 1	2	3
12/16	2412/4	1910–14	£25,000	£16,000	£12,000
16/20	4070/4	1910–15	£32,000	£22,000	£15,000
24	4524/6	1919–22	£30,000	£19,000	£11,000
3 Litre	2916/6	1925–30	£48,000	£30,000	£20,000
14/40	2200/4	1925–30	£18,000	£10,000	£8,000
16	2040/6	1927–30	£16,000	£12,500	£10,000
20	2916/6	1927–30	£22,000	£15,000	£10,500
Speed 20	2916/6	1932–35	£15,000	£10,000	£8,000
Dawn	1627/4	1934–35	£8,000	£5,000	£3,500
25	3317/6	1934	£10,000	£8,000	£4,000

Prices can vary depending on replica bodies, provenance, coachbuilder, drophead, twin cam etc.

1935 Sunbeam 25hp Estate Car, 3318cc overhead-valve 6-cylinder engine, 4-speed manual gearbox with synchromesh on top 3 ratios, Lockheed hydraulic drum brakes, converted from a saloon 1940s, restored 1998, engine overhauled, finished in black, blue leather interior, 1 owner for almost 50 years.
£13,000–16,000 / $18,850–23,200 ⚒ BKS

1959 Sunbeam Rapier Mk II Coupé, 1494cc 4-cylinder engine, manual overdrive gearbox, finished in 2-tone blue, blue and grey interior, original apart from minor electrical upgrades, very good condition.
£2,750–3,250 / $3,900–4,700 ⚒ H&H

1956 Sunbeam-Talbot 90 Mk III Saloon, 2267cc 4-cylinder engine, 4-speed manual gearbox with overdrive, factory-fitted sliding sunroof, finished in green, green interior, good condition.
£3,750–4,500 / $5,400–6,500 ⚒ H&H

1965 Sunbeam Alpine Series IV GT, 1725cc 4-cylinder engine, manual overdrive gearbox, wire wheels, hardtop, tonneau cover, refurbished mid-1990s, finished in blue.
£5,000–6,000 / $7,250–8,700 ⚒ BRIT

Sunbeam Alpine (1959–68)

Production: 69,291.
Body styles: Two-seater roadster and GT hardtop.
Construction: Steel monocoque.
Engine: 1496, 1592 and 1725cc, four-cylinder.
Power output: 1494cc, 78bhp; 1592cc, 82bhp ; 1725cc, 92bhp.
Transmission: Four-speed manual, optional overdrive; optional automatic.
Brakes: Front discs, rear drums.
Maximum speed: 93–99mph.
0–60mph: 13.6–14.2 seconds.

Never a scorching performer or sizzling sales success, the pretty little Sunbeam Alpine lived its life under a long shadow cast by its MG and Triumph rivals. In the first place, the Alpine was perhaps a little too pretty – in a mother's boy kind of way. It also employed humble saloon underpinnings from the Rootes-Hillman-Singer-Sunbeam stable, was softly suspended with a comfortable ride, and its ability to top the magic ton was debatable. Neither did it help that the Alpine adverts often showed a woman at the wheel. Yet in place of outright sporting character, the Sunbeam offered civilised fresh-air motoring, with its wind-up windows, solid build and quality finish. Only in 1961/62, the end of the MGA era and the dawn of the MGB, did Alpine production come near to matching MG numbers, but from its launch in 1962, the faster and cheaper MGB romped ahead. Today, the Alpine remains overshadowed by more obvious classics and can often be bought for less than the price of an MGB. If you're looking to buy one, you'll find little appreciable difference in performance from the three engine options. Engines and other mechanical components are generally tough, but spares support is nowhere near as good as with the ubiquitous MGB.

Alpine fact: In 1959, 'Living Doll' and 'Travelling Light' soared to the top of the charts, and 18-year-old Cliff Richard became the first member of his family ever to own a car, a brand-new pearl grey Sunbeam Alpine.

1968 Sunbeam Alpine Series V, 1725cc 4-cylinder engine, converted to right-hand drive, engine and gearbox reconditioned, alloy wheels, finished in metallic blue.
£2,000–2,400 / $2,900–3,400 BRIT

1966 Sunbeam Tiger, 4.2 litre V8 engine, 164bhp, 4-speed manual gearbox, front disc/rear drum brakes, factory alloy wheels, hard and soft tops, restored, finished in red, black interior.
£12,000–14,000 / $17,400–20,300 RM

▶ **c1969 Sunbeam Stiletto,** 875cc, twin carburettors, 55bhp, Sport running gear, finished in red, very good condition.
£2,250–2,750 / $3,300–3,900 IMP

1966 Sunbeam Tiger Mk I, 4.2 litre V8 engine, left-hand drive, carburettor rebuilt, new clutch and gearbox, Minilite alloy wheels, finished in blue, tonneau cover, Nardi steering wheel, black interior, excellent condition throughout.
£10,500–13,000 / $15,250–18,850 BKS
Inspired by Carroll Shelby's success in shoehorning a Ford V8 into the AC Ace to create the Cobra, Rootes asked the Texan to perform the same trick with its Sunbeam Alpine sports car. Ford's 260cu.in (4.2 litre) engine was chosen, similar to that used in the original Cobra and more than capable of powering a car which began life with a 1.6 litre four. Assembled by Jensen Motors and introduced in 1964, the Tiger featured a stronger gearbox and rear axle, plus rack-and-pinion steering. Vastly superior to its Alpine progenitor in performance terms, the Tiger stormed to 60mph in around seven seconds and peaked at 117mph.

SUNBEAM-TALBOT/ SUNBEAM Model	ENGINE cc/cyl	DATES	CONDITION 1	2	3
Talbot 80	1185/4	1948–50	£3,500	£2,250	£1,000
Talbot 80 DHC	1185/4	1948–50	£6,000	£4,500	£2,000
Talbot 90 Mk I	1944/4	1949–50	£4,000	£2,100	£2,000
Talbot 90 Mk I DHC	1944/4	1949–50	£7,000	£4,750	£750
Talbot 90 II/IIa/III	2267/4	1950–56	£5,000	£3,000	£2,000
Talbot 90 II/IIa/III DHC	2267/4	1950–56	£7,000	£5,000	£1,500
Talbot Alpine I/III	2267/4	1953–55	£11,000	£7,500	£2,250
Talbot Ten	1197/4	1946–48	£3,500	£2,000	£3,750
Talbot Ten Tourer	1197/4	1946–48	£7,000	£4,000	£750
Talbot Ten DHC	1197/4	1946–48	£6,500	£4,000	£2,000
Talbot 2 Litre	1997/4	1946–48	£4,000	£2,500	£2,000
Talbot 2 Litre Tourer	1997/4	1946–48	£7,500	£4,000	£1,000
Rapier I	1392/4	1955–57	£1,200	£700	£2,250
Rapier II	1494/4	1957–59	£1,800	£900	£300
Rapier II Conv	1494/4	1957–59	£3,000	£1,500	£300
Rapier III	1494/4	1959–61	£2,000	£1,200	£450
Rapier III Conv	1494/4	1959–61	£3,500	£1,600	£400
Rapier IIIA	1592/4	1961–63	£2,000	£1,200	£600
Rapier IIIA Conv	1592/4	1961–63	£3,600	£1,700	£400
Rapier IV/V	1592/ 1725/4	1963–67	£2,000	£700	£650
Alpine I-II	1494/4	1959–62	£6,000	£3,500	£250
Alpine III	1592/4	1963	£6,500	£4,000	£1,800
Alpine IV	1592/4	1964	£5,500	£3,500	£1,250
Alpine V	1725/4	1965–68	£6,000	£4,000	£1,250
Harrington Alpine	1592/4	1961	£8,000	£4,750	£1,250
Harrington Le Mans	1592/4	1962–63	£10,000	£6,500	£1,250
Tiger Mk 1	4261/8	1964–67	£12,000	£10,000	£3,000
Tiger Mk 2	4700/8	1967	£13,000	£8,000	£6,000
Rapier Fastback	1725/4	1967–76	£1,100	£700	£6,000
Rapier H120	1725/4	1968–76	£1,500	£800	£250
					£300

Syrena

◄ **1976 Syrena 105S Two-Door Saloon,** 2-stroke engine, finished in pale grey, unrestored, low mileage.
£750–900 / $1,050–1,300 ⊞ Now
The Syrena was built in Poland.

Talbot

► **1916 Talbot 15/20hp Two-Seater,** older restoration, original mechanical specification in all major respects, dual-action brakes, detachable wheels, side-mounted spare, rewired, alternator, electric lighting, brake lights, flashing indicators, folding windscreen and hood, brass bugle horn, finished in white and burgundy, black leather buttoned upholstery, VCC dating certificate.
£11,000–13,000 / $16,000–19,000 ⚒ BKS
With the technical expertise of Adolphe Clément and substantial financial backing from the Earl of Shrewsbury and Talbot, Clément Talbot became a major force in the British motor car industry as early as 1903. Talbots established an excellent reputation in the then fashionable reliability trials and hill climbs and, prior to the outbreak of WWI, the company built thoroughly reliable and quite quick four- and six-cylinder motor cars. The 15/20hp car had a conventional four-cylinder engine with a capacity of 3561cc and found favour, especially in Colonial markets.

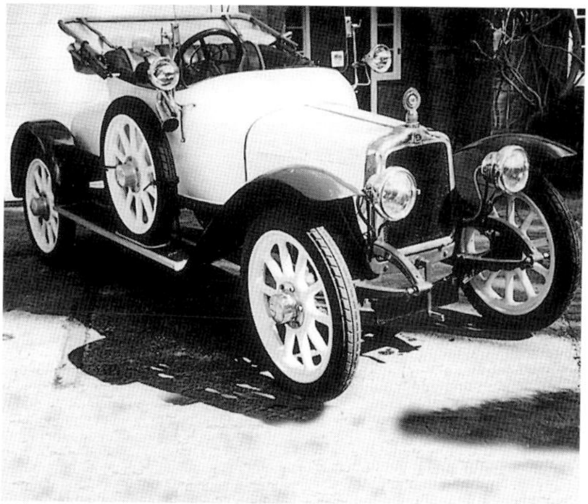

◄ **1932 Talbot Type 20/70 Cabriolet,** coachwork by Carlton, 2276cc 6-cylinder engine, 4-speed manual gearbox, 4-wheel cable-operated drum brakes, Rudge wire wheels, finished in 2-tone green.
£16,000–19,000
$23,200–27,500 ⚒ Pou

A known continuous history can add value to and enhance the enjoyment of a car.

► **c1937 Talbot Ten Drophead Coupé,** partially restored, all panelwork stripped and resprayed, front and rear seats reupholstered in cream hide, dashboard and dash surround not installed, in need of further work.
£1,000–1,200 / $1,500–1,800 ⚒ BKS

TALBOT Model	ENGINE cc/cyl	DATES	CONDITION 1	2	3
25hp and 25/50	4155/4	1907–16	£35,000	£25,000	£15,000
12hp	2409/4	1909–15	£22,000	£15,000	£9,000
8/18	960/4	1922–25	£8,000	£5,000	£2,000
14/45	1666/6	1926–35	£16,000	£10,000	£5,000
75	2276/6	1930–37	£22,000	£12,000	£7,000
105	2969/6	1935–37	£30,000	£20,000+	£15,000

Higher value for tourers and coachbuilt cars.

Talbot-Lago

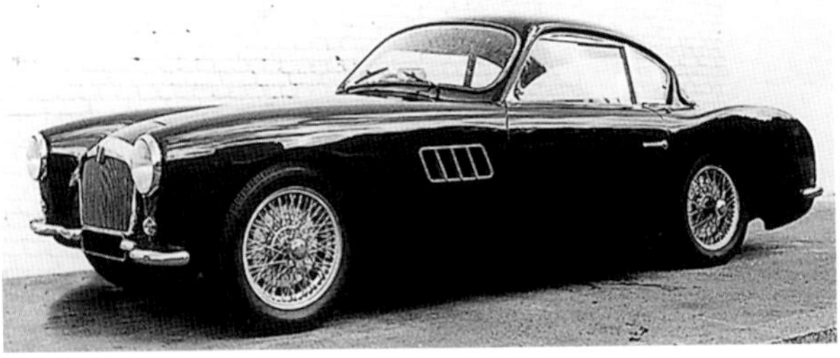

1956 Talbot-Lago Sport 2500 Coupé, 2491cc 4-cylinder engine, twin Zenith Stromberg carburettors, 120bhp, 4-speed manual gearbox, transverse leaf-spring independent front suspension, 4-wheel hydraulic drum brakes, Rudge wire wheels, finished in dark green.
£27,000–32,000 / $39,000–46,400 Pou

► **1957 Talbot-Lago America Coupé,** BMW 2.3 litre V8 engine, 150bhp, 4-speed ZF manual gearbox, 4-wheel drum brakes, restored at a cost of over £68,000, finished in red, black interior, matching numbers, fewer than 69,000 miles from new.
£55,000–65,000 / $79,750–94,250 RM

Toyota

TOYOTA Model	ENGINE cc/cyl	DATES	CONDITION 1	2	3
Celica TA22 & TA23 Coupé	1588/4	1971–78	£2,500	£1,800	£500
RA28 Liftback	1968/4	1971–78	£3,500	£1,500	£400

Plus a premium of £200 to £500 for a Twin-Cam GT.

1967 Toyota 2000GT, left-hand drive, engine and gearbox rebuilt 1993, resprayed in original Solar red 1995, complete with factory tool bag, jack and emergency light, 1 of only 62 cars (53 twin-cams and 9 later single-cam models) imported to USA, excellent condition.
£95,000–110,000 / $137,750–159,500 BKS
Beneath the 2000GT's aerodynamic coupé bodywork was a Lotus Elan-inspired backbone chassis equipped with double-wishbone independent suspension and disc brakes all-round. A five-speed all-synchromesh gearbox, rack-and-pinion steering, oil cooler, heated rear screen and magnesium-alloy knock-off wheels were all state-of-the-art features. Based on the Toyota Crown's cast-iron block, the Yamaha-built twin-cam six displaced 1998cc and produced 150bhp at 6,600rpm. Up to 200bhp was available in race tune. With a top speed of around 130mph in road trim, the 2000GT was one of the fastest 2 litre production cars of its day. However, the 2000GT was handicapped from the start by its cost, which exceeded that of the Jaguar E-Type and Porsche 911. Only 337 were made between 1967 and 1970; 335 coupés plus the two special roadsters that starred in the James Bond movie *You Only Live Twice*.

◄ **1981 Toyota Celica XT Coupé,** 1968cc, alloy wheels, finished in metallic gold, air conditioning, 1 owner and 14,000 miles from new, excellent condition throughout.
£2,500–3,000
$3,600–4,400 H&H

TOYOTA Model	ENGINE cc/cyl	DATES	CONDITION 1	2	3
Crown MS65, MS63, MS75, Saloon, Estate, Coupé	2563/6	1972–75	£2,000	£1,000	£500

Plus a premium of £200 to £400 for the Coupé.

Trabant

Condition Guide

1. A vehicle in top class condition but not 'concours d'elegance standard, either fully restored or in very good original condition.
2. A good, clean, roadworthy vehicle, both mechanically and bodily sound.
3. A runner, but in need of attention, probably both to bodywork and mechanics. Must have current MoT.

◀ **1963 Trabant P600 Saloon,** restored, finished in green and white.
£1,000–1,200 / $1,500–1,750 ⊞ Now

Triumph

From the immediate post-war era to the end of the line in 1980, no other single British marque amassed such a comprehensive portfolio of mainstream sports cars and saloons. On the sporting side, the variety and range of the Triumph TR series far outstripped MG's offerings and even nudged into the lower end of the luxury grand tourer market with the Triumph Stag. On the saloon side, the 1960s were particularly rich with the cheap, capable and pretty Herald, the sporting Vitesse (both available in convertible form), the later Dolomite and Toledo, and the larger saloons, which offered appealing alternatives to Rovers. Today, all Triumphs of the post-war era remain affordable, and most rate highly as durable and stylish starter classics.

1947 Triumph 1800 Roadster, 1800cc, subject of no-expense-spared restoration 1985,engine, gearbox, brakes, radiator and heater reconditioned, body stripped and all damaged areas replaced with new metal, rust proofed, resprayed in grey, blue interior trim, concours winner.
£12,500–15,000 / $18,150–21,750 ⚒ H&H

1949 Triumph 2000 Roadster, 2088cc 4-cylinder engine, restored in Australia, finished in metallic bottle green, beige duck hood, beige Connolly leather interior trim to original specification, concours winner.
£15,000–17,000 / $21,750–24,500 ⚒ BRIT

As private car production slowly got back into its stride following WWII, the recently merged Standard and Triumph motor companies announced their proposed new offerings: a handsome saloon featuring 'razor-edge' body styling – a throwback to the mid-1930s designs by coachbuilders such as Mulliner, together with an attractive Roadster. Early models of the Roadster utilised a 1776cc overhead-valve engine derived from the Standard 14. This model will probably always be remembered as the last British car to be equipped with a dickey seat, and a rather unusual one at that, for the front section of the two-piece boot lid incorporated a windscreen for the rear passengers. From 1948 to 1950, the Roadster was powered by the 2088cc engine from the contemporary Standard Vanguard.

◀ **1959 Triumph TR3A,** 1991cc 4-cylinder engine, restored, finished in cream, black hardtop, excellent condition.
£11,500–13,000 / $16,700–18,850 ⚒ BARO

TRIUMPH Model	ENGINE cc/cyl	DATES	CONDITION 1	2	3
TLC	1393/4	1923–25	£6,000	£4,000	£1,500
TPC	2169/4	1926–30	£6,000	£4,000	£2,000
K	832/4	1928–34	£4,000	£2,000	£1,000
S	1203/6	1931–33	£5,000	£3,000	£1,500
G12 Gloria	1232/4	1935–37	£6,000	£4,000	£2,000
G16 Gloria 6	1991/6	1935–39	£7,000	£4,500	£2,000
Vitesse/Dolomite	1767/4	1937–39	£14,000	£10,000	£6,000
Dolomite	1496/4	1938–39	£7,000	£4,000	£2,000

1960 Triumph TR3A, 2 litre 4-cylinder engine, front disc brakes, Vanguard Phase III rear axle, left-hand drive, restored 1993, converted to unleaded fuel, twin 40DCOE Weber carburettors, A-Type overdrive, Minilite-type aluminium wheels, aeroscreens, Moto Lita leather-rimmed steering wheel, safety harnesses, new black leather interior, approximately 1,000km since completion, excellent condition.
£14,000–17,000 / $20,300–24,650 ⚒ BKS

1963 Triumph TR4, 2138cc 4-cylinder engine, manual overdrive gearbox, engine reconditioned, new stainless-steel exhaust, chrome trim replated, finished in red, black interior, seats reupholstered, new carpets.
£4,000–5,000 / $5,800–7,250 ⚒ H&H

1967 Triumph TR4A, 2.1 litre 4-cylinder engine, independent rear suspension.
£9,000–10,000 / $13,000–14,500 ⊞ HMM

1968 Triumph TR6, originally exported to the USA, completely restored, converted to right-hand drive, fitted with overdrive gearbox, chrome wire wheels.
£8,000–9,000 / $11,600–13,000 ⊞ GrM

Triumph TR4/4A (1961–67)

Price new: £1,095.
Production: 68,718.
Engine: 2138cc, overhead-valve, four-cylinder.
Power: 100–104bhp.
0–60mph: 11.4 seconds.
Top speed: 110mph.
Brakes: Front discs, rear drums.
TR stands for Triumph Roadster, but those two letters also stand for TR-adition in a big way. Forget the Michelotti styling, the TR4 evolved directly from the earlier true-Brit TR2 and TR3 roadsters. Sure, the new Italian suit may have sported such technical innovations as real wind-up windows, but this last of the four-cylinder TRs still has that 'vintage' sports car feel – especially in earlier TR4 form – and a contented burble that transfixes anyone with a pair of string-back gloves and a gap-toothed Terry Thomas smile.
Pick of the bunch: There are two choices: the TR4, which ran until 1965; and the TR4A, which was so proud of its independent rear suspension that it bore the letters 'IRS' on its rump. The TR4A is softer and more refined in road manners and appointments. The earlier rigid-axle TR4 is more true-Brit. Overdrive is desirable and, in effect, gives you a seven-speed gearbox.
What to watch: The Michelotti styled body is a real rotter, from an era when little was known of automotive rustproofing. Ironically, the revised chassis layout of the later TR4A is more prone to rust, with a number of complex closing panels to trap water.
TR4 facts: The Porsche 911 popularised the Targa top, but the TR4 was years ahead; Triumph's version was called a Surrey top. A 2+2 hardtop coupé version of the TR4 was offered by Wimbledon Triumph dealer L.F. Dove; about 55 Dove TR4s were built.

TRIUMPH Model	ENGINE cc/cyl	DATES	CONDITION 1	2	3
1800/2000 Roadster	1776/ 2088/4	1946–49	£14,000	£8,000	£5,000
1800	1776/4	1946–49	£4,000	£2,000	£1,000
2000 Renown	2088/4	1949–54	£4,000	£2,000	£1,000
Mayflower	1247/4	1949–53	£2,000	£1,000	£500
TR2 long door	1247/4	1953	£10,000	£8,000	£5,000
TR2	1247/4	1953–55	£9,000	£6,000	£5,000
TR3	1991/4	1955–57	£9,000	£8,500	£3,500
TR3A	1991/4	1958–62	£11,000	£8,500	£3,500
TR4	2138/4	1961–65	£9,000	£6,000	£3,000
TR4A	2138/4	1965–67	£9,000	£6,500	£3,000
TR5	2498/6	1967–68	£9,000	£7,500	£4,000
TR6 (PI)	2498/6	1969–74	£8,000	£7,500	£3,500
Herald	948/4	1959–61	£1,000	£400	£150
Herald FHC	948/4	1959–61	£1,500	£550	£300
Herald DHC	948/4	1960–61	£2,500	£1,000	£350
Herald 'S'	948/4	1961–64	£800	£400	£150
Herald 1200	1147/4	1961–70	£1,100	£500	£200
Herald 1200 FHC	1147/4	1961–64	£1,400	£800	£300
Herald 1200 DHC	1147/4	1961–67	£2,500	£1,000	£350
Herald 1200 Est	1147/4	1961–67	£1,300	£700	£300
Herald 12/50	1147/4	1963–67	£1,800	£1,000	£250
Herald 13/60	1296/4	1967–71	£1,300	£600	£200
Herald 13/60 DHC	1296/4	1967–71	£3,500	£1,500	£500
Herald 13/60 Est	1296/4	1967–71	£1,500	£650	£300
Vitesse 1600	1596/6	1962–66	£2,000	£1,250	£550
Vitesse 1600 Conv	1596/6	1962–66	£3,500	£1,800	£600
Vitesse 2 litre Mk I	1998/6	1966–68	£1,800	£800	£300
Vitesse 2 litre Mk I Conv	1998/6	1966–68	£4,500	£2,200	£1,000
Vitesse 2 litre Mk II	1998/6	1968–71	£2,000	£1,500	£300
Vitesse 2 litre Mk II Conv	1998/6	1968–71	£5,000	£2,500	£600
Spitfire Mk I	1147/4	1962–64	£2,000	£1,750	£300
Spitfire Mk II	1147/4	1965–67	£2,500	£2,000	£350
Spitfire Mk III	1296/4	1967–70	£3,500	£2,500	£450
Spitfire Mk IV	1296/4	1970–74	£5,000	£2,500	£350
Spitfire 1500	1493/4	1975–78	£3,500	£2,500	£750
Spitfire 1500	1493/4	1979–81	£5,000	£3,500	£1,200
GT6 Mk I	1998/6	1966–68	£5,000	£4,000	£1,200
GT6 Mk II	1998/6	1968–70	£6,000	£4,500	£1,400
GT6 Mk III	1998/6	1970–73	£7,000	£5,000	£1,500
2000 Mk I	1998/6	1963–69	£2,000	£1,200	£400
2000 Mk III	1998/6	1969–77	£2,000	£1,200	£500
2.5 PI	2498/6	1968–75	£2,000	£1,500	£900
2500 TC/S	2498/6	1974–77	£1,750	£700	£150
2500S	2498/6	1975–77	£2,500	£1,000	£150
1300 (FWD)	1296/4	1965–70	£800	£400	£150
1300TC (FWD)	1296/4	1967–70	£900	£450	£150
1500 (FWD)	1493/4	1970–73	£700	£450	£125
1500TC (RWD)	1296/4	1973–76	£850	£500	£100
Toledo	1296/4	1970–76	£850	£450	£100
Dolomite 1500	1493/4	1976–80	£1,350	£750	£125
Dolomite 1850	1854/4	1972–80	£1,450	£850	£150
Dolomite Sprint	1998/4	1976–81	£5,000	£4,000	£1,000
Stag	2997/8	1970–77	£9,000	£5,000	£2,000
TR7	1998/4	1975–82	£4,000	£1,200	£500
TR7 DHC	1998/4	1980–82	£5,000	£3,500	£1,500

1973 Triumph TR6, 2498cc 6-cylinder engine, overdrive gearbox, wire wheels, hardtop, finished in red, very good condition throughout.
£8,000–9,000 / $11,600–13,000 ⚒ BRIT

1975 Triumph TR6, overdrive gearbox, completely restored, galvanised chassis, chrome wire wheels, walnut dashboard.
£12,500–14,000 / $18,150–20,300 ⊞ WbC

Miller's Starter Marque

- **Starter Triumphs:** *Herald & Vitesse saloons and convertibles; Spitfire; Dolomite, Toledo and variants.*
- A Triumph Herald's a top-down winner when it comes to budget wind-in-the-hair motoring – an Italian-styled four-seater convertible with a 25ft turning circle that's tighter than a London taxi's, and an engine that's so accessible it's like having your own inspection pit. They are very modestly priced too. Of course, it's not all good news. The Herald's performance is hardly shattering, particularly with the early, rather asthmatic 948cc Standard 10 engine. They're also prone to rust, and the handling was legendary – for being so darned awful, in the earlier models at least. In the wet and in sudden throttle-off conditions, the car's high-pivot, swing-axle rear suspension would pitch it suddenly into unpredictable oversteer. But who'd be daft enough to try to race a Herald on public roads? What's more relevant is the smiles per mile as you and your family potter along over hill and dale burning fossil fuel at a miserly 35–40mpg.
- Heralds do fray quite ferociously, and you'll want to inspect the separate chassis, which provides the structural strength. The front-hinged bonnet is both a strength and weakness. It gives unrivalled access to front running gear and engine, but once the rot sets in, it can flap around like a soggy cardboard box.
- Because of its separate chassis, the Herald saloon is one car that can be safely turned into a convertible. The roof literally unbolts, and there are a number of ragtop conversion kits available.
- **Pick of the bunch:** The Herald's certainly no winged-messenger, so avoid early cars with puny 948cc engine, and go for at least the 1147cc or preferably the last 1296cc cars.
- The Herald's chassis formed the basis of a number of sporting Triumphs, including the twin-headlamp Vitesse. Similar in looks to the Herald, but with 1600 and 2000cc engines, the Vitesse will heave you along with plenty more urge – almost to 100mph in 2 litre form. The Herald chassis also formed the basis of the pretty little two-seater Triumph Spitfire, again with wonderful engine access provided by a front-hinged, one-piece bonnet. The Spitfire ran from 1961 to 1980, and that means there are plenty to choose from.

1968 Triumph Vitesse Convertible, 2 litre 4-cylinder engine, 4-speed manual gearbox, 4-wheel independent suspension, finished in blue and white, good condition.
£1,500–1,800 / $2,150–2,550 ⚒ H&H

1977 Triumph TR7, finished in white, green tartan upholstery, 1 owner until 1999, 31,000 miles from new.
£1,200–1,400 / $1,750–2,100 ⚒ BKS
Triumph built a new factory in Liverpool to manufacture the TR7, successor to the earlier range of TR models that had won such favour in both the home and export markets. The new sports car was built around a unit-construction bodyshell, while the engine, gearbox and rear axle were adopted from the sporting Triumph Dolomite. Its road-holding was significantly better than previous TRs, and overall the car was lighter. It was also cheaper to maintain. The 2 litre four-cylinder engine developed 105bhp at 5,500rpm and propelled the car to a top speed of 109mph.

1971 Triumph Herald 13/60 Convertible, 1296cc, engine rebuilt, approximately 10,000 miles covered since, exchange gearbox, full tonneau cover, finished in pale blue.
£1,700–2,000 / $2,450–2,900 ⚒ BRIT

Triumph Herald (1959–71)

Construction: Separate backbone chassis with bolt-on steel body panels.
Body styles: Saloon, coupé, convertible, estate and van.
Production: 486,000.
Engine: Four-cylinder, 948–1296cc.
Power: 38–61bhp.
0–60mph: 18–28 seconds.
Maximum speed: 70–85mph.

1971 Triumph Vitesse 2 Litre Mk II Convertible, 2 litre engine, 104bhp, wishbone-type independent rear suspension, restored at a cost of over £6,500, all corroded metal replaced, new door skins and sills, Waxoyled, rear suspension and brakes overhauled, new wheel trims, new chrome, bare-metal respray in red, new black vinyl hood, new carpets, 2 owners and 33,000 miles from new, 1 of the last made.
£5,750–6,500 / $8,300–9,400 ⚒ BKS

1971 Triumph Vitesse Convertible, completely restored, Minilite-type wheels, finished in blue, black interior, very good condition.
£5,000–6,000 / $7,250–8,700 ⊞ VIC

1981 Triumph Spitfire 1500, stainless-steel sports exhaust system, hard and soft tops, cooling system overhauled, gearbox and overdrive rebuilt, new door seals, bare-metal respray in blue, excellent condition.
£2,000–2,500 / $2,900–3,600 BARO

1973 Triumph GT6 Mk III, 1998cc 6-cylinder engine, twin exhaust system, overdrive gearbox, chrome-rim wheels, completely restored, finished in magenta.
£3,750–4,500 / $5,400–6,500 BRIT

Announced in 1966, the GT6 was a fastback fixed-head version of the Triumph Spitfire. A six-cylinder engine, from the contemporary Vitesse model, was used, and with a curb weight of around 17cwt, the power-to-weight ratio was excellent. This gave a spirited performance combined with good fuel consumption and, when fitted with the optional overdrive, the car would cruise comfortably at 90+mph. The GT6 was available until 1973.

1979 Triumph Spitfire 1500, 1491cc 4-cylinder engine, finished in green, 2 owners and fewer than 70,000 miles from new, largely original, 1 of the last made.
£3,000–3,500 / $4,400–5,000 BRIT

1972 Triumph GT6, 1998cc, original UK car, chassis and running gear completely restored, body stripped and all corroded panels replaced, new bonnet, finished in red, black interior, runner-up at 1997 Triumph Sports Six Club international concours.
£5,000–6,000 / $7,250–8,700 H&H

1974 Triumph 2500 Saloon, 6-cylinder engine, manual gearbox, 1 owner from new, in need of restoration.
£300–350 / $440–500 CGC

Triumph GT6 (1966–73)

Price in 1966: £985.
Production: 40,926.
Engine: 1998cc, overhead-valve, six-cylinder, twin SU carburettors.
Power output: 95–104bhp.
Transmission: Four-speed manual; optional overdrive.
Maximum speed: 107–112mph.
0–60mph: 10–11 seconds.

The Triumph GT6 has forever been plagued by unfair comparison, both by devotees and detractors of this dinky GT. To be fair, some of the fault must lie with Triumph for claiming GT credentials for its Spitfire-based coupé, when the term 'grand tourer' still had some residual meaning as shorthand for luxury, close-coupled continent-gobbling tin-tops in the mould of Jaguar, Aston, Jensen and Ferrari. The Triumph's trouble even now is the same as when it was new. The MGB GT was a direct counterpart of the MGB roadster. The Triumph GT6 also looked like a direct fixed-head counterpart of the Triumph Spitfire, but it wasn't. In place of the Spitfire's modest four-cylinder engine, the GT6 had beefy 2 litre six-cylinder power that gave it a marginal edge over straight-line MGB performance. On bendy bits though, the GT6 was no match, and the press rounded on its poor handling. Although later improved, the GT6 was never a mountain goat. Today, none of this should matter, but the collective consciousness of the classic-car crowd makes elephants look forgetful. That's why you can buy a very nice Triumph GT6 for less than a comparable MGB GT – and, come to think of it, that's not such a bad idea.

1972 Triumph Stag, restored, fitted with Triumph 2500 PI 6-cylinder engine, bare-metal respray in red, black interior, good condition.
£2,400–2,800 / $3,500–4,000 ⚒ CGC

1972 Triumph Stag, 2997cc V8 engine, finished in white, black interior, 2 owners and 80,100 miles from new, correct and to original specification in all respects, very good condition.
£3,500–4,000 / $5,000–5,800 ⚒ BRIT

1973 Triumph Stag, 2997cc V8 engine, 3-speed automatic transmission, professionally restored early 1990s at a cost of approximately £10,000, 4,000 miles covered since, original engine rebuilt, suspension and steering overhauled, electric fan, bare-metal respray in red, new hood, black interior.
£5,000–6,000 / $7,250–8,700 ⚒ H&H

1973 Triumph Stag, original 2997cc V8 engine, stainless-steel exhaust system, manual gearbox with overdrive, new clutch, correct black painted alloy wheels, hardtop, finished in magenta, black vinyl interior.
£5,000–6,000 / $7,250–8,700 ⚒ CGC

Cross Reference
See Colour Review (page 151)

1974 Triumph Stag, original 2997cc engine and automatic transmission, alloy wheels, hard and soft tops, finished in yellow, dark tan interior, 35,800 miles from new, excellent condition throughout.
£6,000–7,000 / $8,700–10,200 ⚒ H&H

1975 Triumph Stag, 2997cc V8 engine, new oil pump, new exhaust system, manual gearbox with overdrive, hardtop, unused hood, finished in yellow, 1 owner, mostly original, good condition throughout.
£4,800–5,600 / $7,000–8,000 ⚒ BRIT

Triumph Stag (1970–77)

Production: 25,877.
Engine: 2997cc V8, cast-iron block, alloy cylinder heads, double overhead camshafts, twin carburettors.
Power output: 146bhp.
Transmission: Four-speed manual with optional overdrive; three-speed automatic.
Brakes: Front discs, rear drums.
Maximum speed: 115+mph.
0–60mph: 10.5 seconds.
With crisp, convertible four-seater styling and a burbling V8, British Leyland's blueprint for the Triumph Stag must surely have come straight out of Dearborn, Michigan, where Ford's Mustang had created the 'pony car' idiom and galloped off with record-breaking sales. Where the Mustang had a wild stallion on its grille, British Leyland substituted a leaping Stag and a litany of blunders. Instead of the redoubtable 3.5 litre Rover V8, available in-house and off the shelf, Triumph insisted on developing its own 3 litre V8, but as soon as it hit the road, it earned a rotten reputation from which the Stag never recovered. Over the next seven years, fewer than 26,000 Stags were made, and with all the money swallowed up by developing an engine for a single low-selling model, there was nothing left to develop the Stag into the car it could have become.
What to watch: Specialists and enthusiasts have long since found the solution to the Stag's main bugbears of overheating, warped cylinder heads and blown head gaskets, yet there are still rogue Stags out there. Evidence of regular and careful maintenance to engine and radiator is essential; be very wary of a car that overheats on a test run – the damage has probably already been done. Many have done what Triumph should have done originally, by installing Rover's lusty and robust 3.5 litre V8 – this is an acceptable, even desirable practice.
Stag-gering facts: In May 1996, an enthusiast who had stumped up £53,067 to restore his 1974 Triumph Stag sold it at auction for £16,100.
The design of the Stag was executed by Italian styling house Michelotti, which also penned the Triumph TR4, Herald and 2000 saloon.

► **1976 Triumph Stag,** 2997cc V8 engine, automatic transmission, extensively refurbished 1997, electronic ignition, new large-capacity radiator, serviceable hood, finished in blue, good condition throughout.
£3,500–4,000
$5,000–5,800 ⚒ BRIT

◄ **1976 Triumph Stag,** 2997cc V8 engine, automatic transmission, alloy wheels, hard and soft tops, finished in yellow, black interior, 72,000 miles from new, good condition.
£3,750–4,500
$5,400–6,500 ⚒ H&H

► **1978 Triumph Stag,** automatic transmission, hardtop, tonneau, finished in dark green, new tan leather upholstery, excellent condition.
£6,500–7,500 / $9,400–10,875 ⊞ UMC

1977 Triumph Stag, restored, power-assisted steering, electric windows, finished in white, black interior and hood, 47,000 miles from new.
£6,500–7,500 / $9,400–10,875 ⊞ VIC

► **1974 Triumph 2500TC Estate,** automatic transmission, alloy wheels, good condition.
£1,200–1,400 / $1,750–2,100 ⊞ SiC

Turner-Miesse

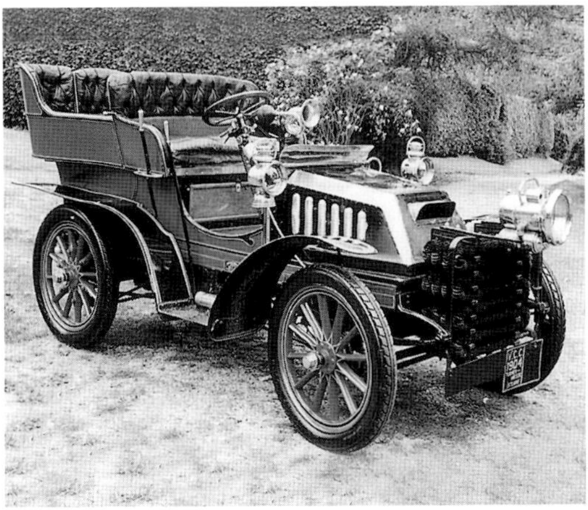

◄ **1904 Turner-Miesse 10hp Steam Car,** new cylinder block, Duplex headlamp, P&H sidelamps, Salisbury rear lamp, bugle horn, 4-seat rear-entrance tonneau coachwork, finished in red, Stewart 0–60mph speedometer, button-back leather upholstery.
£85,000–95,000 / $123,250–137,750 ⚒ BKS

The Turner Motor Manufacturing Company of Wolverhampton began motor car production by adopting steam power at a time when most of the Midlands motor industry had long since switched to the internal-combustion engine. In 1902, Turner acquired the licence to build steam cars from the Belgian company, J. Miesse, and began manufacture of cars powered by a flash-type boiler and a three-cylinder single-acting engine. Miesse had already eight years of experience in developing its motor car, and the design had much in common with the French Serpollet. The engine was mounted horizontally and transversely in the frame, the differential countershaft being geared directly to the crankshaft. Final drive was by side chains.

TVR

1976 TVR 3000M Limited Edition, restored 1999 at a cost of over £17,000, engine rebuilt, converted to unleaded fuel, rewired, electronic ignition, twin electric radiator fans, new chassis, steering, brakes and suspension, finished in fawn and brown, excellent condition.
£8,000–9,000 / $11,600–13,000 COYS
The special-edition 3000M was conceived to commemorate the tenth anniversary of production by TVR Engineering, the concern set up by Arthur and Martin Lilley at the end of 1965. The distinctive paintwork incorporated the name 'Martin', picked out on a contrasting band of paintwork along the flanks. Only ten cars of this type were built, all individually numbered.

TVR Taimar, 2994cc 6-cylinder engine, subject of body-off restoration 1996 at a cost of around £3,000, finished in blue with beige stripe, beige interior, fewer than 60,000 miles from new, very good bodywork and chassis, all major mechanical components in good condition.
£3,500–4,200 / $5,000–6,000 BRIT
Produced between 1976 and 1979, with a run of only 395, the Taimar was basically a restyled 3000M, which featured a practical lift-up hatch in a similar style to the Jensen Interceptor. Powered by the Ford V6 Essex engine, the Taimar was a spirited performer that handled particularly well.

1979 TVR 3000S Convertible, square-tube chassis, 4-wheel independent wishbone suspension, stainless-steel exhaust, Wolfrace alloy wheels, recently resprayed in original metallic dark blue, tan interior, 3 owners from new.
£5,000–6,000 / $7,250–8,700 BKS
The TVR 3000S was powered by the 2994cc Ford Essex V6, which produced 139bhp.

1985 TVR Taimar, 4.7 litre Gurney Eagle V8 engine, ZF manual gearbox, rose-jointed suspension, Jaguar rear axle, Compomotive alloy wheels, FIA fuel tank, full roll-cage, 25,000 miles from new.
£13,000–15,000 / $18,850–21,750 TIHO

TVR Model	ENGINE cc/cyl	DATES	CONDITION 1	2	3
Grantura I	1172/4	1957–62	£4,000	£3,000	£2,000
Grantura II	1558/4	1957–62	£4,500	£3,000	£2,000
Grantura III/1800S	1798/4	1963–67	£5,000	£3,000	£2,200
Tuscan V8	4727/8	1967–70	£12,000	£7,000	£6,000
Vixen S2/3	1599/4	1968–72	£5,000	£3,000	£1,500
3000M	2994/6	1972–79	£7,000	£4,000	£3,000
Taimar	2994/6	1977–79	£7,500	£5,000	£3,500

UNIC

◄ **1912 UNIC 10/12hp Drophead Coupé,** coachwork by Alford & Alder, 4-cylinder engine, electric self-starter, wire wheels, Lucas King of the Road lighting, finished in yellow with black wings and coachlining, Watford speedometer, Smiths 8-day clock, cloth upholstery in good condition, VCC dating certificate.
£14,000–17,000 / $20,300–24,650 BKS
When Georges Richard left the French Brasier company to set up in business at Puteaux in 1905, he called his cars Unic – an allusion to the fact that initially he pursued a one-model policy. This soon went by the board, and the 10/12hp twin-cylinder T-head car was shortly joined on the production line by the 12/14hp four-cylinder model, and later by the highly successful 10/12hp four-cylinder cars. Most commercially successful of all Unics was the 12/14hp model, which found favour as a taxi in many European countries.

Vanden Plas

1970 Vanden Plas Princess 1300, restored, finished in dark green, beige interior, 1 owner and 70,000 miles from new.
£3,500–4,000 / $5,200–5,800 ⊞ VIC

1971 Vanden Plas Princess 1300, 1275cc 4-cylinder engine, finished in dark red, fewer than 22,000 miles from new, very good original condition.
£2,750–3,250 / $3,900–4,700 ⚒ BRIT

Based on the BMC 1100/1300 range, the Vanden Plas version was first seen at the 1963 Motor Show. Equipped and trimmed to exceptionally high standards, the Vanden Plas included a wooden dashboard, sound deadening, and quality cloth headlining. External differences included a distinctive radiator grille and traditional coachlining.

◄ **1973 Vanden Plas Princess 1300,** 1275cc 4-cylinder engine, automatic transmission, recently refurbished, finished in white, blue leather interior, fewer than 37,000 miles from new, good condition.
£1,800–2,100 / $2,600–3,100 ⚒ BRIT

VANDEN PLAS Model	ENGINE cc/cyl	DATES	CONDITION 1	2	3
3 Litre I/II	2912/6	1959–64	£5,000	£3,000	£1,000
4 Litre R	3909/6	1964–67	£4,000	£2,500	£700
1100 Princess	1098/4	1964–67	£2,000	£1,000	£500
1300 Princess	1275/4	1967–74	£2,200	£1,500	£500

Vauxhall

Although owned by General Motors since 1925, Vauxhall has managed to maintain a distinct British identity throughout much of its long life, which began when the first Vauxhall motor car rolled out of the Thames-side Vauxhall Iron Works in 1903. In the Edwardian and vintage eras, the expensive sporting Prince Henry models and the later 30/98 were very highly regarded, but in 1925 poor financial control led to the company's take-over by General Motors. After that, the company moved into the mainstream middle market, which has remained its domain ever since. Throughout the 1950s and into the 1960s, Vauxhalls absorbed American styling influences, but still retained an essentially British character, still more Uncle Stan than Uncle Sam. From the mid-1970s, model lines converged with those of Opel in Germany, also owned since the 1920s by General Motors.

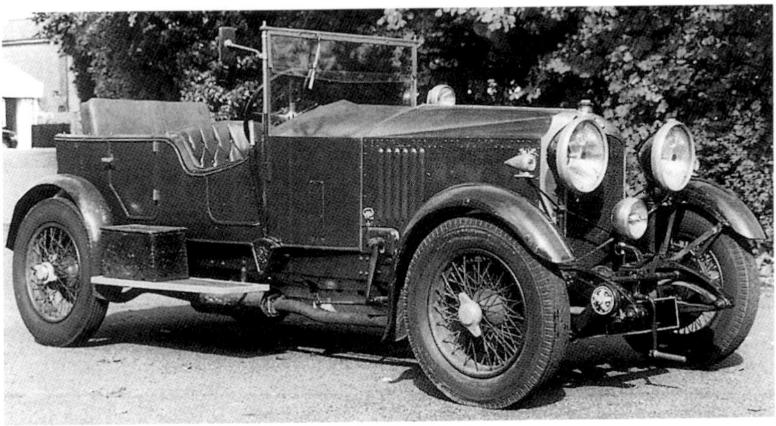

◄ **1923 Vauxhall 30/98 OE Tourer,** coachwork by Mann Egerton, matching numbers, fitted with Lagonda front axle and mechanical brakes, 30 gallon fuel tank, quantity of spares including cylinder head, starter, dynamo, wheel centres, wheels, side screens and parts of the original hood and frame, 1 family ownership for over 66 years, unused since 1974, recently recommissioned to running condition.
£40,000–50,000
$58,000–72,500 ⚒ CGC

VAUXHALL Model	ENGINE cc/cyl	DATES	CONDITION 1	2	3
D/OD	3969/4	1914–26	£35,000	£24,000	£18,000
E/OE	4224/4	1919–28	£80,000	£60,000+	£35,000
Eighty	3317/6	1931–33	£10,000	£8,000	£5,000
Cadet	2048/6	1931–33	£7,000	£5,000	£3,000
Lt Six	1531/6	1934–38	£5,000	£4,000	£1,500
14	1781/6	1934–39	£4,000	£3,000	£1,500
25	3215/6	1937–39	£5,000	£4,000	£1,500
10	1203/4	1938–39	£4,000	£3,000	£1,500
Wyvern LIX	1500/4	1948–51	£2,000	£1,000	£500
Velox LIP	2200/6	1948–51	£2,000	£1,000	£500
Wyvern EIX	1500/4	1951–57	£2,000	£1,320	£400
Velox EIPV	2200/6	1951–57	£3,000	£1,650	£400
Cresta EIPC	2200/6	1954–57	£3,000	£1,650	£400
Velox/Cresta PAS/PAD	2262/6	1957–59	£2,850	£1,300	£300
Velox/Cresta PASY/PADY	2262/6	1959–60	£2,700	£1,500	£300
Velox/Cresta PASX/PADX	2651/6	1960–62	£2,700	£1,300	£300
Velox/Cresta PASX/PADX Est	2651/6	1960–62	£2,700	£1,300	£300
Velox/Cresta PB	2651/6	1962–65	£1,600	£800	£100
Velox/Cresta PB Est	2651/6	1962–65	£1,600	£800	£100
Cresta/Deluxe PC	3294/6	1964–72	£1,500	£800	£100
Cresta PC Est	3294/6	1964–72	£1,500	£800	£100
Viscount	3294/6	1964–72	£1,700	£900	£100
Victor I/II	1507/4	1957–61	£2,000	£1,000	£250
Victor I/II Est	1507/4	1957–61	£2,100	£1,100	£300
Victor FB	1507/4	1961–64	£1,500	£900	£200
Victor FB Est	1507/4	1961–64	£1,600	£1,000	£300
VX4/90	1507/4	1961–64	£2,000	£900	£150
Victor FC101	1594/4	1964–67	£1,600	£900	£150
Victor FC101 Est	1594/4	1964–67	£1,800	£1,000	£200
101 VX4/90	1594/4	1964–67	£2,000	£1,500	£250
VX4/90	1975/4	1969–71	£1,000	£600	£100
Ventora I/II	3294/6	1968–71	£1,000	£375	£100
Viva HA	1057/4	1963–66	£1,000	£350	£100
Viva SL90	1159/4	1966–70	£1,000	£350	£100
Viva Brabham	1159/4	1967–70	£2,000	£1,000	£800
Viva	1600/4	1968–70	£500	£350	£100
Viva Est	1159/4	1967–70	£500	£400	£100

1924 Vauxhall 14/40 Top Hat Saloon, coachwork by Mulliner, 2.2 litre engine, unused since 1960s, original unrestored condition, recently recommissioned to running order.
£11,500–13,500 / $16,700–20,000 ⚒ COYS

A Vauxhall Wyvern stylised bird mascot, WW 367, chrome-plated brass, detachable wings, stamped registration No. 740465, 1927–32.
£400–500 / $580–850 ⚒ RM
This mascot was fitted to the 20/60 Cadet and VX saloons.

1931 Vauxhall Cadet Saloon, 1690cc engine, finished in blue and black, blue and beige interior, fewer than 47,000 miles from new, very good condition throughout.
£6,000–7,000 / $8,700–10,200 ⚒ H&H
This car was previously owned by Sir Freddie Laker.

1933 Vauxhall 14/6 Six-Light Saloon, engine recently rebuilt, original leather upholstery.
£6,000–7,500 / $8,700–10,875 ⊞ GrM

Miller's Starter Marque

Starter Vauxhalls: *PA Cresta/Velox, 1957–62; F-type Victor, 1957–61.*

- As our price table shows, all Vauxhalls of the 1950s and 1960s are affordable, but two models that really stand out for their glamorous styling are the Detroit-inspired PA Cresta/Velox and the F-type Victor, both very appealing to anyone who enjoys nostalgia for the 1950s. They look for all the world like classic Yank tanks, yet their flanks clothe ordinary British mechanicals and running gear, which are generally readily available and easy to maintain. The earlier E-type Cresta, Velox and Wyvern also offer a touch of star-spangled razzmatazz, but their numbers have thinned to a level where they are not quite as practical as the later PA. The PB Cresta and FB Victors are also practical buys; compared to the extravagant PA they are almost muted.
- The glorious PA Cresta is a monster by British standards, a genuine six-seater with enough body rock and roll to please any Elvis fan. Mechanically, they offer little to worry about, with their strong 2.2 and 2.6 litre engines, and ancillaries like front discs, starter motors and dynamos, which are straight out of the MGB.
- **Pick of the PAs:** Some prefer the looks of the pre-1960 model, with its three-piece rear window, although later models have slightly more eager 2.6 litre lumps in place of the earlier 2.2. But the bodies are a different matter. Legend has it that PA Crestas rusted so rapidly that by the time they reached the end of the Luton production line, they would have failed today's MoT test. Actually, their resistance to rust was pretty much in line with other cars of the era. The big difference is that there's just more metal to rust. When you go and look at one, take a metal detector, because a festering rust box will be a labour of love rather than a sound proposition.
- The F-type Victor delivers a Detroit dream in a UK-sized package. Compared to contemporary saloon rivals, it was a fine car to drive, with a tough and flexible engine. The mechanicals are all pretty sturdy, but the early cars really did have a deserved reputation for rusting, as their bodyshells offered more mud traps than a Florida swamp. In fact, by the end of 1959, Vauxhall was already receiving corrosion complaints, and in response added underseal and splash panels.

1953 Vauxhall Velox, 2262cc 6-cylinder engine, finished in grey , grey and red interior trim, stored for 3 years, in need of recommissioning, sound bodywork.
£1,500–1,800 / $2,150–2,550 ⚒ BRIT

1962 Vauxhall Cresta Estate, 2651cc 6-cylinder engine, bodywork restored, finished in 2-tone blue, grey interior, 88,000 miles from new.
£5,000–6,000 / $7,250–8,700 ⚒ H&H
This vehicle was previously owned by Rick Wakeman.

1985 Vauxhall Astra GTE Mk I, finished in black, tinted windows.
£1,500–1,800 / $2,150–2,550 ⚒ MIMI

Voisin

◀ 1936 Voisin C28 Chancellerie Berline Aerodynamique, 4-speed Cotal electro-magnetic gearbox, completely restored early 1980s, engine and gearbox rebuilt, finished in pale yellow and dark green, period-style tartan interior.
£90,000–100,000 / $130,500–145,000 ⚒ BKS
Launched in 1935 to challenge the Bugatti Type 57, the Voisin C28 (codenamed Sprint) was a development of the previous C25 model with the six-cylinder sleeve-valve power unit bored out from 3.0 to 3.3 litres. Five body styles were catalogued: the fastback Aerodyne and Aerosport (the latter the first full-width design with pontoon wings offered in France), and three streamlined saloons. These were the two-door Cimier, and the four-door Clariere and Chancellerie. The saloons were built on a pressed-steel chassis with boxed rear section, while the fastbacks had a chassis that was dropped in the centre with additional sidemembers to carry the bodywork. At its launch in 1935, the Chancellerie retailed at 85,000 francs – a Type 57 Bugatti saloon was relatively affordable by comparison, at 70,000 francs.

Volga

Condition Guide

1. A vehicle in top class condition but not 'concours d'elegance standard, either fully restored or in very good original condition.
2. A good, clean, roadworthy vehicle, both mechanically and bodily sound.
3. A runner, but in need of attention, probably both to bodywork and mechanics. Must have current MoT.

◀ **1965 Volga MZI Four-Door Saloon,** 2445cc in-line 4-cylinder engine, 3-speed transmission, ex-taxi, left-hand drive, partially restored, finished in blue.
£750–900 / $1,100–1,300 ⊞ Now

Volkswagen

1967 Volkswagen 1200 Beetle, 1192cc air-cooled flat-4 engine, finished in grey, 40,000 miles from new, original.
£4,750–5,500 / $6,900–8,000 ⚒ BRIT

1969 Volkswagen Beetle Cabriolet, engine rebuilt, 1,200km covered since, finished in black and white, black interior trim and hood, good condition throughout.
£6,000–7,000 / $8,700–10,200 ⚒ COYS

▶ **1970 Volkswagen Beetle 1300,** new clutch, front wheel cylinders and hoses, finished in royal blue, white vinyl interior, fewer than 33,000 miles from new, very good condition.
£3,250–3,750 / $4,700–5,400 ⚒ BKS

The original VW saloon was intended to be the pre-war German 'people's car', but went on to become an all-time world bestseller and cult classic, with over 21 million having been sold by the late 1970s. It was continuously updated with altered coachwork, improved running gear and larger engines. Larger windows and revised ball-jointed suspension were among the changes for 1965. In 1966, the standard 34bhp 1200 model was joined by the new 1300 with the more powerful 50bhp engine.

VOLKSWAGEN Model	ENGINE cc/cyl	DATES	CONDITION 1	2	3
Beetle (split rear screen)	1131/4	1945–53	£5,000	£3,500	£2,000
Beetle (oval rear screen)	1192/4	1953–57	£4,000	£2,000	£1,000
Beetle (slope headlamps)	1192/4	1957–68	£2,500	£1,000	£600
Beetle DHC	1192/4	1954–60	£6,000	£4,500	£2,000
Beetle 1500	1493/4	1966–70	£3,000	£2,000	£1,000
Beetle 1302 LS	1600/4	1970–72	£2,500	£1,850	£850
Beetle 1303 S	1600/4	1972–79	£3,000	£2,000	£1,500
1500 Variant/1600	1493/ 1584/4	1961–73	£2,000	£1,500	£650
1500/1600	1493/ 1584/4	1961–73	£3,000	£2,000	£800
Karmann Ghia/I	1192/4	1955–59	£5,000	£3,000	£1,000
Karmann Ghia/I DHC	1192/4	1957–59	£8,000	£5,000	£2,500
Karmann Ghia/I	1192/4	1960–74	£5,500	£3,000	£1,800
Karmann Ghia/I DHC	1192/4	1960–74	£7,000	£4,500	£2,000
Karmann Ghia/3	1493/4	1962–69	£4,000	£2,500	£1,250

Miller's Starter Marque

Starter Volkswagens: *Beetle, 1945–on; Karmann Ghia, 1955–74 .*

- The Volkswagen Beetle is one bug they just can't find a cure for. It has been produced continuously from 1945, and every car that rolls off the remaining South American production line adds to a 21 million-plus world production record that's unlikely ever to be beaten.
- Because the Beetle is still in production, cheap spares are readily available for most models, other than very early cars. That buzzing, air-cooled four-cylinder engine is well nigh unburstable too, and in mechanical terms the cars are easy to work on. One fact says it all: the world record for an engine swap – drive up to drive away – is just over three minutes.
- If you're a classic purist, there's the first-of-breed purity of either the 1131cc 1945–53 split-screen cars or the 1953–57 oval-window 1200cc cars. For drivability and less onerous ownership costs, a good mid-way motor is the 1500cc Bug produced from 1966 to 1970. It's old enough to be classic, fast enough to keep up, and still pure in design.
- The body's the Beetle's bugbear, however. Although the wings bolt on and virtually every body panel is available, there are a lot of Beetle bodywork bodges around. Check very closely where the body attaches to the chassis, just behind the front wheels and immediately ahead of the rear wheels. Severe rust here can make the vehicle unsafe.
- The humble Bug turned into the belle of the boulevard when German coachbuilder Karmann clothed the Volkswagen Beetle in debutante designer wear from Italian styling house Ghia. But this Karmann's a chameleon. Its styling is loosely in the sporting idiom, although chubbier and less sharply defined, rather like a novelty bar of soap. As for performance, the cute Karmann Ghia didn't exactly sprout wings when it emerged from its Beetle chrysalis with its spluttering air-cooled engine, all buzz and fury signifying nothing much at all. Needless to say, it was the perfect Beverly Hills boulevardier, a sports car 'mule' that did it all, from the beach to the shopping mall.
- **Pick of the bunch:** The later, the faster. From 1966 on, you get the bigger, faster 1500cc engine with front disc brakes; from 1970, the engine's uprated to 1600cc, but later cars are less pretty with heavy bumpers and large lamp clusters. Also, anything with a steering wheel on the right fetches a premium in the UK.
- **For:** The blend of Beetle basics and sports-car looks makes for a distinctive car with cheap and readily available mechanical components.
- **Against:** Unfortunately, it's also a classic compromise. It's got a better aerodynamic shape than the Beetle, but it's also heavier. That means a slightly higher top speed, but your Karmann will be no Beetle beater away from the lights.
- **What to watch:** The mechanicals may be of that unburstable Beetle breed, but the Karmann coachbuilt body gets costly when it starts to rust – and rust it does.

▶ **1979 Volkswagen 1303 LS Cabriolet,** 1584cc air-cooled flat-4 engine, right-hand drive, fewer than 16,000 miles from new, good condition throughout.
£7,000–8,000 / $10,200–11,600 ⚒ BRIT

1970 Volkswagen Beetle Cabriolet, 1600cc air-cooled engine, original right-hand-drive, period spotlights, new hood, finished in white, grey and red interior, excellent condition.
£6,000–7,000 / $8,700–10,200 ⚒ H&H

1973 Volkswagen 1300 Beetle, 1285cc air-cooled flat-4, new engine fitted 1996, resprayed in red, black vinyl interior, fuel gauge inoperative, in need of new rear brake hoses, sound bodywork and structure.
£1,500–1,800 / $2,150–2,550 ⚒ BRIT

1975 Volkswagen Beetle 1303 Cabriolet, left-hand drive, finished in gunmetal grey, black hood, cream interior, c52,000 miles from new, in need of cosmetic attention.
£3,000–3,600 / $4,400–5,200 ⚒ BKS

1978 Volkswagen Beetle Cabriolet, 1584cc flat-4, engine rebuilt, new clutch, resprayed in metallic blue, sound body and structure.
£3,750–4,500 / $5,400–6,500 ⚒ BRIT

1961 Volkswagen Karmann Ghia Coupé, right-hand drive, completely restored 1989–91 at a cost of over £7,500, c5,000 miles since, new 1.2 litre engine, finished in black with white roof, cream interior.
£3,750–4,250 / $5,700–6,200 BKS
Handbuilt by Karmann at its Osnabrück works, VW's top-of-the-range coupé married a modified export Beetle floorpan, running gear and engine/gearbox to stylish Ghia coachwork. Launched in 1955 in 1192cc-engined form, the Karmann Ghia kept abreast of mainstream Beetle developments, gaining all-synchromesh gearbox, and progressively larger and more powerful engines as time passed. A convertible version appeared in 1957, and in 1959 the car's front end underwent subtle restyling, with raised headlamps and enlarged nose intakes.

1981 Volkswagen GTi Golf Convertible, finished in metallic light blue, black interior and hood, 30,000 miles from new.
£2,500–3,000 / $3,600–4,400 MIMI

1972 Volkswagen 1600E Fastback, 1584cc air-cooled flat-4 engine, fuel-injection, finished in turquoise, black interior, fewer than 27,000 miles from new, concours winner.
£4,750–5,250 / $6,900–7,600 H&H

1972 Volkswagen K70L, 1605cc overhead-camshaft 4-cylinder engine, 90bhp, 1 owner from new.
£500–600 / $720–870 KR

1986 Volkswagen Passat GLS Four-Door Estate, finished in silver, grey cloth upholstery, good condition.
£650–750 / $950–1,100 BKS
First of the new models that ushered in Volkswagen's post-Beetle era, the Passat arrived on the scene in 1973. Introduced in 1980, Series 2 Passats were larger than before and benefited from Audi's new five-cylinder engine.

1966 Volkswagen 21-Window Microbus, 1192cc air-cooled flat-4 engine, 40bhp, 4-speed manual gearbox, 4-wheel drum brakes, canvas moon roof, professionally restored, finished in red and white, concours winner.
£17,000–20,000 / $24,650–29,000 RM

Volvo

In Latin, Volvo means 'I roll', and that's what Volvos are famous for – rolling on and on and on. Although founded in Sweden in 1927, it wasn't really until the 1947 launch of the PV444 that the company's products came to wider international notice. With its quasi-American styling – often compared to the fastback Fords of the 1940s – scaled down to reasonable European proportions, the PV444 was the car that brought Volvo into the mainstream. Its modern unitary construction, high levels of comfort, fine driving dynamics and rugged dependability added up to a winning combination, both in the domestic Swedish market and abroad. The PV544 refined the theme further with a one-piece screen, more powerful engines, optional four-speed gearbox and an emphasis on sensible levels of equipment rather than mere gimmicks. The PV544 featured a padded dash, twin padded sun visors and anti-dazzle rear-view mirror, and self-parking wipers to ease the stress of driving. Seats reclined to form a double bed, and it was also the first car to offer both front and rear seat-belt anchors. In the later 1950s, the 121 continued in the same mould and endured through various model designations (122/131/132/123GT) up to 1970. Today, they are still enjoyed in daily use as a robust and stylish classic workhorse. A little more exotic is the P1800 sports car which, despite its more delicate looks, still possesses Volvo's characteristic robustness, even if body parts aren't as readily available or as cheap. The complex curves can also make repair and renovation quite costly.

1953 Volvo PV444 Special Edition Saloon, stainless-steel wheel rims, stainless-steel decor mouldings to wings, roof-mounted indicators, radiator blind, double sun visors, cigarette lighter, passenger grab handles, starter switch incorporated in ignition lock, left-hand drive, finished in red, red interior, well maintained, good condition throughout.
£3,250–4,250 / $5,700–6,200 ⚒ BKS
Announced in 1944, Volvo's PV444 saloon was the first of the Swedish company's products to sell in significant numbers outside its home market, its quality of construction and good road manners helping to establish the reputation Volvo enjoys to this day. A 1.4 litre, overhead-valve four-cylinder engine, independent front suspension, all-round coil springing, hydraulic brakes and three-speed gearbox formed the basic specification. UK sales did not begin until 1958, by which time the model had developed into the restyled PV544 equipped with 1.6/1.8 litre engines.

1966 Volvo 121 Amazon Estate, Koni adjustable dampers, body and interior refurbished at a cost of £6,000, finished in blue, 1 owner, excellent condition.
£3,000–3,500 / $4,400–5,200 ⚒ BARO

A known continuous history can add value to and enhance the enjoyment of a car.

Miller's Starter Marque

Starter Volvos: *Volvo Amazon, 1957–70.*

- The Amazon is certainly aptly named, because it's a tough old road warrior, armoured like a tank. Built to withstand Swedish winters – and stray reindeer – this capable family four-seater was also the first Volvo to sell in substantial numbers in Britain, and it helped create the reputation for strength and safety that Volvo has traded on ever since (the Amazon had a padded dash top at birth, standard front seat belts from 1958, and dual-circuit brakes the following year). Nearly half of the Amazons sold in Sweden are still on the road, and in Britain they're still more commonly encountered than many of our self-dismantling domestic products of the same period.
- **For:** An everyday classic; rugged long-lasting four-cylinder engines; comprehensive spares support; accomplished ride and handling – the Amazon was a potent rally car in its day; pleasant light steering; fantastic value for money.
- **Against:** Vinyl seating and slightly spartan interior initially disappoint many a potential convert, but they're hardwearing.
- **Pick of the bunch:** All those model numbers are mystifying, signifying two or four doors, single or twin carburettors and different engine sizes. The 123GT is the most powerful, but most expensive. Probably the best combination of price, performance, practicality and comfortable cruising is the 1800cc four-door 122S with overdrive.
- **Amazon appellation:** The Amazon was only so named in Sweden because the German motorcycle manufacturer Kreidler claimed rights to the trademark and only permitted Volvo to use the name in its home market. Elsewhere, Amazons were listed by their model numbers.
- **Body styles:** Two- and four-door saloon, five-door estate.
  Model designations: 121, 131, 122S, 132, 123GT; estates, 221, 222.
  Engine: 1583, 1778, 1986cc overhead-valve, four-cylinder.
  Transmission: Three-speed manual, four-speed manual, four-speed manual with overdrive, three-speed automatic.
  Power output: 60–115bhp.
  Maximum speed: 90–100+mph.

VOLVO Model	ENGINE cc/cyl	DATES	CONDITION 1	2	3
PV444	1800/4	1958–67	£4,000	£1,750	£800
PV544	1800/4	1962–64	£4,000	£1,750	£800
120 (B16)	1583/4	1956–59	£3,000	£1,000	£300
121	1708/4	1960–67	£3,500	£1,500	£350
122S	1780/4	1960–67	£4,500	£1,500	£250
131	1780/4	1962–69	£4,000	£1,500	£350
221/222	1780/4	1962–69	£2,500	£1,500	£300
123Gt	1986/4	1967–69	£3,000	£2,500	£750
P1800	1986/4	1960–70	£4,500	£2,500	£1,000
P1800E	1986/4	1970–71	£4,200	£2,500	£1,000
P1800ES	1986/4	1971–73	£4,800	£3,000	£1,000

Restored values

The cost of a professional restoration will have an influence on, but no direct relation to, a car's market value. A restored car can have a market value lower than the cost of its restoration.

◀ **1971 Volvo P1800ES,** 1986cc 4-cylinder engine, finished in gold, good mechanical condition.
£1,500–1,800
$2,150–2,550 BARO

Westfield

1991 Westfield SEi Wide Body, 1600cc Ford 4-cylinder engine, twin Dellorto carburettors, 4-speed manual gearbox, adjustable suspension, TSW cross-spoke alloy wheels, chrome headlamps, full wet weather equipment, roll-bar, finished in burgundy, VDO instruments, tan interior, individual adjustable seats.
£7,500–8,500 / $10,875–12,300 HMC

White

◀ **1912/15 White-La France Four-Seater Special,** 12 litre La France 6-cylinder engine, triple SU carburettors, restored, new wooden wheels with oak spokes and laminated ash felloes, Great Race-style bodywork, finished in green, red leather upholstered front seats, wicker rear seats.
£9,500–11,500
$13,800–16,700 BKS
This car was built on an American White chassis dating from 1911/12, which almost certainly came from a 60hp six-cylinder Model GF.

Willys

◄ **1928 Willys Overland Whippet 96 Four-Seater Tourer,** 2199cc engine, 4-wheel drum brakes, artillery wheels, original right-hand drive, completely restored, only 2,000 miles covered since, finished in blue with black wings, tonneau and hood covers, new hood sticks and mohair side screens, original instruments, dark brown hide upholstery.
£7,500–9,000
$10,875–13,000 ⚒ H&H

Winton

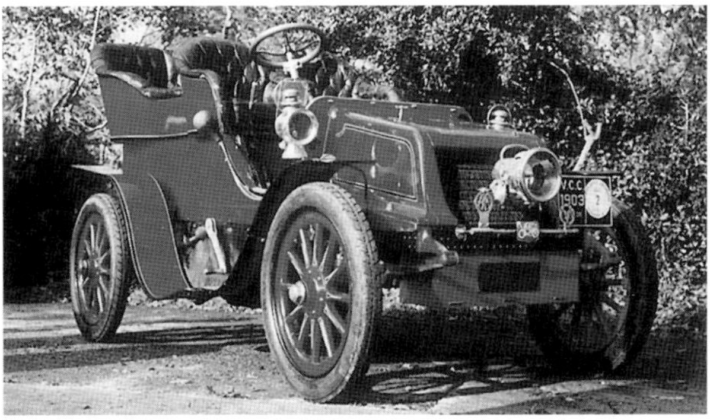

► **1903 Winton 20hp Rear-Entrance Five-Seater Tonneau,** 4.25 litre flat-twin engine, constant-mesh 2-speed gearbox with friction clutches, final drive by chain, open-differential live rear axle, brass lighting, Lucas double-twist bulb horn, finished in maroon, deep-buttoned black leather upholstery, VCC dated.
£75,000–85,000 / $108,750–123,250 ⚒ BKS

Wolseley

Although one of the earlier pioneers of British car manufacturing, Wolseley hardly had an independent existance at all. The company grew out of Frederick Wolseley's Wolseley Sheep Shearing Machine Company, where Herbert Austin was the prime mover in setting the company on the road to motor car manufacture. The first four-wheeled motor car was produced in 1899 or 1900, and in 1901 Wolseley car manufacturing was taken over by armaments firm Vickers. Austin left in 1905 to start his own company. Early Wolseley products were a mixed bag, usually with well engineered power units that didn't always get the chassis and running gear to match. Financial difficulties led to the company's acquisition in 1927 by William Morris, and after 1935 Wolseleys served as upmarket Morrises, with superior interiors and overhead-valve engines. After the 1952 merger of Austin and Morris, Wolseley survived as a BMC brand until 1975.

1923 Wolseley A9 Colonial Model Tourer, restored at a cost of over £25,000, original lights, original thermometer mascot, Auster rear screen, original Wolseley Motors plaque, finished in blue with black wings, double duck hood, full weather equipment, side screens, new blue leather interior, 1 of only 2 examples in UK.
£25,000–28,000 / $36,250–40,000 ⚒ H&H

1935 Wolseley Wasp Saloon, 1073cc engine, 'easy-clean' pressed-steel wheels, older restoration, finished in black over green, green interior, good condition.
£1,800–2,100 / $2,600–3,100 ⚒ CGC

WOLSELEY (Veteran & Vintage) Model	ENGINE cc/cyl	DATES	CONDITION 1	2	3
10	987/2	1909–16	£16,000	£12,500	£9,000
CZ (30hp)	2887/4	1909	£18,000	£13,000	£9,000
15hp and A9	2614/4	1920–27	£12,000	£10,000	£8,000
20 and C8	3921/ 3862/6	1920–27	£11,000	£8,000	£6,000
E4 (10.5hp)	1267/ 1542/4	1925–30	£6,000	£4,000	£3,000
E6 and Viper and 16hp	2025/6	1927–34	£15,000	£12,000	£8,000
E8M	2700/8	1928–31	£18,000	£15,000	£12,000
Hornet	1271/4	1931–35	£10,000	£8,000	£4,500
Hornet Special	1271/ 1604/6	1933–36	£12,000	£8,000	£5,000
Wasp	1069/4	1936	£7,000	£5,000	£3,500
Hornet	1378/6	1936	£8,000	£6,000	£4,000
21/60 and 21hp	2677/ 2916/6	1932–39	£11,000	£6,000	£4,000
25	3485/6	1936–39	£8,500	£5,500	£4,000
12/48	1547/4	1937–39	£5,000	£3,000	£2,000
14/56	1818/6	1937–39	£6,000	£4,000	£2,000
18/80	2322/6	1938–39	£7,500	£5,500	£4,000

Early Wolseley cars are well made and very British, and those with coachbuilt bodies command a premium of at least +25%.

1957 Wolseley Saloon, 1500cc 4-cylinder engine, finished in maroon.
£1,450–1,650 / $2,000–2,400 ⊞ PMo

1961 Wolseley 15/60 Saloon, finished in 2-tone blue, blue leather upholstery, 1 owner and 65,000 miles from new, very original.
£1,800–2,200 / $2,600–3,200 ⊞ UMC

◀ **1969 Wolseley Hornet Mk III,** 998cc 4-cylinder engine, finished in white, black interior, fewer than 61,000 miles from new, largely original, good condition.
£1,000–1,200 / $1,500–1,800 ⚒ BRIT
Introduced in 1961, the Wolseley Hornet took its name from the successful pre-war model, and along with its sister, the Riley Elf, was basically an upmarket, restyled version of the ubiquitous Mini.

WOLSELEY Model	ENGINE cc/cyl	DATES	CONDITION 1	2	3
8	918/4	1939–48	£3,000	£2,000	£1,000
10	1140/4	1939–48	£3,500	£2,000	£1,000
12/48	1548/4	1939–48	£4,000	£2,000	£1,250
14/60	1818/6	1946–48	£4,500	£2,500	£1,500
18/85	2321/6	1946–48	£6,000	£3,000	£2,000
25	3485/6	1946–48	£7,000	£4,000	£2,500
4/50	1476/4	1948–53	£2,500	£1,000	£450
6/80	2215/6	1948–54	£3,000	£1,500	£750
4/44	1250/4	1952–56	£2,500	£1,250	£750
15/50	1489/4	1956–58	£1,850	£850	£500
1500	1489/4	1958–65	£2,500	£1,000	£500
15/60	1489/4	1958–61	£2,000	£700	£400
16/60	1622/4	1961–71	£1,800	£800	£400
6/90	2639/6	1954–57	£2,500	£1,000	£500
6/99	2912/6	1959–61	£3,000	£1,500	£750
6/110 MK I/II	2912/6	1961–68	£2,000	£1,000	£500
Hornet (Mini)	848/4	1961–70	£1,500	£750	£400
1300	1275/4	1967–74	£1,250	£750	£400
18/85	1798/4	1967–72	£950	£500	£250

Commercial Vehicles

1965 AEC Mammoth Major Mk V Six-Wheeler Flatbed Rigid Lorry, Park Royal Cab, originally a military vehicle, restored over 3 years.
£9,000–10,500 / $13,000–15,500 ⚒ CGC

1937 Austin 12/4 Low-Loader London Taxi Cab, restored 1995, taxi meter, roof luggage rack, taxi light, all correct period fittings, finished in blue, blue leather interior, excellent condition throughout.
£15,000–17,000 / $21,750–24,650 ⚒ BKS

Austin produced its first purpose-built taxi in 1929. It was not until April 1930, however, that the design was modified to meet the stringent regulations for London use, laid down by Scotland Yard's Conditions of Fitness. Those requirements included a tight turning circle, which the early cars did not have. Austin's well-tried 12/4 chassis and engine were used as the basis for the new cab. In 1943, the adoption of a worm-drive rear axle allowed a lower body to be fitted, while still keeping a flat floor in the passenger compartment.

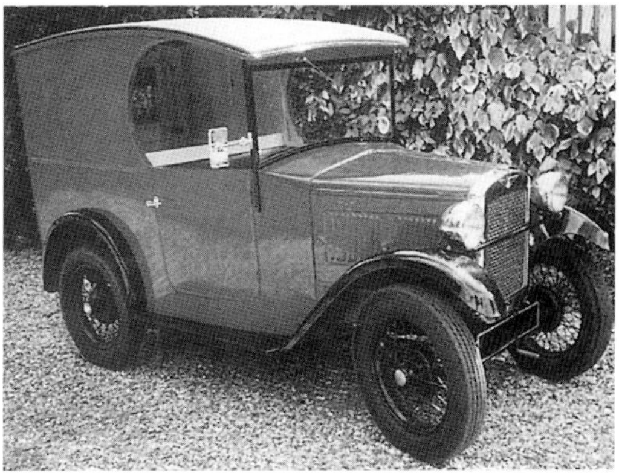

1937 Austin 7 Light van, originally a saloon, rebodied 1980s, older mechanical restoration, finished in red over black, cream interior, excellent condition throughout.
£4,000–5,000 / $5,800–7,250 ⚒ CGC

1979 Austin Mini Pick-up, 1275cc 4-cylinder engine, twin SU carburettors, new rear subframe and petrol tank, wide wheels, glass sunroof, finished in white, Wolseley Hornet leather seats.
£500–600 / $720–860 ⚒ BRIT

Miller's is a price GUIDE not a price LIST

1953 Austin LC-5 Ambulance, coachwork by Smith/Appleyard, restored to original condition, Plymouth & District Ambulance Service livery, 1 of 3 known to exist in UK.
£5,000–6,000 / $7,250–8,700 🚘 BAm

1938 Buick Series 40 Ambulance, in service until 1964, restored, New South Wales Ambulance Transport Service Board livery, 231,000 miles recorded.
£6,000–7,000 / $8,700–10,200 BAm

1926 Chevrolet Superior Taxi Cab, 2500cc 4-cylinder engine, built for Yellow Cab Company, magnetic door signs, finished in yellow and black, beige interior, fewer than 47,000 miles from new, excellent condition throughout.
£10,000–12,000 / $14,500–17,400 H&H

1952 Chevrolet 3100 ½ Ton Pick-up, 3.5 litre overhead-valve 6-cylinder engine, 4-speed manual gearbox, chrome 8-spoke wheels, lighting converted to UK specification, bare-metal respray in green, interior in need of attention, otherwise good condition.
£5,500–6,500 / $8,000–9,500 BKS

1959 Chevrolet Fleetside Apache 3100 Pick-up, V8 engine, wrap-around rear screen, twin headlamp pods, 'bullet' rear lights, 3-seater bench seat, restored at a cost of £25,000, finished in pale blue and white, black interior, very good condition throughout.
£13,000–15,500 / $18,850–22,600 BKS

1918 Ford Model T Pick-up, completely restored to original specification, finished in black, black leather interior, very good condition throughout.
£7,750–9,250 / $11,200–3,350 BKS

◄ **1929 Ford Model AA Dropside Truck,** right-hand drive, completely restored, kingpins, all bushes and brakes renewed, new radiator, new chassis, new body, excellent condition.
£7,500–9,000 / $10,875–13,000 CGC

1931 Ford Model AA Recovery Truck, right-hand drive, completely restored, period Weaver crane, stepside body, excellent condition.
£7,000–8,000 / $10,200–11,600 CGC

1935 Ford Fire Engine, 3622cc sidevalve V8 engine, electric starter, 4-speed manual gearbox, left-hand drive, 2 brass bells, grained wood seating platform, hose and equipment compartments, escape ladder, restored, originally supplied to Dutch Fire Service.
£4,000–4,800 / $5,800–6,900 CGC

1929 Morris Commercial Country Bus, finished in red and cream, good condition throughout.
£8,000–9,500 / $11,600–13,800 BKS

1969 Morris Minor Pick-up, 1098cc overhead-valve 4-cylinder engine, 48bhp, full canvas tilt, lined bed, floorpan renovated, finished in white, black interior.
£2,750–3,300 / $4,000–4,800 BKS

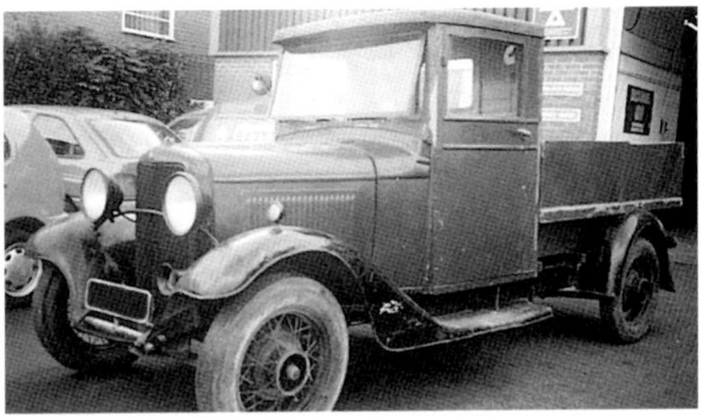

1935 Ford Model BF Pick-up, sidevalve 4-cylinder engine, 1 registered owner, fewer than 8,200 miles from new, unused since 1970, good mechanical condition.
£4,000–5,000 / $5,800–7,250 BKS
This vehicle was supplied new to York Racecourse with ambulance coachwork. It was converted to a pick-up in the mid-1960s.

1974 Ford Granada Estate Ambulance, accommodation for 1 stretcher or 2 sitting patients, ex-Devon Ambulance Service.
£2,000–2,500 / $2,900–3,600 BAm

1954 Morris Minor Van, subject of body-off restoration, side windows, finished in light green, original leather interior.
£2,750–3,300 / $4,000–4,800 COYS

1934 Peugeot 301C Dropside Truck, left-hand drive, disc-type steel wheels, wooden dropside body, finished in grey, original, good condition.
£3,500–4,200 / $5,000–6,000 CGC

◄ **1961 Willys/Wormald FC170 Jeep Q-Van,** 4-wheel drive, 9 forward gears, 4 reverse.
£4,000–5,000 / $5,800–7,250 BAm
This forward-control Jeep was used as a go-anywhere rescue vehicle by the New South Wales ambulance service.

Children's Cars

1950s Austin J40 Pedal Car, battery-powered lights, restored, finished in turquoise, grey interior, paintwork scratched.
£900–1,000 / $1,300–1,500 ⚒ M

c1920 Bugatti Grand Prix Pedal Car, by Eureka, spring front suspension, chrome-plated radiator, electric lights, enamel badge, adjustable seat and pedals, decorative dashboard layout, original, restored.
£1,600–2,000 / $2,300–2,900 ⚒ C

1920 Tri-Ang Brooklands-Type Pedal Car, light pressed-steel construction, windscreen, bulb horn, balloon tyres, large chrome hubcaps, repainted in red.
£225–275 / $325–400 ⊞ CARS

c1930 Bugatti Type 52 'Baby' Children's Car, 12 volt electric motor. 4-wheel hand-operated drum brakes, 16–18km/h top speed.
£15,000–18,000 / $21,750–26,000 ⚒ Pou
Around 90 of these Type 52 'Baby' Bugattis were built, of which 30 or so are thought to survive.

c1960 Citroën DS Pedal Car, by Eureka, pressed-steel construction, working head- and sidelights, integral grille, applied front bumper, rubber-treaded pneumatic tyres, steel wheels, chrome hubcaps, finished in original red, clear plastic windscreen and surround missing.
£600–700 / $1,000–1,150 ⊞ CARS

1920s Eureka-Style Tandem Pedal Car, probably Spanish, poor condition, many parts missing.
£1,500–1,800 / $2,150–2,550 ⊞ CARS

c1990 Ferrari 250 Testa Rossa Children's Car, ⅔ scale, fibreglass body, c400cc Honda petrol engine, electric starter, adjustable suspension, 70km/h top speed, finished in red with white nose band.
£7,000–8,400 / $10,200–12,200 ⚒ BKS

c1924 Two-Seater Pedal Car, by Lines Brothers, wooden body, metal chassis, chain drive, outside gear change, handbrake, lights, dickey seat with faux red leather covers, raised relief tin fascia with dial motifs, 4 wire spoked wheels, solid rubber tyres, finished in brown.
£1,800–2,200 / $2,600–3,200 ⚒ BKS

c1930 Pedal Car, by Lines Brothers, missing 2 cycle wings and steering wheel.
£300–350 / $440–520 ⚒ CGC

1980s MG TD Pedal Car, by Touchwood, plastic construction, treadle driven, electric lights, horn, spare wheel, finished in red.
£400–480 / $580–690 ⚒ BKS

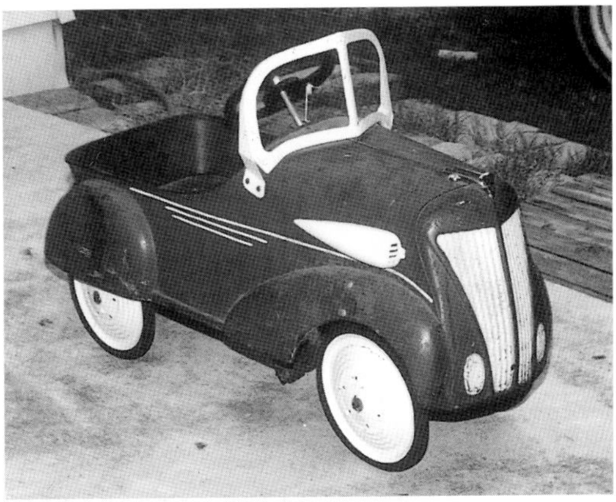

1936 Ford Pedal Car, by Steelcraft, pressed-steel body, integral wings, new windscreen surround, balloon wheels with inserted tyres, original green paintwork.
£850–950 / $1,250–1,375 ⊞ CARS

1920s/1930s Pedal Car and Bicycle Accessories, brass bulb horn, policeman's-helmet brass bell, chrome bulb horn, bell siren in box, battery siren in box.
£20–30 / $30–45 each ⊞ CARS

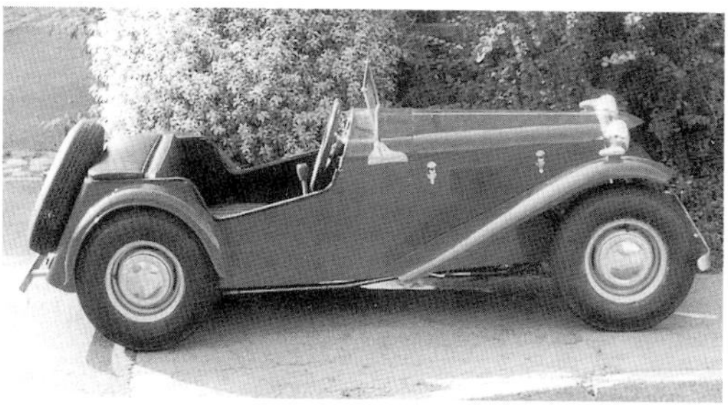

1997 MG TD Children's Car, ¾ scale, 90cc Honda engine, electric starter, Mini wheels, period lights, sidelamps and headlights.
£2,000–2,500 / $2,900–3,600 H&H

l. 1940s Renault-Type Pedal Car, by Eureka, pressed-steel construction, working headlights, balloon steel wheels with inset rubber tyres, chrome hubcaps, unrestored, finished in original dark red.
£950–1,150 / $1,380–1,700
r. 1960s Renault Pedal Car, by Eureka, one-piece pressed-steel body, working headlights, applied grille and front bumper, pressed-steel wheels, rubber treaded tyres, chrome hubcaps, windscreen missing, unrestored, finished in original cream and red.
£520–650 / $760–950 ⊞ CARS

1930s Triang Pedal Car, opening door, aero screen, restored, finished in blue and black.
£350–400 / $520–580 ⊞ JUN

c1955 Vanwall Grand Prix Pedal Car, by Triang, heavy-gauge metal body, wire wheels, rubber tyres, faux aluminium radiator nose, chromed petrol cap, bucket seat, finished in British racing green.
£400–480 / $580–690 BKS

1941 US Army Pursuit Plane Pedal Car, by Murray, pressed-steel construction, large rubber tyres, chrome steel wheels, applied decals, propeller turns when plane is pedalled, completely restored.
£2,000–2,500 / $2,900–3,600 ⊞ CARS
Reproductions of this pedal car are currently being manufactured in China, retailing at about £300.

Rolls-Royce Phantom 1 Child's Car, based on Springfield Roadster version, body formed from aluminium panels on plywood, working front suspension, brakes, rack-and-pinion steering and lights, opening dickey seat, dummy engine, variable-speed electric motor with forward and reverse, touring trunk, finished in cream over black.
£3,500–4,200 / $5,000–6,000 BRIT

1930s Triumph Dolomite Pedal Car, by Triang, opening door, aero screen, finished in cream and blue.
£720–900 / $1,040–1,300 ⊞ JUN

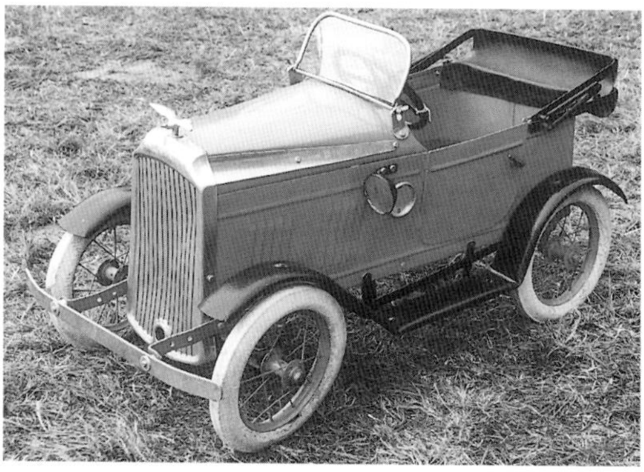

1930s Vauxhall Pedal Car, by Triang, opening door, aero screen, folding hood, flying-bird radiator mascot, wire wheels, finished in green and black.
£500–600 / $720–870 ⊞ JUN

Replica, Kit & Reproduction Cars

1987 Fergus Mosquito Aston Martin Ulster Replica, 1800cc BMC B-series engine, Morris Marina mechanical components including live axle, leaf springs and disc/drum brakes, 18in knock-on wire wheels, steel-tube chassis with built-in roll-cage and front/rear collapse zones, leather bonnet straps, aluminium louvred bonnet, fibreglass body, folding windscreen, aero screens, replica fuel and radiator fillers, Brooklands exhaust system, fluted bucket seats, full weather equipment, 1 of 7 factory-built cars produced by Fergus, very good condition throughout.
£10,000–12,000 / $14,500–17,400 ⚒ BKS

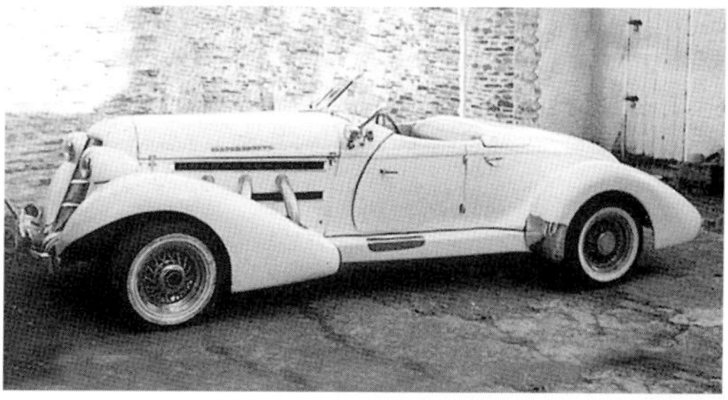

1970s Auburn 851 Speedster Replica, 5.7 litre V8 engine, automatic transmission, left-hand drive, box-section chassis, fibreglass body, golfer's compartment, foldaway hood with cover panel, finished in white, air conditioning, beige interior.
£10,500–13,000 / $15,250–18,850 ⚒ BKS

1981 Aurora GRX Cobra Replica, 4950cc V8 engine, 325bhp, side exhausts, wire wheels, full weather equipment, finished in black.
£11,000–13,000 / $16,000–18,850 ⚒ BRIT
Available as a fully-built vehicle only, the GRX Cobra was produced by Aurora Cars of Toronto. Based on a tubular spaceframe chassis, it was powered by a 5 litre Ford V8 engine, assembled and tested by the well-known tuners Holman and Moody.

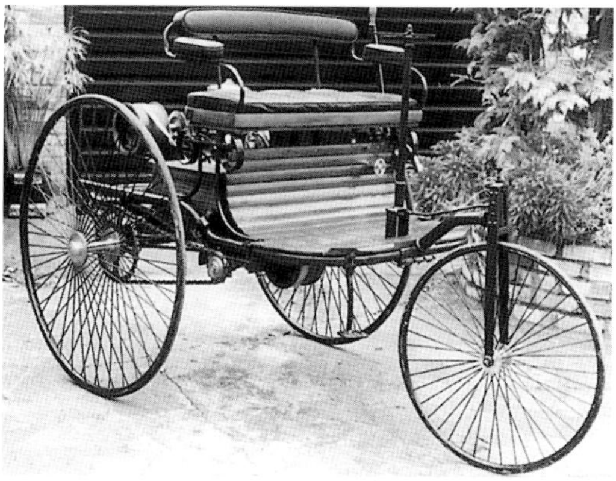

◄ **1986 Bentley Engineering Benz Patent-Motorwagen Centenary Replica,** single-cylinder engine, single-speed drive belt, tubular chassis, 'as-new' condition.
£23,000–26,000 / $33,300–37,700 ⚒ BKS

1960 Ferrari 250 GT California Spyder Replica, 5000cc Ford V8 engine, 300bhp (estimated), 4-speed automatic transmission, Ford running gear, tubular spaceframe chassis, fibreglass body panels, finished in red.
£40,000–45,000 / $58,000–65,250 ⚒ RM

A known continuous history can add value to and enhance the enjoyment of a car.

► **1995 Ferrari 308 GTB Replica,** 2800cc Pontiac V6 engine, fuel injection, automatic transmission, Compomotive split-rim alloy wheels, Ferrari badges, finished in red, electric windows, air conditioning, black leather interior piped in red.
£9,000–10,750 / $13,000–15,600 ⊞ HMC

1999 Ferrari F355 GTS Targa Replica, based on Toyota MR2, 2000cc 16-valve 4-cylinder engine, 5-speed manual gearbox, power steering, split-rim alloy wheels, twin targa roof panels, Ferrari badges, electric mirrors, finished in red, air conditioning, electric windows, remote central locking, cream and black leather interior.
£15,000–17,000 / $21,750–24,650 ⊞ HMC

► **1951 Healey Silverstone Replica,** converted from Tickford saloon, 2796cc Jaguar engine, twin 2in SU carburettors, aluminium bodywork, chromed brass grille, full-width retractable windscreen, aero screens, double duck tonneau cover, finished in green, tan leather upholstery, very good condition.
£9,000–11,000 / $13,000–16,000 ⚒ H&H

c1985 Ford GT40 Replica, 5735cc Chevrolet V8 engine, twin fuel tanks, competition fire extinguishers, finished in red, all instrumentation functional, some crazing evident on fibreglass bodywork.
£10,000–12,000 / $14,500–17,400 ⚒ BRIT

1986 Hutson MG TF Replica, 1.7 litre 4 cylinder engine, 4-speed manual gearbox, front disc/rear drum brakes, body formed from steel panels on ash frame, walnut dashboard, red leather interior.
£10,500–13,000 / $15,100–18,850 🚗 NCC

1969 Jaguar Atlantis A2 Roadster, built at a cost of over £40,000, 7400cc Chevrolet V8 engine, 500+bhp, Hurst shifter, Jaguar XJ6 suspension, Bilstein shock absorbers, automatic fire control system, all aluminium body, finished in white and red, full racing harnesses, red interior.
£6,000–7,000 / $8,700–10,200 ⚒ H&H

Colour Review

1929 Austin 12/4 Van, bodywork original and in very good condition, 1 of only 6 genuine 12/4 vans in existence.
£9,000–10,500 / $13,000–15,250 ⚒ CGC

1937 Foden DG4 4 x 2 Platform Lorry, Gardner 4-cylinder engine, 4-speed gearbox, servo-assisted brakes, 36 x 8 Firestone wheels and tyres, subject of complete chassis-up restoration, engine rebuilt, new cab at a cost of £8,000, excellent condition.
£12,000–15,000 / $17,400–21,750 ⚒ CGC

1909 Ford Model T Fire Chief's Chemical Car, 176.7cu.in 4-cylinder engine, 20bhp, lever gearbox with 2 forward speeds and reverse, contracting-band transmission brake, front and rear leaf springs, metal ribbon-type spring wheels, originally a roadster, converted to a fire chief's chemical car, period firefighting equipment including copper tank, fire hose and basket, twin brass fire extinguishers and lanterns, period bell and axe, correct E&J headlamps, excellent condition.
£25,000–30,000 / $36,250–43,500 ⚒ RM

1925 Ford Model TT Bus, 2890cc, seating for 10, barn find, restored, 12 volt electrics, excellent condition.
£12,000–14,000 / $17,400–19,800 ⚒ H&H

▶ **1931 Ford Model AA Fuel Truck,** 200cu.in, sidevalve 4-cylinder engine, 40bhp, manual gearbox, 4-wheel drum brakes, completely restored, finished in Gilmore Gas Company livery, excellent mechanical condition.
£15,000–18,000 / $21,750–26,000 ⚒ RM

1950 Ford E83W Dropside Truck, 4-cylinder sidevalve engine, partially restored, resprayed in blue and black, original condition.
£3,500–4,000 / $5,000–6,000 ⚒ BKS

▶ **1959 Morris Minor 1000 Van,** completely restored, only 400km covered since, bodywork, interior and chassis in excellent condition.
£6,000–7,000 / $8,700–10,200 ⚒ BKS

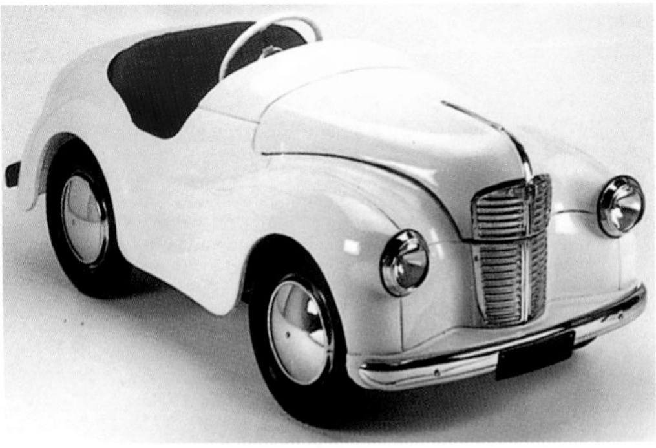

1950s Austin J40 Pedal Car, restored, working lights, pneumatic tyres, working handbrake, chromium-plated radiator, bumpers, headlight trim and wheel covers, finished in cream, red faux leather interior.
£1,200–1,400 / $1,750–2,150 ⚒ BKS

Bugatti Type 43 Pedal Car, by Eureka, chromed radiator, bumper stanchions, passenger grip and wheel nuts, chromed steering wheel and brake lever, wooden running boards, rubber tyres on solid disc wheels, finished in blue, tandem faux leather bucket seats, excellent condition.
£2,300–2,800 / $3,350–4,000 ⚒ BKS

Ford GT40 Junior Half-Scale Child's Car, by Mortarini, built in limited numbers to celebrate Ford's victory at Le Mans, Gulf Racing Team colours representing the 2nd-placed car driven by John Miles and Dennis Hulme, rear-mounted 2-stroke engine, fibreglass bodyshell, knock-off wheels, pneumatic tyres, 40+km/h top speed.
£5,000–6,000 / $7,250–8,700 ⚒ C

c1934 Daimler Pedal Car, by Lines Brothers, steel body, chromium-plated trim, faux soft top hood and black leatherette seat, opening driver's door, pneumatic tyres, spoked wheels, detailed fascia, Lucas King of the Road headlamps.
£1,600–2,000 / $2,300–2,900 ⚒ BKS

Mack Oil Tanker Pedal Car, by Steelcraft, modern reproduction of 1950s original, pressed-steel body, steel wheels, rubber treaded tyres.
£600–750 / $800–1,000 ⊞ CARS

Mercedes 300SL Pedal Car, by Toys-Toys.
£100–120 / $150–180 ⚒ CGC

1930s Triang Hepoch Pedal Car, restored, excellent condition.
£1,200–1,500 / $1,750–2,250 ⊞ JUN

1940s Willys MB Jeep, restored, good condition.
£5,000–6,000 / $7,000–8,700 IMPS

c1942 Canadian Chevrolet C8A Heavy Utility, 6-cylinder engine, 85bhp, 4-speed manual gearbox, single-speed transfer box, personnel carrier bodywork.
£6,000–7,000 / $8,250–10,250 IMPS

1950s Humber 'Pig' 1 Ton Armoured Personnel carrier, 4-wheel drive.
£4,000–4,500 / $5,800–6,500 IMPS

1956 Austin K9 Series II Radio Command Vehicle, 4-wheel drive.
£2,500–3,000 / $3,600–4,300 PC

1942 Diamond Tractor Unit, 529cu.in Rolls-Royce Hercules 6-cylinder engine, 106bhp, fitted with ballast body.
£3,500–4,000 / $5,000–5,800 MVT

1944 Morris Light Reconnaissance Car, 4-wheel drive, restored.
£10,000–12,000 / $14,500–17,500 IMPS

1950s Austin Champ, 2838cc Rolls-Royce 4-cylinder engine, 5-speed all-synchromesh gearbox, 4-wheel drive, restored.
£2,500–3,000 / $3,400–4,250 PC
The Austin Champ was made from January 1952 to December 1955, and just under 13,000 of all variants were built. Of this total, around 12,400 were the standard WN1 military version, such as this example.

1970s Landrover 3/4 Ton Ambulance, suitable for 2–4 stretchers, restored, good condition.
£2,800–3,500 / $4,000–5,000 IMPS

► **A Lancia advertising poster,** by Razzia, signed, linen-backed, c1990, 50 x 29½in (127 x 75cm).
£250–300 / $360–430 ⚒ RM

A Dodge advertising poster, by Fred Coley, linen-backed, fold marks, c1950s, 50 x 38in (127 x 96.5cm).
£300–350 / $430–500 ⚒ RM

A Veedol oil advertising poster, linen-backed, edges restored, French, 1936, 30 x 23in (76 x 58.5cm).
£300–350 / $430–500 ⚒ RM

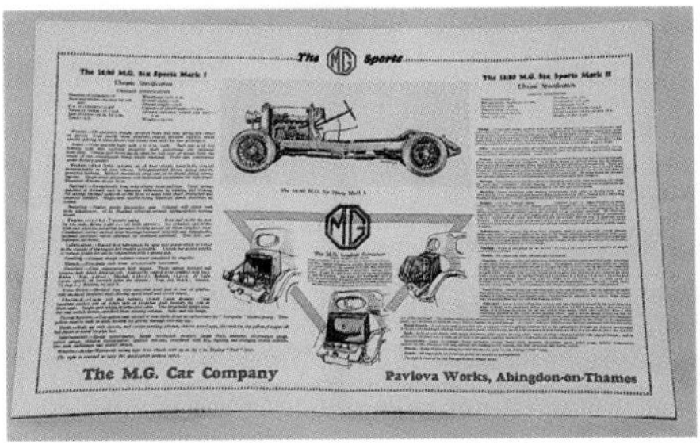

An MG Car Company brochure, for the 18/80 Mk I and Mk II, multi-coloured images of various models by Connolly, slight soiling on edges, otherwise good condition, 9 x 11in (23 x 28cm).
£40–50 / $75–90 ⚒ BKS

◄ **Original artwork for Louis Vuitton Classic advertising poster,** by Razzia, mixed media on canvas, French, 23½ x 31½in (59.5 x 80cm).
£6,000–7,000 / $8,700–10,200 ⚒ RM

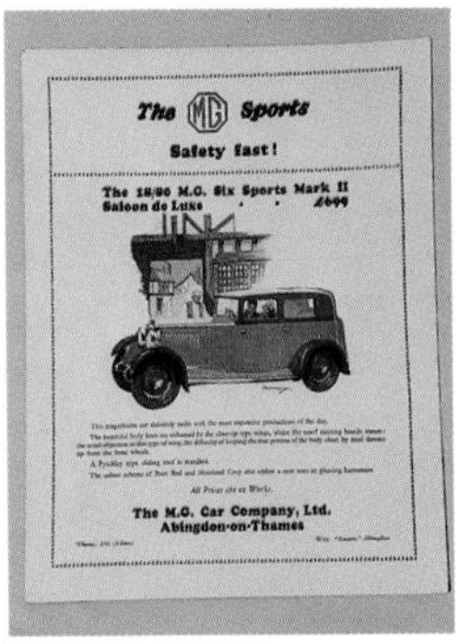

An MG Car Company brochure, for the 18/80 Sports Six Mk II, multi-coloured images of various saloons and touring models by Connolly, slight rubbing to folds, otherwise good condition, 9 x 11in (23 x 28cm).
£40–50 / $75–90 ⚒ BKS

A Gamages Motor Oil tin, 5 gallon capacity, c1930, 20in (51cm) high.
£120–150 / $180–225 ⊞ JUN

1940 Belhved Training Car, 150cc Villiers twin-port single-cylinder engine, kick starter, normal three driving pedals, left-hand drive, in need of some restoration.
£1,000–1,500 / $1,450–2,250 ⚒ H&H
This training car was manufactured in Italy for Alfa Romeo and was used to teach budding drivers the art of vehicle control.

A Jaguar fibreglass showroom figure of a leaping big cat, 1960s.
£350–400 / $500–580 ⊞ JUN

A Brooklands Automobile Racing Club members' badge, No. 69, by Spencers, London, excellent original enamel.
£500–600 / $725–850 ⚒ BKS

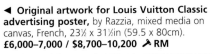

A Francorchamps circuit car badge, 3¼in (8.5cm) diam.
£85–100 / $125–145 ⊞ LE

A Royal Automobile Club of Italy car badge, 4½in (11.5cm) diam.
£90–100 / $130–145 ⊞ BCA

A bronze golfer mascot, by E. Bregeon, original, early 1920s.
£750–900 / $1,150–1,380 ⚒ RM

A silver- or German nickel-plated moon and owl mascot, mounted on a radiator cap, 1920s, 5½in (14cm) high.
£800–1,000 / $1,250–1,450 ⚒ BKS

A Rolls-Royce or Bentley cocktail bar, good-quality veneers, cut-glass drinks decanter, 4 cut-glass champagne glasses, 4 cut-glass whisky tumblers, cocktail shaker, 4 stacking nickel beakers, original condition, 27in (68.5cm) high.
£750–900 / $1,000–1,300 ⚒ BKS

► **A silvered bronze Coureur Automobile mascot,** in the form of a racing car driver behind the wheel, by Bocazzi, impressed full name on back, display mounted.
£2,750–3,250 / $4,000–5,000 ⚒ BKS

A French Sorcière 'Le Zanzibar' mascot, by Hector Planchot, depicting a witch and broomstick above a revolving disc with impressed numbers in red and black enamels, original broom intact, 1921–25.
£1,200–1,500 / $1,750–2,250 ⚒ BKS
This mascot was originally intended for use on a charabanc, where the seat numbers would be indicated where the witch's broom fell. It won a Certificate of Merit in the *L'Auto* magazine competition of 1921.

◄ **A French Croisière Noire African head mascot,** by F. Bazin, made to commemorate the crossing of Africa by a Citroën car in 1924/25, excellent condition, 6in (15cm) high.
£1,800–2,100 / $2,600–3,000 ⚒ RM

► **A monkey seated in a wheel mascot,** by Abit, original silver on bronze finish, c1924.
£750–900 / $1,100–1,300 ⚒ BKS

A Dutch white metal mascot in the form of a dancing woman, silver-plated, by J. Aland, stamped 'Gieteril Holland 'A'Dam', mounted on radiator cap.
£900–1,000 / $1,300–1,450 ⚒ RM

A French hollow-cast brass bulldog mascot, draped in a blanket, mounted on a display base, 1920s.
£1,000–1,200 / $1,450–1,750 ⚒ BKS

A French Bou Bou mascot, in the form of a monkey holding an electric lamp, déposé stamp to base, wired for electricity, original condition, mounted on wooden display base, c1925.
£900–1,100
$1,300–1,600 BKS

A French brass and silver plated Beccasine mascot, signed J. P. Pinchon, head made of composition material and spring mounted, 1930, 5in (12.5cm) high.
£2,750–3,250
$4,000–4,800 RM

A Coq Nain clear glass mascot, by René Lalique, moulded 'R. Lalique' signature to side of base, stencilled 'R. Lalique' under base, original condition, 1930s.
£1,000–1,200
$1,450–1,750 BKS

A Sphinx mascot, with ivory face and wings, by Sertorio, original condition, c1920.
£2,000–2,500
$2,900–3,600 BKS

A French Poisson Tropical tinted green glass fish mascot, c1930, 5½in (14cm) high.
£2,000–2,400
$2,900–3,500 BKS

A clear glass archer mascot, by René Lalique, catalogue No. 1126, etched signature below figure above base, catalogue etched number on base, original, 1920s.
£2,750–3,250
$4,000–4,800 BKS

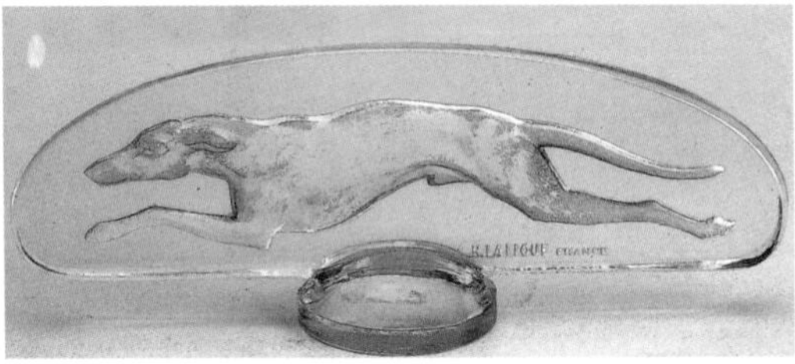

A clear glass Levrier greyhound mascot, by René Lalique, catalogue No. 1141, impressed wording 'R. Lalique', excellent original condition, 1920–30s.
£3,000–3,500 / $4,350–5,000 BKS

An Esso tiger petrol pump globe, 1960s.
£120–150 / $180–225 JUN

► **A scratchbuilt 1/12-scale model of a 1905 Rolls-Royce 20hp,** by G. Combes, made of brass, rubber and wood, leatherette interior, folding canvas top with cover, opening doors and bonnet, detailed engine, working steering, complete, very good condition, 18in (45.5cm) long.
£4,000–4,500
$5,800–6,500 RM

◄ **A BP petrol globe,** Shell petrol globe and Shell flag, 1930s–50s.
£200–250
$290–350 COYS

A Drew & Sons fold-fronted 4-person picnic set, including kettle and stand, burner, saucepan, enamel rectangular plates with gilt edges, stacking glasses, wicker covered condiment bottles, 2 ceramic-based sandwich boxes with nickel lids, 4 glasses, 2 wicker covered drinks bottles, china cups and saucers, preserves and butter jars, milk bottle, vesta case, corkscrew and cutlery.
£2,800–3,400 / $4,000–5,000 BKS

► **A Drew & Sons wicker 4-person picnic set,** including large sandwich box, 2 wicker covered drinks bottles, 2 thermos flasks, enamel plates, preserves jars, condiment bottles, 4 cups, 4 glasses, cutlery, excellent condition.
£1,700–2,000 / $2,450–2,900 BKS

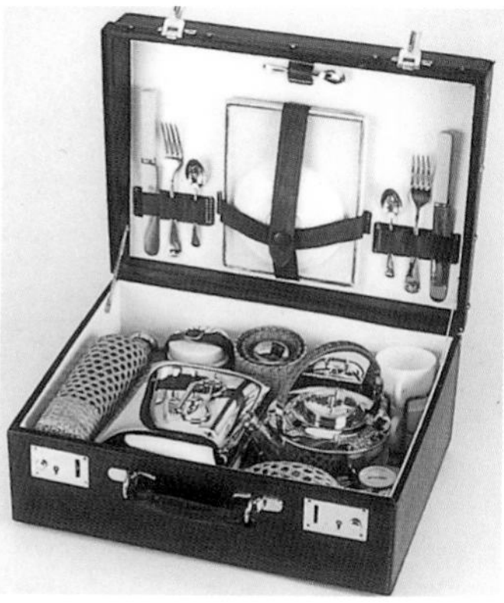

A Drew & Sons 2-person picnic set, including copper kettle and fretwork burner, sandwich box, food box, ceramic preserves jar, china cups, glasses, wicker-covered drinks bottle, wicker-covered milk bottle, ceramic mustard pot, cutlery, enamel plates, 1920s.
£1,500–1,800 / $2,200–2,600 ⚒ BKS

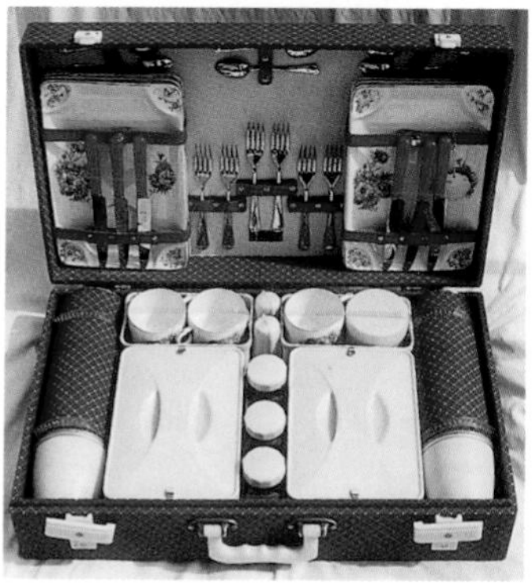

A Brexton tray picnic set, complete, 1950s.
£200–240 / $290–350 ⊞ PPH

A Drew & Sons leather-cased 4-person tea set, including kettle, fretwork burner stand and burner, sandwich box, fine bone china Bisto cups, matching saucers, glass milk bottle, teaspoons, assayed 1903 silver vesta case, interior finished in burr walnut veneer.
£850–1,050 / $1,250–1,550 ⚒ BKS

A leather-cased 6-person picnic set, including spirit kettle, wicker-covered bottles, nickel-plated containers and cups, square plates, beakers, preserve jars, sandwich boxes and salters, cutlery, very good original condition.
£1,300–1,500 / $1,900–2,150 ⚒ BKS

◄ A Coracle 4-person picnic set, including copper kettle and burner, wicker-covered drinks bottle, food boxes, ceramic-based sandwich boxes, glass milk bottles, glasses, 4 fine Bisto cups and saucers with gilt edges, gilt-edged rectangular plates, ceramic butter and preserves jars, glass salt and pepper bottles, original cutlery, 1920s, 34in (86.5cm) wide.
£2,200–2,600 / $3,200–3,800 ⚒ BKS

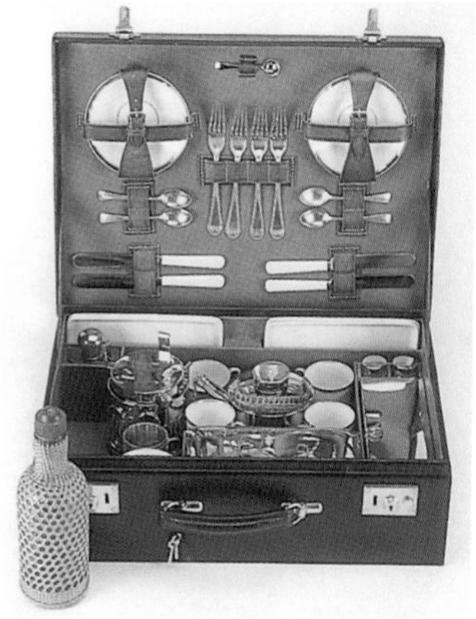

A Drew & Sons leather-cased 4-person picnic set, including kettle, fretwork burner stand and burner, wicker-covered drinks bottle, stacking nickel-plated tumblers, bone china cups and saucers, ceramic plates, milk bottle, ceramic butter jar, ceramic-based sandwich box, food containers, cut-glass condiment bottles, 1920s.
£1,500–1,800 / $2,200–2,600 ⚒ BKS

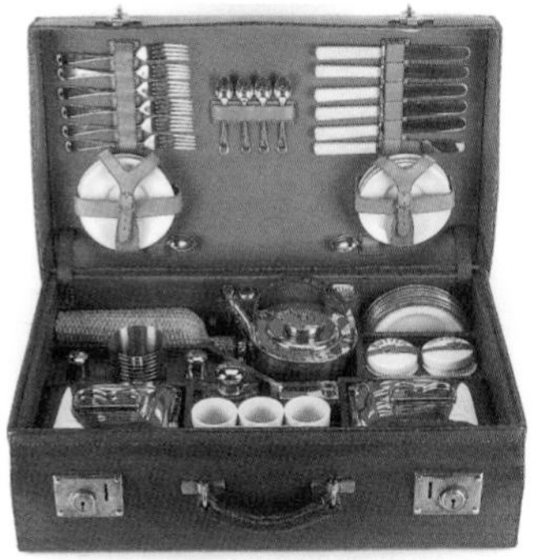

A suitcase-style 6-person picnic set, including copper kettle and burner, 6 cups and saucers, 6 side plates, 2 ceramic sandwich boxes, vesta case, raffia-covered lemonade bottle, 6 nickel-plated beakers, cutlery, 1930s, 36in (91.5cm) wide.
£1,000–1,200 / $1,450–1,700 ⚒ BKS

► A National Benzole enamel sign, 24in (61cm) diam.
£150–200 / $220–290 ⚒ CGC

A Wakefield Castrol Motor Oil enamel sign, 1920s, 16 x 20in (40.5 x 51cm).
£120–150 / $180–220 ⊞ JUN

An original Lagonda Cars agent's enamel sign.
£400–450 / $580–690 ⚒ CGC

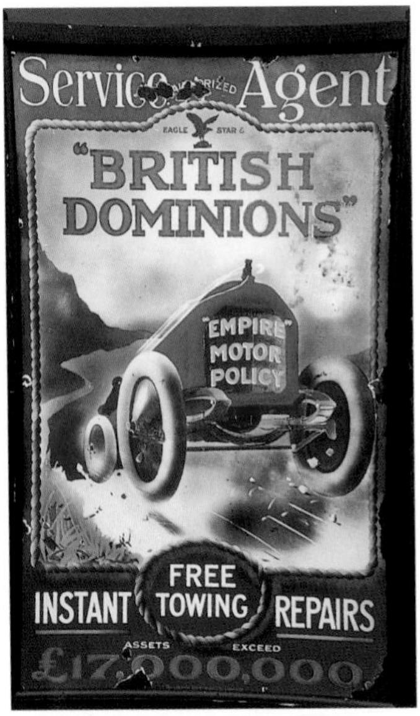

A British Dominions enamel sign, 1920s, 60 x 40in (152.5 x 101.5cm).
£1,400–1,700 / $2,000–2,500 ⊞ JUN

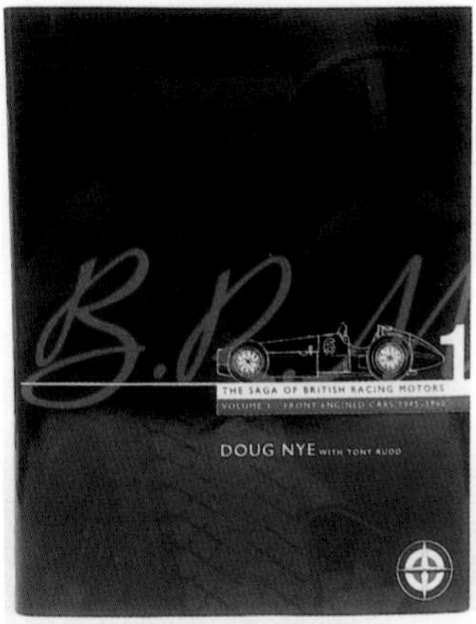

Doug Nye with Tony Rudd, *B.R.M. The Saga of British Racing Motors, Volume 1, Front Engined Cars 1945–1960*, 1994.
£60–75 / $80–100 ⊞ GPCC

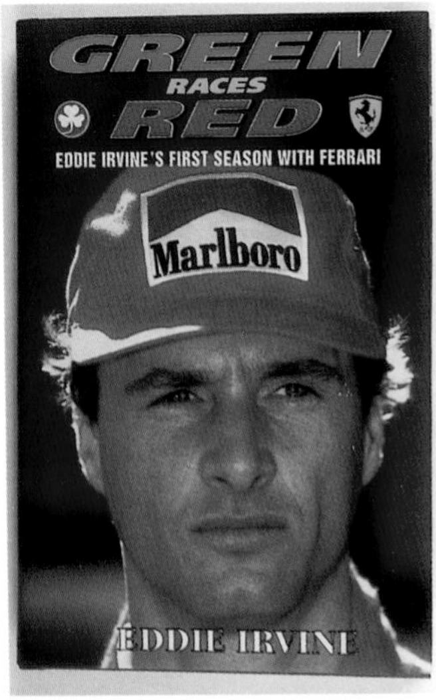

Eddie Irvine and Maurice Hamilton, *Green Races Red – Eddie Irvine's First Season with Ferrari*, signed by Eddie Irvine, 1996.
£40–45 / $60–65 ⊞ GPCC

A Ferrari wall plaque celebrating Ascari's 1949 Swiss Grand Prix win, surrounded by a winner's laurel, 42in (106.5cm) diam.
£1,000–1,200 / $1,450–1,740 ⚒ BKS

Anthony Prichard, *Maserati: a History*, 1976.
£20–25 / $30–35 ⊞ GPCC

Pierre Giorgio, Lancia 037 Ultimo Mito, Italian/English text, limited edition of 1,500 copies, signed by the author.
£75–85 / $110–125 ⊞ DT

A Castrol wall clock, in the form of an oil bottle top, commemorating the 1934 world record of 214.06km/h using Castrol oil.
£400–500 / $580–720 ⚒ BKS

Timothy Collings, *Schumacher – The Life of The New Formula 1 Champion*, signed by Schumacher and Collings, 1994.
£45–55 / $70–80 ⊞ GPCC

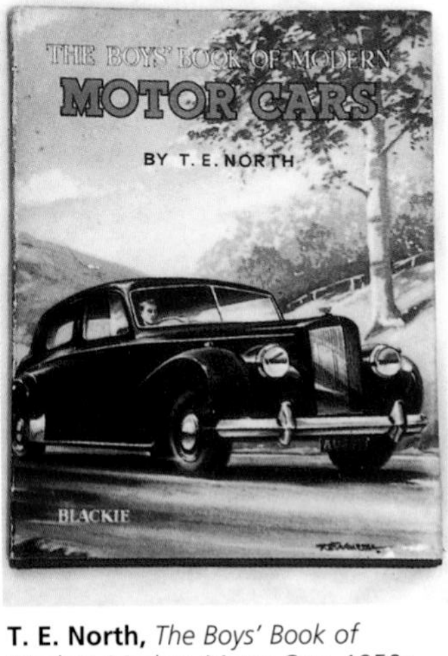

T. E. North, *The Boys' Book of Modern Modern Motor Cars*, 1950s.
£12–15 / $20–25 ⊞ JUN

◄ **Anthony S. Heal,** Sunbeam Racing Cars, with slip case, 1989.
£55–65 / $80–95 ⊞ DT

c1987 Jaguar SS100 Replica, 2786cc Ford 6-cylinder engine, automatic transmission, alloy wheels, full weather equipment, fibreglass bodywork, finished in red, full complement of instruments, wood-rim steering wheel, grey interior.
£3,000–3,500 / $4,400–5,200 ⚒ BRIT

c1968 Jaguar C-Type Replica, XK-type engine, proprietary chassis, alloy bodywork.
£13,000–16,000 / $18,850–23,200 ⚒ COYS
The XK120 did so well on the racetrack and in rallies that it was developed in 1951 into the C-Type for competition. With an uprated XK engine, lightweight tubular chassis and more aerodynamic alloy body, the C-Type promptly won the world's greatest sports car race at Le Mans and, when fitted with revolutionary new disc brakes, went on to win again in 1953.

1987 Autotune Aristocat Jaguar XK120 Replica, 4.2 litre Jaguar XK engine, automatic transmission, spaceframe chassis, finished in cream, red interior, engine in need of service, good condition.
£1,500–1,800 / $2,170–2,550 ⚒ BKS

1976 Heritage Jaguar C-Type Replica, 3.8 litre Jaguar double-overhead-camshaft straight-6 engine, 4-speed manual gearbox, wire wheels, finished in British racing green.
£16,000–18,000 / $23,200–26,000 ⚒ BARO

Cross Reference
See Colour Review (page 152)

1989 LR Roadsters Jaguar D-Type Replica, 4.2 litre Jaguar XK engine, straight-port cylinder head, triple Weber 45DCOE carburettors, overdrive gearbox, tubular-steel backbone spaceframe chassis, steel-braced fibreglass bodywork, full-width windscreen, 10,000 miles covered since built, very good condition throughout.
£18,000–20,000 / $26,00–29,000 ⚒ BKS

► 1990 LR Ram Jaguar D-Type Replica, 3.8 litre Jaguar double-overhead-camshaft 6-cylinder engine, triple 2in Weber carburettors, converted to unleaded fuel, Jaguar 4-speed manual gearbox with overdrive, alloy/steel road wheels, finished in British racing green.
£14,000–16,000
$20,300–23,200 ⚒ BARO

1992 Proteus Jaguar XKSS Replica, 4.2 litre Jaguar straight-6 engine, triple Weber carburettors, 6-branch exhaust manifold, aluminium body tub, finished in Italian racing red, tan leather interior, 3,000 miles from new, 'as-new' condition throughout.
£30,000–35,000 / $43,500–50,750 ⚒ COYS
Jaguar's XKSS, a true supercar of the 1950s, was in essence a lightly road trimmed version of the Le Mans winning D-Type. Only 16 of these machines were built, examples finding their way to the USA, Australia and Cuba.

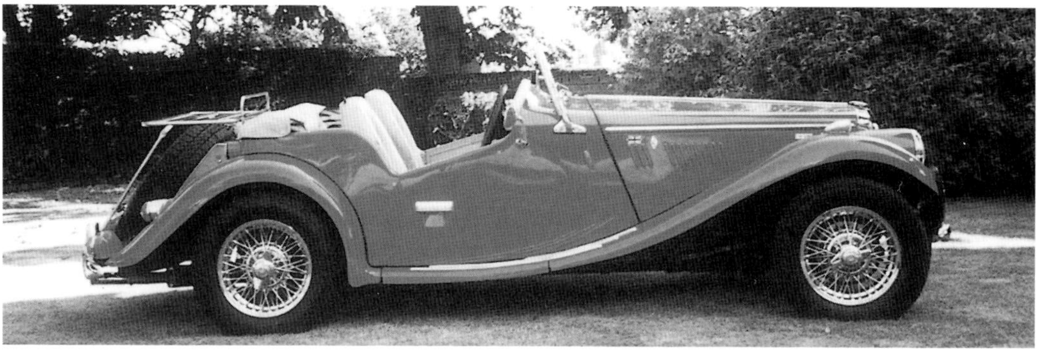

1986 Naylor MG TF Replica, 1.7 litre 4-cylinder engine, 4-speed manual gearbox, front disc/rear drum brakes, chrome wire wheels, body formed from steel panels on ash frame, finished in red, walnut dashboard, leather interior.
£10,500–13,000 / $15,100–18,850 NCC

1970 NG TF, built from new and reconditioned parts, MGB running gear, chrome wheels, finished in red, magnolia interior, walnut dashboard, nominal mileage since completion, 'as-new' condition.
£8,000–9,000 / $11,600–13,000 ⚒ BARO

1955 Benoit Porsche 550 Spyder Replica, professionally built, tuned flat-4 engine, finished in silver, red interior, 2,000 miles since completion, excellent condition throughout.
£14,000–16,000 / $20,300–23,200 ⊞ HCL

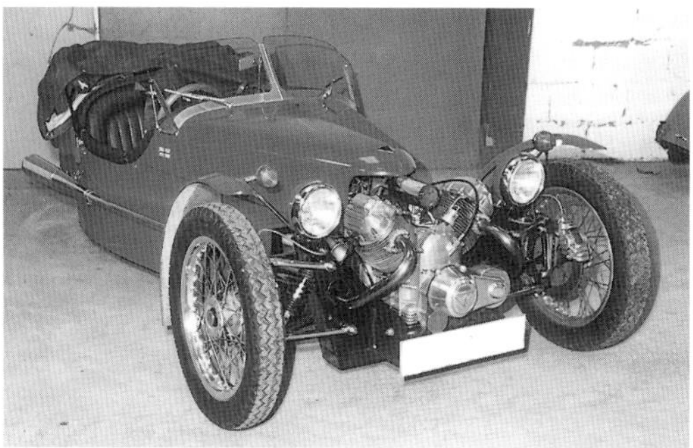

◄ **1984 Triking Sports Three-Wheeler,** 948cc Moto Guzzi V1000 GS air-cooled V-twin engine, 5-speed manual gearbox, detachable hood, tonneau cover, finished in red.
£6,500–7,500 / $9,400–10,875 ⚒ BKS

Restoration Projects

1935 Bentley 3½ Litre Sports Saloon, coachwork by Thrupp & Maberly, partially restored, in need of finishing, wings and running boards need painting and refitting, brown leather interior, sound condition.
£14,000–16,000 / $20,300–23,200 ⊞ RCC

1929 Bugatti Type 46 Two-Door Saloon, 5.5 litre overhead-camshaft straight-8 engine, complete with all ancillary components, original seats and instruments.
£30,000–35,000 / $43,500–50,750 ⚒ COYS
The 46, or Petit-Royal as the model became known, was Bugatti's solution to producing a luxury chassis based on the principles laid down by the Royale. To this end, the smaller car shared much of the mechanical layout of its larger brother. The Type 46 was clothed with all manner of different coachbuilt body styles, from the elegant flowing lines of the Profilée coupé to the practical and stylish British-built saloons. This example is thought to have been bodied for use by the Czechoslovakian Army during the 1930s. It features a 'waterfall' grille, which shrouds the original to give the car a more modern 1930s appearance.

1937 Brough-Superior Drophead Coupé, coachwork by Atcherley, Terraplane engine, minus bonnet, radiator grille and headlamps, finished in green, sound and original.
£4,500–5,400 / $6,500–7,800 ⚒ BARO
Although better known for its motorcycles, Brough-Superior also built cars between 1935 and 1937, originally using a straight-eight Hudson chassis. After some legal wrangling with Railton, however, Brough-Superiors were only produced in six-cylinder form.

1960 Ferrari 250 GTE 2+2 Coupé, coachwork by Pininfarina, chassis no. 3363, chassis, body, blue leather interior and some windows, everything else missing.
£3,000–3,500 / $4,400–5,200 ⚒ BKS
Apparently, this 250 GTE was discovered in an alleyway near the Ferrari factory a few years ago.

1939 Jaguar SS 1½ Litre Saloon, 1 of last SS Jaguar saloons built, complete.
£5,750–6,750 / $5,700–9,500 COYS

1954 Jaguar XK120 SE Drophead Coupé, 3400cc engine to correct specification, but not original, cylinder head overhauled and converted to unleaded fuel, 54-spoke wire wheels, converted to right-hand drive, bodyshell rebuilt and resprayed in grey some years ago, some micro-blistering, red interior, approximately £28,000 spent on parts, in need of finishing.
£16,000–18,000 / $23,200–26,000 H&H

1956 Jaguar XK140 Drophead Coupé, left-hand drive, unrestored, complete.
£15,500–17,500 / $22,800–25,400 TWY

1963 Jaguar Mk II, 3.4 litre engine, manual/overdrive gearbox, in need of complete restoration.
£1,000–1,200 / $1,500–1,750 CGC

Cross Reference
See Colour Review (page 152)

◄ **1958 Land Rover Series 1 LWB Station Wagon,** chassis and bulkhead sound and complete, bodywork straight, finished in deep bronze green with correct grey 'elephanthide' vinyl interior, c72,000 miles from new.
£1,500–1,700 / $2,170–2,450 CGC

1962 Lotus Elite S2 Coupé, 1220cc Coventry Climax engine, twin carburettors, ZF manual gearbox, front screen and steering wheel cracked, bumpers correct and undamaged, finished in red, red interior, paintwork blemishes, barn find, fewer than 25,000 miles from new.
£13,000–16,000 / $18,850–23,200 H&H

◄ **1962 Maserati 5000GT Coupé,** coachwork by Frua, double-overhead-camshaft V8 engine, finished in metallic red, original special-order chamois upholstery, 12,700km from new, complete and running, totally original.
£200,000+
$290,000+ ⚒ BKS
In seven years of production (1959–66), Maserati made only about 34 examples of the 5000GT. It was the last Italian car to be sold only as a chassis. This example is one of only two to be bodied by Frua. According to factory archives, the car was completed in June 1962 and appears to have remained at the works until the 1963 Geneva show, where it adorned the Maserati stand.

1960 Mercedes-Benz 190SL Roadster, 1.9 litre overhead-camshaft 4-cylinder engine, 4-speed manual gearbox, right-hand drive, supplied with new factory front wings and bonnet apron, factory hard and soft tops, steering overhauled 1978, exterior trim replated, stored since 1979, complete.
£5,000–6,000 / $7,250–8,700 ⚒ BKS

1937 MG TA Midget, 1292cc overhead-valve engine, semi-elliptic springing all-round, front hydraulic dampers, Lockheed 9in hydraulic brakes, partly dismantled.
£3,300–3,900 / $4,800–5,700 ⚒ BKS
The TA was introduced in 1936 as a faster successor to the PB Midget, with a pushrod engine derived from that of the contemporary Wolseley Ten. Altogether larger and roomier, it had a wider track and the new 94in-wheelbase chassis was boxed for extra stiffness around the engine and gearbox.

1971 Morgan 4/4 Modsports, engine, gearbox and axle fitted, cylinder head, exhaust system, Weber carburettor and brakes in need of installation, minus camshaft, followers, instruments and lights, 2 boxes of parts including alloy interior panels, fibreglass air dam, brakes and differential.
£2,500–3,000 / $3,600–4,400 ⚒ BKS
This Morgan was built by specialists Rutherford-Berry Engineering as one of a series of three intended solely for Modsports racing. The standard chassis was stiffened by adding a square-tube spaceframe, the increased rigidity enabling superior multi-link rear suspension to be adopted. The standard Morgan sliding-pillar front suspension is braced in the usual fashion, and the steering rack is a 'quick' Hillman Imp item. The engine is a 2 litre overhead-camshaft Ford 4-cylinder unit with a Formula Ford 2000 head.

1936 Morris 12/4 Special Coupé, original engine, leatherette-covered roof, false chrome pram irons, rear-mounted and housed spare wheel, blue leather interior in good condition, 2 owners and 42,000 miles from new, barn find, sound.
£2,750–3,250 / $3,900–5,400 ⚒ CGC

► **1937 Morris Cowley Six Commercial,** aluminium-panelled coachwork over wooden frame, spare wheel housed over cab, radiator calormeter, interior complete with the exception of one instrument, 41,000 miles recorded, barn stored for over 30 years, sound condition throughout.
£700–800 / $1,000–1,150 ⚒ CGC

1953 Porsche 356 1500S Cabriolet, left-hand drive, some restoration carried out to floor, battery pans, bulkhead and sills, new beige leather interior, carpets and mohair hood, engine dismantled, all body parts to complete restoration, over £20,000 spent, 1 of only 150 1500S Cabriolets built.
£8,000–10,000 / $11,600–14,500 BKS

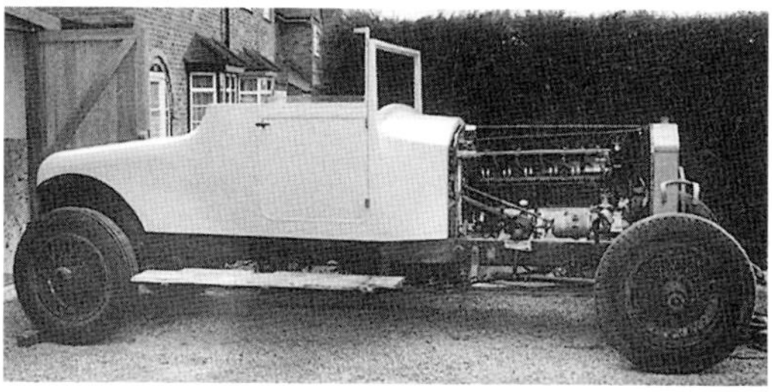

1928 Rolls-Royce Phantom I Golfer's Coupé, originally fitted with Thrupp & Maberly limousine de ville coachwork, new coachwork constructed late 1980s, 4 spare wheels, engine bay/gearbox undershield set, split-type front windscreen, electric klaxon horn, dashboard instruments, stored for last 8 years, substantially complete.
£7,000–9,000 / $10,200–13,000 BKS

1939 Rover 16 Tickford Drophead Coupé, 2147cc engine, finished in cream with beige interior, 1 of 36 built, of which 6 thought to survive, running.
£1,200–1,400 / $1,750–2,000 H&H

1932 Wolseley Hornet Special, rebuilt from chassis up, all mechanical elements refurbished/replaced as necessary, running condition, radiator, scuttle, dashboard and instruments installed, body to be restored, but with some new timber and metal sections, 4 good wings, hood frame.
£5,000–6,000 / $7,250–8,700 BKS

Introduced in 1930, the Hornet featured Wolseley's bevel-driven overhead-camshaft six-cylinder engine in a lengthened Morris Minor chassis. Its power-to-weight ratio was exemplary among contemporary 1.3 litre cars, the smooth and flexible six pulling from walking pace to more than 60mph. The model was revised for 1932 with a shortened, chain-driven overhead-cam engine and a four-speed 'silent third' gearbox. Increased performance was offered by the twin-carburettor Hornet Special, and the latter chassis rapidly became that of choice for the multitude of independent coachbuilders already using the Hornet as the basis for sporting two-seaters.

1951 Sunbeam Talbot 90 Drophead Coupé, finished in metallic blue, substantially complete, in need of complete restoration.
£700–800 / $1,000–1,200 CGC

c1958 Zim Four-Door Limousine, left-hand drive, in need of complete restoration.
£400–500 / $580–720 NOW

Microcars

1961 BMW Isetta 300, 297cc engine, resprayed in red and white, grey interior, recently refurbished, 26,000 miles from new, very good condition throughout.
£2,250–2,700 / $3,300–3,900 H&H
The BMW Isetta was introduced in 1955, and during an eight-year production run a total of 161,000 models were built. Originally, it came with a 247cc engine, but later models had a 297cc unit.

1959 Heinkel Cabin Cruiser, 198cc engine, sunroof, completely restored, finished in blue, blue and grey interior, 27,000 miles from new, excellent condition throughout.
£3,500–4,000 / $5,000–5,800 H&H
A former aircraft company, Heinkel began building engines and scooters after WWII, and in 1955 announced a rear-engined, three-wheeled bubble car. The engine was a single-cylinder, four-stroke air-cooled unit of 175cc, which later was increased to 198cc, when the car was also made available with twin rear wheels. In 1958, the design was sold to Dundalk Engineering in Ireland, and later was built in England by Trojan.

c1962 Velorex 350, Jawa twin two-stroke engine, sequential four-speed gearbox and reverse, chain final drive, left-hand drive, canvas body and seating, restored.
£2,000–2,500 / $2,900–3,600 ⊞ NOW
The Velorex was originally designed for the disabled, but in fact was very hard for the able-bodied to get into!

1962 BMW Isetta 300, 297cc engine, 4-speed manual gearbox with reverse, sunroof, chrome luggage rack, completely restored, finished in red, red and cream interior, fewer than 49,000 miles from new.
£3,750–4,250 / $5,400–6,200 ⊞ HMC

1958 Messerschmitt KR200 Cabriolet, Sachs 200cc engine, 4-speed manual gearbox, completely restored, finished in turquoise, mohair hood, white-piped turquoise interior, original steering wheel, fewer than 11,500 miles from new.
£4,500–5,500 / $6,500–8,000 ⊞ HMC

1958 Messerschmitt KR200 Cabriolet, older restoration, resprayed in metallic red and silver, black hood and interior.
£3,750–4,500 / $5,600–6,500 CGC

Dealer prices

Miller's guide prices for dealer cars take into account the value of any guarantees or warranties that may be included in the purchase. Dealers must also observe additional statutory consumer regulations, which do not apply to private sellers. This is factored into our dealer guide prices. Dealer cars are identified by the ⊞ icon; full details of the dealer can be found on page 330.

Racing & Rallying

1907 Napier 60hp Model T21 7.7 litre Racing Two-Seater, older restoration, brass lighting and acccessories, finished in green, museum displayed since 1972, VCC dated.
£90,000–100,000 / $130,500–145,000 ⚒ BKS
Napiers were the first racing cars to wear British racing green, a works car being fielded as early as 1900 in the Paris-Toulouse-Paris race, driven by salesman Selwyn Francis Edge. However, racing honours were heaped on Napier in 1902, when its 30hp four-cylinder car, again driven by Edge, won the prestigious and previously French-dominated Gordon Bennett race. Sales of Napier cars were buoyed by that success, and the rather pushy Edge did not shy from the publicity. The opening of the Brooklands circuit in 1907 gave Edge a new opportunity to demonstrate the superiority of Napier cars. That year, he drove a 60hp six-cylinder car for 24 hours at that circuit, exceeding an average speed of a mile a minute. This particular car was rebuilt in the 1960s to represent Edge's car. The 60hp 7.7 litre chassis had been one of six ordered by the Nizam of Hyderabad in 1907, and had never been bodied.

◄ **1920 Ford Model T Arnold Thinnes Racer,** 3000cc engine, finished in red, black interior, running condition.
£8,500–9,500 / $12,300–13,800 ⚒ H&H
This car competed in quarter-mile dirt-track races in the USA during the 1920s.

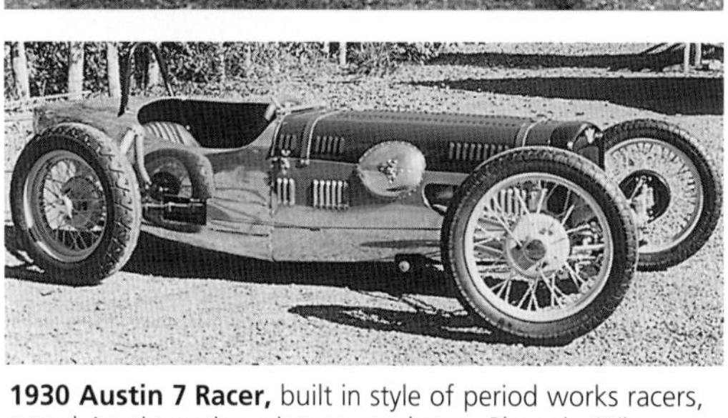

1930 Austin 7 Racer, built in style of period works racers, tuned Austin engine, vintage crankcase, Phoenix 1½in pressure-fed crank, Renault R4 rods and special pistons, oversized valves, high-lift camshaft, reprofiled cam followers, strengthened block, extensive porting, Mk 22 Marshall cabin blower, 4-speed gearbox, suspension by flat springs front and rear, split and widened independent front axle, offset rear axle, 16in racing rear wheels, boxed vintage short chassis, vintage-style aluminium body, polished aluminium finish with British racing green bonnet.
£11,000–13,000 / $16,000–18,850 ⚒ COYS

1931/36 Alvis Silver Eagle Special, modified 1936 Speed 25 engine, 146bhp, Silver Crest gearbox, 12/70 rear axle, Silver Eagle front axle, hydraulically-operated large Alfin drums, adjustable Hartford dampers, original chassis, road registered, demountable cycle wings and lamps, bills for work in excess of £30,000, very good condition.
£44,000–49,000 / $65,000–71,500 ⚒ COYS
This car has been a competition machine all its life, and its hybrid specification includes components from several Alvis models. Supplied new in 1931 as a complete Silver Eagle rolling chassis with shortened wheelbase, it was raced with a single-seater body until WWII, little history being known thereafter until it was purchased in the early 1960s by vintage racer Tony Bianchi. Over the next ten years, Bianchi gradually developed it, fitting first a two-seater body, then, in 1969, a single-seater body. The car's many successes include winning the coveted Brooklands Society Trophy in the 1970s.

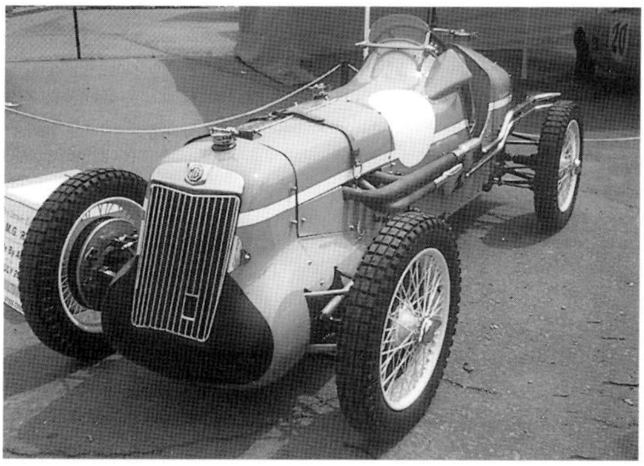

1935 MG R-Type, 750cc engine, restored, original factory-numbered under-trays, many original spares, finished in blue, blue interior.
£125,000–140,000 / $180,000–203,000 ⚒ H&H
The R-Type was the swan song of Abingdon's celebrated designer, H.N. Charles. It had a revolutionary Y-shaped chassis with all-round independent torsion-bar suspension. Power came from a supercharged engine based on the Q-Type, and the whole package was offered for what was then an exceptionally low price – £750. The successful Bellevue Garage – a name synonymous with the MG marque – bought this car originally. It was debuted at the May 1935 Brooklands JCC International Trophy with Doreen Evans behind the wheel. After a gruelling three hours, her tenacious driving brought the car home in seventh place, second in class, immediately behind the R-Type of Sir Malcolm Campbell, at an average speed of 80.63 mph. Later that same year, Doreen broke the Shelsley Walsh hill-climb ladies record with an outstanding 45.4 seconds. She followed this success with a third place in the 1936 Brooklands Outer Circuit handicap race, but her greatest challenge in the R-Type was later that year in the demanding 262 mile International Trophy Race when the car caught fire at half-distance. Doreen baled out of the fiery racer and escaped unscathed, while the R-Type lived to fight another day.

Cross Reference
See Colour Review (page 193)

1950 500cc Two-Way Cooper-Jap Mk IV Formula 3 Racing Single-Seater, JAP engine tuned for methanol fuel, new engine cover, Norton gearbox, original ZF differential, all-aluminium bodywork, red upholstery.
£14,000–16,000 / $20,300–23,200 ⚒ BKS
The long-chassis Two-Way Coopers such as this were intended to provide their owner/drivers with a car that was speedily convertible from running with a 500cc single-cylinder F3 engine to being fitted with anything up to an 1100cc V-twin.

Kieft-Vincent Monoposto Racer, Vincent 1000cc V-twin engine, Manx Norton gearbox and clutch, restored early 1990s, finished in red, excellent condition throughout.
£12,000–14,000 / $17,400–20,300 ⚒ BKS
Kiefts took part in circuit racing, endurance racing, speed hill climbs and sprints, and power units used included MG, Coventry Climax and Vincent V-twin, as used in the Rapide/Shadow range of motorcycles. Kieft enjoyed most success in Formula 3, with the 500cc Norton-engined racing cars that Stirling Moss campaigned.

1957 Cooper-Climax T43 Formula 2/Hill-Climb/Sprint Single-Seater, 1496cc overhead-camshaft Coventry Climax FWB 4-cylinder engine, 2 twin-choke Weber carburettors, 106bhp, complete with alternative final-drive ratio Citroën/ERSA-type gearboxes and 3 spare cast-alloy Cooper wheels, plus an assortment of miscellaneous spare components, museum displayed for many years, 2 owners from new, almost entirely original.
£45,000–50,000 / $65,250–72,500 ⚒ BKS
This Cooper-Climax was campaigned with distinction over many years by Patsy Burt, Britain's leading woman hill-climb and sprint driver of the 1950s–70s. Between 1958 and 1963, she used it to gain 11 fastest times of the day, 14 second-fastest, two course records, 56 Ladies' awards, 24 class wins, 18 second places in class and 17 thirds, two Continental course Ladies' records, one UK class record, and 22 further fourth and fifth placings. She also drove this car to finish fourth overall in the hard-fought 1959 RAC British Hill-Climb Championship.

◀ **1958 PLW Formula Junior,** Type 103m 4-cylinder Fiat engine, twin 40DCO28F carburettors, c80bhp, completely restored, excellent condition throughout.
£17,500–19,500
$25,400–28,300 ⚒ COYS
The Italian Formula Junior racing series was set up in 1958 by Giovani Lurani, with the purpose of finding and cultivating new up-and-coming talent. To keep costs to a minimum, the single-seater cars were to be small – 400kg for 1100cc engines or 360kg for 1000cc engines – and constructed using components from production vehicles. This car, the only example of its type, was built by Renato Cazzulani, Juan Manuel Fangio's mechanic.

1961/96 Ferrari 156 Sharknose Replica, 2 litre Dino 206 engine, dry-sump lubrication, revised ignition system, 180bhp, replica chassis.
£90,00–100,000 / $130,500–145,000 ⚒ COYS
This car was built for Chris Rea's film *La Passione*.

1961 Elva 200 Formula Junior Racing Single-Seater, restored 1988, race-ready condition, believed to be the last example built.
£17,500–19,500 / $25,400–28,300 ⚒ BKS
Following the success of his first, front-engined Formula Junior Elva, designer Frank Nichols turned to a mid-engined layout for its successor, the Elva 200. Although it handled well, the 200 was handicapped by the works' preference for the BMC A-series engine, at a time when the Ford 105E engine was clearly superior. Twenty or so cars are thought to have been built, before the arrival of the Elva 300 in 1961.

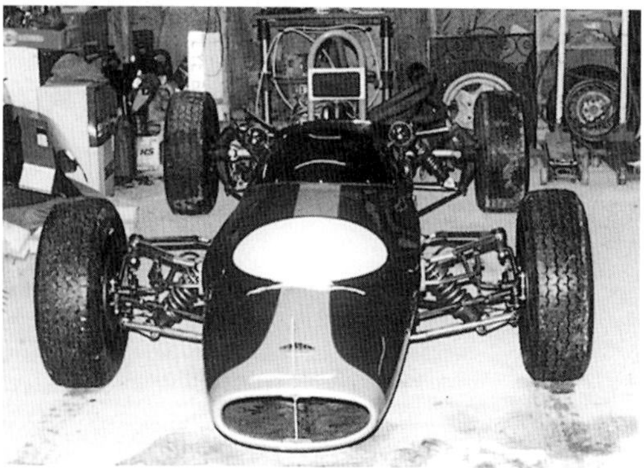

1968 Russell Alexis Mk 14 Formula Ford Single-Seater, stored 20 years, restored, only 2 shakedown runs since, good condition.
£8,000–10,000 / $11,600–14,500 ⚒ BKS

▶ **1968 McLaren M10B,** Formula 5000 Chevrolet engine, 475bhp, older restoration, finished in blue.
£65,000–75,000 / $94,250–108,750 ⚒ COYS

1967 Cooper Maserati T86 V12 Single-Seater, Maserati 36-valve Tipo 10 V12 engine, Hewland transaxle, magnesium-electron-skinned monocoque, unused for almost 30 years, ex-works Jochen Rindt/Jacky Ickx/Ludovico Scarfiotti, last Cooper ever to contest a Formula One Grand Prix, totally original.
£130,000–145,000 / $188,500–210,500 ⚒ COYS
For the British Grand Prix at Silverstone in 1967, Cooper introduced a new car, the T86. This is that first new car, F1–2–67. On its first outing at Silverstone, Jochen Rindt was half a second per lap quicker than team-mate Rodriguez in the T81B, eventually retiring with a sick engine. The car was progressively modified throughout the season, and at the Italian GP at Monza Rindt gave his all to finish a respectable fourth from 11th on the grid. The up-and-coming Jacky Ickx won himself a drive at Monza and, having scored one World Championship point for the team with his sixth place in a T81B, was asked back to drive at the United States Grand Prix in the T86. The car's last appearance for the works was in the hands of the ex-Ferrari driver Ludovico Scarfiotti, in the 1968 South African GP at Kyalami. The T86 was acquired by Colin Crabbe for his Antique Automobiles team and was driven on two occasions by former works Cooper driver Vic Elford. In his hands, it made history as the last Cooper ever to run in a Grand Prix, at Monaco in 1969, when Elford managed to bring the car home in seventh.

1970 Lola T192 Formula A/5000, 305cu.in Chevrolet V8 engine, Hewland DG300 5-speed transmission, front suspension by unequal-length A-arms, rear suspension by lower A-arms and top-links, ex-Mark Donahue/Penske Racing.
£30,000–36,000 / $43,500–52,200 RM
In 1968, Lola introduced the T140, a spaceframe-chassis car using mechanicals from the T70 Mk III sports sports racing car. A year later came the T190, which had a more modern, aluminium monocoque chassis that was riveted and bonded together. A smaller flywheel, relocated starter motor and dry-sump lubrication lowered the centre of gravity, and contributed to a total weight of 1,290lb – 200lb less than the T140. The rear suspension was redesigned to reduce castor and camber variations. A Hewland five-speed gearbox was fitted to the Chevrolet 305cu.in V8. In testing, Mike Hailwood lapped Oulton Park faster than the Formula One record. In the races that took place in the Formula A/5000 series, the T190 had a propensity to swap ends, which was cured by lengthening the wheelbase.

1972 Brabham BT38 Formula Two Single-Seater, minus engine and sundry electrics, restored, 'as-new' condition.
£3,750–4,500 / $5,400–6,500 BKS
The BT38 was Brabham's first monocoque customer car and the first Formula Two Brabham built after the company was bought by Bernie Ecclestone.

1980 Singer Sprint Car, 368cu.in Chevrolet V8 engine, fuel injection, race exhaust headers, electronic ignition, dry-sump lubrication, 500bhp (estimated), Halibrand 'in-and-out' gearbox, tubular steel chassis, coil-over-damper suspension, JFZ disc brakes, Halibrand-style wheels, Goodyear Eagle racing tyres, alloy side-mounted oil tank, restored 1997.
£11,000–13,000 / $16,000–18,850 RM

1973 Vollstedt-Offenhauser Indianapolis Racing Single-Seater, 160cu.in Drake-Offenhauser engine, turbocharger, 850–900bhp at 90in manifold boost pressure or 710–760bhp at 75in boost, over 1000bhp available at maximum manifold pressure, subject of no-expense-spared restoration by original constructor, new main fuel cell, onboard extinguisher system, Simpson five-point driver harness, removable headrest, brake discs, turbocharger and fuel-injection system valves, fewer than 3 hours running since rebuild, accompanied by B29 starter engine, all original body moulds, spare radiator, two sets of tyres, fuel injection system parts and jetting adjusters, plus numerous suspension, brake and structural items, last run 1998.
£23,000–26,000 / $33,300–37,700 BKS
Canadian-born Indianapolis racing car constructor Rolla Vollstedt produced his first rear-engined car – with Offenhauser four-cylinder engine – as a reaction to the invasion of Cooper and Lotus cars during 1963. By 1973, Vollstedt's Champcars were heavily infuenced – as was all American construction – by the proven pace and success of the wedge-shaped McLaren M16s and Eagles, which employed similar turbocharged 2.65 litre Offenhauser four-cylinder engines to the unit in this Indycar.

◀ **1982 Alfa Romeo Tipo 182 Grand Prix Single-Seater,** V12 engine, 540bhp, carbon-composite monocoque, completely rebuilt 1991, used only for demonstration purposes since, starter kit, race-ready.
£70,000–80,000 / $101,500–116,000 BKS
This is the car in which Andrea de Cesaris took his single pole position from 208 Grand Prix starts. It was at long Beach in 1982, and there was no fluke in de Cesaris sitting in the top spot, because he also led the first 14 laps, then tucked in behind Lauda for the next 18, before he crashed. This car was not used again by the works which, during the year, switched to a turbocharged engine.

1986 Ferrari F1/86 Grand Prix Formula One Racing Single-Seater, last run 1992, good condition in all respects.
£130,000–145,000 / $188,500–210,000 ⚒ BKS
This ex-works Formula One Ferrari contested the 1986 Formula One World Championship season. Driving this car – chassis serial 089 – Michele Alboreto secured three World Championship points by finishing fourth behind his team-mate Stefan Johansson in a sister F1/86 at the Belgian Grand Prix on the Francochamps circuit. Subsequently, Johansson scored four more points for Ferrari by bringing this car home to third place in the 1986 Austrian Grand Prix on the Osterreichring.

1986 Benetton-BMW B186 Formula One Single-Seater, 1.5 litre BMW M12/13 4-cylinder engine, turbocharger, c650bhp, accompanied by a substantial quantity of spares including suspension parts, bracketry, remote starter, fuel coupling and two front wheels, unused for a year, complete and runnable.
£40,000–50,000 / $58,000–72,500 ⚒ BKS
This Benetton-BMW B186 was built new for Gerhard Berger to campaign during the 1986 Formula One World Championship season. It is believed to be one of only two surviving B186s.

1990 Swift FR90 Formula Renault, believed never to have been raced and only tested on 2 occasions, suspension never set up for track use, rear wing still mounted in original position (later regulation changes called for wing to be positioned closer to rear wheels), new starter motor, brakes overhauled, finished in white, polished aluminium wings, stored for over 7 years, 'as-new' condition.
£5,000–6,000 / $7,250–8,700 ⚒ COYS

1988 Camel Lotus 100T, fitted with externally complete exhibition engine, excellent condition.
£40,000–50,000 / $58,000–72,500 ⚒ COYS
This car was raced by three-times World Champion Nelson Piquet in the 1988 season. His best race placing came at the beginning of the season – third in the Brazilian and San Marino Grands Prix – and at the end, when again he was third in Australia, against the all-conquering McLaren MP4s of Prost and Senna. Piquet achieved four other scoring finishes, to set against only one outside the top six, and seven retirements.

1965 Iso Bizzarrini 5300 Berlinetta, coachwork by Bertone, restored 1978–80, little use since, 5.4 litre Chevrolet V8 engine rebuilt 1996.
£220,000+ / $320,000+ ⚒ BKS
This Bizzarrini is a veteran of the 1965 Le Mans 24-hour race and, most significantly, it completed the event, taking ninth place overall and winning the over-5 litre category in the hands of Régis Fraissinet and Jean de Mortemart. The distance it completed within the 24 hours was assessed as 4,063.570km, giving an average of 169.313km/h.

◄ **1966 Porsche 906,** 2 litre flat-6 engine, 225bhp, 5-speed manual gearbox, 4-wheel independent suspension, 4-wheel disc brakes, tubular spaceframe chassis, fibreglass bodyshell.
£200,000+ / $290,000+ ⚒ RM
The Porsche 906 won its class first time out at the Daytona 24-hour race, then repeated this feat at the 12-hour Sebring race, beating the main opposition in its class, the Ferrari Dino. In 1966, a 906 won the Targa Florio outright. Three long-tail versions (*Langhecks*), were fitted with fuel injection and longer noses to compete at Le Mans, where one of them came fourth overall, winning the 1600–2000cc class and Index of Performance.

1970 Porsche 917K, 4.5 litre air-cooled flat-12 engine, 4-speed manual gearbox, 4-wheel disc brakes, 4-wheel independent suspension, ex-Steve McQueen.
£900,000+ / $1,305,000 RM
Porsche introduced its 4.5 litre 917 in 1969, to which Ferrari countered with their 512 series. The two represented the fastest and most powerful cars of their era. Both would exceed 140mph on the Mulsanne Straight at Le Mans. At the end of 1969, the factory handed over the responsiblity of running their 917 coupés to the British Gulf Oil sponsored JWA team. At one test session, JWA achieved better handling at speed by cutting the 917 tails short and raking them up at an angle. These coupés were called '*Kurz*' –'short' in English – and the new bodywork was known thereafter as the Type 917K. In 1970, Steve McQueen set out to make a film about Le Mans, and spared no expense to make it as realistic as possible, hiring well-known sports car drivers such as Jo Siffert, David Piper, Richard Attwood, Derek Bell, Brian Redman and Vic Elford. Siffert was also tasked with supplying Porsche 917s and 908s, Ferrari 512s, Lola T70s, Alfa T33s and sundry Porsche 911Ss, a Chevron B16 and even a full-race Corvette. McQueen's production company bought this particular Porsche 917K for the film. It was painted in Gulf colours and played a starring part in the movie, leading the first lap on to the Mulsanne Straight.

1970 Ferrari 512S, 4496cc double-overhead-camshaft light-alloy V12 engine, 550bhp, 5-speed manual gearbox, 4-wheel ventilated disc brakes, double-wishbone independent front suspension, rear suspension by single upper arms and lower wishbones, 1 of of 22 built, of which 16 known to survive.
£900,000+ / $1,305,000+ RM

1948 Veritas Rennsport, modified BMW 328 engine and chassis, completely restored to original specification at a cost of c£100,000, finished in silver, blue upholstery, near concours condition.
£150,000+ / $217,500+ COYS
Veritas was founded in Hausern by three former German soldiers in March 1947. The Allies had restricted German companies to only reconditioning engines with a capacity of over 1 litre. As a result, many pre-war German engines received a new lease of life and were subjected to intense development far beyond that for which they were designed. The most popular unit to receive such attention was the BMW 328. It was to this engine that the Veritas trio turned when constructing their first car. Their experience told, and the car won the 2 litre class at its debut at Hockenheim in 1947.

Auction prices

Miller's only includes cars declared sold. Our guide prices take into account the buyer's premium, VAT on the premium, and the extent of any published catalogue information relating to condition and provenance. Cars sold at auction are identified by the icon; full details of the auction house can be found on page 330.

1990 TWR-Jaguar XJR-11, new 3.5 litre V6 engine, twin turbochargers, not raced since 1991, running order.
£150,000+ / $217,500 BKS
The Tom Walkinshaw Racing series of rear-engined 'Big Cat' Jaguar XJR coupés achieved notable success through the late 1980s/early 1990s. Not only did these carbon-composite-chassis racers add two further great Le Mans victories to Jaguar's record at that venue,, but they also gained Britain three World Championship titles in 1987, 1988 and 1991. This particular car was made by the team as a lighter and more nimble 'short-distance' qualifying-round alternative to the established 7–7.5 litre V12-engined XJR-9s and -10s that the organisation had deployed thus far.

1952 RGS Atalanta-Jaguar, finished in British racing green, good condition.
£80,000–90,000 / $116,000–130,500 COYS
Having competed for four years in his Lea Francis-engined Atalanta Special, for his second car, Major Richard Gaylard Shattock used a similar Atalanta chassis, but replaced the front coil springs with torsion bars and moved the rear brakes inboard. Fitted with the engine and gearbox from the first special, the car was launched in 1952 as the RGS Atalanta-A and offered in kit form. Over the next four years the prototype served as a test-bed, carrying a stark aluminium body with cycle wings. For 1953, the Lea Francis engine was swapped for a 3442cc Jaguar twin-cam six. With over 250bhp on tap, performance was greatly improved, but top speed was limited by the unaerodynamic body. In 1953, however, RGS had begun selling a fibreglass shell, moulded from an alloy HWM body. This was adapted to the existing alloy tub, two prominent fins being added at the rear. It was a solution that worked, the car's top speed increasing from 120 to 138mph.

1955 Moretti 750S Mille Miles Barquette, 750cc 4-cylinder engine, twin Weber carburettors, 75bhp, 4-speed manual gearbox, 4-wheel hydraulic drum brakes, Borrani wire wheels, multi-tubular chassis, aluminium bodywork,
£60,000–70,000 / $87,000–101,500 ⚒ Pou
It is thought that only two or three examples of this car were built.

◄ 1955 Porsche 550RS Spyder, non-original 4-camshaft Typ 547/2 engine, road-car gearbox, all-aluminium body, finished in metallic light blue, black interior trim, 12,500 miles from new, original in most respects, running.
£300,000+ / $435,000 ⚒ BKS

1955 Cisitalia Abarth Boano Spyder, 1248cc, 4-cylinder engine, 90bhp (estimated), 4-speed manual gearbox, 4-wheel drum brakes, completely restored, 1 of only 8 cars produced.
£45,000–50,000 / $65,250–72,500 ⚒ RM

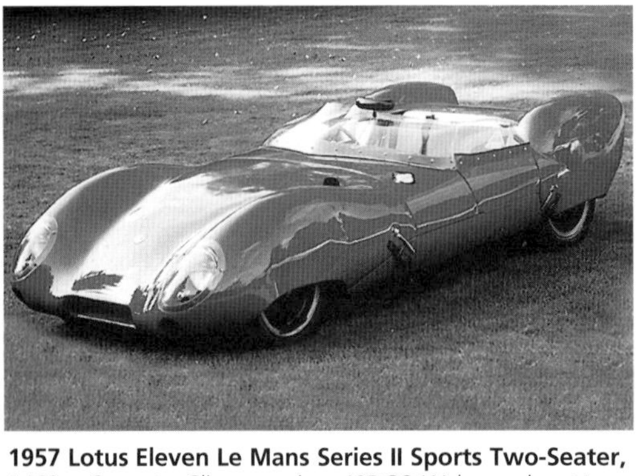

1957 Lotus Eleven Le Mans Series II Sports Two-Seater, 1460cc Coventry Climax engine, 40DCO Weber carburettors, magnesium wheels, stored for 20 years, rebuilt 1989, used only twice a year since, period specification.
£40,000–45,000 / $58,000–65,250 ⚒ BKS
Many customers bought their Lotuses in kit form to save purchase tax and leave more in the kitty to go racing. Top specification in 1957 was the Le Mans Series II with 1460cc FWB Coventry Climax engine, although in its day, this offered only marginal advantage over the 1100cc, 110bhp FWA Coventry Climax engine because of the tendency of the FWB to shed its connecting rods at anything over 6,000rpm.

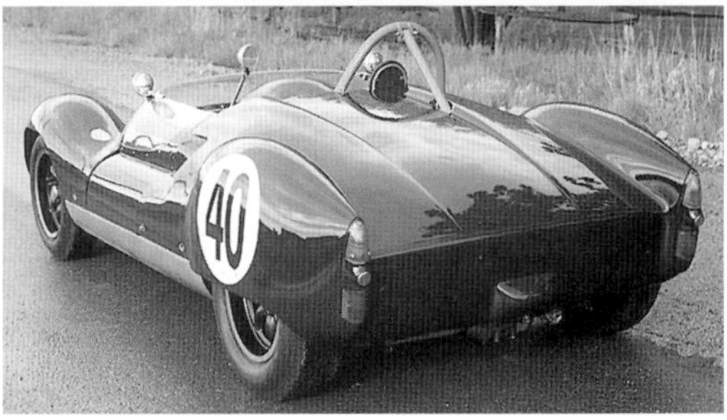

1961 Cooper Monaco-Climax Mk III Sports-Racing Two-Seater, 2.7 litre 'Indy' Coventry Climax FPF 4-cylinder engine, 4-wheel coil-spring suspension, original chassis, equipped originally with pointed-fin 1961-type Monaco Mk III bodyshell, subsequently replaced by Mk II-type bodywork, running condition.
£62,000–69,000 / $90,000–99,000 ⚒ BKS
It was in November 1958 that the original Cooper Monaco Mk I sports-racing car, with its offset driving position, was announced to replace the centre-seat 'bobtail' small-capacity models. The new design was named Monaco after Maurice Trintignant's victory there in the 1958 Grand Prix, driving a Rob Walker Formula One Cooper. The original Mk I model combined coil-and-wishbone front suspension with a transverse-leaf rear end, and was clothed in stubby aluminium bodywork. During 1959, the new Monacos were immediately successful, displaying a slight advantage over the contemporary front-engined Lotus 15s. The Monaco Mk IIs of 1960 featured longer-nosed bodywork, but retained the transverse leaf-spring rear suspension, while the Mk IIIs emerged for 1961, based upon the World Championship-winning Formula One 'Lowline' running gear with all-coil-spring suspension.

1963 Elva Porsche Mk VII, 1679cc double-overhead-camshaft Porsche 547 4-cylinder engine, 183bhp, 5-speed transaxle, 4-wheel independent suspension, tubular spaceframe chassis, only left-hand-drive example built.
£60,000–70,000 / $87,000–101,500 ⚒ RM
The Elva Porsche was born of an idea by an American Porsche distributor, Oliver Schmidt. In late 1962, Schmidt and his team laid down plans for a high power-to-weight-ratio race car, enlisting Porsche's support for the project. The factory supplied a modified 1679cc engine with a horizontal fan. It was dubbed the Type 547/5A. For the lightweight chassis, they chose the British Elva Mk VII sports-racer. The engine generated more than 180bhp, and Porsche engineers feared that the chassis would not be able to handle the power. To avoid problems, the Mk VII's rear chassis was widened and reinforced to accept the Porsche powerplant. Schmidt took delivery of his prototype Elva Porsche in August 1963. After a trial run, it was entered in the 500 mile race at Road America in September. Driven by Bill Wuesthoff and Augie Pabst, the car finished first on the podium, beating Cobras, RS-60s and Ferrari GTOs, to the surprise of everyone.

1968 Abarth OT1600, rear-mounted double-overhead-camshaft engine, modified Fiat 850 transaxle, Fiat 850 floorpan, fibreglass body, finished in Italian racing red, in need of recommissioning, original condition.
£35,000–40,000 / $50,750–58,000 ⚒ COYS

► 1971 McLaren M8C Can Am Car, 5490cc GM V8 engine, fuel injection, Hewland LG600 5-speed transaxle, front suspension by upper and lower A-arms, rear suspension by lower A-arms, top links and radius arms, restored.
£100,000–120,000 / $145,000–174,000 ⚒ RM
The M8C was the customer version of McLaren's all-conquering 1969 works cars. It featured a riveted and bonded aluminium monocoque chassis with four-wheel independent suspension and Chevrolet V8 engine driving the rear wheels through a Hewland transaxle. Steering was by rack-and-pinion, and the entire assembly was clothed in fibreglass open two-seater bodywork.

1964 Crusader VSR, 1600cc flat-4 engine, 85bhp, 4-speed manual gearbox, torsion-bar front suspension, rear swing-axles, EMPI magnesium wheels, 1 of only 7 built, restored 1999, race-ready.
£9,000–10,800 / $13,000–15,600 ⚒ RM
Designed by Chuck Tatum, the Crusader VSR – Volkswagen Sports Racer – was a joint project between Joe Vittone, owner of Engineered Motor Products, Inc. (EMPI) and Tatum, co-owner of Crusader Cars. At the time, EMPI was the world's largest producer of speed equipment for Volkswagens and had a reputation for making them go fast. Vittone wanted a robust chassis in which to demonstrate the possibilities of large-displacement VW engines in SCCA racing. By basing the racer on inexpensive, yet reliable, VW components, it was hoped that once the Crusader VSR proved itself, the SCCA would create a new class of sports-racing cars. In fact, rules were proposed based predominantly on the Formula Vee rulebook, specifying two-seat bodywork and mid-engine location. Any VW transaxle could be used, and wheels and tyres were open.

1969 Lola T163A Can Am Car, 510cu.in Chevrolet V8 engine, fuel injection, 810bhp, Hewland 5-speed manual gearbox, 4-wheel independent suspension, 4-wheel ventilated disc brakes, completely restored, spare set of body panels, four gear sets, race ready, 3rd overall in 1969 Championship, race winner in Vintage Can Am events.
£160,000–180,000 / $232,000–261,000 ⚒ BKS

◄ 1971 Gypsy Dino P271, Ferrari 206 Dino engine, Lucas slide-throttle fuel injection, dry-sump lubrication, 230bhp, Hewland FT200 gearbox, steel monocoque, completely restored, excellent condition throughout.
£45,000–50,000
$65,250–72,500 ⚒ COYS

1973 Chevron B23/36 Sports-Racer, 2 litre Ford BDA engine, Lucas fuel injection, B23 chassis, lightweight body from later B36, chassis completely restored with many new panels, Lockheed brake system rebuilt, new wiring harness, new starter, new Aeroquip plumbing all-round, new Bilstein shock absorbers, set of original Chevron wheels, set of Speedline wheels, 'as-new' condition.
£53,000–59,000 / $77,000–85,500 ⚒ BKS

▶ **1974 Abarth Sport 2000 SE027 Racing Sports Prototype,** 2 litre double-overhead-camshaft 4-cylinder engine, 4-valves per cylinder, fuel injection, 5-speed transaxle, restored, correct factory specification, thought to be 1 of 3 built.
£60,000–70,000 / $87,000–101,500 ⚒ BKS

1948 Connaught L2 Road-Racing Sports Two-Seater, 1.8 litre engine, completely restored.
£44,000–50,000 / $63,500–72,500 ⚒ BKS
The L-Type Connaught was built to accommodate the 1767cc Lea-Francis four-cylinder engine. Its sports bodywork was fashioned by Leacroft of Egham, and the engine was super-tuned with high-lift camshafts, special pistons, quadruple Amal carburettors and dry-sump lubrication to produce some 102bhp.

▶ **1955 Alfa Romeo 1900 Super Sprint Competition Berlinetta,** coachwork by Zagato, completely restored, high-compression race engine, finished in dark red, grey leather interior, concours condition.
£140,000–160,000 / $203,000–232,000 ⚒ BKS
Launched in 1951, the 1900 Sprint utilised the 100bhp engine of the 1900TI sports saloon. The model was upgraded for 1954 as the Series 2, gaining a 1975cc engine and five-speed gearbox. It was joined by the Super Sprint featuring revised styling and a 115bhp engine. Although Pinin Farina and Touring between them accounted for the bulk of 1900 Sprint and Super Sprint production, other coachbuilders could not resist the attractive package from Alfa Romeo. This Competition Berlinetta is the work of Zagato.

1972 UOP Shadow Mk III, 509cu.in Chevrolet V8, fuel injection, Hewland LG600 5-speed transaxle, front suspension by upper and lower A-arms, rear suspension by lower A-arms, top links and radius arms, riveted and bonded aluminium monocoque, restored 1995, race-ready.
£140,000–160,000 / $203,000–232,000 ⚒ RM
The trend toward more powerful and faster Can Am cars was a hallmark of the series since its start in 1966. By 1972, neck-snapping acceleration and speeds in excess of 200mph were not unheard of. From the word go, the UOP Shadow Mk III was quick. Despite its battles with the Porsche 917/10s, which had close to 1,000hp, the Shadow (driven by the likes of Jackie Oliver) scored several top-five finishes and a second place at Mid Ohio. For the last race of the 1972 season, in an attempt to emulate the turbocharged Porsches, the Shadow was fitted with a twin-turbo big-block Chevrolet engine, which produced in excess of 1,000hp.

1949 OSCA MT4, 1350cc engine, finished in Italian racing red, original instrumentation, tan interior, 3rd car built, original, good condition.
£90,000–100,000 / $130,500–145,000 ⚒ COYS
OSCA was founded late in 1947 by the remaining Maserati brothers once their commitments to Officine Alfieri Maserati SpA Modena had been fulfilled. They began constructing their first new car early in the new year, designating it MT4 (Maserati Tipo 4).

1952 Jaguar C-Type, 3442cc double-overhead-camshaft 6-cylinder engine, twin 2in SU carburettors, 210bhp, 4-speed manual gearbox, independent front suspension by torsion bars with telescopic dampers, live rear axle located by torsion-bar-sprung trailing arms, torque-reaction link and telescopic dampers, 4-wheel drum brakes, restored, finished in metallic bronze, ex-Juan Manuel Fangio, completely original condition.
£550,000+ / $217,000+ ⚒ RM
The C-Type was an astounding success in its first race, Le Mans 1951. Stirling Moss set the fastest race lap; Peter Walker and Peter Whitehead scored a dominant victory, breaking the old distance record with over an hour to go and finishing 75 miles in front of the second-place Talbot. Later, C-Types swept the podium in the Dundrod Tourist Trophy, and Moss captured two events at Goodwood. The C-Type's success set up a clamour for customer cars, and production began in 1952. Its combination of competitiveness and reliability made it the ideal sports-racer, and demand far exceeded supply. This particular example was owned originally by Juan Manuel Fangio and enjoyed an active racing career in South America.

1956 Alfa Romeo Giulietta Sprint Veloce Zagato, rebodied by Zagato 1958, older restoration, finished in red, correct black vinyl upholstery, very good condition.
£47,000–54,000 / $69,500–79,500 ⚒ BKS
The Bertone-styled Giulietta Sprint coupé debuted in 1954 and was powered by a 1.3 litre twin-cam four. To satisfy demands for increased performance, upgraded Veloce versions of the Sprint and Spider were introduced for 1956. The new Sprint Veloce was soon being raced with outstanding success, winning its class in the 23rd Mille Miglia and finishing 11th overall, while the Alpine Rally was won outright. Despite its many competition successes, the Giulietta SV remained a modified production car and, as such, was considered by some to be overweight. Zagato had already established itself as a champion of lightweight coachwork when it got the chance to put that experience into practice on a crashed Giulietta SV. Zagato's new aluminium coachwork combined low-drag functionality with beautiful lines and reduced weight. On the SV Zagato's debut at Monza, in 1956, Leto won the Intereuropa Cup. For the next few years, Zagato produced several more special SVs for private customers, later examples featuring lower roofs and faired-in headlamps. Production of SV Zagatos is thought to have numbered 19.

◀ **1959 Austin-Healey Mk I Sprite,** built specifically for Austin-Healey Owners' Club Class C races for road-going cars, A-series engine enlarged to 1340cc, Special Tuning 649-profile camshaft, Stage 3 head, c100bhp, Jack Knight straight-cut gearbox, uprated braking system, converted to right-hand drive, full roll-cage, fire extinguisher system.
£7,500–9,000
$10,875–13,000 ⚒ COYS

1961 Austin-Healey 3000 Works Rally Car, cast-iron block, 12-port cylinder head, correct triple SU HD8 carburettors, Girling and Dunlop disc brakes, works hardtop, restored 1995, resprayed in original red, black interior, Motolita wood-rim steering wheel, 39,000 miles from new, largely original.
£54,000–62,000 / $79,500–90,000 ⚒ BKS
This car was first used competitively by works drivers Peter Riley and Tony Ambrose in the Swedish Midnight Sun Rally. Confounding the Scandinavians' scepticism about its suitability, the Big Healey proved more than a match for the forest stages, finishing second in class and 12th overall. Later, it was crewed by works drivers Pat Moss and Ann Wisdom to a class win in the Tour of Corsica, before serving as Peter Riley and Ann Wisdom's 'wedding car' when the couple married in March 1962.

1961 3.8 Litre Jaguar E-Type Competition Roadster, 1 of 7 factory-prepared competition-specification right-hand-drive roadsters, 310bhp, 4.2 Series I close-ratio gearbox, period competition suspension with bronze alloy bushes, front suspension pick-ups revised to maintain geometry at race ride heights, steering rack solidly mounted and repositioned to eliminate bump-steer, rear radius arms cranked and fitted with rose joints, rear cradle solidly mounted to monocoque, front and rear adjustable dampers, anti-roll bars, aluminium foam-filled fuel tank, final-drive oil cooler, aluminium doors, bonnet, boot lid, boot floor and hardtop, engine and gearbox rebuilt, rear subframe overhauled, new brakes, new alloy radiator, new exhaust system, new camshaft, rebuilt differential, new fire extinguisher system, c£27,000 spent on rebuild, race-ready.
£275,000+ / $399,000+ ⚒ BKS

1964 Porsche 904 Carrera GTS, 1966cc aluminium 4-camshaft flat-4 engine, 180bhp, 5-speed manual gearbox, independent wishbone suspension with coil-spring/damper units, 4-wheel disc brakes, rack-and-pinion steering, fibreglass body, mechanics refurbished, finished in black, 1 of c110 made, museum-displayed for many years.
£180,000–200,000 / $261,000–290,000 ⚒ RM

1961 Ferrari 250 GT SWB Comp/61 Speciale, coachwork by Pininfarina, chassis no. 2429 GT, engine no. 2429 GT, V12 engine, Weber 40DCOE carburettors, left-hand drive, recently restored including extensive work on engine, gearbox, brakes, cooling system and differential, thin-gauge aluminium fuel tank, aluminium-skinned lightweight Berlinetta Aerodinamica bodywork, recessed door handles, covered headlights, finished in red, original dark blue leather interior, original.
£900,000+ / $1,305,000 ⚒ BKS

1963 Fiat Abarth 1000 Bialbero, rear-mounted double-overhead-camshaft, 4-cylinder engine, front-mounted radiator, Fiat 600D floorpan, restored 1985 including complete rebuild of engine, further work 1992, fewer than 300km since, finished in Abarth red, not raced or rallied in recent years, accompanied by spare gearbox, bonnet frame and racing exhaust, good condition.
£21,000–24,000 / $30,500–34,800 ⚒ COYS

1964 Cobra Daytona Coupé, ex-Carroll Shelby/Bob Bondurant, 289cu.in overhead-valve Ford V8 engine, 4 Weber 48IDA carburettors, 390bhp, 4-speed manual gearbox, 4-wheel independent suspension, 4-wheel disc brakes, left-hand drive, alloy body, restored.
£3,000,000+ / $4,350,000 ⚒ RM
The Cobra coupés were conceived in late 1963 as an answer to the more aerodynamic 1962/63 Ferrari GTO. Carroll Shelby's Cobra roadsters had run close to the GTO during 1963, surprising many. In fact, the roadster was faster on short circuits like Sebring and Bridgehampton, but was at an insurmountable disadvantage on the long circuits like Le Mans and Daytona. Shelby asked Pete Brock, his do-it-all first employee, to design a more aerodynamic coupé body on the existing roadster chassis. After construction began on the first car, Ken Miles triangulated the body/interior panel support tubing to increase chassis torsional rigidity. The finished product ran away from the field on its first outing at the 1964 Daytona Continental, only to suffer mechanical failure. The coupé's new body increased top speed by 25mph and fuel economy by 33 per cent, while the stiffer chassis improved handling. Daytona was where the car acquired its name. Shelby quickly contracted with a coachbuilder in Modena, Italy, to construct five more coupé bodies. This example was the second of those cars. It was one of two to race on both the 1964 and 1965 Shelby American and 1965 Alan Mann teams, contributing to Shelby's World Championship win in 1965.

1964 Lotus 37, engine bored to 1600cc, Elan parallel-link-style rear suspension system mounted on subframe, stored last 18 years, restored, finished in green and yellow, road registered, would benefit from refurbishment, purpose-made trailer.
£55,000–61,000 / $79,750–87,750 ⚒ COYS
In 1964, Lotus' Colin Chapman decided that a modified version of his Lotus 7 design could take on the Mallocks and other Clubmans racers and win. He developed a car in time for the 1965 Racing Car Show. Soon after, Chapman agreed that John Berry, the Lotus Home Sales Manager, could have the car in lieu of sales commission. After much set-up work, the 37 finally made its Clubmans debut, proving to be a sound design and the car to beat for several seasons. Berry sold it to rising star Tim Goss who, in 1967, used it to take four wins, seven seconds, seven thirds, seven lap records and the runner-up position in the Clubmans Championship.

1965 Sunbeam Tiger Mk I, 4260cc engine, single Holley 4-barrel carburettor, left-hand drive, works hardtop, finished in red and white, black interior, accompanied by substantial quantity of spares, ex-works.
£40,000–45,000 / $58,000–65,250 ⚒ H&H
This works team car was driven by Andrew Cowan and Brian Coyle in the 1966 Monte Carlo Rally.

1968 Matra Jet 6 Group 4, 1255cc 4-cylinder engine, twin Weber DCOE40 carburettors, 105bhp, 4-speed manual gearbox, 4-wheel independent suspension, 4-wheel Lockheed disc brakes, magnesium wheels, finished in blue.
£13,000–15,000 / $18,850–21,750 ⚒ Pou

1973 Porsche 1991 Carrera RSR, 2806cc overhead-camshaft air-cooled flat-6 engine, fuel injection, dual ignition with 2 plugs per cylinder, 340bhp (estimated), 5-speed manual gearbox, limited-slip differential, 4-wheel independent suspension, Bilstein shock absorbers, 4-wheel ventilated disc brakes, BBS 15in light alloy wheels.
£85,000–95,000 / $123,250–137,750 ⚒ RM

1965 Abarth 1000TC Group 5 Replica, based on Fiat 600D, 1000cc 4-cylinder Abarth A112 engine, 75bhp, 5-speed manual gearbox, 4-wheel disc brakes, alloy wheels, finished in silver and yellow.
£7,000–8,400 / $10,200–12,200 ⚒ Pou

1968 Lotus 47 GT Group 4 Grand Tourer, 1500cc double-overhead-camshaft Ford Cosworth engine, Hewland 4-speed gearbox, 4-wheel independent suspension, 4-wheel disc brakes, reinforced steel box-section chassis, lightweight fibreglass bodywork, completely restored, original.
£30,000–35,000 / $43,500–50,750 ⚒ RM
The first production run of the Lotus 47 totalled 50 units, to homologate the car in FIA Group 4. It was based on the Lotus 46 (Europa) chassis, but constructed of lighter-gauge metal. The rear was modified to accept a Lotus Ford Cosworth twin-cam engine and a Hewland gearbox. The rear suspension came from the Lotus 59 Formula One single-seater – cast magnesium rear uprights were combined with four trailing links, inverted lower wishbones and single top links. Up front, the Triumph Vitesse suspension remained as standard, apart from springs, shock absorbers and pick-up points.

1969 TVR Vixen, prepared to comply with HSCC road-going sports car championship regulations, all parts replaced or refurbished as necessary, rebuilt 100bhp engine, adjustable suspension with new Leda coil-spring/damper units all-round, standard rear aluminium uprights replaced by uprated steel versions, new tubular backbone chassis.
£12,500–15,000 / $18,150–21,750 ⚒ COYS

1973 Clan Crusader, full race specification, engine rebuilt, 110+bhp, fewer than 400 miles since, recent mechanical rebuild, 1 of 5 factory built cars, race-ready.
£6,000–7,000 / $8,700–10,200 ⊞ TSG

Military Vehicles

◀ **1941 Ford GPW Jeep,** finished in olive drab, drab canvas seating, good condition.
£4,000–5,000 / $5,800–7,250 ⚒ CGC
On 10 November, 1941 Ford signed a contract in which it agreed to manufacture the MB utility vehicle to Willys's specifications, known as the Ford GPW or General Purpose Willys. By 1945, Ford had produced nearly 280,000 Jeeps, although Willys production exceeded that by 100,000 units.

c1941 Demag 1 ton Half-Track, left-hand drive, folding hood, restored.
£35,000–40,000 / $50,750–58,000 W&P

1942 NSU HK101 Kettenkrad, 1478cc 4-cylinder water-cooled engine, restored.
£15,000–18,000 / $21,750–26,000 W&P

Miller's is a price GUIDE not a price LIST

▶ **1942 Chevrolet 1½ Ton Cargo/Troop Carrier,** 6-cylinder engine, canvas tilt, left-hand drive, US Navy markings, restored.
£4,500–5,000 / $6,500–7,250 🚘 IMPS

c1942 Mack NM5 6 Ton 6x6 Cargo Truck, 707cu.in 6-cylinder engine, 159bhp, canvas hood, side screens and tilt.
£2,500–3,750 / $3,600–5,475 🚘 MVT

1943 Austin Tilly Truck, completely restored.
£4,000–5,000 / $5,800–7,250 IMPS

c1943 Dodge ¾ Ton 4x4 Command Car, 3.7 litre 6-cylinder petrol engine, 93bhp, 4-speed gearbox, single-speed transfer box, 4-wheel drive, left-hand drive, restored.
£8,000–10,000 / $11,600–14,500 MVT

► **c1944 Albion CX22 6x4 Heavy Artillery Tractor,** 9080cc 6-cylinder engine, 100bhp, 4-speed gearbox, 2-speed auxiliary box, good condition.
£4,000–5,000 / $5,800–7,250 MVT

1944 Canadian Ford F60S LAA 4x2 Truck, built to tow Bofors anti-aircraft gun, fitted with integral ammunition locker, excellent condition.
£1,500–1,800 / $2,150–2,550 CGC

► **1944 Daimler Dingo Mk II Scout Car,** 2520cc 6-cylinder engine, restored, good condition.
£7,000–8,000 / $10,200–11,600 RRM

1943 Bedford QLR 3 Ton Y-Service Wireless Mobile Interceptor Unit, restored, only example known to survive, very good condition.
£7,000–8,000 / $10,200 -11,600 IMPS
This vehicle fought throughout north-western Europe, intercepting German radio traffic and relaying it to Bletchley Park (Station X), where it was decoded.

1944 Fordson WOT2H 15 Cwt 4x2 GS Truck, 3600cc sidevalve V8 engine, 60bhp, canvas hood and tilt, restored.
£4,000–5,000 / $5,800–7,250 MVT

► **1945 Morris C8 Mk II No. 5 Truck,** 3519cc 4-cylinder engine, 70bhp, restored.
£2,800–3,500 / $4,000–5,000 MVT

1944 Austin K6 3 Ton 6x4 Truck, 3995cc 6-cylinder petrol engine, 82bhp, hydraulic drum brakes, suspension by semi-elliptic leaf springs, inverted at rear, fitted with office body.
£3,600–4,500 / $5,200–6,500 MVT
The bulk of K6 production went to the RAF, being fitted with a wide variety of bodies.

1947 Dodge WC53 Carryall, 230cu.in 6-cylinder engine, 4-speed gearbox, single-speed transfer gearbox, 4-wheel drive, restored, very good condition.
£12,000–13,000 / $17,400–18,850 IMPS

► **1955 Leyland Martian 10 Ton 6x6 Truck,** Rolls-Royce B81 6490cc 8-cylinder engine, 215bhp, 4-speed gearbox, 3-speed transfer box, air brakes, leaf-spring suspension, 10 ton winch.
£2,000–2,500 / $2,900–3,600 MVT

1952 Austin Champ ¼ Ton 4x4 FFW, Rolls-Royce B40 engine, hood, original aerial mounts, rear-mounted jerry can, side-mounted pick and shovel, finished in bronze-green, green vinyl interior, original condition.
£1,250–1,500 / $1,875–2,250 CGC

1956 Willys M274 Mechanical Mule, air-cooled 4-cylinder engine, 15bhp, 3-speed gearbox, 4-wheel drive, restored.
£1,200–1,500 / $1,750–2,150 MVT
This vehicle could be operated by someone on foot.

1958 Daimler Ferret Scout Car, 4258cc Rolls-Royce engine, 5-speed pre-selector gearbox, deactivated machine-gun, restored, good condition.
£4,000–4,500 / $5,800–6,500 W&P

1964 Abbot 105mm Self-Propelled Gun, Rolls-Royce K60 engine, 105mm cannon, 33mph top speed.
£10,500–12,000 / $15,600–17,400 W&P

1970 Land Rover LWB Series III 'Pink Panther', deactivated machine-guns, sand channels, finished in pink desert camouflage, restored.
£7,000–9,000 / $10,200–13,000 ⊞ IMPS

1975 Land Rover 101 1 Ton GS Truck, 4-wheel drive, forward control, canvas tilt, finished in olive green.
£3,600–4,500 / $5,200–6,500 ⊞ IMPS

1962 Alvis Saladin 6x6 FV601 Armoured Car, 5675cc rear-mounted Rolls-Royce 8-cylinder engine, 5-speed pre-selector gearbox with forward and reverse transfer, deactivated 76mm cannon and machine-gun.
£4,400–5,500 / $6,400–8,000 ⊞ MVT
The Saladin armoured car appeared in the 1950s and continued in production until 1972. Its chassis was also used as the basis for the Stalwart amphibious vehicle.

1965 Ford/Kaiser M151A2 Military Utility Tactical Truck (Mutt), 141.5cu.in 4-cylinder engine, 71bhp, left-hand drive, canvas tilt and doors, restored, very good condition.
£3,250–3,750 / $4700–5,420 ⊞ MVT
Introduced in 1964, the M151A1 Mutt was built by both Ford and Kaiser. It was superseded by the A2 model with improved suspension in 1970. Bodies were built by Fruehauf, the trailer makers.

1970 Volkswagen 181 Trekker, detuned air-cooled 1500cc flat-4 engine, 44bhp, 4-speed gearbox, 2-wheel drive, left-hand drive, folding hood, in need of respray.
£1,500–2,000 / $2150–2,900 ⊞ MVT

Dealer prices

Miller's guide prices for dealer cars take into account the value of any guarantees or warranties that may be included in the purchase. Dealers must also observe additional statutory consumer regulations, which do not apply to private sellers. This is factored into our dealer guide prices. Dealer cars are identified by the ⊞ icon; full details of the dealer can be found on page 330.

Tractors & Traction Engines

1899 McLaren Agricultural Traction Engine, single-cylinder motion, 8hp, unrestored.
£25,000–30,000 / $36,250–43,500 ⊞ PSS

1901 Burrell Agricultural Old Glory Traction Engine, single-cylinder motion, 7hp
£35,000–40,000 / $50,750–58,000 ⊞ PSS

1907 Wallis & Steevens Agricultural Traction Engine, single-cylinder expansion-type engine, 8hp, restored, good condition.
£40,000–45,000 / $58,000–65,250 ⊞ PSS

Dealer prices

Miller's guide prices for dealer cars take into account the value of any guarantees or warranties that may be included in the purchase. Dealers must also observe additional statutory consumer regulations, which do not apply to private sellers. This is factored into our dealer guide prices. Dealer cars are identified by the ⊞ icon; full details of the dealer can be found on page 330.

1919 International Junior 8-16 Tractor, 4-cylinder overhead-valve engine, IHC magneto, 3 forward and reverse gears, all-steel wheels, exposed chain and sprocket drive.
£10,000–12,000 / $14,500–17,400 ⚒ CGC
Large numbers of the Junior tractor were exported to Britain at the end of WWI, although many of the design features were already outdated. Production ceased in 1922 after only five years.

◀ **1924 Robey Tandem 6 Ton Steam Roller,** restored, good condition.
£14,000–16,000 / $20,300–23,200 ⚒ PSS

1927 Wallis & Steevens Simplicity 3 Ton Steam Roller, single-cylinder motion, angled pistol-type boiler and belly tanks, full driver's canopy, not in steam for several years, no boiler or hydraulic test reports.
£23,000–26,000 / $33,300–37,700 ⚒ CGC

1943 Case Model DEX Tractor, 4-cylinder petrol/tvo engine, 4 forward gears and reverse, belt pulley, rear pto, pedal operated brakes.
£2,700–3,200 / $3,900–4,650 ⚒ CGC

1948 Oliver Model 70 Standard Tractor, Chrysler 6-cylinder petrol/tvo engine, 4 forward and reverse gears, electric starter, lighting set, belt pulley, independent rear brakes.
£2,500–3,000 / $3,600–4,400 ⚒ CGC

1930 Fordson Standard Model N Tractor, 4-cylinder petrol/tvo engine, 25hp, 3 forward and reverse gears, all-steel wheels, rear mudguards with integral tool boxes, Irish built for export with French instruction plates.
£3,250–3,750 / $4,700–5,420 ⚒ CGC

1946 John Deere Model D Tractor, 2-cylinder engine, 30hp, 4 forward and reverse gears, electric starter, belt pulley, rear pto, pneumatic tyres.
£2,500–3,000 / $3,600–4,400 ⚒ CGC

1959 Porsche Tractor, 1374cc 2-cylinder diesel engine, 20hp, restored, very good condition.
£6,000–7,200 / $8,700–10,400 ⚒ RM

Restored values

The cost of a professional restoration will have an influence on, but no direct relation to, a car's market value. A restored car can have a market value lower than the cost of its restoration.

◀ **1960s Burrell-Type ¼ Scale Traction Engine,** single-cylinder piston head, steel-clad, wheel hubs and roof support, pressure gauge with copper piping, handbrake, forward and reverse gearing knob, chain-link steering, pierced artillery-style wheels, working brass whistle, manually operated ember drawer, water tank, coal reserve to rear, brackets for lamps to front, finished in maroon with brass strapwork.
£6,000–7,200 / $8,700–10,400 ⚒ BKS

Horse-Drawn Vehicles

1850 Brougham Coach, complete with harness for 2 horses, original condition.
£1,000–1,200 / $1,500–1,800 ⚒ WILP

1890 Panel Boot Victoria, by Fairbridge and Sons, London, elliptic springs, leather mudguards, side panels with wicker inserts, finished in black with green coachlining, deep-buttoned dark leather interior trimmed in brocade, front seat covered in blue wool cloth.
£3,250–3,750 / $4700–5,420 ⚒ TSh

c1900 Ralli Car, by William Moore, Bath, to fit 14.2–15.2hh, adjustable seat, 14-spoke warner wheels, finished in black with red and gold coachlining, buttoned beige cord interior.
£700–840 / $1,000–1,200 ⚒ TSh

c1900 Spindle Back Show Phaeton, by Fischer & Fuchs, to fit 13.2–14.2hh, single or pair, pole and shafts, finished in dark green with light green coachlining, black upholstery.
£1,500–1,800 / $2,150-2,550 ⚒ TSh

◄ **1980s Phaeton,** by Morgan Davies, to fit 15–16hh, handbrake, finished in varnished natural wood and maroon with red coachlining, dark blue interior.
£525–625 / $760–910 ⚒ TSh

c1910 Norfolk Cart, to fit 14–14.2hh, recently refurbished, body in varnished natural wood, blue shafts and wheels with red coachlining, blue vinyl interior, show condition.
£1,700–2,000 / $2,450–2,900 ⚒ TSh

◄ **1930s London Trolley,** to fit a horse or pony, 2 sets of shafts, body profusely carved, scalloped and highlighted in cream, red and gold, whitemetal fittings, pneumatic tyres, driver's seat on twisted stainless-steel uprights, footbrake, drop tailboard, finished in varnished natural wood, cream undercarriage, lined in red.
£3,000–3,500 / $4,400-5,000 ⚒ TSh

Automobile Art

Juan Manuel Fangio, a print depicting the famous driver, signed by Fangio, 1984, 11 x 15in (30 x 38cm).
£600–700 / $870–1,000 ⊞ SMW

George Lane, a crayon and chalk drawing, depicting Featherstonhaugh possibly driving ERA 'RIB' at speed and entering a corner in front of a Bugatti, signed and dated, mounted, framed, glazed, 17 x 15in (43 x 38cm).
£325–390 / $470–560 ⚒ BKS

A cartoon, 'What are you worried about Mac, that thing's got an ejector seat ain't it!', depicting the James Bond Aston Martin DB5 at the corner of Pine and California Streets, San Francisco, 1966, 22 x 28in (56 x 71cm).
£900–1,100 / $1,300–1,600 ⚒ BKS

Sparkes, Ringmaster, depicting Fangio driving his Ferrari in the 1959 German Grand Prix, oil on canvas, framed, 15 x 30in (38 x 76cm).
£175–210 / $255–305 ⚒ BKS

Ernest Montaut, Pour la Coupe 1904, hand coloured lithograph of 2 racing cars speeding through the French countryside, 37 x 19in (94 x 48.5cm).
£450–550 / $650–800 ⚒ RM

Tony Upson, large mural, depicting a Ferrari 250 GTO at night during the Le Mans 24-hour race, acrylic on board, 96 x 36in (244 x 91.5cm).
£550–650 / $800–950 ⚒ BKS

Bryan de Grineau, The Highway of the future, charcoal heightened with white, the reverse applied with a cutting from *The Motor*, 11 December, 1934, illustration bearing the caption 'The Minister of Transport saved us this system of roads with a physical central division as depicted in this impression of the highway of the future', signed and dated 1934, 13½ x 21¼in (34 x 54cm).
£450–550 / $650–800 ⚒ BKS

◄ **A print, Monaco Meets Monza,** depicting a scene from the 1932 Monaco Grand Prix, on paper, 27 x 33in (68.5 x 84cm).
£90–100 / $130–145 ⊞ MPG

John Oxford, Alfa Romeo Road Racing 1930s, pencil heightened with white, signed and dated 1930, 21 x 30in (53 x 76cm).
£1,000–1,200 / $1,500–1,800 ⚒ BKS

Ray Goldsbrough, Burn Up, limited-edition print, signed by artist and driver Richard Burns, 1999, 22 x 16in (56 x 40.5cm).
£200–250 / $290–360 ⊞ SMW

Gordon Horner, Driver's Briefing, pen and Indian ink heightened with white, signed and dated 1951, 21 x 30½in (54 x 78cm).
£1,000–1,200 / $1,500–1,800 ⚒ BKS

D. Waugh, The Grand Prix Tyrrells, depicting 001, 005 and 007, grey wash heightened with white, signed and dated 1974, 21¼ x 31½in (54 x 80cm).
£325–375 / $470–560 ⚒ BKS

Michael Turner, VSCC Club Meeting, depicting an Austin A35 taking the chequered flag ahead of veteran and vintage machinery, pencil, reverse applied with 1962 date stamp, signed, 10 x 24½in (26 x 62cm).
£400–500 / $580–720 ⚒ BKS

A print, Monaco Magic, depicting a scene from the 1955 Monaco Grand Prix, limited edition of 850, on canvas, 30½ x 44in (77.5 x 112cm).
£1,000–1,250 / $1,500–1875 ⊞ MPG

Antonio de Guasti, Le Ferrari Mondiali, a set of 9 lithographic prints, depicting the Maranello marque's World Championship winning Grand Prix cars, colour on paper, each signed by the artist, enclosed in grey silk cloth portfolio, gold embosssed lettering, limited edition, numbered 85/110, 'as-new' condition.
£550–650 / $800–950 ⚒ BKS

Lucien Faure, En Panne, depicting early motorists at a roadside picnic, lithograph, linen backed, restored in margin, 24 x 18in (61 x 45.5cm).
£160–180 / $230–260 ⚒ RM

Russell Brockbank, The Jolly Waggoner, a Christmas card, prepared for *The Motor* December 1946, pen and indian ink, signed, damage to edges, 16½ x 11½in (42 x 29cm).
£400–500 / $580–720 BKS

Bryan de Grineau, Dieppe 1934, depicting A.H. Lindsay Eccles crashing his Bugatti on a downhill run through the Bal Gosset, charcoal heightened with white, the reverse applied with a cutting from *The Motor* 24 July, 1934, 15 x 21½in (38 x 55cm).
£350–400
$500–580 BKS

Frederick Gordon Crosby, Frazer-Nash single-seater at speed, Shelsley Walsh, 1930s, charcoal heightened with white, framed, glazed, 21 x 15½in (53 x 40cm).
£1,500–1,700 / $2,150-2,450 BKS

Leslie Creswell, ERA R2B 'Romulus', a cut-away drawing, pen and Indian ink heightened with white, signed, dated and applied with *The Motor* copyright stamp, 1935, 12 x 22 (30 x 56cm).
£700–800 / $1,000–1,150 BKS

A print, Le Pur Sang des Automobiles, depicting a scene from the 1931 Monaco Grand Prix, on paper, 27 x 32in (68.5 x 81.5cm).
£90–100 / $130-145 MPG

► **Max Millar, Bugatti 3.3 litre Grand Prix engine,** exploded and part cut-away drawing, pen and ink, applied with *The Autocar* copyright label, pencil date on front '21 May 1943', signed, 25 x 21in (65 x 54cm).
£500–600 / $720–870 BKS

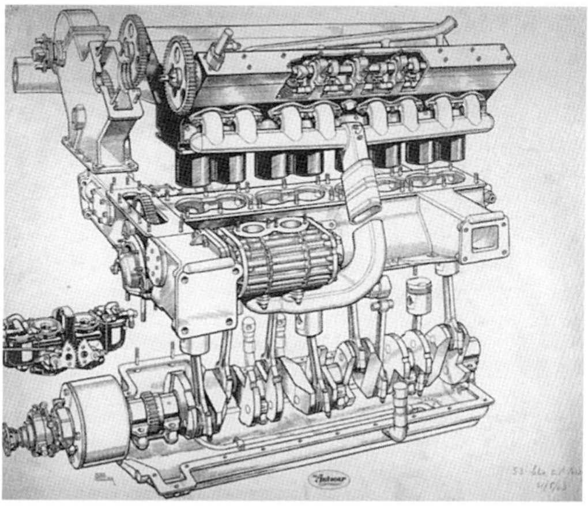

Roy Nockolds, 1932 Brooklands, depicting Tim Birkin racing his 4.5 litre single-seater 'Blower Bentley' on the banking at Brooklands, charcoal sketch, heightened in white, to the reverse an inscription to Rusty Russ Turner 'To Rusty. With very great admiration, an example to be followed', signed and dated 1932, framed, 20 x 12in (51 x 30.5cm).
£800–900 / $1,150–1,300 BKS

► **Roy Nockolds, Alan Hess, with passenger,** driving the famous 4.5 litre works Lagonda at speed on the Brooklands Circuit, 7 October, 1937, oil on board, framed.
£17,000–20,000 / $24,650–29,000 BKS
Subsequently, from this RAC observed run, the Lagonda became the first British sports car to exceed 100mph in one hour from a standing start, the average speed being 104.4mph.

H. J. Moser, a Mercedes W125 driven by Stuck and Carracciola, mixed media, signed and framed, 1939, 17 x 21in (43 x 53.5cm).
£2,300–2,700 / $3,350–3,900 ⚒ BKS

Tony Upson, a mural, depicting a 1953 Ferrari 375 Plus, acrylic on board, 94½ x 47¼in (240 x 120cm).
£500–600 / $720–860 ⚒ BKS

► **Gerald Coulson, No Contest,** limited-edition print, signed by artist and David Coulthard, 26 x 15in (66 x 38cm).
£225–275 / $325–400 ⊞ SMW

Posters

The 49th Indianapolis 500 1965, closed-circuit TV advertising poster, linen-backed, 60 x 40in (152.5 x 101.5cm).
£275–325
$400–470 ⚒ RM

A BMC poster, celebrating the land-speed records gained by Stirling Moss in the MG EX 181 at Utah, 1957, some creasing, 35 x 25in (89 x 63.5cm).
£275–325 / $400–470 ⚒ BKS

Grosser Preis von Deutschland, Nürburgring 3 August 1958, an original advertising poster, colour lithograph, unframed, 34 x 22in (86 x 56cm).
£175–210
$255–305 ⚒ C

Fangio, an original Italian film advertising poster, c1972, 48 x 68in (122 x 172.5cm).
£800–950
$1,150–1,380 ⊞ VEY

Sunbeam Cycles, original artwork for an advertising poster, depicting a cyclist riding toward a sunset, surface cracked and creased, c1908, 60 x 40in (152.5 x 101.5cm).
£350–400 / $500–580 ⚒ BKS

► **A Clément Cycles and Automobiles poster,** framed, 48 x 30in (122 x 76cm).
£60–70 / $90–105 ⚒ CGC

Automobilia

◀ **A solid silver rotating pencil,** bearing the inscribed initials of G.H. Lanchester, engine turned on all three sides, hallmarked London, slightly rubbed.
£575–675
$850–$975 ⚒ BKS

A leather-cased set of 37 Bartholomew's maps, with map of England fitted in its own compartment, hard bound, linen-backed, leather case with embossed 'Mr Bibendum' logo, good condition, c1909.
£300–350 / $440–520 ⚒ BKS

A leather-cased set of motoring maps by Harrods, comprising folded linen-backed motoring maps and contour road book, with front brass spring lock, thick carrying handle and brass clips, c1910.
£750–900 / $1,100–1,300 ⚒ BKS

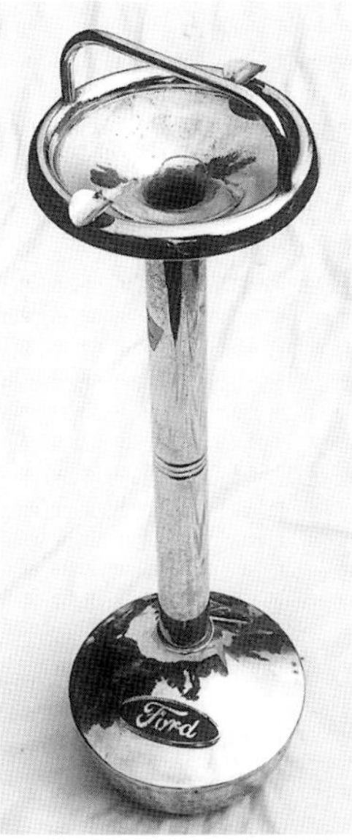

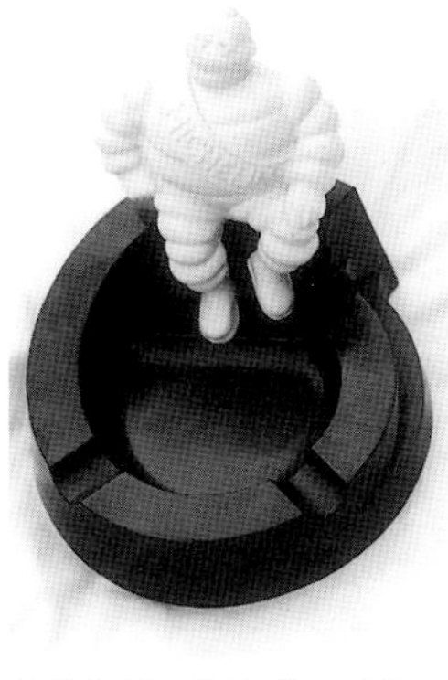

A Bakelite Michelin ashtray, 1930, 5 x 5in (12.5 x 12.5cm).
£120–150
$180–220 ⊞ JUN

◀ **A chrome Ford ashtray,** 1950s, 23in (58.5cm) high.
£40–50 / $60–75 ⊞ JUN

A Shell Motor Oils forecourt oil dispenser, restored, c1920.
£200–250 / $290–360 ⊞ PC

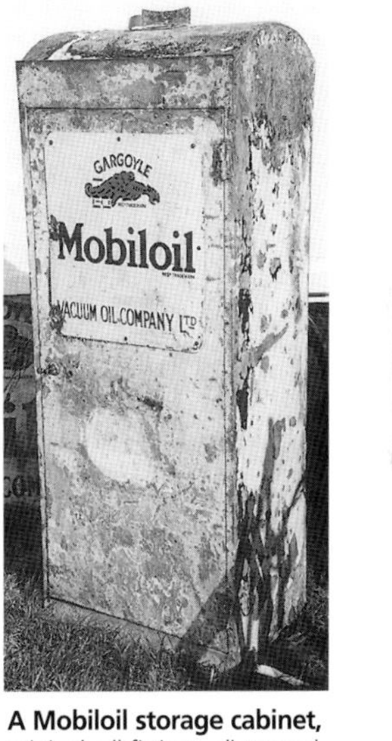

A Mobiloil storage cabinet, original, all fittings, distressed condition, 1920s–30s.
£175–200 / $255–290 ⊞ PC

◀ **An Art Deco St Christopher medal,** blue enamel, 2½in (6.5cm) long.
£120–150 / $180–220 ⊞ DRJ

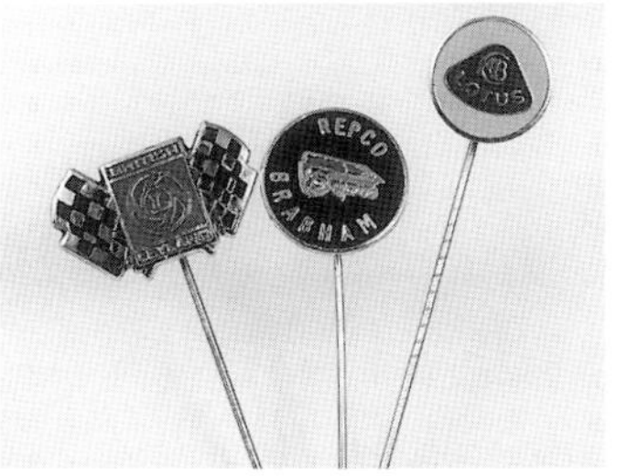

◀ **A collection of tie pins,** British Leyland Special Tuning, Repco Brabham, Lotus, 1960s.
£30–35 each
$45–50 ⊞ LE

An Art Deco St Christopher medal, red enamel and chrome.
£90–100 / $130–145 ⊞ DRJ

A set of 40 Piggott, Son & Weathers motoring maps, with Index and reference book, in a leather case with drop-down front, the lid with a leather handle, 1923.
£250–300 / $360–440 ⚒ BKS

► **The MG Broadsheet,** 10 advertising broadsheets sent to distributors and agents, printed on thick newsprint paper apart from issue 7 which is on glossy art paper, issue 10 imaged on art paper and printed in a combination of gold and dark blue, some folds and scuffing, 1934–36, 17 x 22in (43 x 56cm).
£1,000–1,200
$1,500–1,750 ⚒ BKS

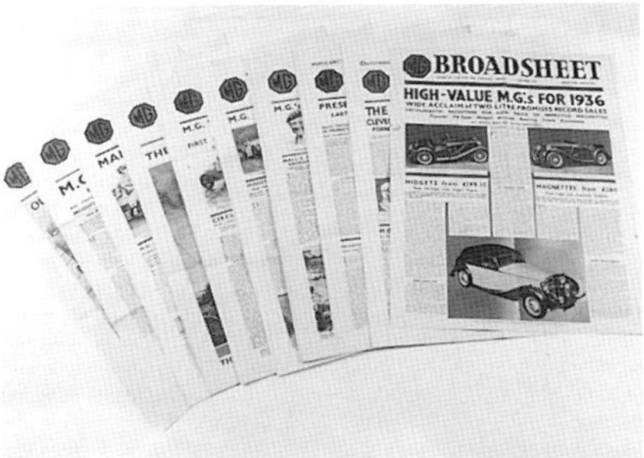

A Mobil quart oil pourer, c1950, 10in (25.5cm) high.
£16–20 / $24–30 ⊞ BLM

A Wesco forced oil can, 1950, 12in (30.5cm) high.
£4–5 / $6–7 ⊞ BLM

An embossed Shell petrol can, 1920–30, 11in (27.9cm) high.
£10–12 / $15–18 ⊞ BLM

A BP lamp oil tin, 1930–50, 10in (25.5cm) high.
£8–10 / $12–15 ⊞ BLM

► **An Ace petrol can,** 13in (33cm) high.
£90–100 / $130–145 ⊞ LE

A Pratts oil can, 2 gallon capacity, repainted black with gold lettering, 1920s, 12½in (32cm) high.
£12–15 / $15–20 ⊞ TPS

► **A Regent Oil Company oil can,** 5 gallon capacity, repainted red, good condition, 22in (56cm).
£20–25 / $30–35 ⊞ TPS

A Racing Shell oil can, repainted red and black, 12½in (32cm) high.
£160–200 / $240–290 ⊞ LE

A Wakefield Castrol Motor Oil can, 5 gallon capacity, repainted green with red lettering, new cap, 1930s–40s, 22in (56cm) high.
£25–30 / $35–45 ⊞ TPS

A Shell oil can, 2 gallon capacity, repainted red, fair condition, 1940, 12½in (32cm) high.
£8–10 / $12–15 ⊞ TPS

A Romac Lightgrade Lubricating Oil can, 1950, 6in (15cm) high.
£2–3 / $5 ⊞ BLM

► **A Luvax shock absorber fluid can,** 1930s, original condition, 22in (56cm) high.
£12–15 / $16–20 ⊞ SW

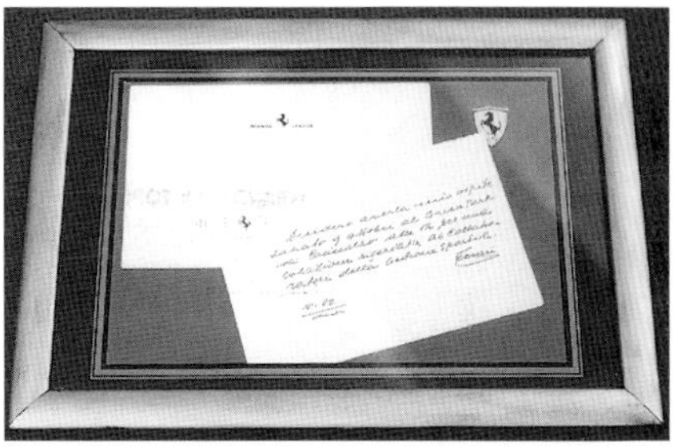

Enzo Ferrari, a hand written invitation to dinner, at the Cavalino restaurant opposite the factory, framed.
£700–800 / $1,000–1,150 ⊞ GPT

◄ **A Jaguar tea tray,** depicting a Mk II saloon at speed, leaping Jaguar handles.
£45–50
$65–75 ⚒ CGC

Clive Ellis, a bronze sculpture of a Ferrari 250 California, at speed with woman driver, red patina on a marble base, limited edition, 11¼ x 11in (28.5 x 28cm).
£2,200–2,600 / $3,200–3,800 ⚒ RM

◄ **A pair of gauze and glass motoring goggles.**
£40–45
$60–65 ⚒ CGC

► **A Ferrari yellow showroom tile,** commissioned by Ferrari factory, signed by René Arnoux, excellent condition, 1970s, 13in (33cm) square.
£120–135
$175–200 ⚒ RM

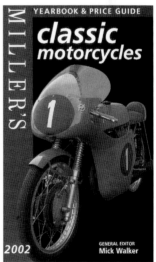

Badges

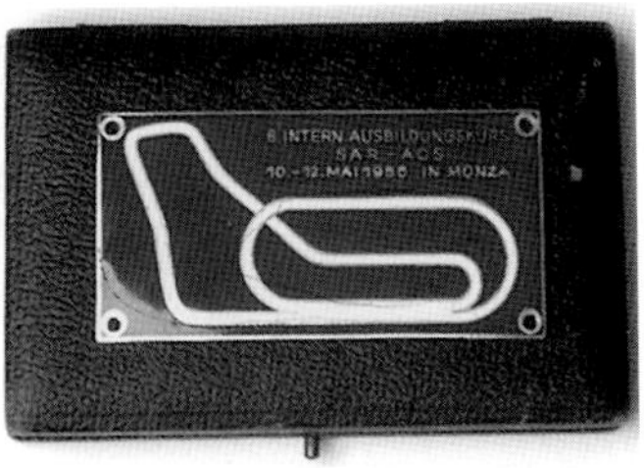

A Monza participant's badge, red and white cloisonné enamel on silver metal, in presentation case, given to Herrn Neubauer, chief instructor, 1956, 3¼in (8.5cm) long.
£200–220 / $290–320 ⚒ RM

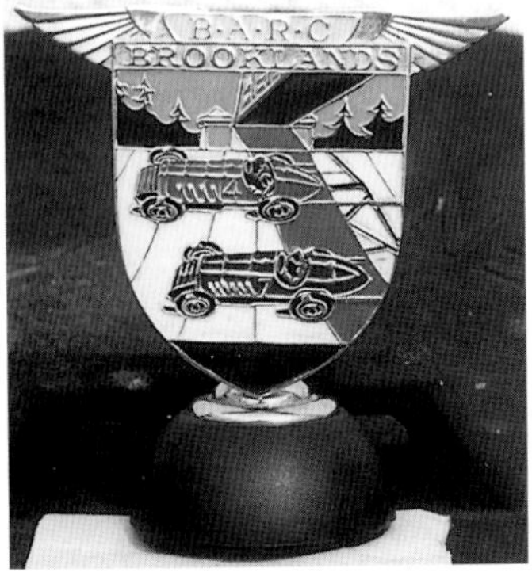

A BARC Brooklands badge, repainted rather than glass enamelled as originally made, 1920s–40s.
£300–350 / $440–500 ⊞ CARS

An Automobile Association pierced brass badge, with correct inscribed Stenson Cooke signature and membership No. 42, c1906.
£400–500 / $580–720 ⚒ BKS

A Brooklands 130mph speed award badge, engraved to 'Charles Brakenbury 10.6.35', un-enamelled for use on car.
£1,500–1,800 / $2,150–2,600 ⊞ CARS

Miller's is a price GUIDE not a price LIST

◀ **A set of 10 enamelled Goodwood members' lapel badges,** 1948–66, each c1in (2.5cm) wide.
£32–40 each
$48–60 each ⊞ LE

◀ **A Kieft lapel badge,** 1in (2.5cm) wide.
£55–65
$75–95 ⊞ LE

▶ **A pair of Silverstone passes,** 1973, 4in (10cm) high.
£6–7
$9–10 ⊞ LE

A Royal Automobile Club Centenary badge, 1997, 5in (12.5cm) high.
£60–75 / $90–110 ⊞ CARS

A Royal Automobile Club Queen's Silver Jubilee badge, 4½in (11.5cm) high.
£80–100 / $120–145 ⊞ CARS

A Royal Irish Automobile Club member's badge, 3¾in (9.5cm) high.
£120–150 / $180–220 ⊞ CARS

A British Racing & Sports Car Club enamel badge, 1960s.
£100–120 / $145–175 ⊞ LE

A set of Brooklands members' lapel badges, 1907–42, each c1in (2.5cm) wide.
£50–100 each / $75–145 ⊞ LE

A Royal Automobile Club badge, with original box and telephone-box key, 1960s, 4in (10cm) high.
£20–25 / $30–35 ⊞ COB

An American Rolls-Royce Owners' Club badge, coloured enamels on chrome, 1950s–present day.
£55–65 / $76–95 ⊞ CARS

An Automobile Club De La Vendée badge, 1930s, 3½in (9cm) wide.
£45–50 / $65–75 ⊞ GIRA

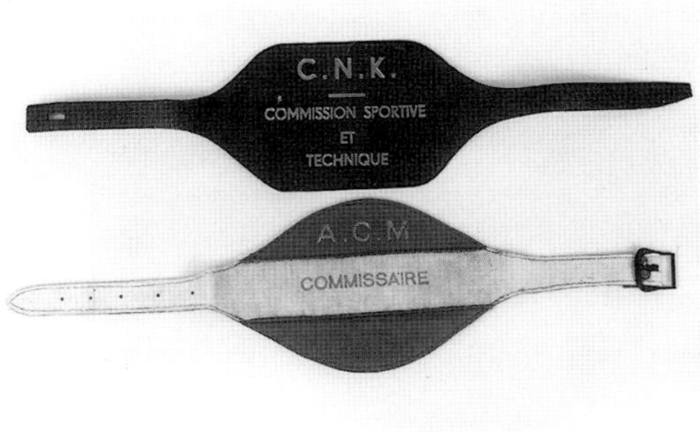

A pair of marshal's leather armbands, French, each 17in (43cm) long.
£32–38 / $45–60 ⊞ LE

Cross Reference
See Colour Review (page 276)

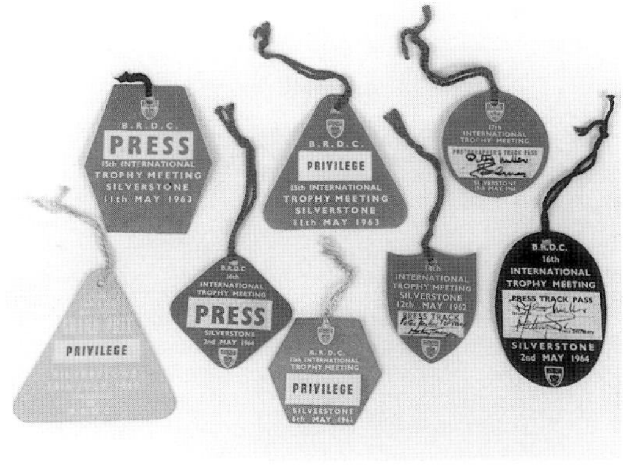

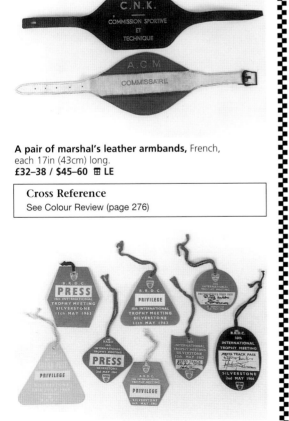

A set of 8 Silverstone passes, 1963–64.
£35–40 / $50–60 ⊞ LE

► **A Monza participant's badge,** multi-colour cloisonné enamel on circular gear-shaped silver metal, in a presentation case, given to Herrn Neubauer as Mercedes-Benz team manager, 1953, 2in (5cm) diam.
£325–375 / $470–560 ⚒ RM

A Brooklands School of Flying membership car badge, probably by Spencer, London, 1920s.
£1,200–1,400 / $1,750–2,000 ⊞ CARS

Three boxed sets of Brooklands annual entry pass brooches, for members and their guests, each comprising 1 paid-up member's badge on a cord and 2 guest brooches, 1910, 1911 and 1920.
£125–150 each / $180–220 each ⊞ CARS

A 2000km Durch Deutschland 1933 participant's badge, presented to Alfred Neubauer, Mercedes-Benz team manager, pewter finish, shows course and emblems of sponsoring car clubs, 6in (15cm) high.
£1,200–1,400
$1,750–2,000 ⚒ RM

◄ **An Automobile Club 1000 Miles Trial 1900 lapel badge,** in the form of a shield, by Spencers, London.
£500–600
$720–870 ⚒ BKS
The badge was awarded to the Lanchester Motor Company for entering the 8hp Gold Medal Phaeton No. 22. Subseqently, the car won the award for Perfection in Design.

Components

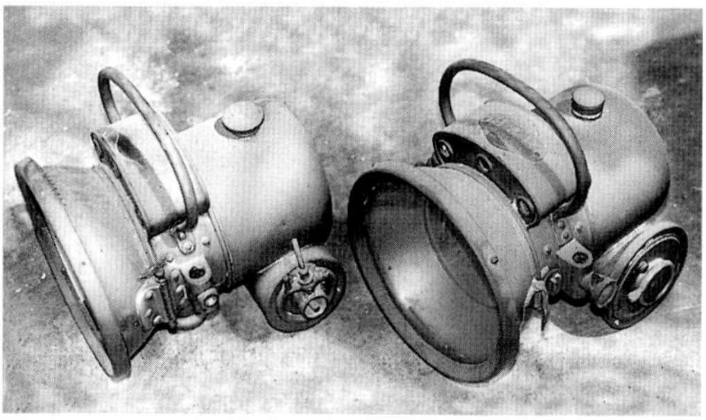

A pair of H & B single-burner self-generating headlamps, No. 1130, one glass missing and burners with non-matching fill plug.
£300–350 / $440–500 ⚒ CGC

A brass single-turn Desmo bulb horn, complete with fly gauze, good working condition, 17in (43cm) long.
£50–60 / $75–90 ⚒ BKS

A pair of Marchal nickel-plated projectors, restored, unmarked bodies and reflectors, 10in (25.5cm) diam.
£600–800 / $870–1,150 ⚒ BKS

◄ **A brass car headlamp,** c1908, 11in (28cm) high.
£100–120 / $140–175 ⊞ CoHA

A pair of nickel-plated Powell & Hanmer acetylene gas headlamps, manufactured for Morris Oxford, fork-mounted side brackets, water control valve, transverse carbide container, locking arm, threaded condenser bowl, rear reflector, parabolic bezel reflector, heat vent, P & H name plate inscribed 'The Morris Oxford', c1913.
£900–1,100 / $1,300–1,600 ⚒ BKS

Mascots

A French nickel-plated pewter marabou mascot, marked 'Artus', used on Lorraine Dietrich cars, 1923–26, 7in (18cm) high.
£1,000–1,200
$1,500–1,750 ⚒ RM

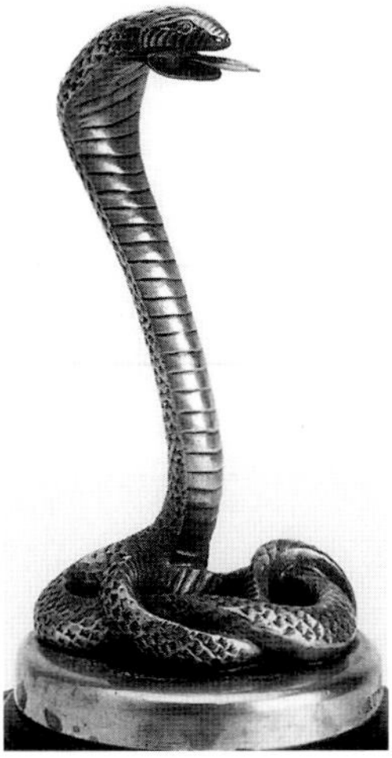

A cobra mascot, by Sasportas, offered exclusively by the French magazine *Auto-Omnia*, No. 0, full Sasportas and *Auto Omnia* stamped markings to base, original forked tongue intact, 1925.
£1,250–1,500
$1,875–2,250 ⚒ BKS

A French bronze mermaid with trumpet mascot, signed H. Briand, good original condition, 1920–25.
£1,100–1,250
$1,600–1,875 ⚒ RM

A French bronze dancers mascot, Danseurs Tête à Tête, by Ruffony, stamped 'A.N. Paris' foundry mark, 1925, 6½in (16.5cm) high.
£1,100–1,250
$1,600–1,875 ⚒ RM

A nickel-plated St George and Dragon mascot, by Miesse, the English patron saint in traditional pose with Turkish sword raised and the dragon underfoot, sword intact, on wooden display base, mid-1920s.
£700–800
$1,000–1,150 ⚒ BKS

A nickel-plated bronze leaping panther mascot, by Casimir Brau, offered by Hermès as mascot No. 2016, correct and original, 1928.
£2,500–3,000
$3,600–4,400 ⚒ BKS

An Old Bill car mascot, by Bruce Bairnsfather, c1918, 5in (12.5cm) high.
£250–300
$360–440 ⊞ COB

A French bronze patiné diving frog mascot, signed A. Renevey, 1915.
£1,000–1,200
$1,500–1,750 ⚒ RM

Miller's is a price GUIDE not a price LIST

A bronze standing Indian nude mascot, Femme Indienne, by Binmoran, mounted on a Renault radiator cap, the artist's name stamped on the base, 1920s, 6½in (16.5cm) high.
£1,200–1,400
$1,750–2,000 ⚒ BKS

A silver nickel on bronze Alfred the Penguin mascot, by Jacques Cartier, created by Alain Saint Ogan to promote the popular cartoon character, original Alfred neck pendant intact, signed, original condition, 1925, 6¼in (16cm) high.
£2,700–3,200
$3,900–4,650 ⚒ BKS

A bronze Nostradamus mascot, by A. Loir, depicting the fabled character in a long cloak and holding a telescope to his eye, c1920.
£4,200–4,800
$620–700 ⚒ BKS

A French woman with umbrella mascot, La Bourraszue, by Julianne, mounted on cap, 1930, 6in (15cm) high.
£1,800–2,000
$2,600–2,900 ⚒ RM

A chrome-plated Mr Therm sprite mascot, numbered, on a plastic base, 1930s.
£325–375
$470–560 RM

A metallo-bronze-finished Peugeot Lion mascot, inscribed R. Baudichon, mounted, c1924, 5½in (14cm) high.
£1,400–1,650
$2,000–2,400 BKS

An Art Deco-style sitting Alsation mascot, by Jacques Cartier, original plated finish, designer's name, foundry name, retailer's name and copyright socle, 1920s.
£1,400–1,600
$2,000–2,300 BKS

► A silvered bronze horse's head mascot, by Eugene Bregeon, mounted on a turned ebonised wooden display base, 1920s.
£775–875
$1,125–1,250 BKS

A French bronze Catalonian man mascot, by Lou Caddetou and Bire Baqui, marked 'Lou Cadde Tou Bire Baqui', arm moves as car is driven, mounted on radiator cap, 1920s.
£1,400–1,600
$2,000–2,300 RM

A French bronze sea nymph mascot, signed by A. Renevey, mounted on cap, 1915–20.
£850–950
$1,250–1,380 RM

A silver-plated bronze winged goddess mascot, Le Génie, by M. Virot, adopted by the Doriot Flandrin Parant automobile company, probably manufactured by Augustine Emile Lejeune in England, believed to be a limited edition, signed, c1922.
£1,400–1,650
$2,000–2,400 BKS

A bronze elephant mascot, by L. Carvin, designer's scripted name on the rock, 'Susse Fres' foundry socle and retailer's name, c1915.
£1,500–1,700
$2,150–2,450 BKS

◄ A French bronze Pierrot mascot, signed A. Bofill, original cap, 1920s.
£750–850
$1,100–1,250 RM

A bronze panther trying to get hedgehog mascot, signed by Bourcart, mounted on cap.
£800–900
$1,150–1,300 RM

A French gilded bronze frog playing a mandolin mascot, signed by A. Renevey, mounted on cap, 1930s.
£1,100–1,250
$1,600–1,800 RM

A bronze female archer mascot, Amazone, by C. Win, stamped foundry mark, original bow and arrow, 1920–25, 7½in (19cm) high.
£1,150–1,300
$1,675-1900 RM

◄ A French silver-plated bronze girl with teddy bear mascot, by Frecourt, 1925.
£1,100–1,250
$1,600–1875 RM

A French nickel on bronze bulldog mascot, Bouledogue à la chaîne, by Duges & Jouenne, created by Editions Marvel, excellent condition, 1923.
£1,400–1,600
$2,000–2,300 BKS

A French monkey with flag pole mascot, signed LeVerrier, 10in (25cm) high.
£1,150–1,250
$1,675–1,875 RM

A French bronze kangaroo mascot, by Bofill, foundry mark 'MAM', 1910, 64¾in (164.5cm) high.
£1,700–1,900
$2,450–2,750 RM

A reproduction nickel-plated Mr Bibendum mascot, excellent condition, 5in (12.5cm) high.
£150–180
$220–260 BKS

A pair of Bentley winged 'B' mascots, both from the 3½ Litre model, by Jos. Fray, Birmingham.
l. £760–950 / $1,110–1,380
r. £800–1,000 / $1,160–1,450 CARS

A glass perch mascot, by R. Lalique, mounted on correct Brevette base.
£460–520
$670–755 BKS

A reproduction Old Bill mascot.
£50–60
$75–90 CGC

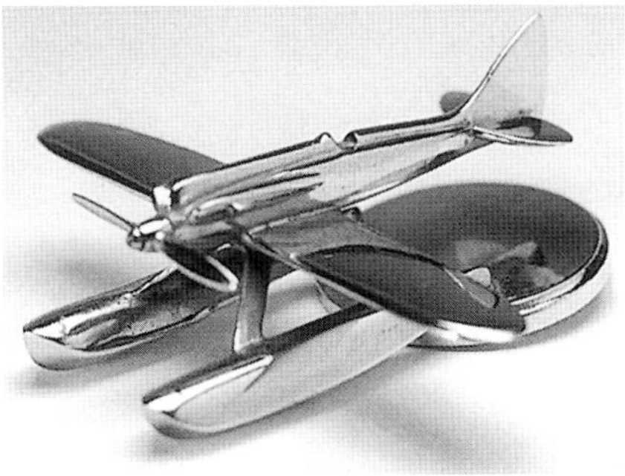

A chrome-plated Schneider seaplane mascot, by A.E. LeJeune, excellent condition, 3½in (9cm) high.
£1,100–1,350
$1,600–1,900 RM

A nickel-plated Britannia mascot, marked 'Vivat Rex', 1914, 5½in (14cm) high.
£500–600
$720–870 RM

A nickel-plated Mic Satyr mascot, signed Le Verrier, 1920s, 7in (18cm) high.
£275–330
$400–480 BKS

A French nickel-plated Lorraine Dietrich greyhound mascot, 1925–30, 6in (15cm) high.
£1,100–1,350
$1,600–1,900 RM

◄ **A silver-plated bronze prancing bull mascot,** inscribed 'Bravo Torro', by H. Payen, marked 'H.P.', 4in (10cm) high.
£1,200–1,350
$1,750–1,930 RM

Models

A 1/43-scale model of a 1996 McLaren F1 Le Mans racer.
£25–30 / $35–45 ⊞ DRAK

◄ A 1/43-scale Minichamps model of a BMW 635 CSi Group A racer.
£20–25 / $30–35 ⊞ DRAK

A 1/8-scale scratchbuilt resin model of a Ferrari 246 SP, as driven by Olivier Gendebien in the 1962 Targa Florio, pierced gauze-style radiator grille, solid aluminium petrol cap, spoked racing wheels, wrap-around screen, faux leather cockpit trim, aluminium-finish dashboard with chrome-rimmed dials and controls.
£2,000–2,400 / $2,900–3,500 ⚒ BKS

A 1/6-scale model of a Ferrari 500 F2, die-cast alloy and tinplate by Fonderpress for the Italian company Toschi, given as a trade gift to their clients, originally housing a bottle of Nocino liqueur and a jar of cherries, usable as a working toy, rubber-band powered, replica Pirelli tyres, chromed faux spoke wheels, wood-finish steering wheel, finished in red, c1950, 22in (56cm) long.
£1,700–1,900 / $2,450–2,750 ⚒ BKS

A 1/24-scale handbuilt white-metal model of a 1.5 litre Alfa Romeo Type 158, removable bonnet, detailed engine, cockpit with detailed dashboard, angled gear stick and faux leather seat, real rubber tyres, chrome spoked wheels, finished in red.
£230–280 / $330–410 ⚒ BKS

A French model of an Alfa Romeo P2, by CIJ, treaded tyres, André brake drums, fully operational steering, opening petrol, oil and radiator caps, faux rusted exhaust, working clockwork motor, finished in original blue, 1926.
£1,500–1,700 / $2,170–2,450 ⚒ BKS

A 1/8-scale handbuilt model of a Ferrari F40, by Maranello Miniatures/Pochet, opening doors, bonnet and boot, detailed engine, authentic wheels and tyres, correct interior, cased in glass and faux mahogany, title to front and F40 number plate, finished in red.
£400–480 / $580–690 ⚒ BKS

► An Italian model of a Ferrari 500/F2 racing car, by Toschi, die-cast body, rubber-band powered, finished in red, excellent condition with original tag still attached, 22in (55.9 cm) long.
£1,800–2,000
$2,600–2,900 ⚒ RM

► A set of 3 1/14-scale handbuilt models of Ferrari racing cars, comprising a 1972 312 B2 as driven by Jackie Ickx and Gianclaudio Regazzoni, a 1975 312 T2 as driven by Nikki Lauda, and a 1982 126 V6 as driven by Gilles Villeneuve, detailed engines, full rubber tyres.
£225–275 / $325–400 ⚒ BKS

Petrol Pumps

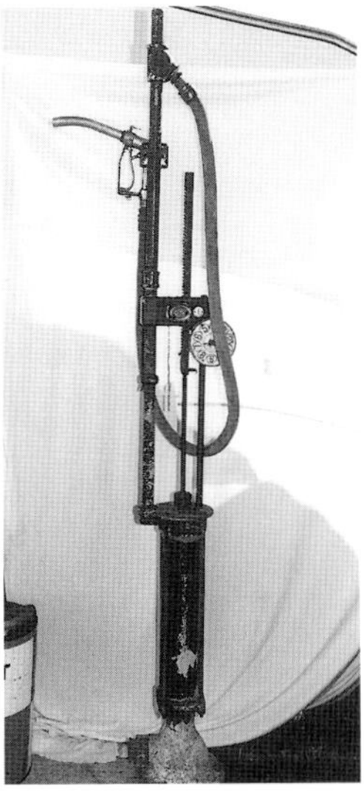

◄ **A Gilbert & Barker hand-operated single-gallon petrol pump,** 1920s, 56in (142cm) high.
£250–300 / $360–440 PC

Miller's is a price GUIDE not a price LIST

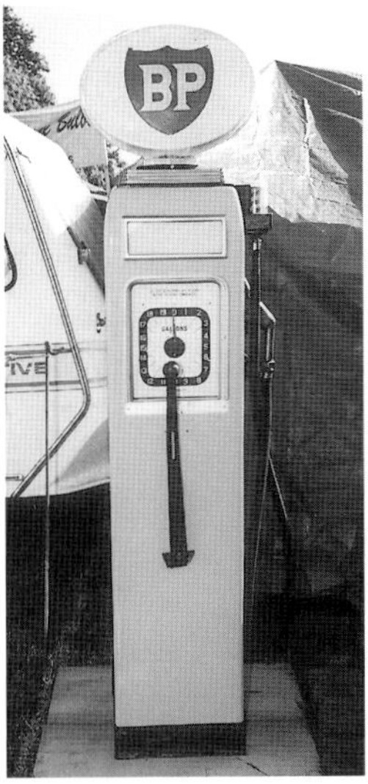

► **An Avery Hardoll BP petrol pump,** 1950s, 84in (213.5cm) high.
£500–600 / $770–870 PC

An Avery Hardoll Mobil 598 type petrol pump, 1950s, 84in (213cm) high.
£450–550 / $650–800 PC

Globes

A set of 5 Shell oil pump globes, 1930s, each 8in (20.5cm) high.
£350–400 / $520–580 ⊞ MSMP

A diamond-shaped Not for Resale glass petrol pump globe, lettered in blue.
£95–110
$140–160 ⚒ CGC

An Esso glass petrol pump globe, lettered in red and blue, some over-painting for Pool petrol, faded, 1930s.
£95–110
$140–160 ⚒ CGC

Picnic Sets, Vanity Cases & Travel Goods

A Gladstone crocodile-skin bag, 1950s, 16in (40.5cm) wide.
£550–650 / $800–950 ⚒ CGC

A set of 3 travelling perfume bottles, in an ostrich-skin-covered box, 1930s, case 9in (23cm) wide.
£190–230 / $275–330 ⚒ BKS

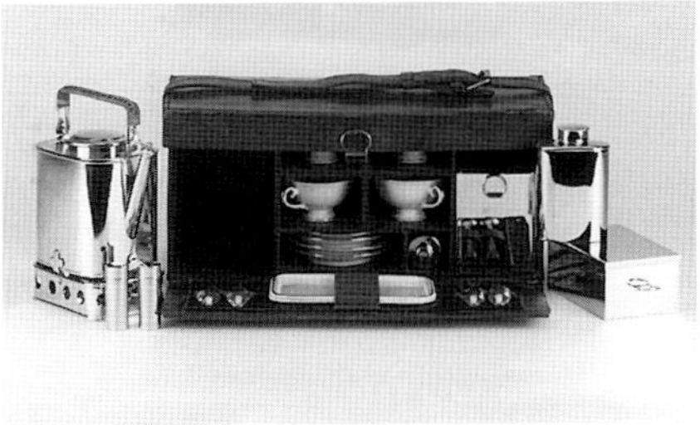

◄ **A Drew & Co leather-cased fold-fronted 4-person picnic set,** rectangular kettle and burner, sandwich boxes, milk flask, condiment bottles, cutlery housed in lid, enamel plates, 4 cups and saucers, 24in (61cm) wide.
£950–1,100
$1,380–1,600 ⚒ BKS

An Asprey leather-cased sandwich box, with leather-covered Thermos flask, original carrying strap, interior cream felt lining, c1905, good condition, 14in (35.5cm) high.
£1,600–1,900 / $2,300–2,750 ⚒ BKS

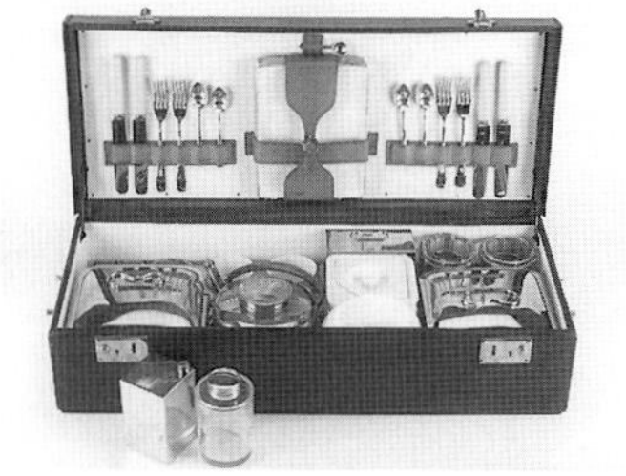

A Coracle 4-person picnic set, kettle and burner, square plates, cutlery in lid, sandwich boxes, cups and saucers, condiment and preserve jars, black Rexene covered case, brass-plated handles and locks, good condition, 1920s, 36in (91.5cm) wide.
£650–750 / $950–1,100 ⚒ BKS

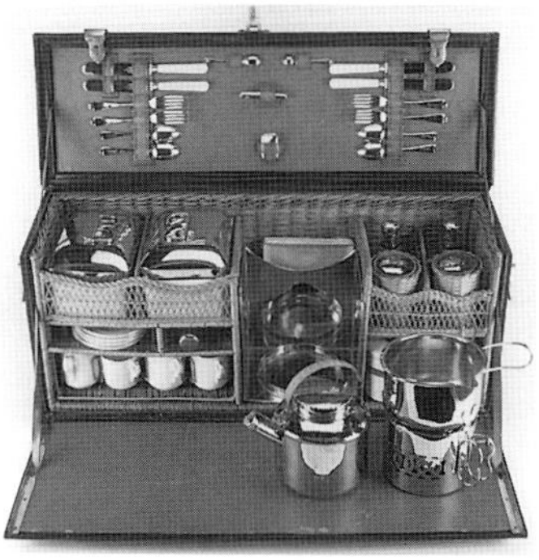

A Drew & Sons 4-person picnic set, drop-fronted, partitioned sections in wicker covering, sandwich boxes, kettle and burner, cups, plates, bottles, condiment and preserve jars, cutlery, corkscrews, lined in brown, brass locks and handles.
£1,250–1,450 / $1,825–2,075 ⚒ BKS

A Finnigans 4-person picnic set, drop-fronted, kettle and burner, cutlery, square plates, bottles and condiment sets, sandwich box, preserve jars, finished in black Rexene, original condition.
£750–900 / $1,100–1,300 ⚒ BKS

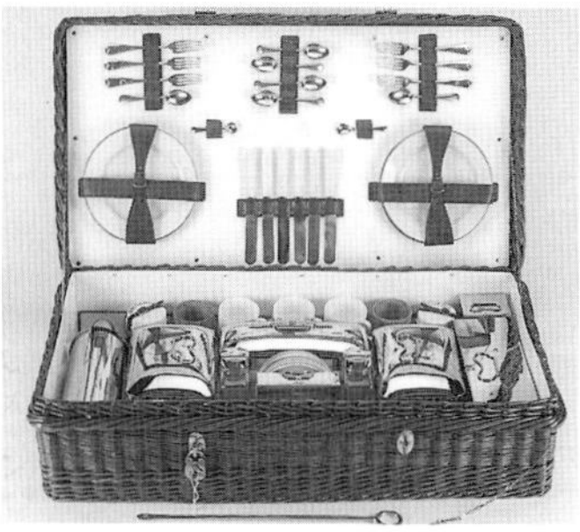

A Scott & Son 6-person wicker suitcase picnic set, fully fitted interior, ceramic-based sandwich boxes, food boxes, china cups and saucers, nest of drinking tumblers, 6 plates, cutlery, Autotherm leather-covered flask, preserves jars, condiment bottles, milk bottles, 1909.
£2,300–2,700 / $3,350–3,900 ⚒ BKS

◄ **A Thermos flask,** tubular brown leather carrying case, 1904, 13in (33cm) high.
£325–375 / $470–560 ⚒ BKS

A Vickery 2-person picnic set, fold-fronted leather case, kettle and burner, cups, saucers, sandwich boxes, milk bottle, red lining, c1910.
£550–650 / $800–950 ⚒ BKS

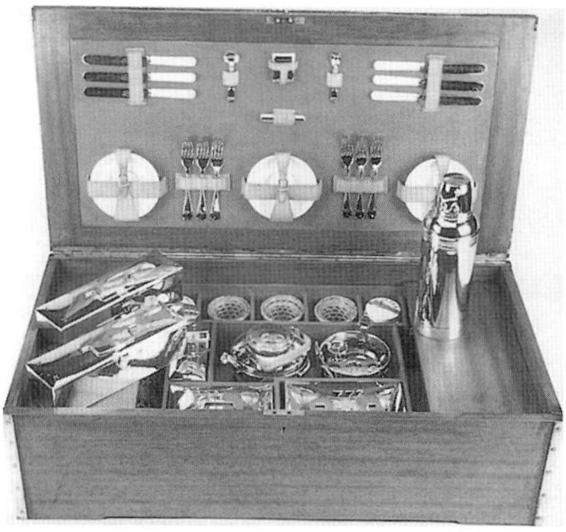

A polished wood and brass-edged combination 6-person games table and picnic set, leather lined, Barratt kettle with original wicker covered handle, matching burner, oil container, leather-covered Thermos flask, wicker-covered drinks bottle, 6 drinking glasses, 6 china cups and saucers, ceramic butter and preserves jars with lids, wicker-covered spirit flask, milk bottle, sandwich boxes, cutlery, vesta case, gilt-edged enamel plates, lid opens to reveal green baize card table, legs can be unfolded to form a standing games unit or picnic table, unused set of period playing cards.
£2,200–2,600 / $3,200–3,800 ⚒ BKS

◄ **A James Dixon & Sons cylindrical travelling cocktail set,** 3 drinking flasks surrounded by an ice flask, 6 stacking beakers, glass container, lemon squeezer, honey pigskin travelling case.
£1,700–2,000
$2,450–2,900 ⚒ BKS

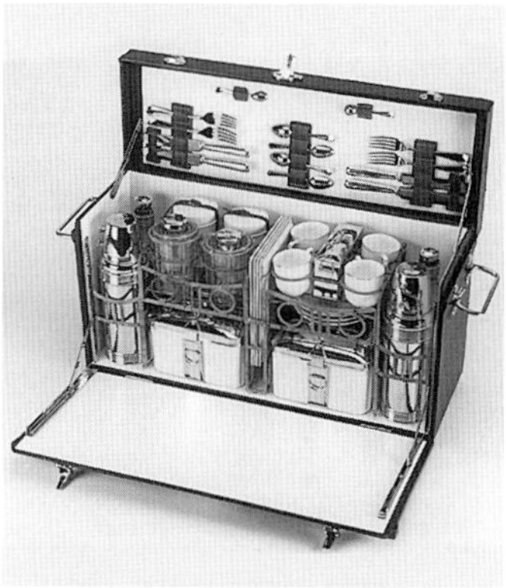

A Scott & Son fold-fronted 4-person picnic set, black case with nickel-plated central lock, nickel carrying handles, wicker-covered drinks bottles, matching Thermos flasks, stacking glasses, gilt-edged enamel plates, gilt-edged bone china cups and saucers, ceramic-based sandwich box, ceramic butter and preserves jar, cutlery, condiment bottles, milk bottle, oil container, gilt-edged rectangular enamel serving plates, food storage box.
£1,900–2,300 / $2,750–3,350 ⚒ BKS

► **A French leather-cased gentleman's vanity set,** 2 heavy cut-glass scent bottles with silver tops, leather-cased manicure set, leather-cased comb, brushes, razor and various boxes, signed, c1905.
£450–540 / $650–780 ⚒ BKS

A Drew & Sons wooden and brass-edged 6-person combination games and picnic set, leather-lined interior, kettle with original wicker covered handle, burner, stand and oil container, vesta case, wicker-covered drinks bottles, drinking glasses, fine china cups and saucers, ceramic butter and preserves jars, wicker-covered spirit flask, milk bottle, fine ceramic-based sandwich boxes, tea and sugar boxes, cutlery, rectangular enamel plates, lid opens to reveal green baize card table, legs can be unfolded to form a games table or simple picnic table, pack of early playing cards.
£5,000–6,000 / $7,250–8,700 ⚒ BKS

A Vickery 6-person suitcase-style picnic set, copper kettle, burner, ceramic cups and saucers, sandwich boxes, wicker-covered drinks flasks, sandwich boxes, glasses, wicker-covered condiment bottles, full complement of early cutlery, heavy gilt-edged rectangular enamel plates, brass carrying handles, c1914.
£2,400–2,800
$3,500–4,000 ⚒ BKS

A Thornhill & Co brown leather-cased picnic set, half-fold front, lock to front flap, satchel back original carrying strap, fitted interior, leather wallet containing a full set of Thornhill cutlery, silver-plated plates, silver cut-glass decanter, sandwich and food boxes, cut-glass tot drinking tumblers, nickel preserves pot, 1910.
£800–950
$1,150–1,380 ⚒ BKS

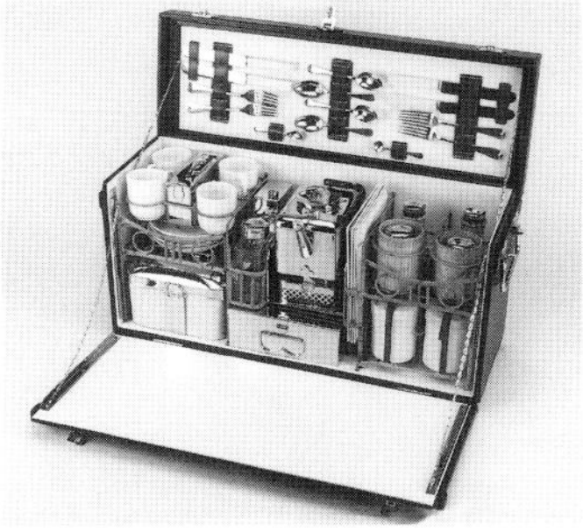

◀ **A Scott & Son fold-fronted 4-person picnic set,** black case, nickel central lock, nickel carrying handles, rectangular kettle and burner within ornate stand, wicker-covered drinks bottles, stacking glasses, bone china Bisto cups and saucers, ceramic-based sandwich box, ceramic butter and preserves jars, milk bottle, oil container, cutlery, condiment bottles, gilt-edged rectangular enamel serving plates, food storage box, 1912.
£3,100–3,600 / $4,550–5,145 ⚒ BKS

Advertising Signs

An illuminated double-sided Alfa Romeo sign, plastic in metal frame, metal wall fixing bracket, 1970s.
£120–150
$180–220 ⊞ CARS

An enamel RAC hanging sign, 1950, 25 x 40in (63.5 x 101.5cm).
£160–200
$240–290 ⊞ JUN

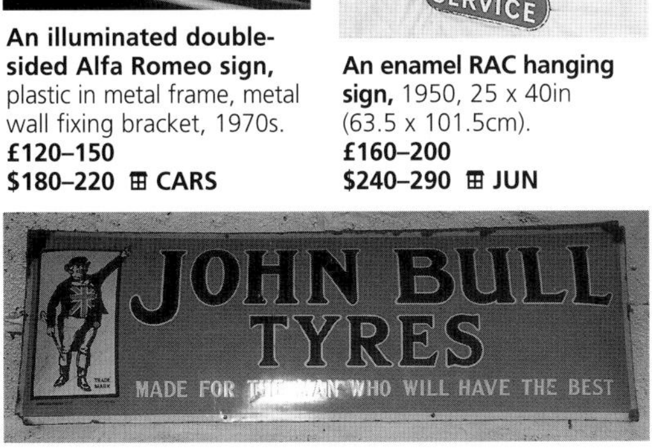

An enamel John Bull sign, 1920s, 41 x 120in (104 x 305cm).
£120–150 / $180–220 ⊞ CRC

A Maserati wall plaque, commemorating the Maserati 250F's victory at the 1956 Monaco Grand Prix, surrounded by a winner's laurel, 42in (106.5cm) diam.
£250–300 / $360–440 ⚒ BKS

> **Cross Reference**
> See Colour Review (page 280)

◄ An enamel No Racing at Fontwell AA sign, c1950, 30 x 42in (76.2 x 106.7cm).
£250–300 / $360–440 ⊞ WAB

► A Ferrari wall plaque, commemorating the marque's victory in the 1962 Le Mans 24-hour race, surrounded by a gold laurel wreath, painted in acrylic and varnish.
£400–500 / $580–720 ⚒ BKS

A Shell Motor Spirit and Motor Oils sign, 48½ x 82½in (123 x 209cm).
£45–55 / $65–80 ⚒ CGC

◄ A British Leyland cloth Motor Show display banner, for Austin, Morris, MG, Jaguar, Triumph and Rover.
£150–170
$220–250 ⚒ CGC

► A double-sided Lion Motor Oils enamel sign, unused, 1918, 12 x 24in (30.5 x 61cm).
£1,100–1,200
$1,600–1,750
⊞ BRUM

Watches & Clocks

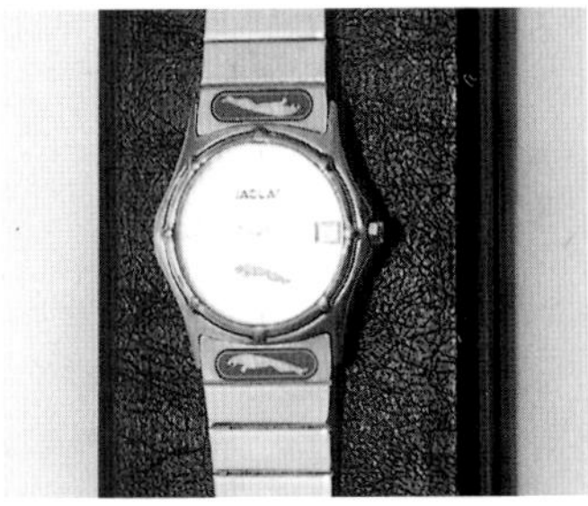

A Jaguar limited-edition watch, issued free to buyers who spent £15,000 on a new Jaguar, 1976.
£430–480 / $630–695 ⊞ TIC

A Hunts angled cased mechanical car clock, nickel-plated case, rear-wind movement, white dial with Roman numerals, mounted on a wooden base, late 1920s, dial 4in (10cm) diam.
£250–300 / $360–440 ⚒ BKS

A Swiss silver-cased split-time pocket stopwatch, white dial with Arabic numerals and sweeping hands, counter-clockwise 30-minute subsidiary dial with sweeping movement, inscribed 'Lanchester Engine Company Ltd' to the reverse, Swiss movement, silver case with marks for Zurich, excellent condition, early 20thC.
£575–680 / $1,000 ⚒ BKS

A wall-hanging Castrol clock. in the form of an oil bottle top, commemorating the 1933 world record of 213.842km/h set by a Bugatti, using Castrol oils.
£350–400 / $500–580 ⚒ BKS

◄ A Heuer Roadster mechanical dashboard stopwatch, c1970.
£160–200 / $240–290 ⊞ HARP

Books

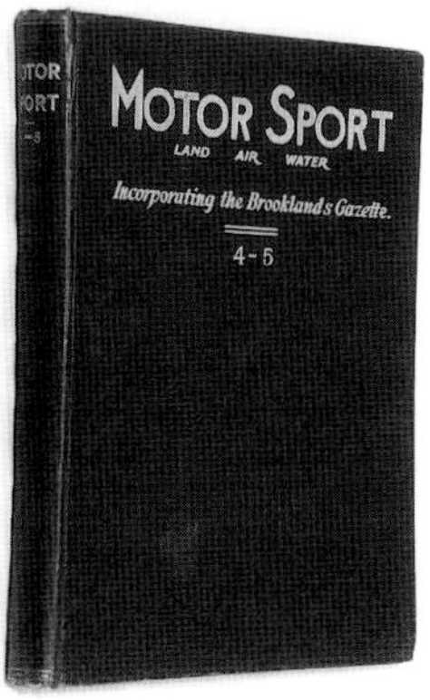

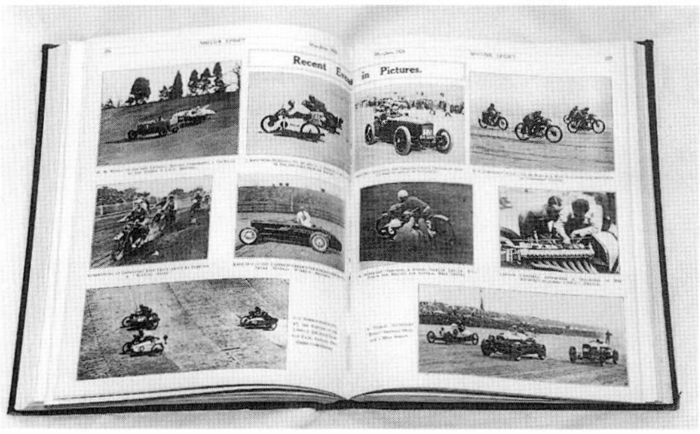

Motor Sport **Volumes 4 and 5,** bound in 1 volume, July 1927–June 1929, Volume 4 incorporating numbers 1–12, and Volume 5 numbers 1–3, bound without covers, black with gold lettering, includes advertisements.
£6,000–7,000 / $8,750–10,250 ⚒ BKS

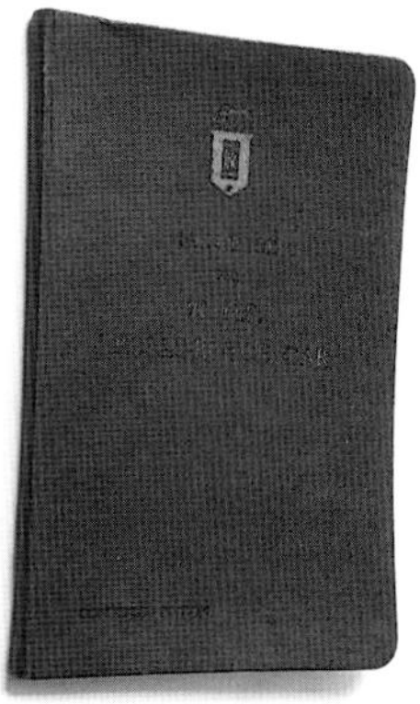

Handbook for 20hp Rolls-Royce Car, 1927, 6 x 9in (15 x 23cm).
£50–60 / $75–90 ⊞ COB

▶ **Mario Andretti and Nigel Roebuck, *Mario Andretti World Champion,*** signed by Mario Andretti, 1979, 9¾ x 7in (25 x 18cm).
£45–50 / $65–75 ⊞ GPCC

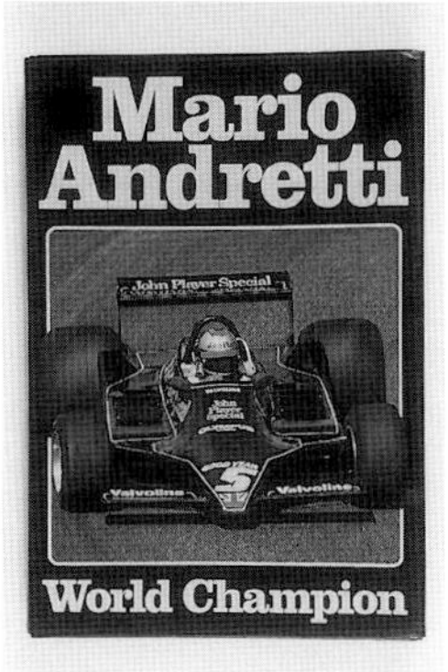

Pole Position, Celebrating The Diamond Jubilee of the British Racing Drivers' Club, 1987, 11 x 8½in (28 x 22cm).
£30–35 / $45–50 ⊞ GPCC

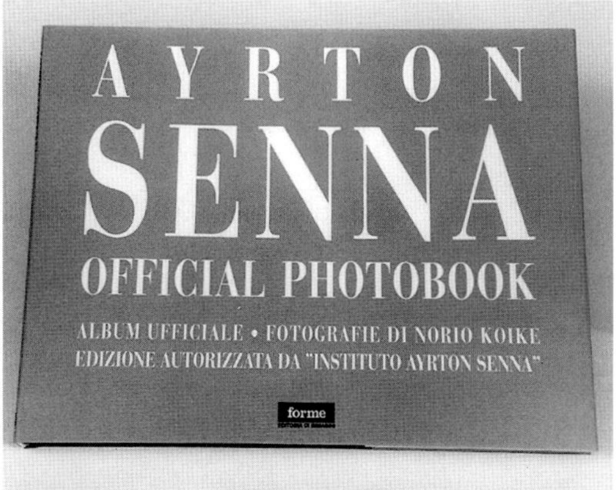

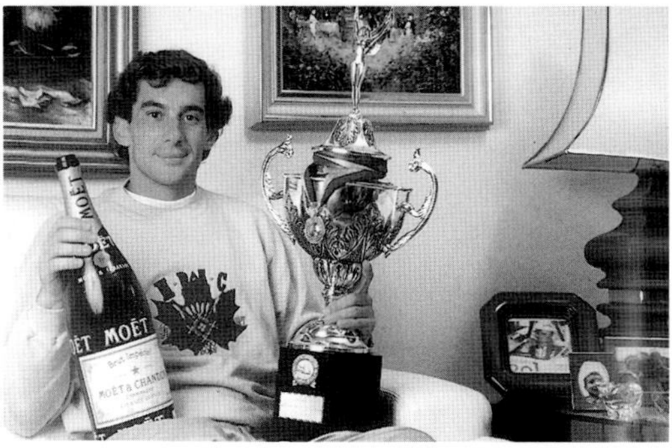

Ayrton Senna Official Photobook, 1994, 12¼ x 9in (31 x 23cm).
£50–55 / $75–80 ⊞ GPCC

The Glamorous World of Grand Prix, 1988.
£10–12 / $14–17 ⊞ GPCC

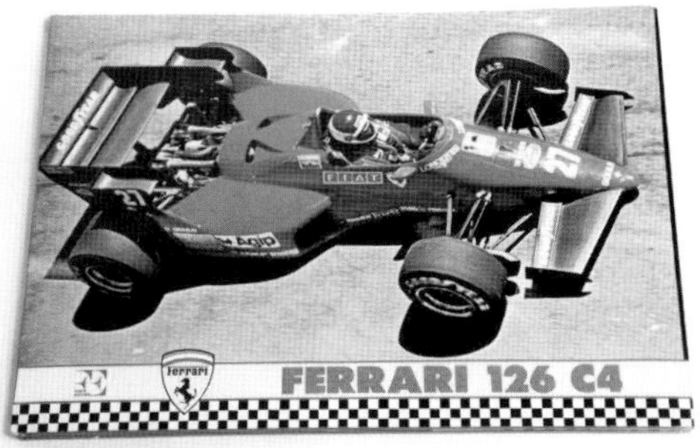

◀ Chiavegato and Colombo, ***Ferrari 126 C4,*** signed by René Arnoux, 1984,13 x 9in (33 x 23cm).
£90–110 / $130–160 ⊞ GPCC

Michael Cooper-Evans, *Rob Walker,* signed by Rob Walker, 1993, 10 x 11in (25.5 x 28cm).
£80–100
$115–145 ⊞ GPCC

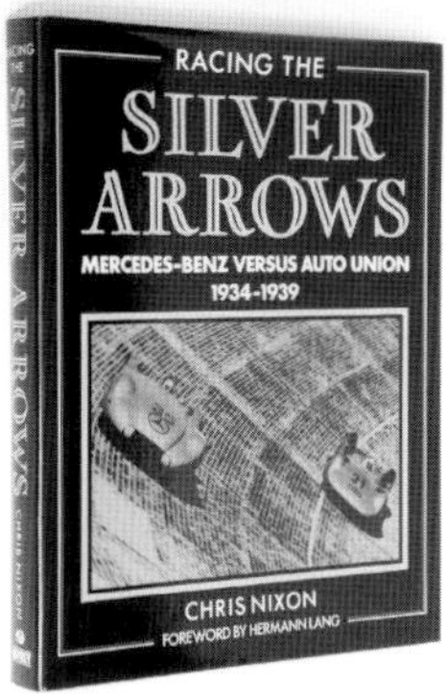

Chris Nixon, *Racing the Silver Arrows, Mercedes-Benz Versus Auto Union 1934–1939,* signed by the author, 1986, 9 x 11in (23 x 28cm).
£95–115
$135–165 ⊞ GPCC

Ferrari Formula 1 Annual 1994, edited by Bruno Alfieri, signed by Jean Alesi and Gerhard Berger, Italy, 10 x 11in (25.5 x 28cm).
£170–200
$250–290 ⊞ GPCC

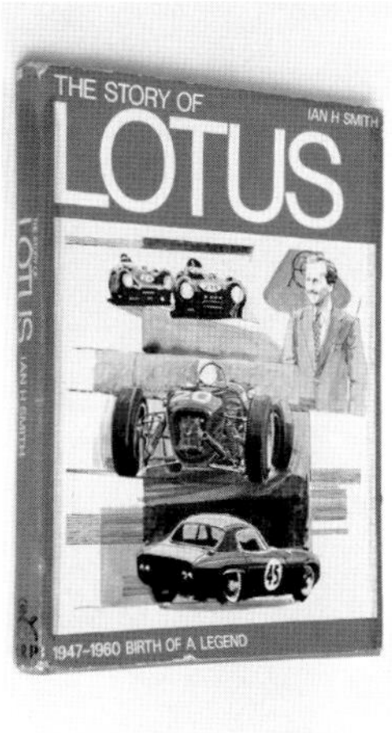

Ian H. Smith, *The Story of Lotus, 1947–1960 Birth of a Legend,* 1970, 10 x 8in (25.5 x 20.5cm).
£85–100
$125–145 ⊞ GPCC

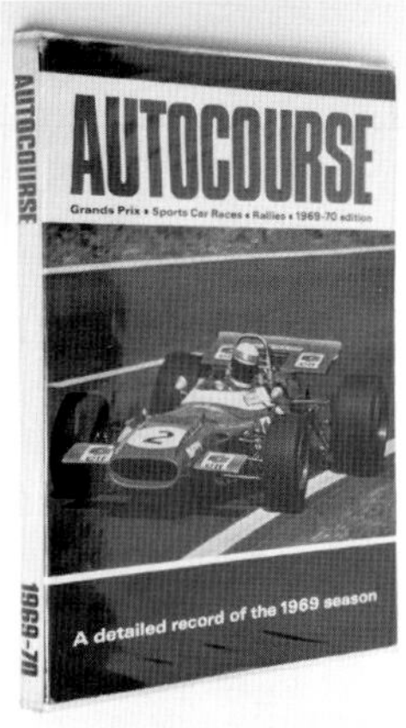

Autocourse 1969–1970, edited by David Phipps, signed by 1969 World Champion Jackie Stewart and Ken Tyrrell, 9 x 13in (23 x 33cm).
£280–320
$410–470 ⊞ GPCC

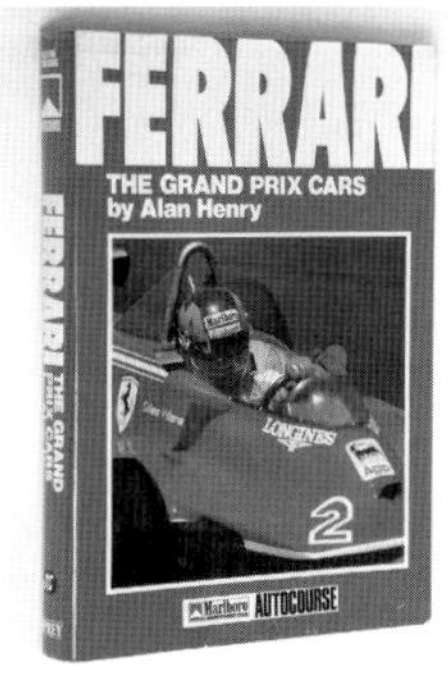

Alan Henry, *Ferrari The Grand Prix Cars,* signed by Ferrari drivers Surtees, Perger, Gonzalez and de Adamich, and Alan Henry, 1984, 7 x 9½in (18 x 24cm).
£140–165
$200–240 ⊞ GPCC

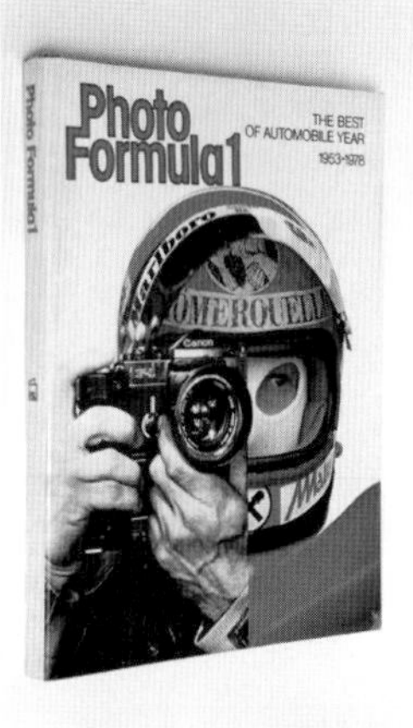

Photo Formula 1, The Best of Automobile Year 1953–1978, signed by Phil Hill and Stirling Moss, 1979, 13 x 10in (33 x 25.5cm).
£150–170
$220–250 ⊞ GPCC

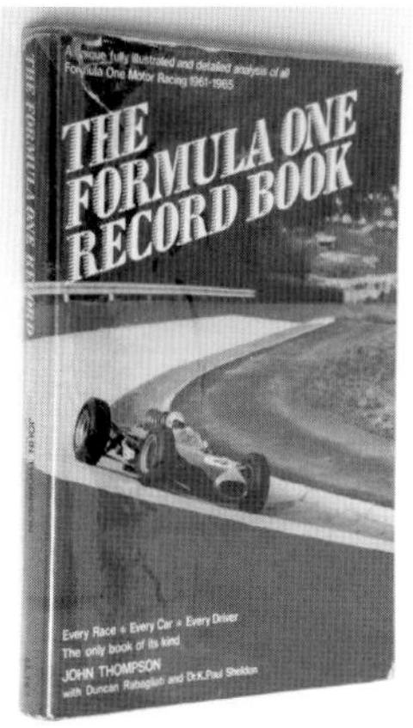

John Thompson, *The Formula One Record Book,* signed by Jack Fairman, 1974, 12 x 9in (30.5 x 23cm).
£75–90
$105–130 ⊞ GPCC

Akira Mase, *Great Drivers,* 1981, 15 x 11in (38 x 28cm).
£140–160 / $200–230 ⊞ GPCC

Doug Nye, *BRM The Saga of British Racing Motors, Volume 1, 1945–1960,* 1st edition, signed by Doug Nye and BMW drivers Jack Fairman and Les Leston, 1994, 9 x 11in (23 x 28cm).
£290–320
$425–470 ⊞ GPCC

Gordon Kirby, *Emerson Fittipaldi,* signed by Fittipaldi, 1990, 12 x9in (30.5 x 23cm).
£44–55 / $65–80 ⊞ GPCC

Motor Racing Memorabilia

A bronze sculpture of an Alfa Romeo P3, showing Tazio Nuvolari at the steering wheel, red and brown patina, mounted on a wooden base, c15¾in (40cm) long.
£1,000–1,200 / $1,500–1,800 ⚒ COYS

A set of 4 Bakelite ashtrays from the Brooklands Clubhouse, all marked B.A.R.C, chrome tops, unique to Brooklands.
£50–75 each / $75–110 ⊞ CARS

An MG Christmas card, embossed silver Gardner class record car on the front, printed message from Cecil Kimber on the inside, 1938.
£250–300 / $360–440 ⚒ BKS

Clive Ellis, a bronze sculpture of a Ferrari 335S at speed, No. 12 of 35 made, mounted on a marble base, 26¾in (68cm) long.
£3,000–3,600 / $4,400–5,200 ⚒ RM

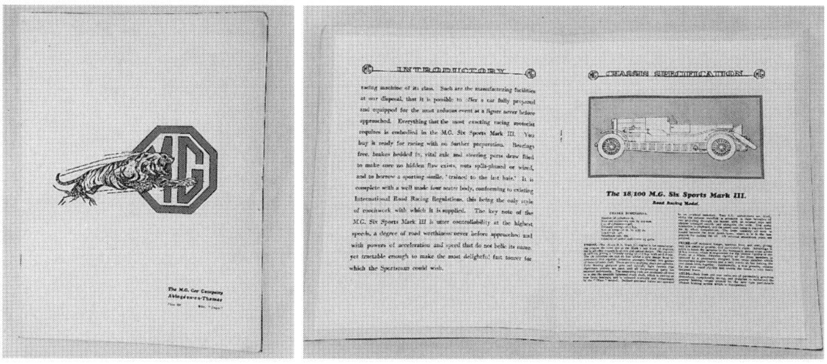

An MG brochure for the Six Sports Mk III racing model, referred to as the 18/100 and Tigress, cream outer cover overprinted with red MG motif and leaping tiger, 4 printed pages including a line profile of the car, introduction and technical specifications.
£600–700 / $870–1,000 ⚒ BKS

A Momo steering wheel, used by Ayrton Senna during the 1986 season with Team Lotus, black suede grip, central logo, signed in gold.
£3,000–3,600 / $4,400–5,200 ⚒ BKS

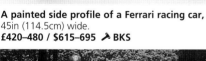

A painted side profile of a Ferrari racing car, 45in (114.5cm) wide.
£420–480 / $615–695 ⚒ BKS

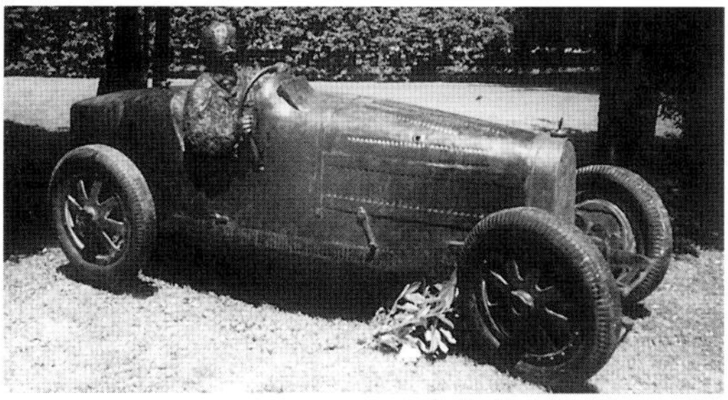

François Chevallier, a full-scale bronze sculpture of the 1929 Monaco Grand Prix winning Bugatti Type 35B, finished with green patina, driver positioned as if entering a right-hand corner at speed, 12ft (3.7m) long.
£50,000–60,000 / $72,500–87,000 ⚒ BKS

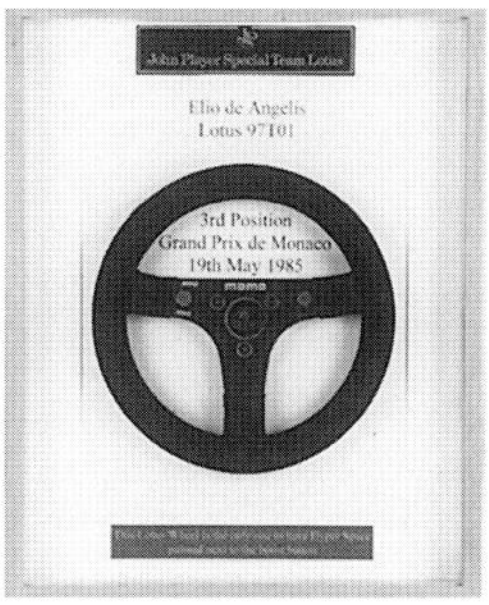

A Momo steering wheel, used by Elio de Angelis in the 3rd-placed Lotus at the 1985 Monaco Grand Prix, together with Team Lotus travel itineraries for the race, the tests at Nogaro and Paul Ricard in France, and the programme for the Monaco race, wheel framed and glazed.
£1,150–1,350
$1,675–2,000 ⚒ BKS
This wheel was the centre of much amusement at the time due to the 'Hyper Space' button label, painted by Team Lotus signwriter Paul Crowland as a joke.

A Bentley Motors Le Mans Victory dinner menu, from the Lyons Corner House, London W1, dated 'Friday, July 27th, 1928', given to the employees by the directors of Bentley Motors, 4-page booklet, signed by 11 personalities including Barnato, Rubin, W.O. Bentley, Birkin, Clement and Pike, slight soiling, otherwise good overall condition, 10 x 7in (25.4 x 17.8cm).
£2,500–2,800
$3,600–4,000 ⚒ BKS

Race Suits & Helmets

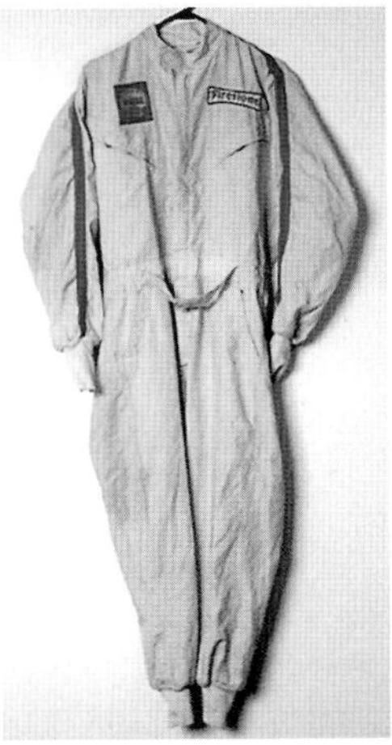

A Nomex race suit, worn by Chris Amon, in the colours of Scuderia Ferrari, letter of authenticity, 1967–69.
£2,250–2,500
$3,300–3,600 RM

► **A Shoei Formula 1 helmet,** worn by Bertrand Gachot while driving for the Pacific Team, signed in gold pen on the visor, 1994.
£1,000–1,200
$1,500–1,750 BKS

A Stand 21 race suit, worn by Nelson Piquet during his 1987 World Championship winning year with Williams, good clean condition.
£1,200–1,400
$1,750–2,000 BKS

An Arai Formula 1 helmet, worn by David Brabham while driving for the MTV Simtex Ford Team, black padded lining and crown vent, tinted visor, 1994.
£1,400–1,600
$2,000–2,300 BKS

An Arai Formula 1 helmet, worn by Jan Magnussen, black padded interior, original chin strap, tinted reflective visor and N/C duct, 1997.
£1,500–1,700
$2,150–2,450 BKS

Miller's is a price GUIDE not a price LIST

◄ **An Arai Formula 1 helmet,** worn by Andrea Montermini, black padded interior, chin strap, clear visor signed in gold by the driver, attached tear-off strip, helmet bag.
£1,200–1,350
$1,750–1,930 BKS

Photographs

A signed colour photograph of Ayrton Senna, framed, 1980, 18 x 11in (45.5 x 28cm).
£1,400–1,600
$2,000–2,300 SMW

A signed colour photograph of Michael Schumacher, driving a Ferrari, 1999, 6 x 10in (15 x 25.5cm).
£160–200 / $240–290 SMW

A signed colour photograph of Damon Hill, framed, c1998, 10 x 8in (25.5 x 20.5cm).
£80–100
$120–145 SMW

A signed photograph of Juan Manuel Fangio, showing the famous driver in the lead (pre-accident) at Le Mans in 1955, by Bernard Cahier, signed by Fangio, slight creasing, 24 x 32in (61 x 81.5cm).
£500–600 / $720–870 RM

A signed photograph of Stirling Moss, showing the famous driver in his Jaguar C-Type in 1952, by Peter McCall, signed by Moss and the photographer, mounted on board.
£260–320 / $380–470 BKS

Trophies

An A. C. Salerno II' Circuito Salerno-Paeustum trophy, presented to 'Gigi' Villoresi, sterling silver shell on a marble base, 11in (28cm) high.
£1,400–1,600
$2,000–2,300 ⚒ RM

The Class I 1937 RSAC Scottish Rally Trophy, presented to MG driver A.B. Langley by *The Autocar*, Art Deco style with striding female holding a shield and sword, on a dark green marble base, engraved plaque, sword in need of repair, 11in (28cm) high.
£650–750
$950–1,100 ⚒ BKS

A chrome Giro Automobilistico Dell'Umbria trophy, awarded to 'Gigi' Villoresi for 2nd place in category at Sport Nazionale, 13 June, 1952, on a wooden base, 13¼in (33.5cm) high.
£500–600
$720–870 ⚒ RM

An Alfa Romeo award plaque, presented to drivers and VIPs, cast bronze relief by Paolo de Leonibus, mounted on a wooden frame, 1969, 9 x 8¼in (23 x 21cm).
£800–900
$1,150–1,300 ⚒ RM

An A.H.M. silver motor racing trophy, by Elkington, the fitted lid terminating in an ivory finial, relief-moulded Spirit of Ecstacy grasping a laurel wreath below a plain body with twin wreath handles, vacant shield, on a circular stepped base, Birmingham 1913, 9½in (24cm) high, 24oz.
£600–700
$870–1,000 ⚒ BWe

A New Zealand International Grand Prix 1959 trophy, presented to Stirling Moss/Cooper-Climax for the fastest estimated lap, silver-plated pitcher, 9in (23cm) high.
£700–800
$1,000–1,150 ⚒ RM

A nickel-plated silver Junior and Light Car Club award plate, 1920s.
£60–75
$90–110 ⊞ CARS

An Automobile Club of Italy trophy, Italian Driver Champion 1948, presented to Luigi 'Gigi' Villoresi, sterling silver cup on a wooden base, 24½in (62cm) high.
£2,200–2,500
$3,200–3,600 ⚒ RM

◄ **A cast bronze prancing horse statue,** presented by Enzo Ferrari to 'Gigi' Villoresi as a token of appreciation, on a dark marble base with Ferrari emblem and World Championship plaque for 1952–53–56 with interlocked rings.
£2,700–3,200
$3,900–4,600 ⚒ RM

Key to Illustrations

**Each illustration and descriptive caption is accompanied by a letter code.
By referring to the following list of Auctioneers (denoted by *), dealers (•), Clubs, Museums and Trusts (§), the source of any item may be immediately determined. Inclusion in this edition no way constitutes or implies a contract or binding offer on the part of any of our contributors to supply or sell the goods illustrated, or similar articles, at the prices stated. Advertisers in this year's directory are denoted by †.
If you require a valuation, it is advisable to check whether the dealer or specialist will carry out this service and if there is a charge. Please mention *Miller's* when making an enquiry. A valuation by telephone is not possible. Most dealers are willing to help you with your enquiry; however, they are very busy people and consideration of the above points would be welcomed.**

AS • Ashted Service Station of Kenilworth, The Willows, Meer End Road, Kenilworth, Warwickshire CV8 1PU Tel: 01676 532289

ASOC § Armstrong Siddeley Owners Club Ltd, Peter Sheppard, 57 Berberry Close, Bournville, Birmingham, West Midlands B30 1TB

BAm § British Ambulance Society, Paul M Tona, 5 Cormorant Drive, Hythe, Hampshire SO45 3GG Tel: 023 8084 1999

BARO *† Barons, Brooklands House, 33 New Road, Hythe, Southampton, Hampshire SO45 6BN Tel: 023 8084 0081 info@barons-auctions.com www.barons-auctions.com

BC •† Beaulieu Garage Ltd, Beaulieu, Brockenhurst, Hampshire SO42 7YE Tel: 01590 612999

BCA • Beaulieu Cars Automobilia, c/o 1 Castle Mews, Castle Way, Southampton, Hampshire SO14 2AW

BJ *† Barrett-Jackson Auction Company, LLC, 3020 N Scottsdale Road, Scottsdale, Arizona U.S.A. Tel: 480-421-6694 www.barrett-jackson.com

BKS *† Bonhams & Brooks, Montpelier Street, Knightsbridge, London SW7 1HH Tel: 020 7393 3900 www.bonhams.com

BLE • Ivor Bleaney, PO Box 60, Salisbury, Wiltshire SP5 2DH Tel: 01794 390895

BLM • Bill Little Motorcycles, Oak Farm, Braydon, Swindon, Wiltshire SN5 0AG Tel: 01666 860577

BRIT * British Car Auctions Ltd, Classic & Historic Automobile Division, Auction Centre, Blackbushe Airport, Blackwater, Camberley, Surrey GU17 9LG Tel: 01252 878555

BRUM • Fred Brumby

BWe * Biddle and Webb Ltd, Ladywood, Middleway, Birmingham, West Midlands B16 0PP Tel: 0121 455 8042 antiques@biddleandwebb.freeserve.co.uk

C * Christie, Manson & Woods Ltd, The Jack Barclay Showroom, 2-4 Ponton Road, Nine Elms, London SW8 5BA Tel: 020 73892217

CARS •† C.A.R.S. (Classic Automobilia & Regalia Specialists), 4-4a Chapel Terrace Mews, Kemp Town, Brighton, East Sussex BN2 1HU Tel: 01273 60 1960

CGC *† Cheffins, 49/53 Regent Street, Cambridge CB2 1AF Tel: 01223 358731 www.chefins.co.uk

COB • Cobwebs, 78-80 Northam Road, Southampton, Hampshire SO14 0PB Tel: 023 8022 7458 www.cobwebs.uk.com

CoHA • Corner House Antiques and Ffoxe Antiques, High Street, Lechlade, Gloucestershire GL7 3AE Tel: 01367 252007

COHN • Terry Cohn, Rotherwood Lodge, Jumps Road, Churt, Surrey GU10 2JZ Tel: 01252 795000

COR •† Claremont Corvette, Snodland, Kent ME6 5NA Tel: 01634 244444

COYS * Coys of Kensington, 2/4 Queens Gate Mews, London SW7 5QJ Tel: 020 7584 7444

CRC § Craven Collection of Classic Motorcycles, Brockfield Villa, Stockton-on-the-Forest, Yorkshire YO3 9UE Tel: 01904 488461/400493

DRAK • John Drake, 5 Fox Field, Everton, Lymington, Hampshire SO41 0LR Tel: 01590 645623

DRJ • The Motorhouse, DS & RG Johnson, Thorton Hall, Thorton, Buckinghamshire MK17 0HB Tel: 01280 812280

DT • David Thomas, 1 The Mews, Orchard Lane, Ledbury, Herefordshire HR8 1DX Tel: 01531 635114 www.allautobooks.com

FCO § Ford Cortina 1600E Owners' Club, Membership Secretary Dave Johnson, 16 Woodland Close, Sarisbury Green, Nr Southampton, Hampshire SO31 7AQ davejohnson1600e@yahoo.com www.ford-cortina-16ooe-club.org.uk

FEO § Ford Executive Owners Register, George Young, 31 Brian Road, Chadwell Heath, Romford, Essex RM6 5DA

FHD •† F. H. Douglass, 1a South Ealing Road, Ealing, London W5 4OT Tel: 020 8567 0570

FIA § Fiat 500 Club, Membership Secretary Janet Westcott, 33 Lionel Avenue, Wendover, Aylesbury, Buckinghamshire HP22 6LP Tel: 01296 622880

FOS • Foskers, U5 Brands Hatch Circuit, Scratchers Lane, Fawkham, Kent DA3 8NG Tel: 01474 874777

GIRA • Girauto, Porte d'Orange, 84860 Caderousse, France Tel: 04 90 51 93 72

GPCC • Grand Prix World Book Service, 43 New Barn Lane, Ridgewood, Uckfield, East Sussex TN22 5EL Tel: 01825 764918 Mobile: 07850 230257 dhl@gpworld.fsnet.co.uk www.GrandPrixWorld.co.uk

GPT •† Grand Prix Top Gear, The Old Mill, Mill End, Standon, Hertfordshire SG11 1LR Tel: 01279 843999

GrM • Grundy Mack Classic Cars, Corner Farm, West Napton, Malton, Yorkshire YO17 8JB Tel: 01484 450446 Nick@grundy-mack-classic-cars.co.uk

H&H *† H & H Classic Auctions Ltd, Whitegate Farm, Hatton Lane, Hatton, Warrington, Cheshire WA4 4BZ Tel: 01925 730630 www.classic-auctions.co.uk

HARP • Harpers Jewellers Ltd, 2/6 Minster Gates, York YO1 7HL Tel: 01904 632634 harpers@talk21.com www.vintage-watches.co.uk

HCL • Heritage Classics Motor Company, 8980 Santa Monica Boulevard, West Hollywood, California 90069, U.S.A. Tel: 310 657 9699 sales@heritageclassics.com www.heritageclassics.com

HMC • Hallmark Cars, 1 Connaught Avenue, North Chingford, London E4 7AE Tel: 020 8529 7474

HMM §† Haynes Motor Museum, Sparkford, Yeovil, Somerset BA22 7LH Tel: 01963 440804

IMP § Imp Club, 27 Brookside Road, Stratford-on-Avon, Warwickshire CV37 9PH

IMPS § Invicta Military Vehicle Preservation Society, Andrew Tizzard, 4 Hanbury Close, Wateringbury, Kent ME18 5DP www.warandpeace.uk.com

JUN •† Junktion, The Old Railway Station, New Bolingbroke, Boston, Lincolnshire PE22 7LB Tel: 01205 480068

KHP • Kent High Performance Cars, Unit 1-2, Target Business Centre, Bircholt Road, Parkwood Industrial Estate, Maidstone, Kent ME15 9YY Tel: 01622 663308

KR § Mr Bood, K70 Register, 25 Cedar Grove, Penn Fields, Wolverhampton WV3 7EB

LE • Laurence Edscer, 91 Sea Road, Carlyon Bay, St. Austell, Cornwall PL25 3SH Tel: 01726 810070 Mobile: 07836 594714 homeusers.prestel.co.uk/edscer

M * Morphets of Harrogate, 6 Albert Street, Harrogate, Yorkshire HG1 1JL Tel: 01423 530030

MIMI * Mimi's Antiques, 8763 Carriage Hills Drive, Columbia MD 21046, USA Tel: 001 410 381 6862 mimis1@erols.com www.mimisantiques.com

MINI § Mini Cooper Register, Public Relations Officer Philip Splett, Burtons Farm, Barling Road, Barling Magna, Southend, Essex SS3 0LZ

MPG • MotorPost Gallery, 5 Shadwell Park Court, Leeds, Yorkshire LS17 8TS Tel: 0113 225 3525

MSMP • Mike Smith Motoring Past, Chiltern House, Ashendon, Aylesbury, Buckinghamshire HP18 0HB Tel: 01296 651283

MUN •† Munich Legends Ltd, The Ashdown Garage, Chelwood Gate, East Sussex RH17 7DE Tel: 01825 740456

MVT § Military Vehicle Trust, PO Box 6, Fleet, Hampshire GU52 6GE

NCC § Naylor Car Club, Registrar Mrs F. R. Taylor, 21 Anglesey Place, Great Barton, Nr Bury St. Edmunds, Suffolk IP31 2TW Tel: 01284 788094

Now • Julian Nowill, Earlsland House, Bradninch, Exeter, Devon EX5 4QP Tel: 01392 453600 www.gerrard.com

PALM *† Palm Springs Exotic Car Auctions, 602 East Sunny Dunes Road, Palm Springs, California 92264, USA Tel: 760 320 3290 www.classic-carauction.com

PC Private Collection

PCr Peter Crisp

PMo • Planet Motorcycles, 44-45 Tamworth Road, Croydon, Surrey CRO 1XU Tel: 020 86865650

Pou * Poulain Le Fur, Commissaires Priseurs Associes, 20 rue de Provence, 75009 Paris, France Tel: 01 42 46 81 81

PPH • Period Picnic Hampers Tel: 0115 937 2934

PSS • Preston Steam Services, Preston, Canterbury, Kent CT3 1DH Tel: 01227 722502 MLB@SteamServices.co.uk www.steamservices.co.uk

RBB * Brightwells Ltd Fine Art Salerooms, Ryelands Road, Leominster, Herefordshire HR6 8NZ Tel: 01568 611122

RCC •† Real Car Co Ltd, Snowdonia Business Park, Coed y Parc, Bethesda, Gwynedd LL57 4YS Tel: 01248 602649 mail@realcar.co.uk

RIL § Riley RM Club, Mrs J. Morris, Y Fachell, Ruthin Road, Gwernymynydd, North Wales CH7 5LQ

RM * RM Auctions, Inc, One Classic Car Drive, Ontario NOP 1AO, Canada Tel: 00 519 352 4575

RRM • RR Motor Services Ltd, Bethersden, Ashford, Kent TN26 3DN Tel: 01233 820219

RSW • R. S. Williams Ltd, Protech House, Copse Road, Cobham, Surrey KT11 2TW Tel: 01932 868377 astons@rswilliams.co.uk www.rswilliams.co.uk

SAAB § Saab Owners Club of GB Ltd, Membership Secretary John Wood, PO Box 900, Durham DH1 2GF Tel: 01923 229945 Membership Hotline: 070 71 71 9000

SiC • Silverstone Classic Cars Tel: 01933 622484 classiccarsales@lineone.net www.classiccarsales.net

SMW • Sporting Memorabilia of Warwick, 13 Market Place, Warwick CV34 4FS Tel: 01926 410600 Mobile: 07860 269340 sales@sportantiques.com www.sportsantiques.com

SW • No longer trading

TEN * Tennants, The Auction Centre, Harmby Road, Leyburn, Yorkshire DL8 5SG Tel: 01969 623780

TEN * Tennants, 34 Montpellier Parade, Harrogate, Yorkshire HG1 2TG Tel: 01423 531661

TIC • Tickers, 31 Old Northam road, Southampton, Hampshire SO14 0NZ Tel: 02380 234431

TIHO •† Titty Ho, Grove Street, Raunds, Northamptonshire Tel: 01933 622206

TPS • Trevor's Pump Shop, 2 Cement Cottages, Station Road, Rainham, Kent ME8 7UF Tel: 01634 361231

TSG •† The School Garage, 47 Buxton Road, Whaley Bridge, High Peak, Derbyshire SK23 7HX Tel: 01663 733209 www.classiccarshop.co.uk

TSh * Thimbleby & Shorland, 31 Great Knollys Street, Reading, Berkshire RG1 7HU Tel: 0118 9508611

TUC •† Tuckett Bros, Marstonfields, North Marston, Buckinghamshire MK18 3PG Tel: 01296 670500

TWY • Twyford Moors Classic Cars, Unit C Burnes Shipyard, Old Bosham, Nr Chichester, West Sussex PO18 8LJ Tel: 01243 576586

UMC •† Unicorn Motor Company, Brian R. Chant, M.I.M.I., Station Road, Stalbridge, Dorset DT10 2RH Tel: 01963 363353

VEY • Paul Veysey Tel: 01452 790672 www.drivepast.com

VIC •† Vicarys of Battle Ltd, 32 High St, Battle, East Sussex TN33 0EH Tel: 01424 772425

W&P § The War & Peace Show, The Hop Farm Country Park, Beltring, Nr. Paddock Wood, Kent

WAB • Warboys Antiques, St Ives, Cambridgeshire Tel: 01480 463891 john.lambden@virgin.net

WbC • Woodbridge Classic Cars, Blomvyle Hall Garage, Easton Road, Hacheston, Suffolk IP13 0DY Tel: 01728 746413 sales@tr6.com www.tr6.com

WCL • Waterside Classics Ltd, 3 Alleysbank Road, Farmeloan Estate, Rutherglen, Glasgow, Scotland G73 1AE Tel: 0141 647 0333

WILM • Wilmington Classic Cars, Lewes Road, Wilmington, Polegate, East Sussex BN26 5JE Tel: 01323 486136

WilP/ WILP * W&H Peacock, 26 Newnham Street, Bedford MK40 3JR Tel: 01234 266366

Glossary

We have attempted to define some of the terms that you will come across in this book. If there are any terms or technical expressions that you would like explained or you feel should be included in future, please let us know.

Aero screen A small, curved windscreen fitted to the scuttle of a sports car in place of the standard full-width screen. Used in competition to reduce wind resistance. Normally fitted in pairs, one each in front of the driver and passenger.

All-weather A term used to describe a vehicle with a more sophisticated folding hood than the normal Cape hood fitted to a touring vehicle. The sides were fitted with metal frames and transparent material, in some cases glass.

Barchetta Italian for 'little boat', an all-enveloping open sports bodywork.

Berline *See* **Sedanca de Ville**.

Boost The amount of pressure applied by a supercharger or turbocharger.

Boxer Engine configuration with horizontally-opposed cylinders.

Brake A term dating from the days of horse-drawn vehicles. Originally the seating was fore and aft, the passengers facing inwards.

Brake horsepower (bhp) This is the amount of power produced by an engine, measured at the flywheel (*See* **Horsepower**).

Cabriolet The term Cabriolet applies to a vehicle with a hood that can be closed, folded half-way or folded right back. A Cabriolet can be distinguished from a Landaulette because the front of the hood reaches the top of the windscreen, whereas on a Landaulette, it only covers the rear half of the car.

Chain drive A transmission system in which the wheels are attached to a sprocket, driven by a chain from an engine-powered sprocket, usually on the output side of a gearbox.

Chassis A framework to which the car body, engine, gearbox, and axles are attached.

Chummy An open-top, two-door body style, usually with a single door on each side, two seats in the front and one at the rear.

Cloverleaf A three-seater, open body style, usually with a single door on each side, two seats in the front and one at the rear.

Concours Concours d'Elegance is a competition in which cars are judged by their condition. Concours has become a byword for a vehicle in excellent condition.

Cone clutch A clutch in which both driving and driven faces form a cone.

Connollising Leather treatment produced by British firm Connolly to rejuvenate and restore suppleness to old and dry leather.

Convertible A general term (post-war) for any car with a folding soft top.

Continental A car specifically designed for high-speed touring, usually on the Continent. Rolls-Royce and Bentley almost exclusively used this term during the 1930s and post-WWII.

Coupé In the early Vintage and Edwardian period, Coupé was only applied to what is now termed a Half Limousine or Doctor's Coupé, which was a two-door two-seater. The term is now usually prefixed by Drophead or Fixed-Head.

Cubic capacity The volume of an engine obtained by multiplying the area of the bore by the stroke. Engine capacity is given in cubic centimetres (cc) in Europe and cubic inches (cu.in) in the USA. 1 cubic inch equals 16.38cc (1 litre = 61.02cu.in).

de Ville A style of coachwork in which the driver/chauffeur occupies an open driving position, and the passengers a closed compartment – thus, Coupé de Ville or Sedanca de Ville. In America, these vehicles are known as Town Cars.

Dickey seat A passenger seat, usually for two people, contained in the boot of the car and without a folding hood (the boot lid forms the backrest). *See* **Rumble seat**.

Doctor's coupé A fixed or drophead coupé without a dickey seat, the passenger seat being slightly staggered back from the driver's to accommodate the famous doctor's bag.

Dog cart A form of horse-drawn vehicle originally designed for transporting beaters and their dogs to a shoot (the dogs were contained in louvred boxes under the seats; the louvres were kept for decoration long after the practice of carrying dogs in this way had ceased).

Dos-à-dos Literally back-to-back, i.e. the passenger seating arrangement.

Double-duck Double-layered fabric used in construction of folding convertible tops.

Drophead coupé Originally a two-door two-seater with a folding roof.

Dry sump A method of lubricating engines in which the oil is contained in a separate reservoir rather than in a sump at the bottom of the cylinder block. Usually, two oil pumps are used, one to remove oil from the engine to the reservoir, the other to pump it back to the engine.

Fender American term used to describe the wing of a car.

F-head An engine design in which the inlet valve is in the cylinder head, while the exhaust valve is in the cylinder block. Also referred to as inlet-over-exhaust.

Fixed-head coupé A coupé with a solid fixed roof.

Golfer's coupé Usually an open two-seater with a square-doored locker behind the driver's seat to accommodate golf clubs.

Hansom As with the famous horse-drawn cab, an enclosed two-seater with the driver out in the elements, either behind or in front of the passenger compartment.

Homologation To qualify for entry into some race series, the rules can require that a minimum number of road-going production versions of the race car are built. These are generally known as 'homologation specials'.

Hood American term used to describe the bonnet of a car.

Horsepower (hp) The unit of measurement of engine power – one horsepower represents the energy expended in raising 33,000lb by one foot in 60 seconds.

Landau An open town carriage for four people with a folding hood at each end, which would meet in the middle when erected.

Landaulette A horse-drawn Landaulette carried two people and was built much like a coupé. The roof line of a Landaulette is always angular, in contrast to a Cabriolet, and the folding hood is very often made of patent leather. A true Landaulette only opens over the rear compartment and not over the front seat at all. (Also Landaulet.)

L-head An engine design in which the inlet and exhaust valves are contained within the cylinder block. *See* **Sidevalve**.
Limousine French in origin and used to describe a closed car equipped with occasional seats and a division between the rear and driver's compartments.
Monobloc engine An engine with all its cylinders cast in a single block.
Monocoque A method of constructing a car without a separate chassis, structural strength being provided by the arrangement of the stressed panels. Most modern, mass-produced cars are built in this way.
Monoposto Single-seater (Italian).
Nitrided Used to describe engine components, particularly crankshafts, that have been specially hardened to withstand the stresses of racing or other high-performance applications.
OHC Overhead camshaft, either single (SOHC) or double (DOHC).
OHV Overhead valves.
Phaeton A term dating back to the days of horse-drawn vehicles and used to describe an open body, sometimes with a dickey or rumble seat for the groom at the rear. It was an owner/driver carriage and designed to be pulled by four horses. A term often misused during the Veteran period, but still in common use, particularly in the USA.
Post Vintage Thoroughbred (PVT) A British term created by the Vintage Sports Car Club (VSCC) to describe selected models made in the vintage tradition between 1931 and 1942.
Roadster A two-seater, open sporting vehicle, the hood of which is removed completely rather than being folded down, as on a drophead coupé. Early versions without side windows.
Roi des Belges A luxurious open touring car with elaborately contoured seat backs, named after King Leopold II of Belgium. The term is sometimes incorrectly used to describe general touring cars.
Rotary engine A unique form of car engine in which the cylinders, pistons and crankshaft of the normal reciprocating engine are replaced by a triangular rotor that rotates about an eccentric shaft within a special waisted chamber. One or more rotor/chamber assemblies may be used. On the whole, the engine has a third of the number of parts of a comparable reciprocating engine. The engine was designed by Dr Felix Wankel and has been used in a range of sports cars by Mazda.
RPM Engine revolutions per minute.
Rumble seat An American term for a folding seat for two passengers, used to increase the carrying capacity of a standard two-passenger car. *See* **Dickey seat**.
Runabout A low-powered, lightweight, open two-seater from the 1900s.
Saloon A two- or four-door car with four or more seats and a fixed roof.
Sedan *See* **Saloon**.
Sedanca de Ville A limousine body with an open driving compartment that can be covered with a folding or sliding roof section, known in America as a Town Car.
Sidevalve Used to describe an engine in which the valves are located in the cylinder block rather than the head.
Sociable A cyclecar term used to describe the side-by-side seating of the driver and passenger.
Spider/Spyder An open two-seater sports car, sometimes a 2+2 (with two small occasional seats behind the two front seats).
Station wagon American term for an estate car.
Supercharger An engine-driven pump for forcing the fuel/air mixture into the cylinders to gain extra power.
Surrey An early 20thC open four-seater with a fringed canopy. A term from the days of horse-drawn vehicles.
Stanhope A single-seat, two-wheeled horse-drawn carriage with a hood. Later, a four-wheeled, two-seater, sometimes with an underfloor engine.
Stroke The distance an engine's piston moves up-and-down within its cylinder. The stroke is invariably measured in millimetres, although in the USA, inches may be used.
Superleggera Italian for 'super lightweight' and used to describe a method of construction devised by Touring of Milan, whereby an aluminium skin was attached to a framework of steel tubes to produce a light, yet strong, structure. One of the best-known proponents of this method was Aston Martin, which employed Superleggera construction in some of its DB series cars.
Tandem A cyclecar term used to describe the fore-and-aft seating of the driver and passenger.
Targa A coupé fitted with a removable central roof section.
Tonneau A rear-entrance tonneau is a four-seater to which access is provided through a centrally-placed rear door. A detachable tonneau meant that the rear seats could be removed to make a two-seater. Today, 'tonneau' usually refers to a waterproof cover that can be fitted over the cockpit of an open car when the roof is detached.
Torpedo An open tourer that has coachwork with an unbroken line from the bonnet to the rear of the body.
Tourer An open four- or five-seater with three or four doors, a folding hood (with or without sidescreens) and seats flush with the body sides. This body style began to appear in about 1910 and, initially, was known as a torpedo (*see above*), but by 1920, the word 'tourer' was being used instead – except in France, where 'torpedo' continued in use until the 1930s.
Turbocharger An exhaust-gas-driven pump for forcing the air/fuel mixture into the engine's cylinders to produce extra power.
Unitary construction Used to describe a vehicle without a separate chassis, structural strength being provided by the arrangement of the stressed panels. *See* **Monocoque**.
Veteran All vehicles manufactured before 31 December 1918; only cars built before 31 March 1904 are eligible for the London to Brighton Commemorative Run.
Victoria Generally an American term for a two- or four-seater with a very large folding hood. If a four-seater, the hood would only cover the rear seats. In some cases, applied to a saloon with a 'bustle' back.
Vintage Any vehicle manufactured between the end of the veteran period and 31 December 1930. *See* **Post Vintage Thoroughbred**.
Vis-à-vis Face-to-face; an open car in which the passengers sit opposite each other.
Voiturette A French term used to describe a very light car, originally coined by Léon Bollée.
Wagonette A large car for six or more passengers, in which the rear seats face each other. Entrance is at the rear, and the vehicle is usually open.
Waxoyled Used to describe a vehicle in which the underside has been treated with Waxoyl, a proprietary oil and wax spray that protects against moisture.
Weymann A system of body construction employing Rexine fabric panels over a Kapok filling to prevent noise and provide insulation.
Wheelbase The distance between the centres of the front and rear wheels of a vehicle.

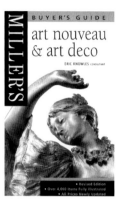

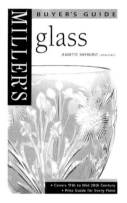

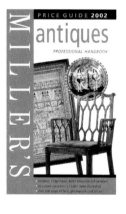

Directory of Car Clubs

If you would like your Club to be included in next year's directory, or have a change of address or telephone number, please inform us by 31 May 2002.

105E Anglia Owners' Club Middlesex Group, 9 Evelyn Avenue, Ruislip, Middlesex HA4 8AR

2CVGB Deux Chevaux Club of GB, PO Box 602, Crick, Northampton, NN6 7UW

750 Motor Club Ltd, Worth Farm, Little Horsted, West Sussex TN22 5TT

AC Owners' Club, P S Tyler, Hopwoods House, Sewards End, Saffron Walden, Essex CB10 2LE

A40 Farina Club, Membership Secretary, 2 Ivy Cottages, Fullers Vale, Headley Down, Bordon, Hampshire GU35 8NR

ABC Owners' Club, D A Hales, The Hedgerows, Sutton St Nicholas, Hereford HR1 3BU

Alexis Racing and Trials Car Register, Duncan Rabagliati, 4 Wool Road, Wimbledon, London SW20 0HW

Alfa Romeo 1900 Register, Peter Marshall, Mariners, Courtlands Avenue, Esher, Surrey KT10 9HZ

Alfa Romeo Owners' Club, Michael Lindsay, 97 High Street, Linton, Cambridge CB1 6JT

Alfa Romeo Section (VSCC Ltd), Allan & Angela Cherrett, Old Forge, Quarr, Nr Gillingham, Dorset SP8 5PA

Allard Owners' Club, Miss P Hulse, 1 Dalmeny Avenue, Tufnell Park, London N7

Alvis Owners' Club, 1 Forge Cottages, Bayham Road, Little Bayham, Lamberhurst, Kent TN3 8BB

Alvis Register, Mr J Willis, The Vinery, Wanborough Hill, Nr Guildford, Surrey GU3 2JR Tel: 01483 810308

American Auto Club UK, 11 Wych Elm, Colchester, Essex CO2 8PR

Amilcar Salmson Register, R A F King, Apple House, Wildmoor Lane, Sherfield on Lodden, Hampshire RG27 0HA

Armstrong Siddeley Owners' Club Ltd, Peter Sheppard, 57 Berberry Close, Bourneville, Birmingham, West Midlands B30 1TB

Association of British Volkswagen Clubs, Dept PC, 76 Eastfield Road, Burnham, Buckinghamshire SL1 7PF

Association of American Car Clubs UK, PO Box 2222, Braintree, Essex CM7 9TW

Association of Healey Owners, John Humphreys, 2 Kingsbury's Lane, Ringwood, Hampshire BH24 1EL

Association of Old Vehicle Clubs in Northern Ireland Ltd, Trevor Mitchell (Secretary), 38 Ballymaconnell Road, Bangor, Co. Down, Northern Ireland BT20 5PS Tel: 028 9146 7886 Fax: 028 91463211 secretary@aovc.co.uk www.aovc.co.uk

Association of Singer Car Owners, Anne Page, 39 Oakfield, Rickmansworth, Hertfordshire WD3 8LR Tel: 01923 778575

Aston Martin Owners' Club Ltd, The Barn, Drayton St. Leonard, Oxon OX10 7BE

Atlas Register, 38 Ridgeway, Southwell, Nottinghamshire NG25 0DJ

Austin 3 Litre OC, Neil Kidby, 78 Croft Street, Ipswich, Suffolk IP2 8EF

Austin A30-35 Owners' Club, Mrs C. Tarsey (Membership Secretary), 3 George Street, Leighton Buzzard, Bedfordshire LU7 8JX www.austin.club.co.uk

Austin Big 7 Register, R E Taylor, 101 Derby Road, Chellaston, Derbyshire DE73 1SB

Austin Cambridge/Westminster Car Club, Arthur Swann, 21 Alexander Terrace, Corsham, Wiltshire SN13 0BW

Austin Counties Car Club, Martin Pickard, 10 George Street, Bedworth, Warwickshire CV12 8EB

Austin Eight Register, Ian Pinniger, 3 La Grange Martin, St Martin, Jersey, Channel Islands JE3 6JB Fax: (44) 01534 859113 mail@pinniger.fsnet.co.uk

Austin Gipsy Register 1958–1968, Mike Gilbert, 24 Green Close, Rixon, Sturminster Newton, Dorset DT10 1BJ

Austin Healey Club, Colleen Holmes, 4 Saxby Street, Leicester LE2 0ND

Austin Healey Club, Mike Ward, Midland Centre, 66 Glascote Lane, Tamworth, Staffordshire B77 2PH

Austin J40 Pedal Car Club, Mary Rowlands, 21 Forest Close, Lickey End, Bromsgrove, Worcestershire B60 1JU

Austin Maxi Club, Mrs C J Jackson, 27 Queen Street, Bardney, Lincolnshire LN3 5XF

Austin Seven Mulliner Register, Mike Tebbett, Little Wyche, Walwyn Road, Upper Colwall, Nr Malvern, Worcestershire WR13 6PL

Austin Seven Van Register 1923–29, N B Baldry, 32 Wentworth Crescent, Maidenhead, Berkshire SL6 4RW

Austin Sheerline & Princess Club, Ian Coombes, 44 Vermeer Crescent, Shoeburyness, Essex S53 9TJ

Austin Swallow Register, G L Walker, School House, Rectory Road, Great Haseley, Oxfordshire OX44 7JP

Austin Taxi Club, A. Thomas, 52 Foss Avenue, Waddon, Croydon, Surrey CR0 4EU Tel: 0208 686 1938 www.taxiclub.freeserve.co.uk

Austin Ten Drivers' Club Ltd, Ian M. Dean, P.O. Box 12, Chichester, West Sussex PO20 7PH Tel: 01243 641284

Battery Vehicle Society, Keith Roberts, 29 Ambergate Drive, North Pentwyn, Cardiff, Wales CF2 7AX

Bentley Drivers' Club, 16 Chearsley Road, Long Crendon, Aylesbury, Buckinghamshire HP18 9AW

Berkeley Enthusiasts Club, M. Rounsville-Smith, 41 Gorsewood Road, Brookwood, Surrey GU21 1UZ Tel: 01483 475330

Biggin Hill Car Club with XJ Register of JDC, Peter Adams, Jasmine House, Jasmine Grove, London SE20 8JY

BMC J2/152 Reg, 10 Sunnyside Cottages, Woodford, Kettering, Northamptonshire NN14 4HX

BMW Drivers' Club, Sue Hicks, Bavaria House, PO Box 8, Dereham, Norfolk NR19 1TF

Bond Owners' Club, Stan Cornock, 42 Beaufort Avenue, Hodge Hill, Birmingham, West Midlands B34 6AE

Borgward Drivers Club, Mr D.C. Farr, 19 Highfield Road, Kettering, Northamptonshire NN15 6HR

Brabham Register, Ed Walker, The Old Bull, 5 Woodmancote, Dursley, Gloucestershire GL11 4AF

Bristol Austin Seven Club, 1 Silsbury Hill Cottages, West Kennett, Marlborough, Wiltshire SN8 1QH

Bristol Microcar Club, 123 Queens Road, Bishopsworth, Bristol, Gloucestershire BS13 8QB

Bristol Owners' Club, John Emery, Vesutor, Marringdean Road, Billingshurst, West Sussex RH14 9HD

British Ambulance Society, Paul M Tona, 5 Cormorant Drive, Hythe, Hampshire SO45 3GG Tel: 023 8084 1999

British Automobile Racing Club, Thruxton Circuit, Andover, Hampshire SP11 8PN Tel: 01264 772607 & 772696/7

The British Hotchkiss Society, Michael R J Edwards,Yew Cottage, Old Boars Hill, Oxford OX1 5JJ

British Saab Enthusiasts, Mr M Hodges, 75 Upper Road, Poole, Dorset BH12 3EN

British Salmson Owners' Club, John Maddison, 86 Broadway North, Walsall, West Midlands WS1 2QF

Brough Superior Club, Justin Wand (Secretary), Flint Cottage, St Paul's Walden, Hitchin, Hertfordshire SG4 8ON

BSA Front Wheel Drive Club, Barry Baker (Membership Secretary), 164 Cottimore Lane, Walton-on-Thames, Surrey KT12 2BL

Bugatti Owners' Club Ltd, Sue Ward, Prescott Hill, Gotherington, Cheltenham, Gloucestershire GL52 4RD

Buick Club UK, PO Box 2222, Braintree, Essex CM7 9TW

CA Bedford Owners' Club, G W Seller, 7 Grasmere Road, Benfleet, Essex SS7 3HF

Cambridge-Oxford Owners' Club, 32 Reservoir Road, Southgate, London N14 4BG

Capri Club International, 18 Arden Business Centre, Arden Road, Alcester B49 6HW

Capri Club International, North London Branch, 12 Chalton Road, Edmonton, London N9 8EG

Capri Drivers Association, Mrs Moira Farrelly (Secretary), 9 Lyndhurst Road, Coulsdon, Surrey CR5 3HT

Citroën Car Club, P O Box 348, Bromley, Kent BR2 2QT Tel: 01689 853999 www.citroencarclub.org.uk

Citroën Traction Owners' Club, Peter Riggs, 2 Appleby Gardens, Dunstable, Bedfordshire LU6 3DB

Clan Owners Club, Chris Clay, 48 Valley Road, Littleover, Derbyshire DE23 6HS

Classic and Historic Motor Club Ltd, Tricia Burridge, Stream Cottage, Yarley Cross, Wells, Somerset BA5 1LS

The Classic Camper Club, PO Box 3, Amlwch, Anglesey LL68 9ZE Tel: 01407 832243 www.ClassicCamperClub.co.uk

Classic Chevrolet Club, PO Box 2222, Braintree, Essex CM7 9TW

Classic Corvette Club (UK), Ashley Pickering, The Gables, Christchurch Road, Tring, Hertfordshire HP23 4EF

Classic Hearse Register, Paul Harris, 121 St Mary's Crescent, Basildon, Essex SS13 2AS Tel: 01268 472313

Classic Z Register, Jon Newlyn, 11 Lawday Link, Upper Hale, Farnham, Surrey GU9 0BS

Club Alpine Renault UK Ltd, 1 Bloomfield Close, Wombourne, Wolverhampton, West Midlands WV5 8HQ

Club Lotus, Lotus Lodge, P O Box 8, Dereham, Norfolk NR19 1TF

Club Peugeot UK, Peter Vaughan, 41 Hazelwood Drive, Bourne, Lincolnshire PE10 9SZ

Club Peugeot UK, Club Regs 504 Cab/Coupe, Beacon View, Forester Road, Soberton Heath, Southampton, Hampshire SO32 3QG

Club Triumph, Derek Pollock, 86 Waggon Road, Hadley Wood, Hertfordshire EN14 0PP

Club Triumph Eastern, Mr D A Davies, 72 Springwater Road, Eastwood, Leigh-on-Sea, Essex SS9 5BJ

Clyno Club, Swallow Cottage, Langton Farm, Elmesthorpe, Leicestershire LE9 7SE

Commercial Vehicle and Road Transport Club, Steven Wimbush, 8 Tachbrook Road, Uxbridge, Middlesex UB8 2QS

Connaught Register, Duncan Rabagliati, 4 Wool Road, Wimbledon, London SW20 0HW

Cortina Mk II Register, Mark Blows, 78 Church Avenue, Broomfield, Chelmsford, Essex CM1 7HA

Cougar Club of America, Barrie S Dixon, 11 Dean Close, Partington, Greater Manchester M31 4BQ

Crayford Convertible Car Club, 58 Geriant Road, Downham, Bromley, Kent BR1 5DX

Crossley Register, 7 Manor Road, Sherborne St John, Nr Basingstoke, Hampshire RG24 9JJ

Crossley Register, Malcolm Jenner, Willow Cottage, Lexham Road, Great Dunham, Kings Lynn, Norfolk PE32 2LS

DAF Owners' Club, S K Bidwell (Club Secretary), 56 Ridgedale Road, Bolsover, Chesterfield, Derbyshire S44 6TX

Daimler and Lanchester Owners' Club, PO Box 276, Sittingbourne, Kent ME9 7GA Tel: 07000 356285 www.dloc.org.uk

Datsun Owners' Club, Jon Rodwell, 26 Langton Park, Wroughton, Wiltshire SN4 0QN Tel: 01793 845271 www.datsunworld.com

De Tomaso Drivers' Club, Phil Stebbings (Founder & Club Secretary), Flint Barn, Malthouse Lane, Ashington, West Sussex RH20 3BU

Delage Section of the VSCC Ltd, Peter Jacobs (Secretary), Clouds' Reach, The Scop, Almondsbury, Bristol BS32 4DU

Delahaye Club GB, A F Harrison, 34 Marine Parade, Hythe, Kent CT21 6AN

Dellow Register, Douglas Temple Design Group, 4 Roumelia Lane, Bournemouth, Dorset BH5 1EU

Delorean Owners' Club, c/o Chris Parnham, 14 Quarndon Heights, Allestree, Derby DE22 2XN www.delorean.co.uk

Diva Register, Steve Pethybridge, 8 Wait End Road, Waterlooville, Hampshire PO7 7DD

DKW Owners' Club, David Simon, Aurelia, Garlogie, Skene, Westhill, Aberdeenshire, Scotland AB32 6RX

Droop Snoot Group, 41 Horsham Avenue, Finchley, London N12 9BG

Dunsfold Land Rover Trust, Dunsfold, Surrey GU8 4NP

Dutton Owners' Club, Rob Powell, 20 Burford Road, Baswich, Stafford ST17 0BT

Early Ford V8 Club, 12 Fairholme Gardens, Cranham, Upminster, Essex RM14 1HJ

East Anglia Fighting Group, 206 Colchester Road, Lawford, Nr Manningtree, Essex

Elva Owners Club, Roger Dunbar, 8 Liverpool Terrace, Worthing, West Sussex BN11 1TA
Tel: 01903 823710
roger.dunbar@elva.com
www.elva.com

Enfield & District Veteran Vehicle Trust, Whitewebbs Museum, Whitewebbs Road, Enfield, Middlesex EN2 9HW

ERA Club, Guy Spollon, Arden Grange, Tanworth-in-Arden, Warwickshire B94 5AE

F and FB Victor Owners' Club, Wayne Parkhouse, 5 Farnell Road, Staines, Middlesex TW18 4HT

F-Victor Owners' Club, Alan Victor Pope, 34 Hawkesbury Drive, Mill Lane, Calcot, Reading, Berkshire RG3 5ZR

Facel Vega Car Club, Mr M. Green (Secretary), 17 Stanley Road, Lymington, Hampshire SO41 3SJ

Fairthorpe Sports Car Club, Tony Hill, 9 Lynhurst Crescent, Uxbridge, Middlesex UB10 9EF

Ferrari Club of GB, Betty Mathias, 7 Swan Close, Blake Down, Kidderminster, Worcestershire DY10 3JT

Ferrari Owners' Club, Peter Everingham, 35 Market Place, Snettisham, Kings Lynn PE31 7LR

Fiat 130 Owners' Club, Michael Reid, 28 Warwick Mansions, Cromwell Crescent, London SW5 9QR

Fiat 500 Club, Janet Westcott (Membership Secretary), 33 Lionel Avenue, Wendover, Aylesbury, Buckinghamshire HP22 6LP

Fiat Motor Club (GB), Mrs S. Robins (Hon. Membership Secretary), 118 Brookland Road, Langport, Somerset TA10 9TH

Fiat Osca Register, Mr M Elliott, 36 Maypole Drive, Chigwell, Essex IG7 6DE

Fiesta Club of GB, S. Church, 145 Chapel Lane, Farnborough, Hampshire GU14 9BN

Fire Service Preservation Group, Andrew Scott, 50 Old Slade Lane, Iver, Buckinghamshire SL0 9DR

Five Hundred Owners' Club Association, David Docherty, Oakley, 68 Upton Park, Chester CH2 1DQ

Ford 105E Owners' Club, Sally Harris, 30 Gower Road, Sedgley, Dudley, West Midlands DY3 3PN

Ford Avo Owners' Club, D. Hensley, 11 Sycamore Drive, Patchway, Bristol, Gloucestershire BS12 5DH

Ford Capri Enthusiasts' Register, Glyn Watson, 7 Louis Avenue, Bury, Lancashire BL9 5EQ
www.uk-classic-cars.com/fordcapri.htm

Ford Classic and Capri Owners' Club, 1 Verney Close, Covingham, Swindon, Wiltshire SN3 5EF

Ford Corsair Owners Club, Mrs E Checkley, 7 Barnfield, New Malden, Surrey KT3 5RH

Ford Cortina Owners' Club, Mr D Eastwood (Chairman), 52 Woodfield, Bamber Bridge, Preston, Lancashire PR5 8ED Tel: 01772 627004
www.cortinaownersclub.co.uk

Ford Cortina 1600E Owners' Club, Dave Johnson, 16 Woodland Close, Sarisbury Green, Nr Southampton, Hampshire SO31 7AQ davejohnson1600e@yahoo.com
www.ford-cortina-16ooe-club.org.uk

Ford Escort 1300E Owners' Club, Robert Watt, 65 Lindley Road, Walton on Thames, Surrey KT12 3EZ

Ford Executive Owners Register, George Young, 31 Brian Road, Chadwell Heath, Romford, Essex RM6 5DA

Ford GT Owners, c/o Riverside School, Ferry Road, Hullbridge, Hockley, Essex SS5 6ND

Ford Mk II Independent O C International, B & J Enticknap, 173 Sparrow Farm Drive, Feltham, Middlesex TW14 0DG Tel: 020 8384 3559 Fax: 020 8890 3741

Ford Mk III Zephyr and Zodiac Owners' Club, John Wilding, 10 Waltondale, Telford, Shropshire TF7 5NQ

Ford Mk IV Zephyr & Zodiac Owners' Club, Richard Cordle, 29 Ruskin Drive, Worcester Park, Surrey KT4 8LG

Ford Model T Ford Register of GB, Mrs Julia Armer, 3 Strong Close, Keighley, Yorkshire BD21 4JT

Ford Sidevalve Owners Club, Membership Secretary, 30 Earls Close, Bishopstoke, Eastleigh, Hampshire SO50 8HY

Ford Y&C Model Register, Bob Wilkinson, 9 Brambleside, Thrapston, Northamptonshire NN14 4PY

Frazer-Nash Section of the VSCC, Mrs J Blake, Daisy Head Farm, South Street, Caulcott, Bicester, Oxfordshire OX6 3NE

Friends of The British Commercial Vehicle, c/o BCVM, King Street, Leyland, Preston, Lancashire PR5 1LE

The Gentry Register, Barbara Reynolds (General Secretary), Barn Close Cottage, Cromford Road, Woodlinkin, Nottinghamshire NG16 4HD

Gilbern Owners' Club, Richard Jockel, 20 Ivyhouse Road, Ickenham, Middlesex UB10 8NF

Gordon Keeble Owners' Club, Ann Knott, Westminster Road, Helmdon, Brackley, Northamptonshire NN13 5QB

Guernsey Motorcycle & Car Club, c/o Graham Rumens, Glenesk, Sandy Hook, St Sampsons, Guernsey, Channel Islands GY2 4ER

Gwynne Register, H K Good, 9 Lancaster Avenue, Hadley Wood, Barnet, Hertfordshire EN4 0EP

Heinkel Trojan Owners' and Enthusiasts' Club, Y Luty, Carisbrooke, Wood End Lane, Fillongley, Coventry, Warwickshire CV7 8DF

Heinz 57 Register, Barry Priestman (Secretary), 58 Geriant Road, Downham, Bromley, Kent BR1 5DX

Hermon Enthusiasts' Club, 6 Westleton Way, Felixstowe, Suffolk IP11 2YG

Hillman, Commer & Karrier Club, A Freakes, Capri House, Walton-on-Thames, Surrey KT12 2LY

Historic Caravan Club, Barbara Bissell (Secretary), 29 Linnet Close, Lodgefield Park, Halesowen, West Midlands B62 8TW Tel: 0121 561 5742

Historic Commercial Vehicle Society, Iden Grange, Cranbrook Road, Staplehurst, Kent TN12 0ET

Historic Grand Prix Cars Association, 106 Gifford Street, London N1 0DF Tel: 020 7607 4887

Historic Lotus Register, Victor Thomas (Secretary), Badgers Farm, Short Green, Winfarthing, Norfolk IP22 2EE
Tel: 01953 860508

Historic Rally Car Register RAC, Martin Jubb, 38 Longfield Road, Bristol, Gloucestershire BS7 9AG

Historic Sports Car Club, Silverstone Circuit, Nr Towcester, Northants NN12 8TN

Historic Volkswagen Club, Rod Sleigh, 28 Longnor Road, Brooklands, Telford, Shropshire TF1 3NY www.historicvws.org

Holden UK Register, 39 Roebuck Road, Chessington, Surrey KT9 1JY holdenuk@ndirect.co.uk

HRG Association, I J Dussek, Churcher, Church Road, Upper Farringdon, Alton, Hampshire GU34 3EG

Humber Register, R N Arman, Northbrook Cottage, 175 York Road, Broadstone, Dorset BH18 8ES

Imp Club, 27 Brookside Road, Stratford-on-Avon, Warwickshire CV37 9PH

Invicta Military Vehicle Preservation Society, Andrew Tizzard, 4 Hanbury Close, Wateringbury, Kent ME18 5DP www.warandpeace.uk.com

Isetta Owners' Club, 19 Towcester Road, Old Stratford, Milton Keynes, Buckinghamshire MK19 6AH

Jaguar Car Club, R Pugh, 19 Eldorado Crescent, Cheltenham, Gloucestershire GL50 2PY

Jaguar Drivers' Club, JDC, Jaguar House, 18 Stuart Street, Luton, Bedfordshire LU1 2SL

Jaguar Enthusiasts' Club, 176 Whittington Way, Pinner, Middlesex HA5 5JY

Jaguar/Daimler Owners' Club, 130/132 Bordesley Green, Birmingham, West Midlands B9 4SU

Jensen Owners' Club, Brian Morrey, Selwood, Howley, Nr Chard, Somerset TA20 3DX

Jowett Car Club, Mrs Pauline Winteringham, 33 Woodlands Road, Gomersall, Cleckheaton, Yorkshire

JU 250 Register, Stuart Cooke, 34 Thorncliffe Drive, Darwen, Lancashire BB3 3QA

Junior Zagato Register, Kenfield Hall, Petham, Nr Canterbury, Kent CT4 5RN

Jupiter Owners' Auto Club, Steve Keil, 16 Empress Avenue, Woodford Green, Essex IG8 9EA

K70 Register, SAE to: Mr Bood, 25 Cedar Grove, Penn Fields, Wolverhampton WV3 7EB

Karmann Ghia Owners' Club, Astrid Kelly (Membership Secretary), 7 Keble Road, Maidenhead, Berkshire SL6 6BB

Kieft Racing and Sports Car Club, Duncan Rabagliati, 4 Wool Road, Wimbledon, London SW20 0HW

Lagonda Club, Colin Bugler (Hon. Secretary), Wintney House, London Road, Hartley Wintney, Hook, Hampshire RG27 8RN

Lancia Motor Club, Dave Baker (Membership Secretary), Mount Pleasant, Penrhos, Brymbo, Wrexham, Clwyd, Wales LL11 5LY

Land Rover Register (1947—1951), Membership Secretary, High House, Ladbrooke, Leamington Spa, Warwickshire CV33 0BT

Land Rover Series 3 Owners' Club Ltd, 23 Deidre Avenue, Wickford, Essex SS12 0AX

Land Rover Series One Club, David Bowyer, East Foldhay, Zeal Monachorum, Crediton, Devon EX17 6DH

Land Rover Series Two Club Ltd, Laurence Mitchell Esq, PO Box 251, Barnsley S70 5YN series2club@freenetname.co.uk www.series2club.org.uk

Landcrab Owners' Club International, 5 Rolston Avenue, Huntington, York YO31 9JD

Lea Francis Owners' Club, R Sawers, French's, High Street, Long Wittenham, Abingdon, Oxfordshire OX14 4QQ

Lincoln-Zephyr Owners' Club, Colin Spong, 22 New North Road, Hainault, Ilford, Essex IG6 2XG

London Bus Preservation Trust, Mike Nash, 43 Stroudwater Park, Weybridge, Surrey KT13 0DT

London Vintage Taxi Association, Steve Dimmock, 51 Ferndale Crescent, Cowley, Uxbridge, Berkshire UB8 2AY

Lotus Cortina Register, Andy Morrell, 64 The Queens Drive, Chorleywood, Rickmansworth, Hertfordshire WD3 2LT

Lotus Drivers' Club, Lee Barton, 15 Pleasant Way, Leamington Spa, Warwickshire CV32 5XA

Lotus Seven Club, Julie Richens, PO Box 137, Alton GU34 5YH Tel: 07000 L7CLUB (572582) www.lotus7club.co.uk

Manta A Series Register, Mark Kinnon, 112 Northwood Avenue, Purley, Surrey CR8 2EQ www.mantaclub.org

Marcos Owners' Club, 62 Culverley Road, Catford, London SE6 2LA

Marendaz Special Car Register, John Shaw, 107 Old Bath Road, Cheltenham, Gloucestershire GL53 7DA

Marina/Ital Drivers' Club, Mr J G Lawson, 12 Nithsdale Road, Liverpool L15 5AX

Maserati Club, Michael Miles, The Paddock, Old Salisbury Road, Abbotts Ann, Andover, Hampshire SP11 7NT

Masters Club, Barry Knight, 2 Ranmore Avenue, East Croydon, Surrey CR0 5QA

Matra Enthusiasts' Club MEC, 19 Abbotsbury, Orton Goldhay, Peterborough, Cambridgeshire PE2 5PS

The Mechanical Horse Club, The Secretary, 2 The Poplars, Horsham, East Sussex RH13 5RH

Mercedes-Benz Owners' Association, Langton Road,Langton Green, Tunbridge Wells, Kent TN3 0EG Tel: 01892 860922 www.mercedesclub.org.uk

Mercedes-Benz Owners' Club, Trevor Mitchell (Northern Ireland Area Organiser), 38 Ballymaconell Road, Bangor, Co Down, Northern Ireland BT20 5PS

Messerschmitt Owners' Club, Mrs Eileen Hallam, Birches, Ashmores Lane, Rusper, West Sussex RH12 4PS

Metropolitan Owners' Club, Nick Savage, The Old Pump House, Nutbourne Common, Pulborough, West Sussex RH20 2HB

MG Car Club, 7 Chequer Lane, Ash, Canterbury, Kent CT3 2ET

MG Octagon Car Club, Unit 1/2 Parchfields Enterprise Park, Colton Road, Trent Valley, Rugeley, Staffordshire WS15 3HB Tel: 01889 574666 Fax: 01889 574555

MG Owners Club, Octagon House, Swavesey, Cambridgeshire CB4 5QZ

MG Y Type Register, Mr J G Lawson, 12 Nithsdale Road, Liverpool L15 5AX

Midas Owners' Club, c/o Steve Evans, 8 Mill Road, Holyhead, Anglesey LL65 2TA Tel: 01407 769544 MIDAS.MEMBERS@tinyworld.co.uk

Midget & Sprite Club, Nigel Williams, 15 Foxcote, Kingswood, Bristol, Gloucestershire BS15 2TX

Military Vehicle Trust, PO Box 6, Fleet, Hampshire GU52 6GE

Mini Cooper Club, Mary Fowler, 59 Giraud Street, Poplar, London E14 6EE

Mini Cooper Register, Philip Splett (Public Relations Officer), Burtons Farm, Barling Road, Barling Magna, Southend, Essex SS3 0LZ

Mini Marcos Owners' Club, Roger Garland, 28 Meadow Road, Worcester WR3 7PP Tel: 01905 458533

Mini Moke Club, Paul Beard, 13 Ashdene Close, Hartlebury, Herefordshire DY11 7TN

Mini Owners' Club, 15 Birchwood Road, Lichfield, Staffordshire WS14 9UN

Mini Seven Racing Club, Mick Jackson, 345 Clay Lane, South Yardley, Birmingham, West Midlands B26 1ES

MK I Consul, Zephyr and Zodiac Club, James T Indermaur, 41 Shaftesbury Avenue, Vicars Cross, Chester CH3 5LH Tel: 01244 327643

Mk I Cortina Owners' Club, Karen Clarke, 6 Hobsons Acre, Gunthorpe, Nottinghamshire NG14 7FF

Mk II Consul, Zephyr and Zodiac Club, Bryn Gwyn Farm, Carmel, Cearnarfon, Gwynedd LL54 7AP

Mk II Granada Owners' Club, Paul Farrer, 58 Jevington Way, Lee, London SE12 9NQ

Model A Ford Club of Great Britain, Mr S J Shepherd, 32 Portland Street, Clifton, Bristol, Gloucestershire BS8 4JB

Morgan Sports Car Club, Carol Kennett, Old Ford Lodge, Ogston, Higham, Derbyshire DE55 6EL

Morgan Three-Wheeler Club Ltd, Dennis Plater (Membership Secretary), Holbrooks, Thoby Lane, Mountnessing, Brentwood, Essex CM15 0TA

Morris Cowley and Oxford Club (1954–60), Derek Andrews, 202 Chantry Gardens, Southwick, Trowbridge, Wiltshire BA14 9QX

Morris Marina Owners' Club, Nigel Butler, Llys-Aled, 63 Junction Road, Stourbridge, West Midlands DY8 4YJ

Morris Minor Owners' Club, Mrs E. Saxon, PO Box 1098, Derby DE23 8ZX Tel: 01332 291675

Morris Minor Owners' Club, N. Ireland Branch, Mrs Joanne Jeffery (Secretary), 116 Oakdale, Ballygowan, Newtownards, Co. Down, Northern Ireland BT23 5TT

Morris Register, Michael Thomas (Secretary), 14 Meadow Rise, Horam, East Sussex TN21 0LZ Tel: 01435 810133 www.morrisregister.co.uk

Moss Owners' Club, David Pegler, Pinewood, Weston Lane, Bath, Somerset BA1 4AG

Motorvatin' USA American CC, T. Lynn, PO Box 2222, Braintree, Essex CM7 6TW

Naylor Car Club, Mrs F. Taylor (Registrar/Membership Secretary), 21 Anglesey Place, Great Barton, Nr Bury St. Edmunds, Suffolk IP31 2TW Tel/Fax: 01284 788094

Nobel Register, Mike Ayriss, 29 Oak Drive, Syston, Leicester LE7 2PX michael.ayriss@virgin.net

Norfolk Military Vehicle Group, Fakenham Road, Stanhoe, King's Lynn, Norfolk PE31 8PX

North East Club for Pre War Austins, Tom Gatenby, 9 Townsend Crescent, Morpeth, Northumberland NE61 2XW

North London MG Club, 2 Duckett Road, Harringey, London N4 1BN

North Thames Military Vehicle Preservation Society, 22 Victoria Avenue, Grays, Essex RM16 2RP

Nova Owners' Club, Ray Nicholls, 19 Bute Avenue, Hathershaw, Oldham, Lancashire OL8 2AQ

NSU Owners' Club, Rosemary Crowley, Nutleigh, Rabies Heath Road, Bletchingley, Surrey RH1 4LX

Ogle Register, Chris Gow, 108 Potters Lane, Burgess Hill, West Sussex RH15 9JN

Old Bean Society, P P Cole, 165 Denbigh Drive, Hately Heath, West Bromwich, West Midlands B71 2SP

Opel GT UK Owners Club, Dean Hayes, 11 Thrale Way, Parkwood, Rainham, Kent ME8 9LX

Opel Vauxhall Drivers Club, The Old Mill, Dereham, Norfolk NR20 5RT

Panhard et Levassor Club GB, Martin McLarence, 18 Dovedale Road, Offerton, Stockport, Cheshire SK2 5DY

Panther Enthusiasts' Club UK, George Newell (Secretary), 91 Fleet Road, Farnborough, Hampshire GU14 9RE www.pantherclub.co.uk

Pedal Car Collectors Club, c/o A P Gayler, 4/4a Chapel Terrace Mews, Kemp Town, Brighton, East Sussex BN2 1HU Tel/Fax: 01273 601960 www.brmmbrmm.com/pedalcars

Piper (Sports and Racing Car) Club, Clive Davies, Pipers Oak, Lopham Rd, East Harling, Norfolk NR16 2PE

Porsche Club Great Britain, Robin Walker, c/o Cornbury House, Cotswold Business Village, London Road, Moreton-in-Marsh, Gloucestershire GL56 0JQ

Post Office Vehicle Club, 7 Bignal Rand Drive, Wells, Somerset BA5 2EU

Post War Thoroughbred Car Club, 87 London Street, Chertsey, Surrey KT16 8AN

Post-Vintage Humber Car Club, Neil Gibbins, 32 Walsh Crescent, New Addington, Croydon, Surrey CR0 0BX

Potteries Vintage and Classic Car Club, B Theobald, 78 Reeves Avenue, Cross Heath, Newcastle, Staffordshire ST5 9LA

Pre-1940 Triumph Owners' Club, Jon Quiney, 2 Duncroft Close, Reigate, Surrey RH2 9DE

Pre-67 Ford Owners' Club, Alistair Cuninghame, 13 Drum Brae Gardens, Edinburgh, Scotland EH12 8SY

Pre-50 American Auto Club, Alan Murphy, 41 Eastham Rake, Wirral, Merseyside L62 9AN

Pre-War Austin Seven Club Ltd, Stephen Jones, 1 The Fold, Doncaster Road, Whitley, Nr Goole, Yorkshire DN14 0HZ

Radford Register, Chris Gow, 108 Potters Lane, Burgess Hill, West Sussex RH15 9JN

Railton Owners' Club, Barrie McKenzie, Fairmiles, Barnes Hall Road, Burncross, Sheffied, Yorkshire S35 1RF

Range Rover Register, Chris Tomley, Cwm/Cochen, Bettws, Newtown, Powys, Wales SY16 3LQ

Rapier Register, D C H Williams, Smithy, Tregynon, Newtown, Powys, Wales SY16 3EH

Register of Unusual Micro-Cars, Jean Hammond, School House Farm, Boarden Lane, Hawkenbury, Staplehurst, Kent TN12 0EB

Reliant Kitten Register, Brian Marshall, 16 Glendee Gardens, Renfrew PA4 0AL

Reliant Owners' Club, Graham Close, 19 Smithey Close, High Green, Sheffield, Yorkshire S35 4FQ

Reliant Sabre and Scimitar Owners Club, P O Box 67, Teddington, Middlesex TW11 8QR

Renault Frères, J G Kemsley, Yew Tree House, Jubliee Road, Chelsfield, Kent BR6 7QZ

Renault Owners' Club, J. Henderson, 24 Long Meadow, Mansfield Woodhouse, Mansfield, Nottinghamshire NG19 9QW

Riley MC Ltd, J. Hall, Treelands, 127 Penn Road, Wolverhampton WV3 0DU

Riley Register, J A Clarke, 56 Cheltenham Road, Bishops Cleeve, Cheltenham, Gloucestershire GL52 8LY

Riley RM Club, Mrs J. Morris, Y Fachell, Ruthin Road, Gwernymynydd, North Wales CH7 5LQ

Ro80 Club GB, Mr Alec Coutts, 46 Molivers Lane, Bromham, Bedfordshire MK43 8LD

Rochdale Owners' Club, Alaric Spendlove, 7 Whitleigh Avenue, Crownhill, Plymouth, Devon PL5 3BQ Tel: 01752 791409 alaric@onetel.net.uk www.rochdale-owners-club.com

Rolls-Royce Enthusiasts' Club, Peter Baines, The Hunt House, Paulerspury, Northamptonshire NN12 7NA

Ronart Drivers' Club, Simon Sutton (Membership Secretary), Orchard Cottage, Allan Lane, Fritchley, Belper, Derbyshire DE56 2FX

Rover P4 Drivers' Guild, Colin Blowers, 32 Arundel Road, Luton, Bedfordshire LU4 8DY

Rover P5 Owners' Club, G Moorshead, 13 Glen Avenue, Ashford, Middlesex TW15 2JE

Rover P6 Owners' Club, M Jones, 48 Upper Aughton Road, Birkdale, Southport PR8 5NH

Rover Sports Register, Cliff Evans, 8 Hilary Close, Great Boughton, Chester CH3 5QP

Royal Automobile Club, PO Box 700, Bristol, Gloucestershire BS99 1RB

Saab Enthusiasts' Club, PO Box 96, Harrow, Middlesex HA3 7DW

Saab Owners' Club of GB Ltd, John Wood (Membership Secretary), PO Box 900, Durham DH1 2GF Tel: 01923 229945 Membership Hotline: 070 71 71 9000

Scimitar Drivers' Club International, Steve Lloyd, 45 Kingshill Park, Dursley, Gloucestershire GL11 4DG

Scootacar Register, Stephen Boyd, Pamanste, 18 Holman Close, Aylsham, Norwich NR11 6DD

Sebring OC, D. Soundy, Hill House, Water Lane, Chelveston, Northamptonshire NN9 6AP

Simca Owners' Register, David Chapman, 18 Cavendish Gardens, Redhill, Surrey RH1 4AQ

Singer Owners' Club, Martyn Wray (Secretary), 11 Ermine Rise, Great Casterton, Stamford, Lincolnshire PE9 4AJ

Small Ford Club, 115 Woodland Gardens, Isleworth, Middlesex TW7 6LU

Solent Austin Seven Club Ltd, F Claxton, 185 Warsash Road, Warsash, Hampshire SO31 9JE

South Devon Commercial Vehicle Club, Bob Gale, Avonwick Station, Diptford, Totnes, Devon TQ9 7LU

South Hants Model Auto Club, C Derbyshire, 21 Aintree Road, Calmore, Southampton, Hampshire SO40 2TL

South Wales Austin Seven Club, Mr H Morgan, 'Glynteg', 90 Ammanford Road, Llandybie, Ammanford, Wales SA18 2JY

Spartan Owners' Club, Steve Andrews, 28 Ashford Drive, Ravenhead, Nottinghamshire NG15 9DE

Split Screen Van Club, Mike & Sue Mundy, The Homestead, Valebridge Road, Burgess Hill, West Sussex RH15 0RT

Sporting Escort Owners' Club, 26 Huntingdon Crescent, Off Madresfield Drive, Halesowen, West Midlands B63 3DJ

Sporting Fiats Club (Formerly Fiat Twin-Cam Register), Freepost (MID D2062), Leamington Spa, Warwickshire CV33 9BR

Stag Owners' Club, c/o The Old Rectory, Aslacton, Norfolk NR15 2JN

Standard Motor Club, Tony Pingriff (Membership Secretary), 57 Main Road, Meriden, Coventry, West Midlands CV7 0LP

Star, Starling, Stuart and Briton Register, D E A Evans, New Wood Lodge, 2A Hyperion Rd, Stourton, Stourbridge, West Midlands DY7 6SB

Sunbeam Alpine Owners' Club, Pauline Leese, 53 Wood Street, Mow Cop, Stoke-on-Trent, Staffordshire ST7 3PF

Sunbeam Rapier Owners' Club, Ruth Kingston, Wayside, Depmore Lane, Kingsley, Nr Warrington, Cheshire WA6 6UD

Sunbeam Talbot Alpine Register, Derek Cook (Membership Secretary), 8 Warwick Court, South Park, Sevenoaks, Kent TN13 1EQ

Sunbeam Talbot Darracq Register, R Lawson, West Emlett Cottage, Black Dog, Crediton, Devon EX17 4QB

Sunbeam Tiger Owners' Club, Brian Postle, Beechwood, 8 Villa Real Estate, Consett, Co Durham DH8 6BJ

Surrey Classic Vehicle Club, 55a Ditton Road, Surbiton, Surrey KT6 6RF

Swift Club and Swift Register for Coventry-built Swifts 1901–31, John Harrison, 70 Eastwick Drive, Bookham, Leatherhead, Surrey KT23 3NX

Tame Valley Vintage and Classic Car Club, Mrs S Ogden, 13 Valley New Road, Royton, Oldham, Lancashire OL2 6BP

Tornado Register, Dave Malins, 48 St Monica's Avenue, Luton, Bedfordshire LU3 1PN Tel: 01582 37641

Toyota Enthusiasts' Club, c/o Billy Wells (Secretary/Treasurer), 28 Park Road, Feltham, Middlesex TW13 6PW Tel: 020 8898 0740

TR Register, 1B Hawksworth, Southmead Industrial Park, Didcot, Oxfordshire OX10 7HR Tel: 01235 818866

Trident Car Club, David Rowlinson, 23 Matlock Crescent, Cheam, Sutton, Surrey SM3 9SS trident.carclub@virgin.net www.tridentcarclub.fsnet.co.uk

Triumph 2000/2500/2.5 Register, Alan Crussell, 10 Gables Close, Chalfont St Peter, Buckinghamshire SL9 0PR www.kvaleberg.com/t2000.html

Triumph Dolomite Club, 39 Mill Lane, Upper Arncott, Bicester, Oxfordshire OX6 0PB

Triumph Mayflower Club, T Gordon, 12 Manor Close, Hoghton, Preston, Lancashire PR5 0EN

Triumph Mayflower Club, John Oaker, 19 Broadway North, Walsall, West Midlands WS1 2QG

Triumph Razoredge Owners' Club, Stewart Langton, 62 Seaward Avenue, Barton-on-Sea, Hampshire BH25 7HP

Triumph Roadster Club, J Cattaway, 59 Cowdray Park Road, Little Common, Bexhill-on-Sea, East Sussex TN39 4EZ

Triumph Spitfire Club, Mr Cor Gent, Anemoon 41, 7483 AC Haaksbergen, The Netherlands

Triumph Sporting Owners' Club, G R King, 16 Windsor Road, Hazel Grove, Stockport, Cheshire SK7 4SW

Triumph Sports Six Club Ltd, 121B St Mary's Road, Market Harborough, Leicestershire LE16 7DT

Triumph Stag Register, M. Wattam, 18 Hazel Close, Highcliffe, Dorset BH23 4PS

Trojan Owners Club, Derrick Graham (President), Troylands, St Johns, Earlswood Common, Redhill, Surrey RH1 6QF

Turner Register, Dave Scott, 21 Ellsworth Road, High Wycombe, Buckinghamshire HP11 2TU

TVR Car Club, c/o David Gerald, TVR Sports Cars Tel: 01386 793239

United States Army Vehicle Club, Dave Boocock, 31 Valley View Close, Bogthorn, Oakworth Rd, Keighley, Yorkshire BD22 7LZ

United States Army Vehicle Club, Simon Johnson, 7 Carter Fold, Mellor, Lancashire BB2 7ER

Unloved Soviet Socialist Register, Julian Nowill, Earlsland House, Bradninch, Exeter, Devon EX5 4QP Tel: 01392 453600(W) 01392 881748(H) julian.nowill@gerrard.com

Vanden Plas Owners' Club, Mr B. Hill, 33 Rectory Lane, Houghton Conquest, Bedfordshire MK45 3LD

Vanguard 1&2 Owners' Club, R Jones, The Villa, The Down, Alviston, Avon BS12 2TQ

Vauxhall Cavalier Convertible Club, Ron Goddard, 47 Brooklands Close, Luton, Bedfordshire LU4 9EH

Vauxhall Owners' Club, Roy Childers (Membership Secretary), 31 Greenbanks, Melbourn, Nr Royston, Cambridgeshire SG8 6AS

Vauxhall PA/PB/PC/E Owners' Club, G Lonsdale, 77 Pilling Lane, Preesall, Lancashire FY6 0HB

Vauxhall Viva OC, Adrian Miller, The Thatches, Snetterton North End, Snetterton, Norwich NR16 2LD Tel/Fax: 01953 498818 adrian@vivaclub.freeserve.co.uk www.vivaclub@freeserve.co.uk

Vauxhall VX4/90 Drivers' Club for enthusiasts of all FD & FE Series Vauxhalls, Richard Bragg (Membership Secretary & Treasurer), 25 Chichester Close, Beckton, London E6 5QJ

Vectis Historic Vehicle Club, Nigel Offer, 10 Paddock Drive, Bembridge, Isle of Wight PO35 5TL

Veteran Car Club Of Great Britain, Jessamine Court, 15 High Street, Ashwell, Hertfordshire SG7 5NL Tel: 01462 742818

Vintage Austin Register, Frank Smith (Hon Secretary), The Briars, Four Lane Ends, Oakerthorpe, Alfreton, Derbyshire DE55 7LH

Vintage Sports-Car Club Ltd, Sadie Wigglesworth (Press & PR Manager), The Old Post Office, West Street, Chipping Norton, Oxon OX7 5EL Tel: 01608 644777

Volkswagen '50-67' Transporter Club, Peter Nicholson, 11 Lowton Road, Lytham St Annes, Lancashire FY8 3JD

Volkswagen Cabriolet Owners' Club (GB), Emma Palfreyman (Secretary), Dishley Mill, Derby Road, Loughborough, Leicestershire LE11 0SF

Volkswagen Owners' Club (GB), PO Box 7, Burntwood, Walsall, West Midlands WS7 8SB

Volvo Enthusiasts' Club, Kevin Price, 4 Goonbell, St Agnes, Cornwall TR5 0PH

Vulcan Register, D Hales, The Hedgerows, Sutton St Nicholas, Herefordshire HR1 3BU

VW Type 3 and 4 Club, Jane Terry, Pear Tree Bungalow, Exted, Elham, Canterbury, Kent CT4 6YG

Wartburg Owners Club, Bernard Trevena, 55 Spiceall Estate, Compton, Guildford, Surrey GU31

Wolseley 6/80 and Morris Oxford MO Club, Don Gould, 2 Barleyfield Close, Heighington, Lincoln LN4 1TX

Wolseley Hornet Special Club, Wolseley Hornet, Sports & Specials 1930–35, Ms Chris Hyde, Kylemor, Crown Gardens, Fleet, Hampshire GU51 3LT whsc.sec@btinternet.com www.whsc.co.uk

Wolseley Register, M. Stanley (Chairman), 1 Flashgate, Higher Ramsgreave Road, Ramsgreave, Nr Blackburn, Lancashire BB1 9DH

XR Owners Club, Les Gent (National Co-ordinator), PO Box 47, Loughborough, Leicestershire LE11 1XS Tel: 01509 882300 www.xroc.co.uk

Yankee Jeep Club, 8 Chew Brook Drive, Greenfield, Saddleworth, Lancashire OL3 7PD

Directory of Auctioneers

Auction Team Köln, Postfach 50 11 19, 50971 Köln, Germany Tel: 00 49 0221 38 70 49
Barons, Brooklands House, 33 New Road, Hythe, Southampton, Hampshire SO45 6BN Tel: 023 8084 0081 www.barons-auctions.com
Barrett-Jackson Auction Company, LLC, 3020 N Scottsdale Road, Scottsdale, Arizona USA Tel: 480-421-6694 www.barrett-jackson.com
Bernaerts, Verlatstraat 18-22, 2000 Antwerpen/Anvers Tel: +32 (0)3 248 19 21 www.auction-bernaerts.com
C Boisgirard, 2 rue de Provence, Paris, France 75009 Tel: 00 33 147708136
Bonhams & Brooks, Montpelier Street, Knightsbridge, London SW7 1HH Tel: 020 7393 3900 www.bonhams.com
Brightwells Ltd, Ryelands Road, Leominster, Herefordshire HR6 8NZ Tel: 01568 611122
British Car Auctions Ltd, Classic & Historic Automobile Division, Auction Centre, Blackbushe Airport, Blackwater, Camberley, Surrey GU17 9LG Tel: 01252 878555
Butterfields, 220 San Bruno Avenue, San Francisco, CA 94103 U.S.A. Tel: 00 1 415 861 7500
Mervyn Carey, Twysden Cottage, Benenden, Cranbrook, Kent TN17 4LD Tel: 01580 240283
Central Motor Auctions Plc, Central House, Pontefract Road, Rothwell, Leeds, Yorkshire LS26 0JE Tel: 0113 282 0707
Cheffins, 49/53 Regent Street, Cambridge CB2 1AF Tel: 01223 358731 www.chefins.co.uk
Christie, Manson & Woods Ltd, The Jack Barclay Showroom, 2-4 Ponton Road, Nine Elms, London SW8 5BA Tel: 020 73892217 www.christies.com
Classic Automobile Auctions B.V, Goethestrasse 10, 6000 Frankfurt 1, Germany Tel: 010 49 69 28666/8
Coys of Kensington, 2/4 Queens Gate Mews, London SW7 5QJ Tel: 020 7584 7444
Dickinson Davy and Markham, Wrawby Street, Brigg, Humberside DN20 8JJ Tel: 01652 653666
Evans & Partridge, Agriculture House, High Street, Stockbridge, Hampshire SO20 6HF Tel: 01264 810702
Thomas Wm Gaze & Son, 10 Market Hill, Diss, Norfolk IP22 3JZ Tel: 01379 651931 www.twgaze.com
Greens (UK) Ltd, Worcestershire WR14 2AY Tel: 01684 575902
H & H Classic Auctions Ltd, Whitegate Farm, Hatton Lane, Hatton, Warrington, Cheshire WA4 4BZ Tel: 01925 730630 www.classic-auctions.co.uk
Andrew Hartley, Victoria Hall Salerooms, Little Lane, Ilkley, Yorkshire LS29 8EA Tel: 01943 816363
Kidson Trigg, Estate Office, Friars Farm, Sevenhampton, Highworth, Swindon, Wiltshire SN6 7PZ Tel: 01793 861000
Kruse International, PO Box 190, 5400 County Road 11A, Auburn, Indiana 46706, USA Tel: 219 925 5600
Lambert & Foster, 77 Commercial Road, Paddock Wood, Kent TN12 6DR Tel: 01892 832325
Lawrences Auctioneers, Norfolk House, 80 High Street, Bletchingley, Surrey RH1 4PA Tel: 01883 743323 www.lawrencesbletchingley.co.uk
Thomas Mawer & Son, The Lincoln Saleroom, 63 Monks Road, Lincoln LN2 5HP Tel: 01522 524984
Mealy's, Chatsworth Street, Castle Comer, Co Kilkenny, Republic of Ireland Tel: 00 353 56 41229 www.mealys.com
Morphets of Harrogate, 6 Albert Street, Harrogate, Yorkshire HG1 1JL Tel: 01423 530030
Neales, 192-194 Mansfield Road, Nottingham NG1 3HU Tel: 0115 962 4141
John Nicholson, The Auction Rooms, Longfield, Midhurst Road, Fernhurst, Surrey GU27 3HA Tel: 01428 653727
Onslow's, The Depot, 2 Michael Road, London SW6 2AD Tel: 020 7371 0505
Palm Springs Exotic Car Auctions, 602 East Sunny Dunes Road, Palm Springs, California 92264, USA Tel: 760 320 3290 www.classic-carauction.com
Palmer Snell, 65 Cheap Street, Sherborne, Dorset DT9 3BATel: 01935 812218
J R Parkinson Son & Hamer Auctions, The Auction Rooms, Rochdale Road (Kershaw Street), Bury, Lancashire BL9 7HH Tel: 0161 761 1612/761 7372
Phillips, Blenstock House, 101 New Bond Street, London W1Y 0AS Tel: 020 7629 6602 www.phillips-auctions.com
Poulain Le Fur, Commissaires Priseurs Associés, 20 rue de Provence, 75009 Paris, France Tel: 01 42 46 81 81
RM Auctions, Inc, One Classic Car Drive, Ontario NOP 1AO, Canada Tel: 00 519 352 4575
Rogers Jones & Co, The Saleroom, 33 Abergele Road, Colwyn Bay, Wales LL29 7RU Tel: 01492 532176 www.rogersjones.ukauctioneers.com
Martyn Rowe, The Truro Auction Centre, Calenick Street, Truro, Cornwall TR1 2SG Tel: 01892 260020
RTS Auctions Ltd, Unit 1 Alston Road, Hellesden Park Industrial Estate, Norwich NR6 5OS Tel: 01603 418200
Silver Collector Car Auctions, E204, Spokane, Washington, USA 99207 Tel: 0101 509 326 4485
Sloan's Auctioneers & Appraisers, Miami Gallery, 8861 NW 18th Terrace, Suite 100, Miami, Florida 33172, USA Tel: (305) 592-2575
Sotheby's, 34-35 New Bond Street, London W1A 2AA Tel: 020 7293 5000 www.sothebys.com
Sworders, 14 Cambridge Road, Stansted Mountfitchet, Essex CM24 8BZ Tel: 01279 817778 www.sworder.co.uk
Taylors, Honiton Galleries, 205 High Street, Honiton, Devon EX14 8LF Tel: 01404 42404
Tennants, 34 Montpellier Parade, Harrogate, Yorkshire HG1 2TG Tel: 01423 531661
'The Auction', 3535 Las Vegas Boulevard, South Las Vegas, Nevada, USA 89101 Tel: 0101 702 794 3174
Thimbleby & Shorland, 31 Great Knollys Street, Reading, Berkshire RG1 7HU Tel: 0118 9508611
Wealden Auction Galleries, Desmond Judd, 23 Hendly Drive, Cranbrook, Kent TN17 3DY Tel: 01580 714522
Wellers Auctioneers, 70/70a Guildford Street, Chertsey, Surrey KT16 9BB Tel: 01932 568678
World Classic Auction & Exposition Co, 3600 Blackhawk Plaza Circle, Danville, California, USA 94506

Directory of Museums

Bedfordshire

Shuttleworth Collection,
Old Warden Aerodrome, Nr Biggleswade
SG18 9EP Tel: 01767 627288
Europe's biggest collection of flying pre-1940 aircraft, also veteran and vintage vehicles including 15 motorcycles. Restaurant, gift shop. Open daily 10–3pm (4pm Mar–Oct).

Stondon Museum,
Station Road, Lower Stondon, Henlow SG16 6JN
Tel: 01462 850339
Over 320 transport exhibits including Bentleys and over 30 motorcycles. Coffee shop. Open daily 10–5pm.

Cheshire

Mouldsworth Motor Museum,
Smithy Lane, Mouldsworth, Chester CH3 8AR
Tel: 01928 731781
Over 60 cars, motorcycles and early bicycles in a 1937 Art Deco building. Open Sundays March–end November 12–5pm inc Bank Holidays & weekends, also Wednesdays 1–5pm, all July and August.

Cornwall

Automobilia Motor Museum,
The Old Mill, Terras Road, St Stephen,
St Austell PL26 7RX
Tel: 01726 823092
Around 50 vehicles from 1900 to 1966, plus about ten motorcycles. Café, shop and autojumble. Open daily except Saturday in April, May and October 10–4pm, daily in June–September 10–5pm.

Cumbria

Cars of the Stars Motor Museum,
Standish Street, Keswick CA12 5LS
Tel: 01768 73757

Lakeland Motor Museum,
Holker Hall & Gardens, Cark-in-Cartmel,
Nr Grange-over-Sands, South Lakeland LA11 7PL
150 classic and vintage cars, tractors, cycles and engines including about 40 motorcycles. A collection of rare models and replicas of Donald Campbell's Bluebird cars and boats. Open end March to end October, Sunday–Friday 10.30–4.45pm, closed Saturday. Hall, gardens and grounds.

Western Lakes Motor Museum,
The Maltings, Brewery Lane, Cockermouth
Tel: 01900 824448
Located in Jennings Castle Brewery beneath the walls of Cockermouth Castle. Some 45 cars and 17 motorcycles from Vintage to Formula 3. Coffee shop, parking in town. Open March–October, daily 10–5pm. Closed January, other dates weekends only.

Derbyshire

The Donnington Collection,
Donnington Park, Castle Donnington
DE74 2RP Tel: 01332 810048

Gloucestershire

Bristol Industrial Museum,
Princes Wharf, City Docks, Bristol BS1 4RN
Tel: 0117 925 1470
Railway exhibits, boats, workshops plus lorries and cars made at Bristol. Open Tuesday–Sunday 10–5pm.

The Bugatti Trust,
Prescott Hill, Gotherington, Cheltenham GL52 4RD
Tel: 01242 677201

Cotswold Motoring Museum & Toy Collection,
Sherbourne Street, Bourton-on-the-Water,
Nr Cheltenham GL54 2BY
Tel: 01451 821 255 Largest collection of advertising signs in the world, plus toys and motorcycles. The home of the Brough-Superior Co and of 'Brum', the small, open 1920s car that has a TV series. Disabled entrance, museum shop and café. Open daily February–November 10–6pm.

Greater Manchester

Manchester Museum of Transport,
Boyle Street M8 8UW Tel: 0161 205 2122

Hampshire

National Motor Museum,
Brockenhurst, Beaulieu SO42 7ZN
Tel: 01590 612123/612345
Over 200 cars, 60 motorcycles and memorabilia. Gardens, information centre, monorail, veteran bus and car rides, model railway, special events including the world famous autojumbles. Restaurant, shops and facilities. Open daily from 10am, closed December 25.

Humberside

Bradford Industrial Museum,
Moorside Mills, Moorside Road, Bradford BD2 3HP
Tel: 01274 631756
General industrial museum including many engineering items, Jowett cars, Panther and Scott motorcycles, a steam roller and Bradford's last tram. Open Tuesday–Friday and Bank Holidays 10–5pm.

Northern Ireland

Ulster Folk and Transport Museum,
Cultra Manor, Holywood, Co Down BT18 0EU
Tel: 028 90 428 428
Folk museum, railway collection and road transport galleries featuring every kind of road vehicle. Tearooms, gift shop, and free parking. Open all year round 10.30–5/6pm, Sundays 12–6pm, closed Christmas.

Republic of Ireland

Kilgarvan Motor Museum,
Kilgarvan, Co Kerry
Tel: 00 353 64 85346

Isle of Man

Manx Motor Museum,
Crosby Tel: 01624 851236

Port Erin Motor Museum,
High Street, Port Erin Tel: 01624 832964

Kent

Historic Vehicles Collection of C M Booth,
Falstaff Antiques, 63–67 High Street,
Rolvenden TN17 4LP
Tel: 01580 241234
A private museum consisting mainly of Morgan three-wheelers but some motorbikes. An interesting collection plus memorabilia, at the rear of the antique shop. Open Monday–Saturday 10–6pm.

Ramsgate Motor Museum,
West Cliff Hall, Ramsgate CT11 9JX
Tel: 01843 581948
Founded 1982, dedicated to the history of motoring, every vehicle set out in scenes depicting the past. Open April–November 10.30–5.30pm, winter Sundays 10–5pm.

Lancashire

British Commercial Vehicles Museum,
King Street, Leyland, Preston PR5 1LE
Tel: 01772 451011 Fax: 01772 423404

Bury Transport Museum,
Castlecroft Road, off Bolton Street, Bury
Tel: 0161 764 7790

Middlesex

Whitewebbs Museum of Transport,
Whitewebbs Road, Enfield EN2 9HW
Tel: 020 8367 1898
Collection of commercial vehicles, cars and 20–30 motorcycles. Telephone for opening times.

Norfolk

Caister Castle Motor Museum,
Caister-on-Sea, Nr Great Yarmouth
Tel: 01572 787251
Private collection of cars and motorcycles from 1893. Tearoom, free car park. Open daily mid-May to end September, closed Saturday.

Nottinghamshire

Nottingham Industrial Museum,
Courtyard Buildings, Wallaton Park Tel: 0115 915 3910

Scotland

Grampian Transport Museum,
Alford, Aberdeenshire AB33 8AE
Tel: 019755 62292 Fax: 019755 62180
email: info@gtm.org.uk
Displays and working exhibits tracing the history of travel and transport in the locality. Open April 2–Oct 31 10–5pm.

Moray Motor Museum,
Bridge Street, Elgin IV30 2DE Tel: 01343 544933
Interesting collection of cars and motorcycles, memorabilia and diecast models. Open daily Easter–October 11–5pm.

Museum of Transport,
Kelvin Hall, 1 Bunhouse Road, Glasgow G3 8DP
Tel: 0141 357 3929
A museum devoted to the history of transport on the land. Café, gift shop, disabled access. Open daily 10–5pm, Sunday 11–5pm except December 25 and January 1.

Myreton Motor Museum,
Aberlady, Longniddry, East Lothian EH32 0PZ
Tel: 01875 870288
Collection of cars, motorcycles, commercials and WWII military vehicles. Established 1966. Open daily at 10am except Christmas Day. Parties and coaches welcome.

National Museum of Scotland,
Granton Centre, 242 West Granton Road, Edinburgh EH1 1JF Tel: 0131 225 7534

Shropshire

Midland Motor Museum,
Stanmore Hall, Stourbridge Road,
Bridgnorth WV15 6DT Tel: 01746 762992
Collection of 60 cars and 30 motorcycles. Museum shop. Open daily 10.30–5pm except December 25–26.

Somerset

Haynes Motor Museum,
Sparkford, Yeovil BA22 7LH
Tel: 01963 440804
Haynes Publishing Co museum with vintage, veteran and classic cars and motorcycles. 250 cars and 50 motorcycles. Café, shop. Open daily summer 9.30–5.30pm, winter 10–4pm except December 25–26, January 1.

Surrey

Brooklands Museum,
Brooklands Road, Weybridge KT13 0QN
Tel: 01932 857381
Motorsport and aviation museum including historic racing cars and aircraft. About 20 motorcycles pre-WWII. Monthly auction events. Tearooms and museum shop. Open daily except Mondays, Good Friday and Christmas 10–5pm summer, 10–4pm winter.

Dunsfold Land Rover Museum,
Dunsfold GU8 4NP Tel: 01483 200567

East Sussex

Bentley Motor Museum,
Bentley Wild Fowl Trust, Harvey's Lane, Ringmer, Lewes BN8 5AF Tel: 01825 840573

Foulkes-Halbard of Filching,
Filching Manor, Filching, Wannock, Polegate BN26 5QA Tel: 01323 487838
Fax: 01323 486331
About 100 cars dating from 1893 to 1993, also 30 motorcycles including American pre-1940s bikes ex-Steve McQueen. Open Easter–October Thursday, Friday, Saturday and Sunday 10.30–4pm.

Tyne & Wear

Newburn Hall Motor Museum,
35 Townfield Gardens, Newburn NE15 8PY
Tel: 0191 264 2977
Private museum of about 50 cars and ten motorcycles. Restaurant. Open daily 10–6pm, closed Mondays.

Wales

Llangollen Motor Museum,
Pentrefelin, Llangollen LL20 8EE
Tel: 01978 860324
20-plus cars and approx ten motorcycles. Model vehicles, signs, tools and parts. Reference library, shop. Open every day 10–5pm Easter–September.

Madog Car & Motorcycle Museum,
Snowdon Street, Porthmadog Tel: 01758 713618
15 cars and nearly 70 motorcycles plus memorabilia. Open Monday–Saturday 10–5 May–September.

Warwickshire

Heritage Motor Centre,
Banbury Road, Gaydon CV35 0BJ
Tel: 01926 641188 web: www.heritage.org.uk

Museum of British Road Transport,
St Agnes Lane, Hales Street, Coventry CV1 1PN
Tel: 024 7683 2425 Fax: 024 7683 2465
email: museum@mbrt.co.uk
web: www.mbrt.co.uk

West Midlands

Black Country Living Museum,
Tipton Road, Dudley DY1 4SQ Tel: 0121 557 9643

Wiltshire

Atwell-Wilson Motor Museum,
Downside, Stockley Lane, Calne SN11 0QX
Tel: 01249 813119
Over 60 cars plus vintage, post vintage and classic motorcycles. Open Monday–Thursday and Sunday, April–October 11–5pm, November–March 11–4pm and Good Friday.

Science Museum Transport Museum,
Red Barn Gate, Wroughton, Nr Swindon SN4 9NS
Tel: 01793 814466

Index to Advertisers

Bibliography

Baldwin, Nick; Georgano, G. N.; Sedgwick, Michael; and Laban, Brian; *The World Guide to Automobiles*, Guild Publishing, London, 1987

Colin Chapman Lotus Engineering, Osprey, 1993.

Flammang, James M; *Standard Catalog of Imported Cars*, Krause Publications Inc, 1992.

Georgano, G. N.; ed: *Encyclopedia of Sports Cars*, Bison Books, 1985.

Georgano, Nick; *Military Vehicles of World War II*, Osprey 1994.

Harding, Anthony; Allport, Warren; Hodges, David; Davenport, John; *The Guinness Book of the Car*, Guinness Superlatives Ltd, 1987

Hay, Michael; *Bentley Factory Cars*, Osprey, 1993.

Hough, Richard; *A History of the World's Sports Cars*, Allen & Unwin, 1961.

Isaac, Rowan; *Morgan*, Osprey, 1994.

McComb, F. Wilson; *MG by McComb*, Osprey, 1978.

Nye, Doug; *Autocourse History of the Grand Prix Car 1966–1991*, Hazleton Publishing, 1992.

Posthumus, Cyril, and Hodges, David; *Classic Sportscars*, Ivy Leaf, 1991.

Robson, Graham; *Classic and Sportscar A–Z of Cars of the 1970s*, Bay View Books, 1990.

Sedgwick, Michael; Gillies, Mark; *Classic and Sportscar A–Z of Cars of the 1930s*, Bay View Books, 1989.

Sedgwick, Michael, Gillies, Mark; *Classic and Sportscar A–Z of Cars 1945–70*, Bay View Books, 1990.

Sieff, Theo; *Mercedes-Benz*, Gallery Books, 1989.

Vanderveen, Bart; *Historic Military Vehicles Directory*, After the Battle Publications, 1989.

Willson, Quentin; Selby David, *The Ultimate Classic Car Book*, Dorling Kindersley, 1995.

PRATTS

150 GPL

Index

Italic page numbers denote colour pages, **bold** numbers refer to information and pointer boxes